THE PUBLICATIONS
OF THE
𝕾𝖊𝖑𝖉𝖊𝖓 𝕾𝖔𝖈𝖎𝖊𝖙𝖞

περὶ παντὸς τὴν ἐλευθερίαν

VOLUME CXXVIII
FOR THE YEAR 2011

Selden Society

FOUNDED 1887
To Encourage the Study and Advance the Knowledge of the History of English Law
2011

Patron
HIS ROYAL HIGHNESS THE PRINCE PHILLIP, DUKE OF EDINBURGH, K.G.

President
The Right Honourable LORD JUDGE, C.J.

Vice-Presidents
Dr PAUL BRAND, F.B.A.
The Right Honourable BEVERLEY MCLACHLIN, C.J.
The Honourable B. H. MCPHERSON, C.B.E.

Council

Mr DAVID AINGER	The Revd Professor A. D. E. LEWIS
The Hon. MORRIS S. ARNOLD	Professor MICHAEL LOBBAN
Mr RICHARD BAGLEY	Professor JANET LOENGARD
Professor C. W. BROOKS	Dr MICHAEL MACNAIR
The late Mrs MARJORIE CHIBNALL, F.B.A.	Dr JOHN MADDICOTT, F.B.A.
Professor M. T. CLANCHY, F.B.A.	His Honour E. F. MONIER-WILLIAMS
Professor W. R. CORNISH, Q.C., F.B.A.	The Rt Hon. LORD MUSTILL, F.B.A.
Dr DAVID CROOK	Mr M. J. PRICHARD
Professor CHARLES DONAHUE, JR.	Professor REBECCA PROBERT
Sir MATTHEW FARRER, G.C.V.O.	The late Rt Hon. LORD RODGER OF EARLSFERRY, F.B.A.
Professor RICHARD H. HELMHOLZ, F.B.A.	The late Professor A. W. B. SIMPSON, F.B.A.
Professor Sir JAMES HOLT, F.B.A.	Professor P. G. STEIN, Q.C., F.B.A.
Mr JOHN HOWELL, Q.C.	Mr A. C. TAUSSIG
Professor J. G. HUDSON	Professor Dr R. C. BARON VAN CAENEGEM, F.B.A.
Professor D. J. IBBETSON, F.B.A.	The Revd Professor T. G. WATKIN
Dr SUSANNE JENKS	Mr D. E. C. YALE, Q.C., F.B.A.
Mr NICHOLAS LE POIDEVIN, Q.C.	

Literary Director
Professor Sir JOHN BAKER, Q.C., F.B.A.

Assistant Literary Director
Dr N. G. JONES

Honorary Treasurer
Mr CHRISTOPHER WRIGHT (Edwin Coe, 2 Stone Buildings, Lincoln's Inn)

Secretary
Mr VICTOR TUNKEL (School of Law, Queen Mary, Mile End Road, London E1 4NS)

Trustees
Professor M. T. CLANCHY, F.B.A.   Mr P. W. E. TAYLOR, Q.C.
Mr CHRISTOPHER WRIGHT

Honorary Secretaries and Treasurers Overseas
Australia: Mr ALADIN RAHEMTULA, Supreme Court Library, Brisbane, Queensland 4000
Canada: Professor MARGARET MCGLYNN, University of Western Ontario, London N6A 5C2
New Zealand: Mr FRANCIS DAWSON, Dawson Harford & Partners, 48 Courthouse Lane, Auckland
United States: Professor CHARLES DONAHUE JR (Treasurer),
Mr DAVID WARRINGTON (Secretary)
Harvard Law School, Cambridge MA 02138

Sir Soulden Lawrence in 1808

In this portrait by John Hoppner RA, Lawrence is wearing the violet summer robes, with scarlet casting hood and black scarf, which he would have worn as a trial judge at *nisi prius*.

By kind permission of the Anne Howard Gallery, New York City, NY. Photograph by David Aronstein.

CASE NOTES OF
SIR SOULDEN LAWRENCE

1787–1800

EDITED FOR
THE SELDEN SOCIETY
BY

JAMES OLDHAM

St Thomas More Professor of Law and Legal History
Georgetown Law Center, Washington D.C.

LONDON
SELDEN SOCIETY
2013

© Selden Society 2013

ISBN 978 0 85423 212 3

Typeset by Anne Joshua & Associates, Oxford
Printed in Great Britain by
Berforts Information Press, Eynsham, Oxford

CONTENTS

PREFACE vii

ABBREVIATIONS xi

INTRODUCTION xiii
   I. Manuscript Case-Notes in Practice xiv
      The Gaps xv
      (a) The Court of Exchequer xvi
      (b) The Court of Common Pleas xvii
      (c) The Court of King's Bench xix
      Selectivity xxi
      Sources of Case Reports in the Nominate Reports xxi
      Manuscript Case-Notes in the Court Room xxiii
      (a) Favoured Manuscript Sources xxiii
          (i) Judges' Notes xxiii
          (ii) Notes Taken or Collected by Practitioners and Others xxvii
          (iii) Anonymous Manuscript Notes of Previously
              Unreported Cases xxxii
          (iv) Manuscript Case-Notes used to Corroborate,
              Elaborate, or Contradict Printed Reports . . . xxxiv
      (b) Bad Law xxxvii
      Summary xxxviii
  II. Lawrence's Notes of Cases xxxix
      The Court of Common Pleas xxxix
      (a) *Hurry* v. *Watson* xl
          (i) Excessive Damages xl
          (ii) Juror Affidavits xliii
          (iii) The Outcome xlv
      The Judicial Years on the King's Bench xlvi
      (a) Counsel and the Pace of Trials xlvi
      (b) The Court of King's Bench under Lord Kenyon . . . xlix
          (i) Kenyon the Outspoken xlix
          (ii) Frustration with the Lawyers liii
      (c) Lawrence's Case-Notes and Espinasse's Reports . . . lviii
  III. Conclusion lx

MANUSCRIPTS OF SIR SOULDEN LAWRENCE

MIDDLE TEMPLE LIBRARY, MS. 49

Part I: Cases in the Common Pleas, 27, 34 Geo. III, Lawrence Volume 5 1

Part II: Cases in the King's Bench, 34–36 Geo. III, Lawrence Volume 5   45

Cases in the King's Bench, 36–40 Geo. III, Lawrence Volume 6   109

LINCOLN'S INN LIBRARY, DAMPIER MANUSCRIPTS

Part III: Selected Paper Books, The Court of King's Bench, 36–40 Geo. III 209
   Introduction 211
   Marshall v. *Rutton* 216
   Morton v. *Lamb* 233
   Brooke v. *Crowther* 243
   Roe v. *Langford* 248
   Bischoff v. *Agar* 264
   Collet v. *Keith* 273
   Pollard v. *Bell* 290

APPENDIX 313

BIBLIOGRAPHY 385

TABLE OF STATUTES 389

TABLE OF CASES 391

INDEX OF PERSONS AND PLACES 411

INDEX OF SUBJECTS 426

PREFACE

This book is the product of many summer visits to the libraries of Lincoln's Inn and the Middle Temple. Among the Middle Temple Library's varied manuscript holdings are notebooks kept by barristers and judges from the late eighteenth and early nineteenth centuries, including Henry Dampier, Vicary Gibbs, Henry Gould, and Soulden Lawrence. At Lincoln's Inn Library, the Dampier Manuscripts comprise almost two thousand Paper Books used and annotated by four common law judges from the same period—chronologically, William Ashhurst, Francis Buller, Soulden Lawrence, and Henry Dampier. The Dampier Manuscripts are not available outside the confines of the Lincoln's Inn Library. Until recently, the manuscript holdings of the Middle Temple Library were likewise inaccessible externally, but in late 2008 the Middle Temple manuscripts were published in microform as Stage VIII of the English Legal Manuscripts Project edited by Sir John Baker (see note 1 to the introduction, below). As is explained more fully in the introduction to this work, the cases transcribed for the present volume were taken from two of Mr Justice Lawrence's case notebooks at the Middle Temple, together with seven representative Paper Books from the Dampier Manuscripts at Lincoln's Inn.

A brief summary of Soulden Lawrence's education and professional career, as given in the *Oxford Dictionary of National Biography*, is as follows:

> He was educated at St Paul's School and at St John's College, Cambridge, where he graduated BA in 1771 as seventh wrangler, and proceeded MA and was elected fellow in 1774. At Cambridge he was a contemporary of Edward Law, afterwards Lord Ellenborough, Vicary Gibbs, who would later take Lawrence's place on the court of common pleas upon Lawrence's resignation, and Simon Le Blanc, who would later join Lawrence on the court of king's bench. He was called to the bar at the Inner Temple in June 1784, and quickly established himself as a leader on the western circuit. He was raised to the degree of serjeant-at-law on 9 February 1787. He was described by Lord Campbell as 'one of the best lawyers that have appeared at Westminster Hall in my time'. In March 1794 Lawrence was knighted and succeeded Sir Henry Gould as a puisne justice of common pleas. Three months later, on the resignation of Sir Francis Buller, he transferred to king's bench, where he served for fourteen years. Reportedly because of a disagreement with Lord Ellenborough he returned in March 1808 to common pleas, where he remained until Easter term 1812 when poor health brought on his retirement.

Editorial Conventions

Most of the manuscript notes transcribed for this volume were taken down in haste by Mr Justice Lawrence while arguments of counsel and opinions of brother judges were being delivered. As a result, there are numerous inconsistencies of punctuation, paragraph breaks, and sentence structure. Also, as was true generally of handwritten prose in late eighteenth-century England, the choice of words to capitalize was far from uniform, seeming at times almost random. Adjustments have been made as necessary to render the case notes intelligible, but not at the cost of substantive content. In the main, modern British practice for spelling, punctuation, and capitalisation has been adopted.

Lawrence often underscored words or phrases in his margin headnotes and in the formal pleadings in his copy of the Paper Book for a given case. These spontaneous underscorings have not been retained. Otherwise, however, the Paper Books in Part III are reproduced verbatim. Quotations from printed sources are likewise reproduced verbatim, with occasional exceptions for case names. Since the names of the litigating parties were often spelled phonetically, variations were frequent. Thus, for example, the name of a case as given in *The Times* might be spelled differently when the same case later appeared in the standard printed reports. In this volume, the plaintiff in all Crown cases has, for the sake of consistency, been shown as 'R.', but otherwise case names for all cases that appeared in the standard printed reports are spelled as they appeared in print. Most of the notes transcribed in this volume, however, are of unreported cases, and case names as given in the manuscripts are adopted.

Throughout Parts I and II, italicized page numbers in brackets are interspersed. These reproduce the pagination in the two Lawrence notebooks (volumes 5 and 6) containing the cases that have been transcribed.

Acknowledgements

This book would not have been possible without the generous access extended to me to the manuscript collections held by the Middle Temple Library and Lincoln's Inn Library. At the Middle Temple, I acknowledge with gratitude the support of the late Mrs Janet Edgell, Librarian and Keeper of the Records, and of her successor, Ms Vanessa Hayward, Keeper of the Library. Extremely helpful also were Senior Librarians Stuart Adams and Renae Satterley. At Lincoln's Inn, Librarian Guy Holborn, Deputy Librarian Catherine McArdle, and their staff provided me with steady encouragement and assistance as I made my way through the Dampier Manuscripts across the years. I am indebted to the Library Committee of the Middle Temple and to the Masters of the Bench of Lincoln's Inn for permission to publish transcriptions of the selected case notes and Paper Books presented in this book. I should also state that an abridged version of Part I of the Introduction ('Manuscript Case Notes in Practice') was first given as a lecture at the Nineteenth British Legal History Conference at the University of Exeter in July 2009 and has since appeared in the conference volume published by Cambridge University Press (J. Oldham, 'The Indispensability of Manuscript Case Notes to Eighteenth-Century Barristers and Judges', in A. Musson and C. Stebbings eds., *Making Legal History* (2012), 30–52).

My research in London was facilitated by regular research grants from Georgetown University Law Center. I am grateful to Deans Judith Areen, Alex

PREFACE

Aleinikoff, and William Treanor for their steadfast support. I had excellent help from late Special Collections Librarian Laura Bedard, Historical Collections Specialist Erin Kidwell, Research Fellow Su Jin Kim, and from research assistants Amanda Bowen, Scott Schweitzer, Natalie DeBoer, and Laura Brookover. Indispensable in the transcription process was Faculty Assistant Mary Ann De Rosa. I am grateful also to Barbara Wilcie Kern for preparing the meticulous indexes that will give readers easy access to this book. I thank David Aronstein for providing the photograph of the Hoppner painting of Sir Soulden Lawrence that is displayed as the frontispiece to this volume. Finally, I am indebted to the Literary Director of the Selden Society, Dr Neil Jones, and to his predecessor, Sir John Baker, for the generous attention they gave to the concept and contents of this volume. In addition to correcting countless errors, both Dr Jones and Professor Baker offered invaluable assistance in sorting out barely decipherable Latin passages, solving puzzles of words and phrases that could be understood only in historical context, and interpreting cryptic citations to cases and sources.

The Stenton Fund of the British Academy made a generous subvention towards this volume.

J.O.

ABBREVIATIONS

The following abbreviations are used throughout. Standard law reports cited in this work are abbreviated as in the *English Reports* and therefore are not included in this list.

[. . .]	Indecipherable word or words in the text
APB	Ashhurst Paper Books, Dampier MSS., Lincoln's Inn Library, London
BPB	Buller Paper Books, Dampier MSS., Lincoln's Inn Library, London
B.R.	*Banco Regis*: 'in the King's Bench'
C.P.	Common Pleas
ca. sa.	*capias ad satisfaciendum*: 'that you take to satisfy'; a post-judgment writ commanding the sheriff to imprison the defendant until the judgment is satisfied
cur. adv. vult	*curia advisari vult*: 'the court will advise'; signals a court's decision to delay judgment pending further consideration
Dom. Proc.	*Domus Procerum*: House of Lords
dub.	*dubitante*: 'doubting'; this term was usually placed in a law report next to a judge's name, indicating that the judge doubted a legal point but was unwilling to state that it was wrong
et al.	*et alia*: 'and others'
ex dim.	*ex dimissione*: 'upon the demise'; a phrase forming a part of the title of the old action of ejectment
fi. fa.	*fieri facias*: 'that you cause to be done'; a writ of execution that directs a marshal or sheriff to seize and sell a defendant's property to satisfy a money judgment
Holdsworth, *HEL*	Holdsworth, *History of English Law*, 17 vols. (London, 1903–72), reprint, 16 vols. (London, 1966)
K.B.	King's Bench
LPB	Lawrence Paper Books, Dampier MSS., Lincoln's Inn Library, London
M.H.	margin headnote
M.N.	margin note
MS.	manuscript
N.B.	*nota bene*: 'note well'
Nil cap.	*nihil capiat per breve*: 'let him take nothing by his writ'; a judgment against the plaintiff in an action at bar or in abatement

nolle pros.	*nolle prosequi*: 'not to wish to prosecute'; to abandon a suit or have it dismissed
non cul.	*non culpabilis*: 'not guilty'
ODNB	*Oxford Dictionary of National Biography*, H. C. G. Matthew and B. Harrison eds., 61 vols. (Oxford, 2004)
OED	*Oxford English Dictionary*
Oldham, *MMSS*	Oldham, *The Mansfield Manuscripts and the Growth of English Law in the Eighteenth Century*, 2 vols. (Chapel Hill, 1992)
q.i.	*quare impedit*: 'why he hinders'; a writ or action to enforce a patron's right to present a person to fill a vacant benefice (ecclesiastical law)
qui tam	*qui tam pro domino rege quam pro se ipso in hac parte sequitur*: 'who as well for the king as for himself sues in this behalf'; an action brought under a statute that allows a private person to sue for a penalty, part of which the government or some specified public institution will receive
Scacc.	*Curia Scaccarium*, or Court of Exchequer, named after the *Scaccarium*, the chequered cloth covering the table, with counters, used originally to keep track of the King's accounts
sci. fa.	*scire facias*: 'you are to make known'; a writ requiring the person against whom it is issued to appear and show cause why some matter of record should not be annulled or vacated, or why a dormant judgment against that person should not be revived
ss. (or *sc.* or *scil.*)	*scilicet*: 'that you may know'; namely, to wit
S.T.	State Trials
ult. concilium	*ulterius concilium*: 'further argument'
ut semb.	*ut semble*: 'as it seems'
viz.	*videlicet*: 'namely'
&c.	Et cetera

INTRODUCTION

During the eighteenth century in England, keeping abreast of decisions by the common law courts was no easy task. Printed reports of cases appeared only sporadically, usually whenever a barrister or court officer was moved to find a publisher to print and market the notes of cases he had taken or collected. A survey is given below of the gaps and delays in the printed reports of the activities of the three common law courts, but it is useful at the outset to state the conclusion that the survey yields: it was absolutely essential for active barristers and judges to keep, collect, or have access to manuscript notes of decided cases.

Many collections of manuscript case notes survive, as is abundantly demonstrated by the English Legal Manuscripts Project edited by Sir John Baker.[1] The substantial collection of case notes from the late eighteenth and early nineteenth centuries held by the Middle Temple Library, London, includes twelve notebooks kept by Sir Soulden Lawrence (1751–1814).[2] Lawrence was a well-respected barrister who became a puisne justice of the Court of Common Pleas in March 1794, transferring three months later to the Court of King's Bench, where he served for fourteen years. Lord Campbell described Lawrence as 'a most learned judge' who exuded 'great acuteness and determination'.[3]

Two parts only of Lawrence's extensive case notes are presented in Parts I and II of this volume. The first part contains Common Pleas cases from 1787 (a year for which no nominate reports of Common Pleas cases were ever published[4]), one case decided in the House of Lords, one case from the

[1] The English Legal Manuscripts Project (ELMP) is an extensive collection on microfiche of legal history manuscripts held by selected repositories in England, Wales, and the United States. Published by Inter Documentation Company, Zug, Switzerland, in 1975 and 1978, the project initially contained manuscripts from the Harvard Law School Library, the Bodleian Library, Lincoln's Inn, and Gray's Inn. It was accompanied by catalogue descriptions by Professor J. H. Baker. Addenda were published subsequently (also accompanied by catalogue descriptions by Professor Baker) containing additional manuscripts from the Harvard Law School Library, the Cambridge University Library and the Middle Temple Library.

[2] Ten of the twelve notebooks are included in the Middle Temple manuscripts that comprise the most recent addendum (Stage VIII) to the ELMP. Five of the ten, Library MSS. 20–24, contain crown cases; the other five, collectively designated as Library MS. 49, contain cases on the plea side, predominantly from the King's Bench. The case notes transcribed in the present volume are from two of the plea side notebooks, labelled by Lawrence as volume 5, Cases in King's Bench 24–28 Geo. 3, 35–36 Geo. 3, and volume 6, Cases in King's Bench, 17–40 Geo. 3. The two remaining Lawrence notebooks at Middle Temple Library are a two-volume set designated as Library MS. 48, labelled on the spines as volume I, Cases in the King's Bench & Chancery 7 & 8 Geo. 2, 23 & 24 Geo. 2, 20–22 Geo. 2, and volume II, Notes of Cases 13–16 Geo. 2. Due to fragile bindings, this two-volume set was not photographed and is not included in Stage VIII of the ELMP.

[3] *ODNB*, quoting from, respectively, *Life of John, Lord Campbell, lord high chancellor of Great Britain*, M. S. Hardcastle ed., 2 vols. (1881), i. 250, and John, Lord Campbell, *Lives of the Chief Justices of England*, 3 vols. (1857), iii. 58.

[4] See below, p. xvii.

xiii

Court of Chancery, and five cases from Lawrence's three months in 1794 as a Common Pleas judge. The second part, considerably larger, comprises King's Bench case notes from Trinity 1794 to Michaelmas 1799, introduced by Lawrence in his notebook by the following:

> Memorandum: The only notes entered in this book are either of matters which are not found in Messr. Durnford and East's Reports, or which did not come on upon special argument, when Paper Books were delivered to the judges. The notes of those cases will be found on the back of the Paper Books themselves.[5]

Durnford and East's reports covered cases in the Court of King's Bench from 1785 to 1800. Sir William Holdsworth quotes from the preface to volume one of Durnford and East that 'the primary object of their reports was "to remedy the inconveniences felt by every part of the profession of waiting two or three years, till some gentleman of experience and ability has collected matter sufficient to form a complete volume"'.[6] Durnford and East's reports were of very high quality,[7] but as Lawrence's memorandum indicates, his notes did not report everything that took place. Also, they did not always report all phases of a case to its conclusion; thus, some of the cases in Lawrence's notes ultimately appeared in *Term Reports* subsequent to the intermediate phases captured by Lawrence. Further, ten cases in the Lawrence notes that are transcribed below appeared in Isaac Espinasse's *Reports of Cases Argued and Ruled at* Nisi Prius, and several others found their way into print, as noted in the transcriptions that follow.

In Part III of this volume, seven representative Paper Books are reproduced from the collection of nearly nine hundred Lawrence Paper Books held by Lincoln's Inn Library. The issues addressed in the cases include limitations on the property rights of married women, principles governing executory bilateral contracts, the permissible scope of a covenant not to compete, interpretation of a testamentary disposition of property by an illiterate testator, and questions of international trade during wartime.

I. MANUSCRIPT CASE NOTES IN PRACTICE

Little thought is given by modern legal historians to the dates of publication of the printed reports, yet for practitioners in the eighteenth century this was a matter of real importance. Consider the four-volume set of reports by Sylvester

---

[5] See below, p. 47. Lawrence's Paper Books survive as part of the Dampier Manuscripts at Lincoln's Inn Library, London. See E. Heward, 'Dampier Manuscripts at Lincoln's Inn', *Journal of Legal History* 9 (1988), p. 357. See also p. 211, below.

[6] Holdsworth, *HEL*, xii. 116.

[7] According to Wallace, 'None of the modern Reports exceed these for the care and accuracy of finish, including great propriety of style, which they everywhere maintain. They are equally distinguished by the terseness and comprehensive accuracy with which the point adjudged is given in the reporters' syllabus, and by the care with which the references to cases cited have been verified before the work went through the press.' J. W. Wallace, *The Reporters Arranged and Characterized with Incidental Remarks*, 4th ed. (1882), pp. 529–530, n. 2.

INTRODUCTION

Douglas, covering cases in the Court of King's Bench from Michaelmas Term 1778 to Trinity Term 1785. The first edition of *Douglas's Reports* was two volumes only, published in 1782, covering decisions up to Trinity Term 1781. John Wallace in his mid-nineteenth-century book, *The Reporters*, observed: 'It is generally known, I presume, that the third and fourth volumes of Douglas's Reports were published long after the first two.'[8] It was not until 1831, almost a half-century after the fact, that volumes three and four of *Douglas's Reports* appeared, published posthumously under the editorship of Henry Roscoe.[9]

Despite the long lapse until the appearance of Douglas's volumes three and four, the Court of King's Bench was the best-reported of the three common law courts in the eighteenth century. The quality of the eighteenth-century King's Bench reports was generally high, especially after Sir James Burrow set the standard.[10] Yet in any given eighteenth-century year, as elaborated below, much activity in the central common law courts, the King's Bench included, was not reflected in a printed record.

Sir William Holdsworth gives a thorough review, both in prose and in tabular display, of the eighteenth-century printed reports, and there is no need to traverse the same ground.[11] Holdsworth does not, however, say much about the *absence* of printed reports, or the extent to which the practising Bar, of necessity, had to rely on manuscript notes of decided cases. There were significant eighteenth-century gaps in the printed reports of the decisions of the three central common law courts. Further, nearly all of the reporters were selective, so that even for the years covered by the printed reports, much remained unreported. It was therefore extremely common for both bench and Bar to rely in arguments and opinions on manuscript reports of cases.

THE GAPS

In evaluating the use of manuscript case notes in practice, the starting point is to assess what would have been available in print while a case was being litigated. Assuming adequate funds to purchase or opportunity to borrow, what printed

---

[8] Ibid., p. 529, n. 1.

[9] The second edition of the first two volumes was issued in 1786 in folio, and according to the preface, 'the new cases, notes, and references, have been printed in a detached pamphlet, on paper of the same size as with the first edition'. The third edition was but a reprint, in octavo, of the second, issued in 1791. The fourth edition of the first two volumes was printed in 1813 with additions by the editor, William Frere, serjeant-at-law. When the first edition of volumes 3 and 4 appeared in 1831, editor Henry Roscoe explained in his preface that he had completed the last two volumes that had been left unfinished by both Douglas and Serjeant Frere. See pp. xxi–xxii, below, for a fuller explanation.

[10] See generally Wallace, *The Reporters*, pp. 446–452. Burrow at the end of his fourth volume, expressed the wish that a person of ability might succeed him, observing: 'It would be great pity to leave the decisions of a court so filled, to the ignorant, erroneous and false reports of newspapers, monthly historians, and collectors for book sellers; or, (what is perhaps still worse,) to the posthumous publication of defective and imperfect notes of gentlemen who cursorily took them, merely for their own use and as helps to their own memories, without any thoughts of making them public.' 4 Burr. 2584.

[11] See generally Holdsworth, *HEL*, xii. 102–162.

reports of decisions by the common law courts would have been available to an eighteenth-century barrister or sitting judge in any given year?[12]

(a) The Court of Exchequer

The least active of the three common law courts in England in the eighteenth century, the Court of Exchequer, was also the least reported. Prior to 1730, the number of eighteenth-century Exchequer cases in the nominate reports was a grand total of one, in the first edition of *Salkeld's Reports*.[13] Three more cases appeared in volumes nine and ten of *Modern Reports* published in 1730, and six more were published by Fitzgibbon in 1732.

Collectively, then, only ten eighteenth-century Exchequer cases were reported in print during the first third of the century, and some of the ten may not have counted for much. James Burrow, for example, noted in his copy of Fitzgibbon that when Fitzgibbon's book was published, 'it was treated with the utmost contempt, both by the Bench and Bar'.[14]

During the middle decades of the eighteenth century, the quantity of Exchequer case reporting increased although the quality of the reports was mixed.[15] Not until 1770, however, was any Exchequer case decided beyond the year 1740 printed.[16] Thus for three mid-century decades, Exchequer practitioners had to attend court or resort to word-of-mouth or manuscript notes in order to stay abreast of the activity of the court. The situation improved significantly in 1776, when retired Chief Baron Parker published his own notes of cases running from 1743 to 1767.[17] Another dry spell followed, with only nine new Exchequer cases appearing until *Anstruther's Reports* were published in 1796.[18] Anstruther, in his preface, declared that, 'while the modern decisions of the other Courts in *Westminster-Hall* have been regularly published, no one has taken notes in that of the Exchequer for a similar purpose; and ... since the publication of *Bunbury's Reports*, during the space of more than fifty years, the determinations of that Court have remained wholly unknown to the Profession

---

[12] In order to stay within a manageable compass, this survey is limited to the three common law courts, thus excluding the status of reporting of cases in the Court of Chancery and the House of Lords.

[13] *Archbishop of York* v. *Duke of Newcastle* (1705) 2 Salk. 656.

[14] See Wallace, *The Reporters*, pp. 427–428, quoting from the *Dublin University Magazine* for December 1847. Burrow went on to explain that Fitzgibbon was an Irish law student who published his notes almost immediately after they were taken to get money for rent or other expenses. Burrow said that Lord Raymond, Chief Justice of the King's Bench, called Fitzgibbon's performance 'a libel upon the Bar and the Bench, and said that it had made the Judges, and particularly himself, to talk nonsense by wholesale'. Burrow himself, however, examined Fitzgibbon's reports of King's Bench cases and concluded that they were, on the whole, accurate.

[15] Exchequer cases appeared in reports by Gilbert (1734), vol. 11 Modern (1737), Barnardiston (1742), Lord Raymond (1743), Comyns (1744), Fortescue (1748), Bunbury (1755), and Strange (1755).

[16] *Wilson's Reports*, published in 1770, contain four Exchequer cases, one each from the years 1747, 1749, 1751 and 1752.

[17] Parker also included an Appendix with cases from 1678 to 1718. See p. xxi, below.

[18] Two Exchequer cases appear in *William Blackstone's Reports*, published in 1780, and seven are in *Ambler's Reports* (1790).

at large'.[19] This was an exaggeration, yet it was not far off the mark. Looking back over the entire eighteenth century, no printed Exchequer reports existed for thirty-seven of the one hundred years.

(b) The Court of Common Pleas

Although less pronounced than in the Court of Exchequer, the gaps in reported Common Pleas cases during the eighteenth century were nevertheless substantial.[20] In 1704, Lutwyche published reports that included sixty Common Pleas cases from the years 1700 to 1703, but as is shown in Table I, the number of printed Common Pleas cases over the period from 1705 to 1726 averaged just over eleven per year.

Table I: Common Pleas Decisions in Printed Reports, 1705–26

Year of Decisions	No. of Reports	Year of Decisions	No. of Reports
1705	4	1717	21
1706	7	1718	17
1707	3	1719	17
1708	10	1720	15
1709	15	1721	10
1710	2	1722	10
1711	7	1723	11
1712	14	1724	10
1713	8	1725	13
1714	2	1726	21
1715	13		
1716	7	Total	237

Also, as with *Douglas's Reports* of King's Bench cases, there were gaps between the dates of the cases printed in some of the reports and the years of publication (see Table II). Most pronounced was the delayed publication of notes taken by Common Pleas Chief Justice John Willes of cases over which he presided, between 1737 and 1758, said to be 'the most authoritative [reports] of George II's reign'.[21] They were not available in print until 1799, published posthumously under the careful editorship of Charles Durnford.

During the years covered by Table I, 1705–26, a total of ten of the 237 cases that were eventually reported came into print, and only one more emerged until *Fitzgibbon's Reports* appeared in 1732. Eleven cases in twenty-seven years hardly provided a foundation for a student or counsel to learn the practices and doctrines announced and followed in one of England's principal courts. For the practising barrister or law student during most of the first half of the

---

[19] *Anstruther's Reports*, preface, at iii. Why Anstruther ignored *Parker's Reports* is unclear.

[20] For an expanded treatment of law reporting of Common Pleas cases in the eighteenth century, see J. Oldham, 'Underreported and Underrated: The Court of Common Pleas in the Eighteenth Century', H. Hartog, W. E. Nelson, and B. W. Kern eds., *Law as Culture and Culture as Law* (2000), 119–146.

[21] A. W. B. Simpson ed., *Biographical Dictionary of the Common Law* (1984), p. 539.

Table II: Eighteenth-Century Common Pleas Cases Reported During the Eighteenth Century[22]

Year Printed	Reporter	No. of Cases	Years in Which Decided
1704	Lutwyche	60	1700–03
1713	VI Modern	3	1703
1716	VII Modern (Farresley)	1	1702
1717	Salkeld	6	1702–03, 1708–09
1730	VII Modern	1	1723
1732	Fitzgibbon	16	1729–32
1736	X Modern	1	1712
1737	XI Modern	4	1707–08
1739	XII Modern	13	1701
1740	W. Kelynge	3	1731–33
1741	Barnes	738	1732–41
1742	Barnardiston	7	1729
	Cooke	422	1706–39
	Freeman	1	1702
1743	Practical Register of Common Pleas	615	1704–41
	Lord Raymond	4	1702–04
1744	Comyns	120	1700–37
1747	Cooke, 2nd ed.	1	1747
1748	Fortescue	11	1725–35
1754	Barnes, supp.	455	1742–54
1755	Strange	20	1716–38
1756	Barnes, supp.	48	1755–56
1770	Wilson	242	1750–70
1772	Barnes, supp.	57	1757–69
1775	Wilson, new ed.	70	1774–74
1776	Lofft	15	1763, 1773–74
1780	W. Blackstone	344	1770–79
1790	Ambler	2	1764
1793	H. Blackstone	163	1788–91
1794	XI Modern (Dublin)	1	1712
1795	Espinasse	9	1792–94
1796	H. Blackstone, new ed. VII	112	1792–96
	Modern (Leach)	43	1738–44
1799	Willes	130	1737–58

[22] Some reporters were specialised. Barnes, *Notes of Cases in Points of Practise*, was published in 1754 and was reprinted with supplements several times. Henry Barnes was one of the Secondaries of the Court of Common Pleas, and despite a title page describing the volume as one of cases decided in the Common Pleas, many King's Bench cases were included. The reports, although generally accurate, did not deal with substantive law and were not considered to have much authority. See Wallace, *The Reporters*, pp. 432–433. The high-volume case count for Barnes's reports thus requires discounting. Cooke was also practice-oriented, though he did include some substantive points. *The Practical Register of the Common Pleas* is a scarce book not included in the *English Reports* reprints; it, too, is focused on practice, but it is closer to Cooke than to Barnes.

eighteenth century, and to a substantial degree in the second half, it was simply not possible to know what was happening in the Court of Common Pleas from published reports.

One gap was never filled. The years 1780 to 1787 were, and remain, a blank; no nominate reports of Common Pleas decisions from those years were ever published.

(c) *The Court of King's Bench*

The Court of King's Bench was the dominant common law court in England in the eighteenth century, increasingly so during the years 1756 to 1788 when Lord Mansfield was chief justice. Yet even for the King's Bench, the printed reports were incomplete and erratic.

No King's Bench cases appeared in the nominate reports during the first dozen years of the eighteenth century. A few decisions from 1702 to 1704 were published in 1713 and 1716 in the first editions of volumes six and seven of *Modern Reports*, but the first substantial infusion of King's Bench cases was in 1717 when the first edition of *Salkeld's Reports* was published. Apart from new editions of *Modern Reports*, volume 6, and *Salkeld* (1719 and 1721, respectively), and a few cases from 1700 to 1701 in *Carthew's Reports* (1728), little else appeared until the 1730s and 1740s, when a fairly steady stream of King's Bench cases emerged in new nominate reports and new editions of existing reports.

Table III: Reports, 1730s and 1740s, Containing Eighteenth-Century King's Bench Cases[23]

Year	Reporter	New Editions	Years Covered
1730	Modern VII		1723–27
1731		Salkeld	1689–1712
1732	Fitzgibbon		1728–32
1733	Modern X		1709–25
1737–38	Modern XI		1702–10
1738	Modern XII		1690–1702
1738	Cases t. Holt		1688–1711
1741		Modern X	1710–18
1742	Freeman		1670–1704
1742–43		Salkeld	1689–1712
1743	Lord Raymond		1694–1732
1743		Carthew	1689–1701
1744	Comyns		1695–1741
1744	Barnardiston		1726–35
1748	Fortescue		1694–1738

[23] For details, see Holdsworth, *HEL*, xii. 118–119; Wallace, *The Reporters*, at pp. 347–444.

In mid-century, however, a fifteen-year gap occurred. No King's Bench decisions from 1750 to 1765 other than practice cases in *Barnes's Reports* were published until 1766. Other reports were published during the 1750s and 1760s, but, as is shown in Table IV, all of them except for *Barnes's Reports* and *Barnes's Supplement* contained cases decided prior to 1750.

Table IV: King's Bench Reports Published 1750–66 (before Burrow)

Year	New Reporters	New Editions	Years Covered
1750–54	Sessions Cases		1710–48
1754	Andrews		1738–39
1754	Barnes		1732–54
1755	Strange		1716–49
1756		Barnes Supplement	1754–56
1760		Sessions Cases	1710–46
1760	Gilbert		1713–15
1765		Raymond	1694–1732
1766	Cunningham		1734–36

Nothing from the last five years of the chief justiceship of William Lee (1749–54), or from the two years when Chief Justice Dudley Ryder was in office (1754–56), arrived in print until *Sayer's Reports* were published in 1775.

Further, the first ten years of Lord Mansfield's influential tenure passed without a printed report, even though the legal community was aware that James Burrow, a well-liked court officer (master of the Crown Office) was assiduously taking notes.[24] Burrow's first edition (1766) covered King's Bench decisions from Michaelmas 1756 to Trinity 1761, after which another unpublished ten years passed until Burrow's third volume was printed in 1771 (covering Michaelmas 1761 to Hilary 1770).

This recitation could continue, but the fundamental point has been made. During most of the eighteenth century, the production of printed reports of cases being decided by the King's Bench was irregular, with intermittent gaps, some lasting ten to fifteen years. When Durnford and East began reporting King's Bench cases each term in 1785, however, barristers' habits relaxed. According to a report in *The Times* in August 1789, barrister Edward Bearcroft remarked that 'he had long ago left off taking notes'—'He now rested on the Termly [*sic*] Reports which made business very pleasant.'[25]

---

[24] Burrow did not always have publication in mind. As he peevishly stated in the preface to his first edition, he became 'subject to continual interruption and even persecution, by incessant applications for searches into my notes', and 'this inconvenience grew from bad to worse, till it became quite unsupportable; and from *thence* arises the present publication'.

[25] *The Times*, 24 August 1789, p. 3.

SELECTIVITY

Even the most faithful eighteenth-century note-taker would not report every case argued in every sitting during each term for the court being covered. Family and personal affairs, professional demands, indisposition, and any number of additional interruptions inevitably caused occasional absences. And even while in attendance, some cases or actions would not seem noteworthy.[26] Omissions by the reporters are easily demonstrated by comparing the printed reports to surviving manuscript case notes from the same courts and time periods. The English Legal Manuscripts Project makes available on microfiche hundreds of collections of manuscript case notes. They vary in quality, and the authorship is not always known. Of special interest are notes that are identified as having been taken by sitting judges such as Sir Soulden Lawrence, and notes by prominent barristers, some of whom later received judicial appointments. Certain collections of manuscript case notes gained a reputation of high quality and were copied, recopied, and passed down from one generation to the next.

SOURCES OF CASE REPORTS IN THE NOMINATE REPORTS

Some reporters were the sole authors of their reports of cases—as, for example, James Burrow, Henry Cowper, Capel Lofft, William Blackstone. Yet many reporters incorporated case reports taken by other identified note-takers,[27] or obtained case notes from unnamed 'outside' sources that were simply declared to be trustworthy. Chief Baron Parker, for example, included in his reports an appendix containing cases from the years 1678 to 1718. Parker supplied no information about the source of these reports except to say that they had been 'carefully transcribed from authentic manuscripts'.[28]

Some reporters or editors who included 'outside' case reports were more forthcoming. Henry Roscoe in publishing volumes three and four of *Douglas's Reports* in 1831 wrote in his preface that the statements of the cases in volume four, plus many of the arguments and judgments, had been prepared (though left unfinished) by William Frere, editor of the fourth edition of Douglas's volumes one and two, and that Frere had used Douglas's manuscripts. The

---

[26] In concluding the fourth volume of his reports, Burrow described the court activity that he chose *not* to report as follows:

> My Reports give but a very faint idea of the extent of the whole business which comes before the Court. I only report what I think may be of use, as a determination or illustration of some matter of law. I take no notice of the numerous questions of fact which are heard upon affidavits; (the most tedious and irksome part of the whole business). I take no notice of a variety of contestations, which, after having been fully discussed, are decided without difficulty or doubt. I take no notice of many cases which turn upon a construction so peculiar and particular as not to be likely to form a precedent for any other case.

4 Burr. 2583.

[27] See, e.g., the discussion of Lord Raymond's reports at Wallace, *The Reporters*, pp. 401–403.

[28] Preface to *Parker's Reports*, at iii. See also J. H. Baker, *English Legal Manuscripts in the United States of America* (1990), ii. 276–284.

cases in volume three from Michaelmas 1781 to Michaelmas 1783, 'were, however, left almost untouched' by Douglas and by Serjeant Frere. Roscoe then explained that,

> In this state the MSS. were put into the hands of the writer of this Preface, accompanied by the contemporary note books of Mr. Justice Le Blanc, Mr. Justice Lawrence, and of Mr. George Wilson, through the liberality and kindness of H. P. Standly, Esq., and Thomas Le Blanc, Esq., the present Master of the Court of King's Bench. In addition to these highly valuable sources of information, he was furnished with two small volumes containing notes taken by Mr. Justice Buller and by Lord Glenbervie [Douglas] himself, and also with some of the note-books of Sir Thomas Davenport and of Mr. Bowyer.

Roscoe then stated that, 'Several volumes of notes by an unknown hand, apparently taken with care and accuracy, were also added', and 'From these copious materials the writer has compiled nearly the whole of the third volume, and has supplied the arguments and judgments in the fourth volume not inserted by Mr Serjeant Frere.'[29] The cobbled-together third volume contains a number of important cases, including *Gregson* v. *Gilbert* (the case of the slave ship *Zong*),[30] two reports of the seminal decision on the use of expert testimony, *Folkes* v. *Chad*,[31] two cases in which Lord Mansfield dealt with the persistent issue of when married women could be sued by their creditors,[32] two cases showing the struggle about whether the applicability of a mercantile custom was a question of law or fact,[33] a major prize case,[34] and a dozen or more cases addressing a variety of insurance questions.[35]

Near the end of a long preface to the fifth edition of *Modern Reports* (1796) the editor, Thomas Leach, summarized that he had added 381 cases, of which 137 had never before been printed. About the latter, Leach informed his readers that, 'The greater number of them appear to possess an extraordinary degree of merit; the statement of the facts, the arguments of Counsel, and the judgments of Court being extremely full, and bearing every intrinsic mark of correctness and authenticity.'[36]

In 1795, barrister Michael Nolan issued the third edition of *Strange's Reports*, and he expressed the hope that, 'In the notes which have swelled these volumes so much beyond the size of the former editions the reader will find some which add a value to the book it could not have otherwise possessed.' He said that he was not at liberty 'to declare the quarter from whence they

---

[29] Preface to volume 3, *Douglas's Reports*, at iv. Roscoe said that he relied most heavily on the notes by George Wilson and by Mr Justice Le Blanc.
[30] (1783) 3 Doug. 232.
[31] (1782) 3 Doug. 157; (1783) 3 Doug. 340.
[32] *Ringsted* v. *Lady Lanesborough* (1783) 3 Doug. 197; *Barwell* v. *Brooks* (1784) 3 Doug. 371.
[33] *Medcalf* v. *Hall* (1783) 3 Doug. 113; *Appleton* v. *Sweetapple* (1783) 3 Doug. 137.
[34] *Anthon* v. *Fisher* (1782) 3 Doug. 166.
[35] Among them *Shirley* v. *Wilkinson* (1782) 3 Doug. 41; *Le Cras* v. *Hughes* (1782) 3 Doug. 81; *Barzallai* v. *Lewis* (1782) 3 Doug. 126; *Court* v. *Martineau* (1782) 3 Doug. 161; *London Assurance Co.* v. *Sainsbury* (1783) 3 Doug. 245.
[36] Preface to fifth edition, *Modern Reports*, penultimate page.

INTRODUCTION

originated, and the circumstances under which they were communicated', but he assured his readers that they 'may be relied upon as authority'.[37]

In reports published in the late eighteenth and early nineteenth centuries, no information was given about the provenance of cases that had been obtained from outside sources, but the reporters did at least identify which cases were from their own notes and which were from manuscript sources. At the outset of the tables of cases to volumes four to eight of *Durnford and East's Reports*, and continuing in all fourteen volumes of *East's Reports*, is the following: 'N.B. Those cases to the pages of which the letter n. is prefixed were cited from MS. Notes.'[38] Full reports are given of many of the manuscript cases; others are merely cited by the term and year when they were decided.

Manuscript Case Notes in the Courtroom

Much can be learned from the printed reports about the extent to which counsel and judges relied on manuscript case notes. Certain sets of manuscript case notes became well known and were recognised as having authority equal to or greater than the printed reports, but even when anonymous, the pedigree of manuscript case notes was rarely questioned. At times, manuscript notes were used to corroborate a printed report of the same case; more often they were used to challenge the accuracy or completeness of a printed report of the same case.

(a) Favoured manuscript sources

(i) Judges' Notes

Numerous sets of manuscript case notes taken by judges while on the bench or when serving as counsel in pre-judicial years were in circulation and were relied upon by successive generations of lawyers and judges. The careful case notes kept by Peter King while chief justice of the Court of Common Pleas during the reign of George I were cited by generations of judges and practitioners throughout the eighteenth century.[39] According to a manuscript report of *Moses* v. *Macferlan*, for example, Lord Mansfield said that there were many cases exhibiting the merits of the common count of 'money had & received', adding: 'I will mention only one, which I have from a manuscript of Lord King. It first came on at Guildhall, and was afterwards determined on solemn argument in the Court of Common Pleas, Michaelmas, 7 Geo. I. *Dutch & Warren*.'[40] Other eighteenth-century judges' notes that were authoritatively

---

[37] Preface to third edition, *Strange's Reports*, at vi.
[38] A similar prefatory note appears in volumes one to four (out of six) of George Maule and William Selwyn's King's Bench reports for 1814–17.
[39] See Oldham, 'Underreported', at pp. 131–145.
[40] Misc. MS. 195, Pas. 33 Geo. II, fols. 324–325, Inner Temple Library, London. For additional cases showing reliance on King's manuscripts, see, e.g., *Tasker* v. *Geale* (1733) Cooke C.P. 84; *Case of Constables of Milborn Port* (1740) Sess. Cas. 116; *R.* v. *Boycot* (1789) 1 Keny. 318 (Nares, counsel, stating that he had seen the notes of Lord Raymond and of Lord King of a decision by Holt reported in 5 Modern); *Lowndes* v. *Horne* (1778) 2 W. Bl. 1252 (case from 'Lord King's Manuscript Reports' cited by Mr Justice Nares).

invoked by both bench and Bar included those by Sir John Holt (C.J.K.B. 1689–1710),[41] John Blencowe (B.Ex. 1696–97, J.C.P. 1697–1722),[42] Sir Philip Yorke, Lord Hardwicke (C.J.K.B. 1733–37, L.C. 1737–56),[43] Sir John Willes (C.J.C.P. 1737–61),[44] Thomas Burnet (J.C.P. 1741–53),[45] Sir Thomas Abney (B.Ex. 1740–43, J.C.P. 1743–50),[46] Edward Clive (B.Ex. 1745–53, J.C.P. 1753–70),[47] Sir John Eardley Wilmot (J.K.B. 1755–66, C.J.C.P. 1766–71),[48] Sir Henry Gould (B.Ex. 1761–62, J.C.P. 1762–94),[49] and Francis Buller (J.K.B. 1778–1794, J.C.P. 1794–1800).[50] Sir Matthew Hale's manuscripts from the prior century were also cited.[51]

[41] See e.g., *Lane* v. *Cotton* (1702) 11 Mod. 12, at 18, n. (a); *Pitt's Case* (1733) 7 Mod. 225, at 229 (Lord Hardwicke, giving the opinion of the twelve judges and citing 'a good manuscript report' that he had of Holt's decision in *Lord Banbury's Case*, 2 Salk. 512); *Smith* v. *Parkhouse* (1740) 7 Mod. 366, at 369 (Lee C.J. quoting 'from a manuscript of Lord Holt's of the case of *Hunt* v. *Bourne*, 1 Salk. 339'); *Erving* v. *Peters*, (1790) 3 T.R. 685, at 689 (Mr Justice Buller read a note of the case of *Rock* v. *Leighton*, 1 Salk. 310 'from Lord Holt's manuscript'); *Milbourn* v. *Ewart*, (1793) 5 T.R. 381, at 386 (Mr Justice Buller using Holt's MSS. to refute a suggestion by counsel for the defendant that the case of *Cage* v. *Acton*, 1 Ld. Raym. 515 had been reversed); *Crosby* v. *Wadsworth*, (1805) 6 East 602, at 604 n. (d) (East in a note quotes the opinion in *Cox* v. *Godsalve* from 'Holt's MS, of which I have the following copy from the original'); *Carrington* v. *Taylor*, (1809) 11 East 571, at 573, n. (a) (East quotes the declaration and judgment in a case 'which is taken from a copy of Lord C.J. Holt's own MS in my possession').

[42] See e.g., *Vaspor* v. *Edwards* (1702) 12 Mod. 658 (also reported sub nom. *Vasper* v. *Eddowes*, 1 Ld. Raym. 719); *ex parte French* (1705) 1 Salk. 352; *Matthews* v. *Phillips* (1713) 2 Salk. 424, at 425; *Doe d. Brown* v. *Holme* (1771) 3 Wils. 237, at 240 (reports of *Loddington* v. *Kime* in Levinz and Salkeld corrected by Blencowe's manuscript report of the case 'which the reporter Serjeant Wilson has seen').

[43] See e.g., *R.* v. *Pasmore* (1789) 3 T.R. 199, at 221 (East, counsel for the defendant, refers to the *Corporation of Banbury Case* (1716) 10 Mod. 346 as 'very shortly reported' in Modern, yet the case 'was very deliberately discussed, as appears from a manuscript note of Lord Hardwicke's of that case'); *Hughes* v. *Thomas* (1811) 13 East 474, at 483, n. c(1) (Ellenborough C.J. cites the holding by Hardwicke in *Garth* v. *Cotton*; reporter East cites a report of the case in Dickens 'from Lord Hardwicke's MS.').

[44] On Willes, see Oldham, 'Underreported', pp. 129–130.

[45] See e.g., *Barker* v. *Bishop of London* (1790) 1 H. Bl. 412; *Williamson* v. *Allison* (1802) 2 East 446, at 448, n. (a) (reporter East cites in a note the case of *Sprigwell* v. *Allen*, Aleyn 91, then supplies 'a fuller note [of the case] taken from a MS. in the hand-writing of Mr. Justice Burnet, in the collection of Lord Hardwicke C. and his son the late Mr. Charles Yorke').

[46] Willes (C.J.C.P. 1737–61) often relied on and quoted from Mr Justice Abney's MSS. See e.g., *Karver* v. *James* (1741) Willes 255, at 259, n. c(2); *Mead* v. *Robinson* (1743) Willes 422, at 426, n. a(2); *Atkinson* v. *Settree* (1744) Willes 482, at 483, n. (a); *Blissett* v. *Hart* (1744) Willes 508, at 512, n. (a); *Mayor of Bedford* v. *Bishop of Lincoln* (1745) Willes 608, at 611, n. (a).

[47] See e.g., *Gist* v. *Mason* (1786) 1 T.R. 88, at 89; *Ludford* v. *Barber* (1786) 1 T.R. 90, at 93, n. (a); *R.* v. *Pasmore* (1789) 3 T.R. 199, at 245 (Mr Justice Buller quotes from a case that was 'Among Mr. J. Clive's manuscripts, which are a collection of cases by several judges'); *Ludford*, 1 T.R. at 93 (Lord Hardwicke's opinion on the first argument of *Hornby* v. *Houlditch* is quoted in full by reporter East's note (a)2, from 'MSS. Clive J.').

[48] See e.g., *Blood* v. *Lee* (1769) 3 Wils. 24, and see generally Oldham, 'Underreported', pp. 127–129.

[49] See e.g., *Rust* v. *Cooper* (1777) 2 Cowp. 629, at 631; *Bamford* v. *Burrell* (1799) 2 Bos. and Pul. 1, at 8 n. (b) (the judgment of Chief Justice De Grey in the case of *Goddard* v. *Vanderheyden* was quoted by Mr Justice Buller 'from a manuscript note of the late Mr. J. Gould'); *Robarts* v. *Mason* (1808) 1 Taunt. 254, at 256.

[50] See below, pp. xxv–xxvi.

[51] See e.g., *R.* v. *Bosworth* (1739) 2 Str. 1112, at 1113; *Middleton* v. *Croft* (1736) 2 Str. 1056, at 1061; *The Case of the London Wharfs* (1766) 1 W. Bl. 581, at 589 (Parker C.B. invokes a rule laid down by Lord Hale 'in a MS. in Lincoln's-Inn Library'); *Frogmorton* v. *Wharrey* (1770) 2 W. Bl. 728, at 732 (Wilmot C.J. referring to 'a manuscript of Lord Hale in possession of my brother Bathurst').

There are indications that Lord Mansfield had an extensive collection of manuscript notes—a collection that was presumably incinerated when the rioters in the Gordon Riots of 1780 made a bonfire out of the contents of Lord Mansfield's library. According to the *London Evening Post*, Lord Mansfield's losses included 'three hundred volumes of notes and other valuable professional papers . . . collected with unremitting assiduity and written in his own hand'.[52] In a parliamentary speech shortly afterwards, Mansfield spoke with favour about the government's actions during the riots, and in giving his reasons, he stated, 'I have not consulted books; indeed I have not books to consult!'[53] Also illustrating how unfortunate the loss was to posterity is Lord Mansfield's comment in *Gist* v. *Mason* that he knew of only two cases that prohibited trading with the enemy, one of which 'was a note (which is now burned) which was given to me by Lord Hardwicke, of a reference in King William's time to all the Judges, whether it were a crime at the common law to carry corn to the enemy in time of war; who were of opinion that it was a misdemeanour'.[54]

Mr Justice Buller was Lord Mansfield's protégé in the King's Bench, and the two men worked together with a closeness that resembled a father–son relationship. Mansfield became physically unable to carry out his duties during his last two years in office (1786–88), and during that time Buller was the *de facto* chief justice.[55] Buller's Paper Books survive as part of the Dampier Manuscripts at Lincoln's Inn Library, and they demonstrate that he left no stone unturned in researching pending cases.[56] While at the Bar he had created an extensive manuscript case note collection that he put to effective use later in his judicial opinions. In *Pritchard* v. *Pugh*, for example, counsel Mingay relied on the case of *Waddington* v. *Thellwell*[57] in arguing for a change of venue, and after cases cited in *Waddington* were mentioned, Buller J. 'read several of them from manuscript notes in his possession'.[58]

Mr Justice Buller's manuscript case notes were shared widely and were acknowledged to be authoritative. Thus in announcing the opinion of the twelve judges in *R.* v. *Trapshaw*,[59] Gould J. said that according to his own note, the twelve judges in an earlier case had been unanimous, but, 'I have seen a manuscript of the same case by Mr Justice Buller, in which he takes notice, that

---

[52] *London Evening Post*, 10–13 June 1780. About half of Lord Mansfield's trial notes are missing; presumably they, too, perished in the fire. See Oldham, *MMSS*, i. 161–163.

[53] J. Holliday, *The Life of William Late Earl of Mansfield* (1797), at p. 412.

[54] (1786) 1 T.R. 88, 89.

[55] According to Isaac Espinasse, 'From the time that Lord Mansfield had withdrawn from sitting at *nisi prius*, Mr. Justice Buller took his place, and the business of that court rested entirely upon him.' Ashhurst was the senior puisne justice, but, 'While Mr. Justice Ashhurst presided in the Court of King's Bench, Mr. Justice Buller had, in effect, been the chief justice in every respect but the possession of the title.' I. Espinasse, '"My Contemporaries", From the Note-book of a Retired Barrister', *Fraser's Magazine for Town and Country* (1832), at 6: 220, 225, 227.

[56] Stuffed into many of the Paper Books are copious research notes by Buller in his own handwriting.

[57] (1763) 4 Burr. 2450.

[58] *Pritchard* v. *Pugh* (1779) 1 Doug. 262.

[59] (1786) 1 Leach 427.

only ten of the Twelve Judges were of this opinion; and from the known accuracy of that learned Judge, I must presume that the fact was as he stated it.'[60] Another example is provided by Douglas's endnote to a case discussed below, *Jones* v. *Barkley*.[61] Douglas described further proceedings in the case, during which counsel for the defendants cited the case of *Smith* v. *Bromley*, tried before Lord Mansfield at Guildhall in London after Easter Term 1760. Lord Mansfield's trial notes for the sittings after that term are missing, no doubt burned up during the Gordon Riots. This may explain why in *Jones* v. *Barkley*, Mansfield made no reference to his own notes of the *Smith* case, even though he said he well remembered it. Instead, he stated that Buller J. 'had a very good note of it', which Mansfield desired Buller to read and 'which he accordingly did'.[62] A copy of Buller's manuscript notes of *Smith* v. *Bromley* must have been given to Douglas, who quoted it in full.[63]

Lord Mansfield's *de jure* successor as chief justice of the King's Bench, Lloyd Kenyon, was a hard-working, practical, inelegant lawyer who also came to the bench with an extensive collection of manuscript case notes.[64] Kenyon's judgments, as Douglas Hay describes them, were usually 'relatively short expositions ... of the technical points at issue, with fairly frequent references to manuscript cases in his own possession'.[65] Perhaps due to irritation at those who thought themselves superior, Kenyon often produced a manuscript copy of a precedent that he characterised as fuller or better than what was in print.[66] In several cases, Kenyon's manuscript notes of a case were said to be better than Sir James Burrow's report of the same case.[67] Kenyon also cited and quoted reports in his manuscript case notes as fuller or better than reports of the same cases in *Wilson*[68] and *Strange*.[69]

[60] Ibid., at 429.
[61] (1781) 2 Doug. 684. See pp. xxxii–xxxiii, below.
[62] Ibid., at 695.
[63] Ibid., at 695–698.
[64] In the *Pritchard* case, counsel Mingay read a manuscript copy of the *Waddington* case 'lent him by Kenyon, who was counsel in it'. Ibid.
[65] 'Kenyon, Lloyd', *ODNB*.
[66] See e.g., *Roe d. Crow* v. *Baldwere* (1793) 5 T.R. 104, at 107–108 ('His Lordship then referred to a MS note [b] of that case [*Martin* v. *Strachan*, 2 Str. 1179], which he said was more full and correct than any in print'); *R.* v. *Price* (1795) 6 T.R. 147, at 148 ('His Lordship then read such parts of the following note [of *R.* v. *Fox*] as are applicable to this case from a manuscript of his own, and which is more full than any report of it in print'); *R.* v. *Cole* (1796) 6 T.R. 640, at 642 ('And on this day his Lordship read a manuscript note of *R.* v. *Robinson* (more fully taken than that in print in the note to *R.* v. *Jones*, 1 Str. 704, third edit.')).
[67] See e.g., *Tatlock* v. *Harris* (1789) 3 T.R. 174, at 182 ('Here the Chief Justice read a manuscript note of that case [*Grant* v. *Vaughan*], which was fuller than the report of it in Sir J. Burrow'); *R.* v. *Harris* (1797) 7 T.R. 238 ('I have rather a fuller account of that case [*R.* v. *Vipont*] than is to be found in Burrow's Reports'). See also the discussion of *Jones* v. *Roe* at pp. xxxv–xxxvi, below.
[68] See *Denn d. Webb* v. *Puckey* (1793) 5 T.R. 299, at 304 ('All these observations were made by Lord Ch. J. Wilmot, in the case cited from Wilson, of which I have a fuller manuscript note'); *Creswell* v. *Hoghton* (1795) 6 T.R. 355, at 359 ('of the case of *Witham* v. *Hill*, reported in 2 Wils. 91, I have a fuller report than any in print').
[69] *Bragner* v. *Langmead* (1796) 7 T.R. 20, at 24 ('Lord Kenyon, C.J. added, that since the case had been argued he had again looked through all the cases cited, and also that of *Chancery* v. *Needham*, reported in 2 Str. 1081, but of which his Lordship said he had a better manuscript note, and that they all confirmed his opinion').

In *Doe* v. *Fonnereau*,[70] a complicated case requiring construction of a will creating estates in land, Lord Mansfield announced that after the second argument, the court 'had decided that the devise to the second son was void, on the authority of the case of *Goodman* v. *Goodright*, as reported by Sir James Burrow, but that they had since seen a manuscript note of that case, taken by Kenyon, which assigned a ground for the determination different from that stated by Sir James Burrow'; thus a third argument was ordered, after which the court changed its mind.[71] Douglas added a footnote saying that he had been favoured with a copy by Mr Kenyon of his note of the *Goodman* case, and it was 'much fuller than either the report by Sir *James Burrow*, or that since printed, in the first volume of *Blackstone's* Reports'.[72]

(ii) Notes Taken or Collected by Practitioners and Others

Court officers occasionally adopted the practice of taking notes of court decisions, as was true of Sir James Burrow. Other eighteenth-century officers who took notes that were never published included Charles Short, clerk of the rules on the plea side, Court of King's Bench,[73] and Sir Simon Harcourt, master of the Crown Office, Court of King's Bench.[74]

More commonly, barristers created and collected their own notes of cases. Young men newly called to the Bar did so not only to continue to learn the law but also to become noticed in the courtroom and in hopes of acquiring business.[75] Seasoned barristers also collected and kept careful case notes to sustain proficiency in their practice. One whose notes were never published despite being borrowed, copied, and cited was John Dunning, later Lord Ashburton. In *Combe* v. *Pitt*,[76] Dunning, in argument for the defendant, described the case of *Jackson* v. *Gisling*[77] as 'very ill reported' by Sir John Strange, and then recited from 'a fuller and more accurate MS. Report' of the

---

[70] (1780) 2 Doug. 487.

[71] Ibid., 507–508.

[72] Ibid., 507, n. [3]. Buller's manuscript notes of the case of *Doe* v. *Fonnereau* reveal that it was Buller, not Mansfield, who questioned Burrow's report of *Goodman* v. *Goodright* (1759) 2 Burr. 873. Buller wrote that he was dissatisfied with Burrow's report of *Goodman* after reading it carefully, so he borrowed Kenyon's notes of that case, which clearly provided grounds for distinguishing the case from that before the court in *Fonnereau*. Buller then mentioned this to the other judges, and the case was put over to be argued the next term. Dampier MSS., Buller Paper Books, Bundle 113–142, Lincoln's Inn Library, London.

[73] See e.g., *Brandon* v. *Davis* (1807) 9 East 154, at 155 (in note c: 'This was read from a MS. Note Book of Practise furnished by Mr. Short, the Clerk of the Rules on the civil side'); *Havelock* v. *Geddes*, (1810) 12 East 622, at 625 n. (b); *Glyn* v. *Baker* (1811) 13 East 509, at 515 n. (a).

[74] See *R.* v. *Sharpness* (1787) 2 T.R. 47, at 47 (Mr Justice Buller began his opinion by declaring, 'From a review of all the cases in a MS. notebook, it appears that the prosecutor is not entitled to his costs'. Durnford and East added an explanation (note (b)): 'This appears from some MS. notes of Sir *Simon Harcourt*, when he was master of the *Crown Office*; and which was the same book Mr. Justice *Buller* referred to.').

[75] On John (later Lord) Campbell's youthful scheme to advance his career by publishing his notes of cases at *nisi prius*, see J. Oldham, 'Law-making at *Nisi Prius* in the Early 1800s', *Journal of Legal History* 25 (2004), pp. 221, 224.

[76] (1763) 3 Burr. 1423.

[77] (1742) 2 Str. 1169.

case, which he read verbatim, and 'which may (he vouched) be depended upon for its Correctness'. Lord Mansfield in his opinion said that the case 'is intelligible, as it is reported by Sir J.S.', adding that 'my brother *Denison* says it is rightly taken'. Opposite this in the margin Burrow inserted: 'If it is *rightly* taken, I am sure it is not *fully* taken: At least, I know that my own Note of it employs twice as many *Pages* as his does *Lines*.'[78] Dunning's manuscript notes of cases were passed on to Mansfield's successor, Chief Justice Kenyon, who cited them as authoritative. In a newspaper account of *Cave* v. *Otway*, Kenyon was quoted as saying that he was able 'to give some assistance by the Notes taken by Mr. Dunning', adding, in subtle praise, 'He was a young man when he took them, but that young man was Mr. Dunning.'[79]

Some of the eighteenth-century barristers who kept careful case notes eventually had them published. This group included Sir John Strange,[80] George Wilson,[81] and Edward Hyde East.[82] Wilson's case notes were thorough, though possibly at times self-serving. In *Doe d. Browne* v. *Holmes and Longmore*,[83] Wilson appeared for the defendants, opposing Serjeant Sayer for the plaintiff. Sayer cited the case of *Doe d. Barnard and Fenton* v. *Reason*, Trinity Term 1755, 'which he stated from a MS. report'. Wilson was prepared to argue for the defendants, but was stopped by the court since the court had already decided in Wilson's client's favour. Having prepared a long and careful argument, Wilson printed it anyway, saying that he trusted the candid reader would not be displeased by his presentation of 'what I intended to have offered the court, if they had been pleased to hear me'. Then in his undelivered argument, he included 'a more accurate report' of *Doe d. Barnard and Fenton* v. *Reason* than that quoted to the court by Sayer. Wilson said that he quoted his version of the case verbatim as he had received it 'from my brother Jephson, who heard the argument and judgment given therein, and noted the same with his own hand'.[84]

Among all of the eighteenth-century barristers who were reporting the activity in the common law courts, the best-known collector of manuscript case notes was the eccentric Serjeant George Hill, who came to be known as

---

[78] 3 Burr. at 1428, 1434, 1434 n. (2).

[79] *The Times*, 24 May 1797, p. 3. For other cases in which Kenyon referenced Dunning's notes, see *Doe d. Church and Phillips* v. *Perkins* (1790) 3 T.R. 749, at 752; *Lovelace* v. *Curry* (1798) 7 T.R. 631, at 633; *R.* v. *Stone* (1801) 1 East 639, at 643–644.

[80] Strange's reports were published posthumously by Strange's son in 1755. Before he died, however, Sir John wrote the preface to the first edition in which he explained that, 'Having during the first years of my attendance at *Westminster-hall* been pretty diligent and exact in taking and transcribing notes; I soon found, it introduced me to the honour of having them borrowed and transcribed by several of the Judges, and others', but Strange then discovered that a servant of one of the borrowers secretly made and sold copies of his notes, which 'put me under an apprehension, that I should soon see some of them in print'. Thus he selected the cases that were actually adjudged so that 'I might at ever so short a warning have it in my power, by printing a genuine, to suppress a surreptitious edition.' A 'surreptitious edition' did indeed appear after Strange's death, prompting the publication of the first edition. See 'Strange, Sir John', *ODNB*.

[81] See Wallace, *The Reporters*, at pp. 442–443.

[82] On East, see p. xxxii, below.

[83] (1771) 3 Wils. 241.

[84] Ibid., at 243–444.

'Serjeant Labyrinth' because 'his memory of case law was so extensive that he was utterly confused by his own learning'.[85] Hill put together a huge assemblage of notes taken personally by him over a long career (1741–1808) and obtained from others.[86] The scope of Hill's manuscript collection was well known to the Bar, and he was often called upon for advice.[87] Hill's manuscripts were often cited in court cases as well, but the main presence of Serjeant Hill in the printed reports is in the fifth edition of *Burrow's Reports*, published in 1812.[88] Hill died in 1808, but the first paragraph of the advertisement to the fifth edition provided the following explanation:

> In preparing the present edition of the late Sir James Burrow's Reports, the greatest attention has been paid to the corrections of the errors of the former editions; and the publishers being in possession of the copy of these Reports which belonged to the late Mr. Serjeant Hill, have ventured to add to this edition, a variety of valuable notes, references, and observations, which he had made in his copy, and which are now for the first time presented to the public: These will be found at the bottom of the page, in the shape of notes, or in the margin enclosed in brackets.

Perhaps because Hill's marginal notes in his copy of *Burrow's Reports* were not written with a view to publication, his comments, or those of the publishers of the fifth edition in referring to Hill's manuscript notes, were at times unrestrained. Thus, for example, in *Sadler v. Evans*,[89] Burrow's report states that Lord Mansfield 'mentioned two cases to shew that a non-suit may be set aside by the Court', and to the second case, *Bagshaw v. Wynn*,[90] the publishers attached the following note: 'The non-suit was not set aside in that case, as appears by a very full report of it in Serjeant Hill's MSS. where the whole learning on the subject is exhausted.'[91]

Hill's manuscripts were also used by editors of other reports for supplementary cases or editorial comment,[92] as by Charles Elsley, editor of the second edition (1828) of William Blackstone's reports.[93] *R. v. Inhabitants of St Michael*[94] involved a presentment demanding community repairs to a

---

[85] Simpson, *Biographical Dictionary*, at p. 242. See also H. W. Woolrych, *Lives of Eminent Sergeants-at-Law of the English Bar*, 2 vols. (1869), ii. 634–659.

[86] See J. H. Baker, *English Legal Manuscripts*, 2 vols. (1978), ii. 80–91 for a full itemization of Hill's manuscripts at Lincoln's Inn Library.

[87] See, e.g., the examples from Lord Eldon's *Anecdote Book* in Oldham, 'Underreported', at p. 127.

[88] The fifth is the edition of *Burrow's Reports* that was included in the *English Reports*.

[89] (1766) 4 Burr. 1984, at 1986 (also known as *Lady Windsor's Case*).

[90] Cited as 'Scacc. [Exchequer]: Tr. 13 G.2, 1739'.

[91] 4 Burr. at 1986, n. '(a)'.

[92] Hill's manuscripts appear in reports of dozens of cases decided in the late eighteenth and nineteenth centuries. There is no need to itemize them here.

[93] Elsley in his preface remarked that, 'These reports have been for some time not in the best repute, partly from an observation made upon them by Lord MANSFIELD, and partly from their own loose and imperfect style.' Preface, iv. Coming to Blackstone's defence, Elsley said that the case in *Blackstone's Reports* that prompted Mansfield's criticism was one that Mansfield 'seems not to have perfectly understood'. Also, although 'It would be invidious to make comparisons between the merits of each: the cases collected by Sir J. BURROWS [sic] are reported at very great length, but with such tiresome prolixity and wearisome minuteness, that one is almost inclined to prefer the conciseness and compendiousness of Sir W. BLACKSTONE's notes'.

[94] (1770) 2 Bl. W. 718.

highway, according to custom. On being removed to the King's Bench by *certiorari*, counsel for the defendants argued that the record was imperfect since no jurors were named on the record, and the record did not state that the jurors were twelve in number. According to Blackstone's report of the case, the court (Mansfield C.J., Willes, and Blackstone JJ.) agreed, and, 'without entering into the merits of the custom, reversed the judgment'. To this statement, editor Elsley attached the following note: '*Serj.* Hill in his MSS., says that "this case is wrong reported, and that the judgment was affirmed" '.[95]

One subset of manuscript case notes within Serjeant Hill's collection was that of a 'Mr. Ford', covering cases decided from 1730 to 1751. According to J. H. Baker's guide to English legal manuscripts, Mr Ford 'has not been certainly identified'.[96] Further inquiry makes it virtually certain that the collector was John Ford, a barrister admitted to the Middle Temple on 28 November 1726, who died on 20 June 1753.[97] His manuscript case notes were highly valued by the Bar, though they seem to have fallen out of view after his death until they were rediscovered in the late eighteenth century. Michael Nolan, editor of the third edition of *Strange's Reports* (1795) attached the following note to Strange's report of *R.* v. *Inhabitants of Uttoxeter*:

> [I]t is well known that in Mr. Ford's MSS., in which the above determination is mentioned, a great many of the cases in Strange are reported at much greater length, and more completely than by that author. Mr. Douglas had an opportunity of perusing Ford's account of this case and several others; but although those who have the pleasure of knowing his son, know how ready he is to permit his friends to consult his father's valuable MSS. it is much to be wished that he may some time or other make it publick for the general benefit of the profession.[98]

Some years later, Edward East, in a note to his report of *R.* v. *Bishop of Oxford*,[99] referred to Ford's manuscript version of a case in *Strange's Reports*, and described Ford's manuscripts as 'the best reports of that period, for the use of which I am much indebted to Mr. R. Ford and his son'.[1] East used Ford's

---

[95] Ibid. at 719. Also in *Calze* v. *Lyttelton* (1774) 2 W. Bl. 954, Serjeant Hill's notes demonstrated his familiarity with the intricate rules of pleading. Responding to a rule of 13 Geo. II cited in Blackstone's report of the court's opinion, Serjeant Hill commented: '*Quaere*, whether any argument can be drawn from that rule in favour of the opinion of the court, as here reported, which seems extrajudicial; for, in the principal case, as well as in all the three cases cited, the Judge's summons was not obtained, till after the rules for pleading were expired.' Ibid. n. (g).

[96] Baker, *English Legal Manuscripts*, ii. 81.

[97] I am indebted to Guy Holborn, Lincoln's Inn Librarian, for the discovery of Mr Ford's identity through his examination of the admission registers of the four Inns, *Musgrave's Index to Obituaries Before 1800* (45–49 Harleian Soc., 1900–01), and the *Gentleman's Magazine*, among other sources. John Ford is the only Ford in the admission registers of the four Inns who could have been active as a reporter from 1730 to 1751. It would not have been unusual for him to have begun his reports in 1730 while still at the Middle Temple, before being called to the Bar.

[98] (1732) 2 Str. 932, at 932.

[99] (1806) 7 East 345.

[1] Ibid. at 347, n. b(2). Very likely the son was Randle Ford, admitted to Lincoln's Inn 2 March 1769 and called to the Bar 4 May 1774. He appears in the *Law Lists* beyond 1806 and so would have been able to assist East. Again, I thank Guy Holborn for this information.

manuscript notes to provide fuller and more correct versions of a number of reported cases, especially those in *Strange's Reports*.[2]

As the Ford manuscript cases show, Sir Edward Hyde East was another barrister with an extensive collection of manuscript case notes. He was co-author of the eight volumes of *Durnford and East's Reports* (1785–1800) (also called *Term Reports*) and sole author of the fourteen volumes of *East's Reports* (1800–12). These reports quickly came to be regarded by the Bar as indispensable.[3] Another of East's publications that was much admired was his two-volume *Pleas of the Crown*, published in 1803. In the preliminary matter to that work, East itemized eleven manuscript sources that are referred to throughout the volumes.[4] One was 'Lord Hale's Summary, interleaved with MS. corrections and additions'. East's further description of this source is worth quoting, as it undoubtedly reveals the way many such manuscript collections evolved:

> This MS. compilation, though begun before, (probably by Mr. Stow, a gentleman at the bar) was put into its present form by Mr. Justice Yates, whose son is now in possession of it. Copies of it were communicated to different Judges, who have contributed from time to time the fruits of their own experience. My own copy was taken from one in the possession of the late Mr. Justice Buller. . . . I have added the page of the MS., because copies of it are now in the hands of many gentlemen of the profession.[5]

Also listed, among other manuscript sources, were manuscript compilations by Sir John Holt and Mr Justice Burnet (both 'part of a most valuable collection of law MSS. made by Lord Chancellor Hardwicke: a copy of which was furnished to me by his descendant, my worthy friend, the Right Honourable Charles Yorke'); a 'MS. volume of Crown cases communicated by the late Lord Ashburton to Mr. Justice Heath'; 'MSS. of Mr. Masterman, sometime since Secondary of the Crown Office'; and two volumes of manuscript cases taken by an unknown hand, but which had been inspected by Mr Justice Buller and given 'the praise of accuracy'.[6]

Most of these same manuscript collections turn up in East's footnotes in *Term Reports*. East and Mr Justice Buller developed a close working partnership in maintaining manuscript case notes of King's Bench decisions. Indeed they, much like Buller and Lord Mansfield, appeared to have something like a father–son relationship. This is shown in a number of ways, not the least by the

---

[2] Ford's manuscript report of *Allam v. Heber* (1748) 2 Str. 1270, shows the Court of King's Bench as declaring that *Gilpin's Case* from the prior century was not the law, even though 'this is not noticed in either Strange or Blackstone's report' of *Allam*. Other cases showing the effective use of Ford's manuscripts include *R. v. Luffe* (1807) 8 East 193, at 196; *Birch v. Triste* (1807) 8 East 412, at 414; *Hallet v. Mears* (1810) 13 East 15, at 16; *R. v. Martyr* (1810) 13 East 55, at 57; *R. v. Doherty* (1810) 13 East 171, at 172; *R. v. Bishop of London* (1811) 13 East 419, at 420; *R. v. Inhabitants of County of Oxford* (1811) 13 East 411, at 412; *Legatt v. Tollervey* (1811) 14 East 302, at 306; *R. v. Parry* (1811) 14 East 549, at 558.
[3] See 'East, Edward Hyde', *ODNB*.
[4] East, *Pleas of the Crown* (1802), pp. xiii-xv.
[5] Ibid., at xiii.
[6] Ibid., at xiv.

fact that East's son was named James Buller East.[7] Eighteen years Buller's junior, Edward East started reporting King's Bench cases in 1785, a year before being called to the Bar by the Inner Temple. Buller by then was in his judicial prime and was increasingly taking Lord Mansfield's place in conducting jury trials at Westminster Hall and Guildhall during and after term. At the Inner Temple Library are two notebooks designated as 'MS Notes of Cases by Buller J. and Sir E. H. East, 1754-1792'.[8] From the contents and marginal annotations, it is clear that this was a cooperative effort. The first volume contains notes of cases at *nisi prius*, the first part of which was apparently collected by Buller since the cases run up to 1777, the year before Buller became a judge. Then, with the exception of two inserted cases, the manuscript reports skip to 1786, when Buller was himself conducting *nisi prius* trials and East was publishing *Term Reports*. The notes of jury trials conducted by Buller are valuable since *nisi prius* reporting had not yet begun,[9] and there is no printed record of these sittings. Internal clues indicate that these notes were taken by East.[10]

(iii) Anonymous Manuscript Notes of Previously Unreported Cases

Examples have been given of the incorporation of anonymous case notes into some of the printed reports.[11] During the eighteenth century, the fact that a manuscript case report was anonymous was of little consequence. Far more important were the character and reputation of the barrister or judge who offered the manuscript version as a binding precedent or as superior to a printed report of the same case. Chief Baron Parker's assurance that the case reports in his Appendix had been 'carefully transcribed from authentic manuscripts'[12] was sufficient, because Parker was a highly respected judge.

When in the course of argument, a barrister or judge presented a manuscript case that was then unreported, a copy of the manuscript version stood a good chance of being included in a later-published report of the litigated case. A famous example is the case of *Kingston* v. *Preston*.[13] The *Kingston* case became famous for Mansfield's lucid taxonomy of types of covenants in bilateral contracts. The case was decided in 1773, but what became the standard report of the case was not published until 1782, when the first two volumes of *Douglas's Reports* appeared. In *Jones* v. *Barkley*,[14] the Court of King's Bench decided, according to Douglas's headnote, that, 'Where something is

---

[7] James Buller East was called to the Bar in early 1813 by the Inner Temple, where, like his father, he became a bencher.

[8] Inner Temple Library, London, Misc. MS. 96.

[9] See Oldham, 'Lawmaking at Nisi Prius', at p. 223.

[10] In addition to marginal notations with the initials 'J. E.', some notes recorded in the first person show East's authorship. In the case of *R.* v. *Bowes* (fo. 133v), for example, the following note appears after Buller's instructions to the jury are recorded: 'I was not in court when he summed up, but he told me immediately afterwards [of his reasoning].'

[11] See pp. xxii-xxiii, above.

[12] See p. xxi, above.

[13] (1773) 2 Doug. 689, quoted within the case of *Jones* v. *Barkley* (1781) 2 Doug. 684.

[14] (1781) 2 Doug. 684.

covenanted or agreed to be performed by each of two parties at the same time, he who was ready and offered to perform his part, but was discharged by the other, may maintain an action against the other for not performing his part.'[15] Many precedents were offered by counsel on both sides. Le Blanc, in order to reinforce a directly applicable precedent from volume ten of *Modern Reports* (because 'it may be said that 10 *Modern* is not a book of authority') referred to *Kingston* v. *Preston*, 'a recent case in this court which confirms the doctrine there [in 10 *Modern*] laid down'.[16] The full text of *Kingston* v. *Preston* is quoted within Douglas's report of *Jones* v. *Barkley*, but without a word about the authorship of the manuscript report of *Kingston*. Perhaps it was from Le Blanc's own notes, but in the event, this became the standard version of *Kingston*, and so it continues to this present day.[17]

Occasionally an anonymous manuscript report of a case would be introduced into a court's opinion by one of the sitting judges. In *Beatson* v. *Haworth*,[18] the Court of King's Bench considered whether, under an insurance policy, the insured ship had deviated from the specified voyage. The court's only opinion was its conclusion that there had been a deviation, followed by a reading by Mr Justice Lawrence of an unreported manuscript case, '*Clason* v. *Simmonds*, B.R. Hil. 15 Geo. 2, at Guildhall, Cor. Lee, Ch. J. March 11, 1741'. The manuscript report, as read by Lawrence, was included verbatim in *Term Reports*, though without any information about the source or author of the manuscript notes.

Whether introduced by counsel or a judge, there was simply no objection to the use of anonymous notes of unreported cases. It would have been unthinkable for a manuscript version of a case to be offered without a belief in the manuscript version's authenticity and accuracy. This was ordinarily emphasised by the adjectival description of the manuscript version when it was introduced: 'good', 'full', 'accurate', 'authentic', or the like.[19]

---

[15] Ibid., at head note.

[16] 2 Doug. at 689. Le Blanc cited *Turner* v. *Goodwin* in 10 Modern.

[17] Another report of *Kingston* v. *Preston* was published anonymously by Capel Lofft (*Lofft's Reports*, at 194, under 'Covenant'), but the report was largely ignored by the Bar, no doubt due to its anonymity and to the Bar's disdain for *Lofft's Reports* in general. See Wallace, *The Reporters*, p. 452.

[18] (1795) 6 T.R. 531.

[19] See e.g., *Pitt's Case* (1733) 7 Mod. 225, at 229, at 1208 (Hardwicke: 'I have a good manuscript report of that case [*Lord Banbury's case*, Salk. 512]'); *Attorney General* v. *Lade* (1746) Parker 57, at 62 (Parker: '*Russell's case*, Michaelmas 1684, from an authentic manuscript of an eminent practiser who was counsel in the cause'); *R.* v. *Willes* (1748) Parker 85, at 90 (Parker: 'And I mentioned the settled differences taken by Lord Chief Baron Ward in this court, in Easter Term, 11 W. 3 1699, as to the preference upon outlawries, from a very authentic manuscript'); *Camplin* v. *Bullman* (1761) Parker 198, at 209 (Parker: 'I have a very accurate manuscript report of the case of *Paul and Shaw*, and shall cite some parts of it from thence'); *Potts* v. *Bell* (1800) 8 T.R. 547, at 556 (Sir John Nicholl, the King's advocate: 'He then read the following notes of cases, taken partly from the MS. notes of Sir Edward Simpson, which are a valuable and authentic collection of Admiralty decisions').

(iv) Manuscript Case Notes used to Corroborate, Elaborate, or Contradict Printed Reports

Already demonstrated in several of the cases that have been discussed is the way that manuscript notes of a reported case would be introduced by counsel or a judge to supersede a printed report of the same case.[20] Usually the manuscript version would be cited as 'fuller', 'better', 'more accurate', or words to that effect. In other instances, a manuscript version of a case would be brought out by counsel or a judge merely to corroborate a printed report of the same case.[21]

---

[20] Dozens of examples could be given. See, e.g., the cases cited, pp. xxx, nn. 99 and 1, p. xxxi, n. 2, above, showing Edward East's use of John Ford's MSS. Others include the following: *Cambridge University Case* (1712) 10 Mod. 125, at 128 ('In the report of the case of *Castle* v. *Litchfield* it is said that upon notice (indefinitely) the Court must surcease their plea; from whence it is inferred, that the time of notice is not material: but Mr. Lechmere produced a better report of that case in manuscript, whereby it appeared, that nothing said in that case could warrant such an inference'); *Chichester* v. *Lethbridge* (1738) Willes 71 (Durnford, editor, referred in a note to reports of a case that had been cited, and then added, 'but as the reasons of that opinion are not in print, I have here subjoined the conclusion of a MS. note of that case taken from MS. Coll. Willes Chief Justice'); *Preston* v. *Funnel* (1739) Willes 166 (Willes: '. . . the case of *Nottingham* v. *Jennings*, Tr. 12 Will. B.R. reported in 1 Salk. 233. But I have a fuller manuscript than the report in Salkeld, where it appears . . .'); *Atkinson* v. *Settree* (1744) Willes 482 (referring to the principal case, Durnford added this note: 'The grounds of the judgment do not appear in Lord Chief Justice Willes's books: but the following account is taken from Mr. J. Abney's MS'); *Dyke* v. *Webber* (1745) Willes 584 (Durnford note: 'Thought not stated in either of the printed reports of this case, it came before the Court of King's Bench on a writ of error from the Common Pleas, the judgment of which last Court in favour of the plaintiff was reversed and a repleader awarded. MS. Coll. Willes Ch. J.'); *Layng* v. *Paine* (1745) Willes 576 (Durnford note: 'And 6 Mod. 234, S.C. but the following manuscript's note of that case is more full than either of the printed accounts of it'); *R.* v. *Fonseca* (1757) 1 Burr. 10 (Serjeant Hill note: 'There is nothing new in this case, for the case of *R.* v. *Sidney*, in Strange, 1165 is in point: of this case I have got a MS. note, whereby it appears . . .'); *R.* v. *Taylor* (1765) 3 Burr. 1679, at 1681 (Serjeant Hill note referring to a case at 2 Str. 1120: 'And it appears from a full manuscript note of that case . . . that there she did the act voluntarily'); *R.* v. *May* (1770) 5 Burr. 2681, at 2682 (Serjeant Hill note referring to an election at a public house, and adding: 'See 1 Str. 484. 2 Ld. Raym. 1358, and a fuller MS. note of my own'); *R.* v. *Inhabitants of St Michael's of Bath* (1781) 3 Doug. 630, at 632 (note by William Frere, editor: 'And I find from an MS. note of this case, that this objection was first stated by the Court'); *Silvester d. Law* v. *Wilson* (1788) 2 T.R. 444, at 447 (East note: 'This was read from a manuscript note, and does not appear in the report of it in Brown'); *Hyde* v. *Whiskard* (1800) 8 T.R. 456 (East note added to the principal case: 'The following account of the cases of *Huggins* v. *Bumbridge* and *Newton* v. *Lewis*, taken from the MSS. of Lord Ch. J. Willes, is more full than that given in Barnes 83 and 88', after which the account is quoted in full); *Williamson* v. *Allison* (1802) 2 East 446, at 449 (East note: 'Vide *Sprigwell* v. *Allen*, Aleyn, 91, of which the following is a fuller note taken from a MS. in the hand-writing of Mr. Justice Burnet, in the collection of Lord Hardwicke C. and his son the late Mr. Charles Yorke'); and *Soulsby* v. *Neving* (1808) 9 East 310, at 315 (East note: 'I have a MS. note of the same case by Mr. Justice Buller in which Lord Mansfield is made to say . . .').

[21] See e.g., *R.* v. *Munoes* (1742) 7 Mod. 315, at 316 (Chief Justice Lee: '[T]here was cited the case of *The King* v. *Jones*, reported by Mr. Salkeld, which I take to be a true account of that case, and which agrees with a manuscript I have seen of that case'); *R.* v. *Wakefield* (1758) 1 Burr. 485, at 486, n. 2 (Serjeant Hill note: 'It is right and true; at least I have a MS. note of the same case to the same effect, or stronger'); *Edie* v. *East India Co.* (1761) 2 Burr. 1216, at 1227 (Burrow note, referring to opinion by Mr Justice Wilmot: 'He cited the manuscript report of that same case of *Acheson* v. *Fountain* which is reported by Sir John Strange: which agreed with Sir John's report of it, and with mine exactly'); *Harris* v. *Rene* (1734) 2 Barn. K.B. 420 ('Judge Lee said that he had a manuscript note taken at that time, which directly confirms the case as stated in Salk.'); *Crossley* v. *Shaw* (1776) 2 W. Bl. 1085, at 1088; (Mr Justice Nares: 'I have seen a manuscript note of Chief Justice Eyre of the case of *Rawlings and Parry*, which agrees with Sir George Cooke's'); *Crepps* v. *Durden* (1777) 2

On rare occasions a manuscript report would be used in the course of argument to demonstrate that a printed report was erroneous. In *Cole* v. *Hawkins*,[22] the question was one of pleading, whether defendant's demurrer claiming the Statute of Limitations bar had been properly responded to by the plaintiff. One of the cases cited by the defendant was *Lee* v. *Raynes*, decided in 1663 and reported by Sir Thomas Raymond.[23] Plaintiff's counsel, William Salkeld, argued that, 'The case of *Lee* v. *Raynes* . . . was misreported; for he had in his hand a manuscript report of that case, of Lord Chief Justice Keyling, wherein it appeared, that the opinion of the Court in that case was, that the Statute of Limitations does not take away the liberty of laying the action at any time.'[24] And in a case in *Blackstone's Reports*, *Savage* v. *Smith*,[25] Chief Justice De Grey was shown as stating: 'A difference has been rightly taken between material and impertinent averments', but in the second edition, editor Charles Elsley changed the word 'material' to 'immaterial', adding in a footnote: '"Immaterial" certainly was the word used by De Grey C.J., as appears . . . from a very accurate manuscript note I have seen of *Savage* v. *Smith*, and indeed from the context in Blackstone's own report.'[26]

Occasional examples can be found of counsel's worst nightmare, when precedents in print that were relied upon were shown by the court to be inaccurate or to have been overtaken by other cases not yet in print. In *Jones* v. *Roe*,[27] barrister Joseph Jekyll, counsel for the defendants, argued that a point in Burrow's report of the case of *Selwyn* v. *Selwyn*[28] could be discounted because it 'did not proceed from the Court, and appears to be only the reporter's conjecture'.[29] Mr Justice Kenyon and Mr Justice Buller, however, teamed up to crush Jekyll's argument. Chief Justice Kenyon said that 'the case of *Selwin* v. *Selwin* is a very strong authority on the question in this case. I have a much fuller note of that case than in Burrow or Blackstone; and the grounds of the opinion of the Court, as supposed by Sir J. Burrow, are those which Lord Mansfield actually declared in Court.'[30] Mr Justice Buller agreed,

---

Cowp. 640, at 642 (Buller, counsel for the plaintiff referring to a case at 1 Str. 711: 'He had a manuscript note of the same case, to the same purport'); *Doe d. Candler* v. *Smith* (1798) 7 T.R. 531, at 534, n. a(2) (East note referring to Mr Justice Wilmot's comment about the case of *Roe d. Dodson* v. *Grew*, 2 Wils. 723: 'His Lordship read a manuscript note of this case, but in substance it agreed with the report in Wilson'); and *R.* v. *Stone* (1801) 1 East 639 ('Lord Kenyon C.J. referred to a MS. note of *The King* v. *Jarvis*, which was taken by the late Lord Ashburton when at the Bar, and corroborated the report by Sir James Burrow').

[22] (1714) 10 Mod. 251.
[23] (1633) Raym. T. 86.
[24] 10 Mod. at 251–252.
[25] (1775) 2 Bl. W. 1101, 1104.
[26] Ibid. at n. '(k)', 1104, 767. Elsley also pointed out that in the case of *Bristow* v. *Wright* (1781) 2 Doug. 665, at 668, Lord Mansfield said that Chief Justice De Grey 'expressly went upon the distinction between immaterial and impertinent averments', and that Douglas, in a footnote, attributed the word 'material' in Blackstone's report to a mistake of the press.
[27] (1789) 3 T.R. 88.
[28] (1760) 2 Burr. 1131.
[29] 3 T.R. at 92.
[30] Ibid., at 94. (The *Selwyn* case was also reported as *Selwin* v. *Selwin*, 1 BL. W. 243, 254.)

declaring that, 'It was not the opinion of Sir James Burrow himself, but of the Court', and that

> It has been openly acknowledged by Lord Mansfield, and I have had repeated opportunities of hearing it from him in private, that he has given to Sir J. Burrow his own note and opinion of a case, which he could not deliver publicly in Court, for it was not at that time the practice of this Court to give their opinions here in cases which came from the Court of Chancery.[31]

In *Bennetto* v. *Elvens*,[32] a question arose as to the competency of the defendant's brother as a witness, who had been objected to by the plaintiff because the brother was co-signer of the promissory note on which the action was brought. At the winter assizes in Cornwall, Mr Justice Ashhurst had rejected the defendant's brother as a witness, and the defendant's counsel, Francis Buller, subsequently moved the King's Bench for a new trial, citing a number of cases in support of his motion. Lord Mansfield referred Buller to a manuscript case, *French* v. *Backhouse*, decided by the Court of King's Bench in Easter Term 1771. Buller evidently was unaware of the *French* case, so Lord Mansfield recessed *Bennetto*, to give Buller time to consider it. Buller either was given or found a copy of *French* v. *Backhouse*, and when *Bennetto* came on again a few days later, he gave up his motion 'upon the authority of that case'. Lord Mansfield said 'He did very right: for that case went further than the present.'[33]

A good example of how important manuscript case notes could be in distinguishing an apparently adverse precedent is *Pollard* v. *Bell*.[34] In *Pollard*, the plaintiff sued to collect on a marine insurance policy covering what had been represented to be a Danish ship. The ship had been condemned by the French Admiralty court, and the question for the Court of King's Bench was whether the condemnation by the French court proved that the ship was not in fact Danish, so that the warranty of neutrality was false. Chief Justice Kenyon called the case one 'of great importance to the public', as 'one of the numberless questions that have arisen in consequence of the extraordinary sentences of condemnation passed by the Courts of Admiralty in France during the war'.[35] He considered it to be 'a system of plunder', but 'until the Legislature interferes on this subject, we, sitting in a Court of Law, are

---

[31] Ibid., at 97.

[32] Misc. MS. 96, *MS. Notes by Buller, J. and Sir E. H. East 1754–92*, Inner Temple Library, London, vol. 1, fol. 98 (Easter 1773).

[33] Ibid., fol. 99. A copy of the manuscript report of *French* v. *Backhouse* is contained in the Buller/East Notebook immediately preceding the *Bennetto* case. A report of *French* v. *Backhouse* would later be printed, (1771) 5 Burr. 2727, but volume 5 of Burrow's Reports was not published until years after the *Bennetto* case was resolved. At the end of Burrow's report of *French* v. *Backhouse* is the following: 'V. post, pa.   [sic] a Case of *Bennetto* v. *Henry Evans* [sic], in *Easter* term 1773, 13 G. 3. *B.R. Monday* 3rd *May* 1773: in which, this Case was mentioned and affirmed'. Ibid., 2730. No such report of *Bennetto* appears, however, in Burrow's volume 5 (his last).

[34] (1800) 8 T.R. 434. See Part III below, pp. 290 ff., for a full transcription of Lawrence's Paper Book in the *Pollard* case.

[35] Ibid. at 436–437.

bound to give credit to the sentences of a Court of competent jurisdiction'.[36] He concluded, nevertheless, that the French *arrêt* that had been relied upon by the French Court of Admiralty had been a unilateral act by France that had no binding force on other nations; thus, the French court's condemnation did not stand as a bar to the plaintiff's recovery.

The real problem in *Pollard*, however, was an earlier decision by the Court of King's Bench, *Barzillai* v. *Lewis*,[37] in which Lord Mansfield held that the French Admiralty court's condemnation of the insured ship as English was conclusive evidence that the ship in that case was not Dutch, despite evidence that the ship sailed under a Dutch name with a Dutch sea brief and with Dutch owners.[38] Understandably, counsel for the defendant in *Pollard* relied heavily on *Barzillai*, using the only report of that case then in print, an abridged version in *Park on Insurance*.[39] But Mr Justice Lawrence was able to distinguish *Barzillai* by using 'a manuscript note of that case, taken by Mr J. Buller rather more full than that in print'.[40] According to that manuscript note, Lord Mansfield stated that the ship's sea brief in the *Barzillai* case did not conform to the Treaty of Utrecht, and it was clear that this non-compliance was the basis for the decision by Lord Mansfield and the other judges that the ship was not Dutch property. Thus the case did not stand for the proposition that 'non-compliance with the ordinances of France, not adopted by a treaty, was a forfeiture of neutrality'.[41]

(b) Bad law

Nearly everyone is familiar with Lord Campbell's famous recollection in his autobiography about his case selection method when, as a young man making his way at the Bar, he was publishing notes of *nisi prius* cases presided over by Lord Ellenborough, chief justice of the King's Bench. Campbell said that he had a drawer marked 'bad Ellenborough law' into which he put (and never reported) all the cases he thought wrongly decided.[42]

---

[36] Ibid., at 437.

[37] (1782) 3 Doug. 126. For Lord Mansfield's trial notes in the case see Oldham, *MMSS*, i. 576–577.

[38] A sea brief was a manifest containing a description of the ship's cargo and identifying its ports of departure and destination, as required of all neutral vessels during wartime.

[39] See pp. 305 ff., below, for Lawrence's notes of the arguments of counsel (not included in Durnford and East's report of the case at 8 T.R. 434)—James Allan Park for the plaintiff and Thomas Carr for the defendant at the first argument on 19 November 1799; Vicary Gibbs for the plaintiff and George Rous for the defendant at the second argument on 28 January 1800. J. A. Park, *A System of the Law of Marine Insurances* (1796), at p. 359.

[40] 8 T.R. at 441. Mr Justice Buller was still on the bench when *Pollard* was decided (he died several months later, on 4 June 1800), but he had transferred from King's Bench to Common Pleas in 1794.

[41] Ibid., at 442. Mr Justice Buller's manuscript notes of the judges' opinions in *Barzillai* are in his paper book in the Dampier MSS. at Lincoln's Inn Library (within bundle BPB 214–233), along with many other documents relevant to the case. See Oldham, *MMSS*, at i. 576–577. Buller's Paper Book was undoubtedly the source used by Henry Roscoe for the version of *Barzillai* that he printed in 1831 in volume 3 of *Douglas's Reports*. The version in *Douglas's Reports* tracks closely the language from Buller's manuscript note of the judges' opinion as quoted and transcribed by Lawrence in the *Pollard* case. See pp. 303–304, below; also 8 T.R. at 441–442.

[42] M. S. Hardcastle ed., *Life of John, Lord Campbell*, 2 vols. (1881), i. 215. Unfortunately, the contents of Campbell's drawer were burned, so the 'bad Ellenborough cases' cannot be identified.

Another example of 'bad law', this one much quieter, is shown by a collegial exchange between Lord Mansfield and Chief Baron Parker involving the case of *Attorney-General* v. *Countess of Portland*, decided by the Court of Exchequer when Parker was chief baron. In the case of *Doe d. Bayntun* v. *Watton*[43] the case of *Attorney-General* v. *Portland* was mentioned and was said to have been argued four times in the Court of Exchequer, so that a case in *Wilson's Reports* that seemed contrary 'must be a mistake'.[44] Lord Mansfield agreed, saying, 'I think it must be so, and the other authorities are, I am afraid, too strong to be got over.' Mansfield was sorry about this; he thought it would have been better to have a rule that favoured a construction of a lease that would make it valid, surely the parties' intention, but in *Doe* v. *Watton*, he could not do it.

In *Pugh* v. *Leeds*,[45] Lord Mansfield explained how he changed his mind. The first edition of *Parker's Reports* was published in 1776, the year before the *Pugh* case was decided. Before going to press, Parker asked Lord Mansfield to review the cases that he had ready for publication, *Attorney-General* v. *Portland* among them. Lord Mansfield did so, and in reading *Attorney-General* v. *Portland*, he came to a new understanding of how the lease terms had been understood by the drafters. He told Parker about this, and Parker confessed that he had doubts about his own opinion in the *Attorney-General* v. *Portland* case. As a result, Parker withdrew his report of the case, and it was never printed. This enabled Lord Mansfield in *Pugh* v. *Leeds* to notify the Bar that the case of *Attorney-General* v. *Portland* was no longer authoritative.

Summary

Learning the law in eighteenth-century England was one thing; keeping up-to-date on decided cases was another. The twenty-first-century lawyer, with electronic resources ready at hand, need not be equipped with a capacious memory and need not labour to create and maintain a personal set of notes of decided cases. The eighteenth-century barrister, however, could not look up the law so easily. The printed reports were non-existent for some years, and even for years that were covered (prior to *Term Reports* at least), there was substantial lag time—often decades—between the year when a case was decided and the year when its report was published. Successful barristers simply had no choice. It was essential for them to create their own sets of manuscript case reports, usually a combination of their personal notes from cases in which they participated or which they attended, and notes borrowed from others and copied.

By the turn of the nineteenth century, the quantity and quality of printed reports had sharply increased, especially compared to a century before. King's

---

[43] (1776) 1 Cowp. 189.
[44] Ibid., at 191.
[45] (1777) 2 Cowp. 714.

Bench cases were appearing steadily in *Term Reports*. *Nisi prius* reporting was well-established. The debates and resolutions of the twelve judges in Crown cases reserved were in print and continuing. The time was near when manuscript notes of cases would no longer be brought out as superior to the printed reports, and could even be discounted as inferior, even untrustworthy. Thus in *Pouchee* v. *Lieven*,[46] Samuel Comyn, responding as counsel to John Campbell's argument against granting a new trial, 'said that the cases cited in Tidd's Practice in favour of this practice *were only MSS*'.[47] Again, in *Sayer* v. *Verdenhalm*,[48] Comyn cited the case of *Mills* v. *Head* adding that 'the MS. case to the contrary, quoted in argument in *Mills* v. *Head*, was not treated by the Court as an authority'.[49]

Even Mr Justice Lawrence, despite his extensive collection of manuscript case notes, began in the early 1800s to show a preference for printed reports. In *Martin* v. *Smith*,[50] the Court of King's Bench held that the plaintiff's general allegations of good and satisfactory title and of his readiness to convey property under contract to the defendant were tantamount to performance so as to entitle him to recover for a breach on the defendant's part in not paying the purchase money. Mr Justice Lawrence began his short opinion as follows: 'I cannot find any printed precedents of this sort of action by a vendor against a vendee of an estate for not accepting the title and paying the purchase money. I have manuscript precedents like the present; but those I do not rely upon in the consideration of the question.'[51]

II. LAWRENCE'S NOTES OF CASES

The Court of Common Pleas

Lawrence's notes of cases decided by the Court of Common Pleas begin with Easter Term 1787. This is due to the fact that Lawrence was raised to the degree of serjeant-at-law in February 1787. Despite attempts to end the custom,[52] the Court of Common Pleas continued to require that counsel in cases coming before the court be of the rank of serjeant-at-law. After Michaelmas Term 1787, Lawrence stopped noting Common Pleas cases, making the following entry in his notebook: 'For subsequent cases determined in the Court of Common Pleas, *vide* the Reports of Mr. Henry Blackstone.'[53] There is a gap in Lawrence's notes from Michaelmas Term 1787 until March 1794, when Lawrence was sworn in as a Common Pleas justice, a post he held for only three months, after which he transferred to the

---

[46] (1815) 4 M. & S. 427.
[47] Ibid., at 427 (emphasis added).
[48] (1817) 6 M. & S. 218.
[49] Ibid., at 218–219.
[50] (1805) 6 East 555.
[51] Ibid., at 562.
[52] See Oldham, *MMSS*, i. 125–127.
[53] Lawrence case notes, p. 39, below.

King's Bench.[54] Despite Lawrence's earlier note about relying on Henry Blackstone's reports, he reported five cases during his short stay on the Court of Common Pleas as a puisne justice.[55]

Apart from his own appearances, Lawrence's notes of the 1787 Common Pleas cases, together with reports of some of those cases in *The Times*, show the dominance as counsel in the Common Pleas of Serjeants Simon Le Blanc, James Adair, James Bolton, and George Bond. Also making occasional appearances were Serjeants Thomas Kerby, Giles Rooke, George Hill, and John Scott (later Lord Eldon).

(a) Hurry v. *Watson* (1786 to 1788)

The absence of nominate reports for the Court of Common Pleas from 1780 to 1787 could suggest that nothing noteworthy occurred during those years. Such a supposition, however, would be unwarranted. Manuscript case notes from unreported years show an active Court of Common Pleas dealing competently with a wide variety of issues.[56] This can also be demonstrated by the case of *Hurry* v. *Watson*. In addition to Lawrence's brief notes of the case[57] and several short articles in *The Times*, a verbatim report of most stages of the case was fortuitously published from shorthand notes by a student at Lincoln's Inn, Robert Alderson.[58] Lawrence records only the court's response to the motion

---

[54] According to the memoirs of the barrister Isaac Espinasse, Lawrence 'was a judge of considerable ability and learning', who 'afforded a striking proof, of how little practise at the bar is required to constitute an able judge when called to the bench'. See Espinasse, 'My Contemporaries', pp. 220, 316. Espinasse said that during his practice years, Lawrence's 'talents had not been appreciated as they deserved, and his rank of business bore no proportion to his merits'. Lawrence's practice was in the Court of King's Bench until Hilary Term 1787, when he 'took the Coif', after which, 'until the year 1794, he practised in the Court of Common Pleas, at which time he was made a judge of that court'. After Lawrence obtained the rank of serjeant, 'he necessarily became a leader'. Ibid.

[55] See below, pp. 40–43. The first edition of Henry Blackstone's reports, covering cases in Common Pleas from Easter Term 1788 to Trinity Term 1791, was published in 1793. Possibly Lawrence wrote his note referring to Henry Blackstone's reports in 1794 just as he was going on the bench. More likely, he knew as of Michaelmas Term 1787 or shortly thereafter that Henry Blackstone was taking up Common Pleas reporting. John Wallace, in *The Reporters*, at p. 532, refers to a citation by Mr Baron Perryn in Henry Blackstone's report of the case of *Gibson* v. *Minet* to 'Term Rep. C.P.', and this suggests that Blackstone published his notes of Common Pleas cases after each term ended, in the same manner as King's Bench cases were being reported by Durnford and East (whose reports came to be known as *Term Reports*).

[56] See, e.g. Oldham, 'Underreported', pp. 131–145, for a discussion of the sophisticated opinions of Common Pleas Chief Justice Peter King (from his own case notes) during another set of years when no nominate case reports for that court were published, 1714–22.

[57] See below, p. 10.

[58] See the Appendix, where the entire Alderson transcription is reproduced. I am indebted to John D. Gordan III of New York City for extending to me his personal copy of the Alderson publication. The full title is as follows: 'Proceedings at the Assizes at Thetford, on the 18th of March, 1786 and the 24th of March, 1787, in the Trial of William Hurry, Merchant, of the Borough of Great Yarmouth, on an Indictment Preferred Against Him by John Watson, Attorney at Law, then Mayor-Elect of the said Borough, for Wilful and Corrupt Perjury: And in the Action Against the said John Watson, then Mayor of the said Borough, brought by the said William Hurry, for a *Malicious Prosecution* of Him by the Above Indictment: With the *Substance* of Mr. Partridge's Opening in the *First* Trial: And the Speeches *at Large* of Mess. Erskine and Harding in the *Last*, to Which are Added a Relation of the Nonsuit in the *Latter* Cause at the Norfolk Assizes in August

for a new trial on the ground of excessive damages, yet from Alderson's publication we learn that other issues were argued, including a question whether the jury verdict should be set aside because the jury arrived at its verdict by an improper method.

(i) Excessive Damages[59]

A few days prior to the hearing in *Hurry* v. *Watson* noted by Lawrence, the case of *Monroe* v. *Elliot* came before the Court of Common Pleas.[60] There, the court granted a rule to show cause why the verdict should not be set aside because the £200 verdict of the jury on a writ of inquiry was excessive against the defendant, 'a constable, who during his attending one Aylett, an attorney, while in the pillory for perjury, had given the Plaintiff a violent blow on the head with his mace'.[61] The court set aside the verdict, and a new trial produced a second verdict of £150. In *Hurry* v. *Watson*, the trial jury awarded £3,000 damages in the action for a malicious prosecution for perjury, and a motion was made to set the verdict aside as excessive. According to Lawrence's notes, Chief Justice Loughborough observed that the court had done so in *Monroe* v. *Elliot*, and he said that 'the question was more a question of feeling than reasoning'.[62] He thought £3,000 too much, but £1,000 would not have been excessive. Ultimately, the parties settled for £1,500.

On the merits, this dispute seems to have been much ado about virtually nothing, apparently fuelled by passionate local politics. In summary the facts were these: from time to time in Yarmouth, anchors and cables that had been lost at sea were located by men called 'salvors' and were placed in the Castle Yard under the care of the Admiralty. This property could then be reclaimed by captains and owners on paying salvage fees. This procedure was followed by a Captain Shipley, for whom William Hurry served as agent. John Watson was at the time Register of the Court of Admiralty. In September 1785, several weeks after Captain Shipley recovered his anchors and cables, William Hurry brought an action against Watson in the local Court of Requests, taking an oath that Watson had overcharged Shipley for the salvage, and demanding repayment of eleven shillings. Watson denied the debt and subsequently preferred an indictment against Hurry for perjury due to the oath Hurry had sworn in the Court of Requests. The indictment was tried at the assizes at Thetford on 18 March 1786 before Mr Justice Nares and a special jury. The defendant, William Hurry, was acquitted.

Last; and a Report of the Argument Thereupon in the Court of Common Pleas the Michaelmas Term following; and the Judgment of that Court as Delivered by the Lord Chief Justice, when the Nonsuit was Set Aside, and a New Trial Granted.' For an expanded discussion of the litigation, see J. Oldham, 'Only Eleven Shillings: Abusing Public Justice in England in the Late Eighteenth Century', *The Green Bag* 2nd ser. 15 (2012), pp. 175, 263.

[59] See generally, J. Oldham, *Trial by Jury: The Seventh Amendment and Anglo-American Special Juries* (2006), pp. 64–73.
[60] See below, p. 4.
[61] Ibid.
[62] Below, p. 10.

Hurry then brought a suit against Watson for malicious prosecution, tried at the summer assizes in 1786 at Norfolk before Chief Baron Skynner and a special jury. Hurry was nonsuited, but in Michaelmas Term 1786 the nonsuit was set aside by the Court of Common Pleas and a new trial was granted. The new trial was held at the Thetford assizes on 24 March 1787 before Mr Justice Ashhurst and a special jury. This time, with the costly assistance of counsel Thomas Erskine, Hurry prevailed, obtaining a verdict of £3,000. That verdict was challenged immediately in the Court of Common Pleas, and counsel for the plaintiff showed that the plaintiff's case had sufficient merit 'to induce the Court to call for the Judges Report'.[63] Then on 13 June 1787, the motion to set aside the verdict and grant a new trial was heard, as reflected in Lawrence's notes and in the appendix to this volume. Serjeants Bolton and Rooke appeared for the defendant; Serjeants Adair, Bond and Lawrence were for the plaintiff.

Serjeant Adair noted the 'extreme reluctance which the Court always feels when a verdict is given by a respectable Special Jury'.[64] He commented on the perverseness of Watson's malicious prosecution and argued that the case before the court was 'a matter which it was peculiarly the province of a Jury to decide upon; of a Jury of the county, where the conduct of both the parties were under their consideration; of a Jury, composed of gentlemen, who were acquainted with both the parties, who knew the character and the circumstances of both the parties'.[65]

Counsel for the plaintiff, however, faced some resistance by Lord Loughborough on the question of damages. Loughborough noted the evidence of very heavy expenses for the prosecution, saying, 'This I dislike very much'— 'It is probable that the Jury, in estimating their damages, started from the 600 l. which was proved upon the trial to have been laid out by the present plaintiff.'[66] Serjeant Bond responded by claiming that, 'when I go to a Jury, I have a right to state to that Jury what damages I find sustained in procuring counsel to protect me', and he argued that, in any case, 'If counsel for the defendant thought that the expence of £800 for fees ought not to have been brought in evidence, they ought at the trial to have stated their objections.'

Serjeant Lawrence's abilities are well displayed in his argument on Hurry's behalf. He cited all the relevant cases in which damages that were said to be excessive were upheld. One, *Lord Townsend* v. *Hughes*,[67] upheld a jury verdict for £4,000 in a case for words, but Chief Justice Loughborough put little stock in that case since it was a time 'of high political ferment'. Serjeant Bolton, for the defendant, attributed the jury's award to the effect of Erskine's speech more than anything else, admitting that 'Mr. Erskine earned his fee, for, upon this

---

[63] See Appendix, p. 365, below. The request would go to Mr Justice Ashhurst in the Court of King's Bench, who tried the case at the Thetford assizes, sitting temporarily as a Common Pleas judge. Mr Justice Ashhurst would use his own trial notes to prepare a report for the justices of Common Pleas of the special jury trial that had produced the £3,000 verdict.
[64] Appendix, p. 368, below.
[65] Ibid.
[66] Appendix, p. 370, below.
[67] (1677) 2 Mod. 150.

occasion, he out-Heroded Herod'.[68] The effect, Bolton claimed, was 'to make the Court and Jury madder than a fever'. Serjeant Rooke argued the same: 'there cannot be a doubt, but that these damages are owing more to the speech of Mr. Erskine than to anything that Mr. Hurry actually suffered.'[69]

Lord Loughborough gave his opinion that the plaintiff was entitled to 'substantial and very considerable damages', but if excessive,

> the enquiry is open to another Jury; because from the circumstances of the excess, it is to be inferred, that the verdict was given in the hurry of a Nisi Prius; the Court does not arrogate hereby to itself the right of assessing damages, nor does it affect the credit of a Jury. The Court does nothing more, than direct a cooler enquiry should be made.[70]

In these reflections, Lord Loughborough seems to have been of the same mind as Lord Raymond, Chief Justice of the King's Bench, in *Chambers* v. *Robinson* (1726),[71] a case that also involved an action for malicious prosecution of an indictment for perjury. The jury had awarded damages of £1,000, but the court ordered a new trial, saying that 'it was but reasonable he [the Plaintiff] should try another Jury, before he was finally charged with £1,000'. Later, however, Chief Justice Pratt of the Court of Common Pleas in *Beardmore* v. *Carrington*[72] disapproved the *Chambers* case, calling the reason given by Lord Raymond ('to give the defendant a chance of another jury') 'a very bad reason; for if it was not, it would be a reason for a third and fourth trial, and would be digging up the constitution by the roots; and therefore we are free to say this case is not law'.[73] Lord Loughborough in *Hurry* v. *Watson* made no reference to the *Beardmore* case, even though *Beardmore* was described and relied upon in argument by Lawrence.[74]

(ii) Juror Affidavits

The fourth reason given by Serjeant Le Blanc in *Hurry* v. *Watson* for setting aside the verdict and ordering a new trial was that the special jury had used an improper method of arriving at damages. Le Blanc said that when the jurors had differed in their opinion or opinions, they adopted the foreman's suggestion that each juryman should put down a sum, all the sums would be added together, and the median figure should be their verdict.[75] Lord Loughborough later observed that, 'If that was the mode of estimating the damages, the verdict ought not to stand.'[76]

---

[68] Appendix, p. 374, below.
[69] Appendix, p. 376, below.
[70] Appendix, p. 378, below.
[71] 2 Str. 691.
[72] (1764) 2 Wils. 244.
[73] 2 Wils. at 249. Chief Justice Pratt, who later became Lord Camden, failed to mention the fact that in *Chambers*, a second trial was held in which the verdict was the same as in the first trial, and the defendant's request for a third jury was rejected—the court said 'it was not in their power to grant a third trial'. See generally Oldham, *Trial by Jury*, pp. 65–66.
[74] Appendix, p. 371, below.
[75] Appendix, p. 364, below.
[76] Appendix, p. 368, below.

The problem, however, was how to prove what the jury had done. Counsel for the defendant offered an affidavit of one of the jurors, supported by affidavits from two other persons who allegedly heard the jurymen describe this mode of having reached the verdict. The court said that the question was whether the juror's affidavit could be received; if it were inadmissible, so also were the affidavits of the other two persons.[77]

When the offer of proof was first made by Serjeant Le Blanc, Mr Justice Wilson asked, 'Do you know, Brother Le Blanc, any case where the affidavit of a Juryman has been received in evidence?' Le Blanc responded, 'I know it was refused lately in the Court of King's Bench.'[78] Mr Justice Gould and Mr Justice Heath mentioned possibly contradictory prior cases, and the issue was discussed again at the hearing on 13 June.[79]

The rule against admitting jury affidavits was firmly established in the Court of King's Bench during Lord Mansfield's time as chief justice. In *R.* v. *Thirkell*,[80] eight of the jurors signed a paper disapproving of the verdict that they had just given, and Lord Mansfield 'expressed great dislike of such representations made by jurymen, after the time of delivering their verdict'. It invited a 'very bad consequence, to listen to such subsequent representations contrary to what they had before found upon their oaths; and which might be obtained by improper applications subsequently made to them'. Mr Justice Wilmot agreed, declaring that representations made by jurymen after their departure from the bar 'ought to be totally disregarded'. This view was reaffirmed in 1772 in an unreported decision of the King's Bench,[81] and again in 1788 in *Jackson* v. *Williamson*,[82] while Lord Mansfield was yet chief justice, although inactive.

In the Court of Common Pleas, the issue about the admissibility of juror affidavits remained uncertain until 1805, when the case of *Owen* v. *Warburton* was decided.[83] There, an affidavit of a juryman was offered to show that the verdict had been decided by lot. After argument centering upon the case of

---

[77] Appendix, p. 368, below.
[78] Appendix, p. 364, below. Le Blanc was referring to the case of *Vaise* v. *Delaval* (1785) 1 T.R. 11, in which an affidavit that the jury had 'tossed up' in order to reach a verdict was rejected. Lord Mansfield said that such affidavits were not admissible, 'but in every such case the Court must derive their knowledge on some other source such as from such person having seen the transaction through a window, or by some such other means'. At the hearing in *Hurry* on 13 June, Serjeant Bond, for the plaintiff, relied on *Vaise* v. *Delaval* (see Appendix, p. 369, below), and Serjeant Bolton, for the defendant, responded, although without much conviction (Appendix, p. 375, below).
[79] Appendix, pp. 368–369, 374–375, below.
[80] (1765) 3 Burr. 1696.
[81] In *Priest* v. *Pidgeon*, 17 June 1772, a bankruptcy case, the jury found for the plaintiff apparently on the theory that the plaintiff, a victualler, had nevertheless become a trader in wine and brandy and thus had been properly declared bankrupt. Afterwards, some of the jury filed an affidavit that they did not mean to find that the defendant was a bankrupt, but according to a note by Edward East, 'the court would not hear it read, it being an established practise never to receive such affidavits'. 'MS. Notes by Buller, J. and Sir E. H. East 1754–1792', Part I, fols. 63–64 (Trinity 1769).
[82] (1788) 2 T.R. 281.
[83] (1805) 1 Bos. & Pul. 326.

Vaise v. *Delaval* and other precedents, Chief Justice James Mansfield seemed to have been of two minds about how the issue should be decided, but took the case under advisement since the authorities were contradictory. Later, he delivered the following opinion of the court:

> We have conversed with the other Judges upon this subject, and we are all of opinion that the affidavit of a juryman cannot be received. It is singular indeed that almost the only evidence of which the case admits should be shut out; but, considering the arts which might be used if a contrary rule were to prevail, we think it necessary to exclude such evidence. If it were understood to be the law that a juryman might set aside a verdict by such evidence, it might sometimes happen that a juryman, being a friend to one of the parties, and not being able to bring over his companions to his opinion, might propose a decision by lot, with a view afterwards to set aside the verdict by his own affidavit, if the decision should be against him.[84]

(iii) The Outcome

On 27 June 1787, as reflected in a consent order in the Common Pleas,[85] the parties settled the case for £1,500. The consent order is unclear whether the £1,500 was inclusive of Watson's costs, but according to a later report in *The Times*, Watson was responsible for £800 costs in addition to the £1,500.[86] This was a major victory for Serjeants Adair, Bond, and Lawrence.

At the initial hearing of the case in Easter Term, Serjeant Le Blanc had asserted that the jury's assessed damages, independent of all the costs, were 'more than he [Watson] is worth in the world'.[87] If true, it is unclear how Watson could have financed the settlement value of £1,500, plus £800 costs.

In fact, Watson devised a way to pay nothing at all. Less than ten weeks after the date of the consent order, twenty members of the corporation of Yarmouth (including Mr Watson) voted, on motion of Mr Watson, to reimburse Watson the sum of £2,300 'for the expences incurred by him in preferring a bill of indictment for perjury against Mr. Hurry, and in defending an action brought by the said William Hurry against the said John Watson in consequence thereof'.[88] According to *The Times*, the resolution of the corporation stated, in effect,

> That Mr. Watson was the Register of the Admiralty-Court, and the late Mayor of Yarmouth, and that in consequence of such offices, he had been involved in divers suits and controversies with Mr. Hurry, and had incurred thereby considerable expences; and that the assembly were sensible that Mr. Watson was influenced in

---

[84] Ibid., at 329–330 (Note: the headnote in the printed report is incorrect. It states that the court *will* set aside a verdict on an affidavit by a juror that it was decided by lot. As the quotation above shows, the court's ruling was the opposite.) By 'the other judges' Chief Justice Mansfield referred to the judges of the Court of King's Bench and the Court of Exchequer. On this informal practice of consultation, see J. Oldham 'Informal Lawmaking in England by the Twelve Judges in the Late Eighteenth and Early Nineteenth Centuries', *Law and History Review* 29 (2011), pp. 181–220.
[85] Appendix, p. 380, below.
[86] *The Times*, 28 March 1789, p. 4.
[87] Appendix, p. 364, below.
[88] *The Times*, 28 March 1789, p. 4.

his conduct by motives of public regard for the interests of the Corporation, and the dignity of the Chief Magistrate of Yarmouth, and that he bore no *ill-will* to Mr. Hurry.[89]

John Watson was not, however, completely out of the woods. On 25 January 1788, an order to show cause was heard by the Court of King's Bench on whether an information should not be exhibited against Watson and nineteen other members of the corporation of Yarmouth for having committed a libel on public justice by the action of the defendants in reimbursing Watson.[90] After argument by counsel, Mr Justice Ashhurst said that the reimbursement resolution did indeed import a libel on the public justice of the country. He said that, 'he happened to be the Judge who tried this cause; and in the course of his recollection he did not remember a grosser or stronger case of malice'. He pointed out that, 'The moment Mr. Hurry was acquitted on the charge in that indictment, Mr. Watson puts in a paragraph in the papers, that the cause only went off on account of a flaw in the indictment, and that a new indictment would soon be preferred.' Further, 'this certainly reflects on the Jury that found that verdict, and on the Judge who suffered that verdict to be found'. Mr Justice Buller concurred, as did Mr Justice Grose. The order to show cause was therefore made absolute.

The information against Watson and nineteen other members of the Yarmouth corporation was tried during the winter assizes at Thetford before Mr Justice Grose and a special jury. After two witnesses had been examined by counsel for the prosecution (Thomas Erskine), and the assembly-book of the corporation containing the reimbursement order had been examined, Mr Justice Grose determined that there was a material variance between the order entered in the assembly-book and the libel as laid in the information; thus, 'after several ingenious arguments by the Counsel on each side, the Jury found a verdict of Not Guilty, for all the defendants'.[91]

Mr Justice Lawrence on the King's Bench

(a) Counsel and the pace of trials

Lawrence's notes of appearances of counsel in cases in the Court of King's Bench, together with reports of some of the same cases that appeared in *The Times*, show two striking patterns. Counsel are identified in slightly more than 200 cases, and Thomas Erskine left his fellow barristers in the dust, appearing in nearly one-third of the cases, twice as often as the next most active (Vicary Gibbs). At the other end of the spectrum, thirty-eight different counsel appeared in only one case each; twenty-six others appeared in two to five cases each (see Table V).

---

[89] Ibid.

[90] *The Times*, 26 January 1788, p. 3. This report in *The Times* referred only to the reimbursement of Watson for the £1,500 verdict; a later report, however, made clear that the reimbursement was for the sum of £2,300 to cover the verdict and costs. See *The Times*, 28 March 1789, p. 4.

[91] *The Times*, 28 March 1789, p. 4.

Table V: Counsel Appearing Most Frequently in King's Bench Cases
Noted by Lawrence, 1794–99*

Number of Cases	Counsel
63	Thomas Ersksine
32	Vicary Gibbs
24	William Garrow
23	Edward Law
16	George Wood
15	Samuel Marryat
15	Samuel Shepherd
12	James Mingay
7	John Bayley

* As shown in Lawrence's case notes or in reports in *The Times* of the same cases reported by Lawrence.

As is shown in Table V, most of the King's Bench business was handled by a group of nine barristers. Within that group, Erskine, Gibbs, Garrow, and Law[92] were the leaders. Erskine's dominance is indicated not only by his frequent appearance, but also by the following notice that appeared in *The Times* on 30 May 1796:

Law Report

Court of King's Bench, May 28

The Court only sat about half an hour, and nothing of consequence occurred.

Mr. Erskine being at Portsmouth on his re-election for that place; and as he is retained as usual in all the business that was to have come before the Court, they could not proceed in his absence.[93]

Most of the reports of cases in Lawrence's notes are brief and appear to have involved matters of procedure or motions without much controversy. Motions asking the court to grant a show cause order were common and were commonly granted.

Legal historians have demonstrated the rapid pace of criminal trials in the Old Bailey during the late eighteenth century,[94] due in significant part to the absence or limited role of lawyers for the defence. Less attention has been paid to the pace of trial in the flow of non-criminal cases through the common law courts sitting in London and on assize. Lord Ellenborough, Kenyon's successor as chief justice of the Court of King' Bench, gained some notoriety from the blistering pace with which he conducted jury trials. In the year 1812,

---

[92] Edward Law would later become Lord Ellenborough, Lord Kenyon's successor as Chief Justice of the King's Bench.
[93] *The Times*, 30 May 1796, p. 4.
[94] See J. H. Langbein, *The Origins of Adversary Criminal Trial* (2003), pp. 16–25; J. M. Beattie, *Crime and the Courts in England 1660–1800* (1986), pp. 376–378; G. Durston, *Crime & Justice in Early Modern England 1500–1790* (2004), pp. 524–526.

for example, Ellenborough conducted trials in over 1,100 cases.⁹⁵ Lord Brougham, in his *Historical Sketches*, gave the following explanation:

> The whole City business was in the hands of [barristers] Gibbs, Garrow, and Park ... and it was a main object with them all to facilitate the dispatch of business. This they effected by at once giving up all but the arguable points of law, on which they immediately took the judge's opinion; and the maintainable questions of fact, on which they went to the jury.⁹⁶

In this way, Brougham claimed, 'Fifteen or twenty important causes were thus disposed of in a morning, more to the satisfaction of the Court and the benefit of the Counsel than to the contentment of the parties or their attorneys.'⁹⁷

Lawrence's notes suggest that the pace of trial was also swift during Lord Kenyon's chief justiceship. This is confirmed by occasional newspaper reports of activity in the courts. On 10 February 1791, for example, *The Times* reported that at Westminster Hall, 'Lord Kenyon sat at Nisi Prius at twelve o'clock', and, 'The bulk of the cases that were tried were undefended.'⁹⁸ Several months later, *The Times* reported that at Guildhall, 'Yesterday morning at 9 o'clock, Lord Kenyon sat at nisi prius, and tried about thirty causes before two o'clock.'⁹⁹ If true, this meant that the average time per case was only ten minutes.¹ Even more arresting, *The Times* reported that on 4 July 1791, 'His Lordship sat at Nisi Prius about two o'clock and tried twenty-one issues before four'²—which would have been at the blazing speed of approximately six minutes per case.³

Statistics appeared sporadically in the newspapers that also demonstrated the high volume case-load in the civil trial docket for the Court of King's Bench. On 21 June 1791, *The Times* reported that at Guildhall as of 20 June,

---

⁹⁵ See J. Oldham, 'Law-making at *Nisi Prius*', at pp. 221, 226–227.

⁹⁶ Henry, Lord Brougham, *Historical Sketches of Statesmen Who Flourished in the time of George III*, 3rd ser., 3 vols. (1843), iii. 212.

⁹⁷ Ibid., at p. 284, n. 62. See generally, Oldham, 'Law-making at *Nisi Prius*', at p. 221.

⁹⁸ *The Times*, 11 February 1791, p. 3. Similarly, *Lloyd's Evening Post*, 1 December 1790, reported that, 'The Causes in the Paper of the Sittings on the first entry of the late Term, were of so *trifling* ... a nature, that verdicts were obtained, many of them being even without *defence*, in more than thirty during the day.' See also Oldham, 'Law-making at *Nisi Prius*', at p. 228 for a mid-nineteenth-century recollection by a Lincoln's Inn barrister that, 'Formerly at the sittings during Term at Guildhall, in the City of London, only undefended causes were taken, such as actions on bills of exchange, promissory notes, and other similar inquiries—where, in fact, the proof of the handwriting of the parties constituted the whole of the evidence to be produced.'

⁹⁹ *The Times*, 28 June 1791, p. 3.

¹ Perhaps many of these were also undefended, or perhaps some were passed over because of the non-appearance of attorneys (see Table VI below). *The Times* for 11 November 1803, p. 3 reported that Lord Eldon 'sat precisely at nine o'clock, and disposed of six causes in the course of an hour'. This, too, would have required a blazing pace of ten minutes per case. The report in *The Times* explained, however, that, 'In five of them the parties were not ready, and therefore they were obliged to withdraw the Records.' See in this connection Table VI below and text following.

² *The Times*, 5 July 1791, p. 3.

³ Other reports were less dramatic, showing nevertheless very rapid case handling. See *The Times* for 26 May 1792, p. 3 (twenty-five cases tried by Lord Kenyon by 3.00 p.m., which would be fifteen minutes per case, assuming a 9.00 a.m. start time); 18 July 1800, p. 3 (six special jury causes were disposed of before 11.00 a.m., or twenty minutes per case, again assuming a 9.00 a.m. start time).

'there were 103 causes in his Lordship's paper'.[4] And on 24 June 1791, it was reported that, 'Near 80 Causes remain to be tried at Guildhall.'[5] An even higher volume was reported for 22 February 1797—'Lord Kenyon sits this day at Guildhall, where there are 130 Causes entered for Trial'.[6] The case-load did slacken at times, as on 14 February 1800, when it was reported that, 'The number of causes entered at Westminster to be tried by Lord Kenyon is only sixty.'[7]

Occasionally, the number of docketed special jury cases was noted. On 27 June 1796, *The Times* reported that, as of 25 June, 'There are near 40 Special Jury causes to be tried in the course of these sittings at Guildhall.'[8] And on 10 December 1799, *The Times* reported that on that day, 'the Special Jury Causes begin, and fifty-one stand in the paper for trial'.[9]

(b) *The Court of King's Bench under Lord Kenyon*

(i) Kenyon the Outspoken

In his portrayal of Lord Kenyon in the *Oxford Dictionary of National Biography*, Douglas Hay states that, 'Concern for moral principle appeared to govern Kenyon's decisions at least as much as concern for the letter of the law.' In *Haycraft* v. *Creasy*[10] Kenyon declared 'that laws were never so well directed as when they were made to enforce religious, moral, and social duties between man and man'.[11] Hay tells us that, 'Kenyon abhorred adultery, and in criminal conversation actions he allowed more weight to circumstantial evidence and encouraged juries to award huge punitive damages that effectively turned a civil suit into a criminal punishment.'[12] Thus, 'Awards over £2000 increased fourfold while he was chief justice, and the increase in litigation that he encouraged merely reinforced his conviction that sexual misconduct was undermining social order'; indeed 'In 1799 he remarked that he wished adultery was punishable by death.'[13]

Kenyon's moral crusade was not limited to the sanctity of marriage. In *Phipps* v. *Burgess*, for example, Kenyon railed against conspiracies among journeymen to raise wages and told the jury in the case before him not to take account of the fact that the defendants were poor—'If a man who had no property chose to injure his neighbours, provided he could not answer for it in his purse, he must pay in his person.'[14] The jury, accordingly, gave a verdict for

---

[4] *The Times*, 21 June 1791, p. 3.
[5] *The Times*, 24 June 1791, p. 3.
[6] *The Times*, 23 February 1797, p. 4.
[7] *The Times*, 15 February 1800, p. 3.
[8] *The Times*, 27 June 1796, p. 3.
[9] *The Times*, 10 December 1799, p. 3.
[10] (1801) 2 East 92.
[11] Ibid., 103.
[12] *ODNB, sub nom.* 'Lloyd Kenyon'.
[13] Ibid.
[14] *The Times*, 22 July 1790, p. 3, reporting on sittings before Lord Kenyon at Guildhall, Trinity Term 1790. (By 'he must pay in his person', Lord Kenyon was referring to debtors' prison.)

the plaintiff for £500, even though the plaintiff in his declaration had stated his loss at only £300.

Another context that raised Lord Kenyon's indignation was gaming. In *McNeil* v. *Wiltshire*, Kenyon was reported to have said of men who ran gaming establishments, 'One would almost wish, that such men, by the laws of the land, *could be branded in their foreheads*, in order . . . to put the innocent and unwary on their guard against their robbery and plunder.'[15]

Although not regarded as a man of eloquence, Lord Kenyon's preaching from the bench had its effect, as is shown by the verdicts of countless respectful juries. Occasionally, jurors had post-trial remorse. On 26 March 1798, *The Times* published a letter to Lord Kenyon from 'A Juror' in which the writer described his reactions to Lord Kenyon's jury instructions while sitting on the case of *Ricketts* v. *Taylor*. He said that,

> we [the jurors] were informed by your Lordship, that the 'Defendant was hacknied in the ways of vice—that his house was a brothel, kept solely for the seduction of tradesmen's daughters, and virtuous wives', and as a result, 'I went into the consideration of a cause whose issue rested on presumptive evidence, where the criminality was constructive—where a verdict was to be given, not grounded on the incontestable proof of facts, but on the fallibility of human discretion; and, amidst my doubts, I need not blush to own that I thought the well-know sagacity, the unimpeached integrity of your Lordship, a safer guide than the imbecility of my own judgment.[16]

On returning to his 'rank as a private Citizen', the juror (who had consented to exemplary damages) was mortified 'to meet with expostulations upon what men have deemed a preposterous verdict'.[17]

Kenyon's deeply-held moral sentiments were clearly influential. His sermons from the bench, however, should be distinguished from the customary excesses that were standard fare in arguments of counsel and in comments by the judges. Just as Erskine and other counsel would often claim that the case before the court was as important a case as had ever come before the Court of King's Bench, Lord Kenyon was quick to scoff at the nature or potential of a party's claim. In *R.* v. *Crossley and Clarke*,[18] the defendants were attorneys who had been charged with forgery, which they denied in sworn affidavits. The circumstantial evidence against the defendants was quite suspicious, and the question in this first phase of the litigation against them was how much credence was to be given to their sworn affidavits. Erskine and his co-counsel confessed 'that the dead weight which pressed them down, was the blasted character of their clients', but claimed nonetheless that for purposes of an attachment, affidavits were to be regarded as true, and the defendants 'were to be considered in the same light as if they

---

[15] *The Times*, 25 May 1796, p. 3, reporting on the sittings at Guildhall before Lord Kenyon on May 24 (italics as in *The Times*).
[16] *The Times*, 26 March 1798, p. 3.
[17] Ibid.
[18] Below, p. 148.

were men of the purest characters'.[19] Lord Kenyon said that if so, 'a man must be believed who said an angel from heaven or the Pope of Rome brought a paper to him'.[20] He considered the defendant's arguments to be absurd, ridiculous—sufficient 'to turn a court of justice into mockery and ridicule'.[21]

In *Hawkins* v. *Lukin*,[22] the question was whether a man named Westwood had committed an act of bankruptcy when he went abroad on a pleasure trip, thinking that bills that he had drawn before leaving would have been paid by the acceptor. The acceptor, however, did not pay. The question was whether Westwood's going abroad constituted an act of bankruptcy. Lord Kenyon said

> this was one of the most important cases that ever was agitated. That the extent to which the arguments for the plaintiff pressed was shocking. If a man be ill and his creditors can't see him, is that an act of bankruptcy? Or if he goes out, though ever so opulent, and his creditors do not find him at home?

Despite Lord Kenyon's demonstrable influence in encouraging exemplary damages in civil cases, he was not always inflexible or intemperate in rendering judgments against convicted criminal defendants. In several of the cases in Lawrence's notes, for example, Kenyon was willing to take into account post-conviction behaviour by the defendants, but he was careful to make it clear on the record that the court was not trivializing the defendant's offence by a light punishment. In *R.* v. *Ramsay, et al.*,[23] one of the defendants was an overseer of the poor, and the other was beadle of the parish of Woolwich. They were convicted of having forced a pauper, Anne Stewart, who was in the heat of labour, into a boat that took her to London, where she was left destitute, having been delivered of a male bastard child. The court was outraged by 'this almost unparalleled instance of inhumanity', but by the time the defendants were brought up for judgment, the court had received 'very favourable representations from very responsible quarters, of the general good conduct of the defendants'; therefore, the court imposed a fine of only one shilling, recognizing that the defendants had indemnified the parish of Clerkenwell where the child was born from all expenses and had paid the expenses of the prosecution, which amounted to about £500. Lord Kenyon insisted, however, that these circumstances be inserted in the rule of court, so that 'when posterity looked at the record, they might see that the court had not treated this as a light offence'.[24]

Lord Kenyon's outspoken remarks when on his moral crusades or in cases where he thought a party's argument absurd suggested a bold self-confidence undiluted by any recognition of personal limitations or lack of knowledge. This, however, was not the case, as is shown most clearly in insurance

---

[19] *The Times*, 3 June 1796, p. 3.
[20] Below, p. 149.
[21] *The Times*, 3 June 1796, p. 3.
[22] Below, p. 152.
[23] Below, p. 66.
[24] See also, for a similar resolution, the case of *R.* v. *Skelton*, below, p. 157.

litigation. In *Calland* v. *Champion*,[25] for example, Lord Kenyon said that when he had tried the case, 'he told the jury that he did not understand what was meant by an insurable life, the expression made use of in those cases', referring to cases that had been cited by counsel on the motion for a new trial.

Most perplexing to Kenyon, however, were marine insurance cases. The case of *Burnett* v. *Kensington*[26] involved an action to recover on a policy of insurance on a cargo of fruit on board the *Commerce*, at and from Malaga to Plymouth, with liberty to touch at Gibraltar and Cadiz to join a convoy. The standard Lloyd's policy covered loss due to 'perils of the sea', but it also contained a standard exception, that damage to the cargo was not covered unless the ship suffered a general loss, or unless 'the ship be stranded'. The issue in the litigation was what was meant by 'stranding'. Four trials were conducted, each before a special jury. The phase of the case in Lawrence's notes was the motion for a new trial following the initial trial before Lord Kenyon and a special jury of merchants on 18 December 1795. A new trial was ordered, and 'Lord Kenyon said that when they had learnt the meaning of the words [the court] would decide on the construction of the policy.'[27] The case dragged on until May 1797. Along the way, counsel Vicary Gibbs remarked that he and his friend, opposing counsel Erskine, 'would some of these days be entitled to the premium for discovering the perpetual motion'.[28] At the final hearing in the case on 12 May 1797, Lord Kenyon said that the court 'had had an abundant opportunity of considering and reconsidering the case'—he had 'read and puzzled himself with it', and although at times he had wavered, in the end he had not been able 'to anchor on any one ground different from that on which it at first set out'.[29]

Lord Kenyon felt even more unsure of himself on questions of navigation. In *Thwaits* v. *Angerstein*, Lord Kenyon 'said he professed himself totally ignorant of navigation, except in so far as he had learned it from his apprenticeship in his judicial office'; that is, 'He had received a great deal of information from the different classes of merchants by whom he had the honour of being assisted in the administration of justice.'[30] And in *Casey* v. *Donald*, a negligence case involving a ship collision, Lord Kenyon confessed that, 'I am totally incapable of judging questions of this kind', but 'I do not rely on my own opinion; for I have conversed with the two respectable Gentlemen who sit beside me. [These were two of the Elder Brethren of the Trinity House, who were assessors to his Lordship, to give him any information with respect to the navigation.]'[31]

---

[25] Below, p. 171.
[26] Below, p. 104. See p. 105, n. 35, for a history of the litigation.
[27] Below, p. 105.
[28] *The Times*, 11 November 1796, p. 3.
[29] *The Times*, 13 May 1797, p. 3.
[30] *The Times*, 14 November 1798, p. 3.
[31] *The Times*, 18 December 1799, p. 3 (bracketed explanation as it appears in *The Times*).

(ii) Frustrations with the Lawyers

The *Burnett* case demonstrates the extent to which Lord Kenyon and his fellow judges were prepared to grant new trials, especially when urged to do so by Erskine and other leading counsel. The increasing frequency with which new trials were requested troubled the court. It was reported in *The Times* on 12 November 1792 that when a new trial motion was, for once, refused, the 'learned counsel . . . observed, that he had not made the application from having consulted his own judgment, but that he had been asked to do it'. Lord Kenyon responded by saying that since he had known Westminster Hall, 'new trials had increased twenty-fold', and 'he was very uneasy about it'. He said that, 'New trials should not be granted when they can only serve to heap expences on expences, merely to try experiments, without the sober advice of counsel.'[32]

Unsupportable new trial motions nevertheless persisted. In *Brier v. Kay*, a jury had awarded 40 shillings damages for a trivial assault even though the trial judge had told the jury that the case was worth only a farthing, after which Serjeant Cockle moved for a new trial on the ground of excessive damages. Lord Kenyon refused the motion, saying that, 'If they in such a case were to grant a new trial, it would make the granting of new trials ridiculous.'[33]

More troublesome to the court than new trial motions was the persistent practice of some attorneys to pad the pleadings in order to increase their fees. In *Herriot v. Stewart*,[34] Lord Kenyon rejected the argument by counsel for the plaintiff who had moved to set aside a nonsuit, saying that 'there was nothing in it', and complaining, 'Why did they so foolishly stuff their declaration with all these terms?' Mr Justice Ashhurst agreed, stating that inconvenience and expense resulted from 'permitting the parties to stuff their declarations with useless and impertinent matter'.[35]

Occasionally the court tried to check this practice. In a trover action in 1790, *Koops v. Chapman*, the question was whether the plaintiff was subject to the bankrupt laws, and counsel for the plaintiff—Erskine, Mingay, and Lawes—were unable to present a persuasive case. Lord Kenyon said that the jury must find a verdict for the defendants, but 'The Plaintiff wished to be non-suited, and accordingly was non-suited.'[36] The solicitor for the plaintiff was Mr Crossley, and according to *The Times*, the court ordered him 'to pay the costs for delivering a declaration of eighty sheets, when the learned Judge declared, eight would have been sufficient'.[37]

The problem of padded pleadings was not limited to civil cases. Responding to an indictment containing no fewer than forty-two assignments of perjury,

---

[32] *The Times*, 12 November 1792, p. 4.
[33] *The Times*, 18 April 1796, p. 3.
[34] Below, p. 136.
[35] Below, p. 136, n. 85.
[36] *The Times*, 15 December 1790, p. 4. The preference for a nonsuit was strategic, in order to avoid a negative jury verdict so that a new action could be brought if better evidence could be produced.
[37] Ibid.

Lord Kenyon called it 'very shameful', and said that he understood 'that Lord Mansfield had refused to try an indictment for perjury that contained a smaller number of charges than forty-two till they had reduced the number'.[38]

Perhaps the prize-winning case of inflated pleadings was *Cowan v. Berry*, tried in Easter Term 1798,[39] in which the court seemed unable to take control. According to Lawrence's notes, the declaration was 'against the defendant for winning money at play of one who was the plaintiff's clerk and who was afterwards hanged for forgery, which he was induced to commit from distresses brought on him by losses at play'. The penalties claimed by the plaintiff amounted to £1,330,000, and 'it was said the declaration was so long it would cost about £700 to come in to court to meet the plaintiff'.[40] According to a report in *The Times*, counsel for the defendant, James Mingay, claimed that the declaration 'consisted of 480 counts, containing between 2 and 3000 sheets, and measuring in length upwards of 100 yards'.[41] The vast sum of £1,330,000 was achieved by counting each loss suffered at play by each of thirty-two persons with whom the defendant played at the gaming tables as a violation of the statute of Queen Anne (9 Anne, c. 14). These were then assembled, to produce penalties of £1,000 per day per person. Lord Kenyon said, 'If this had been for the purpose of oppression, the court would set their face against it', but he would not 'accede to the doctrine that the more offences a man has committed, that on that account the penalties ought to be remitted'.[42] Lawrence added a *nota bene*, stating that he understood Kenyon's comment to be

> a reference to what Buller, Justice, had said at Salisbury in an action brought by Mr. Petrie against Lord Porchester and others for bribery at Cricklade, when he told the jury that if the plaintiff had no conscience and acted like a Jew in going for every penny that the defendant might be liable to, that the jury might mitigate them and give no more than they thought reasonable.[43]

The *Cowan* case was a *qui tam* action. Until the judges intervened in 1795, *qui tam* actions presented another opportunity for abuse by attorneys. As stated in *Tidd's Practice*, 'On the delivery of the issue, or returning the paper book in the King's Bench, the defendant was formerly obliged to pay for copies of the pleadings . . . , and in a *qui tam* action, he paid double.'[44] This payment was called 'issue money', and if it was not paid, the plaintiff or prosecutor was entitled to a signed judgment which, according to a report in *The Times*, 'could not be set aside without considerable expence'.[45] Thus,

---

[38] *The Times*, 15 November 1796, p. 2.
[39] See below, p. 183.
[40] Ibid.
[41] *The Times*, 28 April 1798, p. 3.
[42] Below, p. 184.
[43] Ibid. The court in the *Cowan* case fretted about whether the case was so unmanageable that it would not be possible for a judge and jury to decide it. In the end, the case was settled. See *The Times*, 13 February 1799, p. 3.
[44] William Tidd, *The Practice of the courts of King's Bench, and Common Pleas: in personal actions; and ejectment: to which are added, the law and practise of extents; and the rules of court, and modern decisions, in the Exchequer of Pleas*, 8th ed., 2 vols. (1828), ii. 784.
[45] Ibid.; also, *The Times*, 4 May 1795, p. 2.

many practisers, who disgraced the profession by their misconduct, often brought *qui tam* actions, for which there was not the least foundation, solely for the purpose of getting the issue-money, which often amounts to a considerable sum, as the pleadings in such actions generally run out to a great length; and the moment they received the issue-money, they dropped the action.[46]

To counteract this abuse, 'Lord Chief Justice Kenyon last Term laid down a new rule from the Bench, which, he said, had been adopted by all the Courts in Westminster Hall', which provided that 'what is called the issue money, in *all penal actions*, should not be paid as formerly, on delivering the issue to the Defendant, but should be taxed with the costs'.[47] As *The Times* editorialized:

> This excellent regulation, therefore, will operate as a powerful check on *Pettifoggers*, who made a livelihood by such dishonourable practices. As the Issue Money is now to continue an *Item* in the taxed Costs, it is to be presumed that *no qui tam action* will be commenced that has not some foundation; as the Attorney can get no money till he comes to the conclusion of the suit, and gets his costs taxed.[47a]

Another problem that continually vexed the courts was the use of delaying tactics by the attorneys. One method came to be known as 'sham pleading'. As reported in *The Times* on 13 February 1798, the Court of King's Bench 'seems to be extremely desirous to put an end to this very disgraceful practise'. Responding to a complaint about sham pleading by counsel Erskine in a case before the court, Lord Kenyon said, 'I am very sorry that the term, *sham-pleading*, is ever used in the language of Courts of Justice.' Mr Justice Ashhurst agreed, declaring that, 'This is certainly a very scandalous subterfuge, and is now looked upon as a justifiable thing.'[48] He said that it would give him great pleasure 'if it could by any means be curtailed'.[49]

Delay could also be achieved by means other than sham pleading. A case in point involved the aftermath following an arbitration of a case brought by Mr Stephen Phillips against Lord Falkland, John King, and others. Phillips prevailed in the arbitration, but the defendants refused to honour the award. Phillips then sought an attachment against the defendants for contempt since the award had been made a rule of court. Lawrence's case notes explain that the case against Falkland was dropped since he invoked the privilege of the peerage as a Scottish peer,[50] but by a variety of motions and stratagems,

---

[46] *The Times*, 4 May 1795, p. 2.
[47] Ibid. The rule is printed at 6 T.R. 218, Hilary Term 1795.
[47a] *The Times*, 4 May 1795, p. 2.
[48] *The Times*, 13 February 1798, p. 3.
[49] Ibid. Nothing appears to have been done until twenty years later. In *Bartley* v. *Godslake* (1818) 2 B. & Ald. 199, the Court of King's Bench held that where a sham plea was such as would make it necessary for the plaintiff's attorney to consult counsel and thereby cause delay and expense, the plaintiff was permitted to sign judgment 'as for want of a plea', and 'to prevent such pleas being pleaded in future, they [the court] directed that the defendant's attorney should pay the costs of the application'. For a like result in a later case, see *Shadbolt* v. *Berthod* (1822) 5 B. & Ald. 750.
[50] Below, p. 131 (13 April 1796).

counsel for the other defendants managed to stretch the case across almost two and one-half years. The dispute originated in 1794 as an indictment for a conspiracy to cheat a tradesman out of a large sum of money, between £3,000 and £4,000. Leading counsel throughout were Mingay for the plaintiff and Erskine for the defendants. On 4 February 1795, a hearing was conducted on Erskine's motion to put off the trial of the indictment because of the absence of a material witness. Lord Kenyon allowed the trial to be put off to the next term, but said that 'then it must peremptorily come on'— 'It must not stand over from June to January and from January to June . . . as long as the parties please.'[51] The trial was held after Trinity Term 1795, and the defendants were acquitted 'on condition that they would enter into a rule to refer it to Alexander Champion, Esq. to say how much money was due from the parties to Mr. Phillips, and in what proportion the defendants should pay that sum'.[52] After more delay, the arbitrator issued his award on 31 December, ordering Lord Falkland and Mr King each to pay specified sums of money, together amounting to £5,543.[53] Erskine then, in Hilary Term 1796, filed a motion to set aside the award. Meanwhile, an attorney for the defendants prepared and filed a bill in Chancery against Phillips, despite the fact that the defendants had undertaken not to do so in the arbitration proceeding. An attachment was then sought against the attorney for contempt.

On and on the litigation continued throughout 1796 and into 1797.[54] At a hearing on 11 June 1796, Mingay complained that his client 'had been obliged to attend the Court from Term to Term, from week to week, and he might say, almost from day to day, in order to recover of Mr. King a sum little short of £6000 which had been awarded to him by Mr. Champion'.[55] Several days later, Lord Kenyon said, 'he had almost lived in this cause', and, 'Speaking either legally or morally, nothing could justify these proceedings.'[56] It proved necessary for Lord Kenyon to live in the cause still longer, as it was not settled until 6 May 1797.[57]

Yet another major frustration experienced by Lord Kenyon was the recurrent failure of attorneys to attend to their cases when they were called. Table VI lists examples that were noted in *The Times*. Lord Kenyon seemed unable to deal effectively with this problem. He grumbled that, 'Attorneys must have it impressed on their minds, that they must attend, and the only effectual way to do that, was *to touch their purses.*'[58] He said 'it was scandalous and infamous for Attorneys to charge their Clients for their non-attendance and he wished with all his heart that Clients would bring actions against such

---

[51] *The Times*, 5 February 1795, p. 4.
[52] *The Times*, 15 February 1796, p. 3.
[53] Ibid. The article in *The Times* describing the proceedings at this stage was captioned, 'Legal Fencing'.
[54] Accounts of the progress of the case appeared regularly in *The Times*.
[55] *The Times*, 13 June 1796, p. 3.
[56] *The Times*, 16 June 1796, p. 3.
[57] *The Times*, 8 May 1797, p. 3.
[58] *The Times*, 21 July 1791, p. 3 (emphasis in the original).

INTRODUCTION   lvii

Table VI: Non-appearance and Unpreparedness of Attorneys and Counsel

Date	*From* The Times
8 July 1789	'Lord Kenyon sat only about an hour, as the attorneys were not prepared to go on with any more Causes.'[59]
11 November 1789	'Yesterday when Lord Kenyon came into the Court of King's Bench, there was not one Counsel present.'[60]
20 July 1791	'Lord Kenyon was obliged this morning to withdraw eight or nine records, because the attorneys did not attend with their witnesses.'[61]
29 July 1791	'As the Attorneys were not ready with their witnesses, Lord Kenyon was obliged to stop at ten o'clock.'[62]
29 November 1791	'Lord Kenyon came into Court at nine o'clock, and was obliged to sit a whole hour before he was able to go on. No Attorney or Witness attended, though the Counsel were all ready.'[63]
24 January 1793	'The Court only sat about half a hour, and heard a few motions.—counsel were not prepared to proceed to business.'[64]
10 December 1795	'This morning the Lord Chief Justice, the Jury, and the Counsel waited almost a whole hour before they could proceed with a single cause, on account of the absence of the Attorneys and their Witnesses.'[65]
9 December 1796	'Lord Kenyon, the Gentlemen of the Jury, and the Counsel attended this morning as usual, precisely at nine o'clock, and remained in Court upwards of an hour, without being able to do any business of consequence, because the Attorneys did not attend with their witnesses.'[66]
22 June 1799	'Lord Kenyon was obliged to stop about half past 11 o'clock as the Attorneys were not ready to proceed in any more causes.'[67]
25 February 1801	'Lord Kenyon sat this morning at Nisi Prius, at Guildhall; from nine till 11 o'clock, when he could proceed no farther, as none of the parties were ready.'[68]
3 December 1801	'Lord Kenyon was punctual to time, as usual; but when the Causes were called on, the Attorneys did not appear. Several Causes were of course struck out of the paper; and when the Defendants were ready, his Lordship directed the Plaintiffs to be nonsuited.'[69]

[59] *The Times*, 9 July 1789, p. 3.
[60] *The Times*, 12 November 1789, p. 3.
[61] *The Times*, 21 July 1791, p. 3.
[62] *The Times*, 30 July 1791, p. 3
[63] *The Times*, 30 November 1791, p. 3.
[64] *The Times*, 8 July 1793, p. 3.
[65] *The Times*, 11 December 1795, p. 4.
[66] *The Times*, 10 December 1796, p. 3
[67] *The Times*, 24 June 1799, p. 3.
[68] *The Times*, 25 February 1801, p. 3.
[69] *The Times*, 4 December 1801.

Attorneys for negligence, who were the ruin of many poor families'.[70] Erskine sympathized, saying 'that the only way of curing Attorneys and Witnesses of this evil, was to strike out every cause where the parties were not ready to proceed'.[71] Kenyon eventually threatened to take such action. When attorneys and witnesses failed to appear at the sittings on 10 December 1795, 'His Lordship gave notice that if the Attorneys were not ready with their witnesses to-morrow morning by nine o'clock, he would strike out one cause after another till he went through the whole list, except the Special Juries.'[72] If this threat had any effect, it was only short-term. A year later, the attorneys and witnesses again were absent, and Lord Kenyon reverted to expressing indignation about 'the expence parties were put to by the carelessness and neglect of those whom they had entrusted with the management of their affairs'.[73] Near the end of his life, he began to take firm action. After the attorneys again failed to appear on 3 December 1801, Kenyon 'stated a case that happened within his own recollection, where a man brought an action against his Attorney for similar negligence, and recovered 1500*l.* damages', after which he reportedly struck 'upwards of twenty cases' out of the paper.[74]

Lord Kenyon's timidity in dealing with this problem stands in contrast to the way his predecessor, Lord Mansfield, dealt with the practising Bar. It was reported in the *Morning Chronicle* for 22 May 1782 that, on the Monday before, Mansfield 'sat in Westminster Hall unattended by any Gentlemen of the Bar'. This was, however, an absence by way of protest, since Mansfield had announced his intention to sit on the first day of Whitsuntide week despite a reminder from barrister James Wallace that it was the custom to adjourn the sittings during the first days of that week. According to the *Chronicle*, 'In consequence of this the Gentlemen of the Bar formed the general agreement not to attend the Court on Monday, notwithstanding which his Lordship proceeded in the business of the day, and made the Attorneys conduct their own causes, and examine their own witnesses.'

Notwithstanding Lord Kenyon's recurrent frustrations with the attorneys, the relationship between Kenyon and the barristers who appeared before him was largely cordial and cooperative. Even so, it was plain that Kenyon had his favourites, and the most favoured of all was Thomas Erskine.

(c) *Lawrence's case notes and Espinasse's reports*

Ten of the cases in Lawrence's case notes that appear in this volume were also reported by Isaac Espinasse in his *nisi prius* reports. Espinasse's reports, in their

---

[70] *The Times*, 30 November 1791, p. 3. Little appears to have changed a decade later, when Kenyon lamented that, 'he had several times prescribed a remedy which; if pursued, he conceived would prove effectual; and that was, that any persons who had suffered from the negligence of those whom they had employed to transact their business, would bring an action against them.' *The Times*, 25 February 1801, p. 3.
[71] Ibid.
[72] *The Times*, 11 December 1795, p. 4.
[73] *The Times*, 10 December 1796, p. 3.
[74] *The Times*, 4 December 1801, p. 3.

day, were held in low esteem. As Lord Denman observed, 'I am tempted to remark for the benefit of the profession that *Espinasse's Reports*, in days nearer their own time, when their want of accuracy was better known than it is now, were never quoted without doubt and hesitation, and a special reason was often given as an apology for citing that particular case.'[75] Lord Denman acknowledged that in his time, Espinasse was cited with approval, but this may have been, as he suggested, because the Bar was no longer aware of the deficiencies.

A comparison of Espinasse's reports of the ten cases printed in this volume with Mr Justice Lawrence's notes of the same cases permits brief comment on the contemporary criticism to which Espinasse's reports were subjected. On the whole, Espinasse's reports of the ten cases and Lawrence's case notes correspond. When the issue before the full court had been reserved at trial or when the motion before the court was for a new trial or to set aside a nonsuit, the phase of the case reported by Espinasse would be related to the phase of the case noted by Lawrence, and a comparison can be made.[76] Where possible, Espinasse included information about post-trial stages of the cases that he reported, as in *Hubert v. Groves*.[77] Espinasse reported that during the term following the trial, Barrow moved for a new trial, citing three precedents, and all three precedents are mentioned in Lawrence's notes.

In *Holman v. Viner*,[78] Espinasse says that the jury found for the defendant, whereas Lawrence states that Lord Kenyon nonsuited the plaintiff. In a crowded courtroom, it would have been hard to tell the difference. Lord Kenyon often instructed the jury to return a verdict for the defendant, telling the jury that there was no basis for the plaintiff to recover. When this happened, counsel for the plaintiff often requested that the plaintiff be nonsuited so that the plaintiff would not suffer an adverse jury verdict and would be able to bring suit again if better evidence could be collected.

In *Withnell v. Gartham*,[79] Lawrence records in some detail the argument on the motion for new trial in Trinity Term 1794, which was granted. The new trial was conducted in Easter Term 1795, and was reported by Espinasse.[80] Another motion for a new trial was then argued in Trinity Term 1795, this time unsuccessfully, as was reported in *Term Reports*.[81] All three accounts of the case are largely consistent, but two discrepancies can be noted. Lawrence's notes show Erskine, Law, and Wood as counsel for the plaintiff, whereas Espinasse names Erskine, Law and Baldwin. The case involved the method of voting of churchwardens in an election of the schoolmaster at Skipton, and

---

[75] *Small v. Nairne* (1849) 13 Q.B. 840, at 844, as quoted in Wallace, *The Reporters*, at p. 541, n.3.
[76] In two of the cases, the issue taken up before the full court was entirely unrelated to the jury trial, so that no meaningful comparison is feasible. See *Doe v. Davis*, below, p. 101; (1795) 1 Esp. 358, and *Sikes v. Marshall*, below, p. 189, (1798) 2 Esp. 705.
[77] Below, p. 50, (1794) 1 Esp. 148.
[78] Below, p. 56, (1794) 1 Esp. 132.
[79] Below, p. 47.
[80] (1795) 1 Esp. 322.
[81] (1795) 6 T.R. 388.

Lawrence's notes show that seven of the eleven churchwardens named the plaintiff as schoolmaster; Espinasse says six of the eleven named the plaintiff; and *Term Reports* say that a majority did.[82]

The trial of *Gordon* v. *Harpur*, in December 1795, was reported by Espinasse,[83] and Lawrence reported the argument on a motion for new trial in Easter Term 1796.[84] A new trial was scheduled for Trinity Term but the phrasing of the issue was faulty,[85] and the case was carried over to Michaelmas Term, as was reported in *Term Reports*.[86] All three accounts of the case are consistent. Other cases that show consistent reporting between Lawrence's notes and Espinasse's reports include *Burnett* v. *Kensington*,[87] *Stonehouse* v. *Elliot*,[88] and *Smith* v. *Bowles*.[89]

There is, moreover, reason to favour Espinasse's versions of the facts of the cases. Espinasse was reporting at *nisi prius*, whereas Lawrence's notes always described the argument and disposition of post-trial phases of cases that were heard by the full four-judge Court of King's Bench. Espinasse would have prepared his reports from his first-hand observations at the trials, whereas Lawrence's summaries were, in most cases, derivative. The vast majority of the trials would have been conducted by Lord Kenyon, the chief justice, and Lawrence's notes would be filtered by Lord Kenyon's descriptions.[90] The sample of cases recorded by both Espinasse and Lawrence is small, but it is fair to conclude that Lawrence's notes in some measure substantiate Espinasse's case reporting.

III. CONCLUSION

By chronicling the unpredictable, sputtering production of the nominate reports during most of the eighteenth century, we can see how pronounced the gaps and delays in case reporting were, especially from the perspective of the active practitioners and judges of the time. There are no printed case reports for the Court of Exchequer for well over one-third of the century. In

---

[82] There were, of course, occasional differences in the spelling of the names of parties and witnesses, as was true in *Withnell* v. *Gartham*. Espinasse very likely spelled names in his notes of the cases phonetically, while Lawrence probably obtained the spelling of most of the names from his copy of the pleadings.

[83] (1796) 2 Esp. 465.

[84] Below, p. 134.

[85] Below, p. 135.

[86] (1796) 7 T.R. 9.

[87] Below, p. 104; (1794) 1 Esp. 416. As the annotations to Lawrence's notes of this case show (below), there were many phases of this litigation that were reported in *Term Reports* and in *The Times*.

[88] Below, p. 62; (1795) 1 Esp. 272.

[89] Below, p. 175, (1797) 2 Esp. 578.

[90] Occasionally, one of the junior justices sat in for Kenyon in conducting jury trials and would become the source of the facts and of any legal issue that may have arisen at trial. Also, the presiding judge in cases that were tried on assize was often a judge from the Court of Common Pleas or the Court of Exchequer, in which case the facts and legal issues would be explained in a written report from the trial judge to the Court of King's Bench, which would then be read aloud when the case came before the full court during term time.

the Court of Common Pleas, the years 1780 to 1787 during the chief justiceship of Alexander Wedderburn, Lord Loughborough, are blank,[91] and some of the reports that were eventually published for that court did not appear until decades after the cases had been decided. Long delays occurred in the publication of King's Bench reports as well, notably the half-century lapse before volumes three and four of *Douglas's Reports* appeared. In these circumstances, it was essential for the practising Bar and the judges to compile and maintain manuscript notes of cases decided by the court or courts in which they practiced or sat.

Change arrived, however, in the late 1780s and in the decades that followed. Among other developments,[92] Charles Durnford and Edward East bestowed a generous gift on the Court of King's Bench by publishing their excellent case reports immediately after each term ended, starting in the year 1785. As noted earlier,[93] this prompted barrister Edward Bearcroft to remark in 1789 that he 'had long ago left off taking notes', instead relying on *Term Reports*, 'which made business very pleasant'.

Even Durnford and East's enterprising reports, however, did not capture all of the activity in the Court of King's Bench. This was the point of Mr Justice Lawrence's explanation of the case notes that comprise the bulk of the present volume.[94] These supplementary notes have several attributes. They augment the printed reports, in some cases supplying previously unknown details about intermediate stages of reported cases. More significantly, they contribute to our understanding of the unreported activity of the court on matters that, as Lawrence explained, did not come up for regularly scheduled arguments during term time (for which Paper Books would be prepared).[95] This understanding is enhanced by reports in *The Times* of many of the same cases recorded by Lawrence. The combination of Lawrence's notes and reporting in *The Times* supplies, moreover, a contemporaneous picture of some of the dominant personalities of legal London of the late eighteenth and early nineteenth centuries and of their interactions. Finally, the persistent frustrations of the judges, Lord Kenyon in particular, in dealing with the excesses and delays thrust into the legal process by the 'pettifogging attorneys', often for no purpose other than increasing legal fees, are displayed in sharp relief.

---

[91] The record is blank except for occasional single cases that found their way into print in pamphlet form, usually from shorthand notes, as in *Hurry* v. *Watson* (pp. xl–xlvi, above; Appendix).
[92] See the summary, pp. xxxviii–xxxix, above.
[93] Above, p. xx.
[94] Lawrence's volume 5, p. 47, below.
[95] Ibid.

MANUSCRIPTS OF SIR SOULDEN LAWRENCE

MIDDLE TEMPLE LIBRARY, MS. 49

PART I
VOLUME 5[1]

CASES IN COMMON PLEAS, 27, 34 GEO. III

---

[1] The cases in Part I are transcribed from one of Lawrence's five notebooks containing plea side cases (see p. xiii, n. 2, above). Despite Lawrence's label on the spine of volume 5 ('Cases in the King's Bench 24–28 Geo. 3; 34–36 Geo. 3'), he included a small number of cases from his practice in the Court of Common Pleas after he was made serjeant-at-law in 1787 and from his first three months as a judge, when he sat in the Common Pleas.

[5:158] [M.N.] In Hilary Term 27 Geo. III, I was called to the degree of Serjeant at law.[2]

Alexander Lord Loughborough C.J.
Sir Henry Gould
John Heath, Esq.   } Justices
Sir John Wilson

MONTIERO v. CLARKE

[M.H.] If a defendant is served with a copy of a process in an action for above £10 no notice is necessary to be subscribed to it.

Bolton moved to set aside a judgment for irregularity, the process not having the notice required by Act of parliament[3] subscribed at the foot of it, and further objected that the writ was returnable on Wednesday next after &c. instead of a general return day.

Le Blanc shewed cause on an affidavit which, *inter alia*, stated that the cause of action exceeded £10, in which case he said the notice was not necessary, and relied on *Willis* v. *Lewis*, 1 Wilson 22.[4] As to the 2nd objection, he said being a mere clerical mistake, it could not be taken advantage of after declaration delivered, plea demanded, and judgment signed. For had the defendant come earlier, it might have been amended. 3rd Wilson 454, *Carty* v. *Ashley*.[5]

GOULD J.: Had this stood only on the objection of the return we should not have created a rule *nisi*. The case in Wilson is a very sensible, good case.[6]

HEATH and WILSON, Justices, same opinion.

Rule discharged.

[5:159] E. 27 Geo. III

GIBSON *et al.* v. HEARNE

[M.H.] If judgment is signed on a warrant of attorney, the court will not grant a rule to carry in the roll.

Judgment having been entered up on a warrant of attorney in which there was a release of errors, defendant moved for a rule on the plaintiff to carry in the roll for the purpose of enabling him to assign his infancy as error.

---

[2] Serjeants-at-law held a monopoly in the Common Pleas in arguments on motions heard by the full four-judge court. See J. H. Baker, *The Order of Serjeants at Law* (1984), at p. 42. Lawrence was appointed to the Court of Common Pleas on 7 March 1794. He transferred to the King's Bench on 18 June 1794.

[3] In the margin: '5 G. 2, c. 24'.

[4] *Willis* v. *Lewis*, 1 Wils. 22 (1743).

[5] *Carty* v. *Ashley*, 3 Wils. 454 (1773), also reported at 2 W. Bl. 918.

[6] Gould refers to *Carty* v. *Ashley*. Wilson's report quotes opinions by Gould and Nares JJ.

GOULD J.: if the warrant of attorney was improperly obtained, the mode of applying is by motion to set it aside, but I never knew a motion to bring in the roll of a judge on a warrant of attorney.

Rule discharged.
Lord LOUGHBOROUGH absent.

WELLER et al., EXECUTORS v. CHEESEMAN

[M.H.] If a person dies to whom a warrant of attorney is given to enter up judgment at his suit, judgment can't be entered up at the suit of his executors.

I moved to enter up a judgment on a warrant of attorney given to the testator to confess a judgment at his suit, but not at the suit of his executors, on the authority of a case with which I had been furnished by the master of the King's Bench Office, of *Executors of Pearce Bradshaw* v. *Bradshaw*, Hilary, 15 Geo. III, where the party to whom the judgment was given, having died in Michaelmas or Hilary term, a rule was made to enter up judgment as of the first day of Michaelmas term—no cause being shewn.

But GOULD J. refused a rule *nisi*, saying the same thing had been refused *Walker*, serjeant, who had been desired to look into the cases and had admitted he had not been able to find any precedents.

[5:160] ## BUSH v. GREEN

[M.H.] Judgment for £566 and £18 costs, *fi. fa.* for £566 and 63s. costs is good.

Bolton moved to set aside a writ of *fieri facias* as not agreeing with the judgment, the judgment being for £566 and £18 costs, and for this he relied on a case of *Baynes* v. *Forrest*, Strange 892.[7]

Le Blanc, *contra*, said they might carry in the roll for 63s. costs, though they had £18 taxed.

The court discharged the rule.

MONROE v. ELLIOT

[M.H.] In Trinity term the court set aside this inquisition for excessive damages, and on a new inquisition exhibited before the CHIEF JUSTICE, £150 were recovered.

Motion the last day of term to set aside an inquisition by which in an action for an assault, £200 damages had been assessed against defendant, a constable, who during his attending one Aylett, an attorney, while in the pillory for perjury, had given the plaintiff a violent blow on the head with his mace.[8]

---

[7] (1731) 2 Str. 892.
[8] On Aylett in the pillory, see Oldham, *MMSS*, ii. 1066–68.

At first the court doubted if the motion could be made on the last day of term, as the inquisition having been taken two days before, an earlier application might have been made. But as the damages appeared very excessive, the court granted a rule to show cause.⁹

SMITH v. IRELAND

[M.H.] Process can't be set aside because the defendant is described by a wrong name.

Bolton moved to set aside a *distringas* for irregularity, the defendant having been served by the name of William Ireland, his real name being John.

Le Blanc shewed cause, and insisted that this ought to be the subject of a plea in abatement.

[*5:161*] GOULD J.: The practice is so we can take no notice of the defendant till he appears. This is a new motion. The defendant must go on in the regular course.

Rule discharged.

GOODTITLE, *ex dim.* BAILEY *et al.* v. PUGH *et al.*¹⁰

[M.H.] *Dom. Proc.* A devise to the first and every other son of the devisor's son and heir at law and for want of heirs in him to my right heirs forever, my said son excepted, is a void devise, as it is in the event of his son dying without heirs of his body and a devise to the testator's right heirs.

Vide vol. 4, fo. 256 for the state of this case and the judgment of the King's Bench on error in parliament.¹¹ The question referred the judges was whether

---

⁹ Lord Loughborough in *Hurry* v. *Watson*, at p. 10 below, confirms that the verdict in *Monroe* v. *Elliot* was set aside due to excessive damages.

¹⁰ The proceeding in the House of Lords is reported as *Pugh* v. *Goodtitle* (1787) 3 Bro. P.C. 454. In Brown's report, the lengthy special verdict found by the jury in the trial before Lord Mansfield on 11 July 1783 is printed verbatim. After argument before the full Court of King's Bench, the court ruled, *per curiam*, for the plaintiff. That phase of the case was reported briefly ('From a Manuscript Note of the late Mr Serjeant Hill') by Charles Fearne in *An Essay on the Learning of Contingent Remainders and Executory Devises*, 7th ed. (1820), pp. 573–574. Lord Mansfield is reported to have said that, 'as to "right heir" being a term of description, where a man gives to his own right heir, he don't take by description, but by his better title, by descent. The meaning here is such as would be my right heir, if my son were dead. There is no difficulty as to that.' Ibid., p. 574. Brown's report of the disposition of the writ of error by the Lords summarizes the arguments of counsel and states the question put to the judges as follows: 'Whether any person, and who, took any and what estate under the will mentioned in the special verdict, by way of devise and purchase?' The only description of the unanimous opinion of the judges present, delivered by the lord chief baron, is 'that no person took any estate under the will mentioned in the special verdict'. 3 Bro. P.C. at 460. It is interesting to note Lawrence's postscript to his notes of this case (below, p. 7), saying that the judges were ready to affirm the King's Bench decision until Lord Thurlow turned them around.

¹¹ The reference is to another of Lawrence's notebooks, *Cases in King's Bench, 23 & 24 Geo. 3*, Middle Temple Library, London, MS. 49. Lawrence's notes of that phase of the case (at fols. 256–258) are as follows:

the lessor of the plaintiff took any, and what estate under the will of Calvert Burn by devise or purchase, and EYRE C.B. delivered the opinion of the judges on the 15th of May 1787, to the following effect:

In construing, or in other words, in inquiring what disposition a testator means, the utmost latitude is allowed, and if it be possible to discover his meaning, no inaccuracies in expression shall prevent its taking effect.

But when the question is, whether that disposition can be effected by the rules of law, there can be no latitude. In this case, the ruling idea in the testator's mind was to disinherit his son. But if he has not followed it up, by disposing of his estate to some other person, the law gives it to his son.

[5:162] This case has been argued as a devise to the right heirs of the testator, the son excepted.

It can't be collected that the testator meant a present devise to anybody. The

Goodtitle *ex dim.* Bayley *& al.* v. Pugh *& al.*

[M.H.] H: 24.G.3. Judg^t reversed in Dom: Proc: May 15th 1787. The Lords being of opinion that when the event happened on which the estate was to go to the right heir, the son excepted, the persons answering that description must be the right heir without any restriction, for till the son died without sons, the limitation over could not take effect, so that the devise was in fact a devise to the testator's right heirs and therefore void.

[M.H. for the judgment in the King's Bench] Devise in case my eldest son dies without sons to my right heirs, my son excepted, is a good devise to the daughters of the devisor. But this judgment was reversed in the House of Lords as a void devise, as in the event it was a devise to the devisor's right heirs.

Ejectment for lands in London.

Special verdict stating: That Calvert Burn being seised of the premises in question, by will dated the 4th of April 1769, devised the premises in question in these words: as to my real estate, after the death of my wife, I give and devise to the eldest son of my eldest son begotten to me or to be begotten, all my estate in London and Middlesex for his life, he being obliged to keep them in good repair, insure them from loss by fire, and pay the annuities left chargeable on them. To the 2nd son all my estates in the County of Hertford for his life subject to pay all the charges of a man I have appointed to look after them [and] keep them in repair, and insure them from fire, and so in the same manner to all the sons my son may have. If but one son then all the real estate to him for life, and for want of heirs in him to the right heirs of me the said Calvert Benn for ever, my son excepted, it being my will that he shall have no part of my estates real or personal.

In 1770 the devisor died leaving William Benn his eldest son and heir at law, and three daughters, the lessors of the plaintiff his only issue him surviving.

The wife died in 1777, when the son entered and conveyed to the defendants and died without issue.

This was argued in Michaelmas Term and again in this, when Lord Mansfield said that till the case of Newcoman and Barkham [*Newcoman* v. *Bethlem Hospital* (1741) Amb. 8, 785 (testator Sir Edward Barkham)] it was contended that in the case of a devise to a man's heir male, that the person to take must be heir general as well as heir male. But that Lord Cowper had settled that to be otherwise, which opinion Lord Hardwicke had confirmed on a bill of review. That the description in the case before the court was to such person as would be his heir if his eldest son were dead. In finding him out there could be no difficulty. That heir was a term of description, and that the meaning of the word depended on the subject matter. In Burrough English it meant the youngest son. In Gavelkind, all the sons, and the heir at law was the eldest. And the reason a man could not take as purchaser by the word heir generally, was on account of a rule of law, by which he would take by descent and by a better title. He said there was no doubt of it not being too remote. That the point was settled in *Fonnereau* v. *Fonnereau* [(1748) 3 Atk. 645].

Willes and Ashhurst of the same opinion. Buller J. doubted if a 2nd son had been born if he would not have been excluded by this construction from the estates in London and Middlesex.

Judgment for Plaintiff.

whole is future and executory. We are to discover what future interest he intended.

According to Salkeld 233, *Nottingham* v. *Jennings*, the words 'in want of heirs in him' must mean heirs of the body and the sons must take estate tail according to *Walter* v. *Drew*, Comyns Reports 392. And the devise to the right heirs, the son excepted, must have been intended to take effect on the determination of the estate tail in the sons of his son, and must therefore be meant to take effect, as an executory devise after an executory estate tail.

But that is not all. In the event of the testator's own son having no sons, he meant to devise immediately to the person who, at his son's death, should answer the description of his right heir, his son [5:163] excepted. This devise therefore had a double aspect. The question therefore is, who is meant by this description? And he must have meant whoever happened to be his right heir, his son excepted, and not specifically his daughter.

But a devise to the right heirs, the son excepted, to take effect on the son's death, he being the right heir, in the event must necessarily be a devise to the right heirs of the testator without any exception. The daughters, therefore, must now claim as the right heirs of the devisor.

The question will then be, if they can take under this description as purchasers. With other words, 'heir' may be a *descriptio personae*, and therefore while the son was living, this might be[12] a good *descriptio personae*, but not after his death. A man can't limit an estate to his right heirs so as to make them purchasers without parting with the fee. Co. Litt. 22b; 2 Rolle's Ab. 414, c. 45. And this is like the case cited from Salkeld, excepting that that was a remainder, this is a case of an executory devise.

Here the fee was never out of the testator, and the executory devise does not alter the descent. It is but a part of the old use.[13] [5:164] The conclusion therefore is, that this executory devise can't, by the rules of law, take effect, and the answer to the question submitted to us is that no estate was taken by the lessors of the plaintiff by devise or purchase.

Judgment of K.B. reversed.

[*Lawrence note*:] Mr Justice GOULD informed me that the judges were going unanimously to affirm the judgment of the King's Bench till the chancellor, Lord THURLOW, suggested the ground on which it was reversed.

---

[12] In the manuscript, the word 'was' is struck out and replaced by 'might be'.

[13] At this point in the manuscript, the following is struck out: 'and the power of alienation in the heir at law is an insuperable objection to this being a good executory devise'.

SAWBRIDGE, *qui tam* v. BROUGHTON

[M.H.] *Vide Davis* v. *Mazzinghi*, 1 Term Rep., B.R. 705. Supplemental affidavit to hold to bail not to be used in a penal action.

Defendant had been held to bail for offences against the Lottery Acts in pursuance of the 27 Geo. III, by an affidavit stating that diverse pecuniary penalties had been incurred by the defendant, by offending against the Acts of parliament which concern lotteries, some or one of them. That such penalties do amount to £100 and that the plaintiff on behalf of himself and of our sovereign lord the king intends to commence an action for the recovery of the said penalties, and that pursuant to the statute in such case made and provided, the defendant was indebted to our said lord the king and the plaintiff as aforesaid in £100. A motion having been made to discharge defendant on common bail, *Adair* moved to file a supplemental affidavit stating that ten pecuniary penalties of £50 each, amounting to £500, had been incurred by the defendant by reason of his having insured illegally ten numbers of tickets in the last state lottery contrary to the form of an Act passed in the 27th year of his majesty [*5:165*] entitled an Act &c., and that the plaintiff had commenced an action on behalf of our lord the king and himself to recover the said penalties.

In support of his motion to file a supplemental affidavit, he cited 2nd [W.] Blackstone 850 *Roche, Executor of Burnett* v. *Carey*; *Paris* v. *Stroud & ux*, Barnes 95; *Swarbuck* v. *Wheeler*, ibid.: 100; *Stapleton* v. *Baron de Stark*, ibid.: 109; *Manning* v. *Williams*, ibid.: 89; *Shaw* v. *Hawkins*, ibid.: 72.

Bolton, Adair, and *Rooke* showed cause.

Lord LOUGHBOROUGH: It has been laid down much too largely that a supplemental affidavit may be read in this court. It is by no means a matter of course. In the King's Bench they will not receive affidavits on either side on a motion to discharge on filing common bail. This court has under circumstances thought itself at liberty to inquire into the arrest and have allowed supplemental affidavits. Four cases have been cited, but they are not applicable. *Stroud* [...] *of Paris* is one. That was an application to discharge an infant and in his favour the court directed a supplemental affidavit. The case of *Stapleton and Baron de Stark* was a case of the same nature. Not cases of supplemental affidavit to supply defect in the original affidavit. The case from Blackstone is the case of an executor, the others are cases of foreigners, and in one the facts showed that which was equivalent to an affidavit of belief and the court in that determined on the original affidavit. This shows it is by no means to be a matter of course and you must note a case to induce the court to let an additional affidavit be filed. Here the plaintiff had no right but what all the world had and I think the court can't take that liberty in a penal law like this, nor assume a latitude, as in cases of *meum* and *tuum*. We are called upon to dispense with a guard introduced in favour of the liberty of the subject and in aid of the prosecutor which we can't do.

GOULD J.: Same opinion.

HEATH J.: The affidavit is a condition precedent.

WILSON J.: If a supplemental affidavit has not been filed before process there is nothing to authorize us to hold defendant to bail. Supplemental affidavits should be sparingly used. In all the cases cited the cause of action was set out in the affidavits, and the supplemental affidavit was not to supply that. Here the original affidavit does not set out the cause of action.

[5:*166*]   C.B. TRINITY TERM 27 Geo. III

Alexander Lord Loughborough C.J.
Sir Henry Gould
John Heath, Esq.   Justices
Sir John Wilson

WARREN v. HALL

[M.H.] The plea of the want of defendant's addition in the recital part of the declaration pleaded in abatement set aside.

In an action upon the case in that part of the declaration which shortly recites the writ, no addition was given to the defendant.[14] On this he pleaded in abatement of the writ the want of an addition.

Kerby moved to set this plea aside.

Bolton shewed cause.

Lord LOUGHBOROUGH: There is no principle to support this objection. It is not necessary that an original writ should be sued out, but to support this objection we must suppose such writ, and that there is in it a want of addition.

WILSON J.: What would be the replication to this plea? I have seen a replication of drapers stating the original—which might be sued out without this defect. I remember a case where a man having pleaded in abatement he was a carpenter and not a bricklayer, Lord MANSFIELD said he would hold him a bricklayer if he had ever laid a single brick, or employed any to do it. The objection here is that the writ which need not have been recited is recited imperfectly.

                                                                                        Rule absolute.

[5:*167*]   JONES v. EDWARDS

In an action of covenant for not repairing and completing work on a house in Glamorganshire, the venue was changed, though objected that the venue was never changed in covenant.

Adair for plaintiff.

Rooke for defendant.

---

[14] That is, the defendant's title or status (an 'addition') was not stated.

HURRY v. WATSON[15]

[M.H.] Verdict in tort may be set aside for excessive damages.

In an action for a malicious prosecution for perjury the jury gave £3,000 damages.

And on a motion for a new trial on the ground of excessive damages, Lord LOUGHBOROUGH said he had no doubt but that the court might set aside a verdict in cases of torts for excessive damages. That they had done it in the case of inquiry[16] where they thought the sum given exceeded the amount of the inquiry. That the question was more a question of feeling than of reasoning. That the ability of the defendant did not appear to him the measure of damages—and that he wished a few days to say what would be a reasonable sum. That the £3,000 seemed to be owing to the jury being taken by surprise. That £1,000 would not have been too much, what between the £3,000 [and £1,000] he was not prepared to say would not be improper to have given. [*5:168*] On this being thrown out by the court, the plaintiff took £1,500 in full for his damages and costs.[17]

The plaintiff was a merchant at Yarmouth and the perjury was supposed to have been committed in a proceeding in a court of conscience within that borough.

---

[15] See the discussion of this case, Introduction, pp. xl–xlvi, above. In 1786, John Watson, then mayor-elect of the borough of Great Yarmouth, preferred a bill of indictment for perjury against William Hurry, a local merchant. The indictment was filed in the Borough Court of Great Yarmouth, removed by *certiorari* to the Court of King's Bench, then sent to be tried at the Thetford assizes. The trial was held on 18 March 1786 before Mr Justice Nares of the Court of Common Pleas (sitting on assize for this case as a King's Bench judge) and a special jury. The proceedings were attended by a student of Lincoln's Inn, Robert Alderson, who also attended the subsequent proceedings in the suit by Hurry against Watson for malicious prosecution. Using his own shorthand notes, Alderson then published transcripts of all five stages of the litigation: the acquittal of Hurry by the special jury at Thetford on 18 March 1786; the trial of the malicious prosecution action of *Hurry* v. *Watson* at the 1786 summer assizes at Norfolk before Chief Baron Skynner of the Court of Exchequer (sitting as a King's Bench judge) and a special jury, when the plaintiff was nonsuited; the argument in the Court of Common Pleas in Michaelmas Term 1786 when a new trial was granted; the second trial on 24 March 1787 at the Thetford assizes before Mr Justice Ashhurst and a special jury; and the argument in the Common Pleas of a motion to set aside the jury verdict and order a new trial. The last stage (begun in Easter Term 1787, concluded on 13 June 1787) is the phase of the case noted by Lawrence (above). The entire Alderson publication is reproduced in the Appendix to this volume.

[16] In the margin: '*Monroe* v. *Elliot, antea* 160'.

[17] The order implementing the settlement is printed at the end of the Alderson transcript of *Hurry* v. *Watson*. See Appendix. Watson, however, did not pay the £1,500. This sum and £800 costs were paid instead by the Corporation of Great Yarmouth, after which an information was issued by the Court of King's Bench against Watson and nineteen other members of the Corporation for having libelled the public administration of justice in the country. See *The Times*, 26 January 1788. The information was tried at the Thetford assizes on 23 March 1789 by Mr Justice Grose and a special jury, and due to improper wording of the information, the jury returned a not guilty verdict.

SELBY v. TUPPER

[M.H.] Whether the 24 Geo. II respecting prize money be a subsisting law.

In an action by the plaintiff against the defendant to recover the amount of some prize money which had come to the hands of the defendant as agent for a privateer on board which the plaintiff was a seaman, a letter of attorney was produced by the defendant executed by the plaintiff but not according to the formalities required by the sixth section of the 24th of Geo. 2nd, which was contended not to be necessary and that the Act had expired and *Baker* v. *Jardine*, E. 24 Geo. III, B.R., vol. 4, 341, was cited.[18] This point having been saved at the trial at Guildhall before Lord LOUGHBOROUGH was argued this term, when he said, after some days' consideration, that he thought the determination in *Baker* v. *Jardine* right—that the Act was a jumbled Act and that privateers were left out of the fourth section to enable the men to subsist, as they had no wages. But the sixth section was not confined to prize monies then existing, and was, he thought, a continuing clause. That as to the King's ships, there was a provision respecting the letters of attorney of seamen belonging to them in the 31 Geo. II and as to them those two Acts made a complete law.

[5:169] WAGSTAFF, *ex dim.* TUNNENT v. ROOKE and uxor

[M.H.] A devise to A till B attains 23 and then to B, and a similar devise in favour of C, and if B or C die before 23 his share to the next eldest child of A who shall arrive at 23, vests a chattel interest in A, and in case of B's death, the next eldest child is the next eldest, exclusive of C, who shall arrive at 23.

Hester Wooldridge being seised in fee of the premises in question devised to her son William Wooldridge his executors and administrators all those two messuages or tenements &c. upon trust nevertheless to receive the rents, issues, and profits for his own use until his son John Reason Alexander should attain his age of 23 years and when and as soon as her said grandson, J. R. Alexander, should attain his age of 23 years then she gives them to the said J. R. A. She also made a like devise of the lands to Hester, a daughter of her son William Wooldridge, and they proceeded to say that her mind and will was that if the said Hester or J.R. Alexander should die before they or either of them attained the age of 21 years, then in such case, she bequeathed the part and share of the person so dying unto the next eldest child male or female of her said son William Wooldridge, as aforesaid. William Wooldridge had issue, Hester, who

---

[18] The reference is to Lawrence's manuscript notebooks, vol. 4. According to Lawrence's notes of *Baker* v. *Jardine*, a question was raised whether a certain statute, 20 Geo. II, c. 4, was in force, and Lord Mansfield's opinion was that 'the act expired with the then war'—'It does not follow because there has been a land tax this year that there will be one next year, nor does it follow that though the crown gives away the prize money in one year that it will do so in another.' Lawrence MSS., *Cases in King's Bench 23 & 24 Geo. 3*, at p. 341, Middle Temple Library, London.

married the defendant Rooke, J. Reason Alexander who died at 21, William Allen who died an infant, and Mary Ann, still an infant of 12 years.

The lessors of the plaintiff claimed under the father.

[5:170] And the question was whether Hester was the person described under the words of next eldest child, and if not if the father could convey any title to the plaintiffs.

Lord LOUGHBOROUGH: I am very well satisfied that this is a devise of a chattel[19] to the father and that it remains in him till there is some person to take it from him notwithstanding the son's death.

The question then who is the next eldest child as aforesaid.

I do not think it can mean either Hester or J. R. Alexander. The next eldest must be exclusive of either of them and the interest of Hester could never have gone to John. William Allen is gone, Mary Ann is therefore the next eldest, but as she has not arrived at the age of 23 she cannot take it from her father.

GOULD, HEATH, WILSON, Justices, same opinion.

Postea to plaintiff.

NICHOLAS v. BEYER

After rule to rejoin, the plaintiff signed judgment without making a demand of a rejoinder and the court for that reason set it aside as irregular.

LEAKE v. DAY

The court increased the issues to pay the costs, though sufficient [. . .] to pay the debt. On the motion of *Kerby*, serjeant.

[5:171] Trinity 27 Geo. III

SHARMAN v. STRONG

[M.H.] On a reference, the costs to abide the event, if mutual releases only are awarded the defendant is entitled to his costs.

This cause was referred, and the costs of the cause were directed to abide the event. The arbitrator awarded mutual releases and nothing else.

I moved that the prothonotary might be directed to tax the defendant his costs, contending that this was equivalent to a nonsuit and the court made the rule absolute. GOULD J. *dissentiente*, who doubted if the arbitrator intended it, who might probably have given the plaintiff some small sum unless they were equally to pay the costs.

To this it was answered, that as the costs were to abide the event, he had no such power, and therefore could not be presumed to intend it.

---

[19] A 'real chattel', an interest issuing out of real estate.

HOLLAND v. SMITH

[M.H.] Plaintiff is not bound to charge a defendant in execution, pending a writ of error.

Defendant brought a writ of error returnable in Easter term 26th Geo. III and in Michaelmas term surrendered to the warden in discharge of his bail.

I moved to discharge him as the plaintiff had not within two terms proceeded to charge defendant in execution, and might have non-prossed[20] the writ of error. But the court held that the plaintiff could not charge defendant in execution pending a writ of error, and that he was not bound to non-pross it, but that the defendant must get rid of it.

[5:172] ## WHITCHURCH v. EDWARDS

[M.H.] Judgment being signed for the penalty of a bond conditioned for the honesty of a clerk, the plaintiff shall endorse his writ of execution for the damages really sustained.

The defendant being in execution for the penalty of a bond conditioned for his good behaviour as a clerk, the court on a motion of *Kerby*, Serjeant and an affidavit that the plaintiff had said he had sustained damages to the amount of £180 by his embezzling his money, made a rule to show cause why he should not endorse on the writ of execution the amount of damages he had sustained.

Le Blanc, Serjeant, showed cause, and said that the defendant should compel the plaintiff to assess the damages in pursuance of the Statute of Will. III, or the plaintiff might be prevented taking the defendant in execution for further breaches.[21]

WILSON J., said that might be so, if any further damages could be incurred, but that he did not know but that the plaintiff was irregular in charging the defendant in execution before an assessment of damages.

As there was no danger of further breaches, the rule was made absolute.

---

[20] See abbreviations, *nolle pros.*

[21] The statute of 8 & 9 Will. III, c. 11 provided that in all actions upon any bond or penal sum, 'plaintiff or plaintiffs may assign as many breaches as he or they shall think fit', and if successful, a writ should issue to the sheriff to summon a jury 'to enquire of the truth of every one of those Breaches, and to assess the Damages that the plaintiff shall have sustained thereby'. According to A. W. B. Simpson, this meant that although 'judgment could be entered for the whole penalty', the jury was to assess the damages for each breach, and 'the plaintiff could only recover the damages assessed'. A. W. B. Simpson, 'The Penal Bond with Conditional Defeasance', *Law Quarterly Review* 82 (1966), p. 392, at p. 419.

MERCER et al. v. COOKE

[M.H.] Plea of Michaelmas, 27 Geo. III. Parol agreement can't be pleaded in bar of a contract under seal.

Debt on bond dated 26th December 1775 entered into by defendant to plaintiff insurer and one Shenk for 1276:6:6, New York, currency value £717:10:9½ sterling. Declaration, E. 26. Geo. III. Defendant, praying oyer of the condition of the bond which was for the payment of 698–3–3 on the 1st January 1776, pleaded that on the 1st of August 8, 1786 it was agreed at New York by the plaintiff Mercer for the other plaintiff Shenk and himself to assign the bond and the interest due thereon to one John [5:173] Taylor on condition that Taylor should deliver to Mercer for himself and the other plaintiff fifty pieces of black Persian silk as a full consideration for the said debt, and that afterwards on the 2nd of August, Taylor did deliver the silk at New York, and that thereupon the plaintiff did give Taylor an order on Sargeant Chambers & Company, in whose hands the bond was as agents of the plaintiffs, to deliver it up to Taylor. That afterwards on the 5th of August Taylor ordered Sargeant Chambers & Co. to deliver up the said bond to the defendant on his paying a bill of exchange for £168 15s., drawn by Taylor on the defendant in favour of Sargeant Chambers & Co. of which they had notice, that the defendant afterwards tendered and offered to pay to Sargeant Chambers & Co., the said sum of £168 15s. and required them to deliver up the bond, which they refused to do, or to accept the £168 15s., and that the defendant has ever since the tender been ready to pay them[22] that money—and *profert in curiam* to be paid them[23] if they will receive the same. And concluded with praying if the plaintiff should recover more than the said sum of £168 15s. or any damages by reason of the detention of that debt. To this plea the plaintiffs demurred and assigned for causes, that the plea was pleaded in bar of the action and yet the agreement pleaded was made subsequent to the commencement of it.

Secondly, that the money was tendered after the commencement of the action.

[5:174] In support of the demurrer I contended that a parol agreement could not be pleaded to a contract under seal unless it had been carried into execution. Cro. Eliz. 697.[24] Hobart. 68.[25] Cro. Car. 85.[26] Cro. Eliz. 193.[27] That a less sum could not be a satisfaction for a greater. *Richards* v. *Bartlett*, 1 Leon. 14. *Cumber* v. *Wayne*, Strange 426. That the plea being in the nature of a tender should refer to the times of the commencement of the action, and that the plaintiff was entitled to recover damages for any detention if ever so short. That though a refusal to the party might be equivalent to performance, yet such refusal by a stranger could not. That the money was not brought into

---

[22] In the margin: Sargeant Chambers & Co.
[23] Ibid.
[24] *Hayford* v. *Andrews* (1599) Cro. Eliz. 697.
[25] *Richards* v. *Carvamel* (1615) Hob. 68.
[26] *Lovelace* v. *Cocket* (1627) Cro. Car. 85.
[27] *Tassall* v. *Shane* (1590) Cro. Eliz. 193.

court to be paid the defendants, and suppose Sargeant Chambers & Co. should never take the money, was the bond never to be paid?

Le Blanc, contra, argued that the time of the agreement being under a *viz.,* it did not necessarily appear that it was made subsequent to the commencement of the action; and that the plea was not in the nature of a plea of tender, but was a plea of performance, and the fourth August did not apply. That every plea referred to the time of pleadings. *Sullivan* v. *Montague,* [1] Doug. 106. *Reynolds* and *Berling, antea.*[28] He further contended that in this case [*5:175*] the plea amounted to accord and satisfaction executed, by the acceptance of the silk. And that this was a good plea had been laid down in *Peytoe's Case* Cro. Eliz. 193,[29] and that this was not the case of a sum of money paid in discharge of the obligation. That Sargeant Chambers & Co. were but trustees for Taylor, that the plea was not of a tender of the money due by the land, but of what was equivalent performance of the defendant's part of the subsequent agreement which entitled him to have the bond delivered up, and was like the case of *Jones* v. *Barkley,* Doug. 659.[30]

Lord LOUGHBOROUGH: You take it for granted that[31] there has been a discharge of the bond. But that agreement and the delivery of the silk was not in behalf of Cooke, it was as a consideration for the assignment to Taylor.

Le Blanc: If the plaintiffs are trustees for Taylor, as he ought not in equity to recover, the plaintiffs can't at law recover for his benefit according to Winch and Keeley, T.R. 619.[32]

Lord LOUGHBOROUGH: The argument there amounts to this, you the plaintiff are a trustee for a third person who owes me money and therefore you ought not to recover. But I am afraid in this case if Sargeant Chambers & Co. had received the money this action might be maintained. [*5:176*] I see no harm if a parol agreement could be pleaded to one under seal, but the law is not so. There is no consideration as between Taylor and the defendant to afford him a right to have this bond upon payment of a lesser sum. The bill does not appear to have been accepted, what consideration moves from the defendant? It does not appear to me that anything is stated that amounts to a discharge of the bond. And it is material here that the tender was not before the commencement of the suit, but my opinion does not go on that point, but on the ground that the plea is no defence to the action.[33]

Judgment for plaintiffs.

---

[28] A copy of the Demurrer Book for *Reynolds* v. *Berling* is contained in the Ashhurst Paper Books at Lincoln's Inn Library. The description of the case on the Demurrer Book under the caption reads: 'A judgment recovered may be set off though a writ of error is pending and though the judgment be recovered after the action commenced if before plea pleaded.' Dampier MSS., APB 75, Lincoln's Inn Library. A full report of the case is given at 4 Doug. 181 (1794).

[29] The correct citation for *Peytoe's Case* is (1611) 9 Co. Rep. 77b.

[30] The correct citation is (1781) 2 Doug. 695. For Lord Mansfield's trial notes, see Oldham, *MMSS,* i. 435.

[31] In the manuscript, the words 'the agreement' are written and crossed out.

[32] (1787) 1 T.R. 619.

[33] In the margin: '*Heathcote* v. *Crookshanks,* T. Cases, v. 2, p. 24'. This is a reference by Lawrence to a case at (1787) 2 T.R. 24.

PARKE *et al.*, assignees of WILLIAMS v. CARTER

[M.H.] An insurance broker after the bankruptcy of the insured settles a loss and his assignees bring an action of money had and received for the sum received; they shall recover so much as is due on the general balance between the bankrupt and the broker.

This was an action for money had and received to the use of the plaintiffs, in whose favour a verdict was found, subject to the opinion of the court, on a case stating that the defendant acted as the insurance broker and general agent of the bankrupt. That by an account rendered by the defendant to the bankrupt for 1st January 1777 to the 14th of August 1781, a balance was due to them of 320–4–10. That the balance was carried forward to the next account from January 1st 1782 to the 9th of December following, when there was due to the defendant £302.2s. That on the 1st December 1782, Williams ordered [*5:177*] defendant to get an insurance done on 3/4ths of the ship *Providence*, valued in £300, from Portsmouth to Liverpool, which insurance was accordingly effected on the 3rd of December at 5 guineas premium. The ship was afterwards captured by a French privateer, the news of which arrived the 9th of January [1783]. On the 22nd of December 1782, Williams committed an act of bankruptcy, upon which he was declared a bankrupt on a commission which issued the 13th of March 1783. On the 14th of January [1783], the loss was adjusted and paid to the defendant, for the amount of which, deducting the premium, the verdict was given.

This case was argued in last term by *Adair* and *Bond*, and now by *Le Blanc* and *Bolton*. For the plaintiff it was said that the money not having been received until after the bankruptcy formed no article in any account between the defendant and the bankrupt, but was peculiarly received for their use, for the bankrupt himself would never have settled this loss but only his assignees. That the authority of the defendant as general agent was put an end to by the bankruptcy, and therefore he could not receive the money for the bankrupt— and further that a broker had no general authority to settle losses.

[*5:178*] For the defendant it was said that a policy broker was a factor, and that it had been settled that they had a lien for their general balance. *Green* v. *Farmer*, Burr.,[34] and 1 [W.] Blackstone Reports 651. *Goden* v. *Royal Exchange Assurance Company*, Burr. 490.[35] That it was settled that assignees must take the effects of a bankrupt subject to all liens. *Browne* v. *Heathcote*, 1 Atk. 160, 2 Vern. 564. *Ex parte Deeze*, 1 Atk. 228. And that in *Whitehead* v. *Vaughan* it had been laid down by BULLER, Justice, that a broker had a lien on a policy for his general balance. Cooke's *Bankrupt Law* 316.[36]

In reply it was answered that the cases only showed that factors only had a lien for their general balance unless there was some contract for that purpose,

---

[34] *Green* v. *Farmer* (1768) 4 Burr. 2214.
[35] Probably *Godin* v. *London Assurance Co.* (1758) 1 Burr. 489.
[36] W. Cooke, *A Compendious System of the Bankrupt Laws* (1785).

either expressed or implied, from the usage of trade, and that no such contract or usage was found in this case.

After consideration, Lord LOUGHBOROUGH declared the opinion of the court, and said the question had been argued on the point whether a broker had a lien for his general balance. This had been contended, the broker as general agent or factor. But that the question of lien did not come directly before the court. It should more properly arise in trover for the policy. That money had and received was a new form of action for the assignees of a bankrupt and not used by them in the time of HOLT, PARKER and HARDWICKE, and that in a case in *Vesey*,[37] [*5:179*] it was considered as being brought for the first time. But that it had obtained lately for beneficial purposes, but that the assignees could not stand in a better situation than the bankrupt himself. That in *Billon* v. *Hyde*,[38] Lord HARDWICKE had found a difficulty of interfering in a point where the law and equity _____ [*sic*], but held that the assignees ought only to recover the true balance after all allowances. In 2 Burr. 931, *Foxcroft* v. *Devonshire* is a similar case determined on the authority of the case in *Vesey*.[39] That the point had come more directly before the court in the case of _____ [*sic*] assignees of *Thompson* v. *Buchanan*. There Thompson had employed Buchanan as an insurance broker, and he had paid losses to the amount of £1,027 and received premiums to the amount of £1,400 between November 2, 1781 and the February following. Thompson committed an act of bankruptcy on the 17th of November and a commission was sued out in 1782. This being referred, the arbitrator determined that the balance only should be paid and on a motion to set aside the award, the court determined that he had done right.

This is the plain and short ground. If the assignees usher in the acts of the defendant and insist on the money as received to their use, they must admit that the money paid is also for their use, and therefore they can't be in a better situation than the bankrupt and entitle themselves to recover without deducting.

Postea to defendant.

[*5:180*]

[*Lawrence note:*] On the 1st August, HEATH, J., was desirous of having the usage of the trade made a part of the case as to the lien that brokers had, but this was not agreed to by the plaintiffs.

---

[37] In the margin: '1 Vesey 330'. The reference is to *Billon* v. *Hyde* (1749) 1 Ves. sen. 326, 330.
[38] In the manuscript, '2 Vesey 326' is written and crossed out. In the margin: '1 Atk. 126, 1 Vesey 326'. (The *Billon* case was reported by both Atkins and Vesey, Sr.)
[39] The court in *Foxcroft* v. *Devonshire* dealt with the question of a broker as factor and agent, but reliance by the court in *Foxcroft* on the *Billon* case is not apparent.

DIGBY v. FORBES and GRANT

[M.H.] Bond conditioned to account. Plea that defendant has always been ready and willing to account is a bad plea. He should have pleaded that he had accounted. In an action on such bond the plaintiff must assign breaches according to the 8 and 9 W.3. *ut semb.*

Debt on bond and the penalty of £5,000.

Plea craving oyer of the condition which, reciting that the plaintiff had appointed the defendant Forbes to pay the subsistences and contingencies of His Majesty's troops in the island of Minorca, and also to pay the staff and hospital officers pursuant to such orders, directions and instructions as should be delivered to him in writing, was that if defendant Forbes should well and truly pay to the uses and purposes aforesaid all such sums of money as should [5:181] come to his hands, or with which he should become chargeable either by deductions or otherwise according to such orders and directions and instructions as he the said Forbes should from time to time receive from plaintiff, and also if defendant Forbes *should well and truly account with the said Robert Digby* and produce authentic vouchers for all payments made by him for the purchases aforesaid except such monies as might fall into the enemies' hands or be lost at sea, and upon the close of his accounts pay over the balance which shall appear due thereon, then the objection to be void. That he had well and truly paid to and for the uses and purposes in the condition mentioned all such sums of money which had come to his hands, or which he had justly become chargeable with, either by deductions or otherwise, according to such orders, directions and instructions as he had from time to time received from the said plaintiff. And that no account had been closed or settled between the plaintiff and defendant concerning the payments made by him for the purposes aforesaid, but that he, the said defendant, hath always been and still is ready and willing well and truly to account with the said plaintiff and to produce authentic vouchers for all payments which had at any time been made by him for the purposes in the said condition mentioned except such money as had gotten into the enemies' hands or had been lost at sea, and upon the close of his account to pay over to the said plaintiff the balance, if any.

To this the plaintiff replied and assigned three breaches. The first in not paying over the money [that] came to his hands in pursuance of directions sent him by the plaintiff, which directions were set forth in the replication; secondly that he had not always been ready and willing to account, although often requested; thirdly, that although upon the close of the account a large balance was due, yet he had refused to pay it.

To this the defendant demurred, and assigned several causes. First, that by the law, only one breach could be assigned of the condition of the bond, whereas the plaintiff had assigned several. And that the breaches were not alleged with sufficient certainty.

[5:182] *Bond*, Serjeant, for the defendant insisted that the 8th and 9th W. 3.

c. 11, sec. 8 applied only to cases where the covenant for the performance of which the bond was conditioned was contained in another instrument.

Lord LOUGHBOROUGH: Where do you find that the Act requires a separate instrument?

Bond: It is so laid down in *Cornwallis* v. *Savery*, Burr. 772.[40]

Le Blanc contra: The statute is compulsory on the plaintiff to assign breaches, and there is nothing in the statute which says the agreement to be performed must be in a separate instrument. That the statute was to be construed liberally in ease of defendants to prevent the necessity of going into equity. *Dredge* v. *Bland* 2 Wils. 377.[41] In *Philips* v. *Cheki*, sittings after Easter Term 1784 before BULLER, Justice, the jury assessed damages and action on a bond.[42] In *Cornwallis* v. *Savery* the point was not settled, as it was unnecessary to agitate it for the court was of opinion that there was in fact but one breach assigned. But it is no matter what the replication is, for the plea is bad. The condition of the bond is to account, not to account on request. Defendant being bound to account, the defendant must offer to do it. It is like being bound to pay money.

Bond in reply, said that accounting differed from freezing money, as both parties must concur in accounting.

[5:183] WILSON J.: The defendant has undertaken to account, and if he is obstructed, that will be an excuse like a tender and refusal. If the condition had been that the defendant should be ready to account, the plea would have been good, but the condition being to account, the defendant must show that he had accounted, or that he had offered and was prevented, without which that is not shewn which is equivalent to a performance. The first act is to be done by the defendant, and this is not a collateral act, it rests entirely in the agreement of the parties.[43]

Lord LOUGHBOROUGH: The defendant has undertaken to do a certain act, but he does not plead that he has done it, but only that he was ready.

HEATH J.: *Semper paratus* has been determined to be a bad plea.

Judgment for plaintiff.

[*Lawrence note:*] I have omitted taking notice of those parts of the pleadings to which the latter causes of demurrer apply, as nothing was said by the court respecting them.

---

[40] (1759) 2 Burr. 772.
[41] And in the margin: *Goodwin* v. *Crowle*, Cowper 357.
[42] In the margin: '*Vide* Lord Mansfield's judgment in *Collins* v. *Collins*, 2 Burr. 826, in point. *Vide Roles* v. *Rosewell*, 5 T.R. 540. *Hardy* v. *Born, ibid*: 636.'
[43] And in the margin: '6 Mod. 227'. The reference is to *Fitz-Hugh* v. *Dennington* (1704).

NORRIS v. ROZLE

[M.H.] Action will not lie for breaking out a window overlooking the plaintiff's ground.

Action on the case for breaking out a new light in defendant's house which overlooked the plaintiff's.

It was moved in arrest of judgment that no action would lie for this, but that the plaintiff might have obstructed it.

Adair for the plaintiff mentioned *Cherrington* v. *Abney*, 2 Vern. 646.

WILSON, J.: That case was never in a court of law.[44]

Judgment arrested.

[5:184] PYKE, widow v. BISHOP of BATH and WELLS and THOMAS LINDSAY
Quare Impedit

[M.H.] Pending a *quare impedit* and after judgment for the plaintiff, the bishop admitted the defendant's clerk, whom the plaintiff permits to die incumbent and does not get his clerk admitted until after the death of the other. This admission by the bishop shall serve a turn. *ut semb.*

Declaration stated,[45]—That Richard Roberts being seized of the advowson of the vicarage of the church of Chew Magna with the chapel of Dundry presented William Jones—temp. Eliz.

That Richard Roberts died and the advowson descended to his four daughters, *viz.*

> Mary, the wife of Thomas Westcott
> Jane, the wife of William Squire
> Prudence, the wife of John Amory
> Grace, the wife of Francis Isaac

That Jones died and Catherine Babor usurping on Westcott's turn, presented John Babor. Temp. Elizabeth.
   1st Turn

Babor died, and Squire and his wife presented John Fabwin—temp. Chas. I.
   2nd Turn

Fabwin died and Amory and his wife presented Robert Joyner—temp. Chas. I.
   3rd Turn

---

[44] I.e., all of the proceedings in *Cherrington* v. *Abney* were in Chancery. Norris appears to have sought equitable relief, perhaps an injunction, in this common law action, relying on *Cherrington*, a Chancery case in which it was held that when an old house with ancient lights is pulled down and replaced with a new house, the lights (windows) in the new house must be the same size, number, and locations as in the old house if the claim to ancient lights is to be maintained.

[45] The text of this case laying out the pleadings is in a clerical hand. Lawrence inserted several marginal notations, as indicated below, and his handwriting reappears after the joinder in demurrer.

Joyner died and John Washer claiming right in the turn of Grace Isaac presented Michael Cory—temp. Chas. II

4th Turn

That Mary Westcott survived her husband and devised her turn to Edward Hill in fee, from whom it descended to her son Richard Hill.

That Cory died, and Hill presented Buckler temp. Anne.

5th Turn

That Jane Squire survived her husband and on her death descended to Christopher Squire and through him to William Squire and from him to Elizabeth Squire—that Buckler died and Elizabeth Squire presented John Hatch, temp. Geo. II.

6th Turn

That Sylvanus Bond claiming title to the turn of Amory and his wife presented William Smith, temp. Geo. II.

7th Avoidance

That Smith died before which time Francis Isaac and Grace his wife had issue Robert. [5:185] That his turn descended to Elizabeth the wife of Thomas Pyke as the daughter of Robert, who by the death of[46] Smith presented Robert Isaac Pyke, her clerk, who was inducted—temp. Geo. II.

8th Avoidance

That he died and that the Church is still void.

9th and present Avoidance

That Richard Hill by will gave his turn to Mary in fee, and that she by indenture dated 19th January 1740 sold her next avoidance to Robert Smith, that on the 4th of June 1742, Robert Smith by indenture sold that turn to Humphrey Pyke—that Humphrey Pyke made his wife Elizabeth his executrix, that Elizabeth by indenture of 13th February 1771 sold that turn to Robert J. Pyke—that Robert J. Pyke by will dated 22nd May 1784 made plaintiff Rebecca his executrix, who as such claims a right to present.

Bishop pleaded—that he claimed nothing but as ordinary.

Plea: the other defendant Lindsay pleaded 3 pleas. On the two first, issue was joined. By the 3rd he admitted the presentations and title down to the death of Hatch as stated in the declaration and then protesting that Sylvanus Bond had no title to the 7th turn, protesting also that he did not present William Smith upon the said avoidance. Says that after the presentation of Joyner, the perparty of Prudence Amory descended to her son John Amory and from him to William Amory, his brother.

That William Amory, by will dated 18th April 1667, devised his perparty to his two daughters, Frances and Prudence and that they thereby became jointly seized in fee.

[5:186] That Frances died, and Prudence became sole seized.

That she married Samuel Cudmore and survived him and on 3rd of April 1708 by indenture between her, Nathaniel Griffin, and James Ley conveyed her

---

[46] The manuscript reads, 'who on the by the death of', with the words 'the death of' inserted after 'by'. Apparently Lawrence meant to strike out the words 'by the', but failed to do so.

perparty to them to her use for life. Remainder to Serjeant Thomas Gibbon in fee. That she died—and Serjeant Gibbon died, and on her death the said perparty descended to his son Thomas Gibbon who was seized at the death of Hatch of the said perparty and to him it belonged in the 7th turn on the death of Hatch to present a fit person who, before Sylvanus Bond presented Smith, presented Robert Rogers. Temp. Geo. II.[47]

Who died and made the 8th avoidance, that the turn of Grace Isaac descended to Robert Isaac her son, from him to Elizabeth Pyke, the wife of Henry Pyke as daughter of Robert Isaac—to whom on the death of Rogers it belonged to present to a fit person and that Sylvanus Bond having no right *presented* William Smith.[48] That William Smith died and made the 9th avoidance.

That Richard Hill after his presentation of Buckler gave his perparty to Mary Hill his daughter in fee.

That Mary Hill by indenture 19th January 1740 sold the next avoidance to Robert Smith.

4th June 1742, Robert Smith by indenture sold that next avoidance to Humphrey Pyke, who made Elizabeth Pyke his executrix, and that she on the death of Smith presented Robert Isaac Pyke on the 9th avoidance. Temp. Geo. III.

That Robert Isaac Pyke died and made the 10th and present avoidance.

It then states that Elizabeth Squire on the 3rd [*5:187*] January 1732 devised her perparty to Elizabeth Northcote in fee.

That Elizabeth Northcote 15th February 1734 devised her perparty to Mary, the wife of James Pearce, in fee, who surviving her husband on the 25th of August 1751 devised to defendant Lindsay who claimed title to present the present avoidance.

Replication: to this plaintiff replied that after Joyner was instituted on the presentation of Amory and Prudence his wife, that perparty descended to their son John Amory as heir of Prudence and from him to his brother William, and from him to his two daughters, Frances and Prudence as coheiresses by which they became seized in coparcenary.

That Frances married Edward Gibbon.

That they died and the share of Frances descended to her daughter Frances Gibbon whereby she and Prudence Amory became seized in coparcenary.

That Prudence married Samuel Cudmore and survived him and on the 2nd of April 1680 by indenture of lease and release sold her perparty to Nathaniel Griffin and James Ley to her own use for life, remainder to Serjeant Thomas Gibbon in fee. That Gibbon survived her and became seized in fee, and died, and that his perparty descended to his son Thomas Gibbon.

That Frances Gibbon, the daughter, died, on whose death her perparty descended to Sylvanus Bond as cousin and heir at law of the said Frances Gibbon.

That the church then became void by the death of Hatch.

---

[47] In the margin in Lawrence's hand: 'Death of Rogers'.
[48] In the margin in Lawrence's hand: 'Smith presented'.

[*5:188*] That it belonged to Sylvanus Bond to present as he and Thomas Gibbon could not agree.

That Thomas Gibbon attempted to usurp, and Sylvanus Bond obstructed him.

Whereupon Thomas Gibbon in Hilary Term 4th Geo. 2 brought his *Quare Impedit*[49] against the bishop of Bath and Wells and Sylvanus Bond. And therein stated the title and avoidances as above to the death of Hatch.

That Prudence Amory and John Amory having died seized, the perparty of Prudence descended to John Amory their son—from him to William, who on the 18th of April 1667 made his will and gave it to his daughters Frances and Prudence as joint tenants.

That Prudence survived and became entitled to the whole by survivorship. That she married Samuel Cudmore and surviving him, by indenture of 2nd April 1708, conveyed it to Nathaniel Griffin and Ley, to the use of herself for life. Remainder to Thomas Gibbon, serjeant-at-law, in fee. That Prudence died. That Serjeant Gibbon died and his perparty descended to the then plaintiff, Thomas Gibbon and that on the death of Hatch it then belonged to him to present and that Sylvanus Bond obstructed him.

That to this Bond pleaded[50] and stated the presentations and title as above to Hatch. That the perparty of Prudence Amory descended to John Amory her son, from him to his son William, from him to his daughters Frances and Prudence as coheiresses.

That Frances survived Edward Gibbon and had a daughter to whom the share of her mother descended. That Prudence Cudmore sold to Griffin and Ley as above set forth. [*5:189*] That she died. That Serjeant Gibbon died and the share of Prudence descended to Thomas Gibbon the then plaintiff.

That Frances Gibbon died and that her share descended to Sylvanus Bond as her cousin and heir. And that on the avoidance by the death of Hatch, it belonged to him to present as having the share of Frances, the elder of the two daughters of William Amory, and traversed the devise by William Amory to his daughters as joint tenants.

That Thomas Gibbon by his replication[51] took issue on the traverse, and that the jury at the assizes on the 12th month of 6 Geo. II found a special verdict. And judgment for the defendant Sylvanus Bond. With writ awarded to the bishop. Continuances by *Episcopus non misit breve* till Easter Term 8 Geo. II.[52]

And that the bishop by virtue of that writ returnable in the last term did at the presentation of Sylvanus Bond admit and institute the said William Smith. And that pending the said writ the bishop unjustly and without judgment admitted and instituted Robert Rogers to the said vicarage on the presentation of Thomas Gibbon contrary to law, which admission by virtue of the said

---

[49] In the margin in Lawrence's hand: 'Q.I: [. . .] of *Gibbon* v. *Bond*'.

[50] In Lawrence's hand in the margin: 'Bond's plea'.

[51] In Lawrence's hand in the margin: 'Gibbon's replication'.

[52] In the margin in Lawrence's hand: 'Judgment for Bond, E. 6 G. 2. Smith admitted by writ E. 8 G. 2'. The word '*breve*' is also in Lawrence's hand.

judgment became and was void in law, and that before Sylvanus Bond could obtain admission and institution of William Smith, Rogers died.[53]

Rejoinder: protesting that William Amory's turn did not descend to his daughters as coheiresses—protesting that Rogers did not die before Sylvanus Bond could obtain admission, says that Rogers was alive 1 year [5:190] 3 months and 10 days after giving judgment and during that time remained incumbent. Yet the said Sylvanus did not during his life deliver to the Bishop any writ to admit a fit person to vicarage, nor writ whatsoever but wholly neglected so to do until after the death of Rogers, and suffered him to continue incumbent until the time of his death.

To this our rejoinder there was a demurrer and a joinder in demurrer.[54]

For the plaintiff I contended that the institution and induction of Rogers pending the *Q.I.* against Bond was void, or at least that the judgment in *Q.I.* removed Rogers so that from that time there was no plenarty as against Bond. And that the admission of Smith in pursuance of a writ to the bishop could not be an usurpation on the term of Edward Pyke.

This a fraudulent defect, the object of the suit in *Q.I.* and to get admission of Gibbons' clerk without title, and as such void *ab initio*. This the general rule of law. Resignation of an abbot by covin shall not abate the writ. 3 Co. 76(b).[55] Riens per descent pleaded and a fraudulent feoffment of the ancestor found to separate the heirs from the assets. Defendant shouldn't take advantage of his own wrong. Dy. 295, pl. 16.[56] That there were authorities to show [5:191] that pending a writ of *Q.I.* no alteration could be made and that any admission made during that time was void. Co. Litt. 344. If hanging[57] a writ of *Q.I.* [by] the ordinary, a clerk came in by usurpation, the patron should have a writ to remove him for *pendente lite nihil innovetur*.[58] The same doctrine is laid down by Hobart in *Elvis* v. *Archbishop of York*, Hob. Rep. 320,[59] and the reasoning in Savile 89[60] was to the same effect. In *Moore* v. *Bishop of Norwich*, 3 Leon. 138, judgment being given for the plaintiff a writ issued to the bishop, who returned that after judgment the same incumbent against whom the action was brought was instituted and inducted and so the church was filled. And on that occasion ANDERSON C.J. laid it down that what person soever is presented and admitted after the action brought, unless it be that the title of the patron is paramount to that of the plaintiff, upon such recovery he shall be removed. So where in *Q.I.* the defendant pleaded that the plaintiff had filled the church hanging the writ, to which plaintiff demurred, which confessed as much, yet judgment was given of a writ to the bishop, 11 R. 2. *Qu. I.* 144, cited in Hob.

---

[53] In the margin in Lawrence's hand: 'That the bishop unjustly admitted Rogers *pendente lite*, who died before Smith could obtain institution.'
[54] This sentence, and the remainder of the notes of the present case are in Lawrence's hand.
[55] *Fermor's Case* (1602).
[56] The reference is to 3 Dyer 295b, pl. 16.
[57] I.e., pending.
[58] During litigation nothing new should be introduced.
[59] The case report begins at Hobart 315 (1619).
[60] *Milborne* v. *Dunmow Inhabitants* (c. 1586) Savile 83.

194, which is showing that the admission is absolutely void—or there would be no writ *ad admit*.[61] or it would have abated the suit.

That there were cases of a plaintiff's recovering in *Q. Impedit* but that would not make a difference as both were actions *Q.I.* Booth 230[62] and it is expressly [*5:192*] said in *Fitz Natura* 35c[63] that if defendant recover he shall avoid plaintiff's clerk admitting pending the writ.

The question would then be if suffering Rogers to remain in possession after the judgment in *Q.I.* until his death would make any difference as to this *quod initio non valet tractu temporis non convalescet*.[64] The dying in possession did not fill the church.

If the presentation be void there can be no usurpation. *Green's Case*, 6 Co. 29.[65] The incumbent is so removed by the recovery that no writ to the bishop is necessary. 2 *R. Ab*. 350 pl. 6.[66] From that time therefore, if not *ab initio*, the church was void, and the writ might go at any time after during Rogers' life. It might have gone the moment before his death, and if the death prevents it, it would have prevented the effect of the suit if he had died the moment after the recovery, which could not be. In *Winchcombe* v. *Pulleston*, Hob. 165,[67] when one was presented by simony and died, the king was held entitled to present after his death for the presentation being void during the life of the simoniacal clerk. It was absurd to say that his death could alter the case, and death consummate what was never begun.

And that determining for defendant would be determining that Smith who was admitted in consequence of a judgment of this court was an usurper.

[*5:193*] Hill, the king's serjeant, *contra*:

Observed that the question was whether this was the 9th or 10th turn and 9 writs appeared by the pleading to have been sued out before Bond's clerk was admitted and that Rogers had lived a year and three months after the judgment. Which laches he said not ought to affect third persons who were innocent. The cases cited he said were all between the parties to the suit—and that as to all but Bond, Rogers was incumbent in fact, for such incumbent is entitled to all the profits of the living until he be actually removed. Watson's *C. Law*,[68] c. 40, fol. 314.

That Bond by not suing out an *alias* and *pluries*[69] and an attachment against the bishop meant to run two lives, to suffer Rogers to enjoy and then present another clerk.

He admitted that there was no case in point. But there were cases that have an analogy to this.

---

[61] *Ad admittendum clericum*.
[62] George Booth, *The Law of Real Actions* (1704).
[63] Fitzherbert's *Natura Brevium*, fol. 35c.
[64] 'That which is bad from the beginning does not improve by the passage of time.'
[65] (1602) 6 Co. 29a.
[66] *Rolle's Abridgement*, 350, pl. 6.
[67] The correct citation is Hobart 193.
[68] W. Watson, *The Clergy-man's Law* (1725).
[69] In the manuscript, the words 'against the bishop' are here written and struck out.

If an incumbent be deprived or resign to the ordinary he must give notice to the patron, or there will be no lapse. But if the bishop should collate on a vacancy by deprivation, and the collator *should die*, the turn would be lost though the patron had no notice, and though the patron might present living the clerk, yet if he dies he shall lose his turn and the next person shall not [*5:194*] be prejudiced by his negligence. Cro. Eliz. 811.[70] Hob. 318.[71] Noy 65.[72] He said that the bishop could not collate as being a party to the suit even if Bond had not presented at all and the church might have continued still void. In 4 Mod. 212, in the great case of the *commendam*,[73] it was held that if the Crown presents the avoidance he may prevent the lapse, but if the commendatory dies, the turn of the Crown is satisfied. That it was not necessary to say what might have been the case if Rogers had died a day or two after the judgment, as this was a case of wilful laches. The case of *Winchcombe* v. *Pulleston*, he said, did not apply as that was a case of simony and that until the statute of King William[74] which made a simoniacal dying incumbent a server of a turn, he was in no sense incumbent against anybody.

In reply it was said that the cases cited were not all between parties to the suit. That plaintiffs did not claim under Bond and therefore ought not to be prejudiced by his laches more than the defendant. That on the reasoning of Lord HUBBARD in *Brickhead* v. *Archbishop of York*, Hob. 200,[75] the bishop might be allowed to collate on Bond's not presenting within 6 months.

After a few days' consideration Lord LOUGHBOROUGH delivered the opinion of the court and, [*5:195*] having stated the pleadings, observed that neither the replication nor the rejoinder stated when Smith was presented, nor directly that he was presented. That the plea had expressly stated that Bond presented Smith after the death of Rogers.

On the argument it had been said the other rejoinder contained sufficient matter to bar the right of Bond, because he had neglected to get his clerk admitted and that the church being full as to all but Bond, by his neglecting to sue out his writ till the death of Rogers, his turn was satisfied and his neglect should not prejudice the other coparceners, but that another point occurred without giving an opinion as to that argument which was very strongly urged.

That the argument in favour of Bond must rest on a supposition that when it was open to Bond to take his turn, he did it. And therefore it was essential to know when Bond presented Smith. The replication has not stated when Bond presented Smith. That he had stated it to have been after the death of Rogers and if that be so and Rogers died in possession, there was no presentation on the death of Hatch, and it is a [*5:196*] necessary consequence that any presentation after must be an usurpation on the next turn. That Smith was

---

[70] *Leak* v. *Bishop of Coventry and Babington* (1601).
[71] *Elvis* v. *Archbishop of York* (1619) Hobart 315.
[72] *Servein* v. *Bishop of Lincoln* (n.d., *c.* 1597).
[73] *Attorney-General* v. *Bishop of London* (1693) 4 Mod. 200. The case dealt with *commendam*, holding an ecclesiastical benefice in trust to the custody of a patron during a vacancy.
[74] 1 Will. & Mar., c. 16 (1688).
[75] *Brickhead* v. *Archbishop of York* (1617) Hob. 197.

presented after the death of Rogers is not denied by the replication, and we are, therefore, of opinion judgment must be given for the defendant.

[*Lawrence note*:] Upon examining the plea, I do not find that it is there expressly alleged that Smith was presented after the death of Rogers. The words are these: 'And the said Silvanus having no right to present to the vicarage aforesaid with the Chapel aforesaid but usurping upon the said Humphrey Pyke and Eliz. his wife, did present one William Smith as his Clerk to the aforesaid vicarage with the Chapel aforesaid so being void by the death of the said Robert Rogers in the 8th avoidance after the death of the said Richard Roberts, and which said William Smith was on that presentation admitted instituted and inducted into the same in the time of peace &c.'.

[5:*197*] WRIGHT v. NUTT

[M.N.] This case is in print in H. Blackstone's Reports.[76] In Chancery.

The late Sir James Wright resided in Georgia and having a large real estate there became indebted by bond before the commencement of the rebellion in America to Miles Brewton, Esq. of South Carolina in the sum of £1,000.

Sir J. Wright on account of his loyalty was afterwards banished and his property in Georgia confiscated by an Act of the legislature of that province. But the Act declared his property subject to the payment of all his debts.

He is since dead and the plaintiff—Wright—is his executor.

Brewton is dead and Charles Pinckney of South Carolina is his only surviving executor.

Pinckney, the executor, applied to the commissioner of forfeited estates in Georgia for payment of the debt due from Wright to Brewton. The commissioner did not absolutely reject the claim but referred it, on account of some difficulty, to the legislature.

⟨Nutt⟩, the defendant, obtained by virtue of a power of attorney from Pinckney, administration in this country to Brewton, and in 1784, as administrator, commenced an action on the bond against Sir James Wright, which after his death was revived against his executor.[77]

---

[76] Henry Blackstone's report of this case (volume 1 at 136, decided 23 January 1788) runs to nineteen printed pages. The case was inserted by Blackstone following his report of *Folliott* v. *Owen* (1789) 1 H. Bl. 123, due to the similarity of the facts in the two cases and the reference by Lord Loughborough in his opinion in *Folliott* to the *Wright* case. The factual recitation in *Wright* v. *Nutt* is much more extensive in Blackstone's report than in the manuscript version in Lawrence's notebook; also, Blackstone gives the arguments of counsel that are absent in the Lawrence manuscript. The opinions of Lord Chancellor Thurlow and Master of the Rolls Kenyon, however, are very close to the version printed in Blackstone. Lawrence, in another marginal note, indicates that these opinions were 'from a note of Mr. Cox'. Since there are some variations, the Cox version is presented here, and expressions not found in Henry Blackstone's report are identified by angle brackets.

[77] In the Court of King's Bench, Nutt was non-prossed (see abbreviations, *nolle pros*.). See *Wright* v. *Nutt* (1786) 1 T.R. 388.

The plaintiff brought his bill for an injunction against Nutt and Pinckney.

This day (23rd January 1788) the plaintiff moved for an injunction on Nutt's answer, Pinckney's not being yet put in.

Lord THURLOW assisted by KENYON, Master of the Rolls.

LORD CHANCELLOR: I am glad this application happens to be made when I have his honour's assistance, because there are circumstances in this case [5:198] somewhat particular, though I do not take the general principles upon which it must be decided to be altogether new. A great part of the argument has spent itself on this question, ⟨whether the laws of the country to which the creditor belongs⟩ have or have not disabled him from suing in that country. I think the first answer which was given to that was the strongest and the best, that is to say, if he is disabled from suing, this is not the court to say so, but it ought to have been brought in question before the court in which the action depended, and there it should have been decided. I likewise lay out of the case all the observations that relate to hardship either upon one side or the other. It may be a question for private speculation whether such a law made in the province[78] was a wise or an improvident one, whether a barbarous or civilized institution. But here we must take it as the law of an independent country, and the law of every country must be equally regarded in courts of justice here, whether in private speculation they are wise laws or foolish ones. Nor does it at all apply in my judgment whether Sir. J. Wright was or was not capable of paying. For the case would have stood before me precisely in the same situation if it had been worth £100,000 and had been sued in the way in which he has now sued. As a man I might feel differently about it, and compassion might interpose, but as a judge it would be impossible for me to determine on that ground. Nor can I take into consideration how very much it bears with it an approach to fraud.

The circumstance of converting the charity of this country to individuals ruined in their service to the purpose of paying the creditors of those individuals in the other country is a consideration [5:199] which should have belonged to those who thought proper to allow them that charity, and the terms upon which it was afforded should have been regulated accordingly. It is nothing to me, in short, what the situations of the parties are, but I must consider the plaintiff as competent to bring his action at law and the defendant as coming here to state, if he can, some equitable ground upon which such actions ought not to be permitted to proceed. The equitable ground which he has stated differs from all others that I know of that have come before the court, unless there be more similitude between this and the case of *Holditch* v. *Mist* than the short state of the latter case affords.[79] But the circumstances under which this case comes before the court are these: that Sir James Wright, a banished and ⟨confiscated⟩ man disabled to act or to sue in that country[80] had all his property taken away from him and the terms upon which it was taken

---

[78] Instead of 'the province', the word 'Georgia' appears in the printed report.
[79] The *Holditch* case is reported at (1721) 1 P. Wms 695.
[80] In the printed report, 'in America' appears instead of 'that country'.

away were that it should be applicable in the first place to the payment of his debts contracted in that country.

No doubt has been made on either side that the debt sued for by law here was of that description and capable of being made the subject of a claim upon his estate in that country. Under that circumstance, instead of making a claim there (as is suggested by the bill) an action is sued here. There is no doubt in the world but that according to the general principles of a court of equity, a man who has not actual possession of his debt (for if he had actual possession I should conceive it would be payment even though it might be available in a [5:200] court of law, but if not so at law it would be at least in a court of equity considered as actual payment, and that if a man was vexed twice for the same demand upon some formal difficulty of making the fact of payment available at law) but supposing him to have the power[81] of paying the debt ⟨depending upon his own act⟩. Whether he will resort to a particular fund or not, if instead of making use of that power he will pursue the debtor, it would be too much for the court of equity to permit him to sue the person and relinquish the exercise of that power which he has at the time in his own hands.

This case is attended with a circumstance still more peculiar, and that is it is totally impossible for him to assign over that right to the party debtor here, in order for him to make it available ⟨in America⟩. It is clear that neither the hazard, nor the difficulty, nor the expense of making the demand ought to be thrown upon the creditors. In point of natural justice, they ought to be upon the debtor, provided the creditors can put the debtor into a situation to make it as effectual for him as it would be for the creditor himself; but here the creditors cannot clothe the debtor with the same remedy as he himself is in possession of, and therefore the question is whether, whilst he holds that remedy in his hands, the court does not proceed upon principles of natural justice applied by fair analogy to other cases, or if such other cases had not existed, applied by the reason of the thing and the force of those principles of natural justice [5:201] to this case, when it says to a creditor who makes that demand in a court of law, you shall not proceed upon that demand till you have satisfied me that you have taken all the pains you can, to make that other pledge you have there in your hands (I call it a pledge by metaphor, for I do not mean to state that it effectually as a pledge⟨, but till you make that quasi pledge⟩[82]) as effectual and available to yourself as you possibly can. Under circumstances so stated, a court would proceed according to the clearest notions of distributive justice and the fairest principles of natural equity. If it is said to the creditors so circumstanced, you shall proceed to make that available and you shall demonstrate to me that you have proceeded to make it available *bona fide*, and that you have ⟨neither for the fraudulent purpose of obtaining double satisfaction or the malignant purpose of plaguing your debtor⟩ made your claim in this country. I wish to be understood clearly

---

[81] In the printed report, 'has the power' appears instead of 'supposing him to have the power'.

[82] The parenthetical passage as written in the manuscript is unclear. Henry Blackstone clarified it by deleting the words in angle brackets.

upon this point, that this is the utmost extent my judgment at this moment goes to upon this subject. When this subject was introduced into the House of Lords, I had occasion to give my opinion upon it there more particularly in private to those who brought in the bill with the clearest motives in the world and with a great deal of public spirit and public wisdom also. But other motives arose which rendered that project indiscreet and impolitic, and consequently it was not carried into execution as a legislative act. But then, and at all times, it has continually struck me with wonder that principles such as [5:202] I have just stated should not have been regarded from the moment the question arose as fit to be urged in courts of justice, ⟨for the purpose of bringing the demands⟩ to what (I think) is their proper test.

I am therefore of opinion that provided a case is made by which it appears that there is in the hands of the creditor either possession of the estate in fact, or the clear means of effecting that possession, he ought to be called upon so to do and the court should interfere. When I have stated that to be my opinion, I confess that, thinking much of *Holditch* v. *Mist*,[83] I don't know how exactly to reconcile the decision of that case with the principles I have now laid down. The only way I have to deal with it is to avoid it. From the book, nothing more appears but that a bill was filed by the debtor stating that he had been one of the directors of the South Sea Company, and that by audit of parliament his whole fortune had been confiscated, and therefore an absolute disability of paying his debts had been incurred, and that it was contrary to reason and natural justice that he should be called upon to pay his debts under the circumstances of such an Act of parliament. And no more is stated upon the subject. Yet it is clear that the debts of these directors were capable of being paid out of the fund. It also appears by a memorandum that is added to the bottom of that case that by compromise the debt was directed to be paid ⟨not out of the fund, which I wonder at,⟩ but out of that part of the fund by which some regulation [5:203] of the Act appears to have been given to the private persons of the directors themselves. If there is a doubt about that, or if one's opinion turned upon it, it should be a little more inquired into. But I recollect that beyond the payment of the debts and the confiscation, there was a personal allowance made to them who suffered. But still stating the case in that manner, this much seems fairly to be inferred from it, ⟨as the defendant's counsel wished to do in his argument,⟩ namely, that it did not occur at that time to insist that the debt should not be paid out of the fund which was the personal fund of the delinquent, and which according to my principles ought to have been the last fund which was appropriated to the payment of the debts. I wonder much at that, and it brings the case to apply less because under such an Act passed in this country, an act of partial confiscation qualified in the manner in which it was, Holditch had as good a right to insist upon being relieved of that debt out of the fund as any other man. He did not lose all his right as a citizen—all he lost was the fund he had[84] confiscated. There must therefore be a

---

[83] In the margin, '1 P. Wms. 695'.
[84] In the printed report, the words 'that was' appear instead of 'he had'.

great deal more in that case than appears in the report, for it seems impossible to imagine that that debt was not to be forthcoming in some manner or other out of the fund, and if there were allowances made to say that justice of the case was satisfied by making those allowances liable to those debts. He[85] was not in the miserable situation these people [5:204] are, deprived of all their rights. I do not therefore know how to apply that case to the present and I retain the opinion I gave before, namely, that ⟨a creditor will be bound by an application to this court⟩ to use fair, *bona fide* diligence in order to make the most of his debtor's estate in the place where the law of the country has applied the estate to the payment of his debts.[86] I do not think that this law of Georgia meant any mercy to the debtors. The provision was that of pure policy; ⟨that they might not cut each other's fingers, they reserved to each other the payment of their debts out of the fund⟩. But whatever the object and interest[87] of that law might be, I am clearly of opinion that natural justice requires we should see the utmost made that can be made of that matter. Now what does this case come to? This is a debt, which as it now comes before, is sued by the administrator of Mr Brewton, who has claimed and obtained letters of administration upon a double right. He has stated, and it is recorded in the letters of administration that he is a creditor of Mr Brewton to the amount of £1,300.[88] He is also stated to be the attorney of the executor of Mr Brewton, and in that right entitled to the probate. He could not gain a probate as a creditor without the renunciation of the executor. He was therefore obliged to take it up as a temporary administrator subject to the general right [5:205] of the executor to come in for a general representation of the effects of his testator. That executor, therefore, is the person that is generally interested in and entitled to all the testator's effects and the administrator is only entitled to the temporary interest. In this situation, he brings his action.[89] The bill has been filed against him and also against the executor himself, in whom the principal representation of the testator's estate is vested. It cannot indeed be so in our contemplation till the probate of the will is effectively granted to him, but substantially it resides with him. This bill is therefore brought against him, first in respect of the formal title of the plaintiff at law; secondly in respect of the substantial title of the executor who has a right to make it available whenever he thinks proper ⟨to

---

[85] In the printed report, 'Houlditch' appears in place of the word 'he'. Despite this spelling of the name in the text of the opinion, the plaintiff's name in *Peere Williams' Reports* is shown as 'Holditch'.

[86] In the sixth edition of *Peere Williams' Reports*, issued in 1826, a footnote indicates that in *Wright* v. *Simpson* (1801) 6 Ves. jun. 714, Lord Eldon 'recognized the authority of the principal case, and expressed doubt as to the soundness of the decision in *Wright* v. *Nutt*'. 1 P. Wms. 697, n. (1). The case before Lord Eldon involved the same fact situation as that before Thurlow and Kenyon in *Wright* v. *Nutt*. Lord Eldon, in his opinion, discussed the Holditch case at length. He acknowledged that Lord Thurlow professed not to have overruled *Holditch*, but according to Eldon, 'Lord Thurlow has overruled it'. 6 Ves. jun. at 729. Later in his opinion, he stated that he needed to know satisfactorily why *Holditch* should be overruled, but in the end, he distinguished the case on the facts.

[87] In the printed report the word 'intent' appears in place of the word 'interest'.

[88] In the printed report, the figure given is 1,400.

[89] In the printed report, the words 'at law' are added.

make it so⟩. In answer to[90] this action all the passages have intervened which have been mentioned, and which, whether they arose from the uncertainty which belonged to a new case and from the difficulties the parties had in either obtaining[91] advice, in proceeding upon certain advice, or in choice of remedies which the speculation of those they consulted thought proper to offer them ⟨or not⟩, yet they have been attended with these positive mischiefs: that a man who has a clear demand has been delayed for three or four years together by various shifts in the course of law, and at length a bill in equity is filed to restrain his proceeding there at all. In order to make [5:206] a good and effectual bar in equity to a demand at law it will be necessary to show that the estate of Sir James Wright confiscated in America was as great[92] value, not only than the sum now in question but than all the sums claimed upon that estate, and consequently that there is a fund sufficient to have paid the whole. For if it should turn out to be a defective fund, and capable of satisfying but in part, it can only operate a discharge *pro tanto*. In the second place it must be shown that by the justice to be obtained in that country this demand was completely[93] made. For let what will be the faults of their judicature, I can hear no complaints of them. I must understand them to be deciding according to the laws of that country, whatever my private opinion may be. And therefore, if a ⟨formal and final decision had been obtained by which it became impossible⟩ to have obtained a shilling of the whole of that demand, that would likewise be a sufficient answer. But the bill proceeds upon the idea that the fund was ample[94] and that it is still available, or if not so, that it has been owing to the conduct of the other party. I agree that as this case is circumstanced, if you had come recently you might have stated all the actual circumstances of Sir James Wright, all that you know of the proceedings which have obtained there,[95] and the probable evidence of it,[96] and upon that it would have been competent for the court to have taken the [5:207] step now demanded, which is an injunction till the answer of Pinckney comes in. But I confess, after making allowances for the circumstances that have been pleaded, I think it tends to a dangerous example to say that a party who is sued in 1784 or 1785 should come in 1788 to ask for this answer from the party abroad, instead of applying for it in 1784[97] which he ought to have done. He should have made a proper application by affidavit, and then the action should have been stopped till the answer of the party abroad came in. But considering he has stayed so long before any application was made, I have great doubt of stopping the action upon any other terms than upon bringing the debt into court.

MASTER OF THE ROLLS: Upon the general terms of the case, I cannot hope to

---

[90] In the printed report, this sentence begins with 'In the course of', rather than 'In answer to'.
[91] In the printed report, this word is 'procuring'.
[92] In the printed report, this appears as 'a greater'.
[93] In the printed report, this word appears as 'competently'.
[94] In the printed report, this word appears as 'complete'.
[95] Instead of 'there' the words 'in America' appear in the printed report.
[96] In the printed report, 'them' appears instead of 'it'.
[97] The word 'before' appears in the printed report in place of 'in 1784'.

add to what my LORD CHANCELLOR has said. I can only express my full concurrence with every point of what has fallen from his lordship. The great point will be discussed when the whole case is before the court upon the coming of Pinckney['s] answer. It is vain to say the cause does not stand precisely upon the grounds upon which it would do if Mr Pinckney was the plaintiff in the action.[98] Some argument has been used to show that Mr Nutt stands in his own independent situation, arising for his own debt, having a right to retain (if recovered) this money from creditors[99] of an inferior nature. He comes here clothed merely (in the view of this court) with the character of the agent of Mr Pinckney in order that he may put in force the [5:208] authority with which Mr Pinckney armed him. He has obtained another formal legal character, *viz.*, that of an administrator here, because otherwise he could not have proceeded to recover the debt, and in effect he is still to be considered as the person litigating on the part of Pinckney. And when assets get into his hands, they will be considered in his hands in the character, not of the administrator of Brewton, but of attorney for Pinckney. Mr Nutt would not be entitled, as Mr Pinckney would, in case of a creditor of equal degree. Then is it not essential to the interest of justice that the parties should know from Pinckney whether he has proceeded *bona fide* as far as he can to recover payment of this demand out of that fund which ought to be the primary fund to discharge it; or indeed whether he has not actually obtained payment, for the bill suggests that he has, or that he may have, obtained payment. Now it is essential that these facts should be known from the only person who knows what[1] these facts are. I am clearly of opinion that the injunction ought to be granted. Whether upon the defendant's[2] bringing in the money or not depends upon the facts and circumstances of the argument which impute laches to Sir James Wright's executor. They ought to have taken the earliest methods in order to repel this demand, and as they have kept the party at arm's length by using delay, I think the terms my LORD CHANCELLOR imposed are fit to be imposed [5:209] upon them, namely that they should bring the money into court.[3]

---

[98] In the printed report, the words 'at law' are added.

[99] Immediately beneath the word 'creditors' in the Lawrence manuscript, the word 'debtors' is written. In the printed report, only the word 'debtors' appears.

[1] The word 'how' is written in the manuscript immediately above 'what'.

[2] In the printed report, the words 'upon the condition of' appear in place of 'the defendants'.

[3] A footnote is added at the end of the printed report, which reads as follows: 'Pinckney's answer afterwards came in, but contained nothing to induce the Court to order the injunction to be dissolved.' 1 H. Bl. at 155. This case continued to be litigated for several years as is fully reported at (1791) 3 Bro. C.C. 326. Lord Thurlow 'said that he was still of the same opinion as he was before as to the equity in general', and he ordered the cause to stand over so that application could be made to the state of Georgia. 3 Bro. C.C. at 339. In editorial comment, Brown refers to Lord Eldon's contrary opinion in *Wright* v. *Simpson* (see p. 31, n. 86, above), describing it as 'so very convincing, that it seems to supersede the force of the other decisions alluded to'. Ibid., at 341.

ROBINSON v. HOWELL[4]

[M.H.] E. 31 Geo. III, K.B. Memorial of Annuity in pursuance of 17 Geo. III, c. 26 bad, if contains only a recital of the consideration.

Upon a rule *nisi* why the warrant of attorney to confess judgment and the annuity bond should not be set aside and cancelled, one objection appeared to be that the memorial required by 17 Geo. III, c. 26 stated part of the consideration to be in cash, whereas it was by a cheque on a banker. But the court gave no opinion on that, because they thought the 2nd fatal, *viz.* that the memorial only recited that in consideration of such sums &c., the annuity was to be paid, without containing a specific allegation that the consideration had been paid, for which omission *Mingay* and *Garrow* said several annuities had been vacated.

Erskine, contra.

Rule absolute.

[*5:209A*]   The following is a copy of the Memorial:
Swinden and another to Robinson

A Memorial to be enrolled pursuant to an Act of parliament made for that purpose.

Of a bond bearing date 12th day of July 1786 from Philip Swinden of the Parish of Saint Clement Danes in the County of Middlesex, gentleman, to Thomas Robinson of the Middle Temple, London, gentleman, in the penal sum of £192—conditioned for the payment of an annuity of a clear yearly sum of £16 during the life of the said Philip Swinden in consideration of £96 paid to the said Philip Swinden and Richard Howell by the said Thomas Robinson, the receipt thereof is hereby acknowledged.

And also a Warrant of Attorney bearing even date with the above recited bond from the said Philip Swinden and Richard Howell to the said Thomas Robinson to confess judgment thereon in His Majesty's Court of King's Bench for the said sum of £192, which said bond and Warrant of Attorney are respectively witnessed by John Robinson of [*5:209B*] the Middle Temple, London, gentleman, and Ashton [*sic*] of the same place, gentleman, and are hereby required to be enrolled.

Enrolled in His Majesty's High Court of Chancery at ten of the clock in the forenoon of the 12th July 1786.

---

[4] In the margin: 'A note of Mr. East's'.

[5:210] C.P.   MICHAELMAS TERM 28 Geo. III

Alexander, Lord Loughborough, Chief Justice
Sir Henry Gould ⎫
John Heath, Esq. ⎬ Justices
Sir John Wilson ⎭

CHURCH v. EDWARDS

[M.H.] Land settled on A. for life, remainder to the heirs of the body of B. begotten by A., remainder to the right heirs of A. A. and B. died leaving two daughters, C. and D. C. levied a fine of her share. C. by this acquired a fee simple in the moiety of the estate.

Case from the Rolls.

On the marriage settlement of Bezalom Edwards, an estate was settled *ex provisione viri* on Bezalom for life, remainder to the heirs of the body of the wife by the husband. On the death of the husband the surviving issue of the marriage were Hannah and Elizabeth. Hannah levied a fine of her moiety and by will devised it to the plaintiff, and died without issue.

Elizabeth survived and suffered a common recovery of the whole, and died, devising it to the defendant.

Query if Hannah Edwards by the fine acquired a fee simple in any or what part of the settled estate.

Bond, serjeant, for the plaintiff insisted that the estate tail descended to the two daughters as parceners in tail, with remainder to themselves in [5:211] fee—and that Hannah by the fine acquired a fee simple in the whole of one moiety. Of which opinion he said his honour was, as appeared in Brown's Chancery Cases 180.[5]

Hill, serjeant, *contra*: said that Hannah was seized of an estate tail of one moiety, and in fee in remainder of one moiety of that moiety, and of one moiety of Elizabeth's moiety, and that therefore the fine was good only for one-fourth, and therefore the plaintiff could only be entitled to a quarter, and cited Co. Litt. 165, where it is laid down that there can't be a moiety of an heir.

The court without difficulty certified in favour of the plaintiff, being of opinion that Hannah by the fine acquired a fee simple in one moiety of the estate.

---

[5] The reference is to an earlier phase of the instant case, in Chancery, 15 May 1787. At the end of the report is an addition from a manuscript note of reporter Brown, which reads: 'This question being argued in Common Pleas, the Court had no doubt but that she [Hannah] acquired a fee simple in a moiety.'

ANONYMOUS

[M.H.] Bail must be justified within four days after exception, and they have not four days after added bail.

> Writ returned 6th November.
> Bail put in 6th.
> Notice of bail given the 7th.
> Exception—8th.
> 10th, bail added and notice of justification.
> 12, notice again and on 14th the added bail justified.

[5:212] Under these circumstances a motion was made to stay the proceedings on the bail bond—by *Kerby*.

Adair insisted that they might have justified bail within four days after the exception—and that the defendant had not four days after adding fresh bail. Of this opinion the court were, otherwise the defendant would be in a better situation by putting in that bail, than if he had put in good bail. But the court stayed the proceedings on judgment of costs.

MAINWARING v. DEVON

[M.H.] Recovery passed, though one of the vouchers was deaf and dumb. Query if it be possible to make one who is deaf and dumb understand the effects of a recovery and the deed declaring its uses. *Vide Scholar Armed*, p. 138.[6]

Recovery in which William Guest, the elder and Martha his wife, and William Guest, the younger, were the vouchers.

William Guest, the younger, being deaf and dumb, appeared in court, he being the first tenant in tail, and his brother, another remainderman in tail, though not the next, was examined as to the vouchee's understanding the effect of the recovery and what was intended.

The court then inquired what were the uses of the recovery—which were to pay the debts of the father, then for a term of years, which had been created by the original, [5:213] then to such uses as the father, the brother and son or the survivor should appoint. Remainder to the son in tail.

On executing the deed to lead the uses of the recovery in court, which was witnessed by the brother, the recovery passed.

---

[6] The reference is to *The Scholar Armed Against the Errors of the Time* or, *A Collection of Tracts on the Principles and Evidences of Christianity, the Constitution of the Church, and the Authority of the Civil Government*, 2 vols. (1795). In vol. 2 is an essay by John Ellis, D.D., entitled 'An Enquiry Whence cometh Wisdom and Understanding to Man?' On page 138, Ellis maintains that 'till man had language given him he could not be a rational creature'—'he can no more think than speak without words'.

WILLIAMS v. JACQUES

[M.H.] One of two defendants being discharged by the plaintiff out of execution, the other is not to be discharged on motion, but must sue his *Audita Querela*.

The plaintiff having taken defendant and one Griffin in execution on a joint judgment discharged Griffin on a security from him to pay a moiety of the sum for which both defendants were in execution.

Jacques now moved by *Adair* to be discharged out of execution, who insisted that the judgment was completely done away by the discharge of Griffin, that what he had done was tantamount to a release—and cited

> Carth. 302[7]
> Style 387[8]
> Hob. 70[9]
> *Vigers* v. *Aldrich*, 4 Burr. 2482
> *Jacques* v. *Withy*, Term Cases in B.R. 557.[10]

[5:214] For the plaintiff I insisted that all the cases cited were cases of a complete satisfaction—from which this differed, that the taking the body in execution was no satisfaction but only a pledge. *Blumfield's Case* 5th, Co. 86,[11] and that according to the reasoning in that case, if the plaintiff parted with a part of his pledge, he should not thereby lose the remainder, that the authority in Style was expressly to show in such case that the party should not be released on motion but should have recourse to his *Audita Querela*, which was the only direct authority in favour of the defendant, and that only a dictum of the chief justice.

Lord LOUGHBOROUGH said that *Blumfield's Case* went a great way to show the body was no satisfaction but only a pledge and if so he did not see but that it might be a pledge for part. That though the case in Style was of considerable weight, it was but the dictum of the chief justice. That he thought the defendant should be put to his *Audita Querela*.

HEATH J.: Asked if an honest man and a rogue should be taken in execution and the honest man is ready to give up his all—if such man could not be discharged without discharging [5:215] the rogue, who could pay your debt but would rather remain in gaol.

WILSON J.: If this be a satisfaction Jacques would be liable to Griffin for one-half. But I doubt if it be tantamount to a release.

Rule discharged.

---

[7] The only case at Carthew 302 is *Nichols* v. *Pawlett* (1694) which appears to be relevant only by loose analogy.
[8] *Price* v. *Goodrick* (1653) Style 387.
[9] *Parker* v. *Nevil and Wood* (1614) Hobart 70.
[10] The reference is to *Jaques* v. *Withy* (1787) 1 T.R. 557.
[11] *Blumfield's Case* (1596) 5 Co. Rep. 86b.

Afterwards *Adair* moved the court to allow a writ of *Audita Querela* at the suit of the defendant.

GOULD J., said it ought to be brought to a judge to be allowed.

Adair said, according to a case in Bulstrode, it must be allowed in open court, and the prothonotary should endorse the allowance—and that in *Lord Porchester's Case* it was so allowed in B.R.

On this the court directed the prothonotary to allow it.

JONES v. SHERIFFE

[M.H.] Foreigners may be compelled to give security for costs.

Le Blanc moved that the plaintiff who resided in America should give security for costs or proceedings to be stayed.

Adair, contra, said this was against the practice of the [Common Pleas] though [5:216] it was the practice of the King's Bench.[12] And mentioned the case of *Cooper* at the suit of Fitzgerald. And that it was never done but in case of infants who were lessors in ejectment. And that obliging foreigners to give security amounted to an injunction as to them.

Lord LOUGHBOROUGH: This court after refusing to oblige plaintiff, resident abroad, to give security were struck with the case of *Gammon* v. *Contie*, where defendant was arrested and kept in prison a great while and the plaintiff had no pretence to recover—and thought it a thing worth consideration, that the law might not be used by foreigners for the purposes of oppression.

Another case came on last Hilary term, when the court intended to have considered the question, but the rule was made absolute without opposition. In other nations—as France, Holland, &c., you can't sue a subject of those countries without giving security.

WILSON J.: My difficulty is, as to what is the law on the subject. If it be inconvenient as it stands, it must be regulated elsewhere.

Lord LOUGHBOROUGH: By the common law the plaintiff was [5:217] to give pledges—and he was fined *pro falso clamore*—and Lord HALE in a tract lately published by Mr Hargrave speaks of this mischief, and says that the plaintiff should either give security or put in substantial pledges according to the ancient law. It will be on my brother *Le Blanc* to shew that this is a matter of mere practice, for if it is, it is allowable by the court.

Le Blanc: 52 H. 3 c. 6 is the first statute that gives costs to a defendant. From this and the subsequent statutes that give costs, we may date the disuse of pledges. Where a 2nd action has been brought, the costs of a former not being paid, the court has stayed the proceedings. This is the positive act of the court.

GOULD J.: That is on this ground, that the 2nd action is vexatious and an

---

[12] In the manuscript, the words 'of the King's Bench though it was the', at the bottom of p. 216 and top of p. 217, seem to have been inserted into a blank space that had been left when the case notes were taken, as they appear in lighter ink. Undoubtedly Lawrence meant to insert 'of the Common Pleas' rather than 'of the King's Bench'.

abuse of the practice of the court, and when the court requires the place of abode of a common informer, that depends on the 18th of Eliz., [*5:218*] which requires informers to sue *in propria persona*.

    Le Blanc cites: 1 Wilson 266[13]
                  3 Wilson 145[14]
                  2 Strange 1206[15]
                  Ellen v. *Rees*, B.R., Hilary: 24 Geo. III
                  Lindo v. *Corbett*, M., 26 Geo. III, B.R.
                  Strange 697.[16]

And said that the courts of equity require plaintiffs living abroad to give security for costs.

WILSON J. said he doubted if the pledges to prosecute were anything more than for the purpose of securing to the Crown and its officers their fees, which was part of the ordinary revenue of the Crown. That the 23rd H. 8, c. 15 was the statute which enabled the courts to oblige the plaintiff and give security, if any did. That giving costs was [a] matter of positive law, and that there were positive acts requiring security for costs.

                                                        Cur. adv. vult[17]

[*5:219*]

[*Lawrence note*:] Security in this case was directed to be given, and what was offered was approved of by the prothonotary, but not delivered over. The cause came on to be tried and Lord LOUGHBOROUGH notwithstanding heard the cause, when the plaintiff was nonsuited for not proving the handwriting of a witness to an instrument in writing, and Lord LOUGHBOROUGH said had the court known the defendant would have availed himself of that circumstance, no order would have been made for security for costs, without an admission of the instrument. And the plaintiff was never required to deliver over the security.

[*Lawrence note*:] For subsequent cases determined in the Court of Common Pleas, *vide* the Reports of Mr Henry Blackstone.[18]

[*Lawrence note*:] 1794, March 8—I was sworn into the office of one of the Justices of His Majesty's Court of Common Pleas before the Right Honourable ALEXANDER, Lord LOUGHBOROUGH, Lord High Chancellor of Great Britain, and on the first day of Easter term took my seat on the bench.

---

[13] *Lamii* v. *Sewell* (1750).
[14] *Strithorst* v. *Graeme* (1770).
[15] *Real* v. *Macky* (1744).
[16] *Vat* v. *Green* and *Wyatt* v. *Green* (1726) 2 Str. 697.
[17] In the manuscript, the following next appears and is struck out: 'The court did not make any rule in this business, and on the sitting after Term, the plaintiff tried his cause without giving any security.' Also, in the margin, the following is written: '*Vide Lucky* v. *Bradley*, E. 28 G. 3, post'.
[18] Despite this entry, Lawrence recorded five additional Common Pleas cases from Easter Term, 34 Geo. III, after Lawrence had been made a justice of the Court of Common Pleas. These cases follow.

[5:220] C.P. EASTER TERM 34 Geo. III

Right Honourable Sir James Eyre, Chief Justice
John Heath, Esq.
Sir Giles Rooke } Justices
Sir Soulden Lawrence

ROE, *ex dim.* TURNER v. DOE

[M.H.] Mortgagee is not compellable to give the mortgagor a copy of the deeds, although it is for the purpose of enabling the mortgagor to assign the mortgage and pay off the mortgagee.

Le Blanc moved to stay proceedings in this cause, which was an ejectment by a mortgagee, stating that it had been agreed that a 3rd person should pay off mortgage money, and that an application to the lessor of the plaintiff for an abstract of the title to enable the mortgagor to prepare an assignment of the mortgage, he had refused to furnish any abstract, and had [sic] notwithstanding the agreement, was proceeding to recover possession of the premises.

The court refused the rule, being of opinion that a mortgagee was not compellable in any degree to discover his title and put his security in hazard.

HEATH J. said that there were cases to this effect in Chancery.

READ and TAYLOR v. PARSONS

[M.H.] An action of use and occupation will lie against one who hires a home and suffers another to inhabit it.

On a motion for a new trial the CHIEF JUSTICE reported this to have been an action for the use and occupation of a home in Russell Court, that there was contradictory evidence, the witnesses [5:221] for the plaintiff stating that the defendant had entered into a treaty for the house with the plaintiff, having a friend to inhabit it—and proving that he afterwards said he had got the key. That the house was, during the whole time for which the action was brought, was [sic] inhabited by one Banks, who, being called by the defendant, swore that the house was taken by the defendant for him, and that the plaintiff knew it. That on this evidence, he had left it to the jury to decide on the credit of the witnesses, who found for the plaintiff.

Adair contended for the new trial that, as the house was never occupied by defendant but by Banks, although the defendant might be liable, that the action should have been an action on the special agreement and not for use and occupation.

Clayton, contra, relied on the words of 11 Geo. II, c. 19 s. 14, which gives an action on the case for lands held *or* occupied—and insisted that if the defendant could not be said to have occupied, he was liable in this form of action as having held them.

EYRE, Chief Justice: Said the court were not driven to the necessity of determining whether the action would lie if there was no occupation, as there had been an occupation in this case. That he had entertained an opinion that this action would not lie, where there was no occupation, but of that opinion he had since doubted.

That the preamble of this Act was very material, which showed the intent to [5:222] be to enable persons to recover rent when the demise was not by deed and that the enacting part applied to tenements held. And when the case arose it would be proper to consider whether the words use and occupation in the statute may not extend to the case of a holding when there is no occupation.

But the question here was if there was not an use and occupation by Parsons.

That it was an use and occupation by Banks in consequence of defendant's taking and that it was like the case of goods sold and delivered to another under a contract with the defendant in which case you may recover in a common action for goods sold and delivered.

HEATH, Justice: Same opinion. If defendant had recovered rent from Banks, it would have been an occupation by defendant just as if he had let the house to different lodgers.

ROOKE and LAWRENCE, Justices: Same opinion.

Rule discharged.

MORSE v. FOOTE

[M.H.] Peremptory undertaking not a sufficient cause against judgment as in case of a nonsuit.

A peremptory undertaking was refused as a reason for not giving judgment as in case of a nonsuit and HEATH, Justice, said that this had been so settled in conference with the judges of the King's Bench.

[5:223] ## FLEETWOOD v. ELIOT

[M.H.] Lord of a manor may be compelled by rule to grant a tenant inspection of the court rolls.

This cause, which respected a right of common within the manor of Leatherhead, having been referred at the assizes to the arbitration of A. Palmer, Esq.—a gentleman at the Bar—the same made a rule on Mr Boulton, the lord of that manor, and on his steward to permit the plaintiff, who was a freehold tenant of that manor, to inspect such of the court rolls of the said manor as respected the right of common in dispute.

Le Blanc for plaintiff. *Bond* for the lord.

BRANDON, *et al.*, Assignees v. PATE[19]

[M.H.] *Vide* the Paper Book. Assignees of a bankrupt may recover under the 9 Anne money lost by the bankrupt at play.

This was an action on the 9th Anne, c. 14 by the assignees of a bankrupt to recover of the defendant several sums of money lost by the bankrupt to the defendant at play at the game of hazard. The defendant demurred to the declaration and it was argued in Hilary term last by myself for the plaintiff, and by *Runnington* for the defendant.

And again in this term by *Adair* for the plaintiff and by *Bond* for the defendant.

For the defendant it was contended that until action was brought by the loser, no interest vested in him, and as the bankrupt in this case had not brought any action and declared his opinion to recover back the money, he had no interest which could be vested in his assignees.

[5:224] For the plaintiff it was contended that the statute, by giving to the loser an action for money had and received, showed that the transaction was void, and no act [was] necessary to vest an interest in the loser, and that the clause as to the common informer operated as a penalty on the loser if he did not bring his action. That *Bones* v. *Booth* in *Blackstone's Reports*[20] 1226 was in point to show that the transaction was a nullity—and that 2 Strange 1079[21] proved this was not a penal action, but remedial. That the 13 Eliz., c. 7 transferred to the assignees all the money and debt due to the bankrupt, and the statutes of James, (*ss.*) the 1 J. 1, c. 15 and 21 J. 1, c. 19, gave the assignees all the power the bankrupt had, that the statute had vested the property in the loser if he sued within three months. Which condition the assignees might perform.

EYRE, Chief Justice, said, he felt considerable difficulties. If it were to be laid down that a duty had attached in the bankrupt, there would be an end of them. If that were so, the executor of the loser might maintain an action against the executor of the winner. That this action could only be maintained by bringing debt according to the directions of the statute, but if there was a duty, *assumpsit* would lie. That the more simple [5:225] construction was to say there is no duty till action brought.[22]

---

[19] This case is in print at (1794) 2 Bl. H. 308. Henry Blackstone's report of the case is more extensive in presenting arguments of counsel than are Lawrence's notes. Lawrence argued the case as counsel before going on the bench; thus, as later shown, he gave no opinion as a judge. As is also later indicated, Lawrence's notes of the opinions of the judges reflect some remarks that do not appear in Blackstone's report.

[20] The reference is to William Blackstone's reports, not Henry Blackstone's reports. See *Bones* v. *Booth* (1778) 2 Bl. W. 1226.

[21] In the margin: 'It was there held that defendant shall give bail in an action at the suit of the loser.' The case is *Turner* v. *Warren* (1737).

[22] On his copy of the Paper Book for this case (Dampier MSS., LPB 1, Lincoln's Inn Library), Lawrence recorded Eyre's comments slightly differently, *viz*: 'I still feel very considerable difficulties. If we can lay it down that a duty attached in the bankrupt, there will be no difficulty. If we were to say so, then we must say that the Statute, by giving the action, vested a duty in the

HEATH, Justice: The assignee in this case differs from every other assignee, and as to the difficulty of the executors being entitled to sue if this be a duty, they would not be entitled, for the statute gives the remedy to the party himself, and the right either remained in the bankrupt or went to his assignees. Nor if the bankrupt were to sue, it could only be in trust for them.

ROOKE, Justice: The Act of parliament rescinds the contract, and so the courts have considered it. An affidavit to hold to bail must be made before the writ is sued out, and this shews that the property is in the loser before the action is commenced.

EYRE, Chief Justice: I submit to the opinion of my brothers. I do not wish to convert them, it is certainly a very convenient opinion.

Judgment for plaintiff. LAWRENCE J., *tacente*.[23]

HEATH, Justice: There are many statutes on which it could be inconvenient if the assignees could not sue, as if the party were robbed, or his barns burnt and he should afterwards become bankrupt.[24]

[5:226]

[*Lawrence note:*] June 19th 1794—I resigned my office of one of the Justices of the Court of Common Pleas and was the same day appointed one of the judges of the Court of King's Bench in the place of Mr Justice BULLER, who the same day resigned his office of judge of the King's Bench and was appointed a judge of the Court of Common Pleas, where he took precedence as senior puisne judge of that court according to his rank among the judges, taking place of Mr Justice HEATH and Mr Justice ROOKE. *Vide* Sir Thomas Raymond: 251.[25]

We were both sworn into our offices before the chancellor in his room behind the hall at Lincoln's Inn.

---

bankrupt. But considerable difficulties occur. If this [were] so, the executor of the loser might bring the action, or it might be brought *against* the executor of the winner. This action can only be maintained by an action of debt according to the Statute. But if [there is] a duty, *assumpsit* would lie, which can't be [so] here. The more simple construction is that there is no duty till the action [is] brought. This first struck my mind, but I shall hear what my brothers say.'

[23] 'Being silent'. Henry Blackstone explains that, 'Lawrence j. having argued the case while at the bar, gave no opinion.' 2 Bl. H. at 311.

[24] These added comments by Mr Justice Heath do not appear in Henry Blackstone's report.

[25] In a memorandum, Sir Thomas Raymond notes that when he was sworn in as a baron of the Court of Exchequer on 5 May 1679, Sir William Ellis, who had formerly been a Common Pleas judge, was reappointed and was allowed precedency to Sir Thomas Jones and Sir William Dolben, who had been appointed between Ellis's two terms on the bench.

MANUSCRIPTS OF
SIR SOULDEN LAWRENCE
MIDDLE TEMPLE LIBRARY, MS. 49

PART II
VOLUME 5

CASES IN THE KING'S BENCH, 34–40 GEO. III

[5:227] TRINITY TERM 34 Geo. III, B.R.

Lloyd, Lord Kenyon, Chief Justice
Sir W. H. Ashhurst ⎫
Sir N. Grose   ⎬ Justices
Sir S. Lawrence   ⎭

Memorandum: the only notes entered in this book[26] are either of matters which are not found in Messrs. Durnford and East's Reports, or which did not come on upon special argument, when Paper Books were delivered to the judges. The notes of those cases will be found on the back of the Paper Books themselves.[27]

WITHNELL v. GARTHAM

[M.H.] Election: whether by a majority be good under an authority to persons not a body corporate.[28]

Bearcroft moved for a new trial of issues directed to try—first if the plaintiff was duly elected master of the school at Skipton. Secondly, if the defendant was a [*sic*].

The deed of foundation which was in the time of Edw. VI, by a canon residentiary of St Paul's as to election of the master, contained this direction:

Item volo et ordino quod jus nominandi, ordinandi et presentandi idoneum capellanum ad dictum servitium pedagogi &c. pertineat ad predictum vicarium T. Jolye et successores suos et gardianos ecclesiae de Skipton pro tempore existentes.[29]

In case they did not appoint in a certain time, it gave the nomination to Lincoln College in Oxford. In case the college did not appoint in a certain time, it went to the Dean and Chapter of St Paul's, and if they neglected to do

---

[26] From this point forward.
[27] Despite Lawrence's claim, some of the cases that follow did appear in Durnford & East (*Term Reports*), as will be shown. A few cases were also reported by Espinasse.
[28] See (1795) 6 T.R. 388. An editorial note in *Term Reports* states that, 'This case came first before the Court on a motion for a mandamus to the Archbishop of Canterbury to license the plaintiff; and on arguing that rule, the Court directed these issues.' 6 T.R. at 396, n. (a). In Easter Term 1795, a second trial was held, at which the jury again found for the plaintiff. See 1 Esp. 322. Another motion for a new trial (this one unsuccessful) was argued in Trinity term 1795. According to the account in *Term Reports*, 11 June 1795, 'It appeared at the trial that there had always been eleven churchwardens at Skipton; and the jury found as a fact that the usage had been to appoint by the vicar and a majority of the churchwardens; and they accordingly found a verdict for the plaintiff, who claimed under such an appointment' (6 T.R. at 390). Despite the statement by Lord Kenyon recorded in Lawrence's notes that 'at the trial he [Kenyon] had no doubts, but then he entertained great doubts', Kenyon later claimed that 'from the time when this case came before the Court the first time down to the present moment I have had no doubt in my mind about it'. Ibid. 396.
[29] 'Likewise I wish and settle that the right of naming, appointing, and presenting a suitable chaplain to the said service of schoolmaster &c. extends to the aforesaid vicar T. Joyle and his successors and the wardens of the Church of Skipton for the time being.'

it within a certain time, the nomination reverted to the vicar and churchwardens.

The parish has eleven churchwardens, of whom seven named the plaintiff.

[5:228] On the trial before Lord KENYON, this point was made: whether, as this was only a power and not an interest in the vicar and churchwardens, the church members must not concur.

In support of this proposition, Co. Lit. 12b was cited—where it is laid down that if a power be given to executors to sell, they must all join and that the survivor can't sell, and *The Attorney-General* v. *Davy*, cited in 1 Vesey 419,[30] where three persons being to choose a chaplain, Lord HARDWICKE held that without a usage, all three must concur. On the other side, it was observed that the ultimate devolution was to the vicar and churchwardens, and that the court would not adopt such construction as would leave the office unfilled or lay the parties by the heels, and the case of *Eyre* v. *Lady Shaftsbury*, 2 P. Williams 102[31] was cited, where Lord MACCLESFIELD held that the survivor of three guardians should have the guardianship, although it was not given to the survivor, and *R.* v. *Beeston*, 3 T.R. 592, [5:228A] where a contract under the 9 Geo. I, c. 7, sec. 4 made by a majority of the churchwardens was held binding on the others and valid.

Lord KENYON mentioned *Howell* v. *Barnes*, Cro. Car. 382,[32] as having determined that a devise to A for life and that afterwards it be sold by his executors, who should divide the produce, &c., tho' it give no interest to the executors, enabled the survivor to sell—and observed that Co. Litt. 181b distinguished between authorities for private causes and for matters which are *pro bono publico*, which are to be more favourably expounded, as a writ to four coroners to empanel and return a jury might be executed by the others if one died. That this was the case of a public grammar school, which was *pro bono publico*.

That at the trial he had had no doubts, but that he then entertained great doubts.

That it was certain two joint tenants must present.

As to the authority of Co. Litt. 112, he took that not to be law now, that the case in Cro. Car. was against it —and so was one of the first [5:229] pages in Dyer.[33] That he could not accede to what Lord HARDWICKE is stated to have said in *The Attorney-General* v. *Davy*, 2 Atk. 212, when he says that those persons appointed out of twelve to choose a chaplain were a corporation for that purpose, as they were appointed by the same charter that had appointed and incorporated the twelve. But that it could have been otherwise, if it had been by a different charter. That there must have been some mistake.

---

[30] The citation was given by Lord Hardwicke in *Attorney General* v. *Scott* (1749, 1750) 1 Ves. sen. 412, 419.
[31] The correct citation is *Eyre* v. *Countess of Shaftsbury* (1722) 2 P. Wms 103.
[32] *Howell* v. *Barnes* (1634) Cro. Car. 382.
[33] Perhaps *Clotworth* v. *Kingland* (1536) 1 Dyer 6b.

At the trial he had thought that, as all the other bodies acted by a majority, it might be so as to the vicar and churchwardens, and that *noscitur a sociis* was a rule of Lord HALE. That it appeared by Madox's *Firma Burgi*,[34] that inhabitants might be corporations for certain purposes. That in the case [in] *Vesey*, Lord HARDWICKE had thought that usage might make a great difference and that it was fit to inquire into it in this case and that, therefore, there should be a new trial.

Rule absolute.

For plaintiff: *Erskine, Law, Wood.*
[For] defendant: *Bearcroft, Chambré.*

[5:230]
June 26   DAVIS v. BARBOUR

[M.H.] Feme covert taken in execution on warrant of attorney given by her as a feme sole not to be discharged on motion.

Defendant being a married woman gave a warrant of attorney to confess a judgment to secure the debt of one Jacques and being taken in execution, *Erskine* moved to discharge her out of custody, as being a feme covert, and the suit not being adverse, she having no opportunity of pleading her coverture. It appearing by affidavit that she knew perfectly what she was doing and that the plaintiff understood her to be a feme sole.

Lord KENYON said that it was true that the court did generally interfere summarily, but that it shaped its conduct to meet the justice of the case. That the defendant was not entitled to the favourable interposition of the court, that she might see if her husband would join her in a writ of error, or she might bring it alone.

Rule discharged.

June 26   ANONYMOUS[35]

[M.H.] Merits of an award, not to be gone into on motion for an attachment. *Vide*: *Platt* v. *Knowles*, 231

Manley showed cause against an attachment for non-performance of an award, that the arbitrators had done wrong in not receiving evidence offered on behalf of the defendant.

Lord KENYON at first doubted if in such case the party should not be left to his remedy on the award by action, but on consideration, said they might have

---

[34] T. Madox, *Firma Burgi* (1726).
[35] The case is later identified as *Platt* v. *Knowles*. See the report of *Platt* v. *Knowles* almost immediately below, at p. 50.

moved to set award aside, and he believed the best way was to keep the rule[36] immaculate.

Rule absolute.

[5:231]   HARTLEY v. SMITH

[M.H.] Umpire appointed by arbitrators' tossing up vitiates the award.

Lamb shewed cause against a rule to set aside an award, the two referees, not agreeing who should be the umpire, tossed up which should name him, and in consequence of a friend of one of the parties being named, the other side objected and did not attend him.

Lord KENYON said the arbitrators should exercise their judgment in the choice of the umpire. That the mode taken had not been correct and should be stopped *in limine*.

Rule absolute.

PLATT v. KNOWLES

[M.N.] *Vide* ante, 230.

The court refused to suffer the merits of an award to be gone into on a motion for an attachment and said there should have been a motion to set it aside.

June 28   HUBERT v. GROVES[37]

[M.H.] Inconvenience in going round not a damage to support an action for not repairing a highway.

Barrow moved to set aside a nonsuit in an action on the case for a nuisance in obstructing a public highway, and the special damage stated was that the plaintiff could not go so near a way to his house as he otherwise could have gone. In support of his motion he cited *Maynall* v. *Saltmarsh*, 1 Keb. 847. *Hart* v. *Basset*, Sir Thomas Jones 156. *Iveson* v. *Moore*, 1 Lord Raymond 486.

Sed per Lord KENYON, suppose [5:232] a man is bound *ratione tenurae* to repair, can one who lives near to the road, because he has more inconvenience, any more maintain an action, than a man living in Cornwall?

Nil cap.

---

[36] In the margin: '(*ss*.), as I understood, not to go into the goodness of the award on a motion for an attachment'.
[37] The trial in this case was at the sittings after Easter Term at Guildhall, on 11 June 1794, as reported at 1 Esp. 148. The motion argued on 28 June was at the start of Trinity Term. Espinasse's report reveals that the plaintiff was a coal and timber merchant whose business was affected by 'having to carry his coals, timber, &c. by a circuitous and inconvenient way'. Lord Kenyon thought that the private action in trespass on the case was not maintainable, but should have been brought as an indictment for a public nuisance.

July 2   EX PARTE PARKINSON

[M.H.] Bailiff of a corporation may act as an attorney notwithstanding 4 H. 4 c. 19.

Law shewed cause against an attachment against the defendant for acting as an attorney contrary to the 4 H. 4, c. 19, which provides that no bailiff or minister of lords of franchises which has a return of writs shall be an attorney in any plea within the franchise or bailiwick of which he is minister.

The complaint against the defendant was that he was bailiff of the corporation of Lancaster and that in the proceedings in the court of that corporation, the return to the jury process was signed by him.

It appeared on his behalf that all writs from the superior courts were executed within the borough of Lancaster by the sheriff of the county.

Lord KENYON said, it seemed to him that the words of the Act were applicable only to franchises where the lord had the return of writs—those franchises which [5:233] HALE, Chief Justice, in an argument in Levinz, called a feather in the cap, but a thorn in the side.[38]

                                                                                    Rule discharged.

R. v. SHERIFFS of LONDON

[M.H.] Sheriff not bound to return a writ till ruled, nor can he return it but in term.

Shepherd shewed cause against setting aside an attachment for not returning a writ.

Writ return 27 May.

31 [May], the fourth day on which it should have been returned.

31 [May], sheriff ruled to return it and he contended they were bound to return the writ though there were not four days in term.

The master reported that the sheriff was not bound to return the writ until he was ruled, which might have been done the day of the return, and that he could not return the writ but in term.

                                                                                      Rule absolute.

July 3   R. v. MUNDAY

[M.H.] Bail may have a *habeas corpus* to surrender an impressed seaman. But *ut semb*.

Marriot moved to bring up the defendant, an impressed seaman, to surrender him in discharge of his bail, he being under prosecution for offences against the revenue laws.

---

[38] Lord Kenyon appears to have misidentified the reporter. In *Atkins* v. *Holford Clare* (1671) 1 Ventris 399, Hale did use the expression (at 406), ''tis a feather in his cap, but a thorn in his foot'.

Lord KENYON asked what was to be done with him, as the court could not remand him to the man-of-war on board which he was serving, but on consideration granted a rule to show cause and directed it to be served on the solicitor of the Customs.

[5:234] The solicitor for the Admiralty afterwards undertook to produce the defendant to receive the judgment of the court and in Michaelmas term the recognizance of the bail was discharged on affidavit that the defendant had been left on shore on the evacuation of Ostend.

June 27   ANONYMOUS

[M.H.] A protected seaman, if impressed, not entitled to be discharged.

Mr *Alderson* moved for a *habeas corpus* to bring up a man who had been impressed at a time he had a protection from the Admiralty Board and cited *Goldswain's Case* in 2nd Blackstone's reports.[39]

Lord KENYON said that case was different, as the party had entered into the king's service under the faith of the protection, but that here the court could not interfere and the party must apply to the Admiralty.

Nil cap.

R. v. CHANCELLOR of COUNTY of LANCASTER

[M.H.] Chancellor of Duchy not liable to attachment for not returning a writ.

Reader moved for an attachment against the chancellor of county palatine of Lancaster for not returning a writ.

Lord KENYON said this was irregular. The chancellor had nothing to do but to make his mandate to the sheriff, and that being done, [5:235] the sheriff was to be called on to return the writ, and if he did not do it, the attachment was to be moved against him.

Nil cap.

ANONYMOUS

[M.H.] One committed on suspicion of felony not to be bailed if the justification be not light—nor without [that] the informations are returned.

The court refused Mr *Balguy* a writ of *habeas corpus* for a man committed on suspicion of sheep stealing, as the informations were not returned and nothing to induce the court to believe him innocent but his own affidavit.

Mr *Balguy* afterwards renewed his motion on having got the informations returned, but the suspicion not appearing to be light suspicion, the court refused the writ.

---

[39] *Goldswain's Case* (1778) 2 Bl. W. 1205.

July 2   MOSS v. BIRCH

[M.H.] Irregular on a joint writ if bailable to declare separately. Same case 5 T.R. 722.

Holroyd shewed cause against a rule to set aside proceedings for irregularity.

The plaintiff had declared against the defendant as acceptor of a bill of exchange, and had also proceeded against T. Birch, another of the parties on the bill. The affidavit to hold them to bail charged them jointly. The writ and *ac etiam* were joint.

But two separate declarations were delivered. [*5:236*] Which *Holroyd* contended might be done, and that he, by that, only lost his bail—and cited an anonymous case in Comyns 74[40] and *De La Cour* v. *Read*, H. Black. Reports, v. 2, p. 278 [1794].

Wigley, contra, cited *Holland* v. *Johnson*, 4 T.R. 645:[41] 5 T.R. 254, *Hussey* v. *Wilson*.

The court took time to consider the point and determined the plaintiff was irregular.[42]

                                                                                         Rule absolute.

July 4   ANONYMOUS

Judgment signed irregularly. Defendant took out a rule to be present at the taxation of costs. The master reported this to be a waiver.

Shepherd for plaintiff.

                               ANONYMOUS

[M.H.] Plaintiff has the term issue is joined and the next to give notice of trial.

Marriot shewed cause against judgment, as in case of a nonsuit. Issue was joined in last term and he insisted that plaintiff has all the term in which issue is joined and all the next term to give notice of trial.

The master reported this to be the practice.

                                                                                         Rule absolute.

[*5:237*]   R. v. EPPS

[M.H.] Witness in a criminal case liable to attachment for not attending, though the record be withdrawn.

Erskine shewed cause against a rule for an attachment against a witness for not attending at the assizes at Maidstone in a criminal prosecution, and insisted

---

[40] *Anon.* (1700) 1 Comyns 74.
[41] The correct citation is (1792) 4 T.R. 695.
[42] According to the printed report, 5 T.R. 722, the court was persuaded by the cases cited by Wigley, and issued its opinion on 9 July 1794.

that he was not guilty of a contempt, as the record was withdrawn by the Crown and the case was never called on.

Garrow, for the rule, distinguished this case from a civil suit, and said had the record not been withdrawn, the defendant must have been acquitted, which it was probably the witness to effect.

Rule absolute.

July 7   _____ [sic] v. PHILLIPS *et al.*

[M.H.] Award is final if plaintiff be directed to enter a nonsuit.

On a motion to set aside an award, one objection was that it was not final, as the arbitrators to whom the action had been referred directed the plaintiff to enter a nonsuit, after which *Garrow* said he might bring another action. But Lord KENYON said if that had been the only objection, the court might understand it as putting a final end to the cause.

July 8   R. v. MUNTON[43]

[M.H.] Sentence for a fraud as storekeeper in Antigua.

Defendant having been convicted of having defrauded government to the amount of above £10,000 as storekeeper in Antigua, was brought up for judgment. When the solicitor-general having informed the court that the defendant had given security to pay the government the sums he had cheated them of, the court ordered him to be imprisoned in the custody of the marshal for seven months, he having been already in prison five months.[44]

---

[43] The trial in this case is reported at (1793) 1 Esp. 62. Munton was convicted of colluding with a Mr Whitehead, a seller of goods in England, to manipulate the price of supplies bound for Antigua. The sentence described by Lawrence had not been pronounced when Espinasse wrote his report. Erskine argued for the defendant that the court could not take cognizance of a crime committed out of the realm. Lord Kenyon agreed in principle, but said that jurisdiction was justified because a number of the defendant's false charges had been received by the Navy Office in London.

[44] According to a long account of this case in *The Times*, 9 July 1794, Munton refunded to the Navy £10,000 so that no pecuniary punishment was requested by the solicitor-general at the sentencing hearing. Erskine represented the defendant and with his eloquence in full sail endeavoured to show that his client was a man of irreproachable character whose offence was only 'that he had not resisted a voluntary share of the fair profits of a trade carried on between Mr Whitehead and the Government'. Lord Kenyon said that it was 'a very high offence', but that the defendant 'had redeemed a considerable part of his punishment'. Mr Justice Ashhurst agreed, and in pronouncing the sentence said that for the sake of the public, 'it was necessary to pass some punishment on him, in order that others might be deterred from such practices'.

[5:238]   EX PARTE WILLIAM MURRAY

[M.H.] A father has a right to the custody and guardianship of his child and may take it from the mother. *Vide Blisset's Case*, Lofft 748.

Sir William Murray, having been divorced from his wife, who afterwards married a Mr Harrop, brought a writ of *habeas corpus* to have delivered to him his son, a child of the age of 3 years who had been born a little while before the divorce and having been suffered to remain from that time with the mother.

Sir William Murray being resident in Scotland applied by his counsel to have the child delivered to his attorney, that he might be sent down to him—and *Erskine* contended as the father was not living in England, he had not that right to the custody of the child which he admitted he would have had if resident here.

Lord KENYON: There is no question as to the right of guardianship. A father may forego his right, as where a Roman Catholic agrees that the female progeny shall go with the mother. The court in this case has certainly a discretion, but it is within the limits directed by the law. If the court had reason to think that the child would be sacrificed by the father, the court would not deliver the child. In the case of the duke of Beaufort,[45] the Court of Chancery [5:239] took away the guardianship from the duke of Ormond, who had turned rebel. The father may have a writ *de homine replegiando*, and though in the case of a *habeas corpus* we have a discretion, we have no power to refuse if there is no reason to think that the child will be ill used.[46]

The child was directed to be delivered to Sir William Murray's attorney.[47]

July 9   DOE, *ex dim.* _____ [sic] v. ROE

[M.H.] July 9. Sufficient if the declaration is served on one joint tenant in ejectment.

The court gave *Wood* leave to enter judgment against the casual ejector, there being two joint tenants in possession of the house for which the ejectment

---

[45] *Duke of Beaufort* v. *Berty* (1721) 1 P. Wms 703. See also the discussion in *R.* v. *Inhabitants of St Mary in Cardigan* (1794) 6 T.R. 116.

[46] Opposite this sentence in the margin is the following: 'Q? The father may have trespass *quare filium* and *haeredem rapuit*, but the writ *de homine* &c. according to Fitzherbert is at the suit of the party himself who is imprisoned.'

[47] According to *The Times*, 9 July 1794, a writ of *habeas corpus* had issued during the previous term, after which Erskine, counsel for Lady Harrop, proposed that the three-year-old son be placed in the care of a proper person located not more than twenty miles from his client's place of residence, but this was rejected by Sir William. When the marriage of twenty years ended in divorce, two of the couple's three sons had reached adulthood, but the third son was an infant. Reportedly, an agreement was struck to allow the baby to go with the mother, provided that he would be returned whenever Sir William demanded. Lord Kenyon said that 'every attention should be paid to this child', and since the child appeared to have 'a great tenderness for his nurse, she was ordered to accompany it to Scotland'. Mr Justice Grose 'thought it would not have been unreasonable that this child should have remained with his mother till he had attained to the age of seven years', but 'they must decide according to the law'.

was brought, and the copy of the declaration being served on one only, the other not being at home.

ANONYMOUS

[M.H.] View granted in trover for a steam engine.

In trover for a steam engine claimed by the assignees of a bankrupt, the defendant claiming it as being real property and parcel of an estate mortgaged to him. The court, on the motion of *Shepherd*, granted a view.

ANONYMOUS

[M.H.] Order for time waiver of an irregularity.

Mingay had moved to set aside a judgment for irregularity signed against the defendant, who had been sued as an attorney of the King's Bench, when in fact he was an attorney of the C.B. Having obtained an order for him to plead, [5:240] the court held him too late to apply and discharged the rule with costs.

HOLMAN v. VINER[48]

[M.H.] Creditor who signs a composition deed and does not mention his whole debt can't recover the residue, as this is a fraud on the other creditors.

In an action against defendant as acceptor of a bill of exchange drawn by one Hunt, the defendant produced a deed of composition entered into by him with his creditors, of whom the plaintiff was one, by which they consented [to] take a certain sum in satisfaction of their several demands set against their names. Against the plaintiff's name was set the sum of £81 for goods sold, and at the time of the execution of the deed, the bill on which the action was brought was not due.

Lord KENYON was of opinion that the action would not lie and nonsuited the plaintiff.

Shepherd moved for a new trial, contending that the deed was to be confined

---

[48] The trial in this case is reported as *Holmer* v. *Viner* (1794) 1 Esp. 132. The defendant had been indebted to William Hunt for £185 and to the plaintiff for £81 for goods sold. When 'the defendant's affairs became embarrassed, and Hunt was about to make him a bankrupt, the plaintiff prevailed on him not to do so, but to make the defendant execute an assignment of all his effects to trustees, for the benefit of his creditors at large'. This was done. At the time, in addition to the £81, Hunt was indebted to the plaintiff on two bills of exchange that were not yet due, one for £229, the other for £122. The action was brought on these bills of exchange, the plaintiff having only submitted to the creditors' composition his claim for £81 for goods sold. The defendant, as an accommodation to Hunt, had become an acceptor on the two bills of exchange. Lord Kenyon said that even though the two bills were not due, they could have been claimed in the deed of composition 'in the same manner as bills of exchange are provable under a commission of bankruptcy, by Stat. 7 Geo. I, c. 31, by allowing a rebate of interest'. Thus the plaintiff's attempt to recover on the two bills was barred. Lawrence's notes say that Kenyon nonsuited the plaintiff, whereas Espinasse reported a jury verdict for the defendant.

to the sums against the creditors' names, and discharged no other demands, and particularly that it did not discharge this, as it was not due at the time. Lord KENYON with some [*5:241*] difficulty granted a rule *nisi*, and when it came on, without hearing the other side, discharged the rule—saying his opinion was founded on several old cases. By which I understood those cases where a private agreement between a debtor and his creditor to pay the whole of the debt, if the creditor would sign a composition deed, was held to be a fraud on the other creditors. Such are the cases of *Child* v. *Danbridge* 2 Vern. 71,[49] *Small* v. *Brackley*, ibid. 602, *Spurret* v. *Spiller*, 1 Atk. 105. *Vide* Fonblanque's treatise of equity, vol. 1, p. 257, where these cases and others are referred to.[50]

B.R. MICHAELMAS TERM 35 Geo. III

Lloyd, Lord Kenyon, Chief Justice
Sir W. H. Ashhurst
Sir N. Grose } Justices
Sir S. Lawrence

November 24   ROBERTS v. THOMAS

[M.H.] The court will not quash an inquisition *de proprietate probanda* as it is not a proceeding directed by the court.

Bayley moved to quash an inquisition taken by the sheriff,[51] whereby the jury found the goods taken in execution under a *fi. fa.* against the defendant were the goods of a Mrs Margetson, he contending that the evidence did not warrant the conclusion the jury had drawn.

Lord KENYON said, that this was not a proceeding directed by the court,[52] and that he did not know it had ever been carried into practice, though it might be read of in the books,[53] and that it had been mentioned in this court some years ago[54] that there was no ground to infer fraud in point of law, if the jury found no fraud in fact. That the proceeding was purely vicontial and for the sheriff's indemnity.

Nil cap.

---

[49] *Child* v. *Danbridge* (1688) 2 Vern. 71.
[50] J. Fonblanque ed., *A Treatise of Equity* (1793).
[51] At this point in the manuscript, the following is written and struck out: 'On a *fi. fa.* on a writ *de proprietate probanda*.'
[52] In the margin: '6 T.R. 88, same case'. The printed report describes an earlier hearing in this case, 14 November 1794.
[53] In the margin: '*Vide*: Dalton's Sheriff 146, and *Latkow* v. *Eamer*, 2 H. Black 437.'
[54] In the margin: 'query if this was not in *Cooper* v. *Chitty*, [1] Burr. 20 or *Farr* against *Newman*, 4 T.R. [621,] 633'.

COSSER, assignee of BOTTOMLY, a bankrupt v. J. VARNHAM, Treasurer of the Governors of the Poor of St Mary Bermondsey

[M.H.] An order by a trader to buy out of his earnings is not binding upon the party on whom made, though he assents to it, if given after an act of bankruptcy.

This action was brought against the defendant to recover the amount of some carpenter's work done to the workhouse of the parish. Bottomly committed a secret act of bankruptcy in September 179_ [sic], after which he drew[55] bills on the governors in favour of some of his creditors to the amount of £800, which were ordered by the governors to be paid out of the first money which should be due to the bankrupt. On the 30th of March, [£]400 due to the bankrupt was [5:243] paid in discharge of the bills so drawn,[56] before which time the bankrupt had sent an order not to pay the bills he had drawn.

The jury having found a verdict for the plaintiff at the assizes for Surrey before HOTHAM, Justice, *Shepherd* and *Marriot* moved for a new trial, insisting that the defendant should have been allowed in payment the £400 paid by them in discharge of the bills drawn by the bankrupt, and [they] contended that what had been done by the Governors was equivalent to an acceptance, and compared it to the case of *Julian* v. *Showbrooke*, 2 Wils. 9,[57] where a bill accepted by parol when in cash for the ship *Thetis* was held good, and to the case of *Yates* v. *Groves*, [1] Vesey, jun. 280, where the holder of a note having given it up on an order to pay out of money due to arise from the sale of an estate, was held entitled to recover the money, though the person giving the order afterwards became bankrupt.

Lord KENYON said this was no acceptance of a bill of exchange. It was an appropriation of the bankrupt's future earnings. That the case in Vesey was right, for there the order was before the bankruptcy. But this could not be protected, as it was no payment in the course of trade according to the 19 Geo. II.

Rule discharged.

---

[55] The word 'two' is written in the manuscript and crossed out.
[56] Written in the manuscript and crossed out are the words: 'and which had been brought'.
[57] *Julian* v. *Showbrooke* (1753) 2 Wils. 9.

[5:244] November 25   FRANCO v. FRANCO[58]

[M.H.] Question if court can refuse an attachment for non-performance of an award.

Mr *Erskine* shewed cause against an attachment for non-performance of an award and insisted, *inter alia*, that it was not of course to grant an attachment, but that the party might be left to his action on the bond of arbitration. *Shipley* on the same side cited Reports temp. Hardwicke, *Stock & al.* v. *Smith* 106,[59] *Perry* v. *Nicholson*, 1 Burr. 278, *Sir T. Hales* v. *Taylor*, 1 Str. 695.[60]

Lord KENYON said he doubted that if that were so, that [only] if the award be a judgment increasable could the attachment be discretionary, though formerly it was said to be so. But he thought that latterly Lord MANSFIELD doubted if it was discretionary. But he said he wished to avoid deciding the point and the rule was disposed of [on] other ground.

November 26   R. v. CALEB UNDERWOOD

[M.H.] One outlawed for felony on the reversal of the outlawry, to be committed and not held discharged until *nolle pros.* is entered on record.

The defendant was brought to the bar having been outlawed on an indictment against him for the murder of Col. Roper in a duel, as principal in the second degree, and being asked what he had to say why judgment of death should not be passed on him, he pleaded *ore tenus* that he was abroad at the time of the exigent, which the attorney-general confessed, upon which ASHHURST J. gave judgment that the outlawry should be reversed and that he should be restored to all he had lost.

He was then ordered to be committed. The attorney-general then gave in to the court a *nolle prosequi*, but as the record of the indictment remained with the clerk of assize of the Home Circuit, the court refused to discharge him until the *nolle prosequi* was entered on record.

---

[58] On 3 December 1795, a hearing in Chancery on this case was held, as reported at 2 Cox 420. An injunction for want of an answer had been obtained by the defendant in the King's Bench action to restrain the plaintiff in that action (the defendant in the Chancery case) from all proceedings at law on the arbitration award, and the motion before Lord Chancellor Loughborough was to hold the defendant (in Chancery) and his solicitor in contempt for having breached the injunction. Lord Loughborough declined to do so, though he admitted that he did not remember 'any case where the question arose upon an injunction to restrain the proceedings to compel performance of an award'. He analogised to actions at common law, where, if the action had been commenced before the injunction issued, the party could go on to trial and judgment but could not seek execution while the injunction stood. Thus, he thought that 'the making the award a rule of Court, which had been done before the injunction, is to be considered as the commencement of the proceeding, and that the defendant might not only obtain a rule to show cause (as he has done) but might go on to make his rule absolute for the attachment without being guilty of a breach of this injunction'. (Cox concluded the sentence quoted with 'so as he did execute the attachment', but surely he meant 'so long as he did not execute the attachment'.)

[59] The printed report shows the case as *Stock v. De Smith* (1735).

[60] The case is at 2 Str. 695.

[*5:245*] Mr H. Barton, clerk of the rules, said that he might be discharged at a judge's chambers on a certificate from the clerk of assize that the *nolle prosequi* was entered, which the court said might be done.[61]

R. v. BURGESSES of TRURO

[M.H.] November 27: *Mandamus* to elect a mayor refused, one having been elected though not sworn, as his right was disputed and a *mandamus* granted to swear him in, that *quo warranto* might be filed, or *non electus* returned.

Erskine shewed cause against a rule for a *mandamus* to elect a mayor and four aldermen and alleged that one Lawrence had been elected mayor. To this *Adair*, serjeant, answered that he was illegally elected and had not been sworn in.

Lord KENYON said that if the election was not merely colourable, that must be tried in a *quo warranto*, and that a *mandamus* must be granted to swear him in, by which they might, if they thought fit, return *non electus*—and accordingly, a *mandamus* was granted in the first instance.

_____ [*sic*] v. MANNERS

[M.H.] Venue in trespass of attorney not to be changed.

The court refused to change the venue to Lincolnshire in an action of trespass and assault at the suit of an attorney, he having brought the action in Middlesex.

GILES v. HUTCHINGS

[M.H.] After defendant's attorney has agreed to the common bail, he shan't object for want of it. Summons for particular of plaintiff's demand is no waiver of irregularity.

The declaration in this cause was delivered by the defendant's attorney on the 8th of November, when he promised to file common bail. The plaintiff's attorney afterwards demanded a plea and signed judgment for want of a plea. *Shepherd* moved to set aside this judgment as irregular, on the authority of *Cook* v. *Raven*, 1 T.R. 636,[62] where it was irregular to sign a judgment if plea was demanded before common bail filed.

Garrow shewed cause and relied on the promise to file common bail and the court on that ground discharged the rule.

In this case defendant had taken out a particular of the plaintiff's demand, but this the Master said was no waiver.

---

[61] According to *The Times*, 27 November 1794, Underwood had been second to a Mr Purefoy in the duel. Underwood gained a reversal by showing that at the time of his outlawry he was in Flanders, and this was why he had not pleaded to the indictment that had been found against him.

[62] The report of *Cook* v. *Raven* begins at (1787) 1 T.R. 635.

[5:246] November 28   R. v. METCALFE

[M.H.] No additional interrogatories after examination of defendant.

Erskine had moved to file additional interrogatories after the defendant had been examined, but the court doubting if that could be done directed him to inquire whether it had ever been done, and he now informed the court he could find no instance of it, and should not press it.

[*Lawrence note*:] From the 17th of November to the 22nd November I was absent from court on the special commission at the Old Bailey at the trial of J. Horne Tooke, clerk, for high treason.[63]

[5:247]   B.R. HILARY TERM 1795

Lloyd, Lord Kenyon, Chief Justice
Sir W. H. Ashhurst ⎫
Sir N. Grose   ⎬ Justices
Sir S. Lawrence   ⎭

[*Lawrence note*:] I was during the greater part of this term confined to my house with the gout, and took very few notes.

January 29   GLOVER v. STOKES

[M.H.] Judgment entered for too small a sum, by the mistake of the master, set right.

The master by mistake signed judgment for £105 instead of £305, and defendant being in execution for that sum paid the money. And now *Baldwin* moved to set the judgment right, which was done. *Erskine* for the defendant.

January 31   BONSAL v. JONES *et al.*

[M.H.] Trustees in a deed which might be a sufficient ground for a commission of bankruptcy do not, by acting under it, become executors de son tort.

This was an action brought against the defendants as executors de son tort of one Roderick. To prove them such, the evidence was that they, as trustees under deed of assignment executed by Roderick, who was a trader in favour of some creditors, had possessed themselves of divers goods and things which belonged to him and for the plaintiff it was insisted that, as the deed was an act of bankruptcy, the defendants, by acting under it, became executors de son tort.

Lord KENYON said that nothing was clearer than that, *inter vivos*, the deed

---

[63] See *The Trial of John Horne Tooke* (1794) 25 S.T. 1.

would have been an act of bankruptcy if a commission had been taken out. But that it would not, after his death, make his trustees executors de son tort, for who could avoid it. There were no assignees to come forward.

[*Lawrence note*:]
The above are the only two notes I took worth transcribing, which are not to be found in the Term Rep.

[*5:248*] B.R. EASTER TERM 35 Geo. III

Lloyd, Lord Kenyon, Chief Justice
Sir W. H. Ashhurst
Sir N. Grose   } Justices
Sir S. Lawrence

JONES v. SQUIRE

[M.H.] Verdict cures the want of an allegation which is necessarily implied by what is stated.

Assumpsit. In consideration plaintiff would sell a certain mare to defendant, defendant promised if it should win the Hunter's Plate at Worcester, to give the plaintiff a suit of clothes of such colour as he chose. The declaration then stated that the mare did win the Hunter's Plate at Worcester, and that defendant received it, by reason whereof he became liable to furnish plaintiff with a suit of clothes &c. But did not state that he, the plaintiff, sold the mare to defendant.
Verdict for plaintiff.
Leycester moved in arrest of judgment on the ground of the declaration being bad in not stating that plaintiff sold the mare and cited 1 T.R. 144.[64]

On shewing cause, his rule was discharged, the court being of opinion the verdict had cured it.

STONEHOUSE v. ELIOT

[M.H.] Trespass will lie against one who causes another to be taken into custody on a charge of felony though good ground for suspicion. Same case 6 T.R. 315.

Gibbs moved to enter a nonsuit in an action of false imprisonment.
On the trial it appeared that the defendant had her pocket picked in the playhouse, and having good ground to suspect the plaintiff, charged a constable with him, who took him into custody, and nothing being found

---

[64] *Spires v. Parker* (1786) 1 T.R. 141, 144.

upon him discharged him. At the trial Lord KENYON was disposed to nonsuit the plaintiff, thinking that the form of action should have been case for a malicious charge, if any action could be supported.

Gibbs' rule was afterwards discharged, Lord KENYON being satisfied that the action was proper.[65] The jury gave 1s.

Vide: Welch v. Hole, MS. B, 264.[66]

[*Lawrence note*:] Query if this had not been justified specially. 2 H.H.P.C. 78. Rastell's *Entries*, tit. faux impr. pl. 5.[67]

[5:249]   R. v. JODEN

[M.H.] More candidates than one may be put in nomination for a corporate office, if not objected to. If charter directs election to be made at the council house, an election at a new council house will be good.

Mr *Darrel* moved for a new trial of an Information in *Quo Warranto* against the defendant for usurping the office of a freeman of Coventry, which had been tried at the assizes at Warwick before PERRYN [B.]. Two of the grounds of his motion were, first that two persons had been put in nomination together, whereas according to the case of the *R. v. Monday*, [2] Cowper 530, they ought to have been put in nomination one at a time. Another objection was that the plea stated an election of the defendant at the council house which was mentioned in and referred by the charter. Whereas in fact the election was not at the old council house of which the charter spoke, but at a new council house.

As to the first point, Lord KENYON said when this case was tried before him at Guildhall, he had laid it down that if no persons objected to a joint nomination, and did not require the candidates to be divided, the election would be good. The other point was too ridiculous to be made. Suppose the council house should have fallen down—was no election to be made? A rule *nisi* was granted on another ground, (*ss.*) the misdirection of the judge, but discharged on its turning out that what he said was misapprehended.[68]

---

[65] See 6 T.R. 315. The court's decision was issued in Trinity term 1795. The trial on 17 February is also reported, at 1 Esp. 272. The doubt that Lord Kenyon later overcame was due to his fear that allowing a false imprisonment action to be maintainable whenever a victim of a crime mistakenly accused the wrong person 'would deter parties from charging persons really guilty of such offences'. Ibid.

[66] Lawrence's reference is uncertain. This reference and others to follow (see p. 86, n. 99, p. 188, n. 89, and p. 193, n. 97, below) suggest that Lawrence kept another set of manuscript notes of plea side cases in notebooks designated by capital letters. These are not among the Lawrence notebooks at the Middle Temple Library and may not have survived.

[67] Hale's *History of the Pleas of the Crown* (1778); William Rastell, *Collection of Entries* (1566).

[68] The alleged misdirection was evidently that of Baron Perryn at the trial at the Warwick assizes. It is unclear how 'this case' came to be tried before Lord Kenyon at Guildhall. Perhaps there was a separate action involving the same election.

April 25   CONAL *et al.* v. HAWKINS

[M.H.] April 25: Bankrupt having obtained his certificate, *puis darrein continuance exoneretur* entered on the bail piece.

The defendant obtained his certificate as a bankrupt subsequent to the time of pleading, but having omitted to plead it *puis darrein continuance*, a verdict was obtained against him. On judgment of costs, an *exoneretur* was entered on the bail piece.

[5:250]
April 27   R. v. JOSEPH SMITH

[M.H.]: Two years imprisonment and surety for seven years for obstructing a revenue officer.

Defendant was convicted of obstructing an excise officer in the execution of his duty.[69] He had not long before been released from York castle after an imprisonment for two years for a similar offence. The court sentenced him to two years imprisonment in Newgate and to enter into his own recognizance for his good behaviour for seven years in the sum of £100.

April 28   ACKLAND v. DAY

[M.H.] Costs of obliging an insolvent to assign his effects to be paid out of the estate.

The defendant had been obliged under the computing clause in the 32nd Geo. II, c. 28 to assign his effects for the benefit of his creditors. Considerable expense having been incurred in compelling the defendant to make the assignment, a rule was obtained that this expense should be paid out of the estate.

Gibbs shewed cause and relied on the words of the 17th section, which directs that the acceptors of the prisoner's estate after payment of the debt, damages, and costs and the charges of getting in the estate and effects, shall be paid to the prisoner, and contended that there were no words to justify laying the expense of compelling the assignment on the estate of the defendant.

Lord KENYON said, it would be the severest of all severe cases, to say that the expense of bringing up the prisoner &c. should be thrown on the creditor who acts—and referred it to the master to ascertain the costs which were to be paid by the assignees out of the estate.

---

[69] According to *The Times*, 28 April 1795, Smith had 'rescued a quantity of sovereign geneva [Dutch gin] after it had been seized'.

[5:251]   GOODWYN et al. v. DECHAIR

[M.H.] Bail of a defendant sent abroad under the Alien Act not returned but upon payment of such sum as they may have had deposited on their security and costs, if they have suffered proceedings to go on.

The defendant having been sent out of the kingdom under the Alien Act, his bail now moved that an *exoneretur* should be entered on the bail piece on their paying to the plaintiff the sum of £1,000 without costs, that being the amount of what had been deposited in their hands as a security on their becoming bail.

As the defendant was sent away before the trial of the cause, and the bail did not apply till after the expense of the trial, the court refused the rule unless they paid to the plaintiff the £1,000, which did not exceed the sum recovered and costs.[70]

May 1   R. v. OXFORD

[M.H.] Sentence for obstruction and rescue.

Defendant was convicted of obstructing a revenue officer and receiving run goods. In this case, there was a struggle, but no great degree of violence.

The prisoner having been in custody 4 months, the court sentenced him to 12 months imprisonment and ASHHURST, Justice said that for such offences the usual punishment was 2 years' imprisonment.

May 5   THE GOVERNOR and COMPANY of CHELSEA WATERWORKS v. COOPER

[M.H.] If an executor has no demand on him for a debt until he has paid over the residue of the testator's estate to the residuary legatee after waiting a proper time, he may insist on this on the plea of *plene administravit*.

The defendant was sued as executor of Sir George Littleton, and having paid all demands made on him, paid the residue to the residuary legatee twenty two years ago. The action was brought on a bond of the testator by which he became surety for the good behaviour of one of the servants of the company. To this action, he pleaded *plene administravit*, and Lord KENYON on the trial of the cause was of opinion that the facts above stated had proved the plea. He

---

[70] In *The Times*, 1 May 1795, this case is described as *Godwin & Co. v. De Heine*. After counsel for the bail, Mr Reader, explained that the bail had not come forward immediately because the action had been commenced before any application to the court had been made, Lord Kenyon responded: 'You compelled them to proceed; you might have withdrawn your plea.' He said that it was a new case that called for a new rule, but 'in laying down that rule, they had no intention to encourage the bail to be litigious', and 'nothing is clearer' than that the defendant must pay the plaintiff's costs. In an earlier article, the newspaper reported that the plaintiffs had brought the action of debt against De Heine and two other defendants who kept a gaming house in Pall Mall 'and where John King, the plaintiff's clerk, lost several thousand pounds of his master's property at play'. *The Times*, 25 April 1795. The other defendants let judgment against them go by default, and in the action against De Heine, the plaintiffs recovered £1,000.

however reserved the point and now said that upon considering the Statute of Distributions and rules of the ecclesiastical courts and the Court of Chancery, he had no doubt but that the defendant had fully administered.

[5:252]
May 7 R. v. JUSTICES of CAMBRIDGESHIRE

[M.H.] *Mandamus* to hear an appeal, though not lodged according to the rule of the Sessions, if there was not time to lodge it according to the rule.

Lushington shewed cause against a *mandamus* to the Justices of the County of Cambridge to receive and hear an appeal against an appointment of an overseer.

The appointment was made on the 15th. The party had no notice of it until the 16th.

On the 17th, the sessions were held—and no appeal lodged until after the court had adjourned for the morning, before which time by a rule of the court all appeals are to be lodged—and he relied on Strange 315[71] where it is laid down that the Sessions may lay down rules for their practice.

Lord KENYON said the clause in the 9 Geo. I, c. 7 directs that appeals shall be adjourned if there has not been time for due notice, and though that applies only to cases of removals, yet *ubi eadem est ratio*, there should be *eadem lex*. Unless the court sees that injustice will be done, it ought not to trench on the proceedings of the Sessions, which they ought to regulate, but here does not seem to have been time to lodge the appeal earlier.

Rule absolute.

R. v. RAMSAY *et al.*[72]

[M.H.] A small fine imposed for a great misdemeanour under special circumstances inserted in the rule of court to account for the smallness of the fine.

The defendants, one of whom was an overseer of the poor, the other beadle of the parish of Woolwich, having been found guilty of an indictment tried before ASHHURST, Justice, at Maidstone, of forcing one Anne Stewart, a pauper in the heat of labour, into a boat and carrying her to London and there leaving her destitute when she was in a few hours delivered of a male [5:253] bastard child, with a view to exonerate the parish of Woolwich from the burden of maintaining the child—were not brought up for judgment.

The court committed them to the custody of the marshal till the next term, when, upon its appearing from the representation of the most respectable inhabitants of Woolwich that they [the defendants] on every occasion had behaved well and that they had indemnified the parish of Clerkenwell where the

---

[71] *Anon.* (1720) 1 Str. 315.
[72] Another report of this case, virtually identical, is at p. 77, below.

child was born from all expenses and paid the expenses of the prosecution, the whole of which amounted to about £500, the court discharged them on paying a fine of 1s., the above circumstances being inserted in the rule of court as was done in the case of the Cock Lane Ghost.[73]

BRANDER v. ROBSON

[M.H.] No bail in action on bail bond at the suit of the sheriff.

Marriot moved to discharge defendant on filing common bail, he being sued by the sheriff on a bail bond.

Baldwin showed cause, and the doubt was whether the rule which restrained the assignee of a bail bond from holding to bail on the bond, applied to the sheriff.

The court took time to consider, and upon talking with the judges of the C.P. and *Scacc.*[74] agreed in opinion that in such case, there ought to be only common bail, and accordingly in Trinity term, the rule was made absolute.[75]

---

[73] Reports of this case appeared in *The Times* on 2 April, 8 May, 13 May, and 8 June 1795. Counsel for the prosecution at the trial were Garrow, Shepherd, and Const; counsel for the defendants were Fielding, Espinasse, and Knowles. The Cock Lane Ghost affair demonstrated astonishing public gullibility in 1762 when Londoners were duped by parish clerk Richard Parsons into believing that his house in Cock Lane was haunted by the ghost of the deceased wife of Parsons's lodger and creditor, William Kent. See generally, P. Chambers, *The Cock Lane Ghost: Murder, Sex and Haunting in Dr Johnson's London* (2006). The sensation ended up in the law courts, where Parsons and other defendants were prosecuted by Kent and were convicted by circumstantial evidence of common law conspiracy to defraud. *R.* v. *Parsons* (1762) 1 Bl. W. 391. Parsons and his wife were sent to prison, but two others were discharged after having been ordered to pay Parsons £300 'and his costs, which amounted to near as much more'. *R.* v. *Parsons* (1762) 1 Bl. W. 401, 402. According to Lord Kenyon's recollection, the costs were £580. *The Times*, 13 May 1795. Lord Kenyon and his brother judges were at first outraged by the facts of the Ramsay prosecution—'this almost unparalleled instance of inhumanity'. *The Times*, 8 May 1795. In response to testimony and affidavits from character witnesses for the defendants, Kenyon sardonically responded that 'in a certain Criminal Court [the Old Bailey], they constantly heard bellowed out such a one's witnesses to character . . . but to suppose that character in a clear case was to have any effect was absurd'—in fact, 'Good character sometimes enhanced the offence.' Counsel for the prosecution, William Garrow, said that, 'It would be an insult on the understanding of any man of common sense, to suppose these defendants acted from mistake or ignorance.' When Mingay, counsel for the defendants, observed that fortunately the woman had been safely delivered, Lord Kenyon said that was indeed fortunate, because, 'had the mother and child not been alive, it would have been murder'. By the time the defendants were brought up for judgment a month later, the court's temper had cooled. Kenyon said that the court had 'very favourable representations from very responsible quarters, of the general good conduct of the defendants, which had induced them (the calls of justice being satisfied) to consider the rest of the case with a great deal of indulgence and humanity'. But in ordering the circumstances entered as a rule of court, Lord Kenyon said he was following the example of Lord Mansfield in the case of the Cock Lane Ghost, so that 'when posterity looked at the record, they might see that the court had not treated this as a light offence'. *The Times*, 8 June 1795.

[74] *Scaccarium*, (Court of) Exchequer.

[75] The decision of the court in Trinity Term is reported at 6 T.R. 337. Lord Kenyon said that after consulting with the judges of the other two courts, 'we find that by the practice of these courts a person who has become bail for another cannot himself be held to bail', and the Court of King's Bench adopted the practice, even though recognizing that the sheriff was in a more powerful position than others in taking bail.

[5:254]
May 8   FOWLE v. NEWTON

[M.H.] If a stakeholder has paid over the money, he shall not be liable in an action, though he has taken an indemnity.

This was an action to recover a sum of money in the hands of the defendant as a stakeholder on the event of a match at football, and which defendant had paid over to those who he thought had won, taking from them an indemnity.

On the trial before ROOKE, Justice, at the last assizes for Warwick, the plaintiff was nonsuited, he [ROOKE J.] refusing to go into the laws of the game, and being of opinion that the action could not be maintained against the defendant who had paid the money over.

Vaughan moved for a new trial, and as to the first point, he cited *Pope v. St Leger*, Salkeld 344,[76] and in support of the other mentioned a *nisi prius* determination of Mr Justice HEATH's, who, under similar circumstances, said he would consider the stakeholder who was indemnified as still retaining the money.

As to this, Lord KENYON said it might be wise in a man to take an indemnity that would not make his situation the worse. But as to the other point, as it appeared that the case had not been properly brought before the judge, the court, without giving an opinion on the point, directed a new trial.

[5:255]   R. v. HAFFENDEM

[M.H.] Naval stores, two months imprisonment.

Defendant was convicted of having in his possession naval stores with the king's mark to the amount of £20.

The sentence was to be imprisoned two months in Clerkenwell Bridewell and to be whipped for the length of 100 yards on Tower Hill.[77]

[May 12]   ISAAC v. ISAAC

[M.H.] In setting aside an annuity, length of time and other circumstances may be reasons for the court not interfering.

This was a motion to set aside an annuity, the securities for which had been entered into by the defendant and his father so long back as the year 1781.

The objection to the validity of the instruments was that the consideration of the annuity was not money advanced, as stated in the memorial, but the

---

[76] *Pope v. St Leger* (1693) 1 Salk. 344.

[77] An undoubtedly related case, *R. v. Edie*, was mentioned in *The Times*, 11 June 1795, where Thomas Edie was convicted of possessing a large quantity of naval stores and was sentenced to be publicly whipped for 100 yards on Tower Hill, with three months' hard labour in the House of Corrections. Lord Kenyon lamented that the statute left him no discretion to inflict a heavier punishment.

delivery up of a joint bond of the father and son given for money paid on the account of the father.

Myers, who was the grantee of the annuity, had been dead some years in 1781, as well as the attorney who prepared the securities, and the witness to the deeds, and upon a suit in the Court of Chancery, a fund the property of the father was set aside for the payment of the annuity. This was in 1785. These facts, it was said, would appear by letters written by Myers and by the attorney's bill, who prepared the deed.

Lord KENYON said that by the proceedings in Equity, the annuity *transivit in rem judicatum*. That the parties being adults had not insisted in that court upon the present obligations. [5:256] That *Lord Chesterfield* v. *Janssen*[78] was in point. That the grantee having died might have carried out his property as a provision for his family—which might be entirely defeated. That the court should have some mercy on parties who might have honestly advanced their money and not make presumptions against them after a period of fourteen years, and after all persons were dead who could explain the transaction. That the attorney's bill was not evidence. That he would not have it understood that the court acted merely on the lapse of time but on all the circumstances of the case. *Juncta juvant.*[79]

Rule discharged.

May 13   R. v. MUSCLE

[M.H.] Sentence for assault on Custom House officers.

The defendant was convicted of assault on Custom House officers and attempting to rescue goods.

This was accompanied with circumstances of violence and collecting a number of tinners to the amount of forty to rescue the goods which had been seized.

The judgment was two years imprisonment in Newgate and to find security for his good behaviour for seven years, himself in £100 and two sureties in £25 each.

R. v. STEWARD of the MANOR of FOREY

[M.H.] *Mandamus* in the first instance to hold court to elect portreeve.

The court granted a *mandamus* in the first instance to the steward of the Manor of Forey to hold a court to elect a portreeve, on the motion of Mr Lane.

---

[78] *Chesterfield (Earl of)* v. *Janssen* (1750) has several printed reports; the best known is 1 Atk. 301.
[79] 'Things united aid each other.'

[*5:257*] Tuesday, May 15
SHIPWITH v. BLANCHARD

[M.H.] Illegal distress is a conversion.

The defendant having taken the goods of the plaintiff as a distress for rent, which was illegal, and detained them until he was paid a sum of money, plaintiff brought trover and recovered before HEATH, Justice, at York.

On a motion for a new trial, it was contended that this was no conversion—that the proper remedy of the plaintiff was replevin. Lord KENYON at first doubted but afterwards on the authority of Bunbury 67[80] and Burr. 2067[81] was of opinion with the rest of the court that this was a conversion.[82]

R. v. JUSTICES of CUMBERLAND

[M.H.] *Mandamus* may be granted to appoint overseers of the poor, though more than a month after Easter has elapsed and two have been appointed and one of them removes from the parish, a *mandamus* lies to appoint another.

Law moved for *mandamus* to the overseers of the poor of the township of Whitshaven to make a rule for the relief of the poor and to pay over the money collected to the guardians of the poor according to the provisions of the 22nd Geo. II, which regulates the poor of that place. He suggested at the same time that possibly the writ might be defeated by one of the overseers going from the town.

Lord KENYON: Take your writ and if one of the overseers has moved from the town, take a writ to the Justices to appoint another. To obviate any caviling from the circumstance of more than a month having elapsed since Easter, it will be recollected that in the case of Sir George Colebrook a *mandamus* was directed to him to hold a court leet, though after [*5:258*] the time which is directed for the holding of the leet. The 43rd of Eliz. directs that there shall be an appointment of four, three, or two, and though there has been here an appointment of two, we may order a *mandamus* to approve one in the room of him who has removed.

---

[80] *Etriche* v. *Officer of Revenue* (1720).
[81] Lawrence mistakenly repeated the '67' from the Bunbury citation. The case referred to in Burrow was *Cooper* v. *Chitty and Blackiston* (1756) 1 Burr. 20.
[82] This case is reported at 6 T.R. 298 as *Shipwick* v. *Blanchard*. Mr Justice Heath at trial reasoned that the facts were 'equivalent to a sale to a stranger, which had been deemed a conversion, and that trover was the proper action for trying questions of bankruptcy'. Lord Kenyon explained that his doubts had been removed by Lord Mansfield's decision in *Tinkler* v. *Poole* (1770) 5 Burr. 2657, in which Mansfield considered the authority in Bunbury but concluded that trover would lie against a custom house officer for seizing the plaintiff's goods without justification.

[5:259] IN DOM. PROC. CASE of the BARONY of BEAUMONT

[M.H.] A barony in fee descends to coparceners. Both die leaving issue, one of whom is attainted, leaving issue, and two sisters. The abeyance is not determined by the attainders. Abeyance, what it means as applied to the descent of dignities.

Thomas Stapleton of Carlton in the county of York, Esq., having petitioned the Crown to issue a writ of summons to him as Baron Beaumont and his claim having been referred to a committee of privileges of the House of Peers. The case came on to be heard first in the year 1794, and afterwards on the 21st of May, the 9th, 16th, and 22nd of June in the year 1795. Mr *Plumer* and Mr *Topham*, being of counsel with the claimant; Mr Attorney-General, *Sir John Scott*, e contra.

The facts upon which Mr Stapleton rested his claim were shortly these:

John Baron de Beaumont (who was an immediate descendant of Henry de Beaumont who sat in parliament the 2nd of Edward II) was killed at the battle of Northampton, 38 H. 6, and left one son, William (who was Baron and Viscount de Beaumont, and who died without issue 24 H. 7) and Joan, his only daughter, who married John Lord Lovel and died in the life of her brother, leaving a son, Francis, who was slain at the battle of Stoke two years before the death of the Viscount de Beaumont, 3 H. 7. And two daughters: [5:260] Joan, married to Sir Brian Stapleton of Carlton, knight, and died in the life of her uncle, Viscount Beaumont, leaving a son, Brian Stapleton, from whom the claimant, Mr Thomas Stapleton, was descended, being his heir general; and Frideswide, her 2nd daughter, who married Sir Edward Norris and died in the life of her husband, the Viscount Beaumont, leaving four children, Sir John Norris, who died without issue 6 Elizabeth; Henry Norris, attainted and executed 28 H. 8 in the life of his elder brother, and two daughters, Ann and Margaret.

The attainder of Henry Norris was never reversed, but his son, Henry Norris, was restored in blood and summoned to parliament as Lord Norris of Rycote, 14th Elizabeth, from whom the Earl Abingdon is descended.

Ann left issue, from whom the marchioness of Rockingham and others descended. Margaret's issue are extinct.

For the claimant it was contended that on the death of the Viscount of Beaumont, 24 H. 7, the barony fell into abeyance, &c., Brian Stapleton, the son and Sir John Norris being then his heirs. [5:261] That the consequence of its falling in abeyance was that it vested in nobody except the Crown as *custos* of the honour, which was not extinguished but waited till there should be some one person capable of receiving it.

That abeyance obtained only in cases of necessity.

Blackstone's argument in the case of *Perryn* v. *Blake*, Hargrave *Law Tracts* 498.

That during the life of Sir J. Norris, the abeyance continued, but that there had been no forfeiture by the attainder of Henry Norris, as the honour had never vested in him.

But that the attainder had operated so to corrupt his blood as to prevent his descendants ever inheriting to the honour. *Co. Litt.* Sec. 747. Haw. *P.C.* 637.[83] And that the consequence of this was that upon the death of Sir John Norris, 6 Elizabeth, all right in the descendants of Frideswide ceased and at that instant the barony vested in Sir. B. Stapleton.

[5:262] For neither the sisters of Sir J. Norris nor the descendants could take, as it was a settled principle that if a person attainted left issue (as was the case here), it operated as a bar to the claim of any persons standing lower in the pedigree.

That such was the rule as to lands appeared from what was laid down by Lord HALE in *Collingwood* v. *Pace*, Ventris 413:[84] in 2nd Hawk. 637; 2 Black. Commentaries 253–4; 3 Institutes 211.

That the question would then be if a similar rule took place with respect to honours.

That it was so in the case of a sole heir appeared in the case of Lord Northumberland, Dugdale, v.1 p. 283, and from the Acts 1 Geo. I, c. 34, and 6 Geo. II, which were passed to continue the title of duke of Athol to James, Lord Murray, and the other sons of John, duke of Athol in like manner if the elder brother, the marquis of Tullibardine had been dead without issue, he having been attainted, A.D. 1716. As also from the case of Lord Lumley, Collins' *Precedents*, concerning baronies by writ, 373. *Journals*, vol. 22, p. 298.

[5:263] From these premises, the counsel for the claimant contended that it followed that there was an end of the abeyance, which depended on there being too many capable of enjoying the honour, which ceased to be the case on the death of Sir John Norris, for then there was none but the Stapletons to whom the Crown would issue a writ of summons. And there could be no escheat, for had this been the case of lands, one moiety only would have escheated, and that as an honour was not partible, two could not escheat. To show this the case of Lord Powis, 2nd Dugdale 72 was mentioned, where the issue of one sister being attainted, leaving issue, a descendant of another daughter, received a summons to parliament.[85]

As to the act of restitution of the blood of Henry Norris in the 14th Elizabeth, it was said that Act could not divest a right vested in Sir Brian Stapleton several years before.

Scott, Mr Attorney-General, *contra*.

Admitted that if, on the death of Sir. J. Norris, the title vested in Sir. B. Stapleton, that the claimant was entitled. [5:264] But that the fallacy of the argument was in supposing that because Henry Norris was attainted and had no inheritable blood, that on Sir J. Norris's death, Sir B. Stapleton was the sole heir.

---

[83] The references are to *Coke upon Littleton* and to Hawkins's *Pleas of the Crown*.

[84] Reported as *Collingwood and Pace's Case*, 1 Vent. 413 (Exchequer Chamber n.d., but shown in *Keble's Reports* to span 1661–64).

[85] In the margin: 'This might be the election of the Crown in calling the son of the other sister during the abeyance, per Lord Thurlow.' This evidently refers to the barony of Powis.

That this was not true in the case of lands, for the one co-heir ceases to be heir for want of inheritable blood. It does not make the other sole heir. In case of descent, one moiety of the lands escheats. But in the case of purchase, if there be a limitation to the right heirs of A who has two daughters and one is attainted, the other will take nothing. Co. Litt. 163.

Co-heirs make the *unus heres*, they are but one person.

If an honour be granted on condition that the blood shall be faithful, and one coparcener be attainted, the blood is not faithful. Donee in trust on condition not to discontinue his two daughters, one of them discontinues, the donor may re-enter. Hargraves note from Hale's MSS. in Co. Litt. 163a.

Parceners make but one heir, and each is but the moiety of an heir. Co. Litt. 163b.

Case put of daughters, one within age and the other of age. Ibid. 164a. show the two daughters make but one heir.

[5:265] That it was a fallacy to say because the honour can be enjoyed but by one, that therefore it vested in the king.

That the reason why the law abhorred abeyance did not apply to dignities, and the common language of the books was that dignities descend to coparceners, do not vest in the Crown, and that the term abeyance was improperly applied to dignities. That they always exist, but being inheritances incapable of division, and not to be enjoyed in exclusion of the rest, the law had said that the Crown should decide which should exercise them.

That the question was simply that if Mr Stapleton answered the description of the heir of the first grantee.

If the line of Henry Norris was to be considered as naturally dead for the benefit of Mr Stapleton, it must be so considered for the benefit of the issue of Ann and Margaret and then the title is in abeyance again if there be an abeyance, and that there was no grounds to say that the issue of Henry Norris precluded Ann and Margaret and did not preclude Mr Stapleton.

[5:266] And that there was a fallacy in considering H. Norris as naturally dead, of whom it could only be said with truth that his attainder might prevent the descent to Lord Abingdon. For why, if Mr Stapleton's line should fail and Henry Norris's line should fail would not the issue of Ann and Margaret take? That in the case of lands, they certainly would, and if the dignity had been assigned to the line of Norris, Mr Stapleton could not have been entitled until that line had naturally failed, though some had been attainted.

That the case of Lord Powis only proved that the Crown might call up Mr Stapleton, not that it must. That it was a strange argument to say that the attainder of one co-heir put it out of the power of the Crown to grant the dignity to any other of the co-heirs, and that the case of Powis only shewed that the attainder of the one branch was a reason for calling up the other.

That the case of the earl of Northumberland from Dugdale so far from supporting the claim operated the other way, as it proved that a younger son could not [5:267] claim as heir while he had older brothers, though they had no inheritable blood.

That the duke of Athol case proved only that the younger son could not inherit during the life of his attainted brother because he was not heir *secundum formam doni*, and was therefore a case against the claimant.

That Mr Stapleton's claim failed because he was not, in the legal sense of the word, heir of the first grantee. That to insist upon his writ of summons as a right he must be entire heir and not a part of an heir, and that it did not at all assist him that those who would make the entire heir laboured under a disability of claiming.

In reply, it was said that though there are some things in common as to the rules respecting honours and lands, yet that is not so *in omnibus*. For that honours are not alienable nor transferrable, nor does it follow that what will annihilate a common hereditament will have the same effect on an honour. That by means of the attainder, Sir J. Norris died without any heirs capable of inheriting. So that of two co-heirs, one had then died and no person could claim as his heir. That it is true that for some purposes co-heirs make but one heir, but that rule is not uniform, as a different rule [5:268] holds in the case of the descent of lands from that which obtains where they are to be taken by purchase. And if in the case of descent the whole land does not escheat, the rule of *unus heres* does not invariably hold, and therefore ought not to be applied to dignities. That the public had an interest in the office being exercised, and no reason for the abeyance continuing. And if the House should think the abeyance continued, the House were prayed to come to the same resolution as had been done in the case of barony of Bellecourt.

After the arguments were finished, the LORD CHANCELLOR objected to such resolution being come to, as it was beyond the prayer of the petition, and moved, supposing the facts of the case to be as they had been argued by the claimant's counsel. That the judges be asked whether, supposing the claimant to be one of the co-heirs of Henry de Beaumont the first baron, he is entitled as of right to that barony according to the state of pedigree, as delivered in _____ [*sic*].

June 26. EYRE, Chief Justice of the Common Pleas, after having consulted the judges, delivered their opinion to the following effect:

After stating the question which had been submitted to them, he observed [5:269] that the attorney-general had summed up his objection to the claim in a few words (*ss.*) That the claimant was not heir of Henry de Beaumont, that he had no right, as being the moiety of an heir, but could only be entitled as complete heir.

He then referred to *Co. Litt.* tit. Parceners as pointing out the manner in which they claim, that they do it as *unum corpus, unus heres*, and that there is in them but an *unitas juris*, that they must all join to make an heir or to bring a *praecipe*. That such was the situation that no one knew his part in severalty, though he knew his share. Though if the inheritance was partible, each might sue out his writ of partition and take his lot in severalty. But that this did not apply to inheritances which were impartible, which co-heirs must forever hold, as co-heirs do partible inheritances before partition with this difference, that in some impartible inheritances, such as advowsons, they shall be enjoyed in turns.

That a peerage in the eye of the law descended to co-heirs like other hereditaments, but [5:270] must vest in the *corpus unum*, and the coparceners had in it an *unitas juris*. That it stood at the head of impartible inheritances and when it vested in co-heirs it necessarily fell into a dormant state. That no one, nor could the whole body of co-heirs, assert any right to it, as they could not possess it.

That it was in abeyance, not in the ordinary sense of floating and fixing in no one, but merely as being in the co-heirs in a dormant state incapable of being enjoyed.[86]

That the remedy adopted in the case of other impartible inheritances was not applicable to this case, but a remedy of an extraordinary nature was used, (*ss.*) that of the Crown sending its writ of summons to one of the co-heirs, after which, though he will have the dignity to him and the heirs of his body, he still is but a co-heir, and if he should die without issue, the other co-heir, if there be but one, would take it. If there should be more co-heirs, the dignity would be in abeyance again. That the calling one of the co-heirs to sit does not alter his right,[87] nor add anything [5:271] to it, but only confers a title to sit, collateral to the title to the inheritance.

That the argument for the claimant was founded on a supposed plurality of persons capable of taking, and that the necessity of the Crown choosing one depended on that plurality, and that if there was only one person capable of sustaining the dignity, the prerogative of the Crown was at an end, having nothing to act on.

That if this argument had been built on solid ground, it would be a very considerable question, whether the attainder of one was a disability in all the rest. But that on the best consideration, the judges could give the question, they were of opinion that the claim of Mr Stapleton as sole heir was unfounded, he being only a co-heir.

That there was not a plurality of capable persons.

That abeyance determines by uniting the detached parts of the title in one, and restoring it to its activity. And that unless he could show that all the component parts of the title had united on the death of Sir J. Norris, he could not sustain his claim. [5:272] That the *Case of the Barony of Powis* had not been so stated as to enable the judges to form any opinion respecting it. But that the case cited from *Co. Litt.* 163 of the descent of a moiety in the attainder of coparcener shews that in contemplation of law, she who is not attainted is but a co-heir, and that the utmost benefit she can have is that of two.

And that the case of *Reading* v. *Royston* [1702] Salk. 242, was an authority to prove that the title of all the co-heirs must unite to enable anyone to take as sole heir.

[86] In the margin: 'Abeyance *quidquid* as applied to dignities'.
[87] In the margin, a pointing finger, for emphasis.

After the chief justices had given their opinion, Lord THURLOW moved that the committee were of opinion that the claimant has not any title to his writ of summons, which was agreed to.

[5:273]

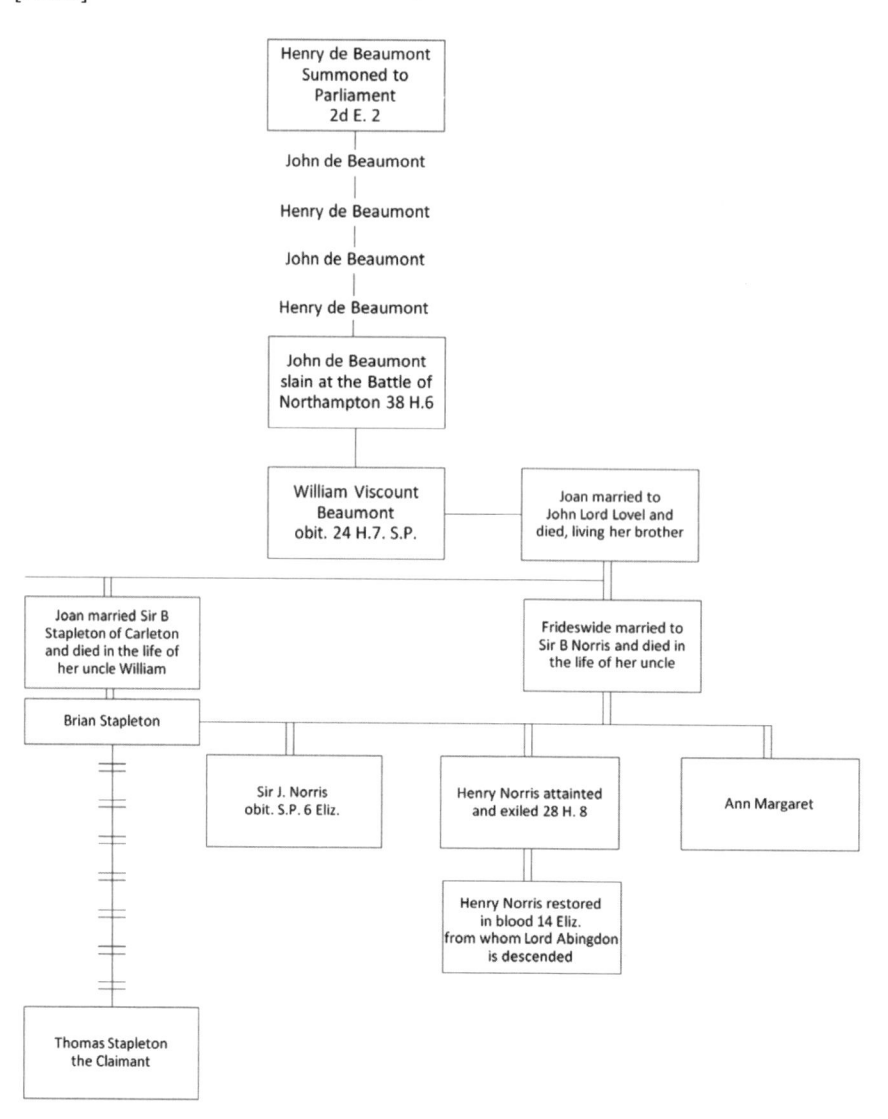

```
                    Henry de Beaumont
                    Summoned to
                    Parliament
                    2d E. 2
                         │
                    John de Beaumont
                         │
                    Henry de Beaumont
                         │
                    John de Beaumont
                         │
                    Henry de Beaumont
                         │
                    John de Beaumont
                    slain at the Battle of
                    Northampton 38 H.6
                         │
           ┌─────────────┴─────────────┐
      William Viscount            Joan married to
      Beaumont                    John Lord Lovel and
      obit. 24 H.7. S.P.          died, living her brother
                                       │
   ┌───────────────────────────────────┴────────────────────┐
Joan married Sir B                              Frideswide married to
Stapleton of Carleton                           Sir B Norris and died in
and died in the life of                         the life of her uncle
her uncle William
      │
Brian Stapleton
      │        ┌──────────────┬──────────────────┬─────────────┐
      │    Sir J. Norris   Henry Norris attainted    Ann Margaret
      │    obit. S.P. 6 Eliz.  and exiled 28 H. 8
      │                          │
      │                    Henry Norris restored
      │                    in blood 14 Eliz.
      │                    from whom Lord Abingdon
      │                    is descended
      │
Thomas Stapleton
the Claimant
```

[5:274]   B.R. TRINITY TERM 35 Geo. III

Lloyd, Lord Kenyon, Chief Justice
Sir W. H. Ashhurst ⎫
Sir N. Grose   ⎬ Justices
Sir S. Lawrence   ⎭

June 5   BLAKELY v. VINCENT

[M.H.] Judgment on an old warrant of attorney twenty years old.

Gibbs moved to enter up a judgment on an old warrant of attorney of twenty years standing. His affidavit stated that the plaintiff was alive the 3rd instant and the defendant the 2nd.

The court, after some hesitation whether there should not be a rule *nisi*, granted the rule in the first instance.

R. v. RAMSAY *et al.*

[M.H.] Circumstances inducing a lenient judgment inserted in the rule for the defendant's discharge. Same case *antea* 252.

Defendants, who were the parish officers of Woolwich, had been convicted of forcibly putting a poor woman on the eve of her being delivered into a boat to be carried to London, and there set ashore where she was delivered the same day, being received into Clerkenwell workhouse as a casual pauper.

It appearing to the court that the defendants had been at an expense of £500 in paying the costs of that prosecution and indemnifying the parish of Clerkenwell, and having been committed to the custody of the marshal, in which they had been from the last term, and having a good account of their general character they were discharged on paying a fine each of 1s. These circumstances being inserted in the rule, that it might not be supposed that persons guilty of so great an offence had only been fined, and that in so small a sum. The same thing was done in the case of some persons convicted for the Cock Lane Ghost conspiracy.

[5:275]
June 13   LANGSTON v. COTTON

[M.H.] Question if a *habeas corpus ad testificandum* grantable for one in custody for high treason. [88]

Erskine moved for a rule to show cause why a *habeas corpus ad testificandum* should not issue, directed to the keeper of Newgate to bring up one Stone, who was in that prison under a commitment of high treason.[89]

Lord KENYON said he doubted if it could be done, that it might be very mischievous that the prisoner might be committed to be kept *in arcta custodia*, and if it would be insisted that a *habeas corpus* must be granted on an affidavit, which any man might make, it would defeat the object of such a commitment, the propriety of which in certain cases all persons admitted. That he trembled for the consequences. That he had spoken to the chief justice of the C[ommon] P[leas], who doubted very much of the propriety of granting the writ. That if a rule to shew cause should be granted, there was a difficultly of saying upon whom it should be served. If upon anybody, it must be the attorney-general, and upon the whole, thought it best to apply to him to consent to a *habeas corpus* being granted.[90]

BEATY v. BEATY

[M.H.] Commitment on *latitat* allowed to the sum recovered. *Vide Judd* v. *Evans*, 6 T.R. 399 [1795].

Knowles showed cause against a rule to alter the commitment on writ of *Latitat* from £1,179 to £912, which was the amount of what had ultimately been recovered against the defendant for damages and costs, the object being to enable the defendant to take advantage of the last Insolvent Act. [5:276] He contended that the original arrest was properly made for £1,179, that being the

---

[88] The first consideration of the issue in this case at the end of the sittings after Easter Term is briefly reported at Peake Add. Cas. 21 (3 June 1795). Lord Kenyon there stated his disinclination 'to go further than the Courts had already gone', and that 'he had mentioned the case to several of the Judges, and they were of opinion that he could not permit him to be brought up without the consent of the Attorney General or the King'. Peake appended an editorial note on the procedure in England, Ireland, and Wales for applying for a *habeas corpus ad testificandum*, citing *Tidd's Practice* and statutes of 43 Geo. III, c. 140, and 44 Geo. III, c. 102.

[89] See p. 93, below.

[90] According to *The Times*, 15 June 1795, Erskine, representing Langston, claimed that Mr Stone was the plaintiff's only witness, and, 'he could not conceive how Civil Justice should be totally disappointed, because of a criminal charge exhibited against any person, whether it was for felony or for a crime against the State'. Lord Kenyon said that perhaps Erskine had no doubts, but 'I entertain doubts', as do others—though he agreed with Erskine that the matter should be settled, 'because it concerns all the Courts at Westminster'. Kenyon asked if Stone might be examined on interrogatories, but Garrow, for the defendant, said that since Stone was a partner in Stone & Co., for whom Langston & Co. acted as security, he would not be a competent witness. The case was tried before Lord Kenyon and a special jury on 24 February 1796. William Stone testified, apparently without objection. The jury verdict was for the defendant. *The Times*, 25 February 1796. A motion for a new trial was heard on 16 April 1796. *The Times*, 18 April 1796.

amount of the debt contracted by the defendant, that reduction of the damages to £912 being occasioned by a plea of set off.

Lord KENYON said that no conscientious man could have sworn to the whole sum, he would have sworn only to the balance, and not to one side of the amount only, and though the defendant might possibly not have pleaded the set off, that made no difference, as that was only a reason for his declaring for the whole sum, to oblige the defendant to plead his set off.

GROSE, Justice, said if the affidavit was to be considered as only a mistake, it should be rectified.

Rule absolute.

WILKINSON v. WILKINSON

[M.H.] Venue can't be changed if the cause of action arises in more counties than one.

Leycester shewed cause against a rule to change the venue to Shropshire on an affidavit that the cause of action arose in Shropshire, Chester, Flint, or one of them. He insisted that the affidavit must be express that the cause of action arose in that county to which the venue should be changed and no other, and cited 1 Wilson 178.[91]

Erskine, contra.

Lord KENYON said he had looked into the books and found that the rule respecting changing the venue must be religiously observed, and that it could not be done in this case. But the rule was enlarged, the parties agreeing to a general reference.[92]

[5:277]
June 15   ANONYMOUS

[M.H.] Execution may be sued out after writ of error, if the bail admits they brought it to gain time to surrender the principal.

Espinasse showed cause against a rule for setting aside an execution for irregularity, it having been sued out after allowance of a writ of error (*ss.*) the bail having admitted that they brought the writ of error to get time to surrender the principal.

---

[91] *Herring* v. *Durant* (1747).
[92] According to *The Times*, 7 October 1795, this case involved a dispute between two brothers who were 'supposed to have sunk near half a million of money in iron works, which they carry on in different parts of the Kingdom to a greater extent than any other in the trade'. The action was brought by one brother against the other 'for breaking up some of these works', and the change of venue motion was made because the witnesses 'were so numerous that Guildhall would be too small for them'. At Lord Kenyon's strong suggestion, the case was referred to the arbitration of 'a number of Iron-Masters that should be elected by the parties'. Kenyon said that the cause 'was so multifarious, that it would be impossible ever to get to the end of it at *Nisi prius*'. There were three bills in Chancery, each several thousand sheets long, and the parties should understand 'that the Court of Chancery would not settle all these accounts for at least these fifty years'.

Shepherd, contra, endeavoured to distinguish this from the case of the defendant in the original action admitting that the writ of error was for delay.

But the court thought there was no ground of distinction.

Rule absolute.

MILLER v. TOSLIN et al.

[M.H.] Old deeds &c. evidence if they do not come out of suspicious custody.

On an issue on an enclosure Act to try the right of the prebendary of [sic] to certain tithes. The CHIEF BARON had refused to receive in evidence a terrier above 100 years old signed by a former prebendary, it not having come out of the proper custody, which was the bishop's Registry.

Lord KENYON said that against the prebendary it was admissible, if it did not come out of a suspicious custody—and that he had known an old instrument in Cromwell's time coming out of a private gentleman's hands received in evidence. That it was another question what weight it might have.

Rule for a new trial.

[5:278]
Wednesday, June 17   [ANONYMOUS]

[M.H.] Belief that A. B. is the proprietor of a newspaper not sufficient for information for a libel.

Russell moved for an information against a printer of the *Morning Post* and Henry Bate Dudley, the proprietor, for a libel. But as the affidavit merely went to the belief of the party from information as to H. B. Dudley being that proprietor, Lord KENYON said the rule would not be granted against him.

EX PARTE ROOSWELL

[M.H.] Attorney struck off the roll for want of due service as a clerk.

Garrow shewed cause against a rule on Rooswell to answer the matters of the affidavit in practising as an attorney, having been improperly admitted as he had not served a regular clerkship, as he had not been employed in the service of the persons to whom he had been articled.

It appeared on the affidavits that on the 4th July 1785 he had been articled to one Elias Jones, a person whose chief business was Crown business, and as Rooswell soon did for him such business [as] he required and was employed by him from time to time. But that Jones did not require his constant attendance and he had acted as a clerk to the magistrates of Shadwell. That Jones died after above a year and ten months, when he was articled to one Findlay, and that he did such business as Findlay required, but that he had during all this time been clerk to the magistrates at Shadwell, and since the Police Act, had been the principal clerk at that office, and that he had been admitted in the usual way.

[5:279] Lord KENYON said if he had any discretion he might leave him in his present situation, but that he had not, being bound by the 22 Geo. II and that he had only to consider if he had the title which the Act of parliament requires for a man to be admitted—and that he was bound to say he had not.

Rule absolute to strike him off the roll, but to be expressed in the rule that it was for want of due service only.

Friday, June 19   DELVES v. FRANCO

[M.H.] If an instalment which has not been paid at the time is afterwards received, plaintiff can't take out execution for the whole sum.

Shepherd showed cause against a rule to discharge defendant out of custody of the sheriff of Middlesex, he having given a bond and warrant of attorney to secure the payment of money in instalments, any one of which not being paid, the plaintiff was to be at liberty to take out execution for the whole sum. On the first of January one instalment of £50 became due which was not paid. But it was paid afterwards, with interest. The defendant designing to go to the East Indies, the plaintiff took out execution for the whole sum which *Shepherd* insisted he had a right to do, as one of the instalments had not been paid at the time.

Sed per Lord KENYON, if you had not received the £50 afterwards you might have insisted on the execution, but this is like the case of a *solvit post diem*.

Rule absolute.

[5:280]   WALWYN v. THOMAS

[M.H.] If a plaintiff takes no steps in an action against the principal but comes in under a commission, he shall not afterwards proceed on the bail bond.

Russel moved to stay proceedings on the bail bond.
The facts of the case were as follows:
In April 1794 there was a commission of bankruptcy issued against the principal. In the September following he was arrested and at the return of the writ put in bail, but did not give notice of it. On the 25th December, the plaintiffs proved their debt under the commission. On the 12th January 1795 the certificate was allowed, and on the 21st took an assignment of the bail bond.

Gibbs shewed cause and contended that proving the debt under the commission did not prevent the plaintiff's going on at law.

Sed per Lord KENYON: This is a very clear case, both in point of law and justice. Instead of going on, you rest on your proceeding, taking steps under the commission in contradiction of what you now are doing. I take no assignment of your bail bond until after the certificate, when you can have no fruit of your action.

Rule absolute.

[5:281] R. v. REED

[M.H.] *Mandamus* not to be granted to the paymaster of the forces to pay out of an officer's pay a penalty due to the party grieved, and which the Mutiny Act directs the paymaster to pay.

Burrough moved for a *mandamus* to be directed to the paymaster of the forces to pay a penalty of £5 in which the defendant, the major of the Wiltshire Militia, had been convicted for not discharging a baggage wagon, which penalty by the Mutiny Act is directed to be paid by the paymaster of the forces to the party aggrieved out of the pay of the officer convicted.

Lord KENYON said that *mandamus* would be multiplied without end—that an action might be brought for the money impressed in the paymaster's hands and that such action had been brought in the Common Pleas against a Mr Courtney.

Nil cap.

SHAW v. MARTIN

[M.H.] No *habeas corpus* on the civil side to bring up the prisoner who is in the King's Bench prison.

The defendant, who was in the custody of the marshal for several debts, being desirous of being brought before the court to make a complaint of some grievances he conceived he laboured under, sued on the civil side the common writ of *habeas corpus ad faciendum et recipiendum*, and served it on the marshal, and for his not returning it moved for an attachment against him.

Erskine shewed cause and upon his statement of the facts, which were not contradicted, Lord KENYON said that such a writ as that had never been sued out from the civil side of the court by a prisoner in the custody of the marshal.

Rule discharged.

[5:282] WYNN v. CROWNINGSHIELD

[M.H.] Where a defendant has been held to bail by a judge's order, affidavits may be received on a motion to discharge defendant on common bail.

The defendant having been held to special bail by a judge's order for negligently stowing *aqua fortis* and oil of vitriol in the hold of a ship, in consequence of which the ship was set on fire and burnt, affidavits were received on a rule to discharge the judge's order, both in support of the rule and against it, though no such affidavits can be received on a motion to discharge the defendant on filing common bail, where he has been held to bail in the ordinary course of proceeding.

ANONYMOUS

[M.H.] After the sheriff is fixed, if a trial be lost, the attachment must stand as a security to bail put in and perfected before attachment.

The master reported the practice to be that after expiration of the rule to bring in the body, an attachment may be moved for against the sheriff, though special bail has been put in and perfected before the attachment was moved—and that in such case, if a bail has been lost, the bail bond must stand as a security.

Rule accordingly.

R. v. JUSTICES of LANCASTER

[M.N.] Query if a constable makes a township.

Erskine shewed cause against a rule for a *mandamus* to appoint overseers for the township of Outhwaite in the county of Lancaster. In this case there was a contradiction in the affidavits whether Outhwaite was a township, or only a hamlet of the township of Pilkington, and what was strongly relied on in support of the rule was it being stated that there had been a constable for Outhwaite [5:283] 130 years, which of itself made a township according to what was laid down by BULLER J., in *R. v. Middleton*, or *R. v. Sir W. Horton*, 1 T.R. 374.[93]

Lord KENYON said that he doubted whether the proposition was true that the appointment of a constable for a district made it a township, but that it appeared the whole parish had had the benefit of the[94] 13th and 14th Chas. II.

The rule was discharged.

Monday, June [15]   R. v. _____ [*sic*]

[M.H.] Information for want of a fair trial directed to be tried in Yorkshire instead of the town of Newcastle.

On the motion of *Gibbs*, a rule was made to enter suggestion that an impartial trial could not be had of their information (which was for a conspiracy to raise and keep up the price of coals to be sent to the London market) either in the county or the town of Newcastle, where the offence had been committed, or in the county of Northumberland, and that it might be held in Yorkshire, being the next English county into which the king's writ of *venire facias* run[s].

Rule absolute.

---

[93] The case of *R. v. Watts Horton* (1786) 1 T.R. 374 involved the parish of Middleton, and townships within.
[94] In the manuscript '43nd of Eliz'. is written and crossed out.

LE MESURIER v. PARRY

[M.H.] Account ordered to be delivered to plaintiff of average.

The court made a rule on the plaintiff to deliver to the defendant an account of his general and particular average.

[5:284]
Thursday, June 18   BIRD v. THOMPSON

[M.H.] A broker is not the person who receives the order to effect the policy, within 29 Geo. III, c. 56.

Law moved for a new trial by the 28 Geo. III, c. 56, that the name of the persons interested &c. shall be inserted in the policy, or the name of the person who shall receive the order for and effect the policy. Bird in this case had no interest whatever in the policy and was merely the broker, and had received the order from the correspondent of the persons interested to effect the policy in effecting the policy. The policy began in this form: In the name of God, Amen, Mr William Bird, agent as well in his own name, &c., as in common cases. And the declaration averred that he was the person who had received the order from the persons interested to effect the policy. This allegation was not proved at the trial, and it was then objected that Bird was not the person meant in the Act as the person receiving the order to effect the policy, as the mere broker's name did not give the underwriter the information the Act of parliament intended, but that it meant the correspondent of the person interested, and the allegation of Bird's being the person who received the order was necessary to be proved. But Lord [5:285] KENYON under some misapprehension at *nisi prius* overruled the objection and now after argument by *Law* and *Gibbs* for the new trial, and *Erskine* and *Giles e contra*, the rule was made absolute.[95]

---

[95] According to *The Times*, 6 October 1795, this case was first tried during Easter term, resulting in a verdict for the plaintiffs. The insurance policy covered goods on board the *Cholmondeley*, travelling from the Bahamas to Liverpool. The plaintiff sought a total loss of the insured interest, £10,000, claiming barratry by the captain (barratry was covered by the policy). A new trial was then ordered after it was claimed that the captain was a part-owner and thus could not commit barratry. At the second trial on 2 June, the defendants attempted to call the captain as a witness, but Lord Kenyon ruled him an incompetent witness because interested. See *Bird* v. *Thompson* (1796) 1 Esp. 339. The plaintiff showed that the sole owner was the ship's captain's father, thus reviving the question of barratry, and argued that the captain committed barratry when, shortly after sailing, he began to cruise and to take prizes. There was a letter of marque on board, but the plaintiff said this was just for show—to quell the fears of the seamen that they might be taken by the French and treated as pirates. Also the ship did not have the certificate required by the most recent prize statute. The defendant underwriters claimed that the captain's cruising and capture of prizes was approved by the ship owner and was therefore a deviation, not covered by the policy; also, the absence of the certificate was because the Act was brand new and the need for the certificate was unknown to the captain and owner. The special jury of merchants at the second trial returned a verdict of £250 for the plaintiff, but on 9 June, a rule was granted to show cause why the case should not be tried a third time, prompting some rambling observations by Lord Kenyon on the singularity of insuring against barratry—where the underwriters insured 'the conduct of people with whom they had nothing to do'. *The Times*, 10 June 1795. The rule was argued on 18 June, as reflected in Lawrence's notes (above), also in *The Times*, 19 June 1795. For the underwriters, Edward Law and Vicary

[*Lawrence note*:] This term would have ended on the 24th of June had it not been a *dies non*, that being the case, the court sat on the 25th.

[*5:286–332*] IN DOM. PROC., HOME v. EARL CAMDEN[96]

[*5:333*]   MICHAELMAS TERM 36 Geo. III

Lloyd, Lord Kenyon, Chief Justice
Sir W. H. Ashhurst ⎫
Sir N. Grose   ⎬ Justices
Sir S. Lawrence   ⎭

SMITH et al. v. SHEPHERD

[M.H.] Water carrier liable on the custom of the realm.

This was an action on case tried at the last assizes for York before ROOKE, Justice, against the defendant as a common carrier of goods by water from Selby to Kingston-upon-Hull, charging the defendant with negligence, by means whereof the goods were wetted and spoiled.

It appeared in evidence that the defendant's vessel had entered the harbour in the night and to avoid a vessel which had been sunk, steered near the shore and there ran on a sandbank which had lately been thrown up and which the

---

Gibbs claimed that the insurance policy was void because it did not identify on its face the person for whom Bird, the agent, acted; nor was it proved at the second trial that Bird had acted as an agent. Further, Law argued that no barratry had occurred. For the plaintiff, Erskine, Garrow, and Giles refuted these claims. Lord Kenyon was indignant, stating that the whole case was reduced to the simple point whether affirmative evidence was required that Mr Bird was the broker and agent who had received the order to insure—a point that was 'most ungracious and unhandsome', even bordering on dishonesty. The court nevertheless ordered a third trial. No record of a further trial has been located in the printed reports or in *The Times*.

[96] Pages 286–332 in Lawrence's notebook contain Lord Chief Justice Eyre's opinion in the case of *Home* v. *Earl Camden*, delivered to the House of Lords on 22 June 1792. The opinion is reported in full at 2 Bl. H. 533, and since the version of Eyre's opinion in Lawrence's notebook is identical to the version in Henry Blackstone's report, Eyre's opinion need not be reprinted here. Lawrence was one of several counsel representing the plaintiff. The litigation commenced in Trinity term 1788, when the plaintiff sought a writ of prohibition to the Lords Commissioners of Appeal in Admiralty (the defendants), claiming that the defendants had exceeded their jurisdiction by issuing a monition to an agent who held residual proceeds from the sale of a Dutch prize taken in July 1781. The claim was that the distribution of proceeds had not complied with the terms of the Dutch Prize Act, 21 Geo. III, c.15. The Court of Common Pleas granted the writ, as is reported at length at (1790) 1 Bl. H. 476. The defendants then filed a writ of error with the Court of King's Bench, and in Michaelmas term 1791, the decision of the Court of Common Pleas was reversed. The King's Bench applied the principle that had been established in a series of earlier cases, 'that the prize courts are the sole judges of questions of prize, as also the question of who are the captors'. See *Lord Camden* v. *Home* (1791) 4 T.R. 382, 394. Counsel for plaintiff then filed a writ of error in the House of Lords, and the sophisticated arguments are fully laid out at 6 Bro. P.C. 215–229. The House of Lords affirmed the ruling of the Court of King's Bench, although on procedural grounds.

defendant had no knowledge of, it having been formed subsequent to the last time he was in the harbour, and that it was safer to go in the night than stay in the road.

The judge was of opinion that no case of negligence was proved and the plaintiff was nonsuited.

Lee moved for a new trial, when Lord KENYON at first doubted if the custom of the realm extended to a water carrier. But upon having been referred to *Dale* v. *Hall*, 1 Wils. 281,[97] Clift's *Entries* 38[98] and the case of the Trent Navigation[99] referred to in the case of *Forward* v. *Pittard*, 1 T.R. 27, he altered his opinion and a new trial was granted that the facts of the case might be more fully inquired into, which had not been sufficiently done at the trial.[1]

[5:*334*]   DOE, *ex dim.* HOWE and *uxor* v. SALTER

[M.H.] One who comes in privity of a tenant's title shan't set up any rights of his own against the landlord.

This was tried before MCDONALD, Chief Baron, at the last assizes for Hertfordshire, when a verdict was found for the defendant, by his direction.

The lessors of the plaintiff's father, one Morgan, had got admitted to the estate, which was copyhold, by fraud and let it to one Lumworth. On Morgan's death, the defendant prevailed on Lumworth to give him the possession, which he did on being paid 15 guineas for his stock.

The court thought the verdict wrong, though the defendant has a title to the estate, and that he could not controvert the title of Lumworth's lessor, as he came in in privity of Lumworth's title and stood in his shoes.

WILLIAMS v. WILLIAMS

[M.H.] Continuances taken off the roll.

The defendant having pleaded the statute of limitations, the plaintiff replied [by] a writ sued out the 14th January 1785 and entered continuances on the roll to connect it with the writ served on the defendant. *Gibbs* moved to take the continuances off the roll on an affidavit that the writ replied was sued out in another action in which the plaintiff had been nonsuit.

Garrow shewed cause, and produced another affidavit, that the writ in the action in which the plaintiff was nonsuit was a writ sued on the 26th November 1785, and was not an alias.

But Lord KENYON said the court could not intend that there were two actions depending at the same time for the same cause, and made the rule absolute.

[97] *Dale* v. *Hall* (1750) 1 Wils. 281.
[98] H. Clift, *A New Book of Declarations, Pleadings, Judgments and Judicial Writs with the Entries thereupon* (1703).
[99] In the margin: '*Vide* book F. 116', apparently another of Lawrence's notebooks (see p. 63, n. 66, above). In the printed reports see *Proprietors of the Trent Navigation* v. *Wood* (1785) 4 Doug. 286.
[1] See p. 132, below, for Lawrence's notes of the new trial.

[5:335] ## ALMACK v. CHAPMAN

[M.H.] Money had and received will not lie against a factor who takes bills when he should have been paid in cash.

Money had and received tried before ROOKE, J. at Newcastle. Nonsuit.

Plaintiff, by defendant his broker, sold goods to one Vesey at three months, when, instead of receiving the money, he took a bill payable at a future day, and before it was paid, the plaintiff brought this action.

Law moved for a new trial, contending that the defendant must be considered as having received the money.

Sed per Lord KENYON: Perhaps an action might have lain against the defendant for his misconduct in not receiving the money, but this nonsuit is right.

DE GARROW v. GALBRAITH

[M.H.] Adjustment of a policy [is] *prima facie* evidence unless there be immediate doubts of the justice of the claim.

This was an action on a policy of assurance. The evidence of the plaintiff was an adjustment of the policy. But the same witness who proved the adjustment proved that almost immediately after doubts arose whether the plaintiff was entitled to recover, when the defendant determined to act as the other underwriter. On this Lord KENYON nonsuited the plaintiff.

Erskine now moved for a new trial, insisting that the adjustment was *prima facie* evidence against the defendant, and that he ought to have gone into his case and mentioned a case of *Rogers* v. *Maylor* tried before Lord KENYON in London at the sittings after Trinity term 1790, where after proof of an adjustment, the defendant was obliged to go into his case.

Lord KENYON distinguished this case from that by the circumstance of the doubts immediately arising, whereas in the case cited, there were none, and he [5:336] said if underwriters were held so strictly, it would put an end to all candour.

Rule refused.

R. v. AITKIN

Defendant was convicted of publishing an indecent libel.

On his affidavit that he had offered to deliver up the plates and all the copies, and was ready to do it, the court fined him £200 and required him to give security for his good behaviour for three years, himself in £300 and two bail in £100 each.

November 26   THOMAS OATES v. CHARLES MILES

[M.H.] *The parties to an indenture of apprenticeship can't give it in evidence without an affidavit that the premium is truly inserted.*

This was an action against the defendant for harbouring the plaintiff's apprentice, tried before PERRYN, Baron, at Chelmsford. The execution of the indentures of apprenticeship and the facts of harbouring the apprentice being proved, the defendant's counsel insisted that there should have been produced an affidavit pursuant to the 8th Anne c. 9, sec. 43, which enacts that such indenture shall be admitted in evidence in any suit to be brought by the parties thereto unless the party on whose behalf the same shall be admitted in evidence do first make oath that the sums therein inserted were really and truly all that was directly or indirectly given or paid.

It was answered that this clause only respected affidavits required by the Stamp Office on stamping the indentures.

The jury found a verdict for the plaintiff, damages £5.

[5:337] *Shepherd*, having obtained a rule for a new trial, *Garrow* showed cause against it.

The court were of opinion that such affidavit should have been produced, but as it might now be made, the damages being only £5, and as it was certain what would be the event of a new trial, the court discharged the rule.

10th, 23rd, and 24th November
MOFFAT *et al.* v. HARGRAVES

[M.H.] *It is usury to secure the payment of more than five per cent, though the parties to the contract did not intend to have more than lawful interest.* Vide same case, post 351.

Erskine moved for a new trial of an issue directed on a motion to set aside an execution, to try whether a bond given by two persons of the name of Nunez and Thorne was in pursuance of an usurious agreement.

The bond was for payment of £616 with interest at five per cent and was dated the 16th May, 1754, on which day:

    250 was advanced in cash
    159 by a note due 31st March 1755
    157 by a note due 1st December 1754
     50 advanced on the 17th of July
    616

It appeared in evidence that Thorne was the son-in-law of the defendant, wanting £600 applied to him for it, which he agreed to let him have. Thorne gave instructions for drawing the bond and it was filled up for £616. When the parties met, the defendant could not produce more than £250, and the notes which Thorne had agreed to take as part of the £600, when it was proposed to alter the bond, but as the defendant was as soon as he could to advance the remaining [5:338] £50, it was thought that the security might as well remain unaltered. Thorne on the trial proved that the defendant had no idea of taking more than five per cent.

In support of the motion, *Nevison* v. *Whitby*, Sir William Jones 396 [1637]; 2 Ventr. 87,[2] Cro. Car. 678,[3] 2 Mod. 307,[4] 2 Blackstone's Reports 864,[5] were cited.

Lord KENYON said he agreed with the cases cited, and if this had appeared to be the mistake of the scrivener, he should have directed for the defendant. And that he believed that the parties, had they known the consequences, would not have done what they had done, but that it was clear that the agreement of the parties was that the bills were to be received as part of the money lent. That being so, it did not depend on the intention of the parties whether this was usury. That the law gave the transaction its denomination, that the parties to the contract need not be asked, for the volume of the law determined what it was. That he was very sorry to say it was the only verdict the jury could give.

Rule discharged.

[5:339]
November 11 EX PARTE JOHN MARTIN

[M.N.] *Habeas corpus ad subjiciendum* irregular if it issues from the plea side, or without a rule of court or judge's signature.

He was brought up on the common writ of *habeas corpus cum causa* directed to the Marshal who returned that he was in his custody charged in execution in diverse civil actions—and he [Martin] would now, would have argued the legality of his commitment.[6] But Lord KENYON told him that upon reading the return he must be remanded, that if it could be to any purpose to hear him he would listen to him as long as he pleased.

LAWRENCE, Justice, asked him if he meant to argue against the legality of his commitment, to which he assented. He then told Martin that he had mistaken the writ, that he should have sued out the *habeas corpus ad subjiciendum*, for that the *habeas corpus cum causa* was only for the purpose for removing actions from inferior courts, for bail to surrender their principal, and other purposes in civil actions different from what he understood to be his object.[7]

---

[2] *Bush* v. *Buckingham* (1689) 2 Vent. 83.
[3] Counsel for plaintiff (Erskine) appears to have meant Cro. Jac. 678, *Buckley* v. *Guildbank* (1623).
[4] *Ballard* v. *Oddey* (1678).
[5] *Murray* v. *Harding* (1773) 2 Bl. W. 859 (C.P.).
[6] That is, he would now have the legality of his commitment argued.
[7] This phase of the case was reported in *The Times* on 12 November 1795. Martin said that he had not been brought up by the plaintiff but by himself under the common law writ, *ad faciendum et recepiendum*. Lord Kenyon said that Martin, who was an attorney, should have known that the court would have to remand him since he was in custody in execution for a civil debt. Martin asked that the writ be read, which was allowed, after which Mr Justice Lawrence explained that the *habeas corpus cum causa* had been improperly sued out—that 'the writ of *Habeas Corpus ad faciendum et*

After this he sued out a writ of *habeas corpus ad subjiciendum* without having first obtained a judge's fiat, and on the 13th of November, wrote a letter to the judges informing them he had served it on the marshal who had refused to obey it, complaining that five counsel had declined moving the court for him and desiring that the court would give orders to the marshal to obey the writ and to assign him counsel [5:340] to move for an attachment against him. He also sent a petition to the same effect, adding that he was illegally confined at the suit of three different plaintiffs.

Lord KENYON upon the court's sitting told the bar what Martin had done, and said if there was any ground to contend that he was illegally imprisoned, he hoped some gentleman at the bar would bring his case before the court. And as it appeared to him the proper way of doing it was by a rule on the plaintiffs to show cause why he should not be discharged. *Gibbs*, on this, said that Martin had applied to him, and he had at first declined to assist him because another gentleman had been previously concerned, but had told Martin what was the proper course for him to pursue, which he had declined to follow.

Gurney said that having in the last term moved for a rule against the Marshal for an attachment for not obeying a writ of *habeas corpus cum causa*, which was discharged, he had been applied to by Martin to move for another writ of *habeas corpus*, which he thought not proper, and had told him he ought to move for the rule Lord KENYON had suggested, but that Martin had declined to do it.

[5:341] On applying to the officers of the court to know how this writ of *habeas corpus ad subjiciendum* had been obtained and what was the practice in obtaining them, Mr Dealtry the clerk of the rules informed me[8] that writs of *habeas corpus* issuing out of the Court of King's Bench are either made out at the Crown Office, if issued on the Crown side, or passed by the signer of the writs if issued on the plea side of the court. That the signer of the writs informed him that he only marks such as are either to testify, to do and receive, or the *habeas corpus cum causa* in some civil suit.

That it appeared that Martin had on the 11th of November got a writ of *habeas corpus ad subjiciendum* passed through the office of the signer of the writs, for which a *praecipe* had been left to this effect: *habeas corpus* being directed to the marshal of the King's Bench prison at the instance of John Martin to submit to do and receive, &c., returnable immediately. John Martin in person, 11 November 1795.

That the signer of the writs says he did not observe the words 'to submit to', otherwise he should not have passed the writ, as he never knew a writ of *habeas corpus* [5:342] of that description pass his office. He only remembered the

---

recepiendum issued when a person was sued in some inferior jurisdiction, and was desirous to remove his action into a superior Court, commanding the inferior Judge to produce the body of the defendant'. The proper writ to complain of illegal imprisonment was a *habeas corpus ad subjiciendum*.

[8] In the manuscript, the words 'the court' and 'judges' are written and struck out. Presumably Lawrence had personally made the inquiry to the officers, and the response had come to him directly.

words 'to do and receive', and passed the writ accordingly. That the writ of *habeas corpus ad subjiciendum* never issues out of the Crown Office until a rule of court has been made for granting it in term time, or a judge's fiat obtained in the vacation, which is signified by the writ being endorsed 'By Rule of Court'— or with a judge's signature. And that the writ of *habeas corpus* was irregular for want of such endorsement and from not having issued from the proper office.
Vide *R. v. Roddam*, Cowp. 672.[9]

EARL OF BARRYMORE, executor of his brother, the late earl v. TAYLOR

[M.H.] A debt after assignment is not liable to foreign attachment.

The defendant being indebted to the late earl in a considerable sum of money directed him to pay it to one Delpini in discharge of a debt the earl owed Delpini. Taylor being accidentally in London, the debt was attached at the suit of another creditor of the earl's. And it was argued that as Taylor did not reside within the jurisdiction, the debt could not be attached, but without determining that point, the court held that by the direction of the late earl for the payment of it to Delpini, it has become his, and on that account was not liable to foreign attachment.

[5:343] ### R. v. the DEAN and CHAPTER OF SARUM

[M.H.] *Mandamus* will not lie where one is not dispossessed of his office, but only disturbed in it.

Gibbs shewed cause against a *mandamus* to restore Daniel Bozter to the privileges of church sexton and bishopry sexton of the cathedral church of Sarum.[10]

As such, he claimed the privilege of showing the church to strangers and of keeping the plate, and complained that the dean and chapter had disturbed him in the exercise of this privilege by taking the keys of the church from him.

Lord KENYON: If the man has seisin of his office, what is a *mandamus* to do?

Erskine admitted he could not support his rule.

Rule discharged.

RIDDING v. HAYES

[M.H.] On an enlarged rule, affidavits not filed can't be read.

This was an enlarged rule, and the affidavits to show cause were not filed within the time directed by a day.

Lord KENYON refused to suffer them to be read, and said the rule was not to

---

[9] *R. v. Roddam* (1777) 2 Cowp. 672.
[10] That is, Salisbury.

be broke through unless the noncompliance with it happened through some accident such as the miscarriage of the post.

Rule absolute against one Hale for an attachment, he being called on to answer the matters of the affidavit.

BOUTFLOWER v. STAFFORD

[M.H.] To make an execution regular after a writ of error, it [the writ of error] must be expressly admitted to be for delay.

The question here was whether the defendant's attorney had confessed a writ of error to be for delay. The attorney's clerk, having said, upon being asked, why he had pleaded so ridiculous a plea, 'what can a man do when he can't pay'?

The court held that not sufficient, that it was an admission that there was not error in the proceeding, and that the rule was that the party or his attorney [*5:344*] must confess it was brought for delay.

Vide: *Masterman v. Grant*, 5 T.R. 714 [1794].

November 17   R. v. RICHARD ENGLAND

[M.H.] Errors assigned on an outlawry for murder. *Vide* page [5:]358.

The defendant was brought to the bar in consequence of a writ of *habeas corpus* directed to the keeper of Newgate, who returned that he had been committed to his custody by a warrant under the hand and seal of Lord KENYON issued on a certificate of his having been outlawed on an indictment for the murder of P. Lee Rolls, found against him before commissioners of oyer and terminer at Hicks Hall.

The clerk of the rules read the record of the outlawry which had been removed here by *certiorari*.

The prisoner was then called on to say why execution should not be awarded against him.

On this he prayed time to consider what he should plead—and it was granted him till Monday the 22nd.

He was afterwards brought up on the 28th, when, it being again demanded of him why execution should not be awarded, he pleaded that he was not in England at the time of the judgment of outlawry. This he delivered in, in parchment. The attorney-general not being present to reply, he was ordered to be brought up again the first day of Hilary term. He was brought up the first day of February, when, being in like manner [*5:345*] called on, he produced a writ of error, and then in person delivered in an assignment of various errors, when the attorney-general delivered a joinder in error.

Vide: Paper Book 95. *Vide* 2 Hawkins. c. 50, Sec. 6.
R. v. Johnson, Str: 824, and 2 H. H. P. C. 209. Post [5:]358.[11]

---

[11] According to *The Times*, 14 November 1795, '*Dick England*, of much notoriety, after an emigration from this country of some years, was discharged at Sablonierre's Hotel, in Leicester

November 19   BICKNELL v. LANGSTAFF

[M.N.] The proceedings not stayed in action on judgment pending unless bail be perfected.

Marriot shewed cause against a rule to stay proceedings on a judgment, pending a writ of error, that though bail had been put in, it was not perfected, and cited 5 T.R. 9.[12]

Rule discharged.

R. v. STONE

[M.H.] Trial for high treason put off on absence of witnesses after copy of indictment, &c. had been delivered.

The prisoner was brought to the bar in pursuance of a writ of *habeas corpus* directed to the keeper of Newgate, to which it was returned that he was committed to his custody by warrant of the secretary of state for high treason.

Mr Attorney-General prayed that the writ and the return might be filed, and that he might be arraigned on an indictment found against him by the grand jury of the county of Middlesex for high treason, which being done, the prisoner pleaded *non cul.*

He then desired that *Adair*, serjeant, and *Erskine* might be assigned to him as his counsel, which was done, when *Adair* moved to put off his trial on account of the absence of two material witnesses, whom he expected to return to England (one being in America and the other in Ireland) before the next term. The attorney-general declined either consenting to or opposing [5:346] this motion, and having stated that the prisoner had had a copy of the indictment, witnesses, and jurors delivered to him ten days in pursuance of the Act of

---

Fields, and apprehended on a warrant of outlawry, not having appeared to plead an indictment long since preferred against him for the murder of Mr Rolles, the brewer of Kingston, whom he killed in a duel.' The bill of indictment against the defendant was for the murder of William Peter Lee Rolls on 18 June 1784. *The Times*, 18 November 1795. Lawrence's notes on his copy of the Paper Book for this case (Dampier MSS., Lincoln's Inn Library, LPB 95) state the disposition of the case as follows: 'Lawes, for the Crown, admitted this case is not to be distinguished from *R.* v. *Barrington*. And Ashhurst J., pronounced judgment that the errors assigned, and other errors appearing, the judgment be reversed. *Procedendo* was awarded and the prisoner remanded.' (This exchange is described somewhat more fully in *The Times*, 8 February 1796.) Lawrence wrote the following summary above the case caption on the Paper Book: 'Writ of Proclamation being returnable the 1st of October at the general quarter sessions, the defendant was by the Sheriff's Proclamation required to appear at the sessions—before which time he was outlawed on the *quinto exactus*. The outlawry for this reason was erroneous.' According to Blackstone, when a prisoner absconds, 'he shall be in the *exigent* in order to his outlawry: that is, he shall be exacted, proclaimed, or required to surrender, at five county courts; and if he be returned *quinto exactus*, and does not appear at the fifth exaction or requisition, then he is adjudged to be *outlawed*, or put out of the protection of the law'. *Blackstone's Commentaries* (1769), iii. 314. In other notes in the Paper Book, Lawrence describes the case of *R.* v. *Johnson*, and lists the procedural steps required in a writ of error upon an outlawry, the last of which is as follows: 'The outlawry being reversed, he is put to answer the indictment and may plead to it, and be tried at the King's Bench bar, or the record may be remitted into the County if it was removed into King's Bench by certiorari, with a command for the justices to proceed, by the statute 6 H. 8, c. 6.'

[12] *Saunders* v. *Hardinge* (1792).

parliament, he thought it proper for the court to decide whether, after that, the trial ought to be put off.

Lord KENYON said applications of this sort ought not to be granted on slight grounds, and that there was great weight in Mr Justice FOSTER's observations as to the consequences of the statute of[13] Queen Anne,[14] but he did not mean to enter into them as he thought the affidavit contained sufficient ground to put off the trial. It was fixed for the first Thursday in Hilary term.[15]

R. v. KIDD WAKE

[M.H.] Bail of one committed for insulting the king.

The defendant was brought up on a *habeas corpus* by the keeper of Tothill Fields Bridewell, having been committed for riotously assembling with others and insulting the king in his way to the parliament, calling out, 'no war'.

On application to bail him, the attorney-general prayed that his bail might be in £500 each. The court directed the recognizance of the principal to be £1,000 and his two bail £250 each.[16]

[5:347] November 20
R. v. THE MASTER AND CLERK OF THE BRAZIERS AND ARMOURERS COMPANY

[M.H.] *Mandamus* not to be granted to [do] a thing until the party has been required to do it, nor to oblige a man to make an entry in a corporate book if it contains a libel on himself.

[M.N.] Query if any person but the presiding officer can put a question if he refuses.

The *mandamus* prayed for in this case was that the master should deliver a book of the company in his possession to the clerk of the company and that the clerk should enter in that book a resolution of the general court of the company

---

[13] The words 'King William' are written in the manuscript and crossed out.

[14] 7 Anne, c. 21, s. 11, referring the delivery to any person indicted for high treason of lists of witnesses and jurors ten days before trial.

[15] The case was tried at bar on 28 and 29 January 1796, and the prisoner was found not guilty. See *R. v. Stone*, 6 T.R. 527. A verbatim account of the case running to 273 printed pages is at 25 S.T. 1155. Full reports also appeared in *The Times* on 28 and 29 January and 1 February 1796. A panel of 178 jurors was summoned by the sheriff, seventy of whom appeared and were called over during *voir dire*. A few were excused by illness or age, but to the distress of Chief Justice Kenyon and Attorney-General Scott, twenty-four of the seventy were dismissed because they were not freeholders, as required by statute. Nineteen were challenged by the defendant. The trial ran until 9.00 p.m. on the first day, when the case was adjourned and the jury sequestered. The case continued on the second day from 9.00 a.m. until 11.00 p.m., when the jury, after almost three hours of deliberation, returned the not guilty verdict.

[16] For the judgment in this case, see p. 138, below.

that the master of the company had acted indecently in not putting a question proposed at such general court.

It appeared by the affidavits that in this company there was a select body consisting of the master, two wardens and twenty-one assistants, and a dispute having arisen whether the body at large had a power to control the expenditures of the revenues of the company. At a general court, it was moved that the master, wardens and assistants submit to the general court the plans, &c. of certain alterations and repairs to be done to their hall.

This question the master refused to put, as being matter not proper for their consideration. On which one *Marriot* moved that it was the opinion of that court that the master had behaved indecently in not putting that question, which motion being seconded by one of his party, was carried without being put by the master. And it was the object of the application for a *mandamus* to have this [5:348] resolution entered in the company's books.

The rule was opposed by *Law*, *Garrow*, and *Luders*, and supported by *Erskine*, *Gibbs* and *Marriot*. The constitution of the Company was a good deal discussed, and the counsel for the rule relied on the determination in the Coventry case as an authority to show that if the presiding officer would not put a question properly proposed, any other member might, where, as was said, Lord KENYON had ruled at Guildhall that an alderman might put the question, the mayor refusing. As to this, Lord KENYON asked if there was any other case than that, as he did not think it was to be taken for granted that in every case any person might put the question, if the presiding officer refused. And took notice of the directions of the Tiverton Act[17] in respect of presiding officers.

After the matter had been much discussed, Lord KENYON said, a *mandamus* is not a writ of right to which a man is entitled on paying his money, but the application for it is to the sound discretion of the court. If it were necessary to discuss the great question which had been made respecting the said company, I should desire further information and should wish to examine all the charters [5:349] and see if by moulding them all together, one consistent exposition can be got from the whole text of them all, always remembering that the charter of Queen Anne is to be the governing charter where it differs from the others.

Nor shall I go into the question whether any person may put the question if the presiding officer does not. That point was not meant to be decided in the Coventry case. Great inconveniences exist on both sides and it is a matter not to be decided, '*stampede in uno*'.

In this case it has not been made [to] appear to us, that any application has been made to the mayor for the books. Before this court will, by *mandamus*, compel a thing to be done, the parties should be applied to for that purpose. And this is not merely matter of form. It saves great expense. Besides here, the application is to make a man enter a libel on himself. It is true the court might

---

[17] 11 Geo. I, c. 4, s. 1.

narrow the *mandamus* and not make that a part of it, but considering the spirit in which this motion has been made, we ought not to do it.

GROSE and LAWRENCE, Justices, same opinion, on the ground of the application being to order a libel.[18]

---

[18] A report of this case in *The Times*, 1 January 1796, gives a fuller version of the arguments of counsel than appears in Lawrence's notes. The report in *The Times* was as follows:

Mr Gibbs had, in a former term, obtained a rule to shew cause why a Mandamus should not be directed to the Master of the Armourers and Braziers company, commanding him to deliver over a book to the Clerk of the Company, that the Clerk might enter in that book certain resolutions.

The real question in this case was, whether the Court of Livery had controlling power over the Court of Assistants.

That question originated in this:—When the Company were about to repair their Common Hall, the Court of the Livery asked the Court of Assistants to shew them the Surveyor's estimate of the expence. The Court of Assistants replied, that they had no objection to shew them that estimate as a favour, but that they were not bound to do it, and that the Livery had no right to ask it, inasmuch as the rule and government of the private domestic economy of the Company belonged exclusively to the Court of Assistants. This was denied by the Livery, and the Master was desired to put the question upon it. Another member put the question, which was seconded, and several resolutions passed, some of which were extremely improper; and it was for the purpose of recording these resolutions, that this Mandamus was sought.

Mr LAW, Mr GARROW, and Mr LUDERS, shewed cause against the rule.

It was observed, that this was a question of immense importance to the tranquility of the City of London, inasmuch as every Livery Company in the City, except the Ironmongers Company, stood precisely in the same situation with the Armourer and Braziers Company.

The original charter of this Company was granted by Henry VI in the year 1450. Queen Elizabeth confirmed that charter. James I. granted them another charter; and the last charter they had received, was from Queen Anne.

It was contended, that by these different charters, the Court of Assistants, composed of the Master, two Wardens, and 18 Assistants, had the power of entering into contracts, for the purpose of repairing or re-building their Common Hall. The same Select Body had also the power of letting their lands, managing their estates, and disposing of their revenues.

The Court of Livery, consisting of the Master, Wardens, Assistants, and 62 Liverymen, had the power of making bye-laws for regulating the trade of the Company. The Court of Assistants had exercised these powers for upwards of three hundred years, without the smallest interruption from the Court of Livery. The private domestic economy of the Company had been directed by the Court of Assistants, without the smallest pretence that the Court of the Livery had any right at all to interfere till the year 1785; and this custom was not only reasonable in itself, but was conformable, as before observed, with one exception, to every other Livery Company in the City.

It was farther observed, that this application to the Court was only a speculation on the theory of Government, a mere attempt to convert this company into a Fraternization Club.

Mr ERSKINE, Mr GIBBS, and Mr MARRYAT, were heard in support of the Rule, and they contended that according to the just construction of the Charters, the Court of Assistants had only a right to *handle, confer, consult, and advise of statutes, ordinances, &c.* They were only to be considered as a previous Council to prepare matters for the Court of the Livery, and it was contended that a majority of the Livery was necessary for carrying any measure legally into execution.

The Court discharged the Rule.

The LORD CHIEF JUSTICE observed, that one of the resolutions which those who made this application to the Court wished the master to insert in their books was, that his own conduct had been highly improper and indecent. Could they compel the Clerk to make an entry to extremely indecent, to further no purpose of public justice upon earth, but merely to record a libel? Was there such an application ever heard of before in a Court of Justice?

[5:350] November 21   ALEXANDER v. LEDWICK

[M.H.] Bill filed in vacation against an attorney as of the preceding term, the memorandum of the issue or Paper Book may be specially made of the day the bill was in fact filed.

Defendant, who was an attorney, was sued as the acceptor of a bill of exchange which, becoming due in the long vacation, was sued by bill, which being filed in the vacation was entitled as of the preceding term. To this declaration, he demurred, assigning for cause that the cause of action arose subsequent to the filing of the bill, and now proved that the Paper Book should be made agreeable to the memorandum of the bill. It having been made up specially stating the day of filing the bill as pointed out in the case of *Dodsworth v. Bowen*, 5 T.R. 325 [1793].

The court discharged the rule with costs.

Wood for plaintiff.

Henderson for defendant.

SPILLER v. WILLIAMS

[M.H.] If plaintiff consents to a writ of execution lying in the sheriff's office, it shall be postponed to subsequent executions coming in before any levy under it.

The plaintiff having sued out a writ of *fi. fa.* against the defendant consented to let it lie in the sheriff's office in hopes the defendant will be able to settle without an actual levy. After which a 2nd writ of execution at the suit of another creditor was delivered to the sheriff, on which the sheriff levied.

Gibbs, for the plaintiff, moved that the sheriff should return the first writ, &c., contending that as no fraud was intended, his client had a priority.

Lord KENYON: I think if a creditor gives this indulgence, he gives it subject it to the executions of other creditors.

[5:351]   R. v. LUCK

Defendant was convicted of obstructing an excise officer.

He was imprisoned six months in Newgate and ordered to find sureties for his good behaviour, himself in £50 and two sureties in £20 each for three years.

MOFFAT v. HARGRAVES and CHAMBERS

[M.H.] An agreement to take above five per cent is usurious, though the parties had no design to recover above legal interest. *Vide* same case, *antea* 337.

This is a motion for a new trial of an issue tried before Lord KENYON at Guildhall to decide whether a bond given to Hargraves was in pursuance of an usurious agreement. A verdict was found for the plaintiff.

The facts of the case were the following: A. J. Nunez and one Thorne, who was the son-in-law of Hargraves, applied to him to lend them a sum of £600, but he not having the whole money, Thorne agreed to take two notes, which had some time to run, as part of the money. Nunez gave directions to an attorney to prepare a bond for the whole sum to be lent and the notes, amounting together to [£]616 with legal interest. According to those directions, a bond was drawn and when it came to be executed on the 16th May 1794, Hargraves could produce in cash only:

	£250 [plus]
One note payable 31 March 1795	159
And one other payable 1 December 1794 for	157
	£566

On this it was proposed that the bond should be allowed, but as Hargraves was likely to advance the money soon, it was argued not to be worthwhile, and Nunez and Thorne executed a bond dated the 16th of May 1794 for £616 for the repayment of the sum with legal interest for the same from the date of the bond. The £50 was paid them the 17th of July 1794. The witnesses all swore that there was no intention of taking more than legal interest, which Lord KENYON stated to have been the case.

[5:352] Mr *Gibbs* and Mr *Marriot* for the new trial contended that this exoneration of usurious interest must be a mistake, and if that were so the issue should have been found for the defendants, and in support of what they contended, they cited *Nevison* v. *Whitby*, Sir William Jones 396 [1637]; Cro. Car. 501, same case; 2 Ventr. 83;[19] Cro. Car. 678;[20] *Ballard* v. *Godby*, 2 Mod. 307;[21] *Booth* v. *Cook*, 1 Freeman 264 [1679]; *Murray* v. *Harding*, 2 Blackstone 864 [1773][22].

Lord KENYON said he agreed with the cases cited, and if it appeared to have been the error of the scrivener, he should have directed the jury to find for the defendant. That he believed that the parties would not have done what they did had they known the consequences. That the agreement was that the bills were to be received as part of the money lent, which being so, whether this amounted to usury or not did not depend on what the parties intended. The law gave to such transactions its denomination. The parties need not be asked, for the volume of the law told him what it was. That he was very sorry to say that the verdict the jury gave was the only verdict they could give.

ASHHURST, Justice, said it would be very mischievous if the parties not conceiving that they were making an usurious bargain could make it not so.

From S. LAWRENCE, Justice, same opinion.

Rule discharged.

---

[19] *Bush* v. *Buckingham* (1689).
[20] The citation should have been to Cro. Jac. 678, *Buckley* v. *Guildbank* (1623).
[21] Styled *Ballard* v. *Oddey* in the printed report.
[22] William Blackstone's reports.

[5:353] HARRIS, *qui tam* v. WOOLFORD

[M.H.] Query if in an action on the Lottery Act, it be necessary to produce an affidavit of the cause of action to prove the regular commencement of the suit.

This was an action on the statute against the defendant for selling goods by lottery.

The plaintiff having proved the facts stated in the declaration produced two writs—the first a *latitat* tested the 13th July Geo. III, returnable on Monday next after the morrow of All Souls; the other an *alias* tested the 28th November 32 Geo. III, returnable on Monday next after the octave of St Hilary.

The memorandum of the declaration was of Hilary term 1795.

It was objected for the defendant that the writ should have specified the cause of action and 4 T.R. 349[23] was relied on. It was also objected that no continuances of the writs appeared.

THOMPSON, Baron, before whom this cause was tried at Oxford, on their objections allowed the plaintiff to move to enter a nonsuit.

Plumer now shewed cause against the rule for a nonsuit.

And in answer to the want of continuances cited *Bates qui tam* v. *Jenkinson*, Easter 24 Geo. III—4 vol. MSS. Cases 349, E 162.[24]

---

[23] *R., qui tam* v. *Horne* (1791).

[24] For Lord Mansfield's notes of three *qui tam* actions brought by Bates against Jenkinson for debt on the Lottery Act, resulting in three verdicts of £500 each, see Oldham, *MMSS*, i. 587–589. *Bates* v. *Jenkinson* is entered at (1784) 3 Doug. 387 with no case report, only cross-references to the description of the case by Lord Kenyon in *Harris* v. *Woolford* and to *Tidd's Practice*. Volumes 3 and 4 of *Douglas's Reports*, however, were not printed until 1831. Evidently after Plumer cited the case and the regnal year, Lawrence added the reference to notes of the case in volume 4 of his own manuscript notebooks, *Cases in King's Bench 23 & 24 Geo. 3*, Middle Temple Library, London, MS. 49. Those notes (vol. 4 at 348–352) are in a neat hand, explained by Lawrence as 'notes copied from Mr Burrow's book'. Very likely the note-taker was Robert Burrow of the Inner Temple, Sir James Burrow's nephew, who was assigned his uncle's chamber after Sir James's death. See *A Calendar of the Inner Temple Records*, R. A. Roberts, ed. (1836), pp. 434–435. Burrow's notes of the *Bates* case are as follows:

Bates *qui tam* v. Jenkinson

This was a qui tam action on the Lottery Act of 1782. The cause of action occurred in December 1782 during the drawing of the Lottery.

Verdict for plaintiff.

Motion for new trial, on the ground of the action not having been commenced within the year under the Statute of Elizabeth. [31 Eliz. c. 5, s. 5 ('Within what Times Suits upon Penal Statutes shall be pursued'.]

At the trial to show the suit was commenced, a *latitat* into London was produced, tested 23rd July 1782, returnable in the term of which tested. This writ was never served. Another writ was produced of a subsequent term (more than a whole term intervening between the *teste* of the 2nd and the return of the 1st). The 2nd was a *latitat* into Surrey and did not appear to be any continuance of the former.

The objection was that the first writ was done away from want of continuance and is too late, and under the Statute of Elizabeth, the action is not maintainable. [Margin note: '*Kinsey* v. *Heyward* 1 Ld. Ray^d 432'.]

On showing cause, it was contended that by the production of the first writ, it appeared the action was brought in time. The first writ was within the year, and previous to the 25 July.

At *nisi prius* it was only necessary to produce the writ. The objection can only be taken on the record. If not regularly made up—if it had been pleaded that the action was not brought within

And as to the other objection insisted that it was not proper at *nisi prius*, and was only a ground to say proceedings.

Leycester, in support of the rule, stated the words of the 27 Geo. III, which in actions for offences against the Lottery Acts require the cause of action to be expressed in the writ—and then urged that the action could not be proved to have been commenced [*5:354*] within six months without producing such writ and affidavit as that statute required. He also mentioned *Goodwin* v. *Parry*, 4 T.R. 577 [1792], in addition to *R.*, *qui tam* v. *Horne*, ibid., 349 [1791], mentioned at the trial.

As to the other point, he cited 2 Lord Raymond 880[25] and 2 T.R. 112[26] to show the writ should be returned.

Higby on the same side mentioned 4 T.R. 577.

Lord KENYON said he did not know to what lengths this would go. Suppose a man were held to bail and there was no *ac etiam* and the Statute of Limitations were pleaded, would it be a good rejoinder to a replication of a *latitat* that there was no *ac etiam*? It is only irregularity in process. In a case

---

the year—plaintiff must have replied [to] the first writ, and then the roll would have been regularly made up down to the 2nd writ.

Lord Mansfield: Continuances are matters of form and matters of record. Writs are never continued on the *nisi prius* roll. I never knew an instance of it. If the party has a right to make up his record with a continuance, he may do it. If the original writ was in time, there is no objection to entering it up.

Mr Justice Ashhurst: The court never grants a new trial when they see it would be nugatory.

It cannot be denied but that it would be competent to the party to enter up the continuances in this case. The entry of them is a thing of course. The *latitat* issued stating a bill of Middlesex. That is conclusive evidence that such writ issued.

The record now made up is regular. It states a bill of Middlesex and *latitat* into London and continuances. The suggestion [is] that the defendant is in Surrey and the *latitat* into Surrey. Every *latitat* is a *testatum* bill of Middlesex.

Mr Justice Buller: The case is somewhat new. There have been two records made up here. The last record shall go on as most consistent with the facts. I don't mean to say the party ought not to sue out a bill of Middlesex if it makes a difference in point of time. But in motions for new trials I take it to be a general rule (except in cases of surprise) never to go a step beyond what happened at the trial.

The defendant first says the action is not in time. The declaration is of a term after the year, upon which the plaintiff produces a *latitat* into London. The defendant says here is the *nisi prius* record [in the margin: 'Query'] which shows that they have been made.

The question is whether these two writs can or cannot be continued. Mr Runnington says the suing out the *latitat* into Surrey was an abandonment of the *latitat* into London. But you cannot sue out an *alias latitat* into another county. But the first writ into a county must be what we call an original *latitat* in opposition to an *alias*. It is admitting that the first was in time. The suggestion on the roll is for suing the writ into Surrey—that defendant is got there—and that plaintiff cannot serve him in London. This shows that it is for the same cause of action. It is not always necessary in this court to sue out the bill of Middlesex. The practice has been to plead the *latitat*. In the case of the Statute of Limitations we rely [on] the suing of the *latitat* and say nothing of the bill of Middlesex. Mr Wood says if the present practice is allowed the party may keep it in his pocket. It is not so, for the writ must be returned. And it may be a question where a man wants to avail himself of an old writ of a year's standing or more, he shall not show it to be returned and filed.

Rule discharged.

[25] *Brown* v. *Babbington* (1703).
[26] *Worley* v. *Lee* (1787).

from Cricklade, *Petrie v. White*, 3 T.R. 5, we stayed the proceedings after trial at *nisi prius*.

Take a rule to show cause why the proceeding should not be stayed.

[M.N.] In Easter term the court were of opinion that the plaintiff should be nonsuited as the first writ was never returned.[27]

November 24   R. v. CUTCLIFFE

[M.H.] Information in the nature of *quo warranto* not to be filed *de bene esse*.

Erskine shewed cause against a rule to enlarge a rule for showing cause against an information on *quo warranto* till next term, as the Statute of Limitations would run—and proposed the Information should be filed *de bene esse*, and taken off if the court should think the ground not sufficient. This Lord KENYON thought improper, and though the time for the defendant answering the affidavits was very short, refused to enlarge the rule, as that would present the possibility of discussing the question.

[5:355]
November 25   DOE v. DAVIS

[M.H.] An encroachment by a tenant can't be claimed by his landlord.

Defendant being lessee of some ground adjoining to a wash, by degrees extended his fence so as to take in part of the wash, and his lease being expired, his landlord, Mr Vaughan, brought an ejectment for the land so taken and recovered. A new trial was now moved for.

Lord KENYON said: did this act of the tenant make the landlord a trespasser? Whatever a villain acquired, he acquired for his lord, but a tenant who trespasses acts for himself only. If he steals, he must suffer.

                                                              Rule absolute.[28]

[*Lawrence note*:] From the Oxford circuit.

---

[27] Lord Kenyon's opinion was delivered on 22 April 1796 and is fully reported at 6 T.R. 617. He relied on opinions by Chief Justice Holt in *Atword v. Burr*, 7 Mod. 3 and *Brown v. Babbington*, 2 Ld. Raym. 883, distinguishing the opinion by Lord Mansfield in *Bates, qui tam v. Jenkinson*, Easter, 24 Geo. III, 6 T.R., at 618–619.

[28] The trial of this trespass action is reported at 1 Esp. 358, Trinity Term 1795. The jury verdict was for the plaintiff with one shilling damages. Mingay, for the defendant, cautioned the jury that if they gave even one shilling damages, their verdict would carry full costs for the plaintiff. Lord Kenyon, however, interrupted to say that in trespass actions, the verdict must be above 40 shillings to carry full costs. (See *Tidd's Practice*, 8th ed. (1828), at p. 998). Consequently, the master of the Court of King's Bench afterward taxed costs at only one shilling. This was challenged before the full Court of King's Bench, as reported at 6 T.R. 593, 12 February 1796, but without success.

November 26   R. v. THE COMMISSIONERS OF THE
              COURT OF REQUESTS OF THE TOWER HAMLETS

[M.H.] Where a certain number are to decide, they must all hear the complaint and can't act on a report of a part, who may have inquired into the business.

Mingay shewed cause against a rule for a *mandamus* to restore one Heretson to the office of beadle of the court, from which he had been dismissed. In order to dismiss for ill behaviour, it was necessary that sixty commissioners should be present.

In this case, thirty-three heard the complaint and then reported what had passed to a court consisting of above sixty commissioners, who dismissed Heretson from his office.

Lord KENYON: This won't do. The persons who decide must hear. It is so in orders of removal. Both justices must be present.

Rule absolute.

[5:356]   WILKINSON v. BROWN

[M.H.] Judgment against a prisoner in custody of the sheriff regular, though no demand of a plea.

The court on the authority of a case of *Brown* v. *Christfield*,[28a] and understanding the practice of the Common Pleas to be so, held a judgment against a prisoner to be regular, he being in the custody of the sheriff, though there was no demand of a plea.

Rule discharged.

R. v. YORKE

[M.N.] As to the power of the King's Bench to commit to any prison, vide 2 Hawk., c. 3, sec. 5.

Defendant had been convicted at the assizes at York for sedition in assembling a great number of people at Sheffield under a pretence of a petition to parliament, and there making a speech tending to incite them to acts of treason.

He had been in prison above twelve months, which the court, having taken into consideration, adjudged him to be imprisoned two years in Dorchester gaol, to pay a fine of £200 and to give security for his good behaviour, himself in £1,000 and two sureties in £250 each for seven years.[29]

[28a] The correct reference should be to *Rose* v. *Christfield* (1781) 1 T.R. 591.

[29] Attorney-General Scott represented the prosecution; Erskine the defendant. The indictment was tried before Mr Justice Rooke at the summer assizes for York. *The Times*, 19 November 1795. Mr Justice Ashhurst's speech in pronouncing the sentence was reported at length in *The Times* on 28 December 1795. According to Ashhurst, defendant Henry Yorke, also known as Henry Redhead, incited a crowd of about 4,000 on Castle Hill with treasonous speeches about elections to and representation in parliament. Among the propositions advocated by Yorke was that members of parliament should be elected by the entire adult population. Ashhurst said that this

[*Lawrence note*:] Subsequent to his conviction, he published his trial with a preface confessing the impropriety of his conduct, &c.[30]

[5:357]   MAY v. SHAFTOE

[M.H.] If a juror is withdrawn, a verdict can't be entered for the money which may awarded by the referee.

Cleaver shewed cause against a rule to enter up a verdict [of] a judgment for a sum of money awarded, which *Barrow* had moved to do, as the defendant had become insane, on which account no writ of attachment could be obtained against him. *Cleaver* insisted that no verdict could be entered up, as a juror had been withdrawn, to which the court agreed, though the arbitrator had directed a verdict to be entered for the sum he awarded.

Rule discharged.

R. v. CROSSLEY[31]

[M.H.] A prisoner in custody on a criminal charge can't remove himself to another gaol by a *habeas corpus*.

Erskine moved for a *habeas corpus* to bring up the defendant, who was in custody in Hereford gaol on a charge of forgery, and that he might be committed to Newgate on an affidavit that he was never in Hereford until he was carried there by the warrant on which he was apprehended, and on the copies of the depositions taken against him.

Lord KENYON said the application was new, that he never heard of an application by a prisoner so committed to remove himself from one gaol to another, that he must wait the event of the gaol delivery. That the bearing of a new case was not always seen, and though he did not immediately see the inconvenience, he was afraid of making a precedent.

GROSE J. said he did not understand the magistrate's granting copies of the depositions.

Rule refused.

---

had been argued and rejected 350 years previously in the reign of Henry VI, and he pointed out how absurd a concept it was in his own time, when the population of the country had increased tenfold—'if the system of universal suffrage were to be adopted, Parliament would be filled with none but the leaders of faction, and sober men would not dare to give their suffrage, but at the peril of their lives'. Yet 'you, Henry Yorke, are rash enough to call out in the most insolent and daring manner, that the people ought to demand Universal Representation as a right'—'O, daring licentiousness of the present times, beyond the example of former ages!'

[30] See *The Trial of Henry Yorke, For a Conspiracy, &c. Before the Hon. Mr Justice Rooke, at the Assizes, Held for the County of York, on Saturday, July 10, 1795* (published by the defendant). Yorke's sixteen-page introduction strives more to justify his actions than to confess impropriety. At the end, however, he states that he had learned 'that useful lesson, so difficult to be acquired in calamitous times, that *moderation is the best policy*'. Ibid., at xxiv (emphasis in the original). See also the report of this case at 20 S.T. 1003.

[31] For reports of further proceedings against Crossley, see pp. 148 and 158 below.

[5:358] ANONYMOUS[32]

[M.H.] What costs an arbitrator may give.

Per Lord KENYON, if costs generally are in the discretion of an arbitrator, he may give costs out of pocket. *Aliter* if he is confined to costs in the cause.

HILARY TERM, 36 Geo. III

Lloyd, Lord Kenyon, Chief Justice
Sir W. H. Ashhurst ⎫
Sir N. Grose   ⎬ Justices
Sir S. Lawrence   ⎭

R. v. HOOPER and ELLISON

The defendants having been convicted of a fraud on the Excise to the amount of £1,600 by using false keys to the locks put upon their stills while they were at work in distilling spirits, in consideration of their having satisfied to the government the sums of which it was defrauded and having lain in gaol several months, were discharged on paying a fine of 6s.8d.

February 1st 1796   R. v. ENGLAND

The defendant, having been outlawed for the murder of P. L. Rolles, was brought to the bar and being called on to say why execution should not be awarded against him produced a writ of error, and *in propria persona* assigned errors. The attorney-general on this delivered into court a joinder in error. *Vide antea*, 344.[33]

R. v. LUI

The defendant being indicted for a conspiracy to prevent administration being granted to one Silva of the effects of one _____ [*sic*], deceased, was bailed, himself in £400, and two sureties £200 each.

BURNETT v. KENSINGTON

[M.H.] A ship runs on shore and afterwards was repaired and reaches its destination. Query if this be a stranding within the usual memorandum in a policy of assurance.

On a motion for new trial in an action on a policy of assurance, the question was if a ship was stranded. The facts were, the ship struck on a rock underwater

---

[32] Lawrence's notes do not indicate that Lord Kenyon's statement about costs in an arbitration proceeding were attached to a specific lawsuit, but presumably there was such a case.
[33] For the outcome, see p. 92, n. 11, above.

between the land's end and Scilly[34] and was run ashore on a sandy beach to prevent her sinking. The cargo was taken out, much damaged, and [5:359] the ship was afterwards repaired and arrived at Portsmouth.

The jury said they thought this no stranding, as the ship had performed her voyage. That stranding was when a vessel was so bulged by taking the ground as to be incapable of finishing her voyage.

Gibbs in support of the new trial relied on what is said in *Nesbitt* v. *Lushington*, 4 T.R. 783.

Erskine, *contra*, insisted on the mischief that would arise to the underwriters if it should be in the power of the captain to make them liable for particular average by putting the ship ashore. And said that they were only liable where the commodities, in consequence of the vessel being bulged and unable to perform the voyage, were sent by some other ship.

The court, as it was a question of great extent, directed a new trial, and Lord KENYON said that when they had learnt the meaning of the words they would decide on the construction of the policy.

On a new trial, the jury found for the plaintiff, saying that they were of opinion that they ought to recover, as what had happened to the ship was attended with all the consequences of stranding. And on a motion for new trial, as the jury had not found directly that the ship was stranded, a 3rd trial was directed in Easter term. [35]

R. v. ISAAC and JACOB

[M.H.] The defendants may be committed by a defective warrant, yet they shall not be discharged without bail, if they have given notice for that purpose.

The defendants having been committed to the county gaol of Hants[36] for uttering counterfeit money to one brought up by *habeas corpus*, gave notice to the prosecutor that they should apply to be discharged, and if the court thought it not proper to discharge them, that they might be permitted to put in bail. The objections to their commitment were that the warrant did not state

---

[34] The Scilly Isles, a group of small islands off the coast of Cornwall.

[35] This case was first tried before Lord Kenyon and a special jury of merchants at Guildhall on 18 December 1795, as reported in *The Times*, 21 December 1795, also at (1795) 1 Esp. 416 and (1795) Peake's Additional Cases 71. As is shown in Lawrence's notes (excepting the last paragraph), a second trial was ordered, which was held on 4 March 1796 (see *The Times*, 5 and 28 March 1796). The last paragraph of Lawrence's notes was a postscript, and as indicated, a third trial was ordered. The rule to show cause for the third trial was granted on 11 April (see *The Times*, 16 and 28 April). The third trial was conducted by Lord Kenyon and a special jury at the Guildhall sittings after Trinity term, on 5 July. *The Times*, 6 July 1796. On 11 November, a show cause rule for a fourth trial was granted, which was conducted by Mr Justice Lawrence and a special jury at the Guildhall sittings after Michaelmas term 1796. At the fourth trial, a special case was reserved for argument, subsequently heard by the full Court of King's Bench on 12 May 1797, as reported in *The Times*, 13 May, and at (1797) 7 T.R. 210. See the Introduction, above, p. lii, for a discussion of this case.

[36] I.e., Hampshire.

[37] In the margin; 'Query if necessary, vide 1 Str. 2.' The reference is to the case of *R.* v.

they had been charged on oath,[37] and did not state to whom the money was [5:360] uttered, nor what sort of money.

Lord KENYON said the warrant was bad, but as the notice might have misled the prosecutor, they could not be discharged without putting in bail. And they gave bail themselves in £100, and two sureties £50 each.

R. v. BOOTH

The defendant was overseer of the poor in a parish in Yorkshire, and was found guilty on an indictment for neglecting a pauper who was brought by him into the workhouse very ill, and for not providing necessary clothes and bedding, and suffering her to lie on the floor till she died.

The court sentenced him to twelve months imprisonment in Newgate.

R. v. SHERIFF of ESSEX

[M.H.] If rule to bring in the body expires in a vacation, the sheriff has the whole of the first day of term to perfect bail.

The defendant having been called on by a rule of the 26th November to bring in the body on the first day of this term, the plaintiff obtained an attachment against him, which the master reported to be irregular, as the sheriff had the whole of the day to perfect his bail.

CLARKE v. CLEMENT *et al.*

[M.H.] If one of two defendants is discharged out of custody on a promise to return, neither of them can afterwards be taken in execution.

Shepherd shewed cause against a rule to discharge the defendant Clement out of execution and to enter satisfaction on the record.

Clement and English gave a warrant of attorney to enter up a judgment jointly against both. A joint writ issued against both, and English was taken in execution, and upon payment of seven guineas, part of the debt, was permitted to go at large on a promise to return into custody if the remainder was not paid by a certain time. This he afterwards refused to do. And on a subsequent writ of execution, Clement was taken in execution.

Dampier in support of his rule insisted that after the discharge of English, notwithstanding his promise to return, no execution could be taken against either of the defendants, and cited Barnes 205,[38] *Vigors* v. *Aldrich*, 4 Burr. 2482,

---

Wyndham (1716) 1 Str. 2, a case in which the Court of King's Bench discussed and acted upon its discretionary power to bail the defendant, Sir William Wyndham, who had been committed by the secretary of state for high treason. One of the exceptions taken to the court's discretionary power was that the charge was said not to be upon oath. The court thought that the fact that the charge was not said to be under oath was not conclusive that it was not in fact upon oath.

[38] *Thompson* v. *Bristow* (1742) Barnes 205.

Jaques v. *Withy* 1 T.R. 577.[39] On the authority of these cases, the court made the rule absolute without costs.[40]

[*5:361*]   R. v. WILLIAM CURTIS

Defendant having been found guilty of a libel on Mr Preston, the recorder of Lynn, charging him with injustice and partiality in his office of recorder, the court adjudged him to be imprisoned three months in the King's Bench, and to find sureties for his good behaviour, himself in £500 and two sureties in £100 each for seven years.[41]

[*Lawrence note*:] N.B., he had been committed to Newgate in the last term.

SCHINOTTI v. BUMSTED *et al.*[42]

[M.H.] Inspection of books of the lottery directed.

A rule was made on the defendants, commissioners of the lottery, to suffer the plaintiff to inspect their books in order to enable him to show he was entitled to a prize as the holder of the last drawn ticket.

---

[39] The correct citation for *Jaques* v. *Withy* is (1787) 1 T.R. 557.

[40] This case is reported at (27 January 1796) 6 T.R. 525. The plaintiff in this action was tangled in his own net. Having initially taken both defendants (Clement and English) on a joint *capias ad satisfaciendum*, and having afterward released English on his promise to pay the debt by a certain date or return to custody, the plaintiff could not then proceed against Clement or English individually.

[41] The defendant was brought up for judgment on 12 February, represented *in absentia* by Erskine, who pleaded for mercy. The defendant, Erskine said, was a family man with numerous dependents who 'had seen better days' but was ready to make (through his counsel) any apology required. Mr Justice Ashhurst in pronouncing judgment said that 'the defendant had been found guilty of publishing a very gross and scandalous libel, accusing the prosecutor of partiality and injustice as a Magistrate', and he had in 'mockery of an apology' published a second libel 'far more atrocious than the first'. *The Times*, 13 February 1796.

[42] Subsequent proceedings in this case were reported at 6 T.R. 646 (28 April 1796). The commissioners had awarded the prize to ticket No. 31,000 after concluding that it was the last-drawn ticket, even though no one had produced it. It was suggested that ticket No. 32,000 remained in the wheel, but after a strict search it was not found. According to *The Times*, 4 March 1796, the following facts were admitted by the parties when the case was tried before Lord Kenyon and a special jury of merchants on 3 March: 'That the plaintiff was possessed of the ticket No. 5278 at the conclusion of the drawing, and that the defendants were the Commissioners of the Lottery. That the plaintiff's ticket was the last numerical ticket drawn out of the wheel, and that upon searching the wheel afterwards, no other numerical ticket was found; but there was *one blank* found in the other wheel' (emphasis in the original). Erskine argued that the plaintiff was entitled to a prize of £1,000, whereas Attorney-General Scott contended for the defendants that 'the Commissioners under the Act of Parliament were called upon to decide, and that in point of law their determination could not be questioned'. As instructed by Lord Kenyon, the jury returned a verdict for the plaintiff for £1,000, subject to the opinion of the Court of King's Bench. On 28 April, the case was argued by Erskine for the plaintiff and by Law and Wood for the defendants, as reported, 6 T.R. 646. Lord Kenyon said that, 'as the plaintiff's ticket was the last drawn, he is entitled to the prize; the only competitor with him was the owner of a ticket which was never drawn, and that person has no claim to it whatever'. The court confirmed the verdict, after concluding that the defendants, as commissioners of the lottery, were mere ministerial officers. See also the report in *The Times*, 29 April 1796.

MANUSCRIPTS OF SIR SOULDEN LAWRENCE
MIDDLE TEMPLE LIBRARY MS. 49

PART II
VOLUME 6

CASES IN THE KING'S BENCH, 17–40 GEO. III[43]

---

[43] Despite Lawrence's label on the spine of volume 6 ('Cases in the King's Bench, 17–40 Geo. 3'), the first case was decided in the House of Lords; the second by the twelve common law judges collectively; the third by the ecclesiastical Court of Delegates. Subsequent cases were heard by the King's Bench.

[Editor's introductory note to *Troward* v. *Calland*

This case was first tried in the Court of Common Pleas, after which it was taken to the King's Bench and the House of Lords on writs of error. All three stages of the case were reported.[44] The Common Pleas opinion delivered by Chief Justice Eyre on 9 July 1794 was summarized in Henry Blackstone's reports as follows: 'The royal prerogative of presenting to a church vacant by the incumbent being promoted to a bishoprick, does not destroy the effect of a prior grant of the next presentation by the owner of the advowsons.'[45] The writ of error from the Common Pleas to the King's Bench recited the jury verdict for the plaintiff, damages of £7,980 and 40 shillings costs,[46] and stated that if the plaintiff ultimately prevailed, and the damages and costs (plus interest) were paid, the plaintiff would reconvey to the defendant the advowson that had been in dispute.[47] Brown's report of the case in the House of Lords quotes the plaintiff's declaration in full, to which the defendant demurred, then presents the arguments for reversing, as given in the printed case for the defendant (counsel John Scott, Thomas Erskine, and John Fonblanque), also the reasons given by the plaintiff's counsel (Edward Law and George Holroyd) for affirming. The report concludes by stating the question that was put to the Law Lords ('Whether the grant to Matthew Kenrick set forth on the record is defeated by the vacancy which has happened by promotion since the grant, which has been filled by the King's prerogative'), and the outcome ('Whereupon, the Lord Chief Justice of the Court of Exchequer delivered the unanimous opinion of the Judges present upon the said question in the negative'). Lawrence's notes of the case in the House of Lords, by contrast, give a narrative summary of the verbal arguments by counsel for the defendant, plus the opinion by the lord chancellor and the judges that the case for the plaintiff-in-error (the defendant at trial) was unpersuasive, so that there was no need to hear from counsel for the defendant-in-error (the plaintiff at trial).

Soulden Lawrence was a justice of the Common Pleas when the demurrer was argued on 14 May 1794. He transferred to King's Bench on 19 June 1794, and on that day, the writ of error in *Calland* v. *Troward* was argued. In deference to counsel for the plaintiff-in-error, a second argument was scheduled for 13 November 1795, but when the case was called, 'his counsel [Erskine] intimated that no farther argument was intended here; and the Court unanimously confirmed the judgment of the Common Pleas'.[48]

Lawrence's Paper Books for both phases of the case are among the Dampier manuscripts at Lincoln's Inn.[49] Lawrence's notes of the arguments of counsel and the opinions of the judges correspond to Henry Blackstone's full report of

---

[44] See *Calland* v. *Troward* (1794) 2 Bl. H. 324; *Troward* v. *Cailland* [sic] (1795) 6 T.R. 439; *Troward* v. *Calland* (1796) 8 Brown P.C. 71.
[45] 2 Bl. H. 324.
[46] Compare £8,059, p. 115, below.
[47] See Bro. P.C. at 76.
[48] 6 T.R. at 441.
[49] Dampier MSS., LPB 72, Lincoln's Inn Library.

the case in the Common Pleas. Lawrence's Paper Book for the writ of error in the King's Bench, however, contains an opinion that he never delivered, at the end of which he wrote: 'I had intended on the 2nd argument to have given my opinion *ut supra* unless the case had been put upon other grounds, but on the 13th November 1795 when this case was to have been argued a 2nd time, Mr Erskine informed the court that the plaintiff-in-error did not mean to trouble the court—from whence it was collected that it was intended to bring error in Dom. Proc.' Lawrence noted that Lord Kenyon then said that the judgment of the Court of Common Pleas must be affirmed, 'and said but little, as he admitted that by the not going into it a 2nd time the case was not so recalled to his memory as to enable him to give the reasons for his judgment so fully as he should have done'.

Mr Justice Lawrence's undelivered opinion was as follows:

> The true point for the court to consider is what was the intent of Sir K. C. [Kenrick Clayton]. If that can be ascertained, the court will put such construction on this deed as will effectuate his intention, if the law permits.
>
> Two different things might be in the contemplation of the grantor, either to give Mr Kenrick the right of presenting at the next vacancy, provided he himself should have that right to exercise, or he might give it to be exercised whenever Sir K. Clayton might first be entitled to exercise it himself.
>
> For plaintiff in error, it is insisted that as this is a grant of the next presentation, it will not entitle the grantee to present after the present incumbency, as that will at best be the 2nd presentation and not the *next*.
>
> This may be true in some sense, but still the question remains, what is the next presentation, in the sense in which it is used in this grant? For if the grantor intended to convey his right to present, when he next should be able to exercise it, a presentment by the Crown on the promotion of the incumbent is not the next presentation intended by this deed.
>
> What then is the meaning of the word next is a matter of uncertainty—and if the words of the deed are sufficient to effect either of these intents, and I think they are full as well adapted to the claim of the defendant in error as of the plaintiff [in error]—and no other rule of construction will remove the doubt, that case of ambiguity arises, which falls within the rule of construction that *verba fortius accipiuntur contra proferentem*.
>
> The expression here used is 'To hold the next presentation to present a fit person as fully and freely as Sir K. Clayton might have done if the deed had not been made.'
>
> Now what is there to confine this to the *next vacancy*?
>
> Had the grant been to hold the said next presentation to present a fit person when the church shall next become void, there would have been words which properly might so have confined it.
>
> Suppose this had been an advowson of which A. & B. had been seized in fee as tenants in common, and that A. had granted the next presentation in the words of this deed—and then a prerogative presentation had taken place. Would not the grantee of the next presentation in such case have been entitled to present?
>
> For A. would have been entitled but for his grant, and against that he could not claim. And B. could not present till A's turn was satisfied.
>
> The operation of the prerogative presentation would be to postpone the turn of

A.'s grantee, just as it would have done A.'s, had he not parted with it. For he would have taken it just as A. had it, and the prerogative presentation would not destroy the grantee's right and revert it in A.

How does this case differ, except that here the grantor is sole seized. But whether one of two past owners separates the next presentation from the larger right of next presentations in endless succession (supposing that to be a true definition) or whether he who is sole seized does it, if the conveyance be in the same words the interest of the grantee must be the same, who will take the thing granted subject to the right of the Crown, which does not supply, but only postpones the right of those who are interested.

One of the arguments of Mr Justice Hutton in the case in Winch is this: 'If the King has the prerogative he (i.e. the grantor) is bound and every derivative title under him, for he (i.e. the grantee) shall not be in a better case than the grantor (this by mistake is printed grantee), for he was bound by the law of the land. And for that it is equity and justice that the estate of the grantee should be bound, and it behooves him to take it as it is bound, with the prerogative of the King.'

Now to apply this reasoning to the present case: it shows that Mr Kenrick took this grant of the next presentation bound as the grantor was by the prerogative. How was he bound? *Viz*: by having his right to present postponed—so far then will his grantee be bound and no further.

Sir K. C. being seized in fee, subject to the right in the Crown, had in him in all events *a* next presentation.

When therefore he granted in general terms *the* next presentation to be exercised as fully as if he had not made the grant, these words must be applied to such presentation as he could certainly exercise, and not be restrained to the next vacancy, for in the construction of grants it is a rule that what is generally spoken shall be generally understood unless qualified by subsequent words. If there is any qualification, it is from this being a grant of *the* next presentation and not of *his* next presentation.

But I do not think that any restriction can be inferred from that form of expression—and that the grant must be construed just as if it had been *his* next presentation.

For the deed must relate to that which Sir K. C. had a power of granting. He had no right to dispose of the interest of the Crown (and if it were his intention that his grantee should not present, unless he could on the next vacancy, still it was his next presentation which the deed conveyed).[50]

If then the grantee has not a right to present when Sir K. C. himself might have exercised the right, it must be because the use of the word *the* next presentation instead of his next presentation must be considered as containing such restriction—and as being a grant of the right upon a condition subsequent, and that the interest granted to Mr K. was liable to be defeated by the contingency which has happened.

But this would, I think, be going much too far.

If then this be considered as a grant of *his* next presentation, the effect of it has been to create an alternate right as far as the two first turns, and the law in such case has been fully settled in the *Case of the Grocers Co*.[51] And if in the case of an alternate right in fee, it would be great injustice, that the prerogative of the Crown should

---

[50] The brackets appear to have been added by Lawrence as an editorial afterthought.
[51] See p. 117, below.

supply the turn of the patron, *a fortiori* it is so, where it would deprive the grantee of the whole fruit of his title.

The authority with which the court has been most pressed is that of *Woodley* v. *the Bishop of Exeter*.

But that was determined where the nature of the right of the Crown on the presentation of an incumbent was doubted by some of the judges, and certainly the nature of it had not been so well considered as it has been since. That authority has been doubted. And the court seem to have considered the right of the Crown as supplying the turn of the patron, and not as suspending it, which it is now settled to do.

But however that may be there is a great difference between that case and this—for the words are very different.

In that case the devise by A. Basset is thus stated in Winch's Entries, 877: *Dedit et legavit primam et proximam advocationem, quae primo et proxime contigeret post mortem ipsius Arthuri.*

Now these words might reasonably be construed as showing that the intention of the devisor was that the devise should present only at the next vacancy—but no such words here.]

16 May 1796   TROWARD v. CALLAND

In Dom. Proc.

[M.H.] If a patron grants the next presentation and the incumbent be made a bishop and the Crown presents, the grantee shall present at the 2nd avoidance. *Vide* 2 H. Blackstone 324, 6 T.R. 439, same case; Paper Book 72 and 4 Printed Cases.

This was a writ of error from a judgment of the Court of King's Bench affirming a judgment of the Court of Common Pleas.

The short state of the case was this: Sir Kenrick Clayton being seized in fee of the advowson of Bletchingley in the County of Surrey on the 30th of May 1745 granted to Matthew Kenrick, Esq. the next presentation, donation, and free disposition of and to the rectory of the said parish church, to hold the next presentation, donation, and free presentation of, &c. to the said Matthew Kenrick, his executors, &c. to present one fit and able person to the said rectory, &c., and all other things which should be necessary to be done about the premises to accomplish as fully, freely and entirely as the said Sir K. Clayton and his heirs might and could do or have done if the said deed poll had not been made.

At this time, John Thomas, clerk, was rector of the rectory who, on the 1st of June 1774 was made bishop of Rochester, upon which Matthew Kenrick, clerk, was instituted and inducted upon the presentation of the Crown.

[6:2] After this, the plaintiff-in-error, having become seized in fee of the advowson, sold the same to the defendant Calland and by indenture of the 26th July 1791 covenanted with him that he, the said Troward, was lawfully, rightfully, and absolutely seized of the said advowson, &c., and the said advowson was free and clear of and from all charges and encumbrances whatsoever.

The defendant-in-error having learnt that this grant of the next presentation had been made by Kenrick Clayton, brought an action of covenant against Troward and stated that grant as a subsisting grant, as a breach of the covenant, and obtained judgment against him in the Common Pleas. Damages and costs were assessed to the amount of £8,059, and judgment given for that sum, the defendant in error obliging himself by rule of court to reconvey the advowson.

Mr *Scott* (the attorney-general) and *Erskine* were counsel for the plaintiff-in-error, and the attorney contended that the true question was, what was intended to be conveyed by the deed of 1745. He stated that the judgment of the King's Bench and Common Pleas had gone on a supposed difference in the construction to be put on the premises in a deed which was voluntary, from that which would be put on them in a deed for valuable consideration. For such distinction, he said there was no authority in any book. That they had proceeded on the ground of the maxim, *quod verba fortius accipiuntur contra proferentem*,[52] which he said had no application to this case, any more than the maxim *quod lex nemini facit injuriam*,[53] which had also been relied on. That the question was whether the grant was not a grant subject to be defeated by the casual contingent right of the Crown, [6:3] and whether the grantee did not take the right of the next presentation, subject to being affected by the interest of the Crown, just as the owner of the fee held the advowson. Or whether the grantor meant to be subject himself to this right of the Crown, but that it was never to affect the grantee.

He then took notice of what EYRE, chief justice of the Common Pleas, says in delivering the judgment of the Common Pleas: 'That grant implies a covenant', which he admitted, but contended that the question still reverted, what was it that the grantor intended to covenant for.

He observed that the chief justice had endeavoured to show that *the* next presentation must be considered as *his* next presentation, and from thence had laid a ground for the judgment of the Common Pleas, but he said so construing the grant, the consequences drawn from it did not follow. For if a man were to grant *his* advowson, it might happen that the grantee might take nothing, as it might happen that the exercise of the right of presentation might be perpetually interrupted by the prerogative of the Crown. And if that be so, he asked what reason there was that the grantee of the next presentation must at all events present.

He said he conceived that the judgment of the King's Bench and Common Pleas had proceeded on a mistake of the case of *Woodley* v. *the Bishop of Exeter*, Cro. Jac. 691, Winch's Reports 94 [1624], contrasted with the cases mentioned in the margin of Dyer 35 and 228. [6:4] He observed that the next

---

[52] That the words are interpreted more strongly against the party offering the document.
[53] That the law causes injury to no one.

presentation subject to a contingent casual right in the Crown is a thing of value, just as the whole advowson is, which is proportionately affected by the interest of the Crown. That the Crown might have forborne to exercise its right, in which case the grantee would have had a right of then presenting as against the grantor,[54] which shows that the first avoidance, however it might happen, was that which the grant respected.

With regard to the authorities from Dyer, he first took notice of the doctrine in that book, p. 35, where Fitzherbert and Shelley differ as to the effect of a grant of *proxima advocatio* after a prior grant by the same person of *proxima advocatio*. Fitzherbert held it void, but Shelley thought it would be good for the 2nd avoidance; this he said was in the 25th of H. 8, but according to a marginal note of a case in the 12 Eliz., it was held by all the justices and serjeants that such 2nd grant was void.[55] So if a man grant the next presentation to A. and afterwards grant the next presentation to the same person, this shall not give him two presentations, but the acceptance of the 2nd shall be a surrender of the 1st. Judgment in margins. As to the note in the margin of the same case of what is stated to have been a determination in the 9th Jac. I[56] [*6:5*] that in the case of the grant of the next avoidance and the incumbent is made a bishop, that the grantee shall have the next after that, a note of the same case is to be found in the same book in the margin of page 228b, where it is said to be have been determined in the 19th Jac. He said this was certainly the case of *Woodley* v. *the Bishop of Exeter*, which appeared to have been differently determined both by the reports in Cro. Jac. and Winch, and by the record, which had been examined. These notes were therefore not to be relied on. He then cited the authority of Brook, tit. Presentment al Eglise, pl. 52, where it is said that if a man grant *proximam advocationem* to A and afterwards *proximam advocationem* to B., the grantee B. shall not have the 2nd turn, or the grant does not impart it. He then read the argument of Hutton J. in *Woodley* v. *the Bishop of Exeter*, Winch 96, and particularly relied on the case there cited of the university of Oxford from 10th Coke's Reports 53,[57] where a man before he was a recusant convict granted the next avoidance, and being afterwards convict, the grantee could not present, when the church became vacant.[58]

He again repeated what he had laid down, that there was no authority for construing a deed differently where it was voluntary from what would be its

---

[54] In the margin: 'Query whether either grantor or grantee could have presented without an usurpation on the Crown.'

[55] In Dyer's report (at 35a), Montague posed the following: 'The patron of a church granted *the next advowson* to one; and afterwards he granted *the next advowson* to another', and then asked whether the second grant be void or not. Fitzherbert thought it void; Shelley thought both grants valid. In the margins alongside their reasons, numerous authorities are cited. At Dyer 228b is the case of *Sidney* v. *Bishop of Gloucester* (1564), involving a *quare impedit* brought against the defendant testing the validity of an avoidance caused by a resignation. Here, too, numerous authorities are cited in the margin.

[56] At this point in the manuscript, the following was written and crossed out: 'where it is said to have been determined'.

[57] *The Case of the Chancellor, Masters, and Scholars of the University of Oxford* (1613) 10 Co. Rep. 53b.

[58] In the margin: 'This determination turned on the words of the statute, 3. J. 1.'

construction if for valuable consideration, that both might be equally enforced as against the grantor, and that the case in Winch was as strong a determination in his favour as if it had been the case of a deed, as every illustration of the doctrine in it was taken from cases on deeds. [6:6] The cases to which this had been likened, he contended, were different. That the *Case of Dower*, Co. Litt. 479 (*viz.*),[59] that if a man grant the 3rd presentation to another and die and his wife present at the 3rd avoidance, that the grantee shall have the 4th depended on this, that the wife's being the older title, such 4th turn was his 3rd presentation. With respect to coparceners, that the right was in the oldest if they disagreed, and that the Crown taking it from the oldest at the first avoidance could not without injustice give it to the youngest at the next avoidance. And with respect to the alternative right to present to churches united subsequent to the fire of London, which was the case of the *Archbishop of Canterbury and the Grocers' Company* in 2 [W.] Blackstone's Reports 770, he said that they depended on the statutes uniting the different parishes, and DE GREY, Chief Justice, in giving judgment in that case, said that *Woodley* v. *the Bishop of Exeter* was a very different case.

As to the words of the devise in *Woodley* v. *the Bishop of Exeter*,[60] which are *primam et proximam advocationem quae primo et proxime contigeret post mortem ipsius Arthuri*, he said that they were material not for the purpose for which they had been mentioned in the Court of King's Bench but to point out which presentation the grantee was to take. For there might be many avoidances before the death of Arthur Bassett[61] but [6:7] the grantee was only to have that which first happened after this death.

As to *Davenport's Case*, 8th Coke 145,[62] he said that could have nothing to do with this case. That only decided that a man should not by an act of his own derogate from his own grant.

Mr *Erskine* on the same side began his argument by stating that an advowson was an incorporeal hereditament consisting in the right to an indefinite number of successive presentations, subject to the prerogative right of the Crown, which is a contingency. That this contingency at the time of the grant must be known both to the grantor and grantee, and worked no injury to either, and was not like a matter lying only in the knowledge of the grantor.

He then put this case: suppose a man grants the 2nd presentation, reserving to himself the first, and the incumbent is made a bishop, shall the grantee not present at the next avoidance?

That *Woodley* v. *the Bishop of Exeter*, having been considered as law, at this distance of time it would be mischievous to overturn it. And though that was said to be a devise that there was no authority to say that a different rule of

---

[59] The reference is to William Hawkins, *An Abridgment of the first part of Lord Coke's Institutes*, 8th ed. (1792), p. 479.

[60] In the margin: '*Vide* as to this, Dyer 35b.'

[61] In the margin: 'A. Bassett was the testator, and his will could only apply to avoidances after his death.'

[62] *Davenport's Case* (1610) 8 Co. Rep. 144b.

construction held between a devise and a deed as to the effect of the premises. That the intention of the parties in the one and in the other was to be looked for and carried into effect. [6:8] That the grant of the next presentation was cutting off the right of presenting at the next avoidance from the series of next presentations in endless succession, which the grantor had. And that the grantee must take it subject and affected by the same contingency, with which each of the presentations remaining in the hands of the grantor were liable to be affected.

That the authority of *Woodley* v. *the Bishop of Exeter* was only affected by the authority of a marginal note in Dyer 35, made by Chief Justice TREBY from some note he had, not of his own taking, for he was not born at the time of that supposed determination, which was contrary to the report in Croke, Winch, and the record.

That this case differed much from the case of a coparcener after having presented granting the next presentation, in which case it is laid down that the grantee shall have the 3rd turn, because in that case the grantor, not having the 2nd, could in no fair construction be understood to intend to grant what belonged to another. But in this case the grantor had in him the next turn and therefore that next turn was a proper object of such grant.

The counsel for the plaintiff-in-error having finished, the LORD CHANCELLOR having himself no doubt, applied to the judges present [ss.] MCDONALD, Chief Baron; THOMPSON, [6:9] Baron; and LAWRENCE, Justice, but learning from them that they did not think the argument of the counsel for the plaintiff-in-error had laid a sufficient ground to revise the judgment of courts below, stopped *Law* and *Holroyd*, who were to have argued for the defendant-in-error, and then proposed that the following questions should be put to the judges who were present: 'Whether the grant of the next presentation to Matthew Kenrick was defeated by the vacancy which had happened by the presentation of J. Thomas to the Bishoprick of Rochester, and the filling of the vacancy by the King's prerogative.'

This question he introduced by shortly observing that though the case was of considerable value, yet it did not appear to him to have much difficulty in it. That it lay in a very narrow compass, and the point to be considered was whether the grant was not of that right which the grantee himself might exercise, and referred to the doctrine of Sir WILLIAM DE GREY in the case of the *Grocers' Co. and the Archbishop of Canterbury*, where he lays it down that the prerogative right of the Crown did not supply, but only suspended or postponed, the turn of the patron, and of all the patrons if more than one.

To this question, the CHIEF BARON answered in the negative without assigning his reasons, on which the chancellor moved that the judgments be affirmed.

[6:10]   [QUARRIER v. ROUSSELET]

[M.H.] Appeals from the vice-admiralty courts in revenue causes must be to the High Court of the Admiralty. *Vide* 8. Geo. III, c. 22.

On the 17th July 1794, the appeal of William Quarrier, master of a ship called the *Hero*, from a sentence of the vice-admiralty court of the Island of Jamaica of the 24th September 1792, pronounced in a cause depending in the said court upon a libel exhibited by John Rousselet, Esq., as well on behalf of the king as for himself, for the recovery of the penalty alleged to have been incurred by the appellant by his having transported from Africa in the said ship into the harbour of Kingston in the said island more male slaves of the height of 4 feet 4 inches than the proportion by law allowed to be carried and transported in the said ship, coming on to be argued before the Privy Council, a question was made touching the jurisdiction of the King in Council in cases of appeal from the courts of vice-admiralty in the plantations in revenue causes and causes instituted for the recovery of penalties and forfeitures created by Acts of parliament. The committee of the Privy Council to whom the same was referred reported to the king that it might be advisable for him to give directions for taking the opinions of the judges upon the question to what court or courts appeals may by law be made in the cases aforesaid arising in the vice- [6:11] admiralty court in the plantations. In consequence of this report, the opinion of the judges was directed to be taken,[63] who on the 23rd of April 1796 sent to the LORD CHANCELLOR (through whom His Majesty's pleasure was communicated in consequence of a letter to him from the duke of Portland, the secretary of state) the following certificate:

We have considered the question on which we have been requested to give our opinions in pursuance of His Majesty's pleasure, communicated to us by the lord chancellor, as to what court appeals may be made from the courts of vice-admiralty in the plantations in revenue causes, and causes instituted for the recovery of forfeitures or penalties created by Act of parliament, and are of opinion that in such cases, appeals must by law be made to the High Court of Admiralty in England.

KENYON	G. ROOKE
JAMES EYRE	S. LAWRENCE
A. McDONALD	April 23, 1796
W. ASHHURST	
B. HOTHAM	
R. PERRYN	
F. BULLER	
J. HEATH	
N. GROSE	
A. THOMPSON	

[63] On this procedure, see J. Oldham, 'Informal Law-Making in England by the Twelve Judges in the late Eighteenth and Early Nineteenth Centuries', *Law and History Review* 29 (2011), p. 181.

[6:12]   At the Delegates: WENMAN v. TAYLOR[64]

[M.H.] An unexecuted paper if proved by circumstantial evidence to have been written by the directions of one deceased must be proved in the ecclesiastical court as a testamentary paper though there be no direct evidence of his having given those directions or having had it read to him.[65]

This was an appeal to the Delegates from a sentence of Sir WILLIAM WYNNE, judge of the Prerogative Court,[66] in a suit there instituted by M. A. Taylor, Esq., son of Sir Robert Taylor, desiring probate of his father's will with two codicils, in which suit a Mr *Pilkington* appeared and prayed that Mr Taylor might take probate also of two other papers, which he contended were codicils and which in the course of the suit were distinguished by the letters A and B. On the 30th of March 1791, the judge being of opinion that neither of the papers were well proved, decreed probate of the will, &c. without either of the papers.

The facts of the case were shortly as follows:

In the beginning of the year 1779, Sir Robert Taylor consulted his solicitor, Mr Hamilton, respecting his will which he had executed and a codicil he had some thoughts of executing for the purpose of disposing of the greatest part of his property in the event of the death of himself and son without issue.

[6:13] In consequence of this consultation, Hamilton went over a copy or draft of the will and made some alterations in it, and read over with Sir Robert Taylor the paper B and laid a copy of it before Mr Pickering, a barrister, to settle on the 24th of March 1779, but this was never done owing to Pickering's disapprobation of the intended disposition, and the paper was found among Pickering's papers on his death in the year 1786.

During the time it lay before Pickering, the testator sometimes spoke of it to Hamilton and said he must execute it.

On the 4th of January 1788 he executed his will and thereby gave the residue of his property in case of failure of issue of himself and his son, to trustees to dispose of as he should by codicil appoint.

Subsequent to the execution of the will, and more than once, he spoke to Hamilton about having the codicil B settled. Part of it was read to the testator,

---

[64] The most informative source on the nature and operation of the Court of Delegates is G. I. O. Duncan, *The High Court of Delegates* (1971). Duncan explains (at p. 178) that the 'Court of Delegates had no permanent judges; a separate commission was issued for each cause appointing judges to hear it, and their authority terminated when the cause was concluded.' The judges were chosen at the lord chancellor's discretion. Ordinarily a mixture of common law judges and civilians was appointed, as in *Wenman v. Taylor*, though sometimes bishops or peers were included. Ibid. at pp. 83, 185–186.

[65] That is, the absence of direct evidence was not determinative; the unexecuted paper could still be proved, but it had to be proved as a testamentary paper in the ecclesiastical court.

[66] The Prerogative Court of Canterbury dealt entirely with testamentary causes. Duncan, *The High Court of Delegates*, p. 32. By a 1653 statute, it was set up as 'a centralised probate court in London for "all and every the counties and cities of England and Wales"'. See R. B. Outhwaite, *The Rise and Fall of the English Ecclesiastical Courts, 1500–1860* (2006), p. 89, quoting C. P. Firth and R. S. Rait eds., *Acts and Ordinances of the Interregnum, 1642–1660* (1911), pp. 564–566.

and Hamilton by his direction made some alterations as to the trustees, and about a month before his death said to Hamilton, who endeavoured to dissuade him from executing the [6:14] codicil, that he did not like his large fortune should go to strangers or to his wife's relations. That he meant to give his son £50,000 to dispose of as he pleased, and that he could not bear to think of his son making no will or giving it to his mother's relations. And on Hamilton's objecting to his intention of giving the money to the university of Oxford to found a college for the teaching and improvement of the European languages as a strange mode of disposing of his property, he said he would adopt any better mode which he, Hamilton, would recommend, who declining to recommend any, the testator said the codicil must be finally settled and talked of having it laid before counsel —which was not done, it continuing in Hamilton's hands till Sir R. Taylor's death.

On the evening of his death, being convinced of his approaching dissolution, he told Mr Devaynes, his apothecary, he wanted Mr Hamilton for the purpose of bequeathing a legacy of £5,000 and upward to make up a sum certain for his son, and that he wished to do something for his young man, [6:15] and desired Devaynes and his physician, Dr Blackburne, in case anything happened, to bear witness that he left his son a further sum of £5,000 and a servant was sent for Mr Hamilton. About an hour before his death, a Mr Westby, an assistant to Devaynes, was called into his bedroom, where he saw the paper A lying by the deceased, and from the discourse which passed, he understood that the testator was going to sign the paper and was only waiting for witnesses, and that after waiting some time, the testator being informed that Westby would be a witness, the deceased said he would sign the paper that night, and accordingly he was, in a very short time, lifted up on his bed for the purpose of signing it. But the agonies of death came upon him, and he was laid down again, and died within the space of twenty minutes without signing it.

During the whole of the day he was of perfect sound mind, memory and understanding, and knew very well what he said and did and what was said and done in his presence, and capable of giving instructions for his will or doing any other serious or rational act that required judgment or reflection.

[6:16] Paper A was in the following form:

26 September 1788

Hasty instructions for the will of Sir Robert Taylor, Knight.

First, whereas, by my books it will appear that I have given to my son absolutely the sum of £45,000, now my pleasure is that the said sum be increased to £50,000 and that the codicil drawn up about the time my will was settled, but for want of counsel's opinion was never executed, be settled according to my instructions expressed in the codicil in every respect as though it had been duly executed, and which instructions are well known to William Hamilton, Esq., who drew the same, and if there should have been any instructions explained to William Hamilton, Esq., who drew the same, though not fully explained in my will and codicil, I direct the same to be carried into execution as if the same was fully explained and signed. All which would have been done if the shortness of my warning had not prevented it, having been taken ill on Monday last. And I desire that my will and codicil and everything relative thereto may be established [*6:17*] in the Court of Chancery by William Hamilton, Esq. He then gave certain legacies, one of which was to Pilkington, and directions for his funeral, and then went on thus, 'I desire that no part of my property do descend or be given to my wife's relations other than what I have heretofore given them by my will.'

This paper was written by a person of the name of Craig, to whom he gave one of the legacies in it. The other persons present, except Westby, were legatees.

Paper B had the names of the trustees struck through and supplied with others in some places, but not in all—and other parts were struck through, and in some places blank spaces were left. The substance of it was a recital of his having devised his estates to his son in strict settlement, &c. and of his desire to execute the ultimate disposition of his property, directed that his trustees in the event of his son dying without issue should lay out the undisposed part of his property in the purchase of lands, &c., to establish a foundation at Oxford for the improvement of the European languages.

[*6:18*] The testator had by his will given to his widow [£]3,000 per annum for life and £2,000 in money to be at her own disposal.

This question came first before Mr Baron HOTHAM, Mr Justice BULLER, Mr Justice WILSON, Dr BATTINE, and Dr ARNOLD as Delegates, and was heard before them, but they gave no judgment before Mr Justice WILSON's death. The matter standing over that Lady Taylor, the widow, might be further examined, which was wished by Mr Justice BULLER, to some facts which he thought should be further inquired into. But this was never done.

On Mr Justice WILSON's death, a commission of adjuncts issued,[67] directed to Mr Justice LAWRENCE, and the cause, &c. came on to be heard the 2nd time before him and the other surviving delegates, when Sir *William Scott*, the king's advocate, Sir *John Scott*, the attorney-general, Dr *Nicholl*, Mr *Erskine*, and Mr *Campbell* were heard for Mr Taylor. And Mr *Hardinge*, Dr *Lawrence*, Dr *Swabey* and Mr *Richards* for the university of Oxford, who carried on the appeal in the name of Dr Wenman. For Mr Taylor it was insisted that though the informality of the papers would not invalidate them if it was clearly showed what was the testator's intention, yet that the presumption of law was against them until proved to be within the intention, [*6:19*] and that not a fluctuating intention, but a fixed, settled intention carried up to the last moment of the testator's capacity. That a man *in extremis* was seldom capable, and not to be presumed, *a priori*, to have the powers he may be proved to possess, and that on this ground, the ecclesiastical court has held it necessary to establish papers not signed or written by the testator, either by proving them to have been read over to him and assented to, or by proving that he had given instructions for

---

[67] Commissions of adjuncts 'were issued whenever it was found necessary to join new judges with those appointed under the original commission'. Duncan, *The High Court of Delegates*, at p. 83, n. 5.

them. That this was no fanciful rule of the ecclesiastical court, but a rule founded in an attention to men's properties, and not to be relaxed in favour of a paper to be established merely by reference, not under the eye of the testator, and of which the testator could only know the contents by recollection, and that in no case the rule should be less relaxed than in the present, where the testament was made to disinherit his nearest relation, when surrounded by persons who took considerable advantage under it, and no relation by at the time. That there should in such case be the strongest proofs of clear volition, capacity, and vigilance of mind, which did not appear in this case. That had this been the settled purpose of the testator's mind, it was very extraordinary that he should not execute a codicil to this effect when he executed his will and codicil in 1788, subsequent to which time he talked of settling it—made alterations a little [6:20] before his death—was ready to adopt any other scheme on Hamilton's remonstrance. That the paper B, being drawn up in the year 1779, could not be considered as a codicil to the will in 1788. Thus the paper A, speaking of a codicil drawn up about the time of making the will, &c., from its incongruity with the will, showed that the testator did not know what he was about. That it professed to be hasty instructions for making a will, which looked more as if his design was to make one anew than to set up any imperfect paper, and in other respects showed a want of composure. And that it might be very mischievous to hold that a paper, however imperfect, should be established as a will, if there was [but] a probability that it contained the intentions of the testator. That to evidence such intention, the law required certain acts, which in case of devises of land were directed by the Statute of Frauds, which had not been extended to the case of personalty, as bequests of that species of property had been sufficiently guarded by the rules of the ecclesiastical court. That regularly, a will of personalty should be signed by the testator, which, if not done, might be supplied by circumstances such as an instrument prepared, but the execution prevented by the act of God. But in such case, the evidence of intention must be clear and satisfactory, such as amounts to the highest degree of moral probability. Secondly it must be clearly shown that testator had come to a resolution [6:21] of executing such will according to the formalities of law, and thirdly you must account for the paper continuing in such imperfect form, to show that the testator's intention continued. And that where a paper was not very imperfect, it might not require much evidence to repel the presumptions in favour of the relations of the deceased, yet very strong evidence was necessary where the paper is very imperfect and has continued in that state a long time, as was the case with paper B. And that it had never been sufficient to show that the intentions of the testator generally speaking went hand in hand with what might be collected from such imperfect paper.

That to establish a paper coming from a man *in extremis*, direct evidence of the knowledge of its contents is necessary, and in that case, signing will not do. That the rule was even in that case that you must prove the deceased gave instructions, or that the instrument was read over to him, and understood—

and if such was the rule in that case, it was the rule, *a fortiori*, when the paper was not signed.

That to say the testator adhered to his intention for several years was talking loosely. The only thing he adhered to was an inability to decide what he was to do with his property. That it was remarkable that he did not speak of his codicil when he mentioned the £5,000 to be given to his son, and of providing for his young man, and that [6:22] was the last act of his life previous to this paper A. And a very strong circumstance against it, that he never mentioned any part of what from that paper was supposed to be his intention when he was in fact making a nuncupative will.

That had he in fact signed the paper which there was no direct evidence of his intention to do, as he did not say what he would sign, it could not, according to the rules of the ecclesiastical court, have been read for want of proof of instructions, or reading over, and that the necessity of the one or the other could not be dispensed with because the instructions were given to a person who, being interested, could not be examined.

That it might be said there was informal evidence from the paper itself, which would be tantamount. But that would be saying that a man who cannot be examined to prove a will, because he has a benefit under it, and in whom the law presumes fraud, shall take the benefit of such will, if he has had art enough to throw in anything which it is probable the testator would have done. In support of the objections to these papers they cited *Nash* v. *Edwards*, 1 Leon. 113, *Wyndham* v. *Chetwind*, 4 Burns' Ecclesiastical Law 80, Swinburne 336, *Doe* v. *Kersey*, Wilson.[68]

[6:23] For the appellant it was contended that the question being whether A and B were testamentary papers, i.e., papers which the testator would have reduced into form if he could, nothing turned upon considering whether the disposition was wise or not. That cases of imperfect instruments were frequently very nice, and that each must stand on its own foundation. And that the judge might pronounce in their favour upon reasonable grounds, to furnish which the court were not confined to the receipt of any particular kind of evidence, of which the giving instructions or reading over the will were only one species. And to restrain the court to that, or to say it was a rule of the testamentary court, no authority whatever could be quoted. To show that circumstantial evidence was sufficient and that the rule contended for on the other side did not obtain, Swinburne 13, 110, and *Sheppard's Touchstone* 408 were cited.[69] And they argued that in this case there was abundant evidence of

---

[68] *Nash* v. *Edwards* (1588) 1 Leon. 113; *Wyndham* v. *Chetwynd* (1757) 1 Bl. W. 95, 2 Keny. 121. The reference to Swinburne is to H. Swinburne, *A briefe treatise of testaments and last willes* (1590). The reference to Wilson is unclear. *Doe* v. *Kersey* does not appear in *Wilson's Reports* or in any of the standard printed reports. It was nonetheless a well-known case, due chiefly to Lord Camden's trenchant criticism of Lord Mansfield's embrace of judicial discretion. The case was decided in 1765 and was reported in full in pamphlet form. See Oldham, *MMSS*, ii. 1356–57.

[69] In the margin: 'Query the reference to Swinburne, and if the first be not part 7, § 13, and *vide* part 4, § 28, and part 2nd, § 25, page 105 of fifth edition.' The Sheppard reference is to W. Sheppard, *The Touch-stone of Common Assurances* (1648).

the disposition in papers A and B, being the deliberate, settled intention of the testator at a time when he was of sound mind and had recollection and discretion sufficient to dispose of his property, and that he persisted in it till the time of his death.

They contended so far from any irresolution being in the testator, as to the disposition of his property, that it was [6:24] owing to the fraud of Hamilton and Pickering, who wished to defeat the intentions of the testator, that the thing had not been formally done long before. That his offer to do what Hamilton might recommend was not a readiness to do anything else, but tantamount to saying, it is impossible I can dispose of it better.

That the internal evidence from the papers themselves was decisive. That paper B having been confided to Hamilton only, it was impossible that Craig, who drew paper A, could know anything of it, unless the testator himself had given instructions for drawing it. Craig could not have referred to a codicil or other paper in Hamilton's hand if Taylor had not instructed him, unless it was supposed that Hamilton had communicated it to Craig, which was not pretended. Who but the testator could tell Craig of the provision he had made for his son and how it would appear? And the recollection of the several matters mentioned in paper A most unquestionably proved not only that the testator gave the instructions, but also his recollection and capacity. That it was evident he did not mean to die intestate, as to the residue of his property, from the anxiety he showed respecting the £5,000 which he desired Devaynes and Dr Blackburne to bear witness he gave to his son, all [6:25] which was unnecessary and idle on any supposition but an intention of giving the rest in such way as that his son should not at all events take it. That in his last illness he could not want Mr Hamilton to give this £5,000, that his son would take by his partial intestacy, though it might be necessary on account of his intended legacies to his young man. His intentions to a certain extent as declared to Devaynes were carried into execution by paper A by the legacies mentioned in that paper, and if so far it was clear that it was the intention of the testator, could it be said that the residue of it was not what he intended?

That the argument on the other side went the length of saying that if Craig had not been a legatee, and had died after the writing paper A of a fit, that this paper could not be proved, and amounted to this because there is no direct proof. There is no proof at all. That what the court had to consider was, is there evidence of the testator's knowledge of the contents of the papers and of his assenting to them sufficient to satisfy their conscience; that if this circumstantial evidence might be as satisfactory as positive proof. That it was an inconsiderable circumstance that the paper A was lying by the testator, that it came from no suspicious custody, and that if the court were [6:26] satisfied on such evidence that the testator intended the disposition in question, and adhered to it to the time of his death, and was prevented by the hand of God from executing it in form, the papers ought to be established as testamentary papers, and that there was such evidence they submitted for the reasons they had assigned.

Sir *William Scott* in reply said:

The question was if there was sufficient proof of the intent of a testator of sufficient capacity. That there might be degrees of testamentary capacity. There might be a capacity adequate to the giving of mourning or a year's wages, but not sufficient for the disposition of large property. And that less evidence of capacity might satisfy the court in the case of an usual and common disposition, such as in favour of children, than where disposition is wild and absurd.

That in the case of a person *in extremis*, the presumption was against his capacity. He was generally in a state of pain, distracted by the apprehensions of his dissolution and leaving all his connections and on that account the testamentary court did not consider the hour of death as an hour of recollection. That an unexecuted paper must prove itself by an adherence to an intent, [6:27] which must depend on external evidence for its support, that it must be shown that the intentions of the testator were that it should take effect in that form, and that the proof should be strong in proportion to the length of time the paper lay in an incomplete state, as the deceased must be presumed in proportion to that time to have receded from his original intention.

That at no one time while the testator was in undoubted possession of his understanding was there evidence of a decided intent to execute the paper B.

That if a paper were left with an attorney by a man a little while before his death, and he were suddenly carried off, that might be set up as a testamentary paper, as there would be no ground to presume that it was abandoned. But where it had been left eight years in an office, the testator all that time in health and walking about the town, the inference of his not continuing in the same mind was much stronger than of his being in such mind, collected from loose declarations. Added to this here, the deceased did not overrule the objections of Hamilton or remonstrate with Pickering for his [6:28] delay of seven years. That it was a strong circumstance (that he executed his will without this disposition) to show at that time he had not come to any settled determination; and his saying it must be finally settled and his talking of laying it before counsel both showed that the paper B did not contain anything which he had been determined to be done in the form and manner contained in that paper. That after it had been settled, the testator might wish to think about it, and consider whether what had been so strongly opposed was fit to be done, and that had the testator died without doing anything, which had been proved the last day of his life, there could have been no pretence to establish paper B as a testamentary paper. And if he was right in that, the question then would be if the evidence of what passed in the last day of his life would establish this paper.

As to which, when his medical friends told him no time was to be lost for settling his affairs, and he solemnly called on them to attest to a legacy of £5,000 to his son, he does not say a word of this paper. [6:29] That saying nothing of it showed he had then departed from his original design. That sending for Hamilton would not be presumed to be to execute this paper, for he had always opposed its execution. And though he might be desirous of concealing his intentions from his relations, that would not account for not mentioning the thing to his physician and the others about him, as he might have done it in as general terms as paper A contained.

That after this conversation with his physician, he must be considered as being in that nimbus state in which no man is to be presumed to be equal to the making of his will; when much might have passed in his room and he did not notice it. That though the paper did in some degree prove that he had given instructions for it, yet the court was completely in the dark as to the degree of faculty he retained at that time, what those instructions were, and what assistance the people about him gave. That the whole the paper proved was that Sir R. Taylor had a confused recollection, and though he was proved sometime before to be in his senses, it was not to be concluded that he was so when *in faucibus orci*.

That it had been said that there was no particular rule as to the mode [6:30] of proof necessary to establish such paper. Now admitting this to be so, and that it was sufficient if the conscience of the court was satisfied by other means, how did it stand?

Here was the testimony of Westby of very loose and uncertain grounds for the court to rest on, opposed by the circumstances of the will not being signed—no proof of the deceased's accurately recollecting this paper, no evidence of its being read over in ten years' deliberation without completion, and no mention of it in a conversation to his intimate friends an hour before, when talking on the settlement of his affairs.

But that the rule of the testamentary court was, in the case of papers to be exhibited as the testamentary papers of a man *in extremis*, that you must prove either that he gave instructions for such papers or that it was read over to him.

[6:31] HOTHAM, Baron: It is clear that paper A refers to paper B, and it is proved that for ten years this disposition to the university of Oxford was the testator's favourite object during a period when there was no incapability on his part, and when he was in the complete enjoyment of his understanding. To the completion of this design, delays are thrown in his way by Pickering and Hamilton till, being at last wearied out by them, he, within a month of his death, says the paper must be settled. Death came upon him. What does he do? He sends for Hamilton. This, Sir *William Scott* says, shows that his intention was not to execute the paper, because Hamilton had always frustrated it. This strikes me just the contrary. He sends for Hamilton as the only man who could do it officially, and on his not coming, he and Craig set about doing it as well as they can. But there is said to be no evidence of instructions. I admit there is no direct evidence, but as there is no proof that this matter was ever communicated to anybody else, it is to me irresistible to show that he gave instructions to Craig. Suppose the subject matter of this paper as to the object of the disposition had been wise and unobjectionable, and all this had passed, can anyone say that under such circumstances, a fair, just and honest will should be arrested?

[*6:32*] I agree that the testator's intention must be made out either by direct proof or circumstantial. It is allowed on all hands that when the testator last spoke he was in his senses. It is pressed that he did not mention this intention in his conversation with Devaynes. But it is to be considered that he was at that time in the house with Lady Taylor and others who might have opposed it, and it is to me a strong circumstance to show his understanding. That he was able to manage with such dexterity and to keep his purpose secret from them all by a reference to his codicil. I think he continued firmly in the intention of making this disposition—that he adhered to it in his last moments and was prevented signing and properly executing a codicil to effectuate his intent by the hand of death, which is the same as if he had done it. And when a paper is seen lying by a man, as this was, the law will presume he knew the contents.

BULLER, Justice: Said four questions in the course of argument had arisen.

The first as to the propriety of a further examination. [*6:33*] The 2nd as to the capacity of the decedent. The 3rd as to the paper A. The 4th as to the paper B.

As to the first, understanding by the rules of the ecclesiastical court that the cause was never concluded *contra judicem*, he had wished for a further examination, but as he understood that was deprecated by Mr Taylor, that if there was no doubt except so far as he might be affected, it would not be necessary to direct a further examination. That as to the capacity of Sir R. Taylor, he had no doubt, his conduct had been uniform for years, and that it was a most mischievous idea to be adopted that a man had capacity *quoad hoc*; that a man must be held to have a disposing mind and to be in a condition to dispose of a million, or he could not dispose of a shilling, otherwise it would be in the power of each judge to say what was too much for a testator to dispose of in this or that state of mind

As to paper A: that there was abundant evidence to support it. [*6:34*] That there was no other paper in the room to which his conversation could refer. That when he said I will execute it, it imported a knowledge of it, else signing the paper would not be evidence of a man's knowledge of its contents. That he did not say he would decide on the internal evidence alone, for an artful man might draw a specious paper, but slight external evidence would be sufficient. As to paper B, there appeared a settled determination for years to execute it, which was prevented only by the fraud of Hamilton,[70] who laid it before Pickering that it might there sleep, on whose death the decedent [Taylor] in effect tells [Hamilton[71]] he can't point out a better mode of disposing of the property, and that the codicil must be finally settled. That on this evidence he had no doubt, that if Sir Robert Taylor had died four hours before the time he did, that the court must establish that as his will. That it came to this, had the deceased when he talked to Devaynes abandoned his intention. As to which he appeared to be ashamed of his [*6:35*] vanity in making such disposition, he makes up his mind as to his son by his nuncupative disposition, but still

---

[70] In the manuscript the words 'and Pickering' are here written and crossed out.
[71] Baron Hotham must have said or meant to say Hamilton here rather than Pickering.

appeared to be hankering after something else. What would that be but this disposition?

LAWRENCE, Justice: agreed that probate should be decreed of these papers. That there did not appear to be any authority in any printed book or manuscript note for the rule insisted on by the counsel for the respondent, 'That in a case like this instructions or the reading of the paper must be directly proved.' That the rule was denied by the other side, who had from Swinburne shown that other proof of intention was sufficient, and that laying such rule out of the question, it was to be considered if there was not from the circumstances of the case sufficient proof to satisfy the court that the deceased had a disposing mind and, knowing its contents, would have executed the paper A had he not been prevented by death. That if he were to direct a jury on this point, he should not hesitate to direct in favour of the codicil. That the argument for the respondent had gone in some measure on considering the two papers distinctly—whereas, they ought to be considered together, and not whether paper B could be established if [6:36] paper A had never been written. Nor whether paper A was an instrument which could be considered as a testamentary paper, without seeing how much it was falsified by its agreement with paper B. That taking both together, there appeared to him strong grounds to decide in favour of the testator's capacity, recollection, unaltered intention, and that he had given instructions to Craig to write the paper A.

Dr BATTINE said he adhered to the opinion he had formed on the first hearing, and that he apprehended the reversing the judgment of[72] Sir WILLIAM WYNNE would overturn the laws respecting testamentary property, open a door to fraud, and lead to difficulties which did not appear to be foreseen. And if he did not feel himself controlled by the rule of law he should agree with the delegates who had given their opinions.

He said that in this case, two questions arose.

The first was, if the rules of the testamentary court could be set aside in any case. The 2nd was, if there was sufficient ground in this case to justify a deviation.

He said the great rule as to unexecuted papers was that the intention of the [6:37] testator should prevail. That such papers need not be signed. But that the intention of the testator would not prevail unless it was reduced into writing by the order of the testator, that such intention must not be merely conjectural, but must be ascertained by some act. Whatever declarations a man may make as to the disposition of his property, a paper consonant to such declarations unless proved to have been written by his orders would not operate as a will, unless the paper was actually read to and approved of by him.

That these rules were wise and proper cautions to guard against fraud. The experiment of an innovation was dangerous. That there were two reasons why the Statute of Frauds did not extend to personal property. The first was that land at that time was most regarded, and secondly because devises of land only

---

[72] In the manuscript, the words 'the Court of King's Bench' are here written and crossed out.

came under the consideration of the courts of common law. That if at that time personal property had been as considerable as it is now, the Statute of Frauds would probably have extended to it. And that unexecuted papers were so various that much mischief would result from weakening the rule. That the presumption was against an unexecuted paper, and as the greater number of wills are made after the death stroke is given, the wisdom of the rule was obvious, which had for its [6:38] object to guard against frauds at a time when they were most likely to be practised.

In questions of sanity, there were no shades of understanding. But that persons *in extremis* had, as had been said by Sir George Hay, seldom more than simple apprehensions enabling them to dispose of a simple legacy. That in the present case, there seems to him nothing more than surmise and inference. That were he a juryman and not considering any rule of law, he should pronounce his verdict as the three judges had their opinion. That if the deceased had signed the paper, it would very much have altered the nature of it. It would then have become perfect, and therefore an attempt to sign it was not equivalent to signing, for after such attempt it remained imperfect. That in looking into the proofs, he did not see any positive and direct evidence that the testator had given any instructions, or that the paper had been read to him. That he was for adhering to the rule of the ecclesiastical court, which he did not think ought to be set aside, and if it were not for those rules, he should have agreed with the Delegates who had delivered their opinion.

[6:39] Dr ARNOLD said he could not consider this case exactly as if it was that of a man in perfect health, who, holding a paper in his hand, is carried off by the hand of God. There he must be taken to know the contents of that paper. But in the last moments of expiring life, when capacity was not to be presumed, a man could not be taken to know the content of a paper near him, and that he did not think Westby's evidence of capacity sufficient.

That he thought in this case that the circumstantial evidence was as strong as possible. That sitting as a juror he should feel himself bound to decide in favour of the will. That the question came to this—can circumstantial evidence be received[?] That it was not the practice of the ecclesiastical court entirely to reject such evidence, and it might be that circumstantial evidence was more strong and more to be depended on than direct and positive evidence. And therefore he concurred with the Delegates who [6:40] were of opinion the judgment of Sir WILLIAM WYNNE should be reversed. At the same time he did not consider himself as deciding a case which could be an authority in any other unless where circumstantial evidence was full and satisfactory.

Sentence of the Prerogative Court reversed, and probate of the papers A and B as testamentary papers decreed. July 4th, 1794.

[*Lawrence note:*] *N.B.* This case took up several days in arguing, and Mr Justice WILSON (as I am told) agreed in the opinion of the majority of the delegates who ultimately decided the case.

[6:41] B.R. EASTER TERM 36 Geo. III

Lloyd, Lord Kenyon, Chief Justice
Sir W. Ashhurst   ⎫
Sir N. Grose   ⎬ Justices
Sir S. Lawrence   ⎭

April 13 R. v. LORD FALKLAND

[M.H.] Attachment not to be granted against a peer for non-performance of an award.[73]

Mingay on the first day of the term moved for an attachment against the defendant for a contempt in not performing an award. *Erskine* objected that as the defendant was a peer of Great Britain he was not liable. At a subsequent day *Erskine* stated that in the case of Lord De Loraine,[73a] the court had refused to grant a rule *nisi*.

Lord KENYON said it required a great deal of discussion, as the question involved the privilege of the peerage.[74]

Afterwards, *Mingay* admitted he could not support the rule he had obtained the first day of the term.[75]

---

[73] The arbitration in this case was between Mr Stephen Phillips and Lord Falkland, John King, and others. A brief report of this case in *The Times*, 12 February 1796, gives the background. In Trinity Term 1795, several indictments stood for trial against Lord Falkland, John King, and other defendants, all prosecuted by Stephen Phillips. The defendants were acquitted 'on condition that they would enter into a rule to refer it to Alexander Champion, Esq. to say how much money was due from the parties to Mr Phillips, and in what proportion the defendants should pay that sum'. This was done, and on 31 December the arbitrator issued his award, 'ordering Lord Falkland and Mr King to pay one sum of money, and Mr King by himself to pay another'. Together the sums amounted to £5,543. Phillips claimed (by affidavit) that he tried unsuccessfully to collect the money, and on the last day of Hilary Term 1796, Phillips's counsel, Mingay, obtained a rule to show cause why an attachment should not issue against the defendants. This led to the hearing described in Lawrence's notes.

Meanwhile, counsel for the defendants, William Garrow, filed a motion to set aside the award, claiming that despite Mr Champion's undoubted integrity and ability, 'he had made an award which could not possibly stand', as it was unsupported by the evidence. *The Times*, 28 January 1796. At the hearing on 27 January, Lord Kenyon said he recalled the case and thought there was no pretence for the motion. He asked his fellow judges whether they would rely on his memory of the facts and join him in denying the motion, but they declined.

[73a] *Hunter v. De Lorraine* (1772) Lofft 49.

[74] According to *The Times*, 14 April 1796, Lord Kenyon observed that Lord Falkland was a Scottish peer, 'yet, by the 23rd Article of the Union between the two Nations, "All Peers of Scotland shall be Peers of Great Britain; and rank next after those of the same degree at the time of the Union, and shall have all the privileges of Parliament, except sitting in the House of Lords, and voting on the trial of a Peer."'

[75] On 26 April, Mingay 'said he had looked into the cases, and was satisfied that he could not attack Lord Falkland'. *The Times*, 27 April 1796. Earlier, Lord Kenyon had acknowledged that 'it was very fit for the honour of the Peerage, that Noble Lords should not entrench themselves behind their *Privileges*, in order to prevent their being amenable to justice', but if this happened, it would be a matter for the legislature. *The Times*, 21 April 1796. The litigation between Phillips and King was not resolved until May 1797, when according to *The Times*, 8 May 1797, 'Mr Mingay informed the Court that Mr King had paid Mr Phillips all his costs, and that consequently there was an end to all the attachments against him.' Reportedly the lawsuits 'had taken out of Mr King's pocket upwards of ten thousand pounds'. Ibid.

Vide: 2 Hawkins, c. 22, sec. 33; 1 Wilson 332; Comyns Digest, tit: Dignity (F3), and what BULLER says in *R. v. Myers*, 1 T.R. 265.[76]

SMITH v. SHEPHERD[77]

[M.H.] Act of God to excuse a carrier must be immediate.

In an action against a common carrier by water, tried before HEATH, Justice, at York for negligently carrying goods, it appeared in evidence that at the entrance of the harbour of Hull, there was a bank on which vessels were used to lie in safety. That in the beginning of March 1795 a great flood swept away a part of the bank, so that it became perfectly steep instead of gradually shelving towards the river. That on the 5th of March, a vessel sank by getting on this bank, and her mast, which was carried away was suffered to float on the river, tied to some part of the vessel. The defendant, upon sailing into the harbour, [6:42] struck against the mast, which, not giving way, forced the vessel towards the bank. There she struck and would have remained safe had it remained in its former situation, but on the tide ebbing, the stern of defendant's vessel sunk into the water and the goods were spoiled.

The defendant tendered evidence to show that there had been no actual negligence, which the judge rejected. And he further ruled that the act of God which would excuse the defendant must be immediate—but this was too remote, and directed the jury to find against the defendant.

Cockell, serjeant, moved for a new trial, insisting that this was such accident as furnished a defence, and that the evidence should have been received.

Lord KENYON said this was hardly the act of God. That is storm, lightning and such like. Had an earthquake removed the bank at the time of the accident, it would have been another thing. I think the judge did right in rejecting the evidence.

Nil cap.

April 14   COLSON *et al.*, assignees of   [*sic*] v. TELLY

[M.H.] If defendant pleads a joint contract in abatement where the plaintiff has delivered a particular of his demand consisting both of joint and separate claims, the plaintiff can't recover for his separate demand.

Plaintiff having delivered to the defendant a bill of particulars of his demand, a part of which had been furnished on the joint contract of the defendant and one Toon, the defendant pleaded that matter in abatement. And at the trial of the issue taken on the plea in abatement, Lord KENYON would

---

[76] *R. v. Bishop of St Asaph* (1752) 1 Wils. 332. In *R. v. Myers* (1786), Mr Justice Buller observed that 'it has been settled of late years that an attachment for non-performance of an award is only in the nature of a civil execution'. 1 T.R. at 266.

[77] See p. 85, above, for an earlier phase of this case.

not suffer the plaintiff to recover only for the thing furnished [6:43] on the sole credit of the defendant, who on that account obtained a verdict.

Atcheson now moved for a new trial and insisted, as the action was well brought for a part, the plaintiff was entitled to recover for such part. But Lord KENYON said there was nothing in it and refused a rule *nisi*.

> [*Lawrence note*:] This matter was mentioned afterwards by *Erskine*, but he obtained no rule. And it seems right on this ground: Had the defendant not pleaded in abatement, the plaintiff would have recovered for the whole, and he ought not, by adding to a separate demand that which is properly the subject of a joint action, to compel the defendant to suffer a recovery against himself alone for that part, or have a verdict against him, as upon an inquisition of damages, for the separate demand if he pleads in abatement. Of this case, I understood some gentleman at the Bar doubted.

R. v. MAWBEY *et al.*

For the statement of this case, *vide* 6 T.R. 619. *Vide* also Paper Book 117, in which are minutes of the several cases furnished by the Crown Office as to granting new trials in criminal cases—and of several cases from printed books not mentioned in the printed report.[78]

BANKS v. MILWARD

[M.H.] No action lies against a man for not fencing a pit into which a horse falls which through fright had run out of the road.

Williams, serjeant, moved for a new trial of an action before THOMPSON, Baron, at Stafford, for not fencing a coal pit, by reason whereon the plaintiff's mare fell in.

The defendant being the lessee of the pits made a road across a common, under [6:44] which the coal was, to the pits. The plaintiff was leading his mare across the common when she took fright and jumped out of the road into the pit. The judge was of opinion the action could not be supported, with which Lord KENYON agreed, saying if an unruly horse leaps out of the road into a pit, the [land-]owner was clearly not liable.

Nil cap.

---

[78] See also p. 151, below, for the judgment entered in this case. The printed report of the case is very full. Lawrence's Paper Book contains a document labeled 'Extracts from the Rule Books in the Crown Office on the Subject of New Trials', prepared by H. Dealtry, clerk of the rules of the Crown Office of the Court of King's Bench. The extracts show that the question in this case was unresolved—whether defendants could be retried when they appeared to have been wrongly convicted by the same jury that acquitted their co-defendants. Dampier MSS., LPB 117, Lincoln's Inn Library.

April 15   BEVER v. TOMLINSON

[M.H.] If loss happening by the act of an enemy is a peril of the sea. *Dub.*

This was an action tried before HEATH, Justice, at Lancaster on a bill of lading of goods from Lisbon to Liverpool, the perils of the sea excepted.

One count charged the defendants generally with a breach of their contract. Other counts charged the defendants with negligent storage of the goods. The loss happened by a French frigate running on board the defendant's ship with a design to sink it, which they contended was within the exception of sea perils.

The judge thought otherwise and the plaintiff recovered.

Chambré now moved for a new trial, and on showing cause, Mr *Law* and Mr *Wood* admitted that by the general law as applicable to the case, the defendant was not liable, but that here the court must look at the special undertaking in the bill of lading. That a peril of the sea [6:45] was an act of God without the intervention of human agency.

Style 132 was mentioned, where it was held that a capture by pirates was a peril of the seas,[79] and *e contra*, 4 Leon 31, p. 86.[80]

Lord KENYON said it appeared to him to be a monstrous construction to say the defendant was liable. That it was a question fit to be put on the record and therefore there should be a new trial.

Rule absolute. *Vide 2 Rolle's Abridgement* 248, pl. 10.

GORDON v. HARPUR

[M.H.] Question if trover will lie for goods tortiously taken at the suit of one who has let them for a certain term. Paper Book 137. The court held that trover would not lie in this case.[81]

Trover tried before HOTHAM, Baron, in Kent. The case was shortly this: one Borrett let his house in which was the furniture, the subject of this action, to the plaintiff, which he purchased at the price of £300. After which he [the plaintiff] let the house and furniture for a term not now expired to J. S. Biscoe, Esq., during whose possession the defendant, the sheriff of Kent, took the goods under an execution against Borrett at the suit of one Broomhead. The jury found for the plaintiff.

Shepherd, serjeant moved for a new trial, insisting that Biscoe ought to have brought the action. On showing cause against the rule, what Lord KENYON is stated to have said in *Ward* v. *McCauley*, 4 T.R. 489, was relied on, and it was insisted that this was a case of general property in the plaintiff, and special

---

[79] *Pickering* v. *Barkley* (1648) Style 132.
[80] *Taylor's Case* (n.d.) 4 Leo. 31.
[81] The trial in this case is reported at (1796) 2 Esp. 465. The Paper Book at Lincoln's Inn Library pertains to argument held in Michaelmas term 1796. That (final) phase of the case is fully reported at 7 T.R. 9. The court's holding was that trover would not lie. The last sentence of Lawrence's margin headnote in his notebook was evidently added later, after the court disposed of the case.

property in Biscoe, and that the tortious taking by the defendant had revested the property in the plaintiff. That strictly speaking Biscoe [6:46] had the mere use of the furniture and not any property in it.

On the other hand it was insisted that trover could not be supported by one who would himself be a trespasser if he took that which was the object of the action, and Cro. Car. 242[82] and 5th Bacon's *Abridgment* 258, tit. Trover, were relied on.

The court directed this be made a case, which came on to be argued in Trinity Term by *Burrough* for the plaintiff and *Best* for the defendant. But it was imperfectly stated to raise the question, and therefore was not argued.

Vide Hudson v. Hudson, Latch 214.

Berry v. Herd, Palmer 327.

Same case Cro. Car. 242.

CALLAHAND v. SKERRET

[M.H.] A seaman entering into the king's service is entitled to the wages he may have earned at the time, though there be an express clause in articles that they shall be forfeited in case of desertion.

Gaselee moved for a new trial of an action brought for seaman's wages, he having entered into articles for a voyage from London to the West Indies and back to the port of London, containing a clause that if he deserted, he should forfeit his wages. While the plaintiff was in the West Indies, he left the ship of the defendant and entered on board a man-of-war and insisted in support of the action that he was entitled to his wages under the provisions of 2nd Geo. II, c. 36.

The plaintiff recovered after the rate[83] of 4£: 15s per month for the time he was on board, that being the rate of wages [6:47] he was to be paid for the whole voyage. Mr *Gaselee* insisted that the 2nd Geo. II did not apply to cases in which, by a clause in the articles, the seaman was to forfeit his wages if he deserted. And if that were not so, yet the verdict was wrong as the plaintiff was not entitled to any wages till the voyage was completed. *Cutter* v. *Powell*, 6 T.R. 320.

On showing cause, *Erskine* insisted that this was precisely the case intended to be provided for by the statute [of] Geo. II, which directs that seamen shall enter into articles.

Lord KENYON said that the question depended entirely on the Act of parliament. That for the defendant it was necessary to contend that the plaintiff was a deserter, but the Act had provided that the entering into the king's service should not be an act of desertion. That the intent of it was that no seaman who entered into the navy should lose any benefit by so doing, and as

---

[82] *Berry* v. *Heard* (1632) Cro. Car. 242.
[83] That is, at the rate.

to the entirety of the contract, it was not an agreement for a gross sum, but for wages at so much per month.

Rule discharged. *Vide* 2 Lord Raymond 1211.[84]

HERRIOT v. STEWART

[M.H.] In an action of tort, question if not sufficient to prove so much as would entitle plaintiff to recover if no more had been stated, though the plaintiff has gone further.

Wood moved to set aside a nonsuit before Lord KENYON in an action against the defendant for a libel on plaintiff, being proprietor, publisher and editor of a newspaper called the *True Briton*. One of the witnesses for the plaintiff proved that he was the editor—and it [6:48] being objected that the plaintiff ought to have proved all the characters he alleged belonged to him, he was nonsuit.

Wood now contended it was sufficient to prove he had any one of those characters if that would be sufficient to maintain the action, if that alone had been stated.

A rule *nisi* was granted, but the point was not determined, as the parties settled it.[85] In support of the motion, *vide* Combe v. Pitt, Burrow 1586;[86] Geary v. Connop, Skinner 333; Roberts v. Herbert, Sid. 5;[87] Smith v. Hickson, Cases temp. Hardwicke 54. Same case 2 Barnardiston 465.[88]

COLLINS v. HOOPER

[M.H.] Land tax is to be deducted out of rent charge in proportion to the value of the estate on which charged. *Aliter* in the case of Crown rents.

Darrel moved for a new trial from Warwick in an action brought for the arrears of a rent charge due to the plaintiff as curate of Lindsay. The question

---

[84] *Wiggins* v. *Ingleton* (1705).

[85] The declaration described the plaintiff as proprietor, editor, and publisher of the newspaper. The defendant was one of the two proprietors of another paper, *The Oracle*. Herriot sued Stewart for libel, but was nonsuited by Lord Kenyon at the sittings after Hilary term at Westminster Hall because Herriot had failed to prove that he was the editor of the *True Briton*. His counsel, Wood, sought a new trial, claiming that Herriot could be construed to be the editor since he hired and paid the person who performed that function. Wood also offered dictionary definitions saying that 'editor' and 'publisher' were synonymous. Lord Kenyon rejected Wood's argument, saying that 'there was nothing in it', but asking, 'Why did they so foolishly stuff their declaration with all these terms?' Mr Justice Ashhurst observed that he remembered many cases in which a party had inserted wholly unnecessary things, but having done so, was required to prove them—even though Ashhurst admitted that 'permitting the parties to stuff their declarations with useless and impertinent matter' caused inconvenience and expense to opposing parties, who had to prepare a defence to everything alleged. Mr Justice Grose was uncertain, and Lawrence 'had doubts', as he 'rather thought there were cases in the books to shew that you need not prove all that was stated in the declaration, and where it was only necessary to prove what was sufficient to maintain the action'. See *The Times*, 18 April 1796. As Lawrence's notes show, Lord Kenyon granted a rule *nisi*, but the case was settled.

[86] *Combe* v. *Pitt* (1763–65) 3 Burr. 1423, 1586, 1682, also reported at 1 Bl. W. 437, 523.

[87] *Roberts* v. *Herbert* (1660, 1662) 1 Sid. 5, 97.

[88] Also (1734) Cun. 52 and 2 Str. 977 (*sub nom. Smith* v. *Hixon*).

being to what extent the deduction for the land tax should be made—whether according to the value of the estate at the present time, or whether there should be a deduction of 4s. in the £ on the rent charge. The judge thought the reduction should be according to the improved value.

Lord KENYON said in the case of Crown rents, he had always understood the party paying was entitled to deduct the whole 4s. in the £ out of them, but in other cases the deduction was to be proportionate. That the districts could not have the amount of the assessments varied, but as between individuals, the rule was that equality was equity.

Nil cap.

[6:49A]   HOLT v. SCHOFIELD

[M.H.] 'Thou art foresworn', not actionable.

Action for slander in which the declaration in various counts charged the defendant with imputing to the plaintiff the crime of perjury, and in one count that he said Holt had foresworn himself (meaning thereby that the plaintiff had committed wilful and corrupt perjury) and that the defendant had three witnesses who would swear it.

Entire damages having been assessed on judgment by default, *Holroyd* moved in arrest of judgment, contending that it is not actionable to say of a man that he is foresworn, as it does not appear that it was in any judicial proceeding. And in support of his objection he cited Cowper 684;[89] 3 Lev 166;[90] 3 Inst. 106; 1 Rolle's Abridgment 39; 4 Coke 17b, 20a;[91] Hardress 151.[92] To which may be added 1 Sid 48.[93]

For the plaintiff, *Erskine, Bayley,* and *Vaughan* insisted that being foresworn was synonymous to being perjured. That the introduction in the declaration that defendant meant that plaintiff should suffer the punishment of perjury showed what short of foreswearing was meant, and they relied upon 1st Bulstrode 40 and 150.[94]

Lord KENYON said he thought the case in Bulstrode was distinguishable, and that he felt himself weighed down by authorities.

Rule absolute.[95]

---

[89] 2 Cowp. 684 is a reference to a portion of Chief Justice De Grey's opinion in *R.* v. *Horne* (1777) 2 Cowp. 672, giving the unanimous view of all the judges that, 'in the case of a libel which does not in itself contain the crime, without some extrinsic aid, it is necessary that it should be put upon the record'.

[90] *Gurneth* v. *Derry* (1684).

[91] *James* v. *Rutlech* (1599) 4 Co. Rep. 17a; *Barham* v. *Nethersal* (1602) 4 Co. Rep., 20a.

[92] *Brunigg* v. *Hanger* (1659).

[93] _____ *Danells Case* [sic] (1661).

[94] The first case is *Smale* v. *Hammon* (1610) 1 Bulst. 40, and the second is *Apthorp* v. *Cockerell* (1615) 3 Bulst. 150.

[95] This case is fully reported as *Holt* v. *Scholefield* (1796) 6 T.R. 691. The verdict for the plaintiff was for £50. Two of the four counts alleged that the defendant had accused the plaintiff of having foresworn himself. Counsel for the plaintiff claimed that the 'obvious and known meaning of the word foresworn is an imputation of perjury', citing not only case authority but also Dr Johnson's

Vide 2nd Black. R. 961;[96] Cowper 275;[97] 3 Lev. 68.[98]

[6:49B]   CHANDLER v. BLUNDELL

[M.H.] Affidavit not necessary to obtain prohibition if the matter has been pleaded in the Admiralty.

Parke shewed cause against a rule for a prohibition to the Court of Admiralty. To the suit there, the defendant had put in a plea by way of responsive allegation that the claim was founded on an instrument under seal. But that there was no affidavit of the truth of it.

Abbot relied on *Buggin* v. *Bennet*, 4 Burrow 2037. He said that it is not necessary to have such affidavit if the matter has been pleaded.

Rule absolute.

R. v. McCAN

Defendant was convicted of an assault upon a Custom House officer and receiving some smuggled tobacco which had been seized by him.

As the prisoner had been in prison five months the court adjudged him to be imprisoned seven months in Newgate.

R. v. KIDD WAKE[99]

The defendant was convicted of a misdemeanour in riotously assembling with a number of persons while the king was going to the parliament house on the 29th October, and hissing, hooting, groaning and calling out 'no war', 'down with George'—'no George'.

The sentence was to be kept at hard labour in the penitentiary house at Gloucester five years, and within the first three months of that time to be put in the pillory in the city of Gloucester on a market day, and at the expiration of the five years to give his own security for his good behaviour for ten years in £1000.[1]

---

dictionary. Thus, they argued, this ordinary meaning was open to the jury by innuendo, especially when coupled with the introductory matter in the declaration. These arguments failed. Lawrence said that if the introductory matter in the declaration could be used in this way, 'none of the objections in the books could have prevailed, because the same sort of introduction is inserted in almost all declarations'. Ibid., at 694. The remaining two counts alleged that the defendant had accused the plaintiff of perjury, but since the damages (by default) were entire, the court held that the judgment should be arrested and no new trial granted. Apparently counsel for the plaintiff asked if the trial judge's notes might be used to amend the declaration, but Lawrence said no, 'because the evidence applied as well to the bad as to the good counts'. Ibid., at 695.

[96] *Oldham* v. *Peake* (1774) 2 Bl. W. 959, 961.
[97] *Peake* v. *Oldham* (1775) 1 Cowp. 275.
[98] *Knightly* v. *Marrow* (1682) 3 Lev. 68.
[99] See p. 94, above, for an earlier phase of this case.
[1] A number of reports of this case appeared in *The Times*. The first, on 31 October 1795, reported on Wake's examination at the Bow Street criminal court. According to that account, the defendant (a journeyman printer) admitted hissing and hooting at the king but denied throwing

[6:49C] R. v. JUSTICES of ANGLESEY

[M.H.] On appeals to the sessions against orders of removal the respondent is to begin.

Gibbs shewed cause against a rule for a *mandamus* to the justices of the county of Anglesey and to enter continuances and at the next sessions to hear an appeal which had come before them, one when the magistrates were equally divided—and had been then adjourned when three justices only met, two of whom had made the original order. At this sessions the respondent refused to begin, when the two justices who had made the order, in the absence of the third who had gone away, affirmed it.

Lord KENYON said it had been determined that the respondent should begin, and intimating strongly his opinion that the Justices must hear the appeal. *Gibbs* said as he saw the inclination of the court, he should advise his clients to do what was wished.

R. v. A. DOLBEN *et al.*

Defendant was convicted of an assault and obstruction of a Custom House officer by throwing him out of a boat and while in the water striking him with a boat-hook.

The sentence was to be imprisoned two years in Newgate, and find security for his good behaviour for three years, himself in £100 and two sureties in £50 each.

EX PARTE HAMILTON

[M.H.] Attorney admitted ten years without serving a clerkship, the court at the distance will not enquire into it.

Erskine moved to strike one Hamilton off the roll of attorneys, he not having served any clerkship.

Lord KENYON understanding that he had been admitted ten years, said it was too long ago for the court to enquire into it.

Nil cap.

---

anything at the carriage, 'and said that he considered every person at liberty to express their disapprobation of the war'. The trial was on 20 February 1796 before Lord Kenyon and a special jury at the Hilary sittings at Westminster Hall. Attorney-General Scott was counsel for the Crown; Erskine, for the defendant. After eyewitness testimony for the prosecution was given, Erskine said that 'it was impossible for the defendant to traverse that evidence'—the defendant was, however, anxious to present character witnesses, even though Erskine acknowledged that 'character could not resist positive facts'. *The Times*, 22 April 1796. At the sentencing hearing on 21 April, the defendant presented an affidavit in mitigation of punishment, among other things claiming that he was near-sighted and had forgotten his glasses on the day when the king passed by, and in squinting to see, 'his features became distorted, and he appeared to strangers to be making wry faces'. He was supported by thirteen character witnesses. *The Times*, 22 April 1796. Mr Justice Ashhurst pronounced the sentence on 6 May. Ashhurst said that even if the defendant were near-sighted as he claimed, this did nothing to explain the words he had shouted at the king. And as to the fact that the defendant had a dependent wife, it was a pity 'that it is the lot of the innocent to suffer with the guilty', but the defendant should have thought of that before he acted. *The Times*, 9 May 1796.

[6:50] [April 25]   R. v. COLLEGE of PHYSICIANS

[M.H.] If a man founds his title to be a member of a corporation under a by-law, he can't dispute any other of the by-laws regulating such admission.

Chambré moved in the last term for a writ of *mandamus* to be directed to the president and fellows of the College of Physicians to admit Christopher Stanger, doctor of physic, to examination in order that he might be admitted into the order of candidates for election into the society or fellowship of the college.

In the affidavit made in support of this motion, the doctor stated his having had the degree of doctor of physic in Edinburgh in 1783. That in 1789 he became a licentiate of the college. And that he had applied to Sir George Baker, the president, and the other fellows of the college desiring to be examined, in order that he might be admitted a candidate, but that they had told him he was not qualified, not being a graduate of the university of Oxford or Cambridge. The validity of which by-law he denied, and he tendered himself at the *Comitia Minora* for examination, but that committee had refused to examine him.

In answer to this application, affidavits were made by Sir George Baker and others by which it appeared by the charter of the college there was no such order as an order of candidates. That the power of determining who were proper persons to be fellows was left to the college, who by their by-laws had directed that before any persons should be admitted fellows, they should be in a probationary state for one year, having been previously examined and found fit by a committee called *Comitia Minora*, [6:51] during which time they were called candidates, and that the by-law provided that no one should be in this order who was not graduate of Oxford or Cambridge. It further appeared that there was another provision for the admission of such persons into the fellowship who had not taken a degree at either of our universities. If they had been licentiates seven years, and were 36 years of age—if they were proposed by any fellow and were found qualified on three examinations.

On these affidavits *Erskine* and *Gibbs* shewed cause and contended that as this was an application to be admitted under a by-law, the doctor could not support his claim to the *mandamus*, unless he showed himself entitled according to the terms of that by-law, and that he could not object to the legality of one part, and found any right upon the other part. And had he meant to controvert the goodness of the by-law, he should have applied to be directed a fellow of the College of Physicians.

Law, *Chambré* and others feebly endeavoured to support the rule.

Lord KENYON: The body at large have under the circumstances remitted the examination of persons desirous of becoming fellows of the college to the *Comitia Minora*, but Dr Stanger does not stand under those circumstances. This is done by one of a body of by-laws made on a supposition that the college have a right to make a distinction between the doctors of Oxford and Cambridge and of other universities. Now you can't sap this distinction [while] admitting the [6:52] by-laws good for other purposes. Now assuming the power of confining the fellowship to the doctors of Oxford and Cambridge is illegal—which I by no means admit—I do not know that it is ill assumed—how can you garble the by-laws and reject a part? I do not know that the by-law is unreasonable. Diplomas from many universities may be got for a small sum of money and what would become of this very learned body if all persons who may have got such degrees should be admitted? The legislature in many instances has not thought it unreasonable to require degrees in the university. What do you say to the rule laid down by bishops that persons ordained shall have been at the university—a rule which it is a pity should have ever been broke through.

Rule discharged.[2]

R. v. SPETTIGUE *et al.*

[M.H.] Question if a mere inhabitant of a town subject to the jurisdiction of the corporation can be a relator in *quo warranto*. Information in *quo warranto* not to be granted if the application be collusive. *Vide* 6 T.R. 504.[3]

In Michaelmas Term last an information in the nature of a *quo warranto* had been moved for against the defendant, one Cutcliffe, and others for exercising the offices of freemen, &c. of Launceston. The duke of Northumberland, the recorder of the borough, being one of the persons joining in the affidavits and the real prosecutor. That rule was discharged in Hilary term, it appearing that the same objection which was made to the defendant's title applied to those who had made the several affidavits.

Erskine this term renewed the application against the defendant William Frost on the affidavit [6:53] of one Tyeth, an inhabitant of the town but no

---

[2] Dr Stanger tried again in 1797. After a three-day hearing, the Court again refused to issue a *mandamus*. The proceeding is extensively reported at 7 T.R. 282, 16 May 1797. In a footnote at the end of the report, a brief description is given of the 1796 attempt noted above by Lawrence. That earlier attempt was also reported by *The Times* summarily on 26 April and at length on 9 September. In the latter version, Erskine's fabled eloquence took flight on behalf of the College in opposing the *mandamus*. Erskine lauded the character of physicians in England as superior to 'any other nation under Heaven', pointed out that the College by-laws were no obstacle to any man practising the profession, but 'no one should have an opportunity of forcing himself into the College, unsanctioned by those by-laws'. Otherwise, a hackney coachman might apply after obtaining a degree of doctor of physic for £5 in Aberdeen—and what would prevent the same thing from happening in the other learned professions of theology and law? Before counsel for Dr Stanger (Law and Chambré) could respond, Lord Kenyon said that he was troubled by Dr Stanger's failure to exhaust his remedies—'You ought to have gone to the *Comitia Minora*, and had your claim rejected by them, before you came into this Court.' Law and Chambré argued nevertheless the pernicious consequences of the Oxford and Cambridge restriction, even invoking Adam Smith's assertion in his *Wealth of Nations* that the teaching of the sciences at the two universities was inferior to that in the public schools. Lord Kenyon responded by saying, 'I know that at Leyden and other Universities on the Continent, a *Diploma* may be purchased for a few shillings, and if such graduates have a right to come here, and to insist on being admitted into the College of Physicians, what is to become of this very learned body, who deserve all that Mr Erskine has said of them?'

[3] *R.* v. *Cudlipp* (1796) 6 T.R. 503. Cudlipp and, in Lawrence's notes, Cutliffe were undoubtedly the same person.

corporator, who swore that if the *quo warranto* were granted he would prosecute it at his own expense, that the application was made at his expense, and that he had no promise or expectation of being reimbursed, and that he as an inhabitant of the town was subject to the jurisdiction of the borough justices, and of the sessions. And as such, interested in the validity of their titles. As to the constitution of the borough, he was joined by Lethbridge, the town clerk, who was liable to the same objection with the persons moved against.

Gibbs, *Law* and *Dampier* showed cause against the rules for Spettigue. No person appeared for Frost, who on the former application had been defended by the attorney of Spettigue and the others, but had on this occasion refused his assistance, and had said he should apply to the attorney for the prosecution. The affidavits they used went to show that in fact the duke was the prosecutor and that Frost had been got over to his interest.

On these they insisted as furnishing an answer to the application—and further that Tyeth, being no member of the corporation, was in no situation to question their titles, and as he could not himself swear to the constitution. There was no relator's affidavit as to that which they contended was necessary, in as much as Lethridge could not be a relator on account of the objection to his title.

[6:54] Erskine, *e contra*, insisted that as Tyeth was interested in the jurisdiction in which he lived, he was in a situation to be a relator, and could by no means be considered as a stranger. That after his affidavit the court could not look upon the duke of Northumberland as the prosecutor. That if he was to be considered as the relator, he had a right to use the evidence of any person, who could not apply himself.

Mr *Bond* on the same side insisted that as it was admitted the elections had been illegal, the court could only further the justice of the case by suffering the inhabitants to be relators, as no corporator could.

Lord KENYON observed that the first objection on behalf of the defendant was that the relator should swear to all the facts to support his rule. This he thought could not be supported. If a man be a *bona fide* relator, though he comes with materials *aliunde* we will hear him.

The next objection is that Tyeth does not stand in the condition of a relator, as not being a member of the corporation.

When this question comes I shall give my best attention to it, but I shall give no opinion on it now. We decided the last question upon the ground that the duke of Northumberland was the relator—is he not now? Tyeth it is true has sworn what meets the ear but we [6:55] must look into the surrounding circumstances to see if he is the real prosecutor, and crave the same indulgence for the court as juries have as to their belief, when witnesses swear positively.

If the question was answered by any reasonable man who is the prosecutor of this application, would he not say *alter* and *idem*. And he thought as to Frost the information ought not to go, as it would be put into the hands of persons dealing collusively.

Per curiam: rule discharged.

R. v. GEE and RICHARDS

They were convicted of assaulting one Lloyd, a revenue officer in the execution of his duty. The defendants with others to the amount of forty assaulted the officer and a party of soldiers who were acting in his assistance.

The judgment on them was two years' imprisonment in Newgate.

R. v. STEWART

[M.H.] Warrants need not be so precise as the convictions on which they are grounded.

Marriot moved for a *habeas corpus* to bring up John Stewart, who had been committed as a vagrant, for an offence contrary to the Lottery Act, 27 Geo. III, c. 1.

The objections he made to the warrant were, first that it did not appear that the committing magistrate was a magistrate of the county where the offence was committed. Secondly that he was committed to the next sessions of the courts, no county being mentioned. Thirdly that it was not negatived that he had not been sued for the penalties.

Lord KENYON on the day of bringing defendant up [6:56] said the objections might be good to the conviction, but is that so to a warrant?

Marriot mentioned *R. v. Rhodes*, 4 T.R. 221[4] as an authority to show that the defendant should be discharged if there had been no previous conviction, and said here was no conviction, except the warrant of commitment could be so considered.

Lord KENYON said that in the case of warrants, the court was not extreme to mark what was done amiss and remanded the defendant. *Marriot* then moved for a *certiorari* to remove the conviction.

R. v. BEARD

Defendant, an attorney in the county of Cornwall, was convicted on an information for challenging and provoking another attorney of the name of Johns to fight a duel. He had done this several times and in the intervals had been seen practising at a target.

The court adjudged him to be imprisoned nine calendar months in the King's Bench—and to enter into a recognizance for his good behaviour, himself in the sum of £500 and two sureties in the sum of £250 each for five years.[5]

[*Lawrence note*:] Hilary 25 Geo. III, Major Brown for a challenge of a Mr Luher was imprisoned six months and fined [£]100, security for five years,

---

[4] *R. v. Rhodes* (1721) 4 T.R. 220.

[5] In delivering judgment, Mr Justice Ashhurst stated that 'it is fit we should pronounce such a sentence as may convince the world we do not chuse to give countenance to this practice'. *The Times*, 4 May 1796.

[£]500, and two sureties [£]250. 33 Geo. III, R. Mackreth for challenging Sir John Scott was imprisoned in B.R. six months and fined £100.

[6:57] R. v. LADY VALENTIA

[M.H.] Affidavits gone into as to the morality of a parent on a writ of *habeas corpus* brought by him for his infant son.

Lord Valentia had moved for a *habeas corpus* to be directed to Lady Valentia to bring up the body of his son, an infant of the age of two years and ½ old, that he might have the child delivered to him, she at that time living in adultery with a gentleman of the name of Gawler.

Gibbs on behalf of Lady Valentia opposed this on affidavits that the husband was a man addicted to unnatural practices, and as such unfit to have the custody of his son.

Erskine desired time to answer the affidavits, and said in the meantime he did not desire that the custody of the child should be changed, which Lord KENYON said was by no means a proper custody, but as it was not desired to be changed, he should give no directions.

Affidavits on 7th May, the affidavits on behalf of Lord Valentia having been read, contradicting the charge, the child was directed to be delivered to the father. Neither Lady Valentia nor the child were in court, but attended in a place adjoining, ready to come into court if it had been required.[6]

As to [the] writ of *habeas corpus* in similar cases, *vide R. v. Clarkson*, Strange

---

[6] Unsurprisingly, the marital discord and custody battle of the Valentias were noticed in the newspapers. Lord Kenyon—who always exhibited 'an uncommon degree of anxiety to restore peace and comfort to unfortunate families'—urged the parties to find 'some common friend of the family under whose care this child might be placed'. Erskine asked for time to respond to Lady Valentia's affidavit, 'for, if the contents of that affidavit were true, it ought to repel him, not only from the custody of this child, but from human society'. *The Times*, 3 May 1796. Lord Kenyon again tried to get the child placed, insisting that, 'At present, the custody of this infant is wholly improper, it must be changed.' *The Times*, 5 May 1796. After receiving and hearing the affidavits from Lord Valentia refuting Lady Valentia's allegations, Lord Kenyon volunteered that he should have been more willing to hear the case, since 'the attack on Lord Valentia appears to be most unwarranted', and he ordered that, 'The child must be delivered over to the father.' Kenyon confessed, though 'perhaps it may be extrajudicial', that he knew 'Lord Valentia as a public character on the Oxford circuit', in 'the most honourable of all situations in which a country gentleman . . . could be engaged', that is, 'at the head of his county at Stafford, as Foreman of the Grand Jury'. *The Times*, 9 May 1796. The last phase in the common law courts of this domestic tempest was the suit by Lord Valentia against John Benjamin Gawler for criminal conversation with Lady Valentia, tried before Lord Kenyon and a special jury on 19 May. Erskine continued to represent Lord Valentia; Gibbs, Lady Valentia. In his speech to the jury, Erskine described the Valentias' marriage when the groom was 20, the bride but 16, and the friendship that developed with two Gawler brothers—the defendant and his brother Henry, a barrister who was one of Lady Valentia's trustees. Gibbs attempted to bring in matters that occurred subsequent to the alleged adultery, but also claimed that Lord Valentia 'was regardless of the virtue of his lady', having publicly and indifferently remarked on the criminal conversation between his wife and Gawler. Lord Kenyon, as was his custom, gave 'a melancholy picture of the times', calling upon the jury to do their duty, 'as the morals of the people were in some measure entrusted to them'. The jury returned a verdict for Lord Valentia, with damages of £1,000, and a subsequent motion for a new trial failed. See *The Times*, 20 May and 1 June 1796.

444; *R.* v. *Johnson*, ibid. 579; *R.* v. *Smith*, ibid. 982; *R.* v. *Sir J. Delaval*, Burrow 1436; and the case of William Murray, Trinity 34 Geo. III, 5 MSS.[7]

[6:58]   PIGOT v. DUNN

[M.H.] Carrier advertising that he will not be liable for jewels or any valuables above £5 unless entered accordingly is not liable for goods above that value if not properly entered though not *ejusdem generis* with jewels, *ut semb.*, and is not liable to the extent of £5. *Vide Clay* v. *Willan*, 1 H. Black 298.

The plaintiff had sent some clothes from Bath to Birmingham from whence they were to be forwarded by the 'Charles' coach of which the defendant was the proprietor. In his coach office, there was a board on which notice was painted, that the proprietor of the coach would not be answerable for money, jewels, writings, or any valuables above £5 unless entered and paid for as such when declared.

There were also advertisements stuck about the town of Birmingham by which the proprietors declared they would not be accountable for any valuables above £5 unless entered and paid for accordingly.

The porter of the Bath coach who carries the clothes from there to the 'Charles' coach was aware that parcels carried by the defendant's coach were to be paid for extra if above the value of £5, and to be entered as such.

Under these circumstances it was contended before me at Shrewsbury[8] that the regulation as to the £5 was to be confined to things *ejusdem generis* with those specialised on the board, e.g. plate, watches &c. And that the plaintiff whose clothes had been lost was entitled to recover at least £5.

These points were saved.

And on a motion to enter a nonsuit, the court were of opinion that upon the whole of the case, there was no doubt [6:59] the plaintiff ought to be nonsuit, and inclined to be of opinion against her had it rested on the notice in the coach office only, and they held her not entitled to recover £5, as her not having entered her parcel as not being above the value of £5. The defendant had not been called on to pay a particular attention to it.

Rule absolute for nonsuit.

R. v. ISABELLA WILLIAMS[9]

Convicted of rescuing a lugger[10] from some revenue officers, throwing stones at them from a cliff thirty feet high and rushing upon them with twenty other persons armed with pistols, cutlasses, &c. and firing at them.

---

[7] *R.* v. *Clarkson* and *R.* v. *Johnson* are in vol. 1 of *Strange's Reports*; *R.* v. *Smith* is in vol. 2, and *R.* v. *Delaval* is in vol. 3 of *Burrow's Reports*. The William Murray case is at p. 55, above.

[8] That is, before Mr Justice Lawrence as the trial judge at the Shrewsbury assizes.

[9] In the manuscript, Lawrence spells the defendant's first name as 'Sebylla'. The spelling given in the report in *The Times*, 5 May 1796, has been adopted.

[10] A small vessel equipped with a lugsail, i.e., a four-cornered sail without a boom.

Many affidavits were read to her character.

Adjudged to one year's imprisonment in the county gaol at Bodmin.[11]

GEORGE v. BAXTER

[M.H.] Verdict not to be set aside to enable defendant to insist on the Statute of Usury against the *bona fide* holder of a negotiable security.

Russel showed cause against a rule for a new trial in which, by some neglect, there had been no defence that the defendant might set up the Statute of Usury against plaintiff, the *bona fide* holder of a bill of exchange for valuable consideration.

The court discharged the rule, Lord KENYON saying the plaintiff had good luck to be formally right, and he would not put him into a situation which the court would regret, adding this could be no precedent in other cases.

[6:60]   ## DALTON v. LAMBERT

[M.H.] Those who are entitled to the effects of an intestate may pay an insolvent his groats before administration granted.

Marriot shewed cause against discharging a man out of custody for non-payment of his groats.[12]

The fact was that the plaintiff had died, and a dispute arose touching the right of administration, and a suit was instituted and is now depending, during which time the groats had been constantly tendered by persons entitled to distribute shares.

Lord KENYON said nothing was more reasonable than that persons concerned in interest should keep the suit alive, and the defendant suffered no inconvenience.

Rule discharged.

---

[11] According to *The Times*, 'Mrs Williams was a woman of very genteel appearance, and it was rather a novel spectacle in the Court of King's Bench, and excited a good deal of surprize, to hear that she had sallied forth at the head of 20 men armed with swords, pistols, and tomahawks, and had assaulted and obstructed two Revenue Officers in the execution of their office, and had rescued a lugger containing uncustomed goods.' Mr Justice Ashhurst observed 'that if this woman were to go unpunished on account of her sex, he was afraid this sort of business would pass into female hands, and that men would withdraw themselves from the danger of punishment'. He nevertheless allowed that the court 'had taken her sex into consideration, and meant to pass a lighter punishment than perhaps, for the sake of example, they ought'.

[12] As explained by Margot Finn, 'By the Lords Act of 1759, debtors imprisoned on final process were eligible to sue for their "groats", a sum of two shillings and fourpence per week paid by the detaining creditor to maintain the debtor in prison.' M. Finn, *The Character of Credit: Personal Debt in English Culture, 1740–1914* (2003), p. 122. She also notes that, 'The amount of "groats" was increased to three shillings and sixpence in 1797.' Ibid., n. 46.

R. v. CORPORATION of SEAFORTH

[M.H.] Rule to show cause only granted and not a *mandamus* in the first instance to elect in a case of doubt on a disclaimer whether another was not elected at the time the party disclaiming took upon himself the office.

The duke of Richmond having been elected a bailiff of the borough of Seaforth, an information in the nature of *quo warranto* was filed against him, on which he disclaimed, and now Serjeant *Shepherd* moved for a writ of *mandamus* to elect a bailiff in his room.

This was opposed by *Erskine*, who alleged that when the duke was pretended to be elected, one Chambers was in fact elected, a number of persons having voted for him and those who did not, but [voted] for the duke, so acted with notice of the duke's disqualification.

No affidavit was produced on either side.

Lord KENYON said in a case of difficulties the safest way was to grant a rule to show cause—which was done.[13]

[6:61] ## PRITCHARD v. STEVENS

[M.H.] Promise to pay a debt by a bankrupt as defendant should be able is no absolute promise.

Defendant, having obtained his certificate, promised to pay the plaintiff's debt if he would take it by instalments, and undertook to pay 10:6 the next Saturday and the rest as he was able.

Lord KENYON held this no absolute promise to pay and made a rule absolute to discharge him on filing common bail.

R. v. HILLS

[M.H.] Though a defendant's recognizance has been respited in consequence of the prosecutor not giving a rule to plead, the prosecutor may move to take off the respite, and compel the defendant to carry down the record to trial.

Marriot shewed cause against reviving a recognizance which had been

---

[13] According to a news report, Erskine and Garrow contended that 'Chambers had five votes, and his Grace sixteen, and those who voted for him [his Grace] had full notice that they were throwing their votes away, as he was no inhabitant'; thus, 'Mr Chambers was Bailiff of Seaforth both *de facto* and *de jure*.' They explained that the duke did not disclaim the office until the previous Saturday night, after post time, so that there was no time to send to Seaforth for affidavits. Leach, as counsel on the same side as Shepherd, contended that the office was empty, and when Lord Kenyon asked for whom he appeared, Leach said, 'a great number of the freemen of Seaforth'. Kenyon lost his patience, stating: 'You could not receive the complaints of these freemen since Saturday last, unless they came by telegraph. I have nothing to do with the politics of Seaforth, nor do I care a farthing about them. One is sorry when such causes get into a Court of Justice.' *The Times*, 10 May 1796. (The non-electric telegraph was invented in 1794 and depended on line-of-sight communication, using semaphore. See G. Holzmann and B. Pehrson, *The Early History of Data Networks* (1995), pp. 62–63.)

respited *quousque*. Defendant had been indicted in the Crown Office. The prosecutor did not order a rule to plead, and in such case, the defendant is not bound to carry down the record—in consequence of which it had been respited for four terms, and then in the ordinary was respited *quousque*.

Marriot contended that the prosecutor might now enter a rule to plead or carry down the record himself.

Lord KENYON said reviving the recognizance is an improper term, but the defendant must comply with the condition of the recognizance, which is that he shall carry down the record.

[6:62]   B.R. TRINITY TERM 36 Geo. III

Lloyd, Lord Kenyon, Chief Justice
Sir W. Ashhurst ⎫
Sir N. Grose   ⎬ Justices
Sir S. Lawrence ⎭

May 30   R. v. HENRY WILLIAM GRIST

Defendant having been convicted of keeping a disorderly house called the Temple of Flora received sentence to be imprisoned six months and to find sureties for his good behaviour for five years, himself in £500 and two sureties in £250 each. He had been committed in the last term.

June 1   R. v. CROSSLEY and CLARKE

[M.H.] How far the positive affidavit of one against a rule for an attachment concludes the court.

A warrant having been obtained to search Crossley's house on a charge of forgery, there was found among his papers a blank paper, at the bottom of which was the name William Clarke written and in the opposite corner a *jurat*, in the usual form in which it is made, to depositions in Chancery with the name of one Brierly, a master extraordinary in Chancery, subscribed. This was found in a private desk of Crossley. Besides this a letter from Clarke to Crossley was found, by which Clarke informed Crossley 'that he had got him four deed stamps, that he could not get a 15s. bond stamp as he promised, that he would try at another place to which he was going, or an old sheet might be stamped, that he had some very choice paper forty years old'.

Crossley having been acquitted of the [6:63] forgery, a rule was made on him and Clarke, they being both attorneys, to answer the matters of the affidavit stating the circumstances of finding the above paper and letter.

Crossley by his affidavit stated this paper had been in his possession seven years and that it had come to his hands in a larger bundle of papers left with him about the business of one Walker of Leicester. And that there being an advertisement from the Stamp Office of counterfeit stamps being in circulation, he applied to Clarke for stamps in order to compare with some that he had, and that he was an utter stranger to what Clarke meant by choice papers forty years old.

Clarke denied that the name subscribed to the paper with the *jurat* was his handwriting, and that the letter respecting the stamps was to satisfy Crossley that a number of stamps Crossley had bought of him were genuine. And that the expression of choice paper forty years old alluded to some India paper given to his wife by Sir Hugh Pallisar to make a fire screen.

The counsel for Crossley and Clarke insisted that however suspicious their clients' case was, the rule must be discharged, [6:64] as they had denied everything that was criminal, and that there was nothing which affected them as officers of this court.

Lord KENYON said it was not in the power of everybody to intrude themselves into the situation of attorneys. That the property of various persons was committed to their care, and that improper persons might not get in, the legislature had taken all the care it could. That if at any time after a man had gotten into the situation of an attorney, those circumstances should appear that made it unfit he should be any longer accredited by the court, it was fit he should no longer continue so accredited.

That the question before the court was, if that which required explanation had been explained. That in answer to a motion for an attachment, every allegation which carried with it its own death's wound would not do. If so a man must be believed who said an angel from heaven or the Pope of Rome brought a paper to him. That the court had every inclination to believe what a man swears, especially when at the peril of perjury. [6:65] That if the question as far as respected Clarke had turned simply on the paper with the *jurat*, the court would have been concluded by his positive affidavit. That as to Crossley, it appeared that he had a paper which could only be used for bad purposes, for about seven years, which he had kept in his own private drawer, when, if his account were true, it was his duty to have destroyed it. That no one would say he had given a satisfactory answer.

The other judges agreeing, the rule was made absolute for the attachment.[14]

---

[14] Colourful details about this case were given in the newspapers. Crossley and Clarke were attorneys of the Court of King's Bench, as was a third defendant, Thomas Brierly, who also held the office of master extraordinary in Chancery. See *The Times*, 30 April, 31 May, and 3 June 1796. Counsel for the defendants (Erskine and Garrow for Crossley; Mingay and Gibbs for Clarke) confessed 'that the dead weight which pressed them down, was the blasted character of their clients', but they gamely contended that for purposes of an attachment, affidavits were to be regarded as true, and since the defendants in their affidavits had denied the allegations of the prosecution (plus the fact that Crossley had been prosecuted for forgery and acquitted), the defendants 'were to be considered in the same light as if they were men of the purest characters'. Lord Kenyon obviously disagreed with their contention, saying (in addition to his comments above) that it was absurd, ridiculous, sufficient 'to turn a Court of Justice into mockery and ridicule'. See *The Times*, 3 June 1796. (Crossley's trial for forgery at the Old Bailey was on 17 February 1796 and a lengthy report of the case is in the Old Bailey Sessions Papers. See Old Bailey

[*Lawrence note*:]: On an affidavit by an officer of the Stamp Office that the stamp on the paper with the *jurat* was not in existence for some years after the time Crossley swore he had it in his possession, the court committed him to Newgate for perjury.[15]

June 4   R. v. GRINDLEY

[M.H.] *Mandamus* to deliver books &c. to the deputy of an infant register of a diocese refused. The application should be in Chancery.

Leicester shewed cause against a rule for a *mandamus* to be directed to one who had been appointed by an infant who was register of the diocese of Bangor to be his deputy, requiring him to deliver up all archives, papers, &c. belonging to that office to one Roberts, who was appointed deputy in his room.
[6:66]
Erskine and *Gibbs* were to support the rule, but Lord KENYON said that the court could not grant the writ, for anything they knew they might be putting the archives, &c. into improper hands. That the Court of Chancery was the proper place to make the application in, where security would be taken from the deputy to account to his principal.

                                                                      Rule discharged.[16]

R. v. GINEVER

[M.H.] Query if the Crown was to take issue and demur to a defendant's plea in *quo warranto*. 6 T.R. 732, same case.[17]

To a *quo warranto* for exercising the office of bailiff of East Retford the plea stated a charter of James I giving the bailiffs and aldermen, or the major part of them, power to choose one of the aldermen to be bailiff. And then stated a bylaw giving the senior bailiff a casting voice, where the votes were equal. That the votes being equal, the senior bailiff gave the defendant his casting voice.

To this there was a replication taking issue upon several parts of the plea, and demurring to that part which stated the bylaw.

Wood moved to quash the demurrer, insisting that the Crown cannot take issue and demur *uno flatu*. He admitted that the Crown might [6:67] traverse several facts, for which Saville 19 was an authority,[18] but said there was no authority for what was done in this case. He cited 10 Mod. 200[19] and Brook's

Proceedings Online, <http://www.oldbaileyonline.org/>, case no. t17960217-70 (accessed 14 October 2012). After deliberating for half an hour from 3.30 to 4.00 am, the Middlesex jury returned a verdict of not guilty.

[15] See p. 103, above; p. 158, below.
[16] See p. 166, below, where, on a second application, the *mandamus* was granted.
[17] The printed report deals with the demurrer on the merits. The point of pleading raised in Lawrence's notes is mentioned in passing in a footnote.
[18] Case XLVII, *Cinque Ports* (1582) Sav. 19.
[19] *R. v. Delme* (1714) 10 Mod. 198.

Abridgment, tit: verdict, pl. 79 to show that the utmost the attorney-general could do was to waive his issue and demur, or *vice versa*, but said that he could not do both any more than assign error in fact and in law at the same time.

Yates, e contra, quoted the pleadings in *R. v. Gibbon*, one of the New Romney corporators, and *R. v. Bayley*, 7 and 8 Geo. II. He also cited Coke's Entries 527b, 4 Burr. 2143, 3 Burr. 1407, 4 Burr. 2515.[20] And the case of the *quo warranto* against the city of London to show that you may take issue and reply, to which there may be a demurrer, so that by a frivolous replication the same thing would be effected as demurring directly to the plea, but as he had no doubt of the validity of the demurrer, offered to withdraw the issues, which was done.

Lord KENYON seemed to think there could be no inconvenience in this mode of pleading, for if there is no demurrer after verdict the goodness of the plea might be discussed on a motion in arrest of judgment or on writ of error.

Vide: *R. v. Amery*, 1 T.R. 575; *R. v. Bellringer*, 4 T.R. 480.[21]

[6:68] June 9   R. v. BAILIFFS &c. of EAST RETFORD

[M.H.] *Mandamus* granted to swear one into an office for the exercise of which an information in *quo warranto* had been filed against him.

Erskine, Gibbs, Perceval, and *Wood* showed cause against a *mandamus* to swear one Clarke into the office of senior bailiff of the town of Retford.

An information had been granted against him for usurping that office, to which he had pleaded, and it was insisted that he ought not to have a *mandamus* to swear him into an office, which it appeared by the records of the court he was then actually exercising.

Sed per Lord KENYON: It may be that the *quo warranto* was because he was not well sworn into his office. By granting the writ we may do a great deal of justice, and we can injure no person whose interest we should attend to.

Rule absolute.

June 13 R. v. SIR JOSEPH MAWBEY and LIPPTROTT, CLERK

The defendants being magistrates of the county of Surrey, having been convicted of conspiracy to pervert the cause of justice in producing at the gaol delivery for that county a certificate under their hands that a road within the parish of Windlesham was in good repair when it was not, received the judgment of the court which was that Mawbey should pay a fine of £100, Lipptrott a fine of £50. The court directed the proceedings against them to be laid before the chancellor, who struck them both out of the commission of the peace.[22]

---

[20] *R. v. Leigh* (1768) 4 Burr. 2143; *Mayor of Yarmouth v. Eaton* (1763) 3 Burr. 1402; *R. v. Head* (1770) 4 Burr. 2515.

[21] *R. v. Bellringer* is reported at (1792) 4 T.R. 810

[22] This case is fully reported at (1796) 6 T.R. 619. The indictment was preferred at the quarter sessions for Surrey in October 1794, and the trial was held at the spring assizes, 1795. Initially there were four defendants; two were acquitted, but Mawbey and Lipptrott were convicted. A motion

[6:69] HAWKINS v. LUKIN

[M.H.] Whether a trader's going abroad without any intent of delaying his creditors be an act of bankruptcy, if they are in fact delayed.

On a motion for a new trial before Lord KENYON, the question was if one Westwood had committed an act of bankruptcy. The facts insisted on to prove an act of bankruptcy were shortly as follows: Westwood, a trader having drawn bills to the amount of [£]300, went abroad on a journey of pleasure, not doubting but that the acceptor would have paid them, relying on which he made no provision for them, and the acceptor did not pay.

Lord KENYON thought this going abroad no act of bankruptcy, as not being done with an intent to delay his creditors.

Law, who moved for a new trial, insisted on the words of the statute of James 1st,[23] which has not the words 'to the intent' but only the word 'whereby', and relied on *Woodyear's Case* in Buller's *Nisi Prius*, who was held to have committed an act of bankruptcy in going abroad in consequence of his having killed a man and not with a view of delaying his creditors, as the effect of it was to delay them.[24] Mr *Wood* on the same side observed that unless the statute of James had a more enlarged construction than the statute of Elizabeth, it would have no effect whatever, as according to the argument for the defendant, the statute of Elizabeth reached every case within the statute of James I.

Erskine, *Garrow*, and *Lawes*, *contra*, insisted on the monstrous mischiefs which would follow if it should be held that every absence from a man's house by which his creditors were delayed in recovering their debts [6:70] so immediately as they otherwise would be able to do should be held an act of bankruptcy when the trader had no intent or suspicion he was delaying his creditors, and they endeavoured to distinguish *Woodyear's Case* from this, as there was no *animus revertendi*.

---

was filed for a new trial for the two defendants who were convicted, and it was decided that a new trial would be legitimate (see p. 133, above). The printed report covers the earlier procedural argument, the hearing on a motion in arrest of judgment, and the argument on 25 April 1796 on a motion for a new trial on the merits. The two defendants lost at every stage. The various proceedings were also covered extensively in the newspapers. See *The Times*, 14 November 1795; 15 and 26 April 1796; 10 and 14 June 1796. At the 9 June hearing when the prosecutor moved for judgment against the defendants, Sir Joseph Mawbey filed an affidavit in mitigation of damages, claiming to having served conscientiously for thirty-six years as a magistrate and for twenty-five years as chairman of the quarter sessions for Surrey; also presented were about twenty supportive affidavits, most from 'Gentlemen of the first rank and consequence in the County of Surrey'. After Mr Justice Ashhurst announced the sentence on 13 June, Sir Joseph asked if he might be permitted to say a word to the court; then, amazingly, said that, 'He had no doubt, that it was in the memory of every gentleman who was present at the trial, that the Learned Judge, who had just spoke, and who tried the cause, did not take any notice to the Jury of the testimony of eight or nine witnesses who appeared on the part of the defendants.' Chief Justice Kenyon interrupted, saying that 'the Court could not hear such an allegation'. *The Times*, 14 June 1796.

[23] 1 Jac. I, c. 15. s. 2.

[24] Buller describes the case of Woodier as having been 'cited by Sir J. Strange in Degolls and Ward, Hil. 12 G. 2'. F. Buller, *An Introduction to the Law Relative to Trials at Nisi Prius*, 5th ed. (1790), at p. 39.

Lord KENYON said this was one of the most important cases that ever was agitated. That the extent to which the arguments for the plaintiff pressed was shocking. If a man be ill and his creditors can't see him, is that an act of bankruptcy? Or if he goes out, though ever so opulent, and his creditors do not find him at home? The whole resolves itself into *Woodyear's Case.* I should think the word *or* in the statute might be rendered *and.* That Lord HARDWICKE in the case *Ex parte Gulston* did not seem to have considered a departure without intent as an act of bankruptcy. He seems aware that the party was delayed, for he says why did they not see him in Barbados. 1 Atk. 139. The cases put by the counsel for the defendant are very alarming, but as there are serious doubts, I wish this to be put on the record.

ASHHURST, GROSE, and LAWRENCE thinking it a proper case for a special verdict, a new trial was granted to that intent.

Vide: Colkett v. Freeman, Cooke's *Bankruptcy Laws* 102.[25]

[6:71]   R. v. BOWES

[M.H.] Satisfaction of a fine entered by consent of the attorney-general.

The defendant having obtained a pardon of that part of the judgment on him which imposed a fine of £300, and satisfaction was entered on the record by the consent of the attorney-general who was present, and His Majesty's warrant under his sign manual being read, dispensing with that part of the judgment which required him to find two sureties for his good behaviour to the amount of £5,000 each, Mr Bowes being present in court entered into his own recognizance in the sum of £10,000 for his good behaviour for the term of fourteen years.[26]

June 15   WHITLEY, one, &c. v. LEARCROFT, one, &c.

[M.H.] Bills between attorneys are not taxable.

The court discharged a rule to tax the plaintiff's bill. Lord KENYON said that they could not do it, as there was an exception in the 12 Geo. II, c. 13 in the case of actions between attorneys. The master said Lord MANSFIELD had done it in an action by an agent against his principal.

---

[25] In the fourth edition (1799) of *The Bankrupt Laws* by William Cooke, the relevant discussion of the *Colkett* case is at p. 79.

[26] Erskine represented Bowes, stating that his client had been imprisoned for ten years, and assuring the court of the 'strict propriety of Mr Bowes's conduct during his long imprisonment'. *The Times*, 14 June 1796 ('*The* KING *on the prosecution of the* COUNTESS OF STRATHMORE, *against* ANDREW ROBINSON BOWES, ESQ'.). Lord Kenyon said 'he was satisfied that Mr Bowes's demeanor had been highly exemplary'. If Bowes's conduct in prison was in fact exemplary, it stood in sharp contrast to his conduct as a husband. The tumultuous and scandalous marriage of the countess and Andrew Bowes, her second husband, enlivened both the newspapers and the law courts for nearly two decades. See W. Moore, *Wedlock: How Georgian Britain's Worst Husband Met his Match* (2009).

[6:72]   B.R. MICHAELMAS TERM 37 Geo. III

Lloyd, Lord Kenyon, Chief Justice
Sir W. Ashhurst ⎫
Sir N. Grose   ⎬ Justices
Sir S. Lawrence ⎭

November 8   LIGHT, *et al.* v. MIDDLETON

[M.H.] In covenant, for not paying a certain sum on a day certain for a consideration to be performed, the jury may give less damages than the sum.

Gazelee moved to enter up the verdict for £340 instead of 1s., the sum for which the verdict was found in an action of covenant on a charter party dated the 24th February 1796, by which the plaintiff covenanted that the ship should be ready the 1st of March to sail to Philadelphia, which voyage she should perform, for which the defendant covenanted on the 29th of February to pay £640. The defendant pleaded two frivolous pleas, and it appearing in evidence that he had paid to the plaintiff [£]300, which was an equivalent for all the damage the plaintiff had sustained by the defendant's not performing his engagement, which he was prevented doing by being arrested and committed to prison, they having sold their ship on 16th of March, the jury found only 1s. damages.

Gazelee on the authority of *Lowe* v. *Peers* in Burrow,[27] contended that he was entitled to the whole sum covenanted to be paid on the 29th of February. But the court being of opinion that this was not like that, a case of stipulated damages, refused him a rule to show cause.

[6:73]   EX PARTE HARRIS

[M.H.] Attorney articled to one whom he never served struck off the roll, as well as the master.[28]

Erskine shewed cause against a rule to strike Harris off the roll of attorneys, he not having duly served his clerkship, it appearing that he was employed as a writer of one Samuel Johnson, an attorney of St Ives, all the time he was under articles of clerkship to one Davenport, an attorney living in London. The cause shown was that Johnson, for some reasons peculiarly operating on him, had refused to take Harris as his articled clerk and had consented to his being articled to Davenport.

Lord KENYON said that it was not possible to get over the Act of parliament, 2 Geo. II, c. 23 sec. 6. And that the court could do no otherwise than strike

---

[27] (1768) 4 Burr. 2225.
[28] A subsequent note was entered in the margin, *viz*: 'Davenport was restored in Trinity Term, 37 G.3, the court thinking his suspension had been sufficiently long.'

both Harris and Davenport off the rolls, as had been done in the case one Sleiber, who had been articled to one Greenwood, both of whom on the application of one Johns, were struck off the rolls, the latter of whom after some time, the court being sensible of his contrition, was restored.[29]

November 9   HIER v. ANGERSTEIN

[M.H.] Security for costs not required of a foreigner who intends going abroad.

The court refused to oblige the plaintiff to give security for costs, on an affidavit that he was a foreigner and about to quit the kingdom.

[6:74]   HANSEL v. EDWARDS

[M.H.] Parol submission to an award can't be made a rule of court.

The court were of opinion that a parol submission to an award could not be made a rule of court under the statute, and refused doing it, though the award which was made directed it to be done.

DOE, *ex dim.* GREEN v. TAYLOR

[M.H.] If the real owner of an estate is turned out by ejectment, he can't, until he recovers the land, convey a title to another.

One Salmon having about twelve years ago died seized of a copyhold estate, the defendant got into possession of the premises by a judgment which he obtained by some mistake against the casual ejector in an ejectment brought by him—after which his son procured himself to be admitted, and surrendered the estate to the lessor.

This case appearing in evidence to HEATH, Justice at the last Worcester assizes, he nonsuited the plaintiff, being of opinion that the son being out of possession could not convey, as his was in law but a pretended title.

On a motion to set this aside, the court refused a rule *nisi*, Lord KENYON saying it was clear that a defeasee could not convey while out of possession.

---

[29] According to *The Times*, Davenport was also a defendant in the case. It was said to be 'admitted on all hands that Mr Harris was a man of irreproachable character', but Lord Kenyon interrupted Erskine to ask 'how the Court, whatever their wishes and inclinations might be, could, consistently with the Act of Parliament, refuse to strike Mr Harris off the roll'. Kenyon explained that 'we have no discretion except a sound discretion to construe the Law, and not to obliterate and cancel it'. He recalled that Lord Mansfield had felt it his duty to remove Sleiber and Greenwood from the roll, though Greenwood was afterwards restored 'upon his shewing to the Court contrition and sorrow for his misconduct'. In the case before it, the court ordered both Harris and Davenport struck off the roll, but said that Davenport might afterwards apply to the court to show cause why he should be restored. *The Times*, 9 November 1796.

November 10 BEST, *et al.*, assignees of MOYSEY v. ISAAC

In trover by the assignees of a bankrupt for a cutter, the question was if a sale by the bankrupt was fraudulent, as the directions of Lord Hawkesbury's Act[30] for the [6:75] registering the sale to the defendant had not been complied with.

It appeared in evidence at the trial before GROSE, Justice at the last assizes for Devon that the defendant, upon the sale of the vessel to him, had taken possession of her for about seven weeks, when Moysey became bankrupt, sent her to Plymouth, and made some alterations in her.

On a motion for new trial, *Atkinson* v. *Maylin*, 4 T.R. 262,[31] was relied on as furnishing arguments applicable to the case of ships not at sea—since Lord Hawkesbury's Act.

Lord KENYON said Lord Hawkesbury's Act had nothing to do with the question. The statute of James I (*ss.*) 21 Jac. I c.19 acted upon the apparent title, not on the real ownership. That it was impossible to pare away a very useful statute, and that in this case, all the indicia of property were in the bankrupt.

Rule for new trial refused.

November 11   DOE *ex* [*dim.*] SHAW v. SHAW

[M.H.] If notice to determine an estate is given for one time and afterwards for a subsequent time, if the tenant continues after the expiration of the time in the first notice, he must quit according to the 2nd.

Law moved for a new trial of an ejectment tried at York. The question turned on a proviso to determine a lease on notice to quit.

The lessor gave notice to quit in 1795 and afterwards gave notice to quit in 1796. This he contended was uncertain, and the power to defeat estates should be strictly construed.

Lord KENYON said there was nothing in it, having continued in possession after the time mentioned in the first notice, he was bound to quit at the time mentioned in the last.

Nil cap.

[6:76]   R. v. KELLY

[M.H.] One against whom interrogatories are filed for a contempt can't answer without taking a copy.

On a motion by counsel for the master's report, he reported the defendant in contempt, he having refused to take copies of the interrogatories exhibited

---

[30] 26 Geo. III, c. 60.
[31] The correct citation is *Atkinson* v. *Maling* (1788) 2 T.R. 462.

against him, without which, according to the practice of the office, he could not be examined.

November 14   COLLIER v. BUTLER DANVERS

[M.H.] If a defendant on a *ca. sa.* pays the sum recovered to the sheriff, the court will not stay it into his hands pending a suit in equity for the purpose of getting rid of the judgment.

Mingay moved that the sheriff of Leicestershire might pay into court a sum of money paid to him by the defendant on being taken upon a *ca. sa.*, who had since given him notice not to pay it over to the plaintiff, against whom he had filed a bill in equity to get rid of the judgment.

But the court refused a rule, being of opinion that the sheriff ran no risk in paying over to the plaintiff money paid to him by the defendant to be discharged out of execution, and that this was a very different case from that of a sheriff who had taken goods in execution, the property of which was disputed, in which case under circumstances they would interfere to protect the sheriff.[32]

Nil cap.

November 21
R. v. SKELTON *et al.*, JUSTICES of CUMBERLAND

Defendants having been found guilty of a conspiracy to appoint one Oyer overseer of the township of Whitehaven after he had filled it many years, that he [6:77] might reimburse himself a balance of many thousand pounds he claimed of the parish. They agreed on the recommendation of Lord KENYON to apply themselves to be struck out of the commission of the peace and to pay the prosecutor the costs as between attorney and client, and to enter in a recognizance of £500 apiece to appear the next term to receive the judgment of the court if they should be called up for that purpose.[33]

---

[32] Mr Justice Grose is reported to have said that, 'If we were to grant this rule, we should have Sheriffs coming to this Court for an indemnity in every case. It is a part of the duty of the Sheriff's office to take care of this money till the bill in equity is disposed of.' *The Times*, 15 November 1796.

[33] The trial was before Mr Justice Lawrence at the Cumberland summer assizes. At the hearing on 21 November Lord Kenyon suggested that the case might be settled if the defendants would cover the costs of the prosecution and would voluntarily remove themselves from their commissions. *The Times*, 22 November 1796. On 27 January 1797, the court ordered the defendants to pay all the costs that had been incurred because of their delinquency, and Mr Law, for the prosecution, said that he only wished to hear that these gentlemen had thrown off a certain robe which they had disgraced. *The Times*, 28 January 1797. On 11 February Law said that the defendants were no longer magistrates and that they had paid 'all the costs of the prosecution as between attorney and client'. Erskine said the costs amounted to £1,291, and he hoped the defendants would be discharged with a nominal fine. The court complied, imposing a fine of 6s. 8d., but Lord Kenyon asked that the proper officer insert into the rule for the nominal fine the facts of the defendants' resignations and the costs they had paid, 'that posterity might see that the court had not allowed an offence of that magnitude to pass unpunished'. *The Times*, 13 February 1797. For a similar resolution, see *R. v. Ramsay*, p. 66, above.

November 22   R. v. CROSSLEY

[M.H.] Bail in perjury.

Being brought up to plead to an indictment for perjury found against him in this court, he imparled till the next term as a matter of course and was remanded to the custody of the keeper of Newgate until he should find bail, himself in £500 and two sureties in £50 each.[34]

---

[34] For earlier phases of this case, see above, pp. 103 and 148. Crossley proved to be nothing but trouble. On 17 November 1796 he appeared in court to plead to his indictment for perjury and read a very long paper to show 'that all the proceedings that had been carried on against him were *irregular, unconstitutional, and against law*'. Lord Kenyon said that Crossley's paper was 'wholly impertinent', and 'almost every allegation was false, within the knowledge of Mr Crossley himself, who had so long practised in that Court with sharpness and keenness'. On 23 January 1797, Crossley attempted bail, and 'a Jew and a German accordingly appeared, who wished to justify for £500, but after examination by Mr Russel, Counsel for the Prosecution, they were rejected as insufficient, and the Prisoner remanded to Newgate'. *The Times*, 24 January 1797. A five-hour trial was held on 14 February. Serjeant Adair and others were counsel for the prosecution; Erskine, Garrow, and Manley appeared for the defendant. Serjeant Adair recounted in detail the history of the discovery of incriminating letters and papers in Crossley's house, and the apparent falsehoods in an affidavit sworn by him. After the evidence for the prosecution was concluded, Erskine gave a flowery speech and said he would prove that Crossley's affidavit had been materially altered after it was sworn. Adair responded that if the affidavit had been altered, Crossley had done it himself. Lord Kenyon gave his usual moral exhortation to the jury, and after twenty minutes' deliberation, the jury returned a guilty verdict. *The Times*, 15 February 1797. On 22 May, counsel for the defendant sought a new trial, presenting another Crossley affidavit, but Serjeant Adair scoffed at the idea that a guilty verdict could be overturned simply on the basis of an affidavit from the defendant who had been convicted. The court ruled against a new trial. *The Times*, 23 May 1797. Crossley then said he planned to move for an arrest of judgment. On 27 May, he was again in court, asking for a continuance. Clearly annoyed, Lord Kenyon grumbled that, 'The Prosecutor has certainly been harassed beyond all bounds', but after listening to Erskine's deferential eloquence, Kenyon agreed to put the case over to the next term. *The Times*, 29 May 1797. Then on 17 June, Erskine argued the motion for an arrest of judgment. He acknowledged the court's indulgences, said he could add nothing to the many objections that Crossley had sent to the court, but felt duty bound to raise one new point—that, although the indictment stated that the defendant had produced a certain affidavit, 'yet the indictment did not go on to state, *that he did in fact exhibit that affidavit*'. He 'contended that it was no crime ... to make a false affidavit before the Court, unless that affidavit was afterwards used', citing precedents. The judges were openly skeptical. Lawrence 'conceived the precedents were the other way'. *The Times*, 19 June 1797. This phase of the litigation is fully reported at 7 T.R. 317 (20 June 1797). When the court sat on 20 June to pronounce judgment on Crossley, according to *The Times*, Erskine tried once more, insisting that the court answer the question, 'whether the crime of Perjury is complete by the bare act of swearing the affidavit before a Court of competent jurisdiction to receive it, without that affidavit being afterwards used for the purpose of obstructing Public Justice'. Lord Kenyon said that the case had been argued and considered again and again, and the objections that had been offered 'had no foundation upon earth'. His brother judges agreed, stating that the crime of perjury did not consist in using the affidavit, but in swearing it—'The moment that a man swears a false affidavit, knowing it to be false, the offence was complete.' Mr Justice Ashhurst committed the defendant to Newgate for six months with a requirement that during that time he stand in the pillory opposite the gate of Westminster Hall for one hour, and he ordered that after Crossley's gaol time ended, he was to be transported for seven years. *The Times*, 21 June 1797.

R. v. WOOSTER

[M.H.] Prisoner indicted for a capital felony bailed, the prosecutrix being a lunatic, and strong affidavits to show the man's innocence.

The defendant was brought up on a *habeas corpus* directed to the keeper of Aylesbury gaol, who returned that he was in his custody by virtue of an order of the court of gaol delivery of that county, the grand jury having found a bill against him for highway robbery.

It was now moved to bail him on an affidavit denying that he was guilty of the crime, and the several circumstances sworn to by T. Nash, the prosecutrix, in her information before a magistrate, in which he was confirmed by other persons [6:78] who joined in the affidavit of the prisoner. And upon affidavits that the prosecutrix was a lunatic confined in St Luke's Hospital, that she was unable to appear on the preceding assizes, and of the prisoner being a man of good character. And that one Gutheridge had confessed that he and one Jesell, who had absconded upon his being taken up for the robbery, was the person who was his accomplice—which Jesell was, by the affidavits, sworn to be like the prisoner.

Under the circumstances the court bailed the prisoner, himself in £80 and four sureties, £40 each.

ANONYMOUS

[M.H.] Attorney's bill not taxed after a settlement of four years standing.

The court refused to refer an attorney's bill to be taxed after it had been settled four years, though *Marriot* pointed out particular articles which were objectionable.

November 23 ## EX PARTE LANG

[M.H.] If writs of *non omittas* have issued for a great number of years, the court will not interfere in a summary way to restrain the issuing them.

Erskine moved on behalf of the coroner of Pomfret, who has the return of writs within that honour, that the officers of this court be directed not to issue writs of *non omittas latitat* to the sheriff of the county of York. This motion *Erskine* said the coroner preferred to bringing an action against the officers. [6:79] But on Master Foster informing the court that such writs had issued for about thirty years, the court refused to interfere and told *Erskine* that his client must act as he should be advised.

[6:80]   HILARY TERM 37 Geo. III

Lloyd, Lord Kenyon, Chief Justice
Sir W. Ashhurst   ⎫
Sir N. Grose   ⎬ Justices
Sir S. Lawrence   ⎭

January 26, 1797   R. v. WEBB, *et al.*

[M.H.] Query if a *mandamus* will lie to the trustees of a vicarage to present a person elected according to the trust deed.

Gibbs shewed cause against a *mandamus* to be directed to the defendant and two others, trustees of the vicarage of Painswick in the county of Gloucester requiring them to present one Jeason to the bishop of Gloucester to be instituted into that living, he having a plurality of voices of the inhabitants of that town, according to which the trustees in whom the right of patronage resided were to present.

As it appeared that Jeason had filed his bill against defendants in the Court of Exchequer, the court discharged the rule.

Vide: *R. v. Marquis of Stafford*, 3 T.R. 646; *R. v. Blooer*, Burr. 1044; *R. v. Baker, et al.*, ibid. 1265.[35]

January 31   R. v. JUSTICES of DORSET

[M.H.] *Mandamus* will not lie to settle an account according to the directions of an Act of parliament if settled, though erroneously.

Erskine moved for a *mandamus* to be directed to the justices of the county of Dorset to state and settle the accounts of the mayor and bailiffs of the borough of Bridport respecting the harbour of Bridport, in pursuance of the 8th Geo. I, which directs that the mayor and bailiffs [are] to keep accounts of the receipts and disbursements of the [6:81] harbour, and to lay them before the justices of the county at the sessions—who are to take, settle and balance the accounts. He stated that from the year 1740, the accounts had been settled without charging the corporation with a sum of £3,000, which Lord Coventry had given toward the support of the harbour—and that at the last sessions, the justices, instead of acting on the balance which had come down to them from the preceding sessions, at which the accounts had passed, had unsettled it by charging the corporation with the £3,000 given by Lord Coventry. This he contended was not settling the balance in pursuance of the Act, but unsettling it.

Lord KENYON said whether the court in any stage of the business can look into the accounts depends on this, whether the case was to be brought before

---

[35] *R. v. Blooer* (1760) 2 Burr. 1043; *R. v. Baker* (1762) 3 Burr. 1265.

the court by *certiorari*—a *mandamus* can only put the justices in motion, it can't prescribe to them the mode of taking the accounts. Whether they ought to be bound by the balance struck by the preceding sessions I am not prepared to say, but it would be going a great way to say that an error can't be corrected. An exception of errors is implied in every account. Would it not be an answer to [6:82] a *mandamus* if the justices should return that they had settled the accounts, though erroneously. A *mandamus* will go to make a rule, or settle overseas accounts, but the court never directs how these things are to be done. We are not warranted by any precedent to do what is asked. If the settlement had been only colourable, it would be another thing.

Nil cap.

February 3   R. v. COOMBE

[M.H.] Commitment in execution bad if it does not appear by the warrant that the party was convicted.

Defendant being brought up on a *habeas corpus* upon a commitment as a rogue and vagabond, it appeared he was committed until the next sessions and not till discharged by due course of law. And it did not appear by the warrant that he had been convicted of being a rogue, &c., and on the authority of *R.* v. *Rhodes*, 4 T.R. 220 he was discharged.[36]

February 6   WEBB v. BROWN

[M.H.] Execution may be taken out by the consent of the defendant without a *sci. fa. Sci. fa.* necessary if plaintiff dies before a *ca. sa.* and before caption. *Ut semb.*

On a motion to discharge the defendant out of custody for irregularity, two objections were made—first that the judgment was of above a year's standing and no writ of *scire facias* had been sued out; second that the plaintiff had died subsequent to the issuing [of] the *capias ad satisfaciendum* and before the executing it, and therefore a *scire facias*, according to the plaintiff and 9th W. 3, should have been sued out. [6:83] The answer to the first objection was that the party had agreed on confessing the judgment that execution should issue in case of nonpayment of the annuity. It was given to secure sufficient any *scire facias*, though the judgment were above a year's standing. And after the last objection, it was said to be sufficient if the plaintiff were alive at the issuing of the *capias ad saisfaciendum*.

In support of the first objection it was said that the congruity of the records made it impossible to waive the *scire facias*, and if this could be done the parties might stipulate that the execution should issue without any judgment—and

---

[36] This case is noted briefly in n. (a) at the end of the report of *R.* v. *Rhodes*, 4 T.R. at 221. See also the additional case there cited, *R.* v. *Cooper* (1796) 6 T.R. 509.

Wynch 100[37] and *Thorpe* v. *Clement et al.*, 6 T.R. 525[38] were cited. And in support of the second objection, *Howel* v. *Hanforth*, 2 [W.] Blackstone 843 was cited, and it was said a *capias ad satisfaciendum* was distinguishable from a *fieri facias*, as there was no commencement of the execution till the party was taken, and therefore the plaintiff must be alive at the time, but it was otherwise in the case of a *fieri facias*, as the goods were bound by the delivery of it to the sheriff.

Lord KENYON said there was nothing in the first objection[39]—but as to the last gave *Gibbs* time to look into it.

Marriot for the defendant.

[6:84] February 10 SMITH v. POOLE

[M.H.] If parties to an award agree that the determination of the arbitrators shall be conclusive, both as to matters of law and fact, the court will not interfere, though they may have mistaken the law.

Gibbs in this case moved to set aside an award, contending that the arbitrators had mistaken in point of law in not giving credit to the house of Louis & Potter for bills to the amount of £12,000, which became due after their bankruptcy and which had been drawn on them by the house of Livesey & Hargrave, between whom there had been bill transactions to the amount of many hundred thousand pounds.

Law on the other side stated that the parties had agreed that the arbitrators should finally decide all questions, both of law and fact, and that they should for this purpose take the legal advice of counsel on such subjects as they thought fit, and that they had consulted two barristers, Mr *Cooke* and Mr *Parke*, and had acted by their advice.

Under the circumstances the court thought the award conclusive and refused to interfere.[40]

Rule discharged.

---

[37] *Hickman* v. *Fish* (1624) Winch 100.
[38] The correct citation is *Clarke* v. *Clement and English* (1796) 6 T.R. 525.
[39] In the margin: '*Vide* p. 85', referring to the anonymous case decided on 13 February (below, p. 163).
[40] In *Assignees of Lewis & Potter* v. *Assignees of Livesey, Hargrave, & Co.*, decided on the same day as *Smith* v. *Poole*, the plaintiffs also sought to set aside an arbitration award in notorious litigation stretching across eight years, involving the bankruptcy of Livesey & Co., a large cotton manufacturer. Erskine and Gibbs represented the plaintiffs, and they claimed that the arbitrators had made improper calculations that cast their clients as debtors of Livesey & Co. to approximately £13,000, whereas they were in fact creditors to the amount of over £30,000. Law and Garrow argued that the arbitration award should stand, having been made, as agreed by the parties, by 'three merchants of the City of London, who were most eminently distinguished for integrity and abilities, to settle the mutual debts and credit of these two houses, and all matters, both of law and fact'. Lord Kenyon said that he could not think of a cause 'in which he felt a greater anxiety to shut the door against all farther litigation', and the court did so by refusing to set aside the award. Kenyon observed that, 'Arbitrations were extremely beneficial in many cases; and in no instance were they more beneficial than in this very case, where there was an immense number of commercial accounts between two houses trading to an extent . . . almost unexampled in the history of the commerce of this country.' *The Times*, 11 February 1797.

[6:85] February 11   R. v. SMITH

[M.H.] A word in a conviction may be rejected to make it sense.

Garrow moved to quash a conviction of the defendant of being a rogue and vagabond under the Lottery Act. The conviction was dated the 9th of February and convicted him of illegally insuring a ticket on the 8th of this *instant* January. This he said was uncertain, what month it was. But the court thought there was nothing in it. That the word 'instant' might be rejected and then it would stand the 8th of January.

Nil cap.

February 13   ANONYMOUS

[M.H.] Execution may be sued out by consent after a year without *scire facias*.

Wood shewed cause against the rule for setting aside a judgment for irregularity, being of more than a year's standing and execution sued out without any *scire facias*. That the defendant had agreed that no *scire facias* should be sued out, and cited *Michel* v. *Cue & ux.*, 2 Burr. 660.

Gibbs, *contra*, said he was concerned for the assignees of the defendant, a bankrupt who by this continuance would prejudice his other creditors. *Sed per* Lord KENYON: If you do not appear for a defendant, you come impertinently into court.

Rule discharged without costs.

[6:86] February 13   RAYNES and HEATH v. SPICER

[M.H.] Judgment as in case of a nonsuit not to be given in a penal action if the reason for not trying be that the limitation had not run so as to enable the plaintiffs to examine one concerned in the transaction.

Erskine shewed cause against a rule for judgment as in case of a nonsuit in an action brought by the assignees of the bankrupt on Sir John Barnard's Act,[41] made to prevent the practice of stock-jobbing.

The cause he shewed was that they could not proceed to trial without the evidence of the broker who had negotiated the business, and who could not be compelled to be a witness until the time had expired during which he himself was liable to an action for the part he had had in the business. This, he contended, showed that there was no affected delay, in which case only such judgment should be given.

Garrow, *Wood*, *Bayley*, and *Lawes*, *contra*, contended that this was in effect prolonging the time of bringing penal actions, and the delay might prejudice the defendant, as his witnesses might die.

Lord KENYON: This application stands on principles allowed every day. The

---

[41] 7 Geo. II, c. 8 (1733).

Act[42] enabling the court to give judgment as in the case of a nonsuit was to discountenance improper delays. [6:87] Is this improper delay? Suppose the witness had been abroad or ill—or insane—he in this case labours under a temporary distress. I am clear there are abundant grounds to put off the trial.[43]

GROSE, Justice, said he thought the Act remedial, and it was not penal.

Rule discharged.[44]

R. v. INHABITANTS OF CHURCH MIDDLETON

[M.H.] No costs under the Highway Act, if the defendants suffer judgment by default.

On an indictment for not repairing a highway, the defendants suffered judgment to go by default. *Manley* applied for costs.

Lord KENYON: There is nothing in this point. The 13 Geo. III, c. 78 does not give costs in this case. All we could do would be to put a large fine on the defendants if they will not do what is right, if in that way you could be helped. But that can't be, as the fine by the directions of the Act is to be paid to the surveyors of the highways.

---

[42] 14 Geo. II, c. 17.

[43] In the margin: 'Same case, 7 T.R. 78'. The citation should be to 7 T.R. 178. In the printed report, Lord Kenyon, after stating that there were abundant grounds to put off the trial, added: 'But it is sufficient for the present to say that this rule for judgment as in case of a nonsuit ought to be discharged.' Lawrence's opinion is also given, *viz*: 'The argument urged in support of this rule tends to shew that in penal actions we have no discretion in determining on such an application as the present: but that proves too much because the Court has always exercised a discretion in granting or refusing these rules in penal as well as other actions.'

[44] The report of this case in *The Times*, 14 February 1797, gives the following background:

Our readers will recollect that in December last, a cause was tried at Guildhall, London, before Lord Kenyon and a Special Jury of Merchants, the name of which was *Raynes and others, Assignees of Kentish against Twogood.*

That action was brought on Sir John Barnard's Act, 7 Geo. II, c. 8. entitled an Act to prevent the infamous practice of Stock-jobbing, to recover a number of penalties of 500l. each. The plaintiffs in that action were nonsuited because the Brokers, who were conversant with the business, could not give evidence without criminating themselves. A number of other actions brought under the same circumstances we understand are still depending.

In *The Times* report of the *Twogood* case (12 December 1796), Lord Kenyon said he hoped 'to put a stop to these nefarious transactions', but that the court must follow the law. Counsel for the prosecution, Mr Reader, suggested that if the Act were amended to take the £500 penalty off the brokers, then they could be compelled to give evidence. Kenyon said that if the Act wanted amendment he was sure it would be done. The report concluded by noting that fifty like actions were pending in the courts. One of these was reported in *The Times* on 16 June 1797, *Raynes and others, Assignees of Kentish v. Chevalier*, tried before Lord Kenyon and a special jury of merchants. Erskine, for the plaintiffs, observed that the part of Sir John Barnard's Act containing the £500 penalty against brokers who violated the act 'had been a dead letter in the Statute Book for many years' because, as penalties attached to the brokers, their 'mouths were shut, and some of these actions were now standing over till the Statute of Limitations . . . expired'.

_____ [sic] v. HIGHMORE

[M.H.] Attorney is not censurable who appeared for an infant and afterwards assigned his infancy for error, he not knowing it when he appeared.

Wood moved that Mr *Parker*, the defendant's attorney, should pay the costs of proceedings in error in which judgment had been reversed because the defendant, an infant, had appeared by attorney, contending that he ought to have known whether his client was an infant or not before he appeared for him as his attorney, and cited 1 Strange 114,[45] where it is laid [6:88] down that if an attorney undertakes to defend for an infant, he shall defend by guardian. And if he acts negligently he ought to pay the party prejudiced by it his costs.

But the court thought there was no ground for the motion and discharged the rule with costs.

R. v. SHERIFF of MIDDLESEX

[M.H.] Sheriff can't surrender after the rule to bring in the body has expired.

On a motion to set aside an attachment against the sheriff, the question was if he could surrender the defendant after the expiration of the rule to bring in the body.

The master certified that formerly an attachment might have been moved for against the sheriff at the rising of the court on the day the rule to bring in the body expired, but since the rule had obtained, the bail put in for the purpose of rendering need not justify. The sheriff had the whole day to render, and could not now surrender after the rule had expired to bring in the body, though no attachment had been moved for.

[6:89] [blank]

---

[45] *Stratton* v. *Burgiss* (1718) 1 Str. 114.

[6:90] EASTER TERM 37 Geo. III

Lloyd, Lord Kenyon, Chief Justice
Sir W. Ashhurst ⎫
Sir N. Grose ⎬ Justices
Sir S. Lawrence ⎭

May 15 STANWAY v. JENNINGS

[M.H.] Note given for an insolvent's groats must be precisely accurate.[46] Query if signed by an agent if there must not be an affidavit of the plaintiff's being abroad.

Marriot moved to discharge an insolvent debtor for the insufficiency of the rate given him for his groats. It was signed by one Hazard as the plaintiff's agent, and undertook to pay the money so long as the 'defendant continues in custody in execution at my suit'.

The objections he made were two. First that there was no affidavit of the plaintiff being abroad, without which he said the note ought to be signed by the party himself.

The second was that the note did not engage for the payment of the money whilst the defendant was in custody at the plaintiff's suit.

Defendant was discharged.

R. v. GRINDLEY[47]

[M.H.] *Mandamus* granted to deliver up the books and papers of the office of the register of a diocese to his committee, he being a lunatic.

Adams shewed cause against a *mandamus* to deliver to J. R., deputy register of the diocese of Bangor, all papers, &c. belonging to their office.

The bishop of Bangor having appointed one Gunning, a minor, to the office of register, he appointed the defendant to be his deputy, and becoming lunatic, his committee, who was by the chancellor directed to administer his office by such persons as he should appoint, appointed J. R. to be the deputy, to whom Grindley refused to deliver up the papers, &c.

[6:91] *Adams* insisted that the parties' remedy was by application to the Court of Chancery and not by *mandamus*.

Lord KENYON said the application appeared to him to be a matter of course. That he remembered the court acting as ancillary to the Court of Chancery in compelling one of the keepers of the seal of Wadham College to affix it to the answer of the college, Lord MANSFIELD holding that the use of the common seal

---

[46] On groats, see *Dalton v. Lambert*, p. 146, above.
[47] See p. 150, above, where Lord Kenyon, on first encounter, denied the *mandamus*.

shall be governed by the majority. That the rule was not so signed, that a *mandamus* was not to be granted in any case where there is a remedy.

Rule absolute.

May 18   R. v. SELECT VESTRY of PRESTON

[M.H.] *Mandamus* will go to a select vestry to make a church rate if there be a custom for the select vestry to make such rate.

Wood moved for a *mandamus* to the select vestry of Preston to make a church rate, stating that there was a custom in the parish to make the rate by a vestry composed of persons returned from three divisions of the parish. This, he said, had been done in 1792 in the case of Bradford, where the custom was for eight different townships to contribute, to which *mandamus* a return had been made and an action tried for a false return.

Lord KENYON, observing that if the custom were admitted, the necessity of a rate might be decided in the ecclesiastical court, which had alone the power to enforce church rates, granted the writ.

May 23   EX PARTE LEACROFT

[M.H.] Attorney compellable by rule to give up court rolls delivered to him as steward.

Gibbs showed cause against a rule on one Leacroft, an attorney, to deliver up the court rolls of a manor to one Wooley, who had been appointed steward. He objected that [6:92] as Leacroft, as steward of the manor, did not act in the character of an attorney, the court had no jurisdiction. But the court made the rule absolute on the authority of two cases—2 [W.] Blackstone 912, 3 T.R. 275.[48]

R. v. BRISTOW

[M.H.] If a county is divided between two treasurers they must be reduced to one, if this division for the convenience of the county interferes with that of the public.

Harvey showed cause against a rule on defendant as treasurer of the county of Kent to pay a sum of 20s for the relief of the poor prisoners in the King's Bench, according to the 43rd Eliz, c. 2. sec.14, and insisted that the defendant, being appointed treasurer only of the eastern division, was not a proper person on whom such a rule could be made, as he could not act out of his division, and the money was to be levied on the whole county.

Lord KENYON: This division may be for the convenience of the county, but

---

[48] *Marshall's Case* (1773) 2 Bl. W. 912; *Hughes* v. *Mayre* (1789) 3 T.R. 275.

other persons are not to be put under inconvenience. If they will not arrange this among themselves, the treasurers must be melted down again into one.

The rule was made absolute.

May 29   GREEN v. MAYOR of LIVERPOOL

[M.H.] *Pone per vadios* is an irregular process against a corporation.

Wood objected to the proceedings as being irregular, the plaintiff having issued a summons into London and then an attachment by gages and [6:93] pledges directed to the chancellor of the duchy. He said the process should be summons and distress.

The court set the proceedings aside.

TRIBE v. GAMAN

[M.H.] Rule *nisi* for attachment for nonpayment of money pursuant to an award the last day of term.

On the motion of Mr *Const*, a rule *nisi* for an attachment for nonpayment of money pursuant to an award was granted on the authority of a case last term, though this was the last day of the term.

[6:94]   TRINITY TERM 37 Geo. III

Lloyd, Lord Kenyon, Chief Justice
Sir W. Ashhurst
Sir N. Grose   } Justices
Sir S. Lawrence

R. v. DR MARIOT

[M.H.] 35 Geo. III, c. 80 relative to the property of Dutch subjects brought into this country does not extend to what is brought in as prize, though it were seized prior to the declaration of hostilities.

Gibbs moved for a prohibition to the Court of Admiralty, who had issued a writ of unlivery to their officer of goods which were Dutch property taken by Sir George Keith at the Cape of Good Hope before the declaration of hostilities, contending that the commissioners appointed in pursuance of the provisions of the 35 Geo. III, c. 80 were entitled to the custody of them, that they had applied for the goods but the court had refused to give them the possession and were proceeding as if they were enemies' property.

Erskine shewed cause and insisted that the 35 Geo. III, c. 15 and 35 Geo. III, c. 80 respected only ships which might come into the port of this country as friends, and not such as were brought in as prize.

The facts of this case were these: the Act passed the 22nd May 1795. Hostilities began at the Cape 7th August. The vessel was taken possession of for safe custody the 15th August, [and] 18th September a proclamation issued for the seizure of Dutch property. In May 1796 the Dutch colours were struck aboard this ship and in December 1796 the cargo was put on board an English vessel and brought to England as prize.

And he insisted that it appeared by the first section of the 35 Geo III, c. 80 to which the [6:95] 21st referred, that his construction was right.

Gibbs, contra, relied on the words of the 21st section which are, 'detained or *brought into the ports*', and provides that such goods shall only be decided on in the way they are presented, and though the goods were brought into the kingdom subsequent to the declaration of hostilities, they were seized before, and as such fell under the provisions of that Act.

Wood, same side: The subsequent declaration of hostilities enables the Admiralty to decide on the question of prize, but the Act has taken the custody of them from the Court of Admiralty.

Lord KENYON said the Act applied to the property of persons in amity with this kingdom brought into the ports of the kingdom. But [as to] others brought in subsequent to hostilities, it made all the difference and gave the Court of Admiralty a jurisdiction, and that it was not a case either within the words or meaning of the Act.

ASHHURST and GROSE, Justices, same opinion.

Rule discharged.

July 1 CHEAP *et al.* v. EAST INDIA COMPANY

[M.H.] Goods sold by them at their sales pursuant to the 33 Geo. III, c. 52, by which the private trade of the East Indies is regulated, can't be retained by them against the persons buying them in as consignees of the goods, to answer a foreign attachment at suit of a creditor of the consignor.

On a motion for a new trial at Guildhall, Lord KENYON stated the case to be this: the action was trover for indigo shipped in the East Indies on board the *Cecilia,* a ship in the defendant's service, on the account and risk of John Cheap, and consigned to the plaintiffs. Cheap and Luftnam, who had accepted bills on the credit of the consignment to the amount of £4,000, on the arrival of the [6:96] goods in the port of London, they were carried to defendant's warehouses, and put up to public sale conformable to the 33 Geo. III, c. 52, and bought in by the plaintiffs. After their arrival in England, John Tasilie, a creditor of John Cheap, attached these goods in the hands of the East India Company, who in consequence of it refused to deliver them to the plaintiffs. The jury found a verdict for the plaintiffs.

Law, who moved for a new trial, contended that as these goods came in the name of the consignor, as the plaintiffs had no bill of lading, and as he was liable for the freight, they were subject to an attachment at suit of Cheap's creditors, contending that till the plaintiff paid their acceptances, the contract was but executory between the consignor and consignee according to the doctrine of EYRE, Chief Justice, in *Kinloch* v. *Craig*, 3 T.R. 115. [49]

Erskine, contra, said the cases were distinguishable, as in the case of *Kinloch* v. *Craig* no possession was taken by the consignee, but in this case the possession of the East India Company was the possession of plaintiffs.

Lord KENYON: How can the East India Company avoid giving up goods they have sold to the plaintiffs?

Rule discharged.

[6:97]   CARR v. SHAW and PRICE

[M.H.] Special *capias* amendable though the proceedings have gone on to outlawry.

Bayley moved to amend a special *capias* against the two defendants, Price by mistake being call John instead of James and outlawed by that name, and the cause ready for trial.

Law and *Espinasse* opposed it as there was nothing to amend by.

But the court made the rule absolute on payment of costs and quashing all the proceedings subsequent to the *capias*.[50]

June 20   R. v. BLYER

[M.H.] Attachment not granted without a rule *nisi* for not obeying a *habeas corpus*.

An attachment was moved for not obeying a writ of *habeas corpus* to bring up her daughter at the instance of her husband.

Lord KENYON said there must be a rule *nisi*, that it [an attachment] had been granted in the first instance in the case Lord Ferrers, but that was under very extraordinary circumstances, and Lady Ferrers' life was sworn to be in danger.

DUNNAGE v. SIR THOMAS TURTON

[M.H.] New trial not be granted for the receipt of evidence not objected to at the trial.

In this case on motion for a new trial, *Perceval* insisted that improper evidence had been received of the contents of some letters which had been destroyed, the witness to the contents not having read them herself but only heard the plaintiff's wife read them.

Lord KENYON said if the objection had been made at the trial he thought he

---

[49] The case appears at (1789) 3 T.R. 119.
[50] This case is reported at (17 June 1797) 7 T.R. 299.

should not have received the evidence, but no objection was then made and the court refused a rule to show cause.[51]

[6:98] CALLAND v. CHAMPION[52]

[M.H.] In a policy on a life if warranted good it is not sufficient to prove it to be tolerably good.

On a motion for a new trial on a policy on the life of Lord Glencairn, who was warranted a good life, it appeared that the witnesses could go no further than to say that he was in tolerable good health, he having a superficial ulcer in one of his legs which diminished his chance of life. But in the opinion of one of the witnesses his life was better than that of John Ross as described in the case of *Ross* v. *Bradshaw*, 1 [W.] Blackstone's Reports 312.

Gibbs, on the authority of this case and that of *Willis* v. *Poole*, Park 439,[53] made the motion.

Lord KENYON said he told the jury that he did not understand what was meant by an insurable life, the expression made use of in those cases. That he did understand what was meant by good health, in which no witness swore Lord Glencairn to have been. And as to his invoking what *Gibbs* called the law in those cases, he said he saw no law in it, it was a question of fact.

Nil cap.

[*Lawrence note*:]: In the Common Pleas the plaintiff obtained verdicts against some of the underwriters. The evidence, I heard, was somewhat different from that given before Lord KENYON.

---

[51] The criminal conversation trial was held before Lord Kenyon and a special jury of merchants on 14 June, as fully reported in *The Times* on 15 June. Dunnage won a jury verdict of £5,000. In this motion for a new trial, Perceval said that he thought the damages excessive, but under all the circumstances, he did not think that a substantial ground for a new trial. He had objected at trial to the witness testimony about the letters, but after it was established that the letters had been destroyed, Lord Kenyon permitted the testimony. In rejecting Perceval's motion at the hearing on 20 June, Kenyon reportedly observed that the letters contained only 'expressions of endearment and affection, and could not weigh a single feather in the cause', and he said that the motion for a new trial was 'very ill-advised'. *The Times*, 21 June 1797.

[52] A change of venue motion in this case was argued in Easter term 1797, reported at 7 T.R. 205 (as *Cailland* v. *Champion*). According to a report in *The Times*, the jury trial was held on 8 May, and the plaintiff sought to recover £250, the face value of the life insurance policy he had taken out. Lord Glencairn owed Cailland 'many thousand pounds at the time of his death', so the plaintiff clearly had an insurable interest. Glencairn was 46 years old at the time the one-year policy was underwritten. The jury verdict was for the defendant. *The Times*, 9 June 1797.

[53] According to Park, *Willis* v. *Poole* was tried before Lord Mansfield at the Guildhall sittings after Easter term 1780. J. A. Park, *A System of the Law of Marine Insurances*, 3rd ed. (1796), p. 439.

[6:99] June 21   R. v. DR MOSELEY

[M.H.] Neither of the parents of a natural child have a right to the custody of it. The great seal is to appoint a guardian. *Vide* post, 107.

Mingay moved for a *habeas corpus* to be directed to a Dr Moseley to bring up the body of a child who was his natural daughter by a woman at whose instance he made the application, insisting that the doctor had no right to the child.

Lord KENYON: A natural child has no guardian by law but the King as *pater patriae*. Before the writ is granted we must look beyond the bringing up the child and see to whom we can deliver it. You should apply to the master of the rolls to be appointed guardian. If you succeed in that, you may come here.[54]

Nil cap.

June 26   SMITH v. WOODGALE

[M.H.] Judgments, though in autre droit, may be set against each other, and execution shall only issue for the difference, but this not to prejudice the attorney's lien for costs.

Defendants having been sued by the plaintiff as the assignee of a bond given to the chancellor on suing out a commission of bankruptcy, and the plaintiff having recovered against them, moved to set off against the judgment against themselves the amount of a judgment recovered against the plaintiff by one Bromhead, whose executors they were, so that upon payment of the difference, satisfaction might be entered on the record.

Erskine opposed this, contending that as the debts claimed of the defendants and payable by them were in different rights, they ought not to be set against each other. That there was no reciprocity, for if the plaintiff had applied it could not be done, as that might disturb the due administration of assets, and that these debts could not have been set off by plea or notice.

Lord KENYON admitted that to be so, but added that the court in the exercise of its equitable jurisdiction would not suffer a sum to be levied on a defendant by its process, when as great [6:100] a sum is due to the party from whom it is levied; but that this must not deprive the attorney of his lien for his costs.

Rule absolute.

[*Lawrence note*]: *Erskine*, alleging that the defendant's judgment was on an usurious contract, the other side waived the judgment *pro hac vice* (*ss.*) that an action might be brought on the bond on which the judgment was entered, that the plaintiff might insist on the usury.

---

[54] For further proceedings in this case, see below, pp. 179 and 181.

July 3   BLACKMORE v. LORD WIGTOWN

[M.H.] The plea in abatement is entitled of the term it is pleaded when it ought to be of the preceding term. The plaintiff may sign judgment and need not demur.

On a motion to set aside a judgment it appeared that after the plaintiff had obtained leave to amend, the defendant pleaded an abatement as of this term, when his plea should have been as of the preceding term, on which the plaintiff signed judgment.

Wood for defendant contended that the defendant ought to have demurred to the plea, and ought not to have signed judgment. But the court discharged his rule. *Vide* 7 T.R. 447.[55]

MICHAELMAS TERM 38 Geo. III

Lloyd, Lord Kenyon, Chief Justice
Sir W. Ashhurst
Sir N. Grose   } Justices
Sir S. Lawrence

November 6   DOE, *ex dim.* FENHOUSE v. CARVER

[M.H.] The court will not grant a new trial where waste is to be taken advantage of, though that which is done be strictly so, if it does not appear that mischief is done to the estate.

Law moved for a new trial of an ejectment in the county of Cumberland. The action was to recover certain customary lands forfeited for waste by laying over the grounds a wagon way raised in some places 2.2 feet above the surface, in other places depressed below it. The jury found a verdict for the defendant under the judge's directions.

In support of the motion, *Law* cited *Cole* v. *Green*, 1 Lev. 311,[56] tried at bar, where HALE ruled the putting down a brew house and erecting new houses by which the rent was increased from £120 to £200 per annum was waste by reason of the alteration of the nature of the thing.

Lord KENYON: How is this waste, it may be an improvement? There are old cases which I will not say are not law, yet they are looked on with a very jealous eye, such as that turning arable into pasture is waste. Is that ever thought of now? I remember an application to the Court of Chancery to stay waste and Lord Northington refused it, saying it appeared to him to be an application for an injunction to stay taste. If you have any appetite, bring another ejectment.

Nil cap.

---

[55] The printed report is of the case of *Blackmore* v. *Flemyng*. The defendant was styled 'Hamilton Flemyng, Esq., commonly called Earl of Wigtown'. In a footnote, the related case noted by Lawrence, above, is described.

[56] *Cole* v. *Green* (1671) 1 Lev. 309.

PATCHETT v. BANCROFT

[M.H.] If collectors of the land tax are sued for what they do in the execution of their duty and the plaintiff is nonsuit, the court has no discretion, but they are of right entitled to double costs.

Topping moved in this case to suggest on the roll that the defendants were sued for what they had done in the execution of their office in collecting the land tax and having obtained a rule *nisi*, Law on the 12th showed cause and stated he had reasons to be submitted to the discretion of the court why such suggestion should not be entered. But Lord KENYON said the court had no discretion—and the rule was made absolute.

Vide 7 T.R. 367.[57]

[6:102]   WEBB v. GOFF

[M.H.] Award under seal not a deed unless it be delivered as such.

The question in this case was whether an award under seal was on a proper stamp, it being written on after having the stamp for deeds and not that directed by the statute for awards, being a 5s. stamp, by the 23 Geo. III, c. 58.

Lord KENYON thought there appeared enough from the attestation of the award for the court to presume it had been delivered as a deed.[58]

After this in Hilary term 38 Geo. III, *Bayley* in answer to the same objection to an award cited cases to shew that an award takes it[s] effect from the signing and sealing and not from the delivery—and was no deed. The cases he cited were Lord Raymond 760–767, 6 Mod. 58, Style 459.[59]

LAWRENCE, Justice, said that the court must not be understood to have determined that an award was necessarily a deed because it was under seal, but that an award might be by deed. And it was a question of fact whether the arbitrator delivered it as a deed or merely put his seal without any delivery. The court told *Bayley* he should have time to put another stamp on the award if on inquiry he found it necessary.

November 8   TENCH v. BELLIS

[M.H.] Infancy is evidence on *non assumpsit* on the warranty of a horse.

In an action of *assumpsit* on the warranty of a horse, PERRYN, Baron, would not suffer the defendant to give infancy in evidence, relying on what fell from

---

[57] The printed report covers prior proceedings in this case in Trinity term 1797 involving the taking by defendants of cattle under a warrant of distress for the aggregate amount of several taxes.

[58] Lawrence margin insert: 'In *Grinham* v. *Horsfield*, the same point came on this term between Wood and Garrow, when Lord Kenyon decided that the court would understand the award to have been delivered as a deed, though that word was not used in the attestation, saying that he should not think it possible for a jury to doubt it.'

[59] *Feltham* v. *Cudworth* (1702) 2 Raym. Ld. 760; *Claxton* v. *Basty* (1703) 6 Mod. 58; *Dod* v. *Herbert* (1655) Style 459.

Lord KENYON in *Bristow* v. *Eastman*, Peake's Cases 223.[60] *Milles* moved for a new trial for this mistake in point of law, and his rule was afterwards made absolute, Lord KENYON saying it was a speculative point and he might be wrong.

[*6:103*] November 9   MAITLAND v. GRAHAM

[M.H.] Query if a grand juror can be arrested during his attendance at sessions.

Park moved to discharge defendant out of custody, he having been arrested while attending at the quarter sessions as a grand juror.
1 H. Blackstone 336.[61]

Rule *nisi*.

SMITH, assignee v. BOWLES, *et al*.

[M.H.] Carrier has no lien if he does not deliver according to order. The right to stop *in transitu* only applies where the price is not paid.

Law moved for a new trial before Lord KENYON at Guildhall.

Trover by plaintiffs, assignees of Staples & Co., bankers, for $3,000 sent by Turner of Penryn by the carrier to Staples & Co., to whom he owed the amount of the dollars. Turner, hearing of the insolvency of Staples & Co. directed the carrier to deliver the goods to the defendants, who paid the carrier for the carriage, and the amount of a bill drawn by Turner on Staples & Co. The plaintiffs had a verdict, and *Law* now moved for a new trial on the ground that Bowles & Co. had a lien for at least the money they had paid for the carriage, which should have been tendered.

Lord KENYON: Has the carrier a lien if he does not deliver according to order? Here the goods were sent to Staples & Co., who had paid value for them, for more was due to them than the amount of the remittance. This case has nothing to do with a stoppage *in transitu*, which only holds where the price is not paid.

Nil cap.[62]

---

[60] In *Bristow* v. *Eastman* (1794) Peake 223, the question was whether an action in *assumpsit* would lie against the defendant, an infant, to recover money embezzled by him. Lord Kenyon said the question was new, but 'he was of opinion that this action, though in form arising *ex contractu*, in fact arose *ex delicto*, and as he could not have defended himself by reason of his infancy if an action of trover had been brought for the money, so he ought not to be permitted to defend himself on that ground in this action'.
[61] The correct reference is *Meekins* v. *Smith* (1791) 1 Bl. H. 636.
[62] This case is reported at 2 Esp. 578. According to Espinasse, the verdict was for £672, the value of the dollars.

FOWLER, *et al.*, assignees of Hunter v. KIMES

[M.H.] Goods can't be stopped as *in transitu* after they have been delivered on board a ship chartered by the vendee, though a receipt may have been given for them as the goods of the vendor.

Trover for tobacco tried before GROSE, Justice, at Bristol. *Bond* moved for a new trial. He stated the question to be if the defendant was not entitled to stop *in transitu*.

[6:104] Hunter, the bankrupt whose assignees the plaintiffs are, bought the tobacco, agreeing to pay for it in three months.

In consequence of which it was put on board a ship chartered by Hunter for Alexander &c., and a receipt given by the mate of the vessel for the tobacco as the goods of defendant, which he said entitled the holder to have a bill of lading made out in his name. The ship afterwards sailed for Portsmouth, and the house having failed on whom the bill was drawn, the goods were reloaded and the defendant took the possession of them. *Bond* said that at the trial it had been contended that the delivery on board the ship was the same as if the tobacco had been delivered into the warehouse of the bankrupt, but he conceived this construction could not obtain, as the mate's receipt prevented the tobacco from being considered as being delivered to the bankrupt.

Lord KENYON: It seems to me as much a delivery to him as if [it][63] had been put under his lock and key in a warehouse.

Nil cap.

R. v. WENFOLD

Prisoner had been committed on a charge for a highway robbery. He was bailed by the consent of the prosecutor, and on reading many affidavits to his character, and it appearing he was drunk at the time so as to induce a doubt if it would turn out to be a robbery.

Bayley for the defendant.

[6:105] Affidavit of debt was made in Ireland but did not negative a tender of the same due in bank notes pursuant to the 37 Geo. III. On this affidavit, an order of a judge was made to hold the defendant to bail.

He was discharged on filing common bail, the court being of opinion that the form of the affidavit must be the same.

---

[63] In the manuscript, Lawrence initially wrote 'as if he had first been', then crossed out 'first' but neglected to change 'he' to 'it'.

RICHARDSON v. COOKE

[M.H.] If one having a house with lights looking over ground of which he is the owner sells the ground and agrees that the vendee may block up the lights, it is not necessary that that right should be expressly given by the deed of conveyance.

Gibbs moved for a new trial of an action before me at Winton[64] against defendant for stopping up the plaintiff's lights by building immediately before them. Lord Mount Edgcumbe being seized of the plaintiff's house and the ground on which the defendant built sold to the defendant the ground without any resolution of the lights in question, which were not absolutely necessary, and at the time of the treaty for the sale, his steward told the defendant he might block them up. After the sale to the defendant, he sold the house to the plaintiff without anything being said about these lights.

At the trial I permitted evidence to be given of this consent of the steward to rebut any presumption that might arise in favour of the plaintiff, and this I did as not being at all contradictory or as enlarging the grant to the defendant, which having no resolution of the lights to Lord Mount Edgecombe I thought carried the power of building as near the lights as the defendant pleased, but for the presumption which might arise from the necessity of the lights to the house.

Verdict for defendant.

Gibbs moved for a new trial on the authority of 2 Sid. 39, Cro., J. 174, 1 Lev. [106] 122, [T.] Ray. 87,[65] contending that the evidence proved only a parol licence and that this interest could not be parted with but by deed.

Praed on the same side quoted Comyn's *Digest*, tit: Suspens: B, Owen 121, Shep: Epitome 158.[66]

Barrow, contra, said the only question was whether Lord Mount Edgecombe might not permit his lessee to build up to close his own windows.

Lord KENYON said he thought it was not necessary to go into the learning of the cases, how far things of necessity might or might not be parted with. That the action was a possessory action and the question was whether a man could not give a licence to do what the defendant had done.

GROSE, Justice, took the same ground I had done at the trial.

Rule discharged.

---

[64] The archaic name for Winchester.

[65] *Packer v. Welsted* (1658) 2 Sid. 39; *Ward v. Walthew* (1607) Cro. Jac. 173; *Palmer v. Fletcher* (1663) 1 Lev. 122; *Palmer v. Fleshees* (1663) Raym. T. 87.

[66] *Jorden v. Atwood* (1605) Ow. 121; W. Sheppard, *An Epitome of All the Common and Statute Laws of This Nation* (1656), at p. 158.

HARPER v. CARR

[M.H.] The judge before whom a cause is tried is to certify for double costs in pursuance of 7 J. I, and not to be directed by the court out of which the record goes.

Law shewed cause against a rule for the Master to tax the defendants their double costs in pursuance of the 7 J. I and 21 J. I, and insisted that this court had no power to do it. That it must be done by the judge who tried the cause, and he cited 2 Ventr. 45, Doug. 294.[67]

Lamb, contra.

Lord KENYON: May not the judge certify now? You should go before him.[68]

[6:107]   HILARY TERM 38 Geo. III

Lloyd, Lord Kenyon, Chief Justice
Sir W. Ashhurst
Sir N. Grose   } Justices
Sir S. Lawrence

WILSON v. KENSINGTON[69]

[M.H.] A natural born subject of this country domiciled in America is an American within the meaning of a warranty that a ship is the property of an American. The written laws of a foreign country cannot be proved by parol.

Law moved for a new trial in an action on a policy on the ship *Argonaut* warranted American. The plaintiff was a natural born subject of Great Britain settled in America.

Law contended he was not such a neutral as satisfied the warranty.

Lord KENYON: This person had been settled in America ever since the treaty of peace and domiciled there. We should make the wildest work in the world if we were not to hold him an American for the purposes of this warranty.

I thought this point had been abandoned.

Law: Another ground is that Mr King, the American minister, was not allowed to give parol evidence of the laws of America because they were in writing, which he should have been permitted to do.

Lord KENYON: I remember it was taken for granted at the Cockpit[70] that the

---

[67] *Anon.* (1689) 2 Ventr. 45 (third anonymous case on page 45); *Barber* v. *French* (1779) 2 Doug. 294.

[68] See the published report of this case at 7 T.R. 448, 27 November 1797. The court said it thought the trial judge was bound to grant the certificate, and it was not necessary that it be granted at the trial.

[69] See p. 181 below for another report of this case, virtually identical.

[70] The Judicial Committee of the Privy Council, named after a venerable room in Whitehall Palace that was occupied as the council chamber.

laws of Spain must be sent over in some form and a copy was procured under seal.[71]

Nil cap.

R. v. DR MOSELEY

[M.H.] The mother is entitled to the custody of her natural child during the age of nurture.

Mingay moved for *habeas corpus* to bring up a natural child of the age of five years, which is within the age of nurture, which child the doctor had by management got out of the possession of the mother. He cited *R. v. Soper* as in point, 5 T.R.[72]

Lord KENYON: Take your writ. If this child had originally been in the [6:108] care of the putative father we would not have changed the custody, but this child is within the age of nurture.[73]

Vide antea 99. *Vide* same case *post* 111.

DOE, *ex dim*. BLACKBOROUGH v. BLACKBOROUGH

[M.H.] Devise to A. and B. in trust for C. and his heirs at 25, and if he does not arrive at that age then to son. Query if in the meantime the legal estate be in the heir at law?

William Blackborough devised certain houses, &c. to his wife Lydia, John Bacon, and Thomas Plugler, their heirs and assigns, to hold to them, their heirs and assigns, upon the trusts and for the intents and purposes following, that is

---

[71] This case was one of several involving the same facts. The first to be reported was tried before Lord Kenyon at the Guildhall sittings after Hilary term 1797, when the plaintiff was nonsuited. See *Wilson v. Backhouse* (1797) Peake's Additional Cases 119. On 15 November, arguments were heard in *Backhouse* on a motion for a new trial, and according to *The Times*: 'This case involves in it a question of as much importance to the trade and commerce of Great Britain, as ever presented itself in an English Court of Justice.' *The Times*, 16 November 1797. After argument, Lord Kenyon 'was of opinion this cause ought to be sent down to another trial, to ascertain the facts, for the purpose of converting it into a special verdict'. The case that facilitated the development of the facts and that was reported at length was *Wilson v. Marryatt* (1798) 8 T.R. 31, also followed closely in *The Times* (31 January (reporting on the trial at Guildhall on 16 December 1797), 5 May, 13 June, 21 November, and 22 November 1798). See also *Wilson v. Marryatt*, p. 198, below, for a ruling on costs in the case. The underwriters had refused to pay, contending that the policy was illegal, and that the loss was due to the negligence of the captain. A special verdict was drawn up and was argued three times. The court's judgment for the plaintiff was finally given on 21 November, as is fully explained in *Term Reports*. According to *The Times*, 7 May 1799, Chief Justice Eyre of the Court of Common Pleas delivered 'an elaborate judgment' in the Court of Exchequer Chamber on 6 May unanimously affirming the King's Bench decision. That opinion is fully reported as *Marryat v. Wilson* (1799) 1 Bos. & Pul. 430. See also the Paper Book for *Collet v. Keith*, p. 273, below.

[72] *R. v. Soper* (1793) 5 T.R. 278.

[73] According to *The Times*, 10 February 1798, the mother swore that the child had been in her possession but Dr Moseley had gone to her house and had taken the child away by force, 'which had been the subject of a prosecution'. The *Soper* case was said to have been cited by Mingay 'to shew that a putative father had no right to the custody of a bastard child'.

to say as to [one] parcel to the use and behoof of his son John Steele Blackborough, his heirs and assigns, when he should attain the age of 25 years, and in case he should happen to die before he attained the age of 25 years then in trust to the use and behoof of his son[s] Henry and William, their heirs and assigns, in equal proportions when they should respectively attain their ages of 25 years, to hold as tenants in common, and in case either should die before he arrived at the age of 25, then in trust to [the] use of the survivor, his heirs and assigns. And as to other part (*ss.* the premises in question) in trust to the use and behoof of his son William and his heirs when he should attain his age of 25 years, but in case his son William should die before he attained his age of 25 years, then in trust to the use and behoof of his sons John Steele and Henry, their heirs and assigns in equal shares when they shall attain their ages of 25 years and in case either should die then in trust for the survivor at 25. And in case all [*6:109*] his sons should die before the age of 25 years then upon trust that they, the said Lydia, John Bacon, and Thomas Pugler and the survivors or survivor and his heirs, should upon the death of his sons dying before 25 make satisfaction of all the said lands and tenements, in trust to divide the produce among his daughters.

J. T. Blackborough the heir at law arrived at his age 25 and was let into the possession of the part devised to him, and brought this ejectment to recover the part devised to his brother William, insisting that until William was 25, that he himself as heir at law was entitled to the estate. On the trial of this cause before Lord KENYON, he nonsuited the plaintiff, being of opinion that the legal estate remained in the trustees. And on a motion for a new trial continues strongly of the same opinion, and said the only case he knew of where the use was executed in the trustees in part only was where an estate is given to trustees and their heirs during the life of A. to preserve contingent remainders, but that in this case the interest the trustees were to take was expressly portioned out. But if that was not so done and it was necessary that the estate should be executed in the trustees for the purposes of the trust, as in this case to sell, it must be executed throughout.

It was, however, ordered to be made a case, so that the court did not decide the point. *Law* said that the master of the rolls had [*6:110*] dismissed the plaintiff's bill, to have an account of the rents, being of opinion that the legal estate was vested in him.

Vide Jones v. *Lord Say and Seal*, 8th Vin. 262.[74]

Broughton v. *Langley*, Salk. 679[75]

Butler's note on Co. Litt. 271b.

[*Lawrence note*:] Query why might not the son take the legal estate subject to be divested by his brothers' arriving at 25 or if none arrived at 25 by all of their deaths, when it might vest in the trustees to sell.

---

[74] *Jones* v. *Say and Seal (Lord)* (1729) 8 Viner's Abridgment 262; also 1 Eq. Ca. Abr. 384, 3 Bro. P. C. 113.

[75] *Broughton* v. *Langley* (1702–03) 2 Salk. 679.

WILSON v. KENSINGTON

[M.H.] A natural born subject domiciled in America is to be considered as a native of America for the purpose of trade. Parol evidence can't be given of the written laws of a foreign country.

In an action on a policy on the *Argonaut*, warranted American and American property, *Law* moved for a new trial on two grounds: first, that the plaintiff was a natural born subject of this country, and though settled in America could not be a neutral within the meaning of the warranty, which the word 'American' implied.

Secondly, that Lord KENYON had rejected parol evidence of the laws of America, which, had Mr King, the American minister, been allowed to give evidence of, the defendant would have shown the ship was not American.

As to the first point, Lord KENYON said, as the plaintiff had been settled in America ever since the treaty of peace, it would be making the wildest work if he were not held to be such, and as to the latter, said that no parol evidence could be given of written laws. That he remembered a case at the Cockpit where it was taken for granted that the written laws of Spain must appear in some form before them, and a copy under seal was procured.[76]

Nil cap.

[6:111] ## R. v. DR MOSELEY[77]

[M.H.] *Habeas corpus* may be granted to restore to the care of its mother a natural born child of the age of nurture, which the putative father has taken from her.

Mingay moved for a *habeas corpus* to bring up the body of a child of the age of five years which Dr Moseley had by a woman of a name of Harriet Kyly, out of whose custody he had taken it, and cited *R.* v. *Soper*, 5 T.R. 278 as in point.

Lord KENYON: Take your writ. If the child had originally been in the care of the father, through the putative father, we would not have changed the custody. But this child is within the age of nurture.

> [*Lawrence note*:]: *N.B.* in Easter term following, the time for returning this writ was enlarged pending an application to the Court of Chancery to appoint a guardian.

VOGHT v. ELGIN

The defendant was held to bail on an affidavit sworn before the praetor of Hamburg, on the motion of Mr *Gibbs*.

---

[76] As is evident, this case is virtually identical in content to the earlier case (see p. 178, above) interpreting the meaning of the warranty.

[77] See earlier versions of this case, pp. 172 and 179, above.

CHRISTIAN v. SELBY

[M.H.] Where a defendant has undertaken to appear and a declaration be delivered *de bene esse*, a plea can't be demanded before the defendant's time has expired.

The defendant having undertaken to file common bail, the plaintiff delivered his declaration *de bene esse* at the return of the recess the 27 January and demanded a plea. On the 6th of February common bail was filed, after which, without any fresh demand of a plea, the plaintiff signed judgment.

Erskine shewed cause against a rule for setting aside the proceedings for irregularity, contending that the plaintiff could pursue no other course, as he could not file common bail himself, as he could not make affidavit that the defendant had been served with process.

Chambré, *contra*, said that the practice required a demand to be made subsequent to the filing common bail—and cited 1 T.R. 635.[78]

The court held that the judgment was irregular, for the demand ought not in any way of considering the question to have been made till after the 4th, when the defendant should have filed common bail.

Rule absolute.

[*6:112*] ANONYMOUS

[M.H.] Injunction does not make the proceedings against the bail irregular.

Judgment having been obtained against the principal in Trinity term, a *capias ad satisfaciendum* was lodged in the office, returnable 6th November.

On the 20th of July, the defendant obtained an injunction.

20th November: plaintiff sued out a *latitat* against the bail.

8th February: the injunction was dissolved.

Marriot moved to set aside the proceedings against the bail as irregular, and compared the injunction to a writ of error pending which a *capias ad satisfaciendum* can't be sued out to fix the bail. *Perry* v. *Campbell*, 3 T.R. 390.

E contra it was said that if the *capias ad satisfaciendum* or the *latitat* were improperly issued pending the injunction, the application to prevent any proceeding ought to have been to the Court of Chancery.

Rule discharged, with costs.

---

[78] *Cook* v. *Raven* (1787) 1 T.R. 635.

EASTER TERM 38 Geo. III

Lloyd, Lord Kenyon, Chief Justice
Sir W. Ashhurst
Sir N. Grose } Justices
Sir S. Lawrence

[6:113]   DOE, *ex dim.* MARTIN v. STUBBS

[M.H.] Parol evidence is admissible that a deed was delivered on a different day than that it bears date.

Shepherd, serjeant, moved for a new trial of an ejectment tried before Mr Baron HOTHAM in Surrey, which was brought by a remainderman to try the validity of a lease made by a tenant for life. The objection was that the lease was a reversionary lease.

The lease was dated the 8th of May and was to commence at Michaelmas. The subscribing witness said he believed the lease was not executed until Michaelmas or after. The judge left it to the jury to say whether the lease was executed on the day it bore date or at Michaelmas.

This, *Shepherd* contended, ought not to have been done, as it was receiving parol evidence against the deed.

Lord KENYON: I have known such evidence admitted. It is like the case mentioned by Lord COKE of livery at a time subsequent to the date of the feoffment.[79]

Nil cap.

COWAN v. BERRY

[M.H.] The court can't restrain an informer from proceeding to recover any number of penalties, however great their amount.

Erskine shewed cause against a rule of *Mingay*'s to compel the plaintiff to choose ten counts out of his declaration brought against the defendant for winning money at play of one who was the plaintiff's clerk and was afterwards hanged for forgery, which he was induced to commit from distresses brought on him by losses at play—and of other people. The penalties claimed amounted to £1,330,000 [6:114] and as it was said the declaration was so long it would cost above £700 to come into court to meet the plaintiff. The cause shown was that the declaration did not charge more offences than the defendant had committed, and that the plaintiff was willing, if the defendant would consent, to divide the cause into several so as to make the trial convenient if he would not insist on the statute of limitations.

---

[79] E. Coke, *The First Part of the Institutes of the Laws of England*, 15th ed. (1794), i. 56b, sec. 70.

Lord KENYON: If this had been for the purpose of oppression, the court would set their face against it. But I will not accede to the doctrine that the more offences a man has committed, that on that account the penalties ought to be remitted.

Rule discharged, with costs.[80]

[*Lawrence note*:] *N.B.* This I understood to be said with reference to what BULLER, Justice, had said at Salisbury in an action brought by Mr Petrie against Lord Porchester and others for bribery at Cricklade, when he told the jury that if the plaintiff had no conscience and acted like a Jew in going for every penny that the defendant might be liable to, that the jury might mitigate them and give no more than they thought reasonable.[81]

R. v. STEVENS *et al.*

[M.H.] If there be a probable ground to question the title of a corporator, the court will grant an information in *quo warranto*. It is no objection to persons applying for such information that they have acted with the defendant in the administration of justice, if they have not concurred in his election.

This was a motion against Stevens for information in the nature of a *quo warranto* for exercising the office of mayor of Harwich, and against Fulham on whose title that of Stevens depended, for having exercised it in the year '97.

---

[80] This case was fully reported in *The Times*, 10 May 1798. Mingay was opposed by a formidable set of counsel for the defendant—Erskine, Garrow, Gibbs, and Onslow. When Erskine said he understood Lord Kenyon's inclination to resist such voluminous pleadings, Kenyon responded, 'I do not know how we can prevent the plaintiff from proceeding for all the offences; but undoubtedly one Declaration ought only to contain so many counts as a Judge and Jury can try.' Erskine explained that the defendant had gambled with thirty-two different persons many different times, and the declaration counted each time one of the thirty-two lost as a separate offence. He offered to cut down the declaration to ten counts as requested if Mingay would agree not to raise the statute of limitations against any of the counts, though Garrow disagreed, asserting that the case was manageable as it stood. Mingay said that if his motion failed, 'there were three other declarations ready to be brought forward against the defendant, each of them consisting of 5,000 sheets, which was double the length of the present declaration, which no Judge or Jury could try'. Further, anyone who read the declaration would see that it was pure fiction—'The defendant was supposed to win 1,000 guineas on one day, 1,000 guineas on another, &c. for 480 days.' Lord Kenyon was torn between his moral condemnation of the defendant's alleged behaviour and the reality that the judge and jury might 'entangle themselves in such a variety of facts, from which they could not be able to extricate themselves'. He said that, 'If it shall appear that all this is done for vexation, the plaintiff will be under the lash of the Court', but absent any such showing, he 'will not smother the offences.' Fearing that if the declaration were to be reduced to ten counts, other lawsuits would then be filed for ten counts each, Mingay abandoned his motion. In another case involving the same facts, *Cowan* v. *Phillips*, Lord Kenyon reportedly said that the court had been unable to divide the record, which was 'immensely long', yet 'Judges and Juries cannot go beyond the strength which it has pleased God Almighty to give them.' Erskine said that the record was so long, that if Lord Kenyon pleased to do it, he could 'walk in procession on it from Westminster Hall to Guildhall in the City'. *The Times*, 4 December 1798. Later, Erskine informed the court that the parties had agreed to compound the causes. *The Times*, 13 February 1799.

[81] On the case of *Petrie* v. *Porchester*, see Oldham, *MMSS*, i. 190–191. As is there noted, the *London Chronicle*, describing bribery cases brought by Petrie against Porchester and tried by Buller at the Salisbury assizes, reported on 2 August 1781 that 'no less than 113 *more actions* were remaining to be tried on the same matter'.

[6:115A] The facts were these: The charter day is the 30th of November when the Mayor and other officers are elected, and it is directed by the charter that in case of the mayor's death after he has been elected and sworn in, the corporation may proceed to the election of a new mayor. The custom was to swear the mayor into office the 21st of December. On the 30th November, 1796 one Dean was elected mayor, and died before he was sworn in, upon which the corporation proceeded to the election of a mayor, at which one Sherman, who was Dean's predecessor, presided, and Fulham was elected and executed his office that year. His election was objected to as bad, on the ground that Sherman could not preside at this second election.

It was said in answer that if this case was not with the words of the charter as described, 'dead before he was sworn in', yet it was within the spirit of it—and that the relators could not be heard to object to Fulham as they had acted with him as mayor. But this only appeared to be in the administration of justice.

Lord KENYON: This question is too much to decide on a motion for an information. If there be a probable ground, the information is the only way of deciding it.

As to the objection *in limine*, the court do not forget that they will not hear persons object to a man's title in whose election they have concurred. But in this case they found him in possession, and have acquiesced in acting under him for the administration of justice.

Rule absolute.

[6:116A] EX PARTE BROOK

[M.H.] An agent has no lien on money received in a cause beyond what he may have laid out in that cause, and can't retain it against the party to satisfy a balance due to him from his client.

The court held in this case that Messrs Ward and Bennet (who had received money on a cause in which Brook was a party, and had carried it to the general account of their client in the county, whose agents they were, he being the person Brook had employed) were liable to pay the balance to Brook after deducting such sums of money as Ward & Co. had laid out in the cause. This Lord KENYON said he remembered had been ruled many years ago in the case of Mr Green of Crane Court.

REES v. ROSE

[M.H.] In the trial of testamentary questions, the ecclesiastical court may incidentally determine on the validity and effect of deeds.

Lawes moved for a prohibition to the spiritual court to restrain them from trying the validity of the will of a feme covert under a deed of trust giving her such power, as the existence of the deed and its effect were both denied by the answer to the libel.

Lord KENYON said the court would not interfere in a question on a testamentary paper. That the ecclesiastical court must examine the points as incident to the principal question, and if it be decided wrong, the parties must go to the Delegates who were the dernier resort.

Nil cap.

[6:115B]   TRINITY TERM 38 Geo. III

Lloyd, Lord Kenyon, Chief Justice
Sir W. Ashhurst ⎫
Sir N. Grose   ⎬ Justices
Sir S. Lawrence ⎭

June 3   ARDESOIF v. ISAAC

[M.H.] The memorial of an annuity deed is not bad for stating as parties to the deed persons who never executed it if they be persons in whom trusts will vest without their execution.

Bayley had moved to set aside a warrant of attorney and judgment to secure an annuity of £40 per annum.

The memorial was of a bond dated 22nd August 1783 for [£]400 from Isaac to the plaintiff, conditioned for payment of [£]40 quarterly; of a warrant of attorney of the same date; and of an indenture 3 partite between Isaac of the first part, Gomport and Stone of the second part, and the plaintiff of the third part, by which the defendant had signed over to the plaintiff £40 parcel of an annuity given him by the will of H. Isaac.

The objection to the memorial was that Gomport and Stone did not appear to have executed the deed, and if they had not, on the authority of *Hart* v. *Lovelace*[82] it was insisted that the memorial was bad, as the memorial would mislead persons by introducing those who had nothing to do with the transaction.

Lord KENYON: In cases of settlements, trusts vest in persons who never execute, e.g. to raise younger children's portions, or secure pin money. They vest *nolens volens*. I take it [in] this case, Stone and Gomport were non-operative parties, made so only for the purpose of giving notice of the assignment of the legacy.

Rule discharged.

[82] (1795) 6 T.R. 471.

[6:116B]   PRESCOT v. PHILLIPS

[M.H.] A possession for a less time than twenty years of the use of a stream can't be connected with a title to such use, not enjoyed for above a century before.

Leycester and *Topping* shewed cause against a new trial of a cause tried before ADAIR, serjeant, chief justice of Chester, which was an action on the case for creating a weir to turn the water of the river Tame to some printing grounds,[83] by which certain meadows which the plaintiffs were interested in as trustees of a Mr Astley, a minor, were overflowed and part of them washed away.

It was proved in support of the plaintiff's case that above twenty years ago a weir was built for the purpose of diverting the water, which stood about seven years and was then washed away. That afterwards another was created, which stood but a little while, when a plank weir was built, which stood within three or four years, when it was washed away. This Mr Astley threatened to pull down. The weir in question was built since, and the meadows were shown to be injured by the weirs.

For the defendant it appeared in evidence that above this weir there were some piles apparently of an old weir, and a gate which was near them, and though Mr Astley had lived there till his death he had never pulled down the weirs defendants had built, but had about twelve years ago threatened an action—and many times made objections.

The defendant contended that there had been an ancient mill to which the remains of the old piles and the old gate belonged, and that the new weir ought to be coupled with the ancient right and would bar the plaintiff's action.

They produced in evidence a deed of release bearing date 4th of March 1650, [6:117] being among the muniments of the defendant's estate, among the parcels of which was mentioned a water corn mill used as a fulling mill, together with all waters, watercourses, water dams, &c. and a deed of covenant to buy a fine dated 1st of March 1680 of, inter alia, one 'fulling mill'.

They also offered evidence of hearsay and reputation that there had been anciently a mill on the defendant's estate, but it was admitted that none had existed in the memory of any living witness.

The court (J. ADAIR, serjeant, and BURTON, justices of Chester) were of opinion that hearsay was not evidence of the fact, and that there having been no possession or exercise of the right for more than sixty years, the ancient right could not be coupled with the recent possession of less than twenty years, so as to give a right against the other landholders on the sides of the river to their damage. And the jury found for the plaintiff.

In support of the verdict, it was said that the prescription would not authorize erecting a weir in another place in support of which 4 Co. 86

---

[83] In the calico preparation process after printing, the cloth is laid on the grass, that is, on 'printing grounds'. See Anon., *A Treatise on Calico Printing* (1792), unpaginated, see 'On Bleaching, Or as it is usually termed Preparation', n. (10).

Luttrel's Case and 4 Mod. 45 were cited.[84] And *Leycester* admitted that if the prescription had been once established, of which he insisted there was not evidence, as no proof of any ancient weir, an interruption for twenty years would not destroy it. Co. Litt. 110. To which Lord KENYON said, 'Is that so? In the case of a road at Brighthelmstone,[85] the court overruled me in that, and held it was gone by non-user, taking the rule from the statute of limitations.'

[6:118] In support of the rule, *Chambré*, *Jervis*, *Vaughan* and *Evance* contended that the right to erect the weir was an incident to the estate, and that the possession of the estate was a possession of the incident. That a possession of the weir for near twenty years without any actual interruption and only verbal opposition was coupled with the other circumstances, evidence of an actual right, that a mill was not a species of property which it was worthwhile to work at all times, and as no adverse mill had been erected, the right continued, though not used, it was not abandoned, and that all these circumstances should have been left to the consideration of the jury. They cited *Eldridge* v. *Knott*,[86] *Cooper Oswald* v. *Legh*, 1 T.R. 270,[87] 2 Blackstone's Commentaries 77, 4 T.R. 682,[88] where conveyances had been presumed in less time than 20 years.

Lord KENYON: That was a case *sui generis*, where I went as far as I could to enable an equitable title to be gone into in ejectment.

If this case were to prevail for the defendants, it would be one of the most dangerous cases that can be determined. For 117 years there is no vestige of the exercise of this right. Mankind in their dealings look at what has been done for the last fifty or sixty years.

[6:119] Admitting the stakes were part of a weir, and the deeds a fair representation of what existed at the time of their execution, here has been a disuser for above 100 years. Is it impossible that this might not have been from the mill, &c. being abated as a nuisance? May not the right to have a mill have been released? If a man has put out windows and enjoyed them for a length of time, shall a man be permitted to say here was once an old house, and I will block them up?

In *Dongel* v. *Wilson*,[89] Mr Justice WILMOT advised the jury to abide by what had been done for the last twenty years.

---

[84] *Luttrel's Case* (1601) 4 Co. Rep. 84b, 86a; *Grimly* v. *Fawlkingham* (1691) 4 Mod. 45.
[85] That is, Brighton.
[86] *Eldridge* v. *Knott* (1774) 1 Cowp. 214.
[87] *Oswald* v. *Legh* (1786) 1 T.R. 270.
[88] *England d. Syburn* v. *Slade* (1792) 4 T.R. 682.
[89] In the margin 'B. 149', evidently another of Lawrence's notebooks (see p. 63, n. 66, above). Otherwise unreported, an account of *Dongal* v. *Wilson* can be found in Misc. MS 96, *MS Notes by Buller, J. & Sir E.H. East 1754–92*, Inner Temple Library, London, vol. 1, fols. 63–64, as follows:
Dongal v. Wilson
Sitting after Trin. 9 G. 3.   *Cor.* Wilmot, C. Justice

In an action for stopping lights, Defendant attempted to show that the lights did not exist more than sixty years.

    Wilmot, C.J. said if a man has been in possession of a house with lights belonging to it fifty or sixty years no man can shut up those lights. Possession for such a time amounts to a grant of the

The learned judges did what I should have done, though perhaps in better terms.

ASHHURST, Justice: The deeds should have been accompanied with some semblance of possession.

Rule discharged.

June 26   SIKES *et al.* v. MARSHALL[90]

[M.H.] No cross interrogatories after publication.

The court refused after the answers to interrogatories had been returned under a commission sent to Elsinore to suffer cross interrogatories to be exhibited to the witness, his examination having been seen. And Lord KENYON said it was the constant practice of the Court of Chancery to refuse cross interrogatories to be administered after publication.

[6:120]   ACTON v. ROBERTS

[M.H.] Proceedings stayed, on affidavit that the action was for 27s., the balance of an account stated.

Proceedings were stayed in this case on an affidavit that the action was brought for 27s., the balance of an account stated. Defendant living within the jurisdiction of the county court of Gloucester. Though *Dauncey* endeavoured to distinguish this from a case in 5th T.R. of *Wellington* v. *Arters*,[91] where the affidavit was that the debt was under 40s., for the balance of an account might involve questions of great amount. But the court said they understood it to be an account stated, as the plaintiff had not sworn it was an action for a greater sum and was not to be reduced by a set off.

---

liberty of making them. It is evidence of an agreement to make them. If I am in possession of an estate for so long a period as sixty years I can't be disturbed even by a writ of right (the highest writ in the law). If my possession of the house itself can't be disturbed, yet shall I be disturbed in my lights, it would be absurd.

But the action can only be maintained for damages so far as the lights originally extended, and not for an increase of lights by enlarging the windows recently. And I should think a *much shorter time* than sixty years must be sufficient, but here there has been a possession that time. Vi: ante 46.

The reference to folio 46 is to the following notes of the case of *Lewis* v. *Price*, Worcester spring assizes 1761:

In an action for stopping and obstructing plaintiff's lights, Wilmot J. said that where a house has been built forty years and has had lights at the end of it, if the owner of the adjoining ground build against them so as to disturb them, an action lies, and this is founded on the same reason as when they have been made immemorial. For this is long enough to induce a presumption that there was originally some agreement between the parties, and he said that as twenty years is sufficient to give a man title in ejectment, on which he may recover the house itself, he saw no reason why it should not be sufficient to entitle him to any easement belonging to his house.

[90] For a report of the trial before Lord Kenyon and a special jury on 18 December 1798, see 2 Esp. 705.
[91] *Wellington* v. *Arters* (1792) 5 T.R. 64.

MICHAELMAS 39 Geo. III

Lloyd, Lord Kenyon, Chief Justice
Sir W. Ashhurst
Sir N. Grose } Justices
Sir S. Lawrence

[6:121] November 8
DOE, ex dim. WILLEY v. HOLMES[92]

[M.H.] 'I give to E. G. my house at a [. . .] and make her my executrix, she pays my debts and legacies', is an estate in fee.

Wood moved for a new trial of an ejectment tried at Durham before me in which the plaintiff had been nonsuit.

The single question was whether Elizabeth Gibson took an estate for life or in fee under the will of Thomas Randall, dated the 20th of December 1774. The words of which were these: 'I gave to Elizabeth Gibson £20. I also give my freehold messuage with the appurtenances (the premises in question) to the said Elizabeth Gibson, whom I make my executrix, she paying all my just debts and funeral expenses and the legacies before mentioned twelve months after my death. Likewise I leave to the said Elizabeth Gibson all the rest of my personal estate except my wearing apparel.'

Wood at the trial contended this was but an estate for life as there were no words of limitation, that the words 'she paying' only pointed out the duty of an executrix and were not directing that it should be paid out of the land. I was of opinion that the words created a charge on the land and gave a fee and nonsuited the plaintiff who claimed under the heir as legatee of the devisor.

And on this motion *Wood* repeated the same argument. But Lord KENYON said that where there was an indefinite charge not restricted to the annual profits, it would create a fee, and it appeared to him to be a charge on the land and in every view of the subject to be a fee.

Nil cap.

[6:122] November 14   DAY v. ALLEN

Erskine shewed cause against a prohibition to the Admiralty Court instituted by Day, a man living at Cowes in the Isle of Wight, for the salvage of a ship which came ashore in Sandown Bay, and of which he claimed the merit of being the salvor.

Three objections were made:

First that the services were not performed at sea.

Secondly if they were, that as there were persons on board, the plaintiff

---

[92] This case is reported at 8 T.R. 1, showing a date of 9 November.

could not sue in the Admiralty for compensation but could only be considered as their assistant, and as such might have a compensation at law.

Thirdly that since the 12 Ann St. 2., c. 18 the amount of the compensation was to be determined by justices of the peace.

Gibbs argued in support of the rule. The court, without giving any opinion, directed the plaintiff to declare in prohibition.

November 15   R. v. BROWN

[M.H.] Conviction on 23 Geo. III, c. 88 stating that defendant was convicted of having implements for housebreaking, instead of stating that he was apprehended with such tools, is bad.

Defendant was brought up on a *habeas corpus* directed to the keeper of the Reading goal, having been committed to that prison by a magistrate of Berks[hire] as a rogue and vagabond under the 23 Geo. [III], c. 88. And it was objected by *Lawes* that the conviction as recited in the warrant, stated that he had been *convicted* of having implements for the breaking open houses, whereas [6:123] according to the words of the Act, it ought to have been stated that at the time *of his apprehension* he had upon him such instruments.

Milles endeavoured to support the commitment but Lord KENYON said he feared the objection was well founded, though he yielded to it with reluctance.

Discharged.

R. v. MARY HENDERSON

[M.H.] In cases of great offences, if [there are] any circumstances of compassion, if a judgment adequate to the crime can't be passed, a slight one ought not.

Convicted of a conspiracy with two others to extort money from Lord Eardley, the woman appearing on many accounts an object of compassion, which was admitted by *Erskine*, counsel for the prosecution. Lord KENYON said it was impossible to inflict a light punishment for such an offence and therefore proposed to take her recognizance in £500 to appear whenever she should be called up for judgment, to which *Erskine*, for the prosecutor, consented.[93]

November 16   DE VIGNIER v. SWANSON

[M.H.] Broker is an agent within 28 Geo. III, c. 56.

This was a policy on ship and goods from St Domingo to London.
One Grandeville having received from the plaintiff, who was resident in

---

[93] This appears to be an act of mercy—a tacit understanding between counsel and the court that the sentencing for such a serious offence was not to be compromised, but the defendant would never be called up for judgment.

England, orders to effect the policy, employed one Clough, a broker, to get the policy subscribed. And his name was used in the policy, and the question was if a policy broker was a person receiving the order for effecting a policy within the meaning of the 28 Geo. III, c. 56. *Erskine*, who had moved for a new trial in order to determine the point, admitted he [Clough] was within [*6:124*] the words of the act, but contended that if that construction was adopted it would introduce all the mischief of blank policies which was the object of the Act of parliament to put an end to.

Garrow and *Park* showed cause against the rule, which without much being said except that a broker was within the words of the Act, was discharged.

November 17   CHATFIELD v. PAXTON *et al.*

[M.H.] Money paid by one supposing himself liable in point of law and not knowing all the circumstances of the case may be recovered back.

This was an action for money had and received tried at Guildhall before Lord KENYON, when a verdict was found for the plaintiff. *Gibbs* moved to enter a nonsuit.

Facts of the case were these according to the report:

The plaintiff being about to go to India drew a bill on a house there of Luard & Co. in favour of the defendants, William Paxton, Cockerell, and A. Paxton, who resided in England, which the defendants discounted and remitted to their correspondents in India, William Paxton, Cockerell and DeLisle, William Paxton and Cockerell being partners in both houses. This bill was done the 2nd of May 1788, and was accepted by Luard & Co., who, not being able to pay it, it was protested on that day, previous to which Luard applied to Paxton & Co., the holders in India, to give him some indulgence, which they did for two months, during part of which time his house made [*6:125*] considerable payments on account of demands, which could not be put off, but stopped payment before the two months expired. In consequence of this, the house of Paxton in India on the 31st of October 1788 wrote to the plaintiff informing him that, as intelligence of the failure of Luard & Co. must have come to him, he would not be surprised at his bill on Luard & Co. coming home under protest, and that they had valued on him for the amount in favour of William Paxton & Co. This bill the plaintiff accepted at six months on 23rd May 1789 and paid when due. And the action was to recover back from the defendants the money he had paid on this bill.

On the 22nd June 1789, plaintiff wrote to the house of Paxton & Co. in India finding fault with them for not having arrested Luard & Co. And on the 16th of August stated in another letter his astonishment that the bill had been kept back, and hoped when he should get to Bengal to be more fully informed of this grievous disaster. And no notice was proved to have been given to the plaintiff when payment of his acceptance was called for, that the indulgence had been given, and he paid the bill under an idea that he was by law liable.

In support of this motion, *Gibbs* and *Burrough* contended that whatever would have been a defence to the action at the suit of Paxton & Co. in India would have been a defence to an action [*6:126*] at the suit of William Paxton & Co. here, and that after a voluntary payment with a knowledge of the facts, which might have furnished an answer to an action on the bill, the plaintiff could not recover what he had so paid. That if he knew the facts, he must decide as to the law and be bound by it, though he be mistaken as to the legal obligation. That there was no pressure on him, which would take off the consequences of his judgment. If he had been arrested and paid he could not have recovered back the money. *Marriot* v. *Hanson* 7 T.R. 269[94], *Fulham* v. *Downer*, *nisi prius*, sittings after Michaelmas term 1788, *coram* Lord KENYON. That the circumstances did not make the plaintiff liable to pay to the house in England, for as there were the same persons partners in both, though not all. Yet each house was in law conversant of what the other did, and that it had so determined in the case of Caldwell's bankruptcy.[95] Consequently as the house in India could not have recovered on the bill for want of consideration, the house in England could not, as they were in law conversant of that objection, which they contended was clearly within the knowledge of the defendant from his letter of the 16th of August.

Erskine, *Law*, and *Gibbs* on the other side insisted [*6:127*] that it was clear the plaintiff accepted the bill without any knowledge of the indulgence given to Luard & Co., and having accepted it it was unreasonable that he should subject himself to the payment of Indian interest at twelve per cent, which runs in the bill, which would have been the consequence of his refusing to pay it, if alternatively the question on the bill had been decided against him. That there was dishonest knowledge of the transaction brought to the plaintiff until after the payment of the bill, as that knowledge was only to be collected from Luard's deposition which had been taken afterwards.[96] And that the facts if known furnished no defence to an action at law of William Paxton & Co. here in England.

Lord KENYON said, if a man is a mere voluntary agent, nothing pressing him, and knowing all the circumstances, makes a payment, shall not recover back if he knows all the circumstances, and is not mistaken in point of law, he shall not change his mind. In *Leake* v. *Lord Pigot*,[97] where the plaintiff paid a copyhold

---

[94] *Marriot* v. *Hampton* (1797) 7 T.R. 269.

[95] Citing four unreported cases, Cooke in his bankruptcy treatise stated: 'Where several persons are partners in trade, and in such character deal with and become creditors of the other firm, and a joint commission issues, proof may be made for such debt, as if they had dealt with strangers.' W. Cooke, *The Bankrupt Laws*, 4th ed. (1799), p. 551.

[96] In the margin: 'This deposition was read at the trial.'

[97] In the margin: 'B. 152', referring to another of Lawrence's manuscript notebooks (see n. 456, above). Otherwise unreported, an account of *Leake* v. *Lord Pigot* can be found in Misc. MS. 96, *MS Notes by Buller, J. & Sir E.H. East 1754–92*, Inner Temple Library, London, vol. 1, fol. 65, as follows:

Stafford Summer Assises 1769   *Cor.* Yates

Action for money had and received. The case was the plaintiff wanting to be admitted a copyhold estate, the yearly value of which was £1,650. The plaintiff offered £120 to the steward (which was

fine of about two years' value without which Lord Pigot would not receipt a surrender protesting against the excess he recovered it back before Mr Justice YATES. Here in this case is a gentleman on whose credit [6:128] his employment depends. Anything that puts that in hazard is no slight pressure. It was of consequence to him to keep his credit as a solvent man perfectly clear. I have not in this case a particle of doubt. Chatfield by his letter of the 16th of August did not mean to acquiesce. It appears to me that he thought himself used exceeding ill. Of the honesty of this case there can be no doubt. I beg to lay out of my consideration all those cases where the Master has passed *in rem* jurisdiction. In *Moses* v. *Macferlan*[98] Lord MANSFIELD was supposed from his moral feelings to have outstepped the line of the law as he set aside a judgment. *Expedit reipublicae ut sit finis litium.*[99] The case of Caldwell's bankruptcy only shows that the knowledge of Forbes and Gregory should bind the others. There the knowledge was against them. Here they would profit by it; could a set off against the house in India be used against the house here? Had the plaintiff facts to furnish a defence? Here has been no judgment; it is but a payment with a claim to set it right and goes no farther than the case determined [6:129] by Sir JOSEPH YATES, which was not decided on a supposition that the judge was giving the law to the country.

ASHHURST, Justice: Where payment is made with a knowledge of all the facts, he who pays shan't recover back, for *volenti non fit injuria*, but that must be a case in which the party from his knowledge could have defended himself.

GROSE, Justice: If the defendant knew all the circumstances so as to have made a defence, I doubt if he could recover back.

LAWRENCE, Justice: It does not appear that the plaintiff had the knowledge.

Rule discharged.[1]

---

two years value). The steward insisted upon £10 per cent (making £165). The plaintiff insisted he was only entitled to two years value, but the steward said he would not admit him unless he would pay £165.

This Mr J. Yates held it to be such an involuntary payment as to the surplus above two years value (supposing defendant was not entitled to receive it) as was sufficient to support the action, and liked it [to] the case of taking a toll at a turnpike where nothing was due. In regard to the principal point, he held the custom to take £10 per cent (supposing the defendant could prove it) in fact was illegal and could not be supported. It was contended this might be good by custom as a fine certain. But (he said) this is no fine certain: had a certain sum in gross been always paid in respect of the particular tenement, that might have made a question, but this is uncertain and always must vary according to the quantum of the purchase money and that no such uncertain price can by law be good if it exceeds two years value.

So Plaintiff had a verdict.

[98] In the margin, 2 Burr. 1005.
[99] It is for the advantage of the state that there be an end to lawsuits.
[1] According to reports in *The Times*, the case was tried before Lord Kenyon and a special jury of merchants on 14 July 1798. The plaintiff, Allan Chatfield, was captain of the *Rodney*, an East Indiaman, and he brought suit to recover the sum of £1,454 14s. 8d. with interest at 12 percent since it became due. The bill that Chatfield paid was for 13,681 rupees. At trial, Erskine contended that 'if the holders of the Bill granted one hour's indulgence to the Acceptors, without the consent of the Drawer, the Drawer was discharged', and he claimed that Luard & Co. after receiving an indulgence of two months from the defendants (of which the plaintiff was wholly unaware) 'made payments in one month only, to the amount of 50,000 rupees'. Lord Kenyon said in

November 23   SIMEON v. THOMPSON

[M.H.] Alien enemy is an issuable plea.

In action on a policy of assurance, a plea that the persons interested in the goods were alien enemies was held an issuable plea within the judge's order.
2 [W.] Black. 1326 and *Brandon* v. *Nesbitt*, T.R., were cited.[2]

DENT v. WESTON[3]

[M.H.] Notice of a declaration filed conditionally need not state that circumstance.

Declaration being filed *conditionally*, notice was delivered without taking notice of that circumstance, as defendant would find it was so filed if he went and searched for the Declaration.

Const, to show it was irregular, cited 1 T.R. 635, 2 T.R. 719.[4]

[6:130] [blank]

HILARY TERM 39 Geo. III

Lloyd, Lord Kenyon, Chief Justice
Sir W. Ashhurst
Sir N. Grose   } Justices
Sir S. Lawrence

[6:131] January 25, 1799   R. v. STEWARD

[M.H.] Information granted against the printer of a newspaper for a libel, though at the time of printing it he supposed the fact true and did not know whom it applied to.

Information having been moved for against the defendant as printer of a paper called *The Oracle* for a libel on a young man of the name of Shuttleworth

---

order for the plaintiff to be held to his payment, it was 'not only necessary that the plaintiff should know all the facts, but that he should also know the legal consequences of them', which, from the tone of the plaintiff's letters, he did not know. The jury returned a verdict for the plaintiff for £2,000, with interest. As Lawrence's notes show, this was upheld by the full court. See *The Times*, 16 July and 19 November 1798.

[2] *Feron* v. *Ladd* (1779) 2 Bl. W. 1326; *Brandon* v. *Nesbitt* (1794) 6 T.R. 23. See the printed report of the *Simeon* case at (24 November 1798) 8 T.R. 71. The court evidently changed its mind, ruling that the alien enemy plan was merely for delay and did not go to the merits, as was required of an issuable plea. Lord Kenyon also observed that 'the money cannot be remitted out of this country without a licence from the Secretary of State'.

[3] An earlier procedural dispute about perfecting bail is reported at 8 T.R. 4, 10 November 1798.

[4] *Cook* v. *Raven* (1787) 1 T.R. 635; *Smith* v. *Painter* (1788) 2 T.R. 719.

who, having been missing from his family some days, and for the discovery of whom his family had offered a considerable reward, the libel consisted in a paragraph that the young man who had been advertised as missing by his friends had been seen coming out of a house of ill fame in Sun Tavern Fields.

Erskine shewed cause against the rule, stating that with respect to informations, he has always entertained a different opinion from many other people who have talked of liberty without knowing what it meant. That the applying to the court was an advantage to the party, as it gave him an opportunity of preventing the law being put in motion against him by exculpating himself by his own oath, and enabled the court to temper justice with mercy. And he admitted this was a fit case for an information unless the defendant could show how the paragraph had got in by mistake, which in this case he said was from a mistake in one Kennet Beal whom he employed to get information for his paper at the police offices. That he believed it true and had no malice against Shuttleworth.

[*6:132*] Lord KENYON said this was a case of general public concern, and that it was no answer to such application that a paragraph furnished by a person employed by a printer to collect them was inserted without any malice against the person to whom it was applicable—as it was to hold up to contempt and ridicule the person to whom it might chance to apply.

Rule absolute.

February 4
R. v. CHURCHWARDENS of ST ANDREW'S[, HOLBORN]

[M.H.] The curate is not the minister of a parish within the meaning of the 26 Geo. III, c. 21, which regulates the slaughtering of horses, and the certificate of that Act is not referable to the place, but to the fitness of the person to carry on that business.

Garrow shewed cause against a rule for a *mandamus* to be directed to the churchwardens and overseers of St Andrew's, Holborn, to hold a vestry, that a meeting of the inhabitants might be convened to appoint an inspector of a house for slaughtering horses in that parish, in pursuance of the 26 Geo. III, c. 21. He objected that no such inspector could be appointed until the party who was to keep a place for the slaughtering horses had obtained a certificate signed by the minister of the parish as to his being a proper person and a licence from the sessions, which in this case was obtained on the certificate of the curate, E. Price, and not of the minister, Mr Barton, who was rector. And the licence obtained was printed at the sessions for Onslow Street and altered surreptitiously to Brew House Yard.

Erskine on the other side contended that the licence having been obtained, it enabled [*6:133*] the party applying (*ss.* one Henry Sills) to keep his slaughtering house anywhere in the parish, the Act applying only to the fitness of the person and not the place.

Lord KENYON: The licence seems only as to the fitness of the person and not of the place, and the person, not the place is the object of the certificate but that must precede the licence, but it must be under the hand of the minister who in this case is the rector, not the curate.

Rule discharged.

PARKINSON v. GILCHRIST

[M.H.] A man not liable to be held to bail abroad shall not be arrested here, if the plaintiff has induced him to come to England by promising not to molest him.

Garrow shewed cause against a rule to discharge the defendant on filing common bail. The application was made on an affidavit of the defendant stating his having agreed to buy a plantation in St Vincent's for £11,000—that afterwards, there being an insurrection of the negroes, many of the plantations were destroyed, and this among others, and that in consequence of the general distress a law passed in April '97 which forbid persons whose property had been so destroyed from being arrested. That in December '97 one Grant brought a power of attorney to the plaintiff to settle accounts with the defendant, and in order that that might be done amicably recommended his returning to England, assuring him that the plaintiff would not molest him.

In answer to this affidavit, it was alleged that the defendant had not done anything towards such amicable settlement, but was arranging his affairs for the advantage of other creditors.

Lord KENYON: As he has altered his situation with [6:134] the concurrence of your agent, I think he ought not to be arrested.

Rule absolute.

February 11   ## EX PARTE SLADE

[M.H.] An attorney struck off the roll restored on the court being satisfied of his contrition, his offence being the promising one to be admitted an attorney who had not regularly served.

Slade, an attorney, had been struck off the roll for procuring a person to be admitted an attorney who had not *bona fide* served him as his clerk, and now was restored at the instance of Mr Rashleigh and other attorneys in Cornwall, they being satisfied of his contrition, they being the persons on whose application he had been struck off the roll.

February 12   CRAWFORD v. HUNTER[5]

[M.H.] Trial of actions on policies not to be put off when a large sum is at stake and any risk of failures without bringing the money into court.

The court refused to put off the trials of several actions on policies of assurance effected by the commissioners for securing Dutch property on the absence of several witnesses unless the money was brought into court, or laid out for the benefit of the parties who should be ultimately entitled, but they added that they did not lay this down as a general rule, but as the sum was very large and there might be danger of bankruptcies, they thought in this case it right to be done. The sum was £108,000.

The plaintiffs also had leave given them to examine such witnesses as were going out of England, but the court would not lay the defendants under the necessity of admitting the subscription to the policy, or that [6:135] the invoices found on board the ship should be evidence of the cargoes.

WILSON v. MARRYATT[6]

[M.H.] Costs of witnesses coming from abroad before the action brought not to be allowed.

In this case, the court refused to allow the costs of persons as witnesses who had come from the Cape of Good Hope, having come over with the plaintiff immediately on the ship being seized, as no person could properly be considered as witnesses until action brought.

---

[5] An earlier phase of this case is reported at 8 T.R. 13 (*sub nom. Craufurd* v. *Hunter*), 13 November 1798. There the court held that commissioners legislatively authorised to appropriate Dutch ships could insure the ships and effects in their own names after the ships were seized abroad and were in transit to England.

[6] For published reports of this case on the merits (involving trade from America to the British settlements in the East Indies, as authorized by the treaty between the United States and Great Britain confirmed by 37 Geo. III, c. 97), see *Wilson* v. *Marryat*, 8 T.R. 31, 21 November 1798, and *Marryat* v. *Wilson*, 1 Bos. & Pul. 430, 6 May 1799. See also *Wilson* v. *Kensington*, pp. 178, 181, above, and the Paper Book for *Collet* v. *Keith*, p. 273, below.

[6:136] EASTER TERM 39 Geo. III

Lloyd, Lord Kenyon, Chief Justice
Sir W. Ashhurst
Sir N. Grose } Justices
Sir S. Lawrence

SYKES v. POTTS

[M.H.] *If money is paid into court on the consolidation rule and plaintiff is nonsuit, he shall pay costs to all the defendants as well as to him against who he tries.*

Erskine showed cause against a rule for the master to review his taxation in several actions on a policy of insurance.

There were three actions in all of which the defendants had paid money into court, and the defendants had entered into the common rule for consolidation.[7]

The plaintiff being nonsuit, he insisted that in the other causes which had not been tried he was entitled to his costs to the time of paying money into court, which the Master refused to allow. And in support of this, *Erskine* cited *Burstall* v. *Horner*, 7 T.R. 372, as in point.

Gibbs, contra, said the uniform practice had been otherwise, and insisted that by the consolidation rule, the plaintiff was only prevented from claiming any costs subsequent to the payment of the premium.

Lord KENYON said, if the plaintiff had stopped and gone no further after payment of money into court, *Gibbs* was right, but that the case had decided the point, and that there must not be *alia lex nunc, alia post hoc.*

LAWRENCE, Justice, said the master informed him that if, in a case where there was no consolidation rule, if the plaintiff took out of court the money paid into court [6:137] and went on and was nonsuited, he paid all costs, and that it seemed to him that this governed the case, for the substance of the rule was, that the trial of the cause tried should be considered as the trial of all the rest, and that the same consequences as to costs, &c. should attend all.

Rule discharged.

April 13 EX PARTE MARNEL

[M.H.] *Affidavits once filed not to be taken off.*

Espinasse moved to take off the file some affidavits filed on a motion against one Marnel for a libel on a man of the name of Rook, the parties having agreed.

But the court refused, and Lord KENYON said he had known motions in the

---

[7] On the consolidation rule, see Oldham, *MMSS*, i. 454–455.

Court of Chancery to take answers off the file, when the parties agreed, which had always been refused.

Nil cap.

HOLLAND v. JARVIS

[M.H.] On an issue, if goods were fraudulently removed to prevent a distress, plaintiff may show the defendant who took them had no title to the premises.

Clifford moved for a new trial on a cause tried before ROOKE, Justice, at Stafford. Trespass for breaking the plaintiff's dwelling house, justification, the taking goods as a distress, which had been fraudulently removed from an estate leased by defendant.

The replication traversed the fraud, admitting the tenure.

ROOKE [J.] admitted evidence that another man and not defendant was the landlord, and that it being a dispute who was entitled to the rent, that this shewed there was no fraud.

Nil cap.

[6:138] ## WATSON v. BINGLEY

[M.H.] Notice of a bill filed against an attorney must be given to defendant himself and not his agent.

Dampier showed cause against a rule for setting aside proceedings against an attorney for irregularity, the notice of the bill being filed being served on the agent and not on the defendant himself.

Lord KENYON: I do not know how we are to make him an agent for this purpose. He is not an agent until he does something in a cause. Why should not an attorney have personal notice as well as any other defendant.

Rule absolute.

April 17
R. v. LORD THANET, ROBERT FERGUSON, Esq. and others[8]

[M.H.] If there are several defendants in an indictment, they must all join in striking it [the special jury], as the whole number can only strike twelve.

Ferguson, who was one of the defendants, objected to the rule for striking a special jury in this case.

The rule was that the attorney for the prosecutor should strike twelve out of the forty-eight and that the attorney for the defendant should strike out the other twelve.

---

[8] After a fifteen-hour trial on 25 April, including one hour of jury deliberation, the earl of Thanet and Robert Ferguson were convicted, and the other defendants acquitted. See *The Times*, 26–27 April 1799. For addresses that Lord Thanet and Mr Ferguson were allowed to read in court on 3 May, see *The Times*, 4 May 1799. For further proceedings, see p. 205, below.

The statute 3 Geo. II, c. 25, he said, did not apply to this case—that each defendant had a right to strike twelve from the panel, the only way of doing which was to try the defendants separately.

Mr Barlow, the secondary, informed the court that the jury in this case had been struck as usual, and when [6:139] there are several defendants, they managed so as to have some person to strike for them all.

Lord KENYON: There is nothing in it.

Nil cap.

[*Lawrence note*:] *Vide*: *Case of the Seven Bishops*, 4 State Trials 332, as to the mode of striking a special jury.[9]

April 19   EARL of CLARE v. PERRY

[M.H.] A writ of enquiry is proper to be executed before a judge, though no question of law, if the rank and situation of the party makes it fit to proceed in it in a solemn way.

Garrow moved for a rule to show cause why a writ of enquiry of damages in an action against the defendant, the printer of a newspaper, for a libel on the plaintiff, the chancellor of Ireland, should not be expounded before the chief justice at *nisi prius*, which was afterwards on the 1st of May made absolute.

Erskine then shewed cause against the rule and relied on the case of *Bodington* v. *Bodington*, where in a case of very aggravated criminal conversation, the court refused it. As they also did in a case of *Bewick* v. *Vaughan*.[10] That in this case, there was no question of law, but only fact. He however admitted it to be a matter in the discretion of the court.

Lord KENYON said he had assisted at many writs of enquiry where there was no law, but the ground he went on was this, that this was a libel on the plaintiff, not as Lord Clare, but on him as chancellor of Ireland [6:140A], as standing in

---

[9] See generally Oldham, *MMSS*, i. 96–97; Oldham, *Trial by Jury*, pp. 142–150.

[10] The *Bodington* and *Bewick* cases were unreported, but *Bodington* was covered in *The Times* (3, 7 July and 9 September 1797), as was an earlier comparable case, also argued by Erskine, *Moulin* v. *Dutton* (5 May 1795). Both were criminal conversation (adultery) actions. In *Moulin*, 'Lord Kenyon said, he did not recollect a case of this sort, where an application had been made to execute a Writ of Enquiry before him; but he could make a rule, that the Sheriff might return a good Jury.' There were, nonetheless, earlier precedents when the chief justice of the Court of King's Bench conducted the writ of inquiry. See Oldham, *Trial by Jury*, p. 50. On the 'good jury' (loosely described in *Tidd's Practice* as 'a better sort of common jury'), see ibid., at pp. 150–151. After argument in *Bodington*, Erskine said the single question was whether the case was 'of that size and moment as to call for the interposition of the dignity of that Court [King's Bench]'. Edward Law, on the other side, argued that there was nothing about the case that called for the 'assistance, and superior wisdom of the Learned Judges of that Court'. The court denied Erskine's motion. Mr Justice Ashhurst said that he 'did not see that they were bound, either in justice or propriety, to grant the motion'—'It would be taking the cause out of the proper channel', and the plaintiff 'had the power of applying to the Court for a good Jury, which was never refused'. Grose and Lawrence JJ. agreed (Chief Justice Kenyon was absent). In the end, Erskine secured an order for a good jury, and that jury, after a hearing before Sheriff Burchall, returned a verdict for Erskine's client, the plaintiff, for £10,000. See *The Times*, 9 September 1797.

the highest situation in the sister kingdom, and charging him with having done that which, if true, is a ground for removing him from his situation and impeaching him. There are different modes of enquiry known to the law, some more, some less solemn, to be adopted according to the nature of the case. On that ground we granted a trial at bar the other day.[11] On this ground, simply that this is an application at the instance of the first law officer in the neighbouring kingdom, I think the rule should be absolute.

GROSE, Justice: An accusation of a high judicial character for his conduct in such character differs very much from cases of criminal conversation.

LAWRENCE, Justice: This case is distinguishable on the grounds mentioned from those cited.

Rule absolute.

April 30   NEWSTEAD v. KEYS

[M.H.] *Prima tonsura*[12] is but evidence of a freehold and is not conclusive.

On a motion for a new trial, the question was if a right to *prima tonsura* supported a plea of the premises in question being the defendant's soil and freehold.

[6:141A] Lord KENYON: *Prima tonsura* may be distinct from the freehold, but it may be evidence whose it is. The case of *Ward* v. *Petifer* in Cro. Char. 362 is not quite accurate in the expression there used. That case must be understood only as laying it down that *prima tonsura* is a degree of evidence whose the freehold is, but it is not decisive. There is an infinite deal of property where one man is entitled to the crop, and other persons to feed the land afterwards.

Rule absolute for a new trial.

Marriot and Serjeant *Shepherd*.

May 3   HOW v. ISAAC *et al.*

[M.H.] Query if a prisoner in King's Bench can be brought up to be charged with a special original.

Wigley moved for a rule on the marshal to bring up the defendant that he might be charged on the special original, that he might be able to outlaw the other defendants, and he cited *Hutchins* v. *Kenrick*, 2 Burr. 1048 and 2 Lilly's *Prac. Register*, tit. Prisoner.

He was ordered to be brought up.

[*Lawrence note:*] *Sed* query what done, and how the sheriff could execute the writ on him in custody.

---

[11] In the margin: 'In Lord Thanet's case'. See the case immediately preceding this one, above. On the grounds for ordering a trial at bar, see Oldham, *Trial by Jury*, pp. 145–148.

[12] The first crop of grass.

[6:140B] TRINITY TERM 39 Geo. III

Lloyd, Lord Kenyon, Chief Justice
Sir N. Grose
Sir S. Lawrence   } Justices
Sir S. Le Blanc

[*Lawrence note*:] On the 6th day of June in this term, Simon *Le Blanc*, one of His Majesty's serjeants-at-law, having been appointed a judge of this court in the place of Sir William Henry AsHHURST, who had resigned his office, took his seat on the bench.

May 31   BIRD v. APPLETON

[M.H.] The court may correct a special verdict after it is drawn up if there be a mistake in it which was left to counsel to settle and not in what the jury have found.

Perceval shewed cause against a rule to amend the special verdict in this case by separating the damages and applying part to the first and other part to the second counts. The motion was made on an affidavit stating that the jury had found the facts which raised the question intended to be argued without any specific sum, the damages being left in blank, and in drawing up the verdict, a sum of [£]400 was inserted generally as the damages without attending to the proper application of part to the count on a policy on goods and the other part to the count on a policy on ship. *Perceval* insisted that there should be a *venire de novo* as the verdict had not fully brought the question before the court, unless the plaintiff would consent to add some facts to the verdict, and he cited *Eddowes* v. *Hopkins*, Doug. 675[13] to shew the court could not alter the findings of a special verdict.

[6:141B] Lord KENYON said, if the jury had exercised their judgment, the court would not interfere, and as the whole rested in blank, he did not think the court would go too far in altering the formal part left to counsel to settle. But he thought under the circumstances of the case, it was fit for reconsideration, and that the proper thing to be done was to award a *venire de novo*.[14]

---

[13] The correct citation is *Eddowes* v. *Hopkins* (1780) 1 Doug. 376.

[14] This case was tried multiple times from 1797 to 1800. The first trial apparently was held in Michaelmas term 1797 with a verdict for the plaintiffs. A show cause rule for a new trial was obtained by Perceval, counsel for the defendant underwriters, opposed by Erskine for the plaintiffs. See *The Times*, 22 November 1797. A new trial was conducted on 2 March 1798 before Lord Kenyon and a special jury of merchants. Erskine said that the case 'most undoubtedly involved property to a very great extent, no less as it concerned the plaintiffs than 50,000l. which had been subscribed by various persons'. *The Times*, 3 March 1798. The case involved a voyage by the ship *Confederacy* from Canton to Hamburg or Copenhagen that had been captured by a French privateer and carried to Nantes, where she was condemned as lawful prize. Afterward the condemnation was confirmed by a French court of appeal on the ground that the ship did not

MUNRO v. SPINKS[15]

[M.H.] Affidavit of belief that no tender was made of bank note is sufficient to hold to bail when made by agent of a plaintiff living abroad.

Garrow shewed cause against a rule of Kidd's to discharge the defendant on filing common bail for a defect in the affidavit in not positively swearing to a tender of bank notes not having been made.

It was an action on a foreign judgment and the party making the affidavit was the plaintiff's agent, he being himself abroad. The affidavit was that defendant was indebted to the plaintiff in the sum of 364–17–3 on a judgment in Jamaica and that no offer had been made to pay that sum in money or in notes of the Governor & Co. of the Bank of England as he the deponent verily believed.

The court thought it sufficient.

Rule discharged.

[6:142] ## GARRELLS v. KENSINGTON

[M.H.] Judgment suspended after argument, the opinion of the court being for the defendant at the instance of the plaintiff, the sentence of a court of vice admiralty, on which the opinion of the court was founded, being appealed from as given without any authority.

The court after argument, having given judgment in this case for the defendant (*vide* the case, 8 T.R. 230), the court suspended its being entered up, on an affidavit that the sentence of the vice admiralty court of St Domingo, which was the ground of the opinion the court had given, was appealed from on the ground that the judge there had proceeded without any authority, that

---

have on board a list of the crew, as required of American ships by two French ordinances. Erskine called this outrageous, contrary to the law of nations, pointing out that the independent nation (America) neither consented to the ordinances nor knew anything about them. The special jury of merchants returned a special verdict that was later found to be faulty. It was corrected, but was challenged again, and yet another trial was ordered. See reports in *The Times*, 23 January, 2 July, and 9 November 1799. That trial resulted in a verdict assessing damages separately on the different counts of the declaration, and finding that the voyage from London to Canton and that from Canton to London were two distinct voyages. This verdict was also challenged in argument on 16 May 1800, as fully reported at 8 T.R. 562. The court concluded, *per curiam*, that the plaintiff was entitled to recover on the first count; the defendant on the second. Yet another opinion of the court was given on 27 November 1800 on entitlement to costs. See 1 East 111. Extensive documentation of the litigation also survives in Lawrence's Paper Books in the Dampier MSS. at Lincoln's Inn Library, including the following: the special verdict as it stood for argument on 15 June 1798; Lawrence's notes of argument of counsel on 22 June 1798, with an appended note of 16 November 1798 stating the court's opinion that the special verdict was incomplete and ordering a new trial, where 'Lord Kenyon's minutes of the last trial [are] to be read'; the special verdict 'altered in consequence of the new trial', with notes on the reverse sides of arguments of counsel on 19 April 1799; the special verdict on the third trial as it stood for argument on 13 May 1800, with notes of argument on the reverse sides, continued on 16 May with brief notes of the judges' opinions (corresponding to those in the printed report at 8 T.R. 366–371); and a copy of the 'Treaty of Amity, Commerce, and Navigation' between Great Britain and the United States, 19 November 1794. Dampier MSS., LPBs 277 and 325.

[15] This case is reported at 8 T.R. 284, 31 May 1799.

the papers had been lodged in the Admiralty Court, and that the appeal was proceeding. But the plaintiff was directed to pay all the costs.

R. v. LORD THANET et al.[16]

[M.H.] Query if an indictment charging an assault and battery in the presence of commissioners of oyer and terminer and gaol delivery, when holding their session, does not require the judgment '*quoad manus amputatus*, &c'. *Nolle prosequi* may be entered on some counts of an information after a verdict of guilty, and judgment prayed on the residue.

The defendants, the earl of Thanet and Robert Ferguson, Esq., a barrister at law, had been found guilty on a trial at bar the last term on an information filed against them by the attorney-general charging them by the first count, that at a special commission of oyer and terminer and gaol delivery holden at Maidstone in the county of Kent on the 21st day of May in the 38th year of the king's reign, Arthur O'Connor Esq. came before the court in the custody of the sheriff of Kent and was then tried for high treason and found not guilty, and that the defendants with diverse other persons unknown, 'in open court and in the presence of the justices and commissioners of oyer and terminer and [6:143] Gaol Delivery and before any order or direction had been made by the said justices &c. for the discharge of the said Arthur O'Connor from the custody of the said sheriff did make a great riot, rant, tumult and disturbance and did attempt and endeavour to rescue said Roger [sic] O'Connor from and out of the custody of the said sheriff, and the better to effect such rescue did in the open court aforesaid and in the presence aforesaid, did make an assault upon John Russell, Edward Tregian and Thomas Adams, and them did then and there beat, incize, wound, and ill treat, and did thereby impede and instruct the said justices and commissioners in the due and lawful holding of the said session and in the execution of their office'.

A second count charged the defendants with assisting O'Connor to rescue himself, not stating it to be in the presence of the judges. A third count charged them with a riot in the presence of the justices and in open court to prevent their due and peaceable holding of the said session and then and there making an assault on and beating therewith, &c.

A fourth count charged them in open court and in the presence of the justices with making a riot and interrupting the holding the sessions.

[6:144] A fifth count charged them with common riot.

The defendants having appeared in court the 3rd of May during the last term and the attorney-general having prayed judgment, Lord KENYON observed to him that he had not prayed any specific punishment. That the case disclosed on the indictment, though new in our times, was not so in our law books, and he wished it to be discussed on a further day whether the charge as laid in the indictment did not take away all discretion as to punishment and require a specific sentence.

---

[16] See the report of this case at 20 S.T. 821.

The attorney-general in answer said that he conceived the punishment was discretionary. He admitted that if the indictment had charged an actual rescue, or that the defendants had struck any person, that the court would have no discretion, and further that the indictment did not charge the thing to be done *coram domino rege*.

As the court wished to take time to consider of their judgment, Mr *Erskine*, the defendants' counsel, prayed that they might in the meantime be bailed, and offered the duke of Bedford and Lord Derby as bail. But the court said they could not do it unless the attorney-general consented, which he refused. And they were committed to the custody of the marshal.

[6:145] Now on the 10th of June, the defendants being brought into court, the attorney-general informed the court that in consequence of the doubt entertained as to a specific punishment, he had his Majesty's commands to enter a *nolle prosequi* on the 1st, 2nd and 3rd counts and to pray judgment only on the 4th and 5th counts, intimating at the same time after a laborious investigation, he was satisfied the others did not require a specific punishment.

On this, GROSE, Justice, pronounced the judgment:

That Lord Thanet should pay a fine of £1,000, be imprisoned in the Tower for one year, give security for his good behaviour for seven years himself in £10,000 and two sureties in £5,000, and be imprisoned till the surety given.

And that Mr Ferguson should pay a fine of £100, be imprisoned in the King's Bench for one year, give security for his good behaviour for seven years, himself in £500 and two sureties in £250, and be imprisoned till fine paid and security given.

As to the necessity of a specific punishment, on talking to Sir John Mitford, the solicitor-general, he thought that [6:146] a specific punishment must be inflicted. Mr *Erskine*, the defendants' counsel told me he had no doubt of it. The authorities as to this point are the following:[17]

Everingham's Case, 6 Edw. III roll 30.
Holbrook's Case, Hilary, 13 Edw. III roll 116.
Karlisle's Case, Trinity, 19 Edw. III roll 30, and note in this case the word
   permissit is not used nor is the assault stated to be *coram domino rege*.
Michaelmas 22 Edw. III 26, *Fitzherbert's Abridgement*, Forfeiture 21.
Aston's Case, Easter, 24 Edw. III roll 56.

---

[17] The reference to *Davy's Case* should be to *Davis's Case*, 2 Dyer 188b. Dyer collected and mentioned several cases in which the punishment of amputation of a hand was imposed, including (in addition to *Davis's Case*) the cases of Elizabeth Girling, Thomas Jones, and Sir William Waller. *Girling's Case* was more fully reported by Coke than by Dyer (see *Oldfield and Gerling's Cases* [sic] (1610) 12 Co. 71), as was *Sir William Waller's Case* by Croke (see *Waller's Case* (1634) Cro. Car. 373). Dyer notes also the case of one Carnes, citing Owen 120, the same case identified by Lawrence as *Carey's Case*, cited mistakenly as Owen 420. Owen presents the case as *Carus Case* (1605) Owen 120. References to other sources in Lawrence's list of authorities should be self-explanatory, excepting perhaps Brook (*Brooke's Abridgment* (1568)), Staunford (*Pleas of the Crown*, (1557)), and Jenkins (probably David Jenkins, *Eight Centuries of Reports*, 3rd ed. (1771), containing translated versions of reports originally published in French and Latin by Sir Leoline Jenkins, a Welsh judge). On the sentence of amputation, see J. H. Baker, 'Le Brickbat Que Narrowly Mist', *Law Quarterly Review* 100 (1984), p. 544.

Davy's Case, 1 E. 4. roll 3, Dyer 188.
Dawson's Case, Michaelmas, 8 and 9 Eliz. roll 20.
Girling's Case, Hilary, 9th Eliz. roll 6. (Dyer 188, 3 Inst. 141, 12 Co. 71).
Jones's case, Hilary, 7th Eliz. roll 6, Dyer 188.
Carey's Case, Trinity, 37 Eliz. roll 3, Cro. Eliz. 405, Owen 420.
Gillingham's Case, Wells summer assizes, 1631.
Sir *William Waller's Case*, Trinity, 10 Car. 1, roll 29, Sir William Jones 343, Cro. Car. 373.
Rockingham's Case, Hilary 15 & 16 Car. 2, roll 73 (Levinz 106, 1 Sid. 21).
Brook, Pain 16, contempt 5.
Fitzherbert: Forfeiture 21, Judgment 174, Coron 280.
2 *Rolle's Abridgement* 76.
Yearbooks, Michaelmas 22 E. 3–26, Michaelmas 19 E. 3, 39 assiz. pl.1, 41 assiz. pl. 25, 42 assiz. 18.
Staunford 38, 2 [Coke's] Inst. 549, 3 [Coke's] Inst. [6:*147*] 140, 218, Jenkyns Contempt 81, 1 Hawkins' P. Crown, c. 21, 2 Hawkins, c. 48.
12 Co. 71, 1 Keil. 751, 4 Blackstone's *Commentaries* 121, Hale's *Summary* 132, 20 Viner, pl. 15, 14 Viner, pl. 365.

A point which occurred in considering this question was, if the specific punishment of amputating the hand was not confined to the person who actually struck, and if that were so, it might have been a ground for a new trial, as the evidence did not prove that either of the defendants gave any blow themselves. The general rule of law would make the stroke of one the stroke of all.

For the indictment and abstracts of record in prosecutions for assaults in courts of justice and other minutes relating to this case, *vide* Bundle of Indictments no. 21.[18]

[6:*148*] MICHAELMAS TERM 40 Geo. III B.R.

Lloyd, Lord Kenyon, Chief Justice
Sir N. Grose
Sir S. Lawrence } Justices
Sir S. Le Blanc

Thursday, November 7   R. v. HAMLYN

Bond moved to take an affidavit off the file, that he might correct a mistake as to the existence of an alderman of the borough of Launceston, who was found to be dead, the party making the affidavit believing him to be alive. The fact, he said, was not material in the dispute, which was on the validity of the defendant's election to a corporate office in the borough.

---

[18] Lawrence's bundles of indictments do not appear to have survived. They are not among the extensive Lawrence MSS. at Lincoln's Inn and the Middle Temple.

Lord KENYON refused the motion, saying he dreaded the precedent, and that he remembered Lord THURLOW refused to suffer an answer to be taken off the file, which had been moved, that a mistake might be corrected, and that it was better for the party to file an explanatory affidavit.

Nil cap.

November 9 HARVEY v. RUGG

Perceval moved for a new trial of a cause tried before HEATH, Justice, at Derby. It was an action of trespass *quare clausum*, called the Yard.

Defendant pleaded a right of way over the *locus in quo* to a close lying beyond it called Paddock Close.

[6:149] To this the plaintiff made a new assignment alleging that the defendant had used the way for other purposes than for the enjoyment and occupation of the close in respect of which it was claimed.

On evidence, it appeared that the defendant beyond his close had a wood, and that he brought trees out of it into Paddock Close, where there was a sawpit, and there shaved them and carried them off after they were sawn over the plaintiff's close, called the Yard.

Mr Justice HEATH thought the manufacturing the wood was an occupation of the Paddock Close, and that defendant was entitled to use the way for the purpose of such occupation, and Lord KENYON said the wood received a melioration in the close, and that there was nothing in it.

Nil cap.

AIKENHEAD v. TAYLOR

Erskine moved for a new trial in an action on a policy of assurance which was not in the common [form], entered into by a society at N. Shields, of which the defendant was the treasurer. In the policy, there was a clause under certain circumstances for a return in proportion to the current premium.

The venue had been retained in London on an understanding to give material evidence regarding [it], to satisfy which *Erskine* had called a witness to prove what, according to the practice in London, was the current premium. But Lord KENYON, being of opinion that this did not satisfy the undertaking, nonsuited the plaintiff and now the court refused a rule to show [cause], [6:150] being of opinion that what was the current premium was not a fact peculiar to London, that it might be proved from what was paid at other places and to be collected from instances in all parts of the kingdom.

Nil cap.

November 11 HEATHFIELD v. CLELAND[19]

---

[19] No notes were recorded for this case.

PART III
PAPER BOOKS, THE COURT OF KING'S BENCH,
36–40 GEO. III

INTRODUCTION

In the tenth edition of Jacob's *Law Dictionary*, Paper Books are defined as follows:

> Paper Books, are the issues at law, &c. upon special pleadings, made up by the clerk of the *papers*, who is an officer for that purpose. And the clerks of the *papers* of the court of *King's Bench*, in all copies of pleas and *paper books* by them made up, shall subscribe to such *paper books*, the names of the counsel who have signed such pleas, as well on the behalf of the plaintiff as defendant; and in all *paper books* delivered to the judges of the court, the names of the counsellors, who did sign those pleas, are to be subscribed to the *books*, by the clerks or attorneys who delivered the same.[20]

The judges of the common law courts were supplied with Paper Books for cases that came on for argument during term time. Lincoln's Inn Library holds a major collection of Paper Books that were delivered to four contemporaneous or successive common law judges during a forty-five year period, from 1771 to 1816.[21]

The Paper Books are made up of copies of the pleadings relevant to the matter being argued, such as a motion for new trial, a special case reserved, a special verdict, or a demurrer and joinder. The earliest Paper Books in the collection are those of Mr Justice William Ashhurst, who retained one hundred Paper Books from 1771 to 1785 that he then passed on to Mr Justice Francis Buller. Buller compiled over 840 Paper Books from the years 1778 to 1794, which, together with the one hundred from Ashhurst, he handed over to his successor, Soulden Lawrence. Lawrence amassed nearly nine hundred Paper Books from 1794 to 1811, and the three collections of Paper Books eventually reached Mr Justice Henry Dampier, who added one hundred and seventy from his short time as a justice of the King's Bench, 1813 to 1816.

In addition to copies of relevant pleadings, many Paper Books are stuffed with additional documents—copies of statutes, treaties, extracts from foreign laws and ordinances, insurance policies, charter parties, and the like. Nearly all of the Paper Books include autograph notes by the judge to whom the Paper Books belonged. These notes encompass arguments of counsel, opinions delivered by brother judges, research notes, and, not infrequently, drafts of opinions. All of the judges whose Paper Books comprise the Dampier manuscripts were puisne justices, and their draft opinions may or may not have been delivered verbally in court, and even if delivered, may or may not have been included in the printed reports. Further, many of the cases in the Dampier manuscripts were unreported, and for these, the Paper Books and the judges' manuscript notes have special value, enlarging our understanding of the substance and scope of the work of the common law courts.

---

[20] G. Jacob, *A New Law Dictionary* 10th ed. (1782).
[21] E. Heward, 'Dampier Manuscripts at Lincoln's Inn', *Journal of Legal History* 9 (1988), p. 357.

In the pages that follow, transcriptions of all or part of seven representative cases from Mr Justice Lawrence's Paper Books are laid out. First is the well-known decision of *Marshall* v. *Rutton*,[22] in which the common law judges followed Chief Justice Kenyon's lead in restoring the 'unity of the persons' theory that prevented married women from obtaining credit or trading in the marketplace on their own behalf. This case and its background are explained in a prefatory note.

The second case, *Morton* v. *Lamb*,[23] involved an issue that had arisen in several prior lawsuits. The question was how explicit or demonstrative a party to a bilateral contract had to be in showing his readiness to perform before being entitled to sue the other party for breach when the promises of both parties to the contract were to be performed simultaneously. Or, to be technically accurate, the question was what had to be stated in the pleadings about the plaintiff's readiness to perform. Mr Justice Lawrence's headnote states: 'In a declaration for not delivering goods, the Plaintiff should state that he tendered the price, unless he shows that the Defendant was not at the appointed time at the place of delivery, unless the promise of the Plaintiff is laid to be the consideration of Defendant's promise.' Details are supplied in a separate introductory note.

The next three cases were unreported. *Brooke* v. *Crowther* dealt with the mixture of contract and anti-trust principles inherent in a covenant not to compete. The issue and resolution of this case are relatively straightforward.

Roe v. *Langford* called upon the court to try to make sense of bequests left in a handwritten will by an illiterate testator. The special case reserved for the court transcribed the will precisely as written by the testator, replete with near-incomprehensible phonetic spelling.[24] An elaborate pedigree chart was attached. The basic question, according to Mr Justice Lawrence, was how far words may be supplied to make sensible a most unintelligible will of a most illiterate person. The testator, Francis Southall, had died twenty years earlier, and the heirs worked out among themselves the disposition of the property until doubts arose in 1790 after the death of the testator's niece, Ann Phillips, formerly Ann Pardoe. The surviving relatives then placed matters in the hands of barrister Richard Geast, instructing him to file either an ejectment action or a feigned issue, and to manage the lawsuit as expeditiously as possible. The parties agreed that,

> no advantage should be taken either by plaintiffs or defendants of any informality or irregularity in the pleadings and that the causes should be fairly tried upon the merits in the shortest and least expensive manner and that both plaintiffs and defendants should be at liberty to give evidence of all such real facts as they should be respectively advised were material and necessary.

Also, 'the verdict to be given on such trial should be final, conclusive, and binding'. The case was tried at the Worcester summer assizes in 1790 before

---

[22] (1800) 8 T.R. 546.
[23] (1797) 7 T.R. 125.
[24] A rendition of the will in modern orthography is attempted after the transcription.

Mr Justice Buller, 'when a verdict was found under his directions for defendants which was not set aside and the subsequent enjoyment has been according to that verdict'. New questions arose in 1797, leading to the action transcribed below.

The third unreported case is *Bischoff* v. *Agar*, a typical marine insurance dispute. According to Lawrence, the question was whether 'an embargo in the port of this Kingdom is within the words "detainment of princes" in policies of assurance'.

The last two Paper Books transcribed below are from lengthy reported cases involving the complexities of international trade during wartime. *Collet* v. *Lord Keith*[25] dealt with an American ship owned by British-born United States citizens attempting a voyage from Philadelphia to the East Indies, with intermediate stops in France and Portugal. That case is fully explained by a separate introductory note.

Finally, *Pollard* v. *Bell*[26] displays the tensions between the English common law courts and the French Admiralty Court during the 1790s. The frustrations of the Court of King's Bench in following the accepted rules of the law of nations during wartime are palpable. Although the decision is reported, full details of the sentences of the French Admiralty Court are not given in the printed report. As stated by reporters Charles Durnford and Edward East, 'These two sentences were set forth at large in the special case: but being unusually long and complicated, introducing a variety of irrelevant matter and false reasoning, they are here omitted, as they could not fail of disgusting every person on whom the task of reading them should be imposed.'[27] The English judges were themselves disgusted by the French Admiralty Court's readiness to condemn ships that did not observe, to the letter, the French requirements of detailed records of the crew and cargo on American ships. In the end, the Court of King's Bench evaded the crew list requirement of the French Admiralty by concluding that the King's Bench was not bound by French ordinances that were not embodied in binding treaties between France and England.

[Editor's introductory note to *Marshall* v. *Rutton*[28]

The report of the *Marshall* case published by Charles Durnford and Edward Hyde East in *Term Reports* is relatively brief, containing only Lord Kenyon's judgment. According to that report, Kenyon described the general question as 'whether by any agreement between a man and his wife, she may be made legally responsible for the contracts she may enter into, and be liable to the actions of those who may have trusted to her engagements, as if she were sole and unmarried'.[29] He then stated that, after two arguments before all the

---

[25] (1802) 2 East 260.
[26] (1800) 8 T.R. 434.
[27] 8 T.R. at 435–436.
[28] For a full discussion, see J. Oldham, 'Creditors and the Feme Covert', in M. Dyson and D. Ibbetson eds., *Law and Legal Process* (2013), ch. 11.
[29] 8 T.R. at 546.

judges, 'and after a very full consideration, the opinion of all the judges who heard the last argument is, that this action cannot be supported'. He tipped his hand early in his opinion by stating that the agreement between husband and wife to live separate and apart from each other was 'a contract supposed to be made between two parties, . . . [who] being in law but one person, are on that account unable to contract with each other; and if the foundation fail, the consequence is, that the whole superstructure must also fail'.[30] He said this would introduce 'all the confusion and inconvenience which must necessarily result from so anomalous and mixed a character', and listed a series of questions that would naturally follow if the plaintiff's argument were to succeed. He claimed that the plaintiff's argument rested only on the simple proposition 'that where the husband ceases to be the protector of his wife, and is not liable to have any claim made on him for her support and maintenance, it necessarily follows that she herself must be her own protectress, make contracts for herself, and be responsible for them'.[31]

Kenyon, having served as master of the rolls in Chancery before becoming chief justice of the King's Bench, acknowledged that a feme covert could protect property to her separate use with a trust, and that courts of equity took notice of such trusts. Trusts, however, were not the province of courts of law. In the law courts, the 'unity of the persons' theory remained the rule, though a limited number of exceptions had crept in. Kenyon mentioned, for example, the situation 'of the husband being considered as dead, and the woman as being in a state of widowhood, or as divorced *a vinculo matrimonii*'. But Kenyon also referred to 'the cases of *Ringsted* v. *Lady Lanesborough*, *Barwell* v. *Brooks*, and some subsequent cases, which we wished to have reconsidered'.[32]

Mr Justice Soulden Lawrence's Paper Book for *Marshall* v. *Rutton* survives at Lincoln's Inn Library, and it contains extensive notes of the two arguments before all the judges.[33] The notes reveal something of a sea-change in judicial attitudes. Certainly the driving force behind the ultimate outcome in *Marshall* v. *Rutton* was Lord Kenyon, but he was aided by fortuitous alterations in the composition of the courts. When the case was first argued in May 1798, two of the justices who had voted with Lord Mansfield in the *Ringsted*, *Corbett*, and *Barwell* cases were still serving—Mr Justice Ashhurst on the King's Bench and Mr Justice Buller, formerly on the King's Bench but who in 1794 had transferred to the Court of Common Pleas. By the time the second argument was held two years later, Mr Justice Ashhurst had resigned and Mr Justice Buller was in failing health (he died a month after the second argument, which

[30] Ibid.
[31] Ibid., at 547.
[32] Ibid., at 548. The most important subsequent case was *Corbett* v. *Poelnitz*. In that case, the King's Bench held that a creditor was allowed to sue a married woman living separately from her husband by agreement and having a large separate maintenance, even though both parties lived in England and the action was not limited to necessaries.
[33] Dampier MSS., Lawrence Paper Book 329, Lincoln's Inn Library, London. Unless otherwise indicated, all quotations from the arguments of counsel and comments or speeches by the judges during the two arguments in the *Marshall* case are taken from Lawrence's handwritten notes in the margins and on the reverse sides of the pages of his copy of the Paper Book.

he did not attend). Also, Chief Justice Eyre of the Court of Common Pleas, who attended the first argument, died in July 1799 and was replaced by the former attorney-general, Sir John Scott, newly created Lord Eldon.

At the first argument, the plaintiff was represented by Josiah-Iles Wathen; the defendant by Stephen Gaselee. Wathen cited most of the cases that have been discussed, relying especially on *Barwell* and *Corbett*. Gaselee, in response, questioned whether the facts of *Marshall* fell within the authority of the cases that were cited, pointing out that it was not within a married woman's power by her own acts to dissolve the civil contract of marriage, and that she could not bring suit by herself.

Lord Kenyon then distinguished the various authorities. Kenyon pointed out that in *Ringsted*, Lord Lanesborough was not in England, and *Barwell* v. *Brooks* involved 'nothing like a permanent fund'. With regard to *Corbett* v. *Poelnitz*, Kenyon said that the first principle (that since the husband was not liable, the wife must be) would not hold, and the old law was 'very immoral'– it 'prevents the breach between husband and wife being healed'.

By the time the second argument before all the judges in *Marshall* took place on 10 May 1800, the plaintiff's position had grown precarious. Mr Justice Ashhurst of the King's Bench had resigned, Common Pleas Chief Justice Eyre had died and been replaced by Lord Eldon, and Mr Justice Buller of the Common Pleas was too ill to participate. Morever the plaintiff's new counsel, Edward Law, was an unfortunate choice. Law later (in 1802) became Lord Ellenborough and succeeded Kenyon as chief justice of the Court of King's Bench. According to Sir William Holdsworth, Ellenborough's fundamental belief was 'that in a changing age it was possible to stand obstinately on the ancient ways' and to stand in 'opposition to all the changes in the law which new ideas and new conditions were making necessary'.[34] It is clear from the colloquies between Law and the judges that Law did not have his heart in the case. After questioning by both Lord Eldon and Lord Kenyon, Law stated: 'I consider *Ringsted* v. *Lady Lanesborough*, &c. as modern revision and therefore do not press them.... And if I can't contend that when the husband is not liable the wife is, I can't succeed.' Later, citing both Lord Coke and the *Carruthers* case,[35] Law declared:

> The effect I contend for at law is that which the courts have given in the cases alluded to and what the courts of equity have given.... Coke [on] Littleton 668 shows that the wife may come in if the husband does not protect her rights. I stand here for a principle. I admit this is not within the cases. If the principle that the husband not being liable is not a ground to charge the wife, I have no pretension to trouble the Court.

After the arguments were concluded by Law for the plaintiff and Serjeant Bayley for the defendant, Lord Kenyon reviewed the authorities once more,

---

[34] *HEL*, xiii. 503.

[35] In response to Law's citation of *Sparrow* v. *Carruthers*, Lord Kenyon interjected: 'That was but a *nisi prius* case and then the party could not come back during the seven years.' Kenyon failed to mention that Yates had taken the opinion of all of the judges in the *Carruthers* case. See p. 223, n. 41, below.

and gave the following unsurprising summary appraisal: 'I was never satisfied and therefore I wish[ed] this case should come to take away all difficulties. I have never had but one opinion about it.']

$$\left.\begin{array}{c}\text{Marshall}\\\text{v.}\\\text{Rutton}^{36}\end{array}\right\}\quad\begin{array}{l}\text{LPB 329}\\\text{Copy Paper Book}\end{array}$$

[*Lawrence headnote*:] Feme covert living separate from her husband is not liable to be sued as a feme sole, although the separation was by the consent of her husband, and a separate maintenance was secured to her by deed.

Judgment for Defendant
May 24, 1800

To be argued on Friday, the 24th November 1797

Ult. Concilium
1st Wednesday in Trinity Term

Gatty

[Demurrer] Michaelmas Term in the 38th year of the reign of King George the Third

Roll   Way[37]

London to wit[38]—Be it remembered that in Michaelmas Term last past before our Lord the King at Westminster came John Marshall by Robert Gatty his attorney and brought into the Court of our said Lord the King before the King himself of a plea of trespass on the case and there are pledges for the prosecution to wit John Doe and Richard Roe which said Bill follows in these words to wit London to wit John Marshall complains of Mary Rutton being in the custody of the Marshal of the Marshalsea of our Lord the now King before the King himself. For that Whereas the said Mary here-

---

[36] (1800) 8 T.R. 545.

[37] In Lawrence's copies of the Paper Books for which there were plea rolls, the word 'Roll' was at times followed by the roll number, entered by hand once obtained. More often, the roll number was never written in, leaving a blank space, as in *Marshall* v. *Rutton*. 'Way' undoubtedly stood for John Way, who held multiple offices in the Court of King's Bench, one being *custos brevium*.

[38] [M.N.] 'A man can't create limitations contrary to the rules of law, because that would be changing the law. *Vide*: 1 *Collecteana Juridica* 388. Shall he by his own act change the law as [to] the marriage relation? He may give up his own rights, but not alter the course of judicial proceedings.' By this Lawrence evidently meant that the consent of the husband to his wife's living as a feme sole under a separation agreement with a separate maintenance, substantiated by deed, could not override a rule of law requiring the husband to be exclusively responsible for his wife's debts.

tofore to wit on the 1st day of June—in the year of our Lord one thousand seven hundred and ninety six to wit at London in the parish of St Mary le Bow in the Ward of Cheap was indebted to the said John in the sum of £500 of lawful money of Great Britain for divers goods wares and merchandises by the said John before that time sold and delivered to the said Mary at her special instance and request and being so indebted she the said Mary in consideration thereof afterwards to wit on the same day and year aforesaid at London aforesaid in the parish and ward aforesaid undertook and then and there faithfully promised the said John to pay him the said sum of money whenever afterwards she the said Mary should be thereto requested. And whereas also afterwards to wit on the same day and year aforesaid at London aforesaid in the parish and ward aforesaid in consideration that the said John at the like special instance and request of the said Mary had before that time sold and delivered to the said Mary divers other goods wares and merchandizes, she the said Mary undertook and then and there faithfully promised the said John to pay him so much money as he therefore reasonably deserved to have. And the said John avers that he therefore reasonably deserved to have of the said Mary other £500 to wit at London aforesaid in the parish and ward aforesaid whereof the said Mary afterwards to wit on the same day and year aforesaid there had notice. And whereas also the said Mary afterwards to wit on the same day and year aforesaid at London aforesaid in the parish and ward aforesaid was indebted to the said John in other £500 for work and labour care and diligence of the said John before that time done performed and bestowed by the said John and his servants in and about the business of the said Mary for the said Mary and at her special instance and request and was for diverse materials and necessary things used and applied in and about that work and labour before that time found and provided by the said John for the said Mary at the like instance and request of the said Mary. And being so indebted she the said Mary in consideration thereof afterwards to wit on the same day and year aforesaid at London aforesaid in the parish and ward aforesaid undertook and then and there faithfully promised the said John to pay him the said last mentioned sum of money whenever afterwards she the said Mary should be thereunto requested. And whereas also afterwards to wit on the same day and year aforesaid at London aforesaid in the parish and ward aforesaid in consideration that the said John at the like instance and request of the said Mary had before that time by himself and his servants done performed and bestowed other work and labour and of diligence in and about other the business of the said Mary and had also before that time at the like instance and request of the said Mary found and provided diverse other materials and necessary things used and applied in and about the said last mentioned work and labour she the said Mary undertook and then and there faithfully promised the said John to pay him so much money as he therefore reasonably deserved to have. And the said John avers that he therefore reasonably deserved to have, [to wit] to have of the said Mary, other £500 to wit at London aforesaid in the parish and ward aforesaid whereof the said

Mary afterwards to wit on the same day and year aforesaid there had notice. And whereas also the said Mary afterwards to wit on the same day and year aforesaid at London aforesaid in the parish and ward aforesaid was indebted to the said John in other £500 of like lawful money of Great Britain for money by the said John before that time laid out expended and paid to and for the use of the said Mary at her special instance and request and being so indebted she the said Mary in consideration thereof afterwards to wit on the same day and year aforesaid at London aforesaid in the parish and ward aforesaid undertook and then and there faithfully promised the said John to pay him the said last mentioned sum of money when afterwards she should be thereto requested. And whereas also the said Mary afterwards to wit on the same day and year aforesaid at London aforesaid in the parish and ward aforesaid accounted together with the said John of and concerning diverse other sums of money before that time were and owing from the said Mary to the said John and then being in arrear and unpaid and upon that account the said Mary was then and there found in arrear and indebted to the said John in other £500 and being so found in arrear and indebted she the said Mary in consideration thereof afterwards to wit on the same day and year aforesaid at London aforesaid in the parish and ward aforesaid undertook and then and there faithfully promised the said John to pay him the said last mentioned sum of money when afterwards she the said Mary should be thereto requested. Yet the said Mary not regarding her aforesaid promises and undertakings but contriving and fraudulently intending craftily and subtilly to deceive and defraud the said John in this respect has not yet paid the said several sums of money or any or either of them or any part thereof to the said John although so to do the said Mary was requested by the said John afterwards to wit on the same day and year aforesaid and often afterwards at London aforesaid in the parish and ward aforesaid. But to pay the said several sums of money or any or either of them or any part thereof to the said John she the said Mary has hitherto wholly refused and still does refuse to the said John his damage of £500 and therefore he brings his suit &c.

Plea—And now at this day that is to say on Monday next after the Morrow of All Souls in this same term until which day the said Mary had leave to imparle to the said Bill and then to answer the same &c. as well the said John by his said Attorney as the said Mary in her own proper person do come before our Lord the King at Westminster and the said Mary defends his aforesaid action thereof against her the said Mary because she says that she the said Mary before and at the time of the making the said several promises and undertakings in the said Declaration above specified was and yet is covert of and married to one Isaac Rutton her now husband which said Isaac Rutton is now living to wit at London aforesaid in the parish and ward aforesaid and this she the said Mary is ready to verify wherefore she prays judgment if the said John ought to have or maintain his aforesaid action thereof against her &c.

Henry Clifford

Replication—And the said John as to the said plea by the said Mary above pleaded in bar says that he by reason of any thing in that plea alledged ought not to be barred from having or maintaining his aforesaid action thereof against her because he says that after the intermarriage of the said Mary with the said Isaac Rutton and before the making of the said several promises and undertakings in the said Declaration specified or of any of them to wit on the 21st day of January in the year of our Lord 1788 to wit at London aforesaid in the parish and ward aforesaid the said Mary and the said Isaac Rutton mutually consented and agreed to live separate and apart from each other and that a separation then and there accordingly took place between the said Mary and the said Isaac who have continually from thenceforth hitherto lived and still do live separate and apart from each other to wit at London aforesaid in the parish and ward aforesaid. And the said John further saith that a competent separate maintenance suitable to the Estate and Degree of the said Mary to wit the yearly sum of £200 p. Anno of lawful money of Great Britain was thereupon then and there to wit on the day and year last aforesaid at London aforesaid in the parish and ward aforesaid in due form of Law settled and secured to the said Mary by Deed to her sole and separate use and benefit to be well and truly paid by the said Isaac Rutton to the use of the said Mary during the joint Lives of the said Mary and the said Isaac Rutton in such manner and form as the said Mary notwithstanding her coverture should direct or appoint which said separate maintenance continually from and after the said time of the making of such separation as aforesaid hitherto hath been and still is duly paid by the said Isaac Rutton to the said Mary and to her sole and separate use and benefit to wit at London aforesaid in the parish and ward aforesaid. And the said John further says that the said several promises and undertakings in the said declaration specified were and each of them was made by the said Mary to the said John after the said Separation between the said Mary and the said Isaac Rutton had taken place in manner aforesaid and whilst they so lived separate and apart from each other and whilst such separate maintenance as aforesaid was secured and paid to the said Mary as aforesaid and that the said several promises and undertakings were respectively made by the said Mary to the said John upon her own separate credit and account in the manner of a feme sole and not upon the account or credit of her said husband in manner and form as in the Declaration aforesaid is above in that behalf alledged. And this the said John is ready to verify therefore he prays judgment and his damages by him sustained on occasion of the non-performing of the said several promises and undertakings in the said declaration mentioned to be adjudged to him &c.

J. I. Wathen

Rejoinder—And as to the said plea of the said John by him above pleaded in reply to the said plea of the said Mary by her above plead [*sic*] in bar—the said Mary says that the said John ought not by reason of any thing therein alledged to have or maintain his aforesaid Action thereof against her because she says that here it is that after the intermarriage of her the said Mary with the said Isaac Rutton and before the making of the several promises and undertakings in the said Declaration mentioned or of any of them she the said Mary and the said Isaac Rutton mutually consented and agreed to live separate and apart from each other and no longer to dwell and cohabit together that a separation accordingly took place between her the said Mary and the said Isaac and that they have continually from thenceforth hitherto lived and still do live separate and apart from each other and that a competent separate maintenance suitable to the Estate and Degree of her the said Mary was settled and secured to her the said Mary by Deed to her sole and separate use and benefit as the said John hath in his said replication alledged. But the said Mary further says that the said Deed whereby the same was so settled and secured was and is a certain Deed or articles of Agreement bearing date the 21st day of January in the year of our Lord 1788 made between the said Isaac Rutton and her the said Mary of the one part and one Thomas Rutton of the other part to wit at London aforesaid in the parish and ward aforesaid which said articles of Agreement sealed with the respective seals of the said Isaac Mary and Thomas the said Mary brings here into court the date whereof is the same day and year last aforesaid. And that by the said deed or articles of Agreement it is provided and declared that such separate maintenance shall be paid for and during such time and for so long only as the said Mary shall permit and suffer the said Isaac Rutton to live continue remain and be separate and apart from her the said Mary according to his own will discretion and pleasure and that without any suit or suits action or actions claims or demands molestation or interruption of or by her the said Mary or any other person or persons whomsoever by her assent consent means or procurement for or by reason of the diet meat drink apparel washing lodging support or maintenance of her the said Mary or for or by reason of any debt or debts whatsoever which she the said Mary shall at any time thereafter during the said separation contract on any account whatsoever or for or by reason of any acts or engagements of what nature or kind soever of her the said Mary and also for and during such time only and so long as she the said Mary shall observe and maintain a chaste due and becoming conduct and demeanour and also for and during such time and so long only as she the said Mary shall and do at her own costs and charges board lodge cloathe educate maintain support and keep Mary Rutton and Elizabeth Rutton the two younger children of the said Isaac and Mary the now Defendant in a good and proper manner so that he the said Isaac Rutton his executors or administrators and his and their goods and chattels lands and tenements shall not thereafter be any ways charged or chargeable or incumbered with any [of] the matters aforesaid or any other matter or thing whatsoever touching or concerning the said Mary the wife of the said Isaac and the said Mary Rutton and Elizabeth Rutton their children which may can or shall arise accrue or happen during the said Separation as by the said articles of Agreement relation being thereunto had will appear without this that the said separate maintenance was or is settled and secured to be paid by the said Isaac Rutton to the use of her the said Mary the now Defendant during the joint lives of her the said Mary and the said Isaac Rutton in manner and form as the said John hath in his said Replication in that behalf alledged and this the said Mary the now Defendant is ready to verify wherefore she prays Judgment if the said John ought to have or maintain his aforesaid action thereof against her &c.

S. Gaselee

Demurrer—And the said John craves oyer of the said articles of Agreement in the said Rejoinder mentioned and they are read to him in these words to wit Articles of Agreement indented made and concluded this twenty first day of January in the year of our Lord 1788 Between Isaac Rutton and Mary his wife of the one part and Thomas Rutton of the other part. Whereas many differences and disputes have unhappily arisen between the above named Isaac Rutton and Mary his wife and do still continue. Whereupon the said Isaac Rutton and Mary his wife for their mutual ease and quiet have come to a final Resolution to live separate and apart from each other and no longer to dwell and cohabit together. Now these presents witness that in consideration of the premises in pursuance of the said recited Agreement the said Isaac Rutton doth covenant promise and agree to and with the said Thomas Rutton his executors administrators and assigns by these presents that he the said Isaac Rutton shall and will yearly and every year during the joint natural lives of the said Isaac Rutton and Mary his wife well and truly pay or cause to be paid unto the said Thomas Rutton his executors or administrators the sum of £200 of lawful money of Great Britain by 4 equal quarterly payments in every year the first of such payments to be made on the fifth day of April now next ensuing. And it is hereby covenanted and agreed by and between all and every the parties hereto that the said payments shall be so made to the said Thomas Rutton in trust to pay and apply the same from time to time to such uses and purposes and in such manner and form as the said Mary the wife of the said Isaac Rutton notwithstanding her coverture shall direct or appoint and in default of such Direction or Appointment then to permit her to receive the same to her sole and separate use and benefit and her receipt notwithstanding her coverture shall be a good discharge to the said Thomas Rutton. And the said Isaac Rutton doth also covenant with the said Thomas Rutton that he will from time to time and at all times hereafter permit and suffer the said Mary his wife to live remain continue and be separate and apart from him the said Isaac Rutton according to her will and pleasure without any suit molestation or interruption of or by him. Provided always and it is hereby declared by and between the said Parties to these presents that the said annual sum of £200 hereinbefore covenanted to be paid as aforesaid shall be so paid for and during such time and for so long only as she the said Mary the wife of the said Isaac Rutton party thereto shall permit and suffer from her the said Mary according to his own will discretion pleasure and that without any suit or suits action or actions claims or demands molestation or interruption of or by her the said Mary or any person or persons whomsoever by her assent consent means or procurement for or by reason of the diet meat drink apparel washing lodging support or maintenance of her the said Mary or for or by reason of any debt or debts whatsoever which she the said Mary shall at any time hereafter during the said separation contract on any account whatsoever or for or by reason of any acts or engagements of what nature or kind soever of her the said Mary and also for and during such time only and so long as the said Mary the wife of the said Isaac Rutton party thereto shall observe and maintain a chaste due and becoming conduct and demeanour and also for and during such time and so long only as she the said Mary shall do at her own costs and charges board lodge cloathe educate maintain support and keep Mary Rutton and Elizabeth Rutton the two younger children of the said Isaac Rutton party hereto and Mary his wife in a good and proper manner so that he the said Isaac Rutton party hereto his executors or administrators and his and their goods and chattels lands and tenements shall not hereafter by anyways charged or chargeable or incumbered with any the matters aforesaid or any other matter or thing whatsoever touching or concerning the said Mary the wife of the said Isaac Rutton party hereto and the said Mary Rutton and Elizabeth Rutton their children which may can or shall arise accrue or happen during their said Separation. In Witness whereof the said parties to these presents have hereunto set their hands and seals the day and year first above written. Isaac Rutton Ls. Mary Rutton Ls. Thomas Rutton Ls. Which being read and heard the said John says that the said Rejoinder of the said Mary and the matters therein contained in manner and form as the same are above pleaded and set forth are not sufficient in Law to bar the said John from having or maintaining his aforesaid action thereof against her in this behalf and that he the said John is not under any necessity nor in any wise bound by the Law of the Land to answer the said Rejoinder and this he is ready to verify. Wherefore for want of a sufficient Rejoinder in this behalf the said John as before prays Judgment and his Damages aforesaid to be adjudged to him and for causes of Demurrer in Law the said John according to the form of the Statute in such case made and provided sets down and shews to the Court here the following to wit For that the said Mary hath in and by her said Rejoinder traversed and denied that the said separate maintenance was settled and secured to be paid by the said Isaac Rutton to her use during the joint lives of herself and of the said Isaac Rutton although it appears in and by the said Deed of Separation that such separate maintenance was settled and secured to be paid by the said Isaac Rutton to the use of the said Mary during the joint lives of herself and of the said Isaac Rutton subject only to be determined in the event of the wilful misconduct or defaults of her the said Mary. And for that although the said Mary in and by her said Rejoinder hath attempted to shew that the said Separate Maintenance was defeazible and determinable upon certain contingencies. Yet the said Mary hath happened to determine or put an end to the payment of her said separate maintenance or that the same hath by any means been defeated or determined. And for that the said Rejoinder attempts to put in Issue an immaterial Averment contained in the said Replication and no material Issue can be taken upon the matter contained in the said Rejoinder and the said Rejoinder is in various other respects uncertain defective and informal &c.

J. I. *Wathen*

Joinder—And the said Mary saith that the said plea in manner and form aforesaid by her the said Mary above pleaded by way of Rejoinder and the matters in the same contained are good and sufficient in Law to bar the said John from having his action aforesaid against her the said Mary which said Rejoinder and the matters in the same contained she the said Mary is ready to verify and prove as the Court shall award and Because the said John hath not answered the said Rejoinder nor hitherto in any manner denied the same she the said Mary as before prays judgment and that the said John may be barred from having his said action against her &c. But because the Court of our Lord the King now here is not yet advised what judgment to give of and concerning the Premises a day is therefore given to the parties aforesaid to come before out Lord the King at Westminster on next after to hear Judgment thereon for that the Court of our said Lord the King now here is not yet advised thereof:—

[*Lawrence's Notes of Argument*]

May 9th 1798 in Exchequer (*Cam. Scacc.*): *coram omnes justiciarios* except PERRYN Baron, to which it was adjourned from the King's Bench.

Mr *Wathen* for the plaintiff:

It appears by these pleadings that the defendant was living under an agreement for separate maintenance for life apart from her husband and that such provision was to be continued for life except in case of some misbehaviour of her own.

I contend she is liable to this action as she has not pleaded in abatement. Women covert by the general rule of law are not liable. But [there are] these exceptions: profession, abjuration, and exile. [See] *Coke on Littleton* 132 for abjuration. *Compton* v. *Collinson* 1 H.B. 334 has all these cases.[39]

The reason of these exceptions—[is] because the husband could not sue with the wife, nor could he be sued with her. And this [is] the reason, and not a civil death. [See] *Duchess of Mazarine*—*1 Salk.* 116 and *Lord Raym.*[40] *Sparrow* v. *Carruthers* 1 *Powell on Contracts*—the case of transportation cited in *Corbett* v. *Poelnitz*.[41]

---

[39] *Compton* v. *Collinson* (1790) 1 Bl. H. 334.

[40] Lawrence interjection: '(That case for a new trial.)'.

[41] See J. J. Powell, *Essay Upon the Law of Contracts and Agreements*, 2 vols. (1790), i. 76 ('And, in the case of *Sparrow and Carruthers*, Mr Justice Yates thought transportation, although but for seven years, to be such an absence of the husband, within the *reason* of the cases of abjuration, &c. as that the wife might, during that period, be sued alone.'). According to a manuscript report of *Pearson* v. *Carruthers* (either the same case as *Sparrow* v. *Carruthers* or a parallel case brought by a different creditor), Mr Justice Yates's opinion was that 'the circumstances of the case dissolved the wife's incapacity to contract', but as a caution, he instructed that the verdict for the plaintiff was to be subject to the opinion of the Court of King's Bench. Afterwards, he reported that, 'the action being for a small sum, and the parties poor, he had not put them to the expence of arguing the point

[In] the action [of] *Franks* v. *Duchess D'Pienne* [it was] held by Lord KENYON that she was liable, as her husband was gone to his own country and never likely to return.

The reasons of the cases of abjuration &c. apply to the cases of separate maintenance. The husband is not suable. The wife has a fund. The husband has renounced his rights over his wife. But [there is] no such renunciation as in the case of abjuration and exile. *R.* v. *Mead—1 Burr.* 542. The disability of coverture is suspended during the separate maintenance. The cases ancient and modern [are] in support of this position.

[See] the cases of account cited from the year books by Lord LOUGHBOROUGH in *Compton* v. *Collinson*.

Cases of bonds to allow feme covert to dispose of her legacies—in Cro. Car. [are] cited in the same case. Another, [is] Cro. Car. 376.[42]

Ringsted v. *Lady Lanesborough*—[see] 1 *Powell on Contracts* 78.
Corbett v. *Poelnitz*. 1 T.R. 5.

Lord KENYON: Lord BATHURST wisely looked forward and held that you must bring the fund before the court in *Tenant* v. *Hulme*.[43]

Wathen: In *Barwell* v. *Brooks*, separate maintenance was not secured by deed. In *Corbett* v. *Poelnitz* it is said that as the husband can't be charged she must.[44] This case [is] stronger than *Corbett* v. *Poelnitz*. That was a case in which it was held that she might bind herself by bond, the action being brought by a co-obligor with her for money he had paid.

EYRE C.J. Suppose he had entered into a bond for her benefit and she had entered into none—it would have been the same case.

Gaselee, contra: [There are] three questions: 1st on the materiality of the traverse; 2nd, if this case is within the authority of the cases cited; 3rdly, if those cases are law.

As to the 1st: The traverse is material because according to the cases cited the maintenance must be permanent.

As to the 2nd: This not a permanent estate. Speaking of estate *dum casta & sola*, Blackstone says so long as it lasts it is considered an estate for life.[45]

Co. Litt. 42: Lord COKE says such estate is an estate for life determinable. *Vide*: Hargrave's note on that part of Lord COKE[46]—where it is said that in pleading it should be stated that the estate *continued*. Therefore on these

---

in court, but would take the opinion of the judges of B.R. upon it, out of court'. Later, he 'declared that all the judges of England were of opinion that the action well lay'. Harvard Law School, MS. 4057 fo. 206 (Carlisle Assizes 1768). Apparently instead of approaching only King's Bench judges, Yates put the case informally to the twelve judges at one of their periodic gatherings to consider questions reserved in crown cases and some civil cases. On this procedure, see J. Oldham, 'Informal Lawmaking'.

[42] *Tylle* v. *Peirce* (1634–35) Cro. Car. 376.
[43] *Hulme* v. *Tenant* (1778) 1 Bro. C.C. 16. According to Brown's report, the case was first heard by Lord Bathurst, who dismissed the bill. The printed report covers rehearings before Lord Thurlow, who became Chancellor on 3 June 1778.
[44] Lawrence note: '(*non sequitur*)'.
[45] 2 Blackstone's *Commentaries* 121.
[46] See Co. Litt. 42a, n.6.

authorities it is not properly alleged that the maintenance is for life. And the court will not presume against the ancient principle of law.

But the maintenance does not depend on chastity, but on her husband not being troubled. On her behaviour being due and becoming, this [is] uncertain. On her maintaining two children. Can all this be presumed—can a woman by her own act dissolve the civil contract? She can't by adultery, 4 T.R. 766.[47]

According to this, if being liable to be sued is an evil, a woman by her own crime gets an advantage which by a separate maintenance she would not have tho' the separation was owing to the husband's fault.

She can't sue by herself. *Caudell* v. *Shaw* 4 T.R. 361.

BULLER J.: That depends on the custom of London not extending to the courts of Westminster.

[*Gaselee*, cont'd]: *Ellah* v. *Leigh*, 5 T.R. 679; *Clayton* v. *Adams*, 6 T.R. 684. The first was the case of alimony and on the ground of no permanent fund. That case rules this, for the maintenance may be determined. She might be taken in execution and then husband and wife might annihilate the maintenance. *Clayton* v. *Adams* [was] an action against executor of a feme covert, who lived separate and carried on trade.

2 Ves. Jun. 195.[48]

The chancellor doubted the doctrine cited as to proceeding against a feme covert. In *Corbett* v. *Poelnitz*, there was a separate maintenance for her life, a fund vested in trustees. Here it rests in the covenant of the husband, and this only for their joint lives.

As to the general question: if there is one principle of law more clear than another it is that a feme covert can't be sued without her husband. Excepted cases: abjuration, profession, and exile. The reason of those cases was that the law considered the husband *civilis mortuus*. He could not sue merely because he was not in this country, but because he could never sue, a person who had abjured the realm could not come here. It was a sort of legal divorce on the same principle.

Sparrow v. *Carruthers* &c.—cases at Maidstone. This in some of the books is called a relegation.[49]

EYRE C.J.: Do you contend that transportation has the same effect as abjuration to create incapacity to sue?

Gaselee: It has the same effect for a time.[50]

[EYRE C.J.]: Legal separations are very different from separations by the agreement of the parties. In the case cited by Lord LOUGHBOROUGH from the year books, the only question was if the husband shall be allowed to contravene his own agreement.

---

[47] *Gilchrist* v. *Brown* (1792) 4 T.R. 766.

[48] *Ball* v. *Montgomery* (1793) 2 Ves. Jun. 191. Lord Chancellor Loughborough said, 'I take it to be now the established law, that no Court, not even the Ecclesiastical Court, has any original jurisdiction to give a wife a separate maintenance.' Ibid., at 195.

[49] See *Coke on Littleton* 133a ('But if the husband, by act of parliament, have judgement to be exiled but for a time, which some call a relegation, that is no civil death.').

[50] Lawrence note: '(He can't come into the country to sue.)'.

Lord KENYON: That goes no farther than very old cases where it is held that if a feme levies a fine and declares this her own, the husband assenting afterwards, it is good. The cases from *Croke Charles* on bonds do not bear on this case.

Duchess of Mazarine's Case: The party was not in the country and was an alien and therefore the law could take no notice of him. [In] the case of *Franks* v. *the Duchess of Pienne*, there it was impossible to sue the husband, and the purposes of justice required that there should be somebody sued.

Ringsted v. *Lady Lanesborough Cooke's Bankrupt Laws* 32, there Lord Lanesborough was not in this country. [In] *Barwell* v. *Brooks*—*[there was]* nothing like a permanent fund, and *[the case was]* overruled by *Ellah* v. *Leigh* and *Clayton* v. *Adams*. [In] *Corbett* v. *Poelnitz* [there were] two principles: 1st that the husband was not liable and therefore the wife must [be]. This will not hold—[see] 6 T.R. 633 *Govier* v. *Hancock*. Another principle, [it is] not decent for me to discuss.[51]

There are contending authorities.

Wathen in reply: As to the first point: The annuity is secured to the Ruttons to be paid to the wife quarterly, so long as she shall be chaste &c. *Coke on Littleton* 42a states that such estate may be alleged to be for life generally. I admit that this maintenance can't be taken in execution, but having a remedy against the person of the wife, it will compel her to pay out of her annuity.

The goods delivered to her and which are the subject of this action might be taken in execution. *Ellah* v. *Leigh* was the case of a provision only *pendente lite*.

Lord KENYON: Do you find any case of an action against a person divorced *a mensa et thoro*?

Wathen: In Moore 466 it is so said, but the facts of the case do not authorize it.[52]

Lord KENYON: I do not think the old law allowed [it]. If she died intestate, the husband would have her effects. Only on execution that against her person. [It was a] very immoral law—prevents the breach between husband and wife being healed.

Lord Chief Justice EYRE: I feel more difficulty from the authorities than from the principles—they [the principles] are with Lord KENYON. I do not know what to do with the authorities.

Ult. Concilium

May 10th 1800

Mr *Law* for plaintiff: [There is] no difficulty in showing the traverse bad as a matter of law. But as that will bring me to the other point, if a woman living separate from her husband having a competent maintenance for life defeasible

---

[51] The case was about adultery.
[52] The reference is unclear. Perhaps it should have been to Moore 665 (see p. 229, n. 66, below, and accompanying text).

by no act of the husband, and not defeated by any act of her own, is capable of being sued as a feme sole. A feme covert can't contract—as [she has] no freedom of will, no property. And because the wife can't be compelled by contract to perform it.

Lord ELDON: Does not the policy go further and settle the relations of the family life, as [far as] the public is concerned? I wish to have it considered if this [is] any deed at all—and if, in a proceeding in the ecclesiastical court for restitution of the conjugal rights, would not this be considered as a nullity. The argument supposes she is in a state of separation—but how is the deed valid that puts her in that state of separation?

Law: I can't find anything in the books as to that last point, but I find from the authority of the books that this separation is taken notice of in our courts, in the Court of Chancery.

Lord ELDON: Do you find any case where the parties themselves applied to the Court of Chancery—that a bill was filed for a specific performance?

Law: *R.* v. *Mead* shows he could renounce any rights to her person.[53]

Lord ELDON: I think as that case has been lately considered, it goes to show that husband and wife can dissolve the matrimonial union.

Law: Cases of abjuration and exile are only instances of the general rule. I take the principle of them to be this: that when the husband can no longer be her protection she shall be allowed to be her own protectress. The husband shall be considered as civilly dead. But this has been expanded to the case of transportation.

Lord KENYON: Lord ELLESMERE in the case of *Posthwaite* observes in *Lady Belknap's Case* it was for life and so it appears in Co. Litt.[54]

Law: There are cases of a temporary absence. *Bracton* B 4. c. 24. s. 2. It is said she may bring an action during a long journey as in *terram sanctam* for trespass or disseisin—in this case Bracton says *Succuritur ei de officio judicis.* *Fleta* B 4. c. 2 s. 10 speaks of suit by husband against wife who holds herself seized against him.

Lord KENYON: Wherever she is seized, the husband is seized and may transfer it—Sir *M. Foster* has cautioned us not to rely much on the authority of either.

Law: These authorities only show the doctrine [is] not so modern as supposed. [Y.B.] 47 Edw. III pl: 43 cited in *Compton* v. *Collinson,* 1 H. Blackstone, shows a feme covert might leave and call on her bailiff to account for the profit of lands for her separate maintenance.

---

[53] *R.* v. *Mead* (1758) 1 Burr. 542. After John Wilkes's cruelty to his wife Mary, he agreed to leave her alone and executed articles of separation in exchange for a large payment from the wife out of her separate estate. In a *habeas corpus* action brought by Wilkes against Mrs Mead, his mother-in-law, to produce Mary Wilkes, the court 'held this agreement to be a formal *renunciation* by the husband, of his marital right to seize her, or force her back to live with him'. Ibid.

[54] *Coke on Littleton*, i. 132b (Sir Thomas Egerton, Baron Ellesmere).

1 Bulstr. 140.[55] Feme covert during her husband's absence maintained [...] Roll 46. Co. Litt. 133. Hargrave's notes—shows a wife may have a writ of deceit against her husband [for] levying a fine in her name.[56]

Deerly v. *Duchess of Mazarine* in Salkeld[57]—she was held liable her husband being abroad.

Duchess of de Pienne Case lately before Lord KENYON.[58] *De Gaillon* v. *de Laigle*.[59]

Lord KENYON: That case came before me with the weight of past authority and I considered the husband as not likely to come here—and I remember on that principle Lord MANSFIELD allowed Mingotti the singer, whose husband was in Italy, to maintain an action for her salary against Mr Drummond.

Law: I consider *Ringsted* v. *Lady Lanesborough* &c. as modern revision and therefore do not press them. The husband [is] not liable in case of the elopement of the wife. *Tod* v. *Stokes* 12 Mod. 244.[60] And if I can't contend that when the husband is not liable the wife is, I can't succeed.

Lord KENYON: How if she takes up more than necessary?

Law: I do not contend this while [she is] under the protection of the husband.

4 Burr. 2177, *Thompson* v. *Hervey*—shows that a temporary maintenance will not do.[61] I infer from the husband ceasing to be liable, that she must [be] or she will starve.

Lord KENYON: She is to pay as she has money—making her liable to an action will not prevent her starving.

Law: *Ex parte Preston, Cooke's Bankrupt Laws* 30.[62]

A feme covert trading was held liable by Lord BATHURST as chancellor. As far as one can turn cases in Chancery, while the husband [is] abroad femes covert have been held liable.

Dubois v. *Hole* 2 Vern. 613.[63] The chancellor held process against a wife good.

Tothills—temp: Eliz.[64]

Lord ELDON: In the Court of Chancery the suit is not against her but is a proceeding against property the subject of the trust.

Law: If you think the cases of the Court of Equity are capable of that answer I will not trouble you on this point.

Lord ELDON: According to ecclesiastical law adultery and cruelty are causes of separation and no other. Suppose a wife who can execute no deed for any

---

[55] *Anon.* (1612). A feme covert whose husband was beyond the sea could sue in her own name for assault and battery against her, but she could not herself be sued for 'divers trespasses, as against the plaintiff' until her husband's return.

[56] *Coke on Littleton*, i. 133b, n.(4).

[57] *Deerly* v. *Duchess of Mazarine* (1696) 1 Salk. 116.

[58] *Duchess of de Pienne Case*, *Franks* v. *Duchess of Pienne* (1797) 2 Esp. 587.

[59] *De Gaillon* v. *L'Aigle* (1798) 1 Bos. & Pul. 357.

[60] *Tod* v. *Stokes* (1699) 12 Mod. 244.

[61] *Thompson* v. *Hervey* (1768) 4 Burr. 2177.

[62] *Ex parte Preston* in the first edition of W. Cooke, *The Bankrupt Laws* (1785) is at p. 22. In the 4th edition (2 vols. 1799), it is at i. 24.

[63] *Dubois* v. *Hole* (1708) 2 Vern. 613.

[64] The reference is unclear.

other purpose, can execute a deed for separation. Now supposing a proceeding then for restitution of conjugal rights after such deed, what courts of common law prohibit—and have you found in a court of equity a proceeding by the parties founded on the deed?

Lord KENYON: *Mary Mead's Case* was a case of cruelty.[65]

Lord ELDON: Could not the wife sue in the ecclesiastical court for restitution of conjugal rights? And *Mary Mead's Case* only decided that after such a deed the husband shall not take back his wife by that which is a breach of the peace. Lord MANSFIELD is there supposed to have said it is a separation between husband and wife, and other court will carry it through all its consequences Now could the court do that, if real estate should descend or a legacy be left her?

Law: Moore 665 shows that after divorce *a mensa et thoro* she may sue.[66]

Lord ELDON: That [is] a separation by act of law.

Law: 2 [W.] Black. 1079. *Hatchett* v. *Baddeley*—decided nothing, as all turned on the word elopement. Blackstone says that proves the husband's not being liable. It does not follow that the wife is. But that was the case with all the excepted cases.

Rolls Parliament, *Tissor's case* is the true name of *Belknap's Case* where the cases fell within the principle.[67] I do not want a [. . .].

M: 20 Geo. III. *Wilson* v. *Campbell* has decided that a feme covert treated as a feme sole may put in Bail. She might part with her bond without fine, for the husband's deed would estop him from controverting it.

Compton v. *Collinson* has all the cases on the subject.

[There is] no case to support *Lean* v. *Schutz*, that it is necessary to join the husband, if his interest can't be affected, except in the case of a feme sole trader, but there the husband has an interest in her person.

Lord ELDON: I believe the lord chancellor has doubted of this giving effect to such articles—and I should be glad to hear this question argued. Can any consideration arise out of such an agreement?

[Lord KENYON, cont'd:] This is universally true, that when a woman has property in the hands of the trustees they will give execution against that property—We have not given effect to deeds against the policy of the law, nor do I know that they have done it in any case where the husband resisted it.

Lord ELDON: If the wife's liability depends on the contract of the husband, how would it be if the husband should engage that notwithstanding the separation she should not be liable?

Law: That could be a contract of indemnity

Lord ELDON: So are all articles of separation— I believe [there are] none that are not contracts of indemnity. In case of exile, the husband compelled to go

---

[65] See p. 227, n. 53, above.
[66] *Stephens* v. *Tot* (1602) Moore 665.
[67] The reference is unclear. Possibly Law had in mind Hargrave's note to Coke's discussion of *Lady Belknap's Case* in which Hargrave refers to parliamentary records that included the case of Matilda, the wife of Robert Cissor. *Coke on Littleton*, 133a n.(2).

abroad. In cases of abjuration—it was then thought it was better for a man to be married to something else than his wife [*sic*].

Bayley, serjeant: The whole basis of the plaintiff's claim is an agreement during the marriage. I need not contend that the acts of the wife are merely void. A wife can't by agreement with her husband be a disseisor. 1 Rolle's Ab. 660—E 2. 1. 2. 3, for the agreement is void.

Perkins sec. 154[68]—if a feme covert after the death of her husband may deliver a deed a 2nd time—and it will be good—if it had been good originally it could not be. If an agreement can't bind her to a stranger it is an additional objection that this is an agreement with the husband. Co. Litt. 112c shows that a wife can't covenant with her husband.

I wish to ask what [is] the effect of this agreement. What operation can it have in a court of law and equity or in ecclesiastical court?

If it can't bind in either, the foundation failing the superstructure, it will fall.

First to consider it at law: if by their agreement they are to be considered as separated persons they could maintain actions against each other and take each other in execution.

And if he does not go that length when will he stop? But if it is not binding at common law how far is it binding in equity?

Legard v. *Johnon*, 3 Ves. Jr. 352. A bill to carry into execution articles of agreement between husband and wife for separation—which the court did not.

Question then how far the ecclesiastical court will give it. The authority to show this, and then for reasons suggested, the ecclesiastical court considers this contract as against the general policy of marriage.

As to authorities: [There is] no case where wife [was] thought liable unless the husband [was] *civilis mortuus* and where the wife was entitled to sue.

Case in Co. Litt. 132b.

In *Lady Belknap's Case* a [. . .] wife sued. [In] another suit against her 1 Hen. IV f. 1 plac. 2, the suit was brought by the king, the exile being during the king's pleasure, which possibly might continue for life—and his bringing that action might so decide the king's pleasure.

In 2 Hen. IV 7a. pl. 26, there the reason given why she was liable was because she was the king's farmer.[69]

In *Weyland's Case*, Co. Litt. 132b stated at large, and Lord COKE says it is to be observed that an abjuration into a foreign life is like profession—a civil death, and so banishment for life, like *Belknap's Case*—but not if the banishment be less than for life.

[In] *Deerly* v. *Duchess of Mazarine* in Salk[eld], Lord HOLT speaks of the husband's absolute disability to live here as making it like *Weyland* and *Lady Belknap's Case,* cases of civil death.

---

[68] J. Perkins, *A Profitable Booke Treating of the Lawes of England* (1545).

[69] The reference is to a year book case from the year 1400, Y.B. Mich. 2 Hen. IV, fo. 7a, pl. 26. Professor David Seipp provides the following abstract: 'A monk could sue without his abbot, if he is the king's farmer by the king's patent. A wife could sue without her husband in the same circumstances, or if her husband is attaint and exiled', <http://www.bu.edu/phpbin/lawyearbooks/display.php?id=15454>, accessed 18 August 2012.

In *Hatchett* v. *Baddeley* [W.] Blackstone says, 'I am clear that the only excepted cases are abjuration and exile, &c.'

As to the case from 1 Bulstrode 140,[70] it is expressly laid down that you can't sue the feme covert in the absence of her husband—and there the action was brought in the name of herself and her husband—and all that the case means is that she does not want his authority to use his name.

4 T.R. 766—has decided that a feme covert living in adultery can't be sued, and certainly the husband not liable.[71]

6 T.R. 603.[72] [2] Str. 706.[73] This shows that the husband not being liable does not prove he is.

As to the case of the king, it admits of this answer, that that is a proceeding *in rem.*

Lavie v. *Phillips*, Burr. 1776,[74] *Caudell* v. *Shaw*, 4 T.R. 361,[75] *Read* v. *Jewson*,[76] these cited [cases] shew the wife can't sue.

[The] case from Moore of the feme covert suing was the case of a suit for a legacy—which it is then said the husband may release.

A better remedy is a court of equity—where a feme covert is considered as a feme sole so as to act on her separate property according to equity.

[See] 2 Williams 199,[77] 2 Ves. 193,[78] 1 Brown Ch. Cas. 16,[79] 1 Ves. 517.[80]

A court of equity could inquire into the return if the debt might marshal the property.

Lord ELDON: Is there any case where a court of equity will give a remedy against the principal of the fund, or only against the property?

Bayley: [Cites] 3 Ves., *Hyde* v. *Price*.[81]

It ought to have been assured that the debt was contracted for her maintenance—for such is the object of the provision.

In *Corbett* v. *Poelnitz* Lord MANSFIELD says a feme covert having a separate maintenance should be liable to the extent of it. Now that case went the length of making her liable to any extent.

Law in reply: A feme covert may be a disseisor—for she may be a trespasser. She may commit waste with her husband and forfeit her estate. The effect I contend for at law is that which the courts have given in the cases alluded to and what the courts of equity have given.

I admit that what I contend for will go the length of taking the husband and wife in execution. Lord COKE observes that relegation is not civil death.

---

[70] *Torrey* v. *Adey* (1611) 1 Buls. 140.
[71] *Gilchrist* v. *Brown* (1792) 4 T.R. 766. See p. 225, n. 47 above.
[72] *Govier* v. *Hancock* (1796) 6 T.R. 603.
[73] *Mainwaring* v. *Sands* (1772–73) 2 Str. 706.
[74] *Lavie* v. *Phillips* (1765) 3 Burr. 1766.
[75] *Caudell* v. *Shaw* (1791) 4 T.R. 361.
[76] Reported as *Jewson* v. *Read* (1773) Lofft 134.
[77] *Marlow* v. *Smith* (1723) 2 P. Wms. 198.
[78] *Ball* v. *Montgomery* (1793) 2 Ves. Jun. 191.
[79] *Hulme* v. *Tenant and wife* (1778) 1 Bro. C.C. 16.
[80] *Master* v. *Fuller* (1792) 1 Ves. Jun. 513.
[81] *Hyde* v. *Price* (1797) 3 Ves. Jun. 437.

Sparrow v. *Carruthers.*

Lord KENYON: That was but a *nisi prius* case and then the party could not come back during the seven years.[82]

Law: Co. Litt. 66b[83] shows that the wife may come in if the husband does not protect her rights. I stand here for a principle. I admit this not within the cases. If the principle that the husband not being liable is not a ground to charge the wife, I have no pretension to trouble the Court.

Lord ELDON: Could she contract to be a witness against her husband? Or that she should not have the benefit of the coverture in an indictment for felony?

Law: I contend the first—the latter would not be the subject of contracts.

Lord KENYON: I was never satisfied and therefore I wish[ed] this case should come to take away all difficulties—I have never had but one opinion about it.

[*Lawrence's Separate Research Notes*]

Ellah v. *Leigh*—5 T.R. 679: A woman to whom alimony was allowed [was] not suable.

Compton v. *Collinson* 1 H. Black. 334: The wife of one who has abjured the realm is suable as a feme sole Co. Litt. 132b.

Quare impedit by the *King* v. *Lady Maltravers*—whose husband was exiled. It [was] the case of *Lady Belknap*—whose husband was exiled.

Duchess of Mazarine's case, 1 Salk. 116.

Ringsted v. *Lady Lanesborough*, Hil. 23 Geo. III.

Corbett v. *Poelnitz*, in *Cooke's Bankrupty Laws* 36, 3rd ed., 1 T.R. 5.

Hatchett v. *Baddeley*, 2 [W.] Black. 1079.

Lean v. *Schutz*, Ibid. 1195.

Vide: 1 H. Black. 347, a case cited from the year books, [Y.B.] 47 Edw. III pl. 43 [*recte* 34] where an action of account was maintained by a feme covert plaintiff against defendant bankrupt of lands assigned for her separate maintenance.

Query if [there is] not a distinction between separations by act of law and by the agreement of the parties?

Can she be considered *partially* as a feme sole for all legacies and gifts to her, and the profits of any real estate she may acquire would belong to the husband?

Is it not against the policy of the marriage contract to allow the parties to dissolve it at pleasure?

Can she be permitted to sue alone?

Because husband not bound, [there is] no legal consequence that the wife is to be sued—e.g. elopement. Voluntary separation does not make a civil widowhood *Lean* v. [*Schutz*] 2 [W.] Black 1195.

Is it more than divorce *a mensa et thoro*?

---

[82] Lord Kenyon failed to mention that Mr Justice Yates had consulted all of his fellow common law judges about the case, and all had agreed with his ruling. See p. 223, n. 41, above.

[83] '"*In the right of another*" as the husband and wife in the right of his wife.'

[Introductory note to *Morton* v. *Lamb*

One of the decisions by Lord Mansfield that continues to be cited and studied in the twenty-first century is *Kingston* v. *Preston*.[84] In that case, Mansfield laid out a taxonomy of the types of covenants typically found in executory bilateral contracts. The black-letter principle that emerged, for which the case has come to stand, is that mutual promises intended to be performed concurrently are constructively conditional upon each other. This means that a party to such a contract who wishes to sue the other for non-performance must either have performed his own promise or must tender that performance.[85]

The *Kingston* v. *Preston* rule provoked another question—what had to be alleged by the plaintiff to show a tender of performance? This was the issue before the Court of King's Bench in *Morton* v. *Lamb*.[86] The plaintiff sued for non-delivery of corn that according to the contract was to be delivered to the plaintiff at a specified location one month from the time of sale. Consistent with the *Kingston* rule, the court held that the delivery of the corn and payment for it were to be concurrent acts, so that each party must aver either performance or an offer to perform before he could sue the other for non-performance. Chief Justice Kenyon said that, 'Speaking of conditions precedent and subsequent in other cases can only lead to confusion', and 'whether covenants be or be not independent of each other, must depend on the good sense of the case'.[87] The court held that, 'as the plaintiff has not averred that he was ready to pay for the corn, he cannot maintain this action against the defendant for not delivering it'.[88]

Among other authorities, counsel for the defendant (George Holroyd) cited *Kingston* v. *Preston*, but none of the judges referred to the case. Two years later, in *Glazebrook* v. *Woodrow*,[89] Mr Justice Grose remarked on the confusion in early cases on the dependency or independency of covenants and then observed that on this subject, 'the case of *Kingston* v. *Preston* was the first strong authority', and 'nothing indeed could exhibit the doctrine which ought to prevail in these instances in a stronger point of view than the circumstances of that case'.[90] This strong endorsement is explained by the fact that Mr Justice Grose, while at the bar, had been counsel for the successful plaintiff in *Kingston*.

Two years after *Glazebrook*, in *Rawson* v. *Johnson*,[91] the question of tendering or averring performance arose again, this time in a suit on a contract

---

[84] (1773) 2 Doug. at 689, quoted within the case of *Jones* v. *Barkley* (1781) 2 Doug. 684.

[85] For full discussion of *Kingston*, including previously unrecovered manuscript reports of the case, see J. Oldham, 'Detecting Non-Fiction: Sleuthing among Manuscript Case Reports for What was Really Said', in *Law Reporting in Britain*, Chantal Stebbings, ed. (1995), pp. 133–168. One of the manuscript sources is Mr Justice Ashhurst's Paper Book 17 from the Dampier MSS., transcribed in the first appendix to 'Detecting Non-Fiction'.

[86] (1797) 7 T.R. 125.

[87] Ibid., at 130.

[88] Ibid.

[89] (1799) 8 T.R. 366.

[90] Ibid., at 371.

[91] (1801) 1 East 203. See also p. 239, n. 8, below.

to deliver a certain quantity of malt at a specified place on request. The plaintiff in his declaration averred that he had made the request and was ready and willing to receive the malt, but he did not aver an actual tender of the price. Counsel for the defendant (George Holroyd again) claimed that the declaration was insufficient, citing *Kingston* v. *Preston*, among other cases. He pointed out that, 'the case of *Morton* v. *Lamb* only decided that a declaration without such an averment was bad: and Lawrence J. there said, that the plaintiff must either aver performance or a tender'.[92] Counsel for the plaintiff (Law and Lambe) argued that, 'the averment that the plaintiffs were ready to pay the defendant is sufficient; and distinguishes this from the case of *Morton* v. *Lamb*'.[93] They said that, 'A readiness to pay implies an ability as well as a willingness to do the act.'[94]

Chief Justice Kenyon in *Rawson* observed that 'in administering justice, we must not lose sight of common sense', and that 'to entitle them [the plaintiffs] to maintain their action that they should have gone through the useless ceremony of laying the money down in order to take it up again' would be 'repugnant to common sense'.[95] But he acknowledged a report that, 'in the case of *Morton* v. *Lamb* that I said that the plaintiff should have averred a performance or a readiness to perform his part of the contract; I do not doubt that I said so, and I think it was rightly said: and if so it would decide this case'.[96] That is, it would decide the case in favour of the defendant. But Kenyon moved sideways and upheld a jury verdict for the plaintiff on the principle that a jury verdict 'will cure a case defectively stated'.[97]

Mr Justice Grose remarked that, 'The doctrine in question was much discussed in the case of *Morton* v. *Lamb*; and we there held that where mutual acts are to be performed, the plaintiff, in order to maintain his action for the non-performance by the other party, must shew that he was ready to do whatever was required to be done by himself.'[98] But in *Morton*, he said, 'the court considered that an averment of a readiness to pay would have been sufficient as well as the actual tender', and he considered the circumstances before the court 'as tantamount to the tender of the money; for the plaintiffs say they were ready to pay for the malt, but the defendant refused to deliver it'.[99]

Lawrence was not comfortable relying on the principle that a verdict cures a faulty declaration, though he recognized that 'so much strictness in the manner of pleading a fact is not necessary after verdict as on demurrer'.[1] He chose, however, to support the declaration by other precedents that he identified, adding that the declaration 'is not impeached by the case of *Morton* v. *Lamb*'.[2]]

---

[92] Ibid., at 207. [93] Ibid., at 204. [94] Ibid., at 204–205.
[95] Ibid., at 208. [96] Ibid., at 209. [97] Ibid.
[98] Ibid.
[99] Ibid. Grose made no mention of either *Kingston* v. *Preston* or *Glazebrook* v. *Woodrow*.
[1] Ibid., at 210.
[2] Ibid., at 210–211.

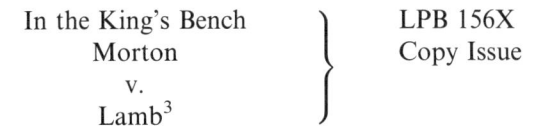

In the King's Bench } LPB 156X
    Morton   Copy Issue
      v.
    Lamb[3]

Motion in Arrest of Judgment, the 22nd Instant.
Judgment Arrested

[*Lawrence headnote*]: In a declaration for not delivering goods, the Plaintiff should state that he tendered the price, unless he shows that the Defendant was not at the appointed time at the place of delivery, unless the promise of the Plaintiff is laid to be the consideration of Defendant's promise.]

Foulkes and *Cooke*, Defendant's Attorneys
Hart Street, Bloomsbury
Mansfield and Way

Trinity Term in the thirty-sixth year of the reign of King George the Third Lancashire to wit: Be it remembered, that on Friday next after the morrow of the Holy Trinity in this same term, before our Lord the King at Westminster comes William Morton by *Richard Walter Paynter*, his attorney, and brings into the court of our said Lord the King before the King himself now here his certain bill against William Lamb, being in the custody of the Marshal of the Marshalsea of the Lord the now King before the King himself of a plea of trespass on the case, and there are pledges for the prosecution, to wit John Doe and Richard Roe, which said bill follows in these words (to wit) Lancashire, to wit, William Morton complains of William Lamb, being in the custody of the Marshal of the Marshalsea of our Sovereign Lord the now King before the King himself, for that whereas, on the tenth day of February in the year of our Lord one thousand seven hundred and ninety-six at Manchester in the County of Lancaster in consideration that the said William Morton at the special instance and request of the said William Lamb had then and there bought of the said William Lamb the corn and grain hereafter mentioned, that is to say, two hundred quarters of wheat at the price of one hundred shillings and sixpence per quarter, likewise one hundred quarters of barley at the price of forty-two shillings and sixpence per quarter, also one hundred quarters of oats, either Poland or what was termed small shorts, at the price of thirty shillings and fourpence per quarter, and also fifty quarters of beans at the price of forty-five shillings per quarter, such prices to be therefore paid by the said William Morton to the said William Lamb, he the said William Lamb undertook and then and there faithfully promised the said William Morton to deliver the said corn and grain to him the said William Morton at Shardlow in the County of Derby in one month from that time, that is to say from the time of such sale as

[3] (1797) 7 T.R. 125.

aforesaid. And the said William Morton in fact says that although he the said William Morton always from the time of making such sale for the space of one month then next following and afterwards was ready and willing to receive the said corn and grain at Shardlow aforesaid, yet the said William Lamb not regarding his said promise and undertaking so made as aforesaid but contriving and fraudulently intending craftily and subtly to deceive and defraud said William Morton in this behalf, did not in one month from the time of the making of such sale as aforesaid or at any other time deliver the said corn and grain or any part thereof to the said William Morton at Shardlow aforesaid or elsewhere, although he the said William Lamb hath been often requested so to do, to wit at Manchester aforesaid, but the said William Lamb to do this hath hitherto wholly refused and still doth refuse. And whereas also on the tenth day of February in the year aforesaid at Manchester aforesaid in the said County of Lancaster, in consideration that the said William Morton at the special instance and request of the said William Lamb had then and there bought of the said William Lamb other the corn and grain hereinafter mentioned, that is to say, two hundred quarters of other wheat at the price of one hundred shillings and sixpence per quarter, likewise one hundred quarters of other barley at the price of forty-two shillings and sixpence per quarter, and also one hundred quarters of other oats, either Poland or what was termed small shorts, at the price of thirty shillings and fourpence per quarter, such prices to be therefor paid by the said William Morton to the said William Lamb, he the said William Lamb undertook and then and there faithfully promised the said William Morton to deliver the said last mentioned corn and grain to him the said William Morton at Shardlow in the said County of Derby in one month from that time, that is to say, from the time of such sale as last aforesaid. And that the said William Morton in fact says that although he the said William Morton always from that time of the making of such last mentioned sale for the space of one month then next following and afterwards was ready and willing to receive the said last mentioned corn or grain at Shardlow aforesaid, yet the said William Lamb not regarding his said promise and undertaking so made as last aforesaid, but contriving and fraudulently intending craftily and subtly to deceive and defraud the said William Morton in this behalf, did not in one month from the time of making of such sale as last aforesaid, or at any other time, deliver the said last mentioned corn and grain, or any part thereof, to the said William Morton at Shardlow aforesaid or elsewhere, although he the said William Lamb hath been often requested so to do, to wit at Manchester aforesaid, but the said William Lamb to do this hath hitherto wholly refused and still doth refuse. And whereas also the said tenth day of February in the year aforesaid at Manchester aforesaid in the said county of Lancaster in consideration that the said William Morton at the special instance and request of the said William Lamb had then and there bought of the said William Lamb fifty quarters of other beans at the price of forty-five shillings per quarter, to be therefor paid by the said William Morton to the said William Lamb, he the said William Lamb undertook and then and there faithfully promised the said William Morton to deliver the last mentioned beans to him the said William Morton at Shardlow in the said County of Derby in one month from that time, that is to say from the time of such sale as last aforesaid. And the said William Morton in fact says that although he the said William Morton always from the time of the making of such sale as last aforesaid for the said space of one month then next following and afterwards was ready and willing to receive the said beans at Shardlow aforesaid, yet the said William Lamb not regarding his said promise and undertaking so made as last aforesaid but the continuing and fraudulent intending craftily and subtly to deceive and defraud the said William Morton in this behalf, did not within one month from the time of the making of such sale as last aforesaid or at any other time deliver the said beans or any part thereof to the said William Morton at Shardlow aforesaid or elsewhere (although he the said William Lamb hath been often requested so to do to wit at Manchester aforesaid). But he the said William Lamb to do this hath hitherto wholly refused and still doth refuse, to the damage of the said William Morton of five hundred pounds and therefore he brings his suit, &c.

Plea: And the said William Lamb by *Edward Foulkes* his attorney comes and defends the wrong and injury when &c. and says he did not undertake and promise in manner and form as the said William Morton hath above thereof complained against him. And of this he puts himself upon the country and the said William Morton doth the like, &c. Therefore &c.

[*Lawrence's Notes of Argument, 1 February 1797*]

On a motion to warrant the judgment in this case made by *Holroyd* which came on February 1st 1797, because it was not stated that the plaintiff had tendered to the defendant the price of the corn:

Law, *Wood*, and *Scarlett* insisted that it was not necessary, *Law* arguing that the substance of the agreement was that of mutual promises, and that the defendant had his remedy against the plaintiff for non-performance of his promise if he did not pay the money. And he [*Law*] alluded to cases of *Thorpe* v. *Thorpe*, Salk. 171, 1 [Wms.] Saund. 319, 1 Vent. 177, 214, Lutwyche 249–51, 496, 565, Str. 712, 535, [Wms.] Saund. 352.[4] *Wood* insisted that there was no grounds to arrest the judgment unless the payment of the money was a condition precedent. That the first act was to be done by the defendant (*ss.*) to deliver the corn. He admitted that the plaintiff was not entitled to the corn without paying, and that the not sending the money might be a good excuse for the plaintiff's not delivering, but if this were so, it ought to come on the part of the defendant as an excuse, and was not necessary to be alleged by the plaintiff.

Scarlett observed that the contract was executory, and that the rule which

---

[4] Respectively, *Thorpe* v. *Thorpe* (1701) 1 Salk. 171; *Pordage* v. *Cole* (1668) 1 Wms. Saund. 319; *Peters* v. *Opie* (1671–1672) 1 Vent. 177, 214; *Thorpe* v. *Thorpe* (1702) 1 Lut. 245; *Hilton* v. *Smith* (1704) 1 Lut. 493; *Chaloner* v. *Davis* (1704) 1 Lut. 565; *Dawson* v. *Myer* (1726) 2 Str. 712; *Blackwell* v. *Nash* (1722) 1 Str. 535; *Peeters* [sic] v. *Opie* (1648) 2 Wms. Saund. 350.

required payment on the delivery of goods sold did not apply to a case where a certain time was fixed for the delivery, as here (*ss.* a month). That this was not a mere contract of bargain and sale, but that the goods were to be carried to Shardlow. That if the delivery and payment were concurrent acts, that there was no ground to say a tender and refusal was necessary, as that admitted there was no precedency in point of time which made it necessary to allege the doing or tender of the thing as a condition precedent.

He relied on *Merrit v. Rane*, 1 Str. 458, to show that the tender should come on the defendant's part as an excuse. That according to *Ughtred's Case*, 7 Coke,[5] the plaintiff could not be called on to allege that which was an excuse for the Defendant.

Mr *Holroyd, contra*:

[He] observed that the action was not brought for not carrying the corn to Shardlow, but for not delivering it, to enable the plaintiff, to which the payment or tender and refusal of the money was necessary, which though not a condition precedent was a concurrent circumstance.

That the rule was laid down in *Goodisson v. Nunn*[6] that in cases of dependent covenants such as this, one party can't maintain an action unless he has done or offered to do all on his part. That if the charge against the defendant had been not carrying the corn to Shardlow, a tender need not have been alleged, but in an action for not delivering it a tender, &c. must be alleged, as that was a part of the plaintiff's title and not an excuse for the defendant. He cited *Callonel v. Briggs*, 1 Salk. 113, as decisive in his favour, and that was the case of an executory contract. And he mentioned *Lancashire v. Killingsworth* in Salk. 623 as establishing this principle, that the plaintiff should have gone so far as to aver that he was at the place, ready to receive on the last day of the time within which the corn was to be delivered, and that he offered the price.

Lord KENYON said he did not pretend to be much used to the niceties of pleading, but that on the true construction of the agreement, there could be no doubt but that payment should be made at the time of delivery. That on this declaration, the corn must be taken to be at Shardlow, the defendant complaining of the non-delivery. That it did not appear to him that the plaintiff had disclosed anything which entitled him to come into a court of justice, for if the acts were concurrent, the plaintiff should show he had been ready to [do] all on his side.

GROSE J. was of the same opinion.

LAWRENCE J: [He] observed that in this case no mutual promises were laid, and therefore this was not the case supposed by *Law*, but that it seemed to him to be like the case of *Callonel v. Briggs*. That it being admitted the payment was to be made at the same time, that *Callonel* was an authority to show that the plaintiff should aver a tender, and prove it.

That the case which seemed strongest for the defendant was that of *Merrit v. Rane*, 1 Str. 358. But that he did not understand what the court meant by

[5] *Ughtred's Case* (1591) 7 Co. Rep. 9b.
[6] *Goodisson v. Nunn* (1792) 4 T.R. 761.

saying that a tender need not be alleged but should have come on the defendant's part, for as plaintiff had alleged there that his agent was ready to receive a transfer of the stock, but that the defendant never attended, it would have been absurd to say that the agent had made a tender, when it appeared that there was no person to whom the tender could be made. He then referred to *Lea* v. *Exelby*, Cro. Eliz. 888 as an authority to show that the plaintiff should have stated a tender and refusal, and as making the distinction between delivering on mutual *assumpsit* and on a promise such as this, to which he conceived this case was very like. For these reasons the court arrested the judgment.

> [*Lawrence note*]: *N.B.* The case of *Merrit* v. *Rane* points out (*ut semble*) the proper mode of declaring, which the plaintiff might have pursued by stating that the defendant appointed no time for the delivery and that the plaintiff attended on the last day in order to receive the said corn and was ready to pay for the same and to receive it, but the defendant did not attend to deliver it, which if he had done, on the authority of that case (if authority was wanting) no tender need have been stated. But upon this declaration, there is nothing stated from whence it can be inferred that the defendant was not at Shardlow, or that any other reason existed by which the defendant had put it out of the plaintiff's power to make a tender, and that he could not receive without a tender being made (and if that be so, there can be no doubt but it must be stated as part of his title). [It] follows not only from the cases cited but from *Noy's Maxims* 88,[7] who lays it down that on a sale of a horse for money, the vendor may keep him until he is paid, but if the vendee tender the money and the vendor refuse, he may have a detinue; plainly implying that without tender, detinue will not lie, and if detinue would not lie, an action to recover damages for not delivering will not.

[*Lawrence's Separate Research Notes*]

Rawson v. *Johnson*.[8] *Assumpsit* in consideration that the plaintiff had agreed to purchase one hundred quarters of malt of defendant and to find sacks. Defendant promised to deliver them at Kiddermarsh. Breach, non-delivery. Objected by *Holroyd* in arrest of judgment that there was no allegation by the plaintiff that he was prepared with or had tendered the money.

Turner v. *Goodwyn*, Fortescue 145. Action on a bond conditioned for payment of 1500, Plaintiff assigning a judgment. Defendant pleaded that plaintiff had not assigned the judgment. Plaintiff replies he was ready and

---

[7] W. Noy, *The Grounds and Maxims, and also An Analysis of the English Laws*, 6th ed. (1794) 88.

[8] (1801) 1 East 203. This separate paper of notes must have been prepared during or after the hearing on 31 January 1801 on the motion in arrest of judgment in *Rawson*, and retained by Lawrence in his Paper Book for *Morton* v. *Lamb* (decided on 1 February 1797). In East's report of *Rawson*, Lawrence begins his opinion by stating that, 'The rule in this case was moved for on the authority of *Morton* v. *Lamb*.'

[filed] demurrer. PARKER, C.J.: The assignment shall neither wait nor precede the payment but accompany it, and both [are] to be done at the same time. The defendant ought to find out the plaintiff and tender him the money, and at the same time demand an assignment, and then if plaintiff refuse, defendant will be excused.

Plowden 180, *Norwood v. Norwood and Reed, Executors of Gray*. The declaration states the agreement with Gray to delivery sixty quarters of wheat at Ramsgate at certain times for £33, to be paid as follows (*ss.*) £16:13:4 immediately after the delivery of the first parcel, and £16:13:4 immediately after the delivery of the residue. It then assigned a breach in not delivering any part of the wheat (although he was often requested and although the plaintiff at the several times afterwards was ready at Ramsgate to have received the same, and to pay the several sums of money which he ought to pay immediately after the several receipts of the wheat in form aforesaid).

Herne 131.[9] Declaration on agreement to deliver barley to be paid for on delivery. Breach in non-delivery. Although plaintiff always was ready upon delivery of the said barley to pay to defendant the aforesaid £20, that is to say eight shillings for every [. . .] according to his promise, &c.

Clift 97.[10] Particular declaration for non-delivery of barley—*licet semper paratus ad hordeum recipiendum et ad denarios predictos per eodem hordeo solubiles ei solvendi.*[11] But there are in this book other precedents without such allegation (*ss.*) 91, for not delivering tallow; 92, for not delivering lupines; 93, for not delivering ox hides.

Lea v. Exelby, Cro. Eliz. 888. *Assumpsit*. Whereas the defendant was possessed of such a lease for grass, the inheritance being in the plaintiff, in consideration the plaintiff promised to pay him such a sum of money [at] such a day and place. That defendant promised *super solutionem inde* to surrender unto him his lease and alleged that he at the day and place tendered the money and the defendant had not surrendered the lease. [After] a *non-assumpsit* verdict for the plaintiff, [there was] a motion in arrest of judgment that the defendant was not to surrender but upon payment of the money or an express tender and refusal, and the plaintiff hath alleged here *quod oblatit*, but he says not that the defendant refused, which is material and issuable, and he might have taken issue on the refusal, if it had been alleged, as *Coke*, Attorney-General, moved that this declaration was good, and that there needed not any tender and refusal to be alleged, for it suffices to allege that in consideration he assumed to pay such a sum, the defendant assumed to surrender, so there being *assumpsit* against *assumpsit*, it is well enough.

---

[9] J. Herne, *The Pleader* (1657).

[10] H. Clift, *A New Book of Declarations, Pleadings, Judgments and Judicial Writs with the Entries thereupon* (1703). In translation, the case referred to states: 'And notwithstanding the same Edward Draper, after the aforesaid promise and undertaking had been made, up until the same festival day had often in that place been prepared to receive the aforesaid barley from the aforesaid Edward Wilson and to pay the aforesaid money for the same barley.'

[11] 'Notwithstanding always having been prepared to receive and pay for the barley.'

But all the court held [was] that if the promise had been in consideration [that] he assumed to pay such a sum, that the defendant had assumed to surrender, that had been sufficient. But here it is that he assumed to pay, and the other assumed to surrender upon payment, so that he would not trust to his promise, but when he had paid, he could surrender it. And in the first case he needed not allege the performance of the promise. But here in this he ought, and when he says that *oblatit* and says not that the other accepted it or refused it, his allegation of the tender is not to any purpose, for he shall never say *quod oblatit* only, but he ought to plead that none was there to receive it, or that he refused it.

Try the case before the court by this. It is not a case of mutual promises. But where the payment was to be concomitant with the delivery, [it] shall neither precede nor wait for it. Had then the plaintiff any cause of action if not ready to pay? If not, that readiness was a part of his case. According to HOLT in *Lancashire* v. *Killingsworth*, a man is required to do all he can to enable himself to an action, and in conformity to this principle is *Lea* v. *Exelby*.

Lancashire v. *Killingsworth* and *Callonel* v. *Briggs*—where the action being on an agreement to pay so much money, the plaintiff transferring stock, HOLT ruled, if either party would sue on this agreement, the plaintiff for not paying or defendant for not transferring, the one must aver and prove a transfer or a tender, and the other a payment or a tender.

Clearly [it was] necessary to aver a tender of what is the consideration of the money in an action for the money; why not equally so state a tender of the money, or a readiness and no one to receive [it], where the action is brought for the thing?

Merrit v. *Rane* in Strange is *contra*, and affirmed both in *Cam. Scacc.* and in *Dom. Proc.*, [though] not in *Brown's Parliamentary Cases*. It is there said that the 'not showing the tender should be by the Defendant by way of excuse, that he was there ready to have transferred if the Plaintiff or anybody for him had been there to have paid the money'.

When cited in *Morton* v. *Lamb*, I misapprehended the case. It struck me as an absurd mode of pleading for the defendant to state that he had tendered and that no person was there to whom a tender could be made. But on looking into the book, I find that what is pointed out is this, that the defendant should by way of excuse have shown he was there, but no one on plaintiff's part to pay; and consequently that the plaintiff had not done his part either by paying or tendering. So that this case has decided that a readiness to pay the money is not a necessary part of the plaintiff's case to be shown by him, though it is so essential a part as to furnish a defence, if alleged by the defendant.

Between these conflicting authorities we must decide.

It is said that no issue can be taken on the readiness to pay. But this does not show it is not to be alleged. It is necessary in a plea of tender, though no issue can be taken on it, for if plaintiff would show defendant not ready, plaintiff must reply a special request to show [that] the defendant [was] not always ready. Salk. 623.

[*Lawrence's Notes, on the face of the caption page*]

Thorpe v. *Thorpe*, Salk. 171. *Pordage* v. *Cole*, 1 Saund. 319, day fixed for the money. 1 Vent. 177, 214.
Lutwyche 249–251.
496. 565.
Doc. Plac. 30ab.
Str. 712, 535. Saund. 352.
Kingston v. *Preston*.[12]
Campbell v. *Jones*, Hil. 36 [Geo. III].[13] Whether mutual covenants are conditions precedent depends on common sense of the case. No mutual promises [were] laid [for] paying and transferring in this case. Question then if Plaintiff must not show his title to recover.

[See] case in Strange.[14]

If I sell my horse for money, I may keep him until I am paid, but I can ____ [*sic*]. But if he (*ss.* the buyer) do personally tender me my money, and I do refuse it, he may take the horse or have an action of detainment. Noy 88.[15] If a man promises to surrender land on payment of so much money, in *assumpsit* the Plaintiff ought to allege payment or tender and refusal. *Lea* v. *Exelby*, Cro. Eliz. 888.

Clift. 91–2–3–9.[16] No tender or readiness to pay the money stated, but in these, the consideration of defendant's promise is [. . .] plaintiff is to pay the money. *Ibid.* 97 *Licet ad denarius solvendus solubiles pro eodem hordeo*[17] *hucusque paratus fuit*.[18] *Vide*: In Cro. Eliz. 888 [there is] a distinction where the *assumpsit* of plaintiff is laid as to consideration, and where the payment [is].

If a man be bound at any time during his life to pay £20 at a place certain, the obligor can't tender the money when he will at the place, for then the obligor would be bound to perpetual attendance, and therefore the obligor in respect to the uncertainty of the time must give the obligee notice that at such a time at the place limited, he will pay the money and that the obligee must attend to receive it. Co. Litt. 211a.

[*Callonel* v. *Briggs*:] The agreement was that the defendant should pay so much, six months after the bargain, the plaintiff transferring stock. The plaintiff gave a note at the same time to transfer the stock, the defendant paying, &c. And *per* HOLT, if either party would sue on this agreement, the plaintiff for not paying, or the defendant for not transferring, the one must aver and prove a transfer or tender, and the other a payment or tender, for transferring in the first bargain was a condition precedent, and though there

---

[12] (1773) 2 Doug. 689, quoted within the case of *Jones* v. *Barkley* (1781) 2 Doug. 684.
[13] *Campbell* v. *Jones* (1796) 6 T.R. 570.
[14] *Merrit* v. *Rane* (1721) 1 Str. 458.
[15] Reference unclear. None of the three cases at Noy 88 seems relevant.
[16] H. Clift, *A New Book of Declarations, Pleadings, Judgments and Judicial Writs with the Entries thereupon* (1703), case nos. 73, 74, 75, and 81, at pp. 91, 92, 93, and 99, respectively.
[17] Lawrence's handwriting is unclear, but *hordeo* seems to have been intended.
[18] Lawrence paraphrases the quotation from Clift. A translation is, 'Although always having been ready to receive the barley and to pay him the money payable for the same barley.'

be mutual promises, yet if one thing be the consideration of the other, there a performance is necessary to be averred unless a certain day be appointed for performance. If I sell you my horse for 10, if you will have the horse I must have the money, or if I will have the money you must have the horse. *Callonel v. Briggs*, 1 Salk. 112.

King's Bench } LPB 85b
Brooke and another, Assignees, &c.
v.
Crowther[19] } Demurrer

To Be Argued on Tuesday, 9 June

[*Lawrence headnote*:] Bond conditioned for performance of covenant not to exercise the business of factoring wool in England, but to forward the interest of A. B. by recommending to him all his customers and not promote any other person in the business.

Query if bond not void, as being in restraint of trade?
Second: if the assignees of obligee, a bankrupt, can sue on this bond.

10 November, '95 *Ult. Concilium*

Sykes, New Inn

[*Lawrence's Notes of Arguments of Counsel*]

June 9, 1795
Holroyd for Defendants:
First objection: this bond [is] to perform covenants, not to pay money.
That, therefore, the action does not lie by the assignees but should have been brought by the bankrupt himself because there may be breaches subsequent to the bankruptcy.
Second: that the two covenants are in restraint of trade.
Third: to the second objection not having stated the particular customers not recommended, as we can't meet them.
Fourth: in not stating to whom he recommended the other persons, and how he promoted them.
As to the first point, [see] *Holt v. Scarisbrig*,[20] 2 Keb. 372, referred to by Comyns, *Bankruptcy*, E 29.

---

[19] Unreported. Brooke was the assignee of Denton, a bankrupt, who had been originally named in the bond.

[20] [*Lawrence footnote*:] 'This was an action to be discharged on a commission of bankruptcy, plaintiff having been bankrupt in regard [to] all debts assigned. Kelyng C.J. [said] the bankrupt may have trespass or covenant when damages are uncertain, which is agreed, but any debt certain is assignable.'

1 Ch. Cas. 71.[21]

3 Wils. 270, *Goddard* v. *Vanderheyden*, what De GREY says:[22]

Lord KENYON: Cases in Atkins, *ex parte Winchester*[23] and *ex parte Groome*[24] touch upon that as a forfeiture of the bond.

Tuesday, November 10, 1795

Holroyd for Defendant:

First objection, that the assignees can't sue, for they cannot sue for uncertain damages. I will hereafter consider if the penalty makes a difference. The Statute of Elizabeth [and] James I do not empower assignment of uncertain damages.

2 Keb. 372.

1 Ch. Cas. 71.

Question then what difference, as a penalty. Suppose a covenant [is] broken after the bankrupt's certificate. By Statute of Will. III he could not have *scire facias* as he was not the plaintiff. They could not, and therefore there would be no remedy.

Suppose a bankrupt [is] bound in a penalty and [there is] a breach by him, could the penalty be proved under the commission?[25]

Suppose a bond for good behaviour—would that go to the assignees?

Lord KENYON: Suppose a lease with a covenant for rent, would not the bankrupt be liable for subsequent rent, so that though the thing be assigned, he would be still liable?

Holroyd: But if [it is] a bond for payment of rent, that would not be assignable. If the covenant itself would pass, the bond might be sued upon by

---

[21] [*Lawrence footnote*:] '*Drake* v. *Mayor of Exon*, 1 Ch. Cas. 71, held that the assignee of a bankrupt should not have the benefit of a covenant to renew a lease. But by 5 G. 2. c. 30. sec. 1, a bankrupt is required to discover all such effects wherein he was interested, or which he hath, or may expect any profit, possibility of profit, benefit, or advantage whatsoever. A contingency in trust in a bankrupt is assignable by the commissioners. *Hodges* v. *Williamson*, 3 P.Wms. 132.' (Pere Williams reported the case as *Higden* v. *Williamson*.)

[22] [*Lawrence footnote*:] 'Cases put by De Grey, C.J.: A has a bond of indemnity from B and the condition terms [are] broken, and afterwards, B becomes a bankrupt before A has been sued or damnified. Though A had a good cause of action against B before the bankruptcy, yet as A had not been damnified by paying any certain sums of money, A can't swear to any debt owing from B at the time of the bankruptcy. Suppose a lessee ploughs up meadowland, for which he is bound to pay a certain sum as a penalty, can that penalty be proved as a debt under the commission of bankruptcy? It certainly cannot. But it does not follow that because it can't be proved, that therefore it is not assignable. 7 G. 1. c. 31 respects debts payable at a future day.

Ex parte Winchester 1 Atk. 116. Bond conditioned to pay £1,000 after the death of the obligor Grant and his wife, and interest at 4 percent. The obligor became a bankrupt and having omitted to pay the interest at the day, Lord Hardwicke directed the commissioners to suffer the bond to be proved.

But where the bankrupt had bound his lessee to pay £400 within two months after his death if M. L. should survive him, the court held this could not be proved, it being uncertain whether the bond would ever be due. *Tully* v. *Sparkes*, 2 Ld. Ray. 1546. *Perkins* v. *Kempland*, 2 Bl. W. 1106. *Wyllie* v. *Wilkes*, [2] Doug. 501 [519]—settled if an annuity bond [was] forfeited by non-payment at the day, though the annuities are afterwards paid, that it might be proved under a commission.'

[23] 1 Atk. 116.

[24] 1 Atk. 115.

[25] [*Lawrence observation*:] 'This difficulty arises from the difficulty of swearing to the debt.'

the intervention of a court of equity. But here the covenant is not assignable to the assignees. The covenant is not a debt in this case.

In the case of a bond to secure rent, the covenant is the real debt and not the penalty of the bond.

In cases of the Statute of Setoff, the penalty is never the debt.[26]

As to the second point:

Covenants on which first and third breaches are assigned are in restraint of trade. *Mitchel* v. *Reynold*, 1 P. Wms. 181. Aleyn 67, *Prugnell* v. *Gosse*. The bankrupt was to carry on trade at Wakefield. This [was] no sufficient consideration for not carrying on his trade anywhere else. Nor is it confined to the time of the bankrupt's carrying on the business, so that if he died or left off, defendant could not carry on the trade. Therefore too general.

As to the third point:

Not naming the customers to whom the bankrupt should have been recommended, he must know these, otherwise we must bring all our customers. *Jansen* v. *Stewart*, 1 T.R. 747.[26a] Libel, charging defendant with acts of fraud. The plea, that he was guilty of diverse acts, held too general—as defendant would be obliged to prove all his own life.

This case of a replication, which requires certainty, to a certain intent, in particular.

This objection holds to the third and last breach.

Mr *Wood* for the Plaintiff:

As to the first objection, that the assignees can't maintain this action, this [is] not an action for uncertain damages, but for a penalty, which at law was a *debt* vested in the bankrupt. The Statute of Elizabeth authorizes the assignment of all *debts*.

The only question then is if this be a debt.

So in the case of 2 Keb. 372, wherever the penalty is forfeited, the debt may be proved, as in the case of annuities—and yet the continuance of the annuity is uncertain. But a value may be put on the annuity.

The argument from the Statute of Setoff does not apply because the Statute of Setoff requires that the penalty shall not be set off.

As to the second objection of this being in restraint of trade, [see] 5 T.R. 118, *Davis* v. *Mason*, a bond not to practise for fourteen years within ten miles of Thetford. The court held that whether it was a reasonable distance was for the jury.

The consideration here is £500 for the defendant's trade.[27] The covenant here, it is to be observed, is an *affirmative* covenant.

Defendant has taken upon himself to prove he recommended *all*. [It is]

---

[26] [*Lawrence observation*:] 'That is so in cases of bonds to pay annuities, &c., and yet they are proved.'

[26a] The correct citation is *J'Anson* v. *Stuart* (1787) 1 T.R. 748.

[27] [*Lawrence observation*:] 'If the law is against the covenant restraining defendant from carrying on his trade, it is at least good so far as [it] restrains him from recommending any other person. As to the time, looking at the context, it is to be understood as confined to the time he carried on the trade.'

sufficient to assign a breach of covenant in the words of the covenant, and [there is] no distinction between an action on the bond and on the covenant.

Holroyd in Reply:

The argument from the case of annuity does not apply, as there is a debt on non-payment of an instalment.

Here, the condition is not to secure sums of money.[28] The case in Douglas as to embezzling money [is] in point as to the not stating the customers. *Jones* v. *Williams*, Doug. 203.

Lord KENYON: If the plaintiff thinks it worth his while to pursue this action, it must be argued again. Mr *Holroyd*'s argument has created considerable difficulty.

Ult. Concilium

[*Lawrence note*:] *Chambré* on Friday, February 4 informed the court that the plaintiff has taken the advice of the court.[29]

[*Lawrence's Draft Opinion*[30]]

The covenant in this case is that the defendant will not exercise or employ himself or any other on his own account or benefit, or for the benefit of any other person in factoring wool in that part of Great Britain called England, but [will] forward the interest of Denton in the said business by recommending him to all and every, the customers of the defendant. And that he would not directly or indirectly recommend or promote any other person in such employment.

Breaches:

1st, that before Denton's bankruptcy, defendant did exercise and employ himself and others on his account in the business of factoring wool.

2nd, that he did not forward the interest of Denton by recommending to all and every, his customers.

3rd, that he did recommend and promote other persons than Denton (*ss.*) John Barker and Peter Richardson in such employment and business.

Demurrer:

To the first breach, general.

To the second, special, for not specifying the names of the customers who were not recommended.

To the third, special, because the covenant is in restraint of trade, because the assignees can maintain no action on the bond, and for not stating the

---

[28] [*Lawrence observation*:] 'As to the answer to this covenant being in restraint of trade, the case in 5 Term Reports does not impeach that case. As to the last breach, that is in restraint of trade as well as the first, for it prevents him from assisting others. He can't act as a servant or become partner with any other. The covenant in its terms is general, and it can't be made good by the mode of assigning the breach.'

[29] Thus the case was discontinued.

[30] Apparently before receiving word that the plaintiff would not continue the case, Lawrence prepared this draft opinion.

persons to whom Barker and Richardson were recommended, or how recommended.

The objection that the assignees cannot maintain the action applies to all the breaches.

That this is an illegal bond, as being in restraint of trade, to the first and third breaches. To the second and third besides the general objections, there is one of form.

If the objection from the bond being in restraint of trade and the formal one to the second and third breaches hold, it is not necessary to decide anything as to the general question whether this action can be maintained by the assignees. But it seems to me that this question is to be decided, as it would have been anterior to the statute of the 8th and 9th William III, which, being intended to prevent defendants being drawn into equity, could not have been meant to deprive the assignees of a bankrupt of any benefit they were entitled to from his estate.[31]

Anterior to the statute by any breach of the conditions, the whole penalty of the bond became a debt at law, and passed to the assignees, subject to have their execution restrained by the Chancery, to the amount of the real damages the bankrupt had sustained. And as the law then stood, possibly they, as trustees for him, might have been permitted to levy on account of subsequent breaches. Whether the Statute of William has deprived the obligee of having that done now it is not necessary to decide, but if he can't assign future damages (if his assignees have the benefit of the bond) it seems to me that he should have the advantage, and not they.

But however this point may be, and taking it for granted that it [is] with the plaintiff, I think on the ground of the other objections the plaintiff cannot recover. And it seemed to me in the course of the first argument to be hardly denied by Mr *Wood*, yet the objection of the bond being in restraint of trade was a good one, for he, on the authority of *Davis* v. *Mason*, 5 T.R. 118, contended that whether the restraint was reasonable or not, should go to a jury.

Supposing it to be so in a case where the restraint was for a certain, definite number of miles. I cannot agree that it is so where the restraint is, as here, throughout all England. That such bond is void, then, is the express opinion of Roll in Aleyn 67, and Lord MACCLESFIELD in Pere Williams.

This then reduces the question to the formal objection to the second and third breach, as to which it is said that it is sufficient to assign the breach in the words of the covenant, and Mr *Wood* said that there is no distinction between

---

[31] As explained by A. W. B. Simspon, the statute, 8 and 9 Will. III, c. 11, allowed 'a plaintiff who sued for a penalty due on a conditioned bond for the performance of covenants to assign as many breaches as he wished', leaving it to the jury to assess the actual damages caused by each breach. Then, 'Judgment would be entered for the whole penalty, but the plaintiffs could only recover for the damages assessed.' A. W. B. Simpson, *A History of the Common Law of Contract* (1975), p. 122. Thus, since only actual damages could be recovered, there was no occasion to go to Chancery for relief from the penal effect that would be created if the face amount of the bond had been assessed.

an action on the bond and of covenant. But that is not so. For there is a distinction between assigning a breach in an action of covenant in the declaration and in a replication to a plea of performance. In the first, it is sufficient to assign the breach according to the covenant. *Aliter* as to the latter.

Syms v. *Smith*, Cro. Car. 176.
Farrow v. *Chevalier*, Salk. 139.
Brigstock v. *Stanion*, Lord Raym. 106.

But further as to the formal objection to the third breach, it seems to me not to be alleged with such certainty as to enable the defendant to meet the plaintiff's case, for Barker and Richardson might not know of their recommendation, and might not be able to disprove that charge, which those to whom it might be said they were recommended would do, or if not true, had their names been stated. The defendant could not have been surprised, and if no particular recommendation, then the mode of recommendation should have been stated.

Jones v. *Williams*, Doug. 203.

Michaelmas Term 1797 LPB 271
Roe *ex dim.* Southall and others
v.
Langford and others[32]

[*Lawrence headnote*]: For the construction of a most unintelligible will of a most illiterate person. Tenancy in common [was] never intended without words to prevent a joint tenancy. Question how far words may be supplied to make a will sensible?

For Defendant
Special Case
To be argued on Friday, the 24th November 1797
Judgment for Plaintiff
The Honourable Mr Justice Lawrence

Neeld and *Aspinall*

Roe on the several Demises of William Southall the younger, Michael Lea, and William Southall the elder [plaintiff]
and
Thomas Langford, John Kynaston, Joseph Clarke, Thomas Harris, Hannah Haines, Thomas Roberts, Richard Jamson and Mary Robeson tenants, and Thomas Southall, Edward Liggins and Elizabeth his wife, and Joseph Southall and Mary his wife landlords [defendants]

[32] Unreported.

Brief for Defendants

Worcestershire (to wit) declaration states 1st that William Southall the younger on the 9th June 1797 demised to let 87 messuages, 87 cottages, 10 barns, 10 stables, 10 orchards, and 20 acres of land with the appurtenances in the parishes of Saint Peter and Saint Andrew Droitwich and Salwarp in the county of Worcester. To hold from 8th said June for ten years and that defendant rejected them.

2nd. Count—On the demise of Michael Lea same date and term and ejectment.

3rd. Count—On the demise of William Southall the elder same date and term and ejectment.

That defendants pleaded the general issue and defended for the undivided 5th parts of the premises, *viz*[t], Thomas Langford, John Kynaston, Joseph Clarke, Thomas Harris, Hannah Haines, Thomas Roberts, Richard Jamson, and Henry Robeson, as tenants of the said 4/5th and also Thomas Southall as landlord of one undivided 5th part of the premises, Edward Liggins and Elizabeth his wife as landlords of another undivided fifth part, and Joseph Southall and Mary his wife as landlords of another undivided fifth part. The cause came on to be heard at the summer assizes 1797 at Worcester before Mr Baron PERRYN when by consent a verdict was found for plaintiff subject to the opinion of the court on the following case.

That Francis Southall late of Droitwich aforesaid being seized in fee of the premises in question and also possessed of divers leasehold houses and cottages for the remainder of different long terms of years on or about the 14th December 1775, made his will of this case written with his own hand duly created and attested in the presence of three subscribing witnesses as follows:

> In the nam of God Amen. I Francis Southall in the parish of Saint Peters in the Bourro of Droitwich in the Counttie of Worcester do mack and ordaine this my last will and testement in maner and faurm followin. Itam, I give and beqeth to Willeam Southall son of my Brouther William Southall five pounds and his wife's ringe and no mor. Itam, I give and beqeth to Franses Southall son of my Brouther Willem Southall five pounds and no mor. Itam, I give and beqeth to Ann Dotter of my Brouther Willeam Southall five pounds and no mor. Itam, I give and beqeth to Henrey Bowin son of my sister Ann Bowin five pounds and no mor. Itam, I give to Marrey Harrison Dotter of my sister Ann Bowin five pounds and no mor. Itam, I give and beqeth to Willem Pardoe son of my sistter Sarra Pardoe five pounds and no mor. Itam, I give and beqeth to John Pardoe son of my sistter Sarra Pardoe five pounds and no more. Itam, I give and give to my neves John and Edward and Charles Southall on gine each and no more. Itam, I give and beqeth to my nies Marre Pridey wife of Routan Pridey on gine and no more. Itam, I give to Bengamin Pridey senor my carpenter on gine and no more. Itam, I give and beqeth to Willeam Willams sene my masune on gine and no more. Itam, I give and beqeth to Bengamon Green my hold gardiner on gine and no more. Itam, I give and beqeth to Francis Nightinner my Barber on gine and no more. And thos legeses to be payd to them 6 muntes hafter my deses if ples god thay may live so long to nesev itt, otherways, Exsecttrifts shall have it to herself. Itam, I

give and beqeth to my nevey and nies Horther Harrison and and [sic] his wife five pounds eche to be paid them att my deses. So by the. And if any purson or pursons should go to lawe or couse any lawe or put forward any lawe or cous any lawe for any thing I diyd posses with exepin my Legesis should not be paid by the time above mentioned my Exsectiriicks hearhafter mentioned to giet in the Deps that was dow to me at my deses that purson or pursons that proseds and further in lowe shall have thay nor thare children no claim nor titel nor intrust to hany thing I diyd posest with, not so long as watter runs nor timber grows hall. The rest of my effects that I diye posest with I give to my nies Ann Pardoe hom I mack my hol and sol Exsectitriets and for she to pay my Jsht Deps and my Legices and my Funeral gharges, and hall the rest of my afects as I diyd posest with I leve to my nies Ann Pardoe Dotter of my Sister Sarra Pardoe provided she never sels nor morgishe nor sels aney part or parsill that I have left her if she dos, then the Baylle or aney of his Magiste Justis of the pes shall tack that part she sels or morgiges of her and givit to the nearist and porist relashon of my siyd and for his trubel the purson he puts in the premises shall give him a giney and so for every such trubel shall have a giney payd him moreover she shall not let nor sel aney part or parsel of land or hous to aney of her Brother or Sistter nor Brother nor Sisters children if she dus then by the [...] of my will any of his Magisty Justittis of the peas shall tack it of her and givit to anuther has above mentioned and if the parson ho itt is given to should morgish or sell itt then itt shall be tacken of them in the maner as above mentioned and so to continu in the Famelle has long has the world indowers thar shal not be no Intayl be cutt off nor morgig nor sell nor tack any monis a ponit aney of wat I diyd posest, if they do then the nearist and porist and nerist Relation of my siyd thoe ever so long standin na even the child that is un bourn if he can prove the nearest relashon to me put in by thos that have sold it he shall havit and turn them out that bout it in the sam maner as above mentioned and watt I have left my nies Ann Pardoe she shall cip the houses in tenantabel repar and reseve the Rents of them drorine her natteral and then go to her children shar and shar a liyck but if she shold have but one then that shall havit and go in that liyn in the sam maner as I have left it still as long as thar is on left of the Brangh or Liyn and if my nies Ann Pardoe should diye without child or childdren then itt shall go to Willeam and Francis and Ann sons and dotter of my Brouthers sons and Dotter of Willem Southal and to Willeam Pardoe and John Pardoe Sons of my Sistter Sarra Pardoe if they har[33] livin itt shall go to thar eldis child to cip the Houses in tenantable prepar in the same maner as I hav let never to be sold nor morged and to let now that I was in Boodle heltf and sound of memerey even this was this was [sic] inacted I Roytit with my hown hands and seld itt with the sam and hall outher wills I revok and to be nul and vaed and of no efect becous this his my last will and testament has witnes my name this fourteen day of December on thousand seven hunderd and seventy five; LS Francis Southall. LS

 Witness: Thomas Jamson,
 E. Parker, X, her mark,
 Mary Jamson.[34]

[33] Lawrence margin note: 'Possibly *not* is omitted.'
[34] Here is a rendition of the will (to the extent possible) in modern orthography:
 In the name of God, amen. I Francis Southall in the parish of St Peters in the borough of Droitwich in the county of Worcester do make and ordain this my last will and testament in manner and form following. Item: I give and bequeath to William Southall, son of my brother William Southall, five pounds and his wife's ring and no more. Item: I give and bequeath to Francis

That the said Francis Southall died 21st August 1777 so seized and possessed of said premises houses and cottages without altering or revoking his said will.

The pedigree of the said Francis Southall as far as relates to the estate in question under which William Southall the younger claims as heir at law of the testator is hereto annexed.

Southall, son of my brother William Southall five pounds and no more. Item: I give and bequeath to Ann, daughter of my brother William Southall, five pounds and no more. Item: I give and bequeath to Henry Bowen, son of my sister Ann Bowen, five pounds and no more. Item: I give to Mary Harrison, daughter of my sister Ann Bowen, five pounds and no more. Item: I give and bequeath to William Pardoe, son of my sister Sarah Pardoe, five pounds and no more. Item: I give and bequeath to John Pardoe, son of my sister Sarah Pardoe five pounds and no more. Item: I give to my nephews John and Edward and Charles Southall one guinea each and no more. Item: I give and bequeath to my niece Mary Pridley, wife of Routan Pridley, one guinea and no more. Item: I give and bequeath to Benjamin Pridley senior, my carpenter, one guinea and no more. Item: I give and bequeath to William Williams, senior, my mason, one guinea and no more. Item: I give and bequeath to Benjamin Green, my old gardener, one guinea and no more. Item: I give and bequeath to Francis Nightinner, my barber, one guinea and no more. And those legacies to be paid to them six months after my decease if [it] please God they live so long to receive it. Otherwise [my] executrix shall have it to herself. Item: I give and bequeath to my nephew and niece Arthur Harrison and his wife five pounds each, to be paid them at my decease. So be they. And if any person or persons should go to law or cause any law or put forward any law or cause any law for any thing I died possessed with, excepting my legacies should not be paid by the time above mentioned, my executrix hereafter mentioned [is] to get in the debts that was due to me at my decease. That person or persons that proceeds any further in law shall have they, nor their children, no claim nor title nor interest to any thing I died possessed with, not so long as water runs nor timber grows tall. The rest of my effects that I died possessed with I give to my niece Ann Pardoe, whom I make my whole and sole executrix, and for she to pay my just debts and my legacies and my funeral charges. And all the rest of my effects as I died possessed with I leave to my niece Ann Pardoe, daughter of my sister Sarah Pardoe, provided she never sells nor mortgages nor sells any part or parcel that I have left her. If she does, then the bailiff or any of His Majesty's justices of the peace shall take that part she sells or mortgages off and give it to the nearest and poorest relation of my side, and for his trouble the person he puts in the premises shall give him a guinea, and so for every such trouble shall have a guinea paid him. Moreover she shall not let nor sell any part or parcel of land or house to any of her brother or sister, nor brother nor sister's children. If she does then by the [. . .] of my will any of His Majesty's justices of the peace shall take it off her and give it to another as above mentioned. And if the person who it is given to should mortgage or sell it, then it shall be taken of them in the manner as above mentioned, and so to continue in the family. As long as the world endures, there shall not be no entail, be cut off, nor mortgage, nor sale, nor take any moneys upon it, any of what I died possessed. If they do then the nearest and poorest and nearest relation of my side, though ever so long standing, nor even the child that is unborn if he can prove the nearest relation to me put in by those that have sold it, he shall have it and turn them out that bought it, in the same manner as above mentioned. And what I have left my niece Ann Pardoe, she shall keep up the houses in tenantable repair and reserve the rents of them during her natural [life], and then go to her children, share and share alike. But if she should have but one, then that shall have it. And go in that line in the same manner as I have left it, still as long as there is one left of the branch or line. And if my niece Ann Pardoe should die without child or children, then it shall go to William and Francis and Ann, sons and daughter of my brothers, sons and daughter of William Southall, and to William Pardoe and John Pardoe, sons of my sister Sarah Pardoe. If they are living it shall go to their eldest child to keep the houses in tenantable repair in the same manner as I have let to she, never to be sold nor mortgaged. And to let [all] know that I was in boodle health and sound of memory even [as] this was this was [sic] enacted. I wrote it with my own hands and sealed it with the same. And all other wills I revoke, and to be null and void and of no effect because this is my last will and testament, as witness my hand this fourteenth day of December one thousand seven hundred and seventy-five.

LS Francis Southall LS
Witness: Thomas Jamson
E. Parker X her mark
Mary Jamson

That Ann Pardo the testator's niece married Joseph Phillips and died in the year 1783 without any child or children.

That Ann Hyam formerly Southall and William Pardo nephew and niece of the testator Francis Southall and devisees named in his will survived the said testator and died in the life time of the said Ann Pardo and that Francis Southall and John Pardo two other of the nephews and devisees of the testator survived the said Ann Pardo and died before the day of the demise laid in the declaration.

That William Southall the elder the 3rd lessor of the plaintiff is the surviving devisee named in the will of the said testator and that William Southall the younger the first lessor of the plaintiff is the testator's heir at law.

That Mary Southall one of the defendants is the eldest child of William Pardo deceased.

That Elizabeth Liggins late Elizabeth Hyam is the eldest child of Ann Southall by William Hyam her husband.

That Elizabeth the eldest child of the said Francis Southall the devisee survived the said Francis Southall but is since dead.

That Mary the eldest child of the said John Pardo is still living.

That on 1st May 1786 by Indenture of Lease said William Southall (the 3rd lessor of plaintiff) Thomas Southall his brother said John Pardo, Mary Southall, and Elizabeth Hyam leased to Henry Robeson a messuage or tenement part of the estates devised by the said testator (but not part of the premises in question) for twenty-one years at £13 a year payable unto the said William Southall, Thomas Southall, John Pardo, Mary Southall, and Elizabeth Hyam and their heirs or unto such of them or such other person or persons to whom the said premises shall from time to time descend to and belong and by the proportions they are entitled to.

That on 16 November 1787 said John Pardo, William Southall 3rd Lessor, and Elizabeth his wife and William Southall his eldest son by indenture reciting that said John Pardo was justly indebted to William Roper of Worcester in £59.16 which was secured by the joint note of said John Pardo and William Southall the elder in consideration thereof and of 10s. paid them and the better to secure same they and each of them did grant bargain sell and demise all those their two third parts or shares the whole into three equal parts to be divided of and in the premises in question amongst others to said William Roper his executors, administrators, and assigns for 1,000 years with a proviso that the same should be determined on payment of the said £59.16 and interest on the 16 May then next with covenant to levy a fine.

That the said principal money and interest was paid on said 16 May whereby said term and estate of the said William Roper was determined.

That after the death of said Ann Philips formerly Pardo vizt 1st May 1790, doubts having arisen with respect to the said estate, William Southall 3rd lessor of plaintiff Francis Southall's brother and John Pardo of the devisees in remainder mentioned in the will with John Southall and Mary his wife formerly Mary Pardo eldest child of William Pardo another of the said devisees and

Elizabeth Hyam now Elizabeth Liggins eldest child of Ann Southall another of the said devisees, came to an agreement under seal whereby after reciting the said will of the said testator his death the death of the said Ann Pardo without child or children and the death of the said Ann Southall and William Pardo in the lifetime of the said Ann Pardo leaving issue as before stated, and that doubts had arisen through the inaccuracy and obscurity of the wording of the said will as to the intention of the testator and legal construction of the same and that it was doubtful whether any and what estate or interest in the real estates of the said testator passed thereby to the children of the said Ann Southall and William Pardo and that the several parties claiming title to the hereditaments and premises in the said will comprised thereby devised being willing and desirous to obtain the opinion and sanction of a court of justice as to the legal intention and construction of the said will had agreed to join in the expense of obtaining such opinion and sanction for their mutual satisfaction upon the terms therein and herein after mentioned and expressed. It is by such agreement witnessed that for clearing up all doubts as far as may be as to the construction, intent, and operation of the said will of the said Francis Southall the testator deceased and for settling and adjusting all claims to the hereditaments and premises in and by the said will devised as aforesaid and for ascertaining the estate and interest which each and every or any of the several parties to the said agreement had or were or was entitled unto in or out of the hereditaments and premises aforesaid or any part thereof and for preventing disputes and litigations between the said parties or any of them relative thereto. It was thereby covenanted, agreed, and declared by and between the said William Southall, Francis Southall, party thereto, John Pardo, Joseph Southall, and Mary his wife, and Elizabeth Hyam for themselves severally and respectively and for their several and respective heirs, executors, administrators, and assigns, that under the direction of Richard Geast Esq. and according to such opinion as he should give upon a case to be for that purpose stated and settled by the attorneys therein after named on behalf of the said parties respectively an ejectment should be forthwith brought and prosecuted by the said William Southall, Francis Southall, and John Pardo against the said Joseph Southall and Mary his wife and Elizabeth Hyam or that a feigned issue should be tried between the said parties upon such terms and under such restrictions as the said Richard Geast should advise and direct for trying the title and ascertaining the estate and interest of the said Joseph Southall and Mary his wife and Elizabeth Hyam to the two undivided fifth shares or parts of and in the hereditaments and premises in and by the said will of the said Francis Southall given and devised or meant or intended so to be of which the said Joseph Southall and Mary his wife and Elizabeth Hyam were therein possessed or to which they claimed to be entitled in which said ejectment or feigned issue. It was agreed that no advantage should be taken either by plaintiffs or defendants of any informality or irregularity in the pleadings and that the causes should be fairly tried upon the merits in the shortest and least expensive manner and that both plaintiffs and defendants should be at liberty to give evidence of all such real facts as they should be respectively advised were material and necessary to the support of their respective claims without being confined or tied down to the precise rules required by law for maintaining and supporting such action or ejectment. And it was thereby further covenanted, agreed, and declared by and between the said parties thereto for themselves severally and respectively and for their several and respective executors, administrators, and assigns that no advantage should be taken by them or any of them by reason of any mortgage or other deed made or executed by the said parties or any of them to any person or persons whomsoever so as to nonsuit the plaintiffs in such action or ejectment or to deprive the said parties or any of them of any benefit or advantage to which they would have been respectively intitled in case no such mortgage or other deed had been made or executed. And likewise that the verdict to be given on such trial should be final, conclusive, and binding on all the said parties thereto, their heirs and assigns, to all intents and purposes and that no new trial should be moved for by the said parties or any of them, their or any of his heirs or assigns, except such verdict should be given contrary to evidence and contrary to the directions of the judge before whom the cause should come on to be tried and that no writ of error or suit in equity should be brought, commenced, or prosecuted by the said parties thereto or any of them their or any of their heirs or assigns for the purpose of reversing or setting aside the said verdict or preventing the same taking effect. And also that the said parties thereto should within the space of six calendar months next after such verdict should be given as aforesaid make do and execute any act, deed, matter, or thing for confirming and carrying the same into effect as should be advised and directed by the said Richard Geast.

On the Execution of the said Articles, the attorneys for the respective parties thereto agreed on a case to be laid before this Richard Geast (a barrister of eminence) and under his direction an ejectment was brought on the demises of William Southall, Francis Southall, and John Pardo, which was defended by Joseph Southall and Mary his wife, and came on to be tried at Worcester summer assizes 1790 before Mr Justice BULLER when a verdict was found under his directions for defendants which was not set aside and the subsequent enjoyment has been according to that verdict.

Question for the opinion of the court:

The question for the consideration of the court is whether William Southall the younger, the first lessor of plaintiff, is intitled to recover as heir at law to the said testator, and if not, whether William Southall the elder, the 3rd lessor is intitled to more than one undivided fifth part of the premises in question, and if the court should be of opinion that the heir at law is entitled to recover or William Southall the elder is entitled to more than one fifth part, the verdict to be entered accordingly. If the court should be of opinion that he is not entitled to more than one fifth part and that the heir at law is not entitled to recover, the verdict to be for the defendants.

[*Lawrence's Notes of Arguments of Counsel*]

Friday, April 27, 1798

Peake for Lessors:[35]

On the demise of the heirs at law, two questions: first, if any part of the real estate passed. Second, that as two of the devisees were dead at the time of the death of Ann Pardo, that the remainder did not take effect.

As to the first point, [there are] no words to carry land. [In] *Grayson* v. *Atkinson*, 1 Wils. 333,[36] [the residuary estate included] goods and chattels real and personal, movable and immovable, as houses, gardens, tenements, &c. But for these explanatory words, Lord HARDWICKE thought 'goods and chattels' would not have carried the land.

Here [there was] no introduction as to all his estate. As to the words 'lands and houses' in this will, that won't help, for he had long leases.

[He cited] 2 Atk. 454[37] and Cro. Car. 292.[38]

The nearest [to] the present is *Hogan* v. *Jackson*, Cowp. 299.[39] The expression there was 'real effects,' but Lord MANSFIELD relied on the introduction in the will. [See] Cowp. 667[40] and ibid. 235.[41]

Heirs [are] not to be disinherited if [it is] problematical what the testator meant. Now that [is] not necessary, as there are other estates to which the words in the will are applicable. [See] Precedents in Chancery, *Piggot* v. *Penrice*.[42] [There] the testator made his niece executrix of his lands. He had no lands but freehold, yet the chancellor held this would not disinherit the heir at law, who was only to be disinherited by express words or necessary implication. [See also] 1 Lev. 130, Sir Thomas Raymond 97, 1 Sid. 191.[43] The devise [was], 'I give all to my mother.' Lands [were] held not to pass, as it had its effect to pass chattels.

On the second point, the estate which passed on Ann Pardo's death, it was either a contingent remainder to all, not to take effect unless all the devisees were then living, or it was a devise to such as were living, and the eldest child of such, as died in her lifetime, as joint tenants for life.

As to the first construction, two died in the lifetime of Ann Pardo, and if the first construction is right, the contingency not having happened, the heir at law is entitled. 1 Fearne 358[44] lays down a rule that shows all the subsequent limitations will be affected (*ss.*) that where there is no apparent distinction in view between the estate first hinged upon the contingency and those which

---

[35] Thomas Peake for the defendants (the lessors).
[36] *Grayson* v. *Atkinson* (1752) 1 Wils. 333.
[37] *Oldham* v. *Hughes* (1742) 2 Atk. 452, 454.
[38] *Rose* v. *Bartlett* (1633) Cro. Car. 292.
[39] *Hogan* v. *Jackson* (1775) 1 Cowp. 299.
[40] The correct citation may be *Denn ex dim. Gaskin* v. *Gaskin* (1777) 2 Cowp. 657.
[41] *Roe, ex dim. Bose* v. *Blackett* (1775) 1 Cowp. 235.
[42] *Piggot* v. *Penrice* (1717) Prec. Ch. 471.
[43] The references are to three reports of the same case, *Bowman* v. *Milbanke* (1664).
[44] C. Fearne, *An Essay on the Learning of Contingent Remainders and Executory Devises* (1772), p. 358.

follow, it will affect the whole train of limitations. *Davis* v. *Norton*, 2 P. Wms. 390,[45] *Doe* v. *Shipphard*, Doug. 74[46] and 3 Burr. 1634.[47]

If the words 'if not' are supplied after the words 'if they are living,' then the eldest child will take, as representing the deceased parents. But as the estate given Ann Pardo [was] only an estate for life, for it is given after her death to her children, share and share alike, the remainders then could only take such estates, i.e., for life.

If [it is] so uncertain that the Court can't say what construction of several [is] to be adopted, the heir must take. Fearne 260.[48]

The lease [is] no severance, as [there is] a reservation to the persons entitled. The mortgage does not sever the jointures, being a mortgage for a term, which won't sever a jointure for life.

Wigley, contra:

Lord KENYON, we may release you from the first point. It appears to us not clearly to relate to his freehold lands. Here the heir at law is noticed and his legacy given him. The estate is given to Ann Pardo, and to the children, share and share alike, &c. The devise to the five is in the same manner as it was given to Ann Pardo. Therefore, his intent was that it should continue in the family of the five, as it was intended to go in the family of Ann Pardo. Each family was the object of the Testator's bounty, and he meant it should continue in the families. 1 Ves. 165.[49] [That case is] authority to show that courts construe wills as giving tenancies in common when the provisions [are] for children.

[Mr Justice] BULLER thought the children [in this case] took estates tail.[50] Ann Pardo certainly took an estate tail. I [say the] intent [was] that Ann Pardo took for life, that her children would have taken as tenants in common and tail, and as she had no children [see] 1 T.R. 632.[51]

Parke: I admit the eldest child is a ward of the purchaser—and that the eldest child an object of the testator's bounty, as the parent was. If that [be] so, there is nothing to extend it beyond an estate for life, for it is given that then as it was given to Ann Pardo, and it was given to her during her natural—which must mean natural life.

Wigley negatives the five devisees by taking the estate of inheritance.

Lord KENYON: This is to be argued again. We are to construe the will of a man who had no meaning at all. The first part may be laid out of the case. [It is] clear [that] the Testator meant that the will should operate on the whole of his property.

I think it an estate tail in Ann Pardo, on the reasoning of *Roe ex dim. Dodson*

---

[45] *Davis* v. *Norton* (1726) 2 P. Wms. 390.
[46] *Doe, Lessee of Watson and others* v. *Shipphard* (1779).
[47] *Chapman* v. *Brown* (1765) 3 Burr. 1626, 1634.
[48] Possibly a reference to *The Posthumous Works of Charles Fearne, Esquire, Barrister at Law*, T. M. Shadwell, ed. (1797), p. 260, but this is far from clear.
[49] *Stones* v. *Huertly* (1748) 1 Ves. Sen. 165.
[50] As indicated in the Special Case, above, the suit was initially tried before Mr Justice Buller at the Worcester summer assizes, 1790.
[51] *Roe d. Nightingale* v. *Quartley* (1787) 1 T.R. 630, 632.

v. *Grew* in 2nd Wils. 322.[52] But a question still remains what estate [is] in the five devisees. [There is] great difficulty to whom you are to apply the words 'if they are living'. A question worth considering [is] if we can supply the word 'not'.

The case of *Brown* v. *Chapman*, Burr. 1626 shows that the court could not insert words to disappoint the intention of a testator, but that they might, to forward it.[53]

If I had despotic power, I would insert 'not'. Then the question is, if it be not given to the children as to Ann Pardo, i.e., in tail. Then the question will be if this [is] a joint tenancy or a tenancy in common.

But another point: Lord Coke says an estate to two of the heirs of their bodies, it is a joint tenancy and several inheritances. That point is worth looking into.

Ult. Concilium

June 12, 1798

Mr *Leycester* for plaintiff:

The heir at law [is] not to be disinherited but by plain words or necessary implication. If the will had stopped at the devise to the five devisees, they would be joint tenants. But then the words come, 'if they are living'. Now if the stop is made at the word 'living', then, as two died, the survivors can't take. If the stop is made before the words 'if they are living', I leave it to the counsel for the defendant to make sense of it. If the words 'if they are not' are inserted, which according to *Chapman* v. *Brown* can't be, yet that will only be untying one knot to make another.

For what child is meant? The construction that the eldest children of those who are dead and the surviving devisees as joint tenants? Or it may be to the survivors and their eldest child.

If the words 'if they are living then to their eldest child' can be rejected, then the question is what estate the five devisees took.

I conceive it is only an estate for life. For [if] these words [are] in the same manner as 'I leave it to them', [they] may mean only to keep up the houses and not to be mortgaged or sold.

But supposing the words meant to give the same interests Ann Pardo had— only an estate for life.

Lord KENYON: The general intention was that it should go forever in branch and line. Now this can't be without giving her an estate tail.

Leycester: It is clear that the testator meant that the estate should be unalienable as long as the law allows, and therefore if the testator was asked if he meant, as [was] said in *Dodson* v. *Grew*, do you give Ann Pardo an estate tail which she may destroy, he would [have] said not that which will enable her to cut off the entail.

---

[52] *Roe ex dim. Dodson* v. *Grew* (1767) 2 Wils. 322.

[53] Reported as *Chapman* v. *Brown* (1765) 3 Burr. 1626 (for an earlier phase of the case, see *Brown* v. *Chapman* (1763) 3 Burr. 1418).

Plumer, contra:

As to the claim of the heir at law, there is sufficient to show that it was not the intent he should take. It is clear [that] he was disposing of his whole estate. And the objects of his bounty are distinctly marked out. Ann Pardo is the first object, and he meant it should go in her line, i.e., to her lineal descendants. And the devisor directs the entail should not be cut off, and at that time no estate was spoke of but that given to Ann Pardo.

The principles in *Dodson* v. *Grew* apply to this case. And not withstanding the difficulties from giving it to her children, share and share alike, and the word 'life' may have to be omitted after the word 'natural', the primary intention must prevail.

The next object of his bounty are his nephews and nieces, and I conceive he meant to give it to them exactly as he had given to Ann Pardo.

Lord KENYON: Supposing it had been given to the five devisees and the heirs of their bodies, what estate would they take?

Plumer: That, I know, would be a joint estate with several inheritances. But if they were all alive, I should contend that each took an estate in common in tail. 1 Ves. 165.[54] Lord HARDWICKE states the reason of the courts preferring tenancies in common. The testator meant, if it had been possible that the children should take, share and share alike. So it is clear that it was in his intention that the children of the five devisees should take. I conceive he meant that the children should take in the place of the parent. 'If living' must be referred to the five devisees, not that he meant that the children should be substituted for the parent, but that the children should be substituted in the place of the parent so dying.[55] Words may be supplied to further the general intent, as in cases of remainders.[56]

Leycester [was] stopped in reply.

Lord KENYON: On reading the will, the document [is] illiterate. I will not look forward to questions that may hereafter arise. We are not bound to say if Ann Pardo took an estate for life or entail. The last construction we can give it, though I have no confidence it will meet with his intention, for he was so ignorant of the laws of descent and of all the questions put to us, that he would have stared about him and could have given no answer till he had made inquiries and got information. If all the remainders were contingent, it would thwart his intentions, for Ann Pardo might have defeated them by forfeiting her estate.

If they were living, I do not think [we can] construct [it] to make it contingent. And I see no reason that we are to take the unintelligible words and refer them to the devise to the five, and defeat what is evidently his intention.

---

[54] *Stones* v. *Huertly* (1748) 1 Ves. Sen. 165.
[55] (Lawrence comment: 'According to this argument, it should be read, "if they are *not* living".')
[56] Lawrence here cross-references to thoughts of his own given separately after giving the judgment in the case (see below).

Tenancy in common [is] never without words to create it, as 'share and share alike'.

I think the probable construction is that this is a joint tenancy for life with several inheritances.

GROSE J.: The last time it was argued that this real property did not pass. But it is impossible to doubt here that the devisor meant that his real property should pass.

The question [is] what interest did pass. [It was] not a fee, for he takes great pains that it should not be alienated. The five devisees must take something. Now they must take as joint tenants, &c.

Judgment on the third demise for the lessees of the Plaintiff.

[Lawrence's Supplementary Note]

If one seized in fee of land make a lease for years of it, or [for] life, on condition that he shall not alien it, or any part of it, during the term, this is a good condition. Shep. T. 131.[57] We cannot from arbitrary conjecture, though founded on the strongest probability, add to a will or supply omissions, *per* Lord MANSFIELD in *Chapman* v. *Brown*, Burr. 1634. But if words are rejected or supplied by construction, it must always be in support of the manifest intent. Ibid.

If a grant be to two men and the heirs of their bodies, they have a joint estate for life, and several inheritances. Co. Litt., Sec. 283. So if it be to a man and woman who can't intermarry, as to a man and his mother, aunt, or sister. Co. Litt. 184a. A devise to a woman and her brother and to the heirs of every of their bodies lawfully begotten [is] a joint tenancy for life and several inheritances. Benloe 226, *Huntley* v. *Roper*. Same case Dyer 326a and Anderson 21.[58]

In the interpretation of words, there are two grounds: first, if the second part contradicts the first, the second shall be good. If the second part expounds the first, both shall stand, per Dodderidge, 1 Roll's Report 376.[59]

[Lawrence's Draft Opinion]

In this case, two questions have been made. First, whether any part of the testator's real estate passed by the will. This may be laid aside, as there can be no doubt of the testator's intention, and the words are sufficient.

Secondly, it has been intended that the devise over was either a contingent remainder to take effect in case all the nephews and nieces were living at the death of Ann Pardo, or that it was a devise to such of them as should be then surviving, and to the eldest child of such as might have died previous to that time, to take as joint tenants for life, the words 'if not' being supplied after the words 'if they are living'.

On the first supposition, William Southall the younger, as heir at law, will be

---
[57] Sheppard's *Touchstone*.
[58] *Huntley* v. *Roper* (1574) Benloe 226, Dyer 326a, 1 Anderson 21.
[59] *Berrie* v. *Perrie* (1615) 1 Rolle 375.

entitled to the whole of the estate. On the second, William Southall the elder will be entitled to one-third part, with William Southall [the younger] and Elizabeth Liggins.

As to the first supposition, the will is, shortly, a devise to Ann Pardo for life, and then to go to her children, share and share alike. If she shall have but one child, that one is to have it, and it is to go in that line, as long as there is one left of the branch or line. And if she shall die without children, then it shall go to William, Francis and Ann Southall, and to William and John Pardo,[60] [and] if they are living it shall go to their eldest child to keep the houses in tenantable repair in the same manner [as] the devisor had left it to them.[61]

The effect of this devise is to give Ann Pardo an estate tail, notwithstanding the devise to the children, share and share alike. It is not unlike the case of *Doe v. Smith* determined last term,[62] where we held that a devise to M. A. and the heirs of her body lawfully to be begotten as tenants in common, and in case she should die without issue, then [the remainder] over, gave her an estate tail.

With respect to the remainder to the nephews and nieces, it does not appear to me that the words 'if they are living' can make a contingent remainder, because it was left to Ann Pardo to continue in the family as long as the world endures and to go in that line as long as there is one left of the branch or line. After her decease without children, it is left to the five devisees in remainder in the same manner as it is left to her, i.e., as long as there is any one of the line or branch. Which is inconsistent with their being intended only to take in the event of their all surviving.

With respect to the last supposition, however probable the conjecture may be that the words 'if not' have been omitted, I find no authority for supplying them. And it has been laid down by Lord MANSFIELD in *Chapman v. Brown*, [3] Burr. 1634, that the court cannot from arbitrary conjecture founded on the strongest probability add to a will or supply omissions.

But I think that William Southall the elder is entitled to the full for his life, to give which I conceive the words 'if they are living it shall go to their oldest child' must be rejected as contradictory to and inconsistent with the prior devise to the parents. It is uncertain that in this devise there is some omission, and it is impossible to say exactly what that omission is. It may be that the word 'not' only has been omitted, and that it should be read 'if they are *not* living it shall go to their eldest child,' which will refer [to] the condition to the devise to the children. And if I am right in supposing that the devise could not intend that the devise to the parents should be conditional, these words must as they stand be referred to the devise to the children, and then the words of the will will give the estate to the parents, and if they are living to the eldest child, which is inconsistent and contradictory.

Now if these words are rejected, the devise will be to the nephews and nieces

---

[60] On the various relationships, see the attached 'Pedigree for Case'.

[61] As Lawrence's opinion later makes clear, it would appear that the testator meant to say, 'if they are *not* living' in this passage in his will.

[62] *Doe d. Candler v. Smith* (1798) 7 T.R. 531.

as joint tenants, with several inheritances, according to which construction William Southall the elder will be entitled as surviving joint tenant to the premises for his life.

[*Supplementary Notes following Lawrence's Draft Opinion*]

Ann Pardo died in 1783 sans issue. Ann Southall and William Pardo died in her life. Francis Southall, John Pardo, and William Southall survived her. William Southall is now the only surviving devisee.

If it could be a tenancy in common, William Southall, the devisee, would be entitled to one-fifth only, as they would be vested remainders. If a joint tenancy in the five devisees only, then he will be entitled to the whole for life, and will have a special inheritance in one-fifth. If in the devisees and their eldest children, then he would have one-third.

Roe ex dim. Southall, and others
against
Langford, and others

Pedigree for Case

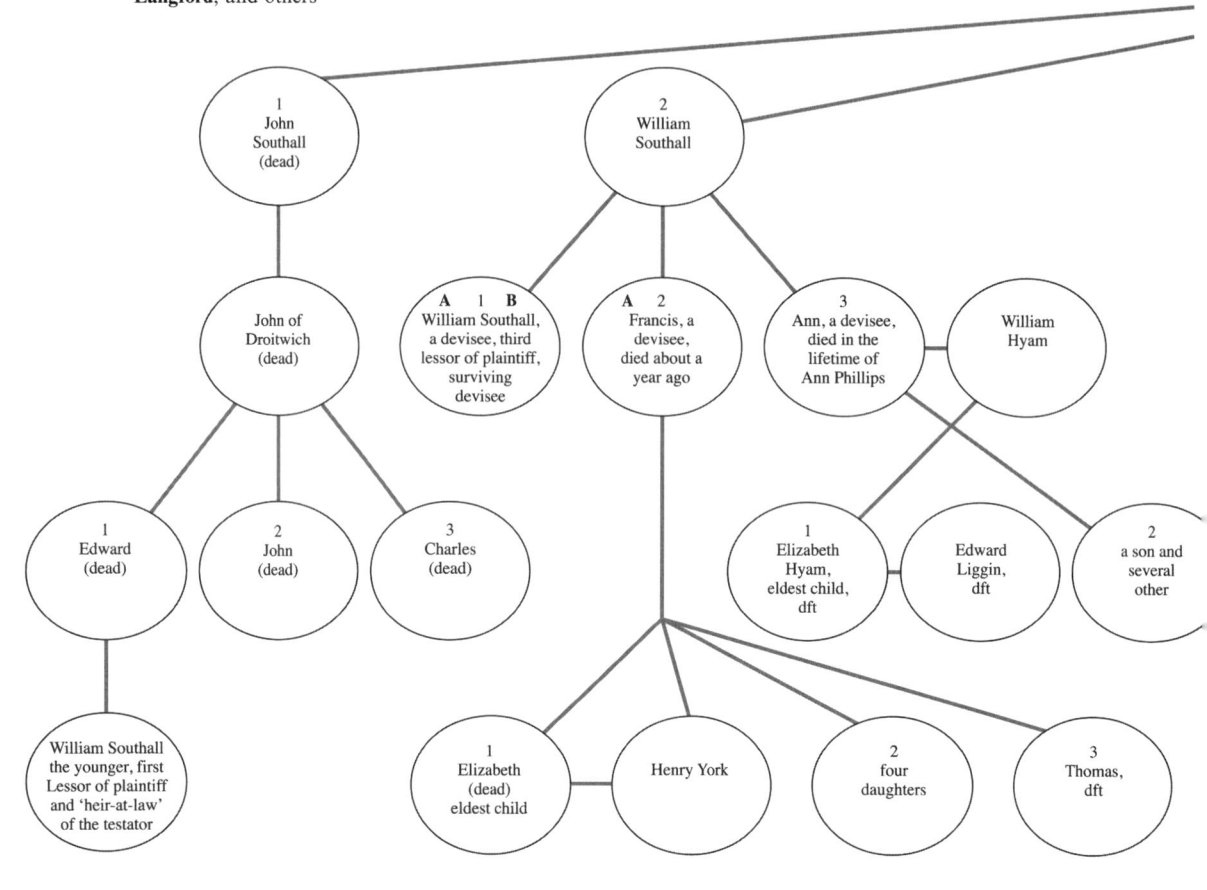

- 1 John Southall (dead)
  - John of Droitwich (dead)
    - 1 Edward (dead)
      - William Southall the younger, first Lessor of plaintiff and 'heir-at-law' of the testator
    - 2 John (dead)
    - 3 Charles (dead)
- 2 William Southall
  - A 1 B William Southall, a devisee, third lessor of plaintiff, surviving devisee
  - A 2 Francis, a devisee, died about a year ago
    - 1 Elizabeth (dead) eldest child — Henry York
    - 2 four daughters
    - 3 Thomas, dft
  - 3 Ann, a devisee, died in the lifetime of Ann Phillips — William Hyam
    - 1 Elizabeth Hyam, eldest child, dft — Edward Liggin, dft
    - 2 a son and several other

Southall, Common Ancestor

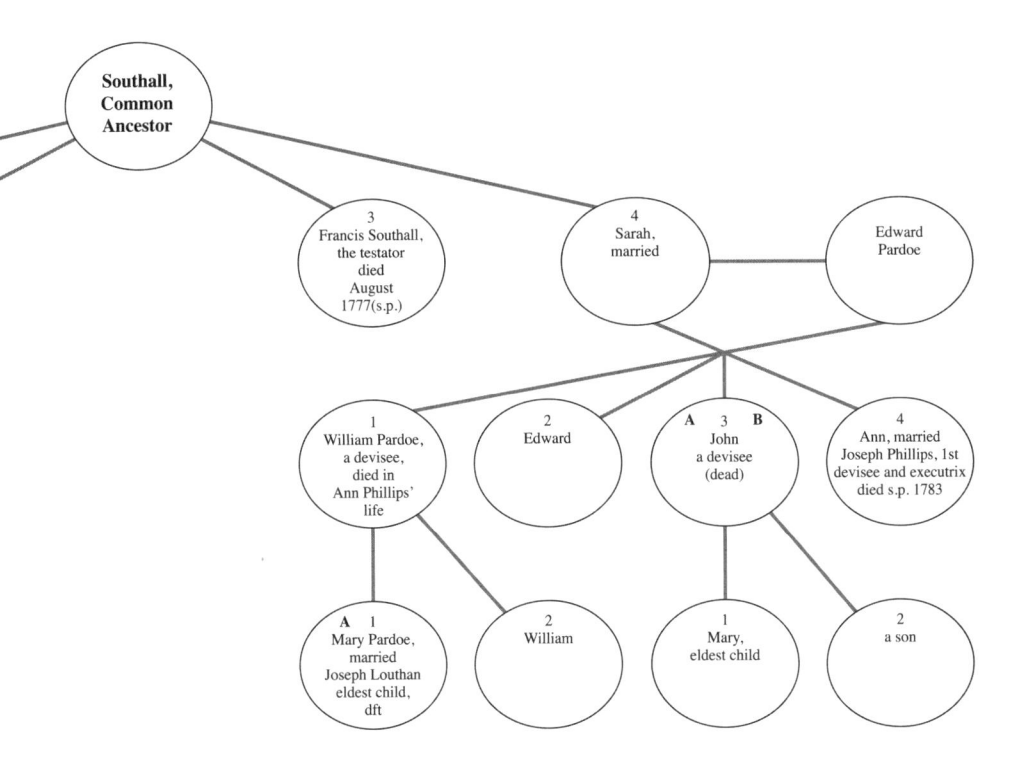

- 3 Francis Southall, the testator died August 1777 (s.p.)
- 4 Sarah, married — Edward Pardoe
  - 1 William Pardoe, a devisee, died in Ann Phillips' life
    - **A** 1 Mary Pardoe, married Joseph Louthan eldest child, dft
    - 2 William
  - 2 Edward
  - **A** 3 **B** John a devisee (dead)
    - 1 Mary, eldest child
    - 2 a son
  - 4 Ann, married Joseph Phillips, 1st devisee and executrix died s.p. 1783

A Lessor in the indenture of 1 May 1786 demising part of the lands to Henry Robeson.
B Mortgagors of part of the premises to William Roper.

In the King's Bench   LPB 167
Bischoff
v.
Agar[63]

[*Lawrence headnote*]: Query: If an embargo in the port of this Kingdom is within the words 'detainment of princes' in policies of assurance? And how soon notice must be given of abandonment.

To be Argued on Friday, 19th May [1797]

Wadeson and *Hardy*, Defendant's Attorneys

George Bischoff and another Plaintiffs
and
Moses Agar Defendant

This is an action on a policy of insurance upon goods shipped on board the *Albion* at and from Hull to Leghorn with liberty to join convoy and take in goods at any port or ports, place or places in the channel and warranted to depart with or join convoy from England or the channel bound for the Mediterranean.

The policy contained the usual perils, among which are 'arrests, restraints, and detainments of all kings, princes and people of what nation, condition or quality so ever'. The defendant for a premium of 7 guineas per cent subscribed the policy for the sum of £200.

The declaration states that the ship sailed from Hull on the 24th June 1796 and arrived at Portsmouth on the 14th July following and there joined a convoy appointed for the Mediterranean. That on the 27th of July the ship with the goods on board was by order and authority of the king and against the will of the plaintiffs arrested, restrained, and detained from farther prosecuting her voyage, and that the ship and the said goods so laden on board have from thence hitherto been restrained and prevented from prosecuting her voyage by virtue of that arrest and restraint, whereby the said voyage hath been defeated and the goods wholly lost to the plaintiffs.

The defendant pleaded the general issue.

This cause came on to be tried before the Right Honourable Lord KENYON at the sittings after last Hilary term at Guildhall. The jury found verdict for the plaintiffs with £200 damages subject to the opinion of this court on the following case:

The plaintiffs being merchants at Leeds in Yorkshire shipped goods consisting of woolen cloths to merchants residing at Leghorn on board the *Albion* there lying at the port of Hull and bound on a voyage to Leghorn and on the 3rd of June they insured them by the policy in question.

On the 24th of June last the ship sailed from Hull to Portsmouth to join

[63] Unreported.

convoy, at which time a convoy under the command of Sir Hyde Parker was lying there, appointed to convoy ships bound to Portugal, Spain, Gibraltar and the Mediterranean. The *Albion* arrived at Spithead on 30th of June last and joined the convoy. While the convoy lay there, intelligence arrived that the French were in possession of Leghorn, between whom and the English government open war prevailed.[64]

Afterwards on the 27th of July an embargo was laid by His Majesty in Council on all ships in the ports of this kingdom bound to any ports within the territories of the grand duke of Tuscany or the dominions of the Ecclesiastical State, which embargo has never yet been taken off.

On the 23rd of August it was ordered by His Majesty in Council that the said embargo be taken off so far as to permit the ships to proceed from the ports where they then were to the ports at which they might have respectively taken in their several cargos, provided the masters of such ships did first give security by bond to the proper officers of the customs at the nearest port, with one able surety to be approved of by such officers. That the ships should return as aforesaid under convoy of such of His Majesty's ships of war as should be appointed to convoy the same, and it was thereby also further ordered that on their return they be permitted to re-land their cargoes and deposit the goods in warehouses to be approved of by the proper officers of the Customs and Excise under the joint locks of the king and the proprietors at the expense of the latter; and that they be at liberty to take the same out of the said warehouses for exportation under the usual regulations if they should so think fit, or for home consumption upon repayment of the drawbacks where any had been obtained.

The convoy appointed for Portugal and the Mediterranean sailed on the 8th of August, but in consequence of the embargo, the *Albion* could not and did not sail with the convoy. The *Albion* still remains at Portsmouth with the goods insured on board.

On the 15th of December the assured gave notice of abandonment to the underwriters and claimed for a total loss.

The question for the opinion of the court is, whether the plaintiffs are entitled to recover. If the court should be of opinion they are, then the verdict to stand; if the contrary, a verdict to be entered for the defendant.

Robert Ward
John Cross

[*Lawrence's Notes*]

May 19, 1797

Mr *Cross* for the plaintiffs:

The question [is] of general consequence, as the merchants at Leeds, Exeter, and Manchester are all interested in this question. The second order of Council makes no difference. The words of the policy [are] sufficiently large.

Rotch v. *Edie*, 6 T.R. 413

---

[64] Leghorn (Livorno, Italy) was invaded by Napoleon in June 1796. See, e.g., Arthur Redford, *Manchester Merchants and Foreign Trade* (1973), pp. 37–38.

Green v. *Young*, Salk. 444, Ld. Raym. 840
Robertson v. *Ewer*, 1 T.R. 127.

So much as to the general question.

Particular objections:

First, that there is a warranty that the ship shall sail with convoy, and that, not having sailed with convoy, the risk did not commence. The answer is, at and from Hull to Leghorn, and the ship had sailed.

Another objection: that the embargo did not prevent the sailing, but the port of Leghorn being in the hands of the enemy [did]. But the masters of the ships had no knowledge of this, and would have sailed but for the embargo. This [is] like jetsam, where the necessity to throw the things overboard always exists before the things are thrown over, which the loss insured against.

Another objection is the lateness of the abandonment.

Lord KENYON: That is a very worthy objection. The rule in *Mitchel* v. *Edie* is that they must in the first instance make their election.

Erskine: Said the question having not been tried, it ought to go down to a jury. The case was made without anything going to the jury.

GROSE J.: It seems very difficult by a new trial to introduce anything which will show that it was abandoned in time.

The court directed the case to go down again to be tried, [so] that any fact which the plaintiff could bring forward material to his case might be stated.

Erskine and *Park* conceived that there was a difference between a loss by the sea or capture, and by an embargo.

To be tried *de novo*.[65]

[Separate Lawrence note: Query, if this [is] a case within the policy, if the notice to abandon [was] in time. *Mitchel* v. *Edie*, 1 T.R. 608. *Allwood* v. *Henckell*, Park 172.]

---

[65] No record of a new trial has been located.

[Introductory note to *Collet v. Keith*

Several cases in Mr Justice Lawrence's Paper Books dealt with the truncated voyage in 1796 of an American ship, the *Argonaut*, intended to sail from Philadelphia to France and Portugal, onward to the East Indies, with a return voyage to Philadelphia.[66] The *Argonaut* was co-owned by Anthony Butler and John Collet, both of whom were British-born residents of the United States. Butler had moved to Pennsylvania before American independence; Collet moved with his family to the United States in July 1784.

The first of the reported cases, *Wilson v. Marryatt*,[67] was brought by Wilson, agent for Collet and Butler, who had insured the voyage (both ship and cargo) by policies underwritten by Marryatt. Wilson claimed a total loss due to the detention and seizure of the ship at the Cape of Good Hope on the order of Sir George Keith Elphinstone (Viscount Keith), then commander of the British sea forces at Cape Colony.[68]

Lord Keith was a witness at the jury trial in *Wilson v. Marryatt*, and a transcription of his testimony, recorded by a shorthand writer, survives as part of Mr Justice Lawrence's Paper Book.[69] As Keith testified, the *Argonaut* arrived at Simon's Bay on 2 August 1796, and within days afterward, anticipating the arrival of the Dutch invasion fleet, Keith and his colleague, General Craig, decided 'to lay a general embargo upon the whole Colony that no vessel should sail for forty days'. The ship, having been removed to a place of safety, was not then under detention, but on inspection of the ship's papers, Keith detained the ship as an illicit trader.[70] Keith testified that the ship fell under the jurisdiction of 'the Court that acted generally under the Capitulation as the Admiralty Court'. He also said that when he seized the ship as an illicit trader, he took off the embargo in order to make the seizure permanent.

According to the printed report, *Wilson v. Marryatt* 'was three times argued at great length; first in Easter term last by Giles for the plaintiff, and Rous for the defendant; next in Trinity term following, by Gibbs for the plaintiff, and Law [later Lord Ellenborough] for the defendant; and in this term, by Erskine for the plaintiff, and Adam for the defendant'.[71] At the hearing on 21 November 1798, counsel for the defendant made five arguments: (1) that allowing the plaintiff to recover would interfere with public policy, in particu-

---

[66] Not all of the cases were reported. See, e.g., Lawrence's notes of *Wilson v. Kensington*, pp. 178, 181, above.

[67] (1798) 8 T.R. 31, (1799) 1 Bos. & Pul. 430.

[68] After the Netherlands had been occupied by France in January 1795, Lord Keith sailed with a squadron of ships to attempt to capture the Dutch Cape Colony in order to prevent it from falling to the French. In September 1795, Cape Town capitulated. Keith then sailed for India, but returned to Simon's Bay at the Cape in May 1796, having received intelligence that the Dutch were attempting to recapture Cape Colony. A Dutch squadron arrived at Cape Colony in August 1796 but surrendered peacefully to Lord Keith in the face of overwhelmingly superior firepower. For details on these events and on Lord Keith's career, see *ODNB*, *sub nom.* Elphinstone, George Keith.

[69] Dampier MSS., LPB 244, Lincoln's Inn Library, London. The transcription of Keith's testimony is reproduced in full below.

[70] See below, letter from G. K. Elphinstone (Lord Keith) to John Collet, 19 September 1796.

[71] 8 T.R. at 37.

lar, the exclusive trading rights extended to the East India Company by parliament; (2) that circuitous commerce through France was not contemplated by the 1796 treaty between Great Britain and the United States;[72] (3) that the treaty incorporated by reference a pre-existing prohibition in British law against trading with the East Indies; (4) that the voyage of the *Argonaut* was illegal throughout because it was commenced before the treaty had been ratified; (5) and that even as a United States citizen, Collet remained a British subject and was bound by the British navigation laws.

The King's Bench opinion by Lord Kenyon in *Wilson* v. *Marryatt* as reported in *Term Reports* was relatively brief and was apparently *per curiam*. Lord Kenyon rejected all of the defendant's arguments. He swept aside as insubstantial the public policy claim, the question of citizenship, and the circuitous voyage claim. As to the alleged illegality, Kenyon reasoned that the inception of the voyage was not to be deemed illegal because, even accepting that the ultimate destination was the East Indies when the *Argonaut* set sail from Philadelphia, the ship was not precluded from trading in the East Indies as long as the British settlements were avoided.[73] Kenyon said that the court must be guided by the specific words of the special verdict, which said only that the ship intended to go to the East Indies; it did not say 'to the British settlements in the East Indies'.[74]

Despite the judgment given by Kenyon for the court, the King's Bench was not unanimous. Mr Justice Lawrence wrote a full opinion that was either not delivered or not reported. After analysing the defendant's arguments, he concluded that the voyage was illegal at its inception, and, perforce, ever after. Thus, he would have held for the defendant. Lawrence's unreported opinion (from his notes in the Paper Book) was as follows:

> [There are] three questions: first, whether this voyage is authorized by the thirteenth article of the treaty. Second, if Collet [is] an American citizen. Third, if the policy be not void, as the voyage began before the ratification of the treaty.
>
> As to the first point, the terms of the treaty in which the question arises furnish some ground for the argument for the defendants, if a very strict, rigid, and literal interpretation is to be adopted. But such mode of construing the treaty ought not to be pursued. It is a rule that the construction of deeds shall be favourable, and as near the minds and intents of the parties as possible. If this be the line to be followed in cases of ordinary contracts, *a fortiori* such liberal rule of exposition should be adopted in the contracts between nations, in the construing of which there should be nothing which savours of narrowness, and which regards the letter rather than the spirit.

---

[72] A treaty of commerce between Great Britain and the United States had been negotiated in November 1794, but it was not ratified until after the *Argonaut* had sailed. According to the opinion by Chief Justice Eyre in the Exchequer Chamber, the treaty was ratified by the United States on 14 August 1795 and by Great Britain on 28 October of that year. See 1 Bos. & Pul. at 432. A copy of the statute confirming the treaty is contained in Lawrence's Paper Book, dated 27 September 1796.

[73] According to the printed report, Collet purchased the ship in Philadelphia in June 1795 and set sail from there on 25 July for France. 8 T.R. at 32. Earlier, on 16 February 1793, the king issued a proclamation forbidding British subjects from serving in any foreign ship or vessel without a special licence from the king. Collet had no such licence.

[74] 8 T.R. at 45.

The argument arising from the stipulation that the vessels of the United States shall not export any articles from the East Indies but to America, has great weight in showing that the true meaning of the treaty is not as the defendants contend[75]—for it is truly said by the plaintiff's counsel that if the construction they contend for is right, it would have been unnecessary to have added the provision, as the grant to the Americans to carry on a trade 'between' the East Indies and the United States would have been sufficient.

And it is no answer to this to say that the provision as to goods exported from the East Indies was introduced in order that regulations might be made in America to enforce the treaty as to the goods brought from the East Indies, for if 'between' necessarily implies that the voyage shall be directly from and to America, it would have been sufficient to have provided that regulations should be adopted to enforce the observance of the stipulation without a repetition of any part of it.

Nor does the argument from the additional clause furnish an answer to it, for though, in that the word 'between' may mean 'to and from', yet it has acquired that sense from a reference to another article (*ss.*) the twelfth, in which 'to and from' are used. But it does not follow from thence that the word 'between' must have the same sense in every clause of the treaty.

Now if the trade be carried on by an American['s] capital—by persons settled in the United States, and by ships sailing from those ports, why is it necessary that the course of the voyage should be in a direct line of communication? Why might not an American ship sail from thence to Europe, and procure a cargo to trade with in the East Indies, when it cannot be contended that the same ship might not have carried those very identical commodities to America and then have sailed with them to the East Indies?

It has been asked by what perversion of language a trade from Great Britain to the East Indies can be held to be a trade from America to the East Indies? The answer to that question is that in this case, no such trade as that from London to the East Indies is found.

It appears from the special verdict that the voyage had its inception in America—that its destination on leaving America was the East Indies, that the object of the ship's coming to Europe was to provide a proper cargo, and that the determination of the voyage, if not interrupted, might have been in America,[76] and that it was carried on by an American credit and on an American's capital.

If a man were to fit out a ship to go to St Giles for salt and from thence to Newfoundland to catch fish to be cured with that salt and to be brought here, can there be a doubt but that this would be a trade between Newfoundland and this country? Is

---

[75] In the treaty at issue, the twelfth article dealt with trade between America and the West Indies, while the thirteenth article governed trade between America and the East Indies. The defendants argued that the thirteenth article barred any circuitous trade between America and the East Indies; that is, all trade had to be directly between the two entities, without any intermediate stops. In support of their argument, the defendants pointed out that language in the twelfth article, which used the words 'to and from' to describe commerce between America and the West Indies, was *not* used in the thirteenth article. According to the defendants, because different trade regulations were required for different voyages to and from America and the West Indies, additional language, such as 'to and from', was necessary. However, for trade between America and the East Indies, the word 'between' was synonymous with 'to and from', because there was allegedly no need for discriminating regulations, and therefore 'between' meant direct trade only (as it was intended to mean in the twelfth article, as well).

[76] That is, the voyage would have terminated in Philadelphia if not interrupted.

the trade between this country and the West Indies carried on by many merchants by sending their ships to Africa to procure a cargo of slaves to go with them to the West Indies?

The argument for the defendant is as strict as if it were a question of deviation.

As to the dangers of the monopoly of the East India Company by Anglo-Americans, by the subjects of this country being the real traders under American names, nothing of that sort is found by this special verdict. If it were, that might be another case, and would deserve a different consideration.

As to the argument drawn from the restriction as to the coasting trade being confined to the original cargoes, which it is insisted this ship had not to traffic with, as it was collected in different parts of Europe,[77] that is without foundation, for the original cargo may be collected either in or out of America if it be the cargo with which the ship sails to the East Indies to trade with. Original cargo means a cargo contradistinguished to that acquired in the East Indies.

As to the argument that the trade shall be subject to the laws of two countries, and that by law the East India Company have the monopoly here, that leaves the case just where it was, for if the treaty and the act confirming it have authorized this trade, it is not against the law. And it is further to be observed that the article which refers to the laws and statutes of the two countries relates only to the trade between the territories of the United States and the king's European dominions.

As to the second question: it is a very different question whether a man can excuse *patriam* from that now under consideration. The question is not what is the natural allegiance of the plaintiff, but whether one who has been domiciled in America between ten and twenty years and who has been received as a citizen of the United States is one of the persons described in the treaty as a citizen of those states.

If Collet be not such a citizen, the natural born subjects of every country foreign to America are incapable of deriving any advantage under this treaty, however long their residence may have been in that country, or however intimately they may have been adopted by the American states. If to enjoy the advantages of a commercial treaty granted to the public of any country, it be necessary that all who claim it must be natives, no naturalized foreigner in a question depending on the general law of nations could be considered as an Englishman.

As to the last question: I think the plaintiff cannot recover. For there is no question but that the voyage insured must be such as is not contrary to the laws of this country. And in this case the adventure from Bordeaux and Madeira to the East Indies can only be consistent with law as part of a voyage begun in America according to the provisions of the treaty and the statute confirming it. That is the foundation upon which the whole depends, and if that fails, the superstructure must fall.

If the ship had sailed from America subsequent to the ratification, it might have completed a voyage legally commenced, and the policy would have protected it throughout. But being entire, if the commencement was illegal, its further prosecution is so also. And the policy can't be applied to the risk from Bordeaux without reference to the earlier part of it, for then it will not be a voyage between territories of the United States and the East Indies.

---

[77] The scheme of the voyage was for the cargo from America to be sold in Brest and Bordeaux, the ship to be re-loaded with French goods, and to proceed to Maderia. There, the *Argonaut* took on a shipment of local wines and additional goods which had been shipped by Collet from London directly to Madeira. The *Argonaut* was then to proceed to the East Indies.

On writ of error to the Exchequer Chamber, Chief Justice Eyre, in a lengthy opinion, affirmed the judgment of the Court of King's Bench. He said nothing about the defendant's claim that the voyage was illegal because it began before the treaty was ratified; presumably, counsel for the defendant did not pursue the argument. Eyre's opinion for the Exchequer Chamber was devoted to a close reading of the words of the treaty and to the question of citizenship. His treaty interpretation was conservative. He said that if the words of the treaty led to an unbalanced conclusion, he could not help it—the judges were not 'the expounders of treaties', but 'are to collect from the nature of the subject, from the words and from the context, the true intent and meaning of the contracting parties'.[78]

Chief Justice Eyre was troubled, however, by the defendant's claim that the plaintiffs, as British subjects, were precluded from trading in the East Indies. He referred to a 1797 opinion by the law officers of the crown and the advocate-general 'that the master of an American vessel a subject of the United States domiciled there, but in fact a natural-born subject of Great Britain was not to be considered as a subject of the United States within the meaning of our navigation laws, founding themselves upon an opinion of Lord Hardwicke when he was Attorney-General'.[79] Eyre said that 'though this was not a judicial decision, (as in the argument at the bar of the Court of King's Bench, it was supposed to be), it was certainly of the highest authority next to a judicial decision'.[80] Yet in the end, he concluded: 'I am not prepared to say, highly as I respect the authority of those who held that opinion, that this character of a natural-born subject will control or suspend the legal operation of that of a subject of the United States.'[81]

Chief Justice Eyre's Exchequer Chamber opinion in *Wilson* v. *Marryatt* was issued on 6 May 1799. In Trinity term following, another action was filed on the loss of the *Argonaut*, this time by Collet and Butler against Lord Keith for a claimed uninsured loss of £100,000. Lawrence's Paper Book for *Collet* v. *Keith* reveals that the parties first intended a jury trial,[82] but the pleadings were subsequently amended to reflect a demurrer and joinder. Lawrence's copy of the Demurrer Book, set for argument on 11 November 1799, is reproduced in full below, together with the testimony of Lord Keith that had been given in *Wilson* v. *Marryatt*, and two brief related letters from Keith to Collet.

According to *The Times*, 'This case is in fact the same with that of *Wilson* v. *Marryatt*, which was an action brought on three Policies of Insurance by the Plaintiff, as Broker for Collet and Butler, against the Underwriters, to recover the amount of their subscriptions', but the *Argonaut* and her cargo 'were only

---

[78] 1 Bos. & Pul., at 438–439.
[79] Ibid., at 440–441. Bosanquet and Puller quote in full the opinion of the advocate-general (William Scott), the attorney-general (John Scott, later Lord Eldon), and the solicitor-general (John Mitford). Ibid., at 440, n. (3).
[80] Ibid., at 441.
[81] Ibid., at 444.
[82] Dampier MSS., LPB 297, Lincoln's Inn Library, London. By the first Copy of the Record in the Paper Book from Trinity term 1799, the parties agreed 'to put themselves upon the country'.

insured for about one-tenth of their value; and therefore, this action of trespass was brought by the Plaintiffs, who were the Gentlemen, really interested, to recover the whole of their loss which arose from this capture'.[83] Counsel for the plaintiffs, Daniel Giles, was deferential, pointing out that, 'Lord Keith was indemnified by Government, and therefore if the Court should give judgment for the Plaintiffs, that judgment would in no degree affect his Lordship.'[84]

In a second argument on 19 December 1799, Thomas Erskine took over as lead counsel for the plaintiffs. He said that, 'The present action was brought to recover the amount of the loss of that part of their property which had not been insured.'[85] The question was, he said, 'whether his Lordship, or rather the Public, were not civilly responsible', and 'whether the Plaintiffs had not a right to be indemnified to the full amount of that property which was lost in consequence of the seizure'.[86] Lord Keith's testimony in *Wilson* v. *Marryatt* was read 'from Mr. Gurney's Short-hand Notes'.[87] William Garrow, counsel for the defendants, attempted to discredit Lord Keith's testimony by claiming 'that Lord Keith was examined in the Case of *Wilson and Marryatt*, for the express purpose of getting from him facts that might be turned against himself in this cause, which the Plaintiffs then contemplated to bring against him'.[88]

According to *The Times*, Lord Kenyon said that he 'must put a fair and liberal construction on the whole of Lord Keith's evidence'—'he must not garble it'—he 'must suppose that Lord Keith acted under the authority of a Court', which Lord Keith 'says over and over, and over again'. Lord Kenyon said he did not know whether the court to which Keith referred was analogous to the Court of King's Bench, but it was enough for him to suppose that Lord Keith 'acted under the authority of some Court', even 'under the authority of a Court of *Hottentots*, if you will'.[89] Consequently, the plaintiffs were nonsuited.

The case was reconsidered on 27 January 1800 on a motion by Erskine but was postponed to July 1800, and was postponed again in May 1801 to permit the parties to amend their pleadings.[90] Re-argument finally occurred on 14 May 1802, as was fully reported by Edward East.[91] Lord Ellenborough recused himself, because he had served as counsel for the defendants in earlier proceedings. The court held that Lord Keith's plea was bad since it justified his actions by saying only that he had acted on the authority of a court of competent jurisdiction, which gave the plaintiffs no way to contest the defendant's claim or to question whether Lord Keith was in fact justified as an officer of the court. Judgment was given, therefore, for the plaintiffs.[92]

[83] *The Times*, 16 November 1799, p. 2.
[84] Ibid.
[85] *The Times*, 20 December 1799, p. 3.
[86] Ibid.
[87] Ibid. Thomas Gurney was a well-known expert on shorthand, author of *Brachygraphy, or, An Easy and Compendious System of Short-Hand, Adapted to the Various Arts, Sciences, and Professions*, 9th ed. (1778).
[88] Ibid. *The Times*, 20 December 1799, p. 3.
[89] Ibid.
[90] See *The Times*, 28 January 1800, p. 3, 6 May 1801, p. 3, and 9 May 1801, p. 3.
[91] (1802) 2 East 260.   [92] Ibid., at 276.

According to *The Times*, the case was tried once more on 20 November 1802 before Mr Justice Le Blanc and a special jury. Noting that there had been several previous trials, the brief report stated that the cause 'again occupied the whole day, and the Jury gave their verdict for the Plaintiff'.[93] The verdict was said to be 'subject to a reference to Mr Inglis, a merchant of the City of London', undoubtedly in order to fix the amount of the damages.

There was a brief epilogue in this case. On 30 November 1802, Garrow challenged the allowance into evidence in the *Collet* case of the examination of Lord Keith that had taken place in *Wilson* v. *Marryatt*.[94] Shorthand writer Thomas Gurney testified about what Lord Keith had said. Garrow's theory was that Keith had not been allowed to speak freely after Lord Kenyon had interrupted him, saying that Keith 'need enter into no defence to vindicate his conduct; all the world will agree with him'. Mr Justice Le Blanc said that Keith's examination was admissible, 'That the manner in which it had been obtained might be matter of observation to make to the jury; but if what was said bore in any way on the issue, he was bound to receive it as evidence of the fact itself.'[95]]

Way

Collet
v.
Lord Keith[96]

LPB 297
Copy
Demurrer Book

Trinity Term 39th George III

[*Lawrence headnote:*] Declaration for taking a ship and converting it to defendant's use. But that defendant, as commander of the King's sea forces, took the ship to prevent its giving information to the enemy, which he had reason to suspect it intended doing. Replication *de injuria absque tali causa*. New assignment that the action was brought for converting the ship to defendant's use as well as for taking. Rejoinder joins issue on the traverse and demurrer to the new assignment as making the replication double. This [is] a good objection to the replication, but the defendant should not have joined issue but have demurred to the whole replication.

To be argued on Monday the 11th of November [1799]

Dann and *Dunn*

[93] *The Times*, 22 November 1801, p. 3.
[94] *Collet* v. *Lord Keith* (1802) 4 Esp. 212.
[95] Ibid., at 213.
[96] (1802) 2 East 260; 4 Esp. 212.

Trinity Term in the thirty-ninth year of the Reign of
King George the third

Roll   Way

London to wit, Be it remembered that in Easter Term last past before our Lord the King at Westminster came John Collet and Anthony Butler by [sic] their attorney and brought in the court of our said Lord the King then there their Bill against George Lord Keith having privilege of Parliament of a plea of trespass and there are pledges for the prosecution (to wit) John Doe and Richard Roe which said Bill follows in these words to wit, London (to wit) John Collet and Anthony Butler complain of George Lord Keith (having privilege of Parliament) in a Plea of Trespass. For that he the said George Lord Keith heretofore (to wit) on the second day of August in the year of our Lord one thousand seven hundred and ninety six (to wit) at London in the Parish of Saint Mary le Bow in the Ward of Cheap with force and arms seized and took a certain ship or vessel of them the said John and Anthony of great value (to wit) of the value of Fifty thousand pounds of lawful money of Great Britain and also divers goods, wares, and merchandizes of them the said John and Anthony of great value (to wit) of the value of fifty thousand pounds of lawful money of Great Britain then and there being on board of the said ship or vessel and converted and disposed of the said ship or vessel and of the said goods, wares, and merchandizes to his own use and other wrongs to them the said John and Anthony then and there did against the peace of our Lord the now King and to the damage of the said John and Anthony of one hundred thousand pounds and therefore they bring suit &c. And the said John and Anthony pray the process of our Lord the King according to the form of the Statute in such case made and provided to him thereon to be made and to him thereon it is granted &c.

Plea—And now at this day (that is to say) on Friday next after the Morrow of the Holy Trinity in this same term until which day the said George Lord Keith had leave to imparle to the said Bill and then to answer the same &c. as well the said John and Anthony by their said attorney as the said George Lord Keith by Richard Dann his attorney do come before our Lord the King at Westminster and the said George defends the force and injury when &c. and says that he is not guilty of the trespasses above laid to his charge in manner and form as the said John and Anthony have above thereof complained against him the said George and of this he puts himself upon the Country &c. And the said George for further Plea as to the seizing and taking of the said ship or vessel and of the said goods, wares, and merchandizes on board of the same in the said declaration mentioned by leave of the court here to him for that purpose first granted according to the form of the statute in such case made and provided says that the said John and Anthony ought not to have or maintain their said action thereof against the said George because he says that before and at the same time when &c. the settlement of the Cape of Good Hope in Africa in foreign parts was in the lawful possession of our Sovereign Lord the now King and was guarded and defended by certain land and sea forces of our said Lord the King by him employed in that behalf of which sea forces the said George before and at the said time when &c. was the Commander in Chief in that behalf duly authorized to wit, at London aforesaid in the parish and ward aforesaid and that before and at the said time when &c. the said George being such Commander in Chief as aforesaid had reasonable ground to believe and did believe that a certain powerful armament of the land and sea forces of certain enemies of our said Lord the King were near to the said settlement and was about to attack the same in an hostile manner and to endeavour to take the same by force from the possession of our said Lord the King and that our said Lord the King's said possession thereof was thereby then and there greatly endangered (to wit) at London aforesaid in the parish and ward aforesaid by reason whereof it then and there became and was the duty of the said George as such Commander in Chief as aforesaid of the said settlement to prevent as far as lay in his power by all due and necessary means any communication or intercourse from being had or made between the said enemies of our said Lord the King and the inhabitants of the said settlement or any intelligence from being had or obtained by the said enemies of our said Lord the King of and concerning the state of the said settlement or of or concerning the said forces of our said Lord the King there and the said George further says that while he was such Commander in Chief as aforesaid and while he was in immediate expectation of such attack as aforesaid the said ship or vessel in the said Declaration mentioned with the said goods, wares, and merchandizes on board of the same a little before the said time when &c. (to wit) on the same day and year in the said Declaration mentioned arrived at a certain place (to wit) a place called Simon's Bay being part of the said settlement and under the command, authority, and defence of the said George as such Commander in Chief as aforesaid (to wit) at London aforesaid in the parish and ward aforesaid. And the said George then and there had reasonable cause to suspect and did in fact suspect that the said ship or vessel had so there arrived as aforesaid and was then and there employed for the purpose of carrying on communication injurious and hostile to our said Lord the King between his said enemies and certain inhabitants of the same settlement or of obtaining intelligence for the said enemies of our said Lord the King of and concerning the state of the said settlement or of and concerning our said Lord the King's said forces there (to wit) at London aforesaid in the parish and ward aforesaid and thereupon the said George being such Commander in Chief as aforesaid and expecting such attack as aforesaid in pursuance of his duty as such Commander in Chief as aforesaid to prevent any communication injurious or hostile to our said Lord the King between his said enemies and any inhabitants of the said settlement from being carried on or any intelligence of and concerning the state of the said settlement or of or concerning the said forces of our said Lord the King there from being obtained by our said Lord the King's said enemies by means of the said ship or vessel did at the said time when &c. for the necessary defence and protection of our said Lord the King's said possession of the said settlement seize and take the said ship or vessel with the said goods, wares, and merchandizes on board of the same as it was lawful for the said George to do for the cause aforesaid which are the same several supposed trespasses in the introductory part of this plea mentioned and whereof the said John and Anthony have in their said Declaration complained against the said George without this that the said George is guilty of the said supposed trespasses or any of them at London or elsewhere than at the said settlement and this he is ready to verify wherefore he prays judgment if the said John and Anthony ought to have or maintain their said action thereof against the said George &c. And the said George for further plea as to the seizing and taking of the said ship or vessel and of the said goods, wares, and merchandizes on board of the same in the said Declaration mentioned by like leave of the Court here to him for that purpose first granted according to the form of the statute in such case made and provided says that the said John and Anthony ought not to have or maintain their said action thereof against the said George because he says that before and at the said time when &c. the said settlement of the said Cape of Good Hope was in the lawful possession of our said Lord the King and was guarded and defended by certain land and sea forces of our said Lord the King by him employed in that behalf of which sea forces the said George before and at the said time when &c. was the Commander in Chief in that behalf duly authorized (to wit) at London aforesaid in the parish and ward aforesaid and that before and at the said time when &c. the said George being such Commander in Chief as last aforesaid had reasonable ground to believe and did believe that a certain other powerful armament of the land and sea forces of certain enemies of our said Lord the King was near to the said settlement and was about to attack the same in an hostile manner and to endeavour to take the same by force from the possession thereof was then and there thereby greatly endangered (to wit) at London aforesaid in the parish and ward aforesaid by reason whereof it then and there became and was the duty of the said George as such Commander in Chief as aforesaid for the necessary defence and protection of our said Lord the King's said possession of the said settlement to prevent as far as lay in his power any communication or intercourse from being had or made between the said last mentioned enemies of our said Lord the King and the inhabitants of the said settlement or any intelligence from being had or obtained by the said last mentioned enemies of our said settlement or of or concerning the said forces of our said Lord the King there. And the said George further says that whilst he was such Commander in Chief as aforesaid and whilst he was in actual expectation of such attack as last aforesaid the said ship or vessel in the said declaration mentioned being a foreign ship or vessel with the said goods, wares, and merchandizes on board of the same a little before the said time when &c. (to wit) on the same day and year in the said Declaration mentioned without the permission or privity of the said George had arrived at a certain place (to wit) a place called Simon's Bay being part of the said settlement and under the command authority and defence of the said George as such Commander in Chief as aforesaid (to wit) at London aforesaid in the parish and ward aforesaid and thereupon the said George being such Commander in Chief as aforesaid and expecting such attack as last aforesaid in pursuance of his duty as such Commander in Chief as aforesaid to prevent any communication injurious or hostile to our said Lord the King between his said last mentioned enemies and any inhabitants of the said settlement from being carried on or any intelligence of or concerning the state of the said settlement or of or concerning the said forces of our said Lord the King there from being had or obtained by our said Lord the King's last mentioned enemies by means of the said ship or vessel did at the said time when &c. for the defence and protection of our said Lord the King's said possession of the said settlement seize and take the said ship or vessel and the said goods, wares, and merchandizes on board of the same as it was lawful for the said George to do for the cause last aforesaid which are the same several supposed trespasses in the introductory part of this plea mentioned and whereof the said John and Anthony have in their said Declaration complained against the said George without this that the said George is guilty of the said supposed trespasses or any of them at London or elsewhere than at the said settlement and this he is ready to verify wherefore he prays judgment if the said John and Anthony ought to have or maintain their said action thereof against the said George &c.

Charles Cowper

Replication and New Assignment—And the said John and Anthony as to the said Plea of the said George by him first above pleaded in Bar and whereof he hath put himself upon the Country do so likewise. And the said John and Anthony as to the said Plea of the said George by him secondly above pleaded in Bar as to the seizing and taking of the said ship or vessel and of the said goods, wares, and merchandizes, on board of the same in the said Declaration mentioned say that they by reason of any thing by the said George in that Plea above alledged ought not to be barred from having or maintaining their aforesaid action thereof against the said George because they say that the said George at the said time when &c. in the said Declaration mentioned seized and took the said ship or vessel and the said goods, wares, and merchandizes on board of the same in the said declaration mentioned in manner and form as the said John and Anthony have above thereof complained against him of his own wrong and without any such cause as he the said George has in his said plea above alledged. And this they pray may be enquired of by the country &c. And the said John and Anthony as to the said Plea of the said George by him lastly above pleaded in Bar as to the seizing and taking of the said ship or vessel and of the said goods, wares, and merchandizes on board of the same in the said Declaration mentioned say that they by reason of any Thing by the said George in that Plea above alledged ought not to be barred from having or maintaining their aforesaid Action thereof against the said George because they say that the said George at the said time when &c. in the said Declaration mentioned, seized and took the said ship or vessel and the said goods, wares, and merchandizes on board of the same in the said Declaration mentioned in manner and form as the said John and Anthony have above thereof complained against him and of his own wrong and without any such cause as the said George has in his said last mentioned Plea above alledged. And this they pray may be enquired of by the Country &c. And the said John and Anthony further say that they the said John and Anthony exhibited their said Bill against the said George as well for the said several Trespasses by the said George in his said pleas by him secondly and lastly above pleaded in Bar acknowledged to have been committed and thereby attempted to be justified as also for that the said George at the said time when &c. in the said Declaration mentioned converted and disposed of the said ship or vessel and of the said goods, wares, and merchandizes to his own use in manner and form as the said John and Anthony have above thereof complained against him (to wit) at London aforesaid in the parish and ward aforesaid which are other and different trespasses than the said trespasses by the said George in his said last mentioned Pleas acknowledged to have been committed. And this the said John and Anthony are ready to verify wherefore in as much as the said George hath not made any Answer to the said several Trespasses herein above newly assigned the said John and Anthony pray Judgment and their Damages by occasion of the committing of these Trespasses to be adjudged to them &c.

Daniel Giles

Rejoinder and Demurrer—And the said George as to the said plea of the said John and Anthony by them above pleaded by way of Reply to the said plea of the said George by him secondly above pleaded in Bar and whereof they have put themselves upon the Country doth so likewise. And the said George as to the said plea of the said John and Anthony by them above pleaded by way of Reply to the said plea of the said George by him lastly above pleaded in Bar and whereof they have put themselves upon the Country doth so likewise. And the said George as to the said new Assignment of the said John and Anthony by them above made and the matters therein contained says that the said new Assignment and the matters therein contained are not sufficient in law for the said John and Anthony to have or maintain their aforesaid Action thereof against him the said George. And that he the said George is not under any necessity nor is he bound by the Law of the Land in any manner to answer the same. And this he the said George is ready to verify wherefore he prays Judgment and that the said John and Anthony may be barred from having and maintaining their aforesaid Action thereof against him and for Causes of Demurrer in Law according to the form of the Statute in that case made and provided the said George sets down and shews to the Court here the following causes (to wit). For that the Matter by the said John and Anthony before pleaded by way of reply and whereon the said Issues are above joined is in itself and exclusive of the said new Assignment a full and compleat Answer to the said Pleas of the said George by him secondly and lastly above pleaded in Bar and will if those Issues should be found for the said John and Anthony intitle them to recover their damages and take their Judgment for all the supposed

Trespasses complained of in their said Declaration and for that the Matter contained in the said New Assignment is another full and compleat Answer to the said pleas and will if pleaded to by the said George and found for the said John and Anthony also intitle the said John and Anthony to recover their damages and take their Judgment for all the Trespasses complained of in their said Declaration and so the said new Assignment is not only superfluous but renders the said Replication double and puts the said George in order to establish either of his said to pleas by him secondly and lastly above pleaded in Bar on the Proof of two Issues each extending to the whole of such plea. Whereas by the law of the Land the said John and Anthony ought to have elected one only of the said two issues and to have relied thereon. And also for that the said new Assignment not being an explanation or specification of the Matters contained in the said Declaration but a compleat Answer to the said Pleas ought to have been pleaded by way of Reply and not by way or new Assignment. And also for that the said supposed conversion in the said new Assignment mentioned is not in itself a substantive Trespass but only a Matter of aggravation of the other supposed Trespasses alledged in the said Declaration and therefore that the said supposed conversion is not fit Matter for a new Assignment but ought to have been alledged by way of Reply.

Charles Cowper

Joinder—And the said John and Anthony say that the said New Assignment in manner and form aforesaid by them the said John and Anthony above made and the Matters in the same contained are sufficient in Law for them the said John and Anthony to have and maintain their said Action thereof against the said George which said new Assignment and the matters in the same contained they the said John and Anthony are ready to verify and prove as the Court shall award and because the said George hath not answered the said New Assignment nor hitherto in any manner denied the same they the said John and Anthony pray Judgment and their damages by reason of the said Trespasses above newly assigned to be adjudged to them &c. but because the Court of our Lord the King now here will advise amongst themselves what Judgment to give in the Premises whereon the said parties have put themselves upon the Judgment of the Court here before they give Judgment thereon a day is therefore given to the parties aforesaid to come before our Lord the King at Westminster on   [sic] next after   [sic] to hear Judgment thereon because that the Court of our said Lord the King now here is not yet fully advised thereof and as well to try the Issues above joined to be tried by the Country as to inquire what damages the said John and Anthony have sustained on occasion of the premises whereof the said parties have put themselves upon the Judgment of the Court in Case Judgment shall be thereon given for the said John and Anthony. Let a Jury come before our Lord the King at Westminster on   [sic] by whom &c. and who neither &c. to recognize &c. because as well &c. the same day is given to the Parties there &c.

[*Lawrence's Notes*[97]]

In an action of trespass and not of trover, the taking away and converting are the same, for every taking is a sufficient conversion to this purpose. *Cooper v. Monk*, Willes 55 [1737]. *Vide*: to the same point *Taylor v. Cole*, 3 T.R. 297 [1789]. There, the defendant justified the taking and converting goods to his own use as a distress for rent, selling sufficient to pay the rest and leaving the residue for the plaintiff, and it was insisted the defendant could not justify converting the whole and then say he only converted a part. But the court said [that] as the defendants had insisted that they took all the goods as a distress, they thought that this was a sufficient conversion of the whole.

Question: if [one is a] trespasser *ab initio* in seizing the ship, that is, if the justification a mere pretence. This to be decided by subsequent conduct. If for the party's own use, this shows it, but [it is] no abuse of authority in law to seize for one good cause and detain for another. *Vide*: *Six Carpenters' Case*.[98]

Lord Keith's examination upon the trial of the cause – *Wilson v. Marryat* upon the 16th December[99]

Wilson v. Marryat—Tried at Guildhall the 16th of December 1797.

The Right Honourable Lord Keith (sworn), examined by Mr *Adam*.

Q. Your lordship commanded the British squadron at the Cape of Good Hope?

A. I commanded the British force at the Cape of Good Hope, and all over the East Indies, at the time that the *Argonaut* arrived at the Cape of Good Hope.

Q. The *Argonaut* came there we understand in the month of August 1795.

A. In the beginning of August 1795.

Q. The vessel was detained by your order as we understand?

A. Not in the first instance. I will state with the permission of the court in a few words the cause of the original detention, prior to the arrival of the *Argonaut*. An American vessel stood in, in the night, and landed three men with money and an information of a large force coming against the Cape of Good Hope. The vessel disappeared before morning.

Lord KENYON, I do verily believe my Lord Keith need not go into any evidence to vindicate his own conduct because all the world are agreed in that question.

---

[97] These brief notes by Lawrence are on the reverse side of the Copy of the Record first filed in the case.

[98] *Six Carpenters' Case* (1610) 8 Co. Rep. 146a. At this point in the manuscript, Lawrence wrote the following and crossed it out: 'Should have replied in such a way as to show the action was brought for the subsequent detention as a substantive injury and not as making the original taking lawful; if that could not be as no fresh taking, the action is mistaken.'

[99] This document was transferred by Lawrence from his Paper Book for *Wilson v. Marryatt* (LPB 244) to the Paper Book for *Collet v. Keith* (LPB 297).

Lord Keith—The colony was filled with uproar and apprehension but we could not trace from whence that information came. The men absconded and got into the country at that time. I found them afterwards. I held a conversation with my colleague Sir James Craig upon the grounds that the French and Dutch force, as we imagined them to be, must have passed the Cape 'ere that time. We consulted upon the measures to be pursued to overtake them. We agreed to embark 6,000 men. I have the agreement signed by Sir James Craig and myself to pursue the French and Dutch force to the island of Mauritius or Batavia supposing they must have passed the Cape by that time the *Argonaut* arrived upon the 2nd of August. To the best of my recollection letters were put into my hand in six hours after her arrival,

Mr *Erskine*—We cannot hear evidence as to any letters.

Mr *Adam*—Mention the fact.

A. Confirming that the Dutch fleet had not passed.

Mr *Erskine*—Tho' it is no evidence against my client, yet I should be sorry to interrupt Lord Keith in any thing which can at all elucidate his reasons for doing that which I have no doubt he did from the best judgment, and which I am not at all questioning.

Mr *Adam*—Your Lordship had reason to believe that the Dutch fleet had not passed?

A. I had.

Q. In consequence of your belief that the Dutch fleet had not passed was any thing done with regard to the detention of the *Argonaut*?

A. General Craig and I agreed to lay a general embargo upon the whole Colony that no vessel should sail for forty days—

Q. That affected the *Argonaut* of course?

A. Yes, and the British East India fleet also and every ship that was there—of all nations whatever. It was a general embargo.

Q. Did you give any particular orders with regard to the *Argonaut*?

A. At that moment no—the Master of the *Argonaut* attended. An officer formerly belonging to the States General and recently to His Majesty went in the course of his duty on board the *Argonaut* and removed her into a situation of safety.

Q. Do you know in point of fact that the *Argonaut* was removed into a state of safety?

A. Yes, and had she remained where she first anchored she must have been drowned in twenty-four hours.

Q. Do you know the fact that your order was obeyed?

A. She was removed merely for safety and not at this time with any view of detention—

Q. What would have been the consequence if she had remained in her original station?

A. In my humble opinion she must have been lost in the course of twenty-four hours, for if the enemy had appeared she must have been struck with our shot. The court will do me the honour to understand that the fleet was in a situation of defence.

Mr *Erskine*—Had your Lordship seen the *Argonaut* at this time or did you trust to report?

A. I had not seen her myself but my orders are upon record and can be proved. I had seen the *Argonaut* at her first arrival, but not in the place to which she was removed.

Mr *Adam*—Did your Lordship take any further steps respecting the *Argonaut*?

A. Yes, the marines and seamen and an officer were sent on board the *Argonaut* as had been the constant practice on board of all ships that had anchored in the Cape from the day the Dutch surrendered it to prevent smuggling or improper communications but not to restrain the liberty of any person that might choose to go on shore to purchase provision and return when they pleased.

Q. Did your lordship give orders to the master attendant and to the adjutant of the fleet or our captain to do any thing respecting the *Argonaut*?

A. Yes, to compliment the ship upon her arrival and to say that every thing that was in the port belonging to His Majesty was at their disposal. A civil thing that is done upon the arrival of every ship into port and particularly those of America. To offer stores and provisions, and I offered to put water on board in my own boats.

Mr *Erskine*—Who was the master attendant?

A. Donald Taite.

Mr *Adam*—Does your lordship know from any communication with Captain Collet himself that these orders were received by him?

A. I repeated to Captain Collet himself more than once, twice or thrice what I have already sworn.

Q. Was any thing further done with respect to the *Argonaut*?

A. Whilst I was consulting with General Craig at the Cape material information came to me from the *Argonaut*, that induced me to apply to the Court of Justice to bring up Captain Collet to the court and his papers that they might be inspected, and upon inspection of the papers I detained the ship as a contraband trader—but not in the first instance. He might have sailed if he had chose in forty-eight hours, and I should have asked no questions. The courts are slow there. I did nothing of this sort by my own authority. I took the law of the place with me.

Q. Have you got the ship's papers here?

A. They are in court. They were sworn to in my presence before a court of justice.

Q. Did you give any directions with respect to controlling the captain in the management of the ship?

Mr *Erskine*—Were not your lordship's orders in writing?

A. Many of them were.

Mr *Adam*—Had you any communication with Mr Collet upon this subject?

A. He was with me at the Cape. He lived at the Cape Town.

Q. How far off is the Cape Town?

A. It is commonly called twenty-five miles, the absolute measure is twenty-two miles and three-quarters.

Q. Was he compelled to remain in the Cape Town?

A. No, the Cape Town is as free as the streets of London to every man.

Q. Can you state how long Captain Collet remained in Cape Town?

A. I cannot positively say because I went to Saldanha Bay. When I returned again I found him where I left him after having repeatedly admonished him to take care of the ship or to relinquish her to me in writing. He always refused, and sometimes not in the civilest terms.

Mr *Erskine*—Was that by letter?

A. In conversation repeatedly and in the presence of witnesses who can put me right if I am wrong—and I had much to do.

Mr *Adam*—Did your Lordship write a letter to Captain Collet of the 20 September 1796?

A. I have not seen the paper since that time. I cannot charge my memory with it.

Mr *Erskine*—Do you call for that letter?

Mr *Adam*—Yes.

Mr *Erskine*—Then I will produce it.

Letter from Lord Keith to Captain Collet dated Table Bay September 20th 1796. Read.

Mr *Adam*—At this time the vessel was detained as a contraband trader?

A. At this time the vessel was in the custody of a court and examination taken.

Q. You had at this time no authority of yourself to release the vessel?

A. No, by the capitulation, the laws of the Cape were to remain as they were before—this Court of Judicature took cognizance of Admiralty causes before.

Q. The ship was under the authority of the court that acted generally under the capitulation as the Admiralty Court?

A. Yes.

Q. At this time had Captain Collet a power of regulating the navigation of his ship in the place in which she was, or was he restrained from so doing?

A. I have said before he was more than five times advised by myself to take proper caution to secure his ship which was in a state of insecurity. He said one time that he would, at another time that he would not, and that the court of England should pay for it.

Q. Do you know any thing of the state of the ship from your own knowledge?

A. No, I never saw the ship's cables—but Captain Collet represented to me in the presence of Mr Jackson the secretary and half a dozen clerks that the ship's ground tackling was bad and the ship in a state of insecurity. I said it is easy to write to me for a cable, and you shall have one, two or three if you please.

Q. What did Captain Collet say upon your offering him cables?

A. He said, I consider that I have nothing more to do with the ship, I do not intend to return to her. I recurred to what I had said before, be so good as write me that and I shall know how to proceed—I shall never dispossess you of your ship, but if you relinquish her, undoubtedly I will take care of her.

Q. Did you receive any letter from him to that effect, giving up the ship?

A. No.

Q. Did he apply for a cable?

A. No, never.

Q. Did he continue to remain at that time at the Cape Town, absent from the ship?

A. Yes, till the loss of the ship. Underwood the second mate sent an express that the ship was lost, which passed through my hands.

Q. Do you know what the number of the crew left on board the *Argonaut* was?

A. I do not, but I know nothing of impressing any of them. Some abandoned the ship and some came to me personally for protection. An Irishman of the name of Barron, I believe, came and asked my protection.

Q. How does your Lordship know that he was an Irishman?

A. He told me so, and he has made oath of it.

Q. Did you know it from his dialect or from any other circumstance?

A. I conversed with the man. He told me he was an Irishman, had served the king.

Q. Did any other of the crew come to your lordship?

A. Yes.

Mr *Erskine*—I object to the statement of any thing which passed between the crew and Lord Keith.

Lord Keith—I conversed with every one of the crew at the Court of Justice when they were examined.

Mr *Erskine*—Was Mr Collet present at that time?

A. Yes.

Mr *Erskine*—Were not all those examinations taken down in writing?

A. The examinations touching the cause were taken down in writing.

Mr *Adam*—Did not there a conversation pass in the presence of Mr Collet which was not taken down in writing?

A. Yes.

Mr *Erskine*—Was not every thing relative to Captain Collet's adventure which you thought material to examine him to, taken down in writing?

A. Yes, the court followed its own practice—

Lord KENYON—Are those proceedings here?

Mr *Erskine*—They are.

Mr *Law*—What Mr Collet says in presence of Lord Keith is undoubtedly evidence.

Mr *Erskine*—No doubt it is.

Lord Keith—I conversed with men from Scotland and from the Isle of Man.

I conversed with no Americans there, save the one that has been examined here.

Mr *Erskine*—I object to that being received.

Lord KENYON—To be sure, that is not evidence, what countrymen the men were.

Mr *Adam*—Did Captain Collet admit to you that he was a native of the Isle of Man?

Mr *Erskine*—That I object to.

Mr *Adam*—Had you any conversation with Captain Collet with respect to the place of his nativity?

A. Yes.

Mr *Erskine*—Was not that an answer given by him upon an interrogatory and committed to writing or was it in familiar conversation with your lordship?

A. In both.

Mr *Adam*—I ask your lordship to [consider] the familiar conversation. In that conversation did Captain Collet say any thing to you where he was born?

A. Upon his arrival at the Cape of Good Hope he told me he was positively bound to China.

Q. Did he say where he was born?

A. Yes, in the Isle of Man.

Q. Did he say any thing with respect to the place of nativity of Barron, his mate?

A. No, Barron, his mate, came to me for the king's protection.

Q. Did any thing pass in the presence of Captain Collet upon the part of Barron with respect to the place of Barron's birth?

A. I believe Collet was present.

Mr *Erskine*—Supposing Barron said that in the presence of Mr Collet, does that bind him?

Lord KENYON: It is not evidence to be sure.

Mr *Adam*—Did any thing pass between Collet and your lordship with respect to the birth of any other of the men?

A. Yes, Bane, a man from Scotland.

Mr *Erskine*—Did Collet say he was from Scotland?

A. Collet heard him say so.

Mr *Law*—Did Collet hear him say so to your lordship in any conversation not in the course of a judicial proceeding?

A. It was in the court he heard him say so. Collet told me he had taken an apprentice to him from an apothecary living, I think, on Snow Hill, that the father was an apothecary on or near Snow Hill. I saw the young man and spoke to him. Captain Collet told me he had met with a relation of his own on Ludgate Hill, I think of the name of Collet and engaged him to go with him as a seaman.

Q. Do you know of your own knowledge to what number the crew was reduced?

A. No, but I know that no man was impressed but British subjects.

Q. Could any man be impressed without your Lordship's knowledge?

A. It was irregular if there was. A fiscal[1] apprehended all strangers about the streets if they were British subjects, in order to go on board the fleet. If they were French subjects in order to go to prison.

Q. Did Captain Collet ever apply to you for assistance of men?

A. No, he might have had what assistance he pleased if he had wrote a note to me for that purpose.

Q. Did he ever make any complaint to your Lordship of his men being improperly impressed and taken away?

A. I never heard it 'till I came to Europe. I heard stories about the Cape of men abandoning the *Argonaut* but I knew nothing of that.

Q. How long was it before the loss of the ship that you offered Captain Collet a cable?

A. From the first of his arrival, particularly once at the door of the house in which he lodged, which was close by my own. I met him early in the morning when I had been taking a view of stores and talked with him familiarly. I meant it civilly and in attention to him, but he was rather enraged. I was very humble and I only bowed and said such things as I had to offer. Perhaps I had done too much.

Q. Could you judge from the situation of the ship whether if proper care had been taken of her the ship might have been saved?

Mr *Erskine*—Did you see her in the berth where she was?

A. Positively, yes, and knew that if she had been properly secured with good anchors and cables she was in the safest and best place in Simon's Bay, without exception. Otherwise I have no knowledge in marine matters.

Mr *Adam*—Simon's Bay is a cove within False Bay?

A. False Bay is the ocean. Symond's [sic] Bay is a cove within it. She was within the men-of-war in the place where merchants' ships are usually put for safety.

Q. I understand that at the time this vessel was lost and indeed at the time you offered a cable and offered to take charge of her if he by letter would give her up that your Lordship was then proceeding in the Court of Admiralty to have the vessel condemned?

A. No, not for condemnation but as to grave authority to send over to this country. I was doing the best I could in case of any accident or of the Cape being taken from us, which might have been in a few days afterwards. I was doing it for my own vindication to government.

The Right Honourable Lord Keith
Cross-examined by Mr *Erskine*

Q. Was this vessel libelled in the Admiralty Court for the purpose of condemnation?

---

[1] In Dutch colonies, 'A magistrate whose duty it is to take cognizance of offences against the revenue,' as in 'fiscal of the Admiralty'. *OED*.

A. No, I did not expect to derive any advantage from her. She was seized for the Crown.

Q. Had you these examinations taken for the purpose of transmitting them to England?

A. Yes.

Q. Was that court exercising any other jurisdiction than that which you conferred upon it by directing those examinations for your own objects, which I admit were proper ones?

A. They were carrying on the legislation of the country in every respect as they had done before.

Q. Was this a voluntary proceeding on their part?

A. I proceeded by a memorial stating to the court the case between the *Argonaut* and the Crown.

Q. Your lordship set this cause in motion by a memorial and in consequence of that these examinations were taken?

A. I applied to the court there, not choosing to interfere with the law myself.

Q. Upon your memorial this was done. Had your lordship written this letter first (showing it to his lordship) or was it written by the authority of the court when your lordship seized upon the vessel as an illicit trader?

A. I wrote this letter certainly.

Q. Your lordship was not a member of the court?

A. No.

Q. Then you did not write this letter as a member of that Supreme Court of Justice or whatever it may be called at the Cape of Good Hope?

A. This is dated the 19th of September.

Q. This is a letter written by your lordship, your lordship acting for the public in seizing this vessel as an illicit trader?

A. Yes. Subsequent to this I applied to the court for their sanction on purpose that the paper might come fairly to this country.

Mr *Erskine*—I wish this letter may be read.

Letter from Lord Keith to Mr John Collet dated 19th September 1796. Read.

Mr *Erskine*—After having written this letter and after the seizure had taken place by your lordship's authority you applied to this Court of Justice for the purpose of having the ship's papers brought before that court?

A. And authenticated.

Q. And for taking all the examinations which afterwards were taken by the Court in consequence of the memorial presented by your lordship?

A. Yes.

Q. You had seized this vessel previous to her being seized as an illicit trader, from reasons of public policy?

A. I had laid an embargo upon her—but I took off the embargo when I seized her as an illicit trader.

Q. Was that done for the purpose of letting her go?

A. Certainly not. It was for the purpose of detaining her.

Q. Had she the liberty of departing from the Cape of Good Hope at any period from the time when you seized her as an illicit trader 'till she went on shore?

A. Certainly not.

Q. Was there any time at which there were no persons on board that vessel belonging to the public?

A. No, and if she had remained there seven years she could not, unless orders had come from England to the contrary. They were merely to prevent smuggling.

Q. Was it by your lordship's orders that the yards and topsails were struck?

A. That was a matter of security. As you must know in bad weather the sails were stored in order to prevent them being destroyed and wasted. They were put down below to keep them from damage.

Q. But if you were disposed to go to sea you would keep your sails to the yard?

A. The moment the ship was detained I did not intend she should go to sea.

Q. Do you know whether the ship was removed from the place where she originally was with your lordship's orders?

A. The master attendant did it as a matter of safety, not by any positive orders from me, for which he receives I believe a fee of ten dollars.

Q. Has he a right to do that without any particular orders?

A. I believe in all parts of the world, in Europe, Asia, Africa and America, it is the duty of the master attendant, who is both a civil and a naval officer to do it.

Q. It was upon the ship's papers that you seized this vessel as an illicit trader?

A. Yes. After examining the American papers I knew of no Act of parliament, allowing this trade for one plain reason, because no Act of parliament had passed.

One of the jury—when did your Lordship first seize her as an illicit trader?

A. I have not the letter before me. The letter will show it.

[*Letters referred to in Lord Keith's Examination*]

To: Mr John Collet, Master of the Ship, *Argonaut*

Sir, In reply to your letter, I am to inform you that the *Argonaut* is detained as an illicit trader, and part of the cargo may be sold, and the value deposited in the hands of such officers of the Court of Justice as may be appointed to receive it, but I cannot permit any other appropriation of the value.

I am, Sir
Your most obedient humble servant.
G. K. Elphinstone.

Monarch 19 September 1796.

To: Mr John Collet, Master of the Ship, *Argonaut*

Sir, If you relinquish the *Argonaut*, it will be my duty to cause her to be taken care of, any part of the cargo may be sold as you shall think proper, the value being secured in the competent court at this place as before signified to you.

You will be pleased to communicate to me a regular statement of the money due and which you are consequently inclined to pay to your officers and crew that I may subjoin thereto my approval of appropriating a sum adequate to the purpose.

Your application for copies of the papers more immediately concerns the Court of Justice to whom I am equally answerable as yourself. You will therefore address the court on the subject.

You have my permission to take from the *Argonaut* any part or the whole of your personal property, including apparel, furniture, and books, but not treasure or any other article not usually requisite for current purposes nor any article of trade.

I am, Sir
Your most obedient humble servant.

Monarch—Table Bay, the 20 September 1796.   G. K. Elphinstone.

In The King's Bench	LPB 311
Pollard	
v.	Special Case
Bell[2]	[*Ult. Concilium*]

[*Lawrence headnote:*] A warranty of neutrality is not falsified by a sentence of a Court of Admiralty condemning a ship for navigating contrary to the ordinances of a belligerent power to which the neutral power has not agreed by treaty.

Mr Justice Lawrence

Stands in the paper for Tuesday the 19th of November 1799.

[28 January 1800, judgment for plaintiff]

Gregg and *Corfield*

In the King's Bench[3]

Between: William Pollard and another, plaintiffs
and
William Bell, defendant

Case for the Opinion of the Court

This is an action upon a policy of assurance on goods on board a ship called the *Juliana*, 'warranted a Dane', on the voyage 'at and from London to Teneriffe with liberty to touch at Guernsey and Madeira'. The defendant subscribed the policy on the 23rd of August 1796 as an underwriter for the sum of £200 at a premium of four guineas per cent. The policy was effected by the plaintiffs as agents on the account and for the benefit of certain persons resident in the island of Teneriffe in whom the interest is averred. There are counts in the declaration for a total loss by capture of the goods on board the *Juliana* for money paid, laid out, and expended, and for money had and received. The defendant pleaded the general issue, non-*assumpsit*, and paid the premium into court, and the cause was tried at the sitting after Trinity Term 1799 before the Right Honourable LLOYD Lord KENYON, lord chief justice of this honourable court, when the jury found a verdict for the plaintiff with damages £____ [*sic*], costs 40s., subject to the opinion of the court upon the following

---

[2] (1800) 8 T.R. 434. See pp. xxxvi–xxxvii above for a discussion of the instrumental use of manuscript case-notes in the *Pollard* case.

[3] In the margin, Lawrence noted the following: 'First question, what is the ground of the sentence. Secondly, if the warranty of neutrality is thereby falsified [by] clear ground of condemnation, acting contrary to French ordinance—was that no impingement of neutrality?'

Case

That the persons for whose benefit and on whose account the said policy was effected at the time of making the said insurance were and still are resident in the island of Teneriffe. That the *Juliana* was a Danish ship and the property of Danish subjects and previous to the voyage insured had obtained a passport signed by the king of Denmark for a voyage from Copenhagen to ports in the East Indies. That Captain Eggleston, the master of the said ship, sailed from Copenhagen on the 23rd of June 1796, having on board a partial cargo of tar, pitch, cordage, cables, trump leather, French brandy, sail cloth, and coals, and in pursuance of the verbal instructions of the owners of the *Juliana* arrived in the Thames on the 23rd of July 1796. That during his stay in the said river, he took on board a quantity of goods on account of the owners of the said ship. That he there also received on board goods upon which the policy mentioned in the declaration is written and having taken out his clearances for Guernsey and Madeira on the 23rd of August 1796, he sailed upon the voyage insured. That after having put into Guernsey and taken on board other additional goods on account of the owners of the said ship on the 27th of August, he proceeded on his voyage and was captured on the 18th of September by a French privateer, *La Dorade*, Captain Ferrand, and carried into Bordeaux.

That at the time of the said capture and during the whole voyage insured the *Juliana* had on board the passport as above described together with every other document usually carried by Danish ships. That she had also a *roll d'equipage* containing the names and places of nativity of the officers, but it did not express the names nor the places nor the nation of the persons composing the crew, but stated them generally to be sixty men of colour.

That Captain Eggleston, the master of the said ship for the said voyage insured, was born in Scotland of British parents under the allegiance of the king. That he was not naturalized in Denmark, but on the 6th October 1794 posterior to the war between England and France had obtained letters of burghership in that country, but that he had no domicile in Denmark, never having resided there.

Upon the ship's arrival at Bordeaux, proceedings were instituted by the captors before the Tribunal of Commerce, and a sentence, whereof the following is an extract, was pronounced in that court.

First Sentence of Condemnation	Extract of the Judgment given by the Tribunal of Commerce at Bordeaux the 14th Nivôse, 5th Year.[4]

---

[4] Between 1792 and 1805 France used what was known as the Republican Calendar. The months were renamed, and the calendar began with the foundation of the republic on 22 September 1792, the autumn equinox. Since the autumn equinox did not always fall on the same day, there could be variation in the start date for a given year. The 4th and 5th years referenced in *Pollard* v. *Bell* were 1795–1796 (starting 23 September) and 1796–1797 (starting 22 September). The months of the Republican Calendar for the years that began on 22 September were as follows:

Vendémiaire   22 September–21 October

The ship *Juliana*, Captain Eggleston, is she Danish property, and are these facts proved by the papers found on board? Are these papers sufficient to establish and warrant the neutrality of the goods loaded at Copenhagen? The merchandises loaded at London, are they accompanied with pieces to establish them to be neutral property?[5]

Considering on the first question—That the certain character of neutrality of a ship is traced in the treaties between the different powers of Europe and in the *Reglements* anterior and posterior to the treaties. That the Treaty of Commerce passed between France and Denmark the 23rd August 1742, article 21, says that the ships of the two powers shall be furnished with a passport containing a special statement of the cargo attested and marked with the signatures and usual seals of the officers of the Admiralty in that place from which they first parted, and with their declaration of the destination. That Captain Eggleston at the time of the capture was furnished with a passport to go from Copenhagen the 20th June 1796, signed by the king of Denmark, by which it appears that the ship *Juliana* went from Copenhagen to sail to places in the East Indies without this passport safeguard being signed and sealed by the officers of the Admiralty at Copenhagen, as it is precisely ordered in the 21st article of the said treaty. Considering that one of the principal characters of neutrality, as ordered in the 2nd article of the *reglements* dated 26 July 1778, is the act of property of the ship. Considering Captain Eggleston has produced no act of property of the ship *Juliana*, not even an act to prove as he pretends that the ship has been built at Frederick-nagore.[6] That the certificate found on board dated 5th November 1794, signed Lars Earsen, declares in expressive terms that he has only repaired the ship and put her in good order, and adds that the ship was not furnished with a letter of construction. Considering that a second character of neutrality as ordered by the *reglement* of July 26, 1778 is that the list of the ship's crew shall be made by public officers of that neutral place the ship parted from, and if not furnished with this piece, the ship shall be declared good prize. That the said 9th article of the said *reglement* make an absolute law of it. Considering the roll of the ship's crew found on board the

Brumaire	22 October–20 November
Frimaire	21 November–20 December
Nivôse	21 December–19 January
Pluviôse	20 January–18 February
Ventôse	19 February–20 March
Germinal	21 March–19 April
Floréal	20 April–19 May
Prairial	20 May–18 June
Messidor	19 June–18 July
Thermidor	19 July–17 August
Fructidor	18 August–21 September

[5] Throughout this extract, Lawrence wrote brief marginal phrases to describe the contents of the paragraphs opposite. These phrases are not reproduced.
[6] Frederick-nagore was a Danish colony in India, near Serampore, West Bengal. It was occupied twice by the British during their war with Denmark, and the colony failed as a commercial venture. The Danish East India Company went bankrupt in 1777, and Serampore became a Danish crown colony. In 1845 Denmark ceded Serampore to Britain.

Juliana do [*sic*] not contain the names of more than the names of the officers and carpenter of the said ship and do not in the least mention the rest of the people; however, Captain Eggleston declared before the justice of the peace when questioned that his ship's crew consisted of sixty or seventy men. Considering there was found among the papers deposited at the secretary's a list taken *per* Extract No. 918 signed by Eggleston and signed underneath Schultz, and visited the 20th June 1796, signed Kaas, nevertheless this list cannot be called a roll of the ship's crew, as it has the same fault with the other in not containing more than the names of the four principal officers with the explanation of their honours and places of nativity. The rest are mentioned in a mass, 'sixty men of colour', without their names and what nation they are. That this omission in the list of the ship's crew is in contravention to the *reglement* because it is impossible to discover from it if more than one-third of the ship *Juliana*'s crew consists of subjects of enemies to France. Considering the 5th article of the same *reglement* 1778 orders that no regard shall be paid to the passports granted by neutral powers if those who obtained them is [*sic*] found to have acted in contravention. That Captain Eggleston had contravened to his passport or letter of safeguard which has been granted him in Copenhagen because by this letter the *Juliana* was destined to places in the East Indies, and he has voluntarily stopped at London and there loaded merchandises for Madeira, Madras and Calcutta, all places belonging to enemies to France. Considering it has been advanced by Captain Eggleston's defender that the ship *Juliana* has been at Guernsey and loaded merchandise there, notwithstanding amongst the papers deposited at the secretary's, not one piece has been found relative to this loading. That all these separate contraventions to the *reglement*s are sufficient to operate the confiscation of the ship *Juliana*.

Considering the second question, that the cargo taken in at Copenhagen consists partly in sail cloth, cordage, pitch, and tar, and is not accompanied with any bill of loading. Considering what Captain Eggleston has mentioned in his pleadings that the general bill of loading of his cargo taken at Copenhagen existed at the time his ship was captured and that with all probability it was suppressed or lost. His attestation on this point is ungrounded because a list was found among the rest of the papers relative to the *Juliana*, signed Jacobson, containing all the ship's papers on which no mention is made about the general bill of loading for the cargo taken at Copenhagen. That the want of such a bill of loading is a formal contravention to the 20th article of the *reglement* of the 26th July 1778, that this contravention against the *reglement* is sufficient reason for declaring good prize the merchandise taken in at Copenhagen.

Considering on the third question that the aforesaid 2nd article of said regulation says that charter-parties and bills of loading not signed are null and of no effect. That a part of the bills of loading found on board the *Juliana* are not signed by Captain Eggleston and that none of all these bills of loading, one excepted, annunciate [*sic*] the neutrality of the property, that the want of this annunciation is a formal contravention to the 2nd article of the *reglement* of

1778. Considering the goods loaded at London in the *Juliana* are destined for Madeira, Madras and Calcutta, are enemies' ports, one bale excepted, addressed to Calcutta, and consigned to Captain Eggleston, of which the bill of loading annuncited to be Danish property.

That this loading is made in contravention not only to the ancient *reglements* but also to the decree of the National Convention of the 9th May and 27th July 1793 against the *arrêts* of the Executive Directory of the 14th and 28th Messidor, the 4th year, and against the letter of the marine minister of the 20th Frimaire, 5th year. That the first article of the decree of the 9th May 1793 orders that the French ships of war and cruisers shall stop and bring into the ports of the Republic the neutral ships found to be loaded in full or partly with combustibles belonging to neutrals and destined to enemies' ports or with merchandises belonging to enemies. That the 2nd article of the said decree orders that the merchandise belonging to enemies shall be declared good prize and be sold for the benefit of the capturers.

That the *arrêt* of the Executive Directory of the 14th Messidor year 4th, orders that it should be notified without delay to all neutral and allied powers that the flag of the French Republic shall behave in the same manner to the neutral vessels as to the confiscations, visitations, and arrestations as these powers suffered themselves to be used by the English in this respect. That in the letter from the marine minister of the 20th Frimaire, 5th year, addressed to the principal commissary of the marine and by him transmitted to the tribunal with the two *arrêts* of the Directory, is decreed the 14th Messidor last. That by the example of the English, the French armateurs shall capture on board the neutral vessels all merchandises dispatched for destination and account of enemies of which the bills of lading do not express the indisputable neutrality. Considering it is constant that the pieces relative to the merchandises loaded on the *Juliana* be in Copenhagen, be it in Copenhagen, be it in London, do not in the least annunciate it to be neutral property, with the exception of the aforesaid bale to the address and consignment of Captain Eggleston, of which the bill of loading announces the Danish or neutral property.

That is likewise constant there exists on board the ship eleven cannon and 150 cannon balls, of which no mention is made in the papers found on board and deposed at the secretary's. That these cannons and balls, agreeable to all laws and *reglements* and even by the treaty between France and Denmark, are one of the number of objects forming contraband, and subject to confiscation. Considering that after an exact research and visitation of the papers, not one piece is found to clear Captain Eggleston from the different contraventions remarked in the procedure. In considerance, the tribunal, without stopping at things said or alleged by Captain Eggleston, declare as good prize the ship *Juliana* and all her cargo with the exception of the one bale aforesaid, the said bale shall be delivered to the captain. In consequence the tribunal confiscated the cargo, the profit of the capturers, Jean Baptiste Ferrand & Co., armateurs of the crusier *La Dorade* of this port, and authorized the said capturers, Ferrand & Co., to dispose of the said ship and cargo as goods belonging to themselves and conforming to what is prescribed by the laws. The tribunal condemn also Captain Eggleston to all expenses, costs for the judgment, procedure, liquidation, &c. pronounced at Bordeaux at the audience of the Tribunal de Commerce in presence of the parties 14th Nivose, 5th year of the Republic, one and indivisible.

Signed Bomner, President

From this sentence Captain Eggleston appeals to the Civil Tribunal of La Gironde, and the following is part of the proceedings on such appeal as reported by Citizen Perrens, the president:

That the Tribunal of Commerce ought not to have decreed the ship *Juliana* a legal capture on the pretext that the list of the crew was not backed by the public officers of the Admiralty of the place of her departure, conformable to the 9th article of the regulation of 1778, and that the list that had been found among his papers, signed by him Eggleston, could not be considered as the list because it contained mention of the superior officers and the number of sixty men without any description of their names, residences, and country to which they belonged. That in this the Tribunal of Commerce were in an error because there were amongst the papers of the ship two ship lists of the crew, the one delivered and signed by the chief of the Office of Classes at Copenhagen, also sealed with the Admiralty seal, and the other approved by the admiral at the head of the marine and by the chief officer of the guard of the port alone entrusted with this employ, and that if these lists did not contain any designation of the names of the sixty men of the crew, nor of the residence, nor of the nation of which they belonged, it was because it was not the usage of Denmark, as he proved from the declarations which he produced of the members of the Royal Council of Direction and of Commerce at Copenhagen, of the consul-general of Denmark at Paris, of the chargé d'affairs of the King of Denmark to the French Republic, of the vice-admiral, and of the counsellor secretary of state at Copenhagen for the affairs of India.

That concerning the last motives for the decree of the Tribunal of Commerce relative as well to the shipment of the goods for Madeira, Madras, and Calcutta, as to the bills of lading of which the larger part were not found signed by the captain and which with the exception of only one did not express their being neutral property, first, that the cannon and balls made part of the ship's stores and that they were expressed in the inventory which was not found on board, not through his fault but that of the captain of *La Dorade*, and that they could not consider arms as a contraband object unless it had been proved (which it was not) that they were to be carried to enemies, as is declared in the first article of the regulation of 1778. Second, that he had orders from the fitters-out of the ship the *Juliana* to buy sail cloth in England which he had purchased as also her supercargo and his lieutenant had bought goods for their own account both at London and at Guernsey, which he proved by the bills of lading and by the invoice, and that this particular property should neither have been seized or confiscated. Third, that the goods shipped for account of certain English merchants neither ought to have been seized any more because the 28th article of the treaty of 1742 positively expresses that the merchandize which shall be found on board a Danish vessel shall be clear and free although the cargo may wholly or partially belong to the enemies of France.

The court then proceeded to pronounce the following sentence:

Sentence of Condemnation: Considering the Treaty of Commerce of 1742 has ceased being in force in 1764, at which time were expired the fifteen years during which it was to be observed between France and Denmark and which had been prorogued the first time, that this delay being expired without a fresh prorogation the treaty no longer formed any contract for these powers that could reciprocally bind them in so much that it could no longer be considered as a law relating to them or any of its provisions.

That there is not in effect, as the Executive Directory has observed to the Tribunals in its Decree of the 12th Ventose in the 5th year, any other than the actual and existing treaties which should claim their attention respecting the validity or invalidity of prizes in the causes that might be brought before them and submitted to their decision. Of course there is no doubt that the Treaty of Commerce of 1742 by that even that [sic], [because] it no longer exists between France and Denmark, cannot be quoted in this process by the Captain Eggleston, as by the same reason the tribunal cannot take it as a basis for it decisions.

That in matters of prize it is on the contrary in the maritime laws as well ancient as modern that should guide, that is to say in the ordinance of the marine of the month of August 1691, in the regulations of 1744 and 1778, the decrees of the National Convention of the 9th of May and 27th of July 1793, especially in the regulation of 1778, for the particular hypothesis of the process, because this regulation is so much more binding for the Danes, that Captain Eggleston is expressly subject thereto by his list of the ship's crew.[7]

Considering that these laws and these regulations have many different provisions that declare as legal capture the ships and their cargo, but of which some only relate to the ships and others to their cargo according to the cases they determine.

That the ordinance of the Marine respecting prizes stipulates the first—that all ships which shall be found to be loaded with effects belonging to the enemies of France shall be legal capture. That the decrees of the 9th of May and 27th of July 1793 permit the men-of-war and French privateers to stop and conduct to the ports of the Republic as well the neutral vessels which shall be found loaded wholly or in part with provisions belonging to neutrals and bound to enemies' ports and the merchandize belonging to enemies.

That the regulation of 1744 in the seventh, tenth, eleventh and twelfth articles, and that of 1778 in the articles of the fifth, sixth, seventh, and eighth contain general stipulations to pronounce neutral vessels a legal capture in the cases hereinafter mentioned.

1st: When these ships are met with at sea navigating under a passport and which has been deviated from by those who obtained it.

---

[7] Opposite this convoluted sentence, Lawrence notes in the margin: 'What does this mean?' He also struck out several iterations of the word 'in'.

2nd: When these passports are granted by neutrals or allied states to the proprietors or masters of ships, subjects of enemies' states, if they have not been naturalized or if they have not transferred the domiciliation of the neutral states before the declaration of war, these regulations stipulating in these cases that no regard should be paid to these passports.

3rd: Whensoever on board these ships shall be found a supercargo, merchant commissary, or chief officer being an enemy.

4th: Whenever the ships being of enemies' building, there shall not be found on board an authentic title of property made to an ally or a neutral before the declaration of war, popularly registered by the public officer or by the principal officer of the place of departure.

That independently of these provisions which are general in all these cases to each of these regulations, that of 1778 has four positive ones in the articles second, third, ninth, and eleventh.

That by the first of these articles it subjects the masters of ships to justify at sea their neutral property by their passport, bills of lading, and invoices and other ship's papers, one at least of which should verify this property or contain a precise declaration thereof. That by the second, it also declares to be legal capture all ships whatsoever nation they may be whether allies or neutrals when there shall have been any of the ship's papers suppressed or made away with. That by the third in like manner it declares to be legal capture every ship whose list of the crew is not approved of by the public officers of the place from whence she took her departure. That by the fourth it is stipulated that no regard shall be paid on any occasion whatever but to the papers only on board.

That the regulation of 1778, the first and second articles giving permission to stop neutral vessels (although they may have liberty to enter enemies' ports and to depart therefrom) at all times when they shall be found to be loaded with contraband goods destined for the enemy, to seize the goods, to confiscate them, even the ships, when they do not compose the three-fourths of the value of their loading, and reputes as such all those goods of which it is not specified their being neutral property, since it is obligatory on the master of the ship to justify this property by passports, bills of lading, invoices, and other ship papers.

That lastly the second article of the decree of the ninth of May 1793 contains expressly that the goods belonging to enemies shall be declared a legal capture and confiscated for the benefit of the captors.

That thus there is no doubt according to the intents of these laws and these regulations that the ships navigating under neutral colours should be declared to be legal captures seized and confiscated, as also their cargoes, if these ships and the goods which compose their cargo shall fall under any of the cases which they have stated and determined.

Considering that if one attends seriously to the series of facts that appears from the documents of the proceedings, one can clearly perceive that there is scarcely one of these cases but which are applicable to the ship *Juliana* and her cargo.

That one must not judge for a certainty of the non-neutrality of this ship for the deficiency of the forms required by the 21st article of the Treaty of 1742, as has been done by the Tribunal of Commerce when it has been determined by the first motive of his sentence that the passports of Captain Eggleston were an infringement of the provision of this article in that it was not authenticated with the signature of the officers of the Admiralty of Copenhagen, and that it was signed by the king of Denmark only, that in effect it is useless to examine whether this passport is or is not conformable to the provisions of this treaty, since it no longer was law between France and Denmark since 1764, the epoch at which it ceased being enforced—it therefore little signifies to know whether the passport was signed by the king of Denmark only, or whether, if authenticated with the signatures that now appear in succession to the first, it so existed previous to the sentence of the Tribunal of Commerce.

That all the arguments that have been entered into on this point in the cause of appeal are absolutely of no consequence since one cannot have recourse to terminate them to what is prescribed by the article in question of the Treaty of 1742.

That consequently that without entering into any of these discussions which would only prolong the decision of this affair at the same time that one would not probably obtain a full proof of the falsities supposed to have been preposterously committed on the passport of Captain Eggleston with reference to the author or authors of these errors, it is easy to decide if one can or cannot pay regard thereto according to the substance of the sixth article of regulation of 1778 conformable in all points to the eleventh article of that of 1744.[8]

That it is sufficient for that purpose by these two certain facts, the first that Captain Eggleston in only considering him as master of the ship *Juliana* is a subject of an enemy of French Republic, and the second that he is not naturalized a Dane. That of course is indisputable. That he is an enemy's subject to the French Republic since according to the examination before the justice of the peace, he was born in Scotland, that he is not the less so. That this Englishman has not obtained of the king of Denmark any letters of naturalization, since he could only produce letters of citizenship, and those even granted eighteen months after the declaration of war, letters which could not afford him at the best but a domicile in a neutral country, this domicile even illegal and of no effect since it was posterior to the declaration of war.

This being the case one cannot according to the precise terms of the sixth article of the regulation of 1778 pay any regard to the passport of Captain Eggleston, [even] had this passport in the beginning been authenticated with all the signatures prescribed by the twenty-first article of the Treaty of Commerce of 1742 and in the supposition that this treaty were still existing, because granted for a neutral port to a master of a ship an enemy's subject and not naturalized in a neutral country.

That one cannot any more decide whether the ship the *Juliana* is of English building although the Captain Eggleston has not openly explained himself

---

[8] In the margin Lawrence notes opposite this sentence: '*Nota Bene*'.

respecting the place of her construction. That there are in truth some strong presumptions that she was not built at Frederick-nagore as well from the declarations of the builders made in presence of the justice of the peace during the verbal process which states this evidence as according with the evidence given in proceedings of the Captains Destronet and Chiend and by the certificate of Lars Lensens, ship builder at Copenhagen, he has therein certified that when he performed the repairs of the *Juliana* he was not furnished with the documents of her building but on the other hand there are not any more positive proofs that she was built at Frederick-nagore or at any other of the English possessions.

That in this state of uncertainty which could not have been cleared up until it had been verified that she had been of English building it is impossible to argue against Captain Eggleston on the provision of the seventh article of the regulation of 1778 relative to the ships of enemies' construction to oblige Eggleston to produce an authentic document of the property of his ship as of an ally or neutral previous to the declaration of war and property registered before or in the presence of the principal officers of the place of her departure for the intent of reputing her a neutral because this article then supposes and evidently so that the ship is proved to be of enemy's building, and that here there is no proof whatever of this construction.

That one cannot in like manner argue against Captain Eggleston in the provision of the third article of the same regulation because it is not any more proved that any of the ship papers have been suppressed or made away with either by him or any one of his officers. That there is not on this point but some very vague circumstances in the verbal process of the 2nd and 8th Vendémiaire in the 5th year, and that on the other hand one finds in that of the 2nd complementary day in the 4th year that vessel delivered up those which he had endeavoured to conceal from the captain of the *Dorade* but although one cannot positively attach to him the provisions of these articles of the regulation of 1778, there are nevertheless others which he naturally falls under in the manner least equivocal:

1st: That it is indisputably proved against him of having had on board his ship an enemy's officer in the person of William Doeg, his first lieutenant, as well before as at the time of the capture of his ship.

2nd: As having acted contrary to his passport by going to London and Guernsey.

3rd: Of not having been able to justify either the property of his ship as a neutral or the property of the goods took on board at Copenhagen.

4th: Of having taken in at London and Guernsey goods belonging to enemies and destined to enemies' ports.

5th: Of not having had the list of the crew approved by the public officers of the place of departure of his ship.

That the first of these facts is as well proved as it can be by the acknowledgement made by William Doeg at his hearing of being born in Scotland and of having been in the service of Captain Eggleston for three years or thereabouts, a circumstance which above was sufficient to cause the ship the *Juliana* being pronounced a legal capture according to the eighth article of the regulation of 1778 and which, evident as it is, has nevertheless been overlooked by the Tribunal of Commerce, since it was not made one of the motives of its sentence.

That the second fact is in like manner proved as well by the confession of the Captain Eggleston of his second, of his first lieutenant, of his master, and of his passengers in their hearings before the justice of the peace as well by the invoices, bills of lading, and other ship papers, that is to say, that it manifestly appears from these accounts and from these documents that the Captain Eggleston, who, according to his passports, ought on sailing from Copenhagen to have gone direct to the East Indies, as to Tranquebar and its dependencies, the place of destination of his ship, has nevertheless touched twice, once at London, and secondly at Guernsey.

That he has in vain attempted to excuse this contravention of his passports by making exceptions, that it was not a touching at but a putting into which he had performed in the enemy's ports, that he had besides express orders from the fitters-out to go there, which nothing justifies:

1st: That he had been obliged to change his course by any casualty at sea, this he would not have omitted verifying by a protest if the fact had been so.

2nd: That there has been given him by his fitters-out orders such as he has stated, yet he does not produce any.

And lastly that if he had met with contrary winds in the manner he has alleged and to have been constrained to have put in both at London and at Guernsey, he would not have stayed in these ports the space of two months. That therefore it appears on the contrary that they voluntarily entered therein for the sole purpose of taking on board goods. That he therefore altered his course for the same intent and that he was consequently by that alone, acted in direct contradiction to his passport.

That the third fact is in like manner verified in the process by the deficiency of producing the document of property of the ship the *Juliana* as a neutral, and of the general bill of lading of the goods shipped at Copenhagen. That without doubt it was impossible for Captain Eggleston to justify at sea the property of both one and the other since he had not produced either any proof to establish that his ship belonged, as he has never ceased pretending, to the heirs of Christopher Hanson presiding at Frederick-nagore, or the general bill of lading of the goods shipped at Copenhagen.

That he has ineffectually rested his plea on these expressions of the second article of the regulation of 1778 in speaking of the ship's papers 'one of which at least shall contain a positive declaration of being neutral property' with intent to apply them to the declaration expressed in sundry documents which he had produced that his ship belonged to the heirs of Hanson and to the invoice of the cargo shipped at Copenhagen by Duntzfield & Co., who had dispatched the ship the *Juliana* for the pretended account of the same heirs. Also to the permits, the Turkish passport, and to the ship's certificate, all which could supply the said (according to him), of the general bill of lading, that the declaration of which he has availed himself, is not expressed with that style of precision to enable the ascertaining the neutral property. That the documents quoted by Captain Eggleston, by that even wherein they declared that the ship *Juliana* belongs to the heirs of Christopher Hanson, contains nothing positive or decisive, but on the contrary there appears a vagueness incompatible with this precision since they do not express who are these heirs, where they reside, and in what manner the ship first came to belong to Christopher Hanson, so that one cannot know whether the persons described under the vague title of heirs of Christopher Hanson, supposing it were proved that he was originally proprietor of the ship *Juliana*, have rightfully succeeded him or whether they are not other individuals and who instead of being domiciliated in a neutral country, they are rather in an enemy's country. That besides this, the invoice of the cargo shipped by Duntzfield & Co. of Copenhagen, the permits, the Turkish passport and the ship's certificate are absolutely in contradiction to the certificate which is more worthy of credit of the tribunals than all the other documents, makes not the least mention of the general bill of lading of the goods shipped at Copenhagen, although it contains in detail all the papers relative to the ship *Juliana*. That [it] is therefore rendered evident by these different circumstances that this ship does not belong to the heirs of Hanson, and that the goods shipped at Copenhagen are contraband. That in consequence one must consider the cannon, cannon balls, and other warlike stores, since they are no more provided with a bill of lading than the cordage, the sail cloth, the pitch and tar, the cables &c., which make part of the cargo taken in at Copenhagen.

That the fourth fact is no more doubtful than the preceding ones since the same confessions made by the Captain Eggleston, his officers and his passengers, as well as the bills of lading, invoices and other ship's papers alike, contain the proof that as well at London as at Guernsey there had been shipped on board the *Juliana* goods belonging to English merchants and destined for enemies' ports such as Madeira, Madras, and Calcutta.

That lastly the fifth fact is not less certain than all the rest, that is to say, that it appears from the inspection of the list of the ship's crew that it has not been approved by the public officers of the place of the departure of the ship *Juliana* as is required by the ninth article of the regulation of 1778. That the list even which was found among the ship's papers signed by Captain Eggleston is in itself imperfect since it only contains the chief officers and the complement of sixty men without any specification of their names, residences, or of the nation they belong to in such manner that one cannot know whether this crew is composed of friends or enemies to the French Republic.

That accordingly by making reference to the provisions of the maritime laws and regulations from which the decrees of the Executive Directory are merely the emanation and to the facts proved by the papers of the proceeding, it is fully decided that the ship *Juliana* and her cargo ought to be pronounced a legal capture to be seized and confiscated for the benefit of the fitters-out of the privateer the *Dorade* as being found nearly to have incurred all the cases they have provided against.

From this sentence Captain Eggleston appealed to the Supreme Tribunal of Cassation at Paris, which decreed as follows:

Final Sentence of Appeal: Having heard the parties by their counsel, the tribunal considering that it hath been fully proved by the confession of Captain Eggleston and ascertained by the judges of La Gironde that the said Captain Eggleston was born in Scotland and an enemy. That his designation in a neutral territory was not justified according to law. That his quality of enemy sufficed to legitimate the prize. That the fact of Captain Eggleston being a Scot and enemy existed independently of the papers on board. That in consequence all remedies of nullity drawn either from the withdrawing of some of the papers on board or from the non-application of the seal to the bag wherein they were included can give any way to *cassation*, rejects the request of Charles Eggleston and condemns him to the fine of 150 francs.

The counsel of each party are with the permission of the court at liberty to refer upon the argument of this case to the proceedings at large in the French courts of Admiralty and to the printed copy of the treaty between France and Denmark of 1742.

The question for the opinion of the court is whether the plaintiffs are entitled to recover in this action.

J.A. Park for the Plaintiffs
Ralph Carr for the Defendant

[Draft of Lawrence's Opinion][9]

Vide: Minute of the first sheet of the Paper Book where I have put down the two questions.[10] A warranty of neutrality does not induce any necessity to comply with the peculiar regulations of the belligerent powers. For if a ship be captured and the question be whether she be neutral or not, the general rule for judging and deciding on that point is the law of nations, subject to such alterations and modifications as may have been introduced by treaties. But where the law of nations has not been varied or departed from by mutual agreement, that is the general rule for deciding all questions in matter of prize. *Vide*: *Collecteana Juridica*, p. 135.[11]

When therefore a state in amity with a belligerent power has by treaty agreed that the ships of their subjects shall only have that character when furnished with certain precise documents, whoever warrants a ship as the property of such subject should provide himself with those evidences which have by the country to which it belongs been agreed to be the necessary proof of that character.

---

[9] This draft corresponds closely to Lawrence's opinion as given at 8 T.R. 339–343. No attempt has been made to decipher words or sentences that were crossed out by Lawrence in his draft.
[10] See p. 290, n. 3, above.
[11] See p. 304, n. 17, below.

In requiring this, no difficulty is imposed, of which the insured is not aware, and which may not be in his power to prevent, but to require of him to furnish himself with every document belligerent powers may require. And to insist that the warranty is not complied with unless according to their ordinances and regulations [by which they claim] the ship is [to be] navigated would be to deprive the insured of his indemnity for the want of papers &c., of the necessity of which he may fairly be presumed ignorant, which papers it may not be in his power to procure, for how can the officers, &c. of one country be called on to grant that which the laws of their own country do not require.

In examining the cases decided on this head, it will not be found that there is any determination of this court to support what is now insisted on, but on the contrary that many cases have settled it. A condemnation on the particular ordinances of a belligerent power is no violation of a warranty of neutrality.

In *Bernardi* v. *Matteux*, Doug. 554,[12] the *Joanna* was warranted neutral. The only doubt was whether the ship was condemned as being enemies' property, or for violating a French *arrêt* in throwing papers overboard.[13] For one or the other she was condemned, but it is not clear that it was as enemies' property. The plaintiff recovered.

The case of *Barzillai* v. *Lewis*, Park 335,[14] relied on by the defendants, was decided by Lord MANSFIELD on the ground of a non-compliance with the Treaty of Utrecht on the sentence having condemned the ship as English by the particular regulations. According to a note of that case taken by Mr Justice BULLER rather more full than that in print,[15] Lord MANSFIELD began his judgment by stating that the sentence of the Court of Admiralty as being inclusive, and that the question was, what did it mean? He afterwards observed that the ship was insured by her Dutch name, and the underwriters take it for granted that she is so, but when this is sifted in France, she appears to have none of the requisites to show that she was neutral property, for she never had been in a Dutch port, and the sea brief was not conformable to the Treaty of Utrecht. And he concluded by saying the condemnation is as an English ship, and it is not open for us to enquire whether it be right or wrong. Mr Justice WILLES, Mr Justice ASHHURST, and Mr Justice BULLER agreed on the ground of the ship not being properly documented, and Mr Justice BULLER's minute of what he said is in these words: 'The first sentence seems to have been on particular *arrêts*. The second appears to go on the ground of property, for the

---

[12] The correct citation is (1781) 2 Doug. 575. Lawrence apparently refers here to an early edition of *Douglas's Reports*. In his notes of Park's argument for the plaintiff (below), he gives the correct citation, referencing the 'last' (latest) edition.

[13] Added in pencil by Lawrence was the following: 'this *arrêt* [was] the same here referred to', i.e., the *arrêt* of the Executive Directory of the 14th Messidor year 4th, referenced in the case for the opinion of the court in *Pollard* v. *Bell*.

[14] The printed report of *Barzillai* v. *Lewis* is at (1782) 3 Doug. 126. Volume 3 of *Douglas's Reports*, however, was not published until 1831. See Introduction, p. xv above. Lawrence cites instead *Park on Insurance* (J. A. Park, *A System on the Law of Marine Insurances*, first published in 1787). As shown below, J. A. Park was counsel for the plaintiff in *Pollard* v. *Bell*.

[15] For a description of Buller's Paper Book in the *Barzillai* case, see Oldham, *MMSS*, i. 576–577, n.1.

name is changed, and they do not go into evidence as to the muster roll or situation of the crew as to their being more than two-thirds English. The other ground is more general, and it makes it immaterial whether it was on the one ground or the other, for if she was not so documented as to have the protection of a neutral ship, the warranty is not complied with.'

Now it is true she was not so documented, as she [had] not a sea brief in conformity to the Treaty of Utrecht. It is certain that Lord MANSFIELD did use in the course of giving his opinion expressions which may be applied to support the defendant's argument, but it is clear that the ground on which he decided was a non-compliance with what was agreed by the Treaty [of] Utrecht, should be a necessary document to evidence Dutch property, and this is the express ground of the other judges.

That Lord MANSFIELD could not intend to lay it down that a non-compliance with the ordinances of France not adopted by any treaty appears from the case of *Mayne* v. *Walter*, where the plaintiff recovered, and he there pointedly marking how such ordinances may become binding, by observing that the whole case turns upon the treaties between France and Portugal, about which both parties were silent, and [he] there held the English supercargo [had] no ground to prevent plaintiff recovering on a ship warranted Portuguese.

In the subsequent case of *Salucci* v. *Johnson*, one ground of condemnation was the want of a charter party. Of this case I have a note of Mr Justice ASHHURST's on the back of his Paper Book speaking of that ground of condemnation.[16] [It] is in these words: 'As to the next question, her not having a charter party, this clearly is not required by the law of nations, and it appears by the case that she was a general ship, and though contrary to a particular ordinance of Spain, other nations are not bound to take notice of such ordinances unless in virtue of some treaty subsisting between two states, by which they submit to be bound by such ordinance. That is not the case here.'

[Separate Research Note by Lawrence]

Question not of documents, therefore *Barzillai*, &c. do not apply.

Before a ship or goods can be disposed by the captor there must be a regular judicial proceeding wherein both parties may be heard, and condemnation thereon as a prize in the Court of Admiralty, judging by the law of nations and treaties. Answer to the Prussian memorial, *Collecteana Juridica* 135.[17] Ibid. 137.

Though the law of nations be the general rule, yet it may by mutual agreement between two powers be varied and departed from, and when there is an alteration or exception introduced by particular treaties, that is the law

---

[16] Mr Justice Ashhurst's Paper Book is at Lincoln's Inn Library, Dampier MSS., APB 82. It includes a lengthy document containing extracts of proceedings from the Spanish courts.

[17] The reference is to a document reprinted in Francis Hargrave's *Collecteana Juridica* (1791–92), *viz.*, the duke of Newcastle's letter (1753), which transmitted a dispositive response to a Prussian memorial attempting to undermine the customary practices in Admiralty for condemning non-neutral ships or cargo. The principal author of the 'masterly' response was Solicitor-General William Murray, later Lord Mansfield. See Oldham, *MMSS*, i. 18.

between the parties to the treaty, and the law of nations only governs so far as it is not derogated from by the treaty.[18]

[*Lawrence's Notes of Arguments of Counsel*][19]

November 19, 1799

Park for Plaintiff: The first sentence [is] on the ground of the passport being contrary to the treaty. Second, for not having an act of property. Third, *roll d'equipage* being irregular.

The question will be if the sentences are conclusive against the ship being a Danish ship. Plaintiff's case does not militate with any decision. For the sentence proceeds on the [. . .] of partial ordinances of the French. The warranty is that the ship is Danish. The last sentence is the only one which in strictness ought to be regarded, and its ground is the only one to be regarded, as it takes no notice of the grounds of the other sentences.

If this sentence had condemned this ship as not being Danish, it would have concluded us. But there is not one ground that negatives its neutrality.

I admit cases go the length of saying that if the sentences proceed on the law of nations or on the construction of treaties, I could not expect to succeed, because as far as the law of nations goes, the decisions of the Court of Admiralty bind. But here the courts have proceeded on bare municipal regulations of their own, not accepted by the court of Denmark, and therefore not binding, and as such, the proceedings are against the law of nations.

The cases that have gone before have rested on the sentences having decided the ships were enemies' property. It is impossible that [we] can take note of the municipal regulations of all states. They may be contradictory. France may enact one thing, Spain another, so that at most a ship is bound to observe laws of the state from which and to which it sails.

Taking it for granted that the sentence proceeds on the violation of the ordinances and not of the law of nations, or of treaties, I shall cite cases to show that the assured is not bound by the decisions on partial regulations. *Bernardi* v. *Matteux*, Doug. 575, last edition. Judgment for the assured, as it did not appear that it was condemned as enemies' property.

Mayne v. *Walter*, Park 362. *Salucci* v. *Johnson*, ibid., 363. I admit that [case is] shaken by *Garrels* and *Kensington*[20] as to its principal point, and I find from a judgment in the Admiralty it is held by the law of nations [that] a ship must be searched. But I cite it for what BULLER says.

Geyer v. *Aguilar*, 7 T.R. 68 [is] distinguishable from this case. There the court decided on the ground of the sentence condemning her as belonging to the enemies of the Republic. First, the sentence in this case first proceeds on the passport not agreeing with the treaty. Second, the sentence states [that] the treaty [is] at an end, it having ceased in 1764. Second ground of the first

---

[18] Ibid., at p. 137.
[19] Arguments of counsel are not given in Durnford and East's report of the *Pollard* case (8 T.R. 434).
[20] *Garrels* v. *Kensington* (1799) 8 T.R. 230.

sentence, the captain not having any act of property according to the *reglement* of 26 July 1778. Another ground [is] the informality of the lists of the crew according to their ordinances. Another ground [is] acting in contradiction to the passport according to the *reglement* of 1778 and, *inter alia*, for being destined to an enemy's port. That [is] no ground of contradiction according to *Calvert* v. *Bovill*, 7 T.R. 526.

To her being destined to Madras, Madeira and Calcutta, [that is] no ground to condemn, if the sentence goes on to state all these acts are in contravention of the *reglement*.

As to the cargo: if the enemies', it does not alter the neutrality. But they proceed on the ground of the bill of loading at Copenhagen, [that it] is in contravention of the *reglement* of 1778, and against the decree of the National Assembly and the Directory of 1793.

As to the second sentence: they say nothing but [that] existing treaties should regulate the court of prize, yet [there was] no adjudication that such treaties are broken. They then proceed to take notice of the ordinance which prohibits neutrals having chief officers and the supercargo of enemies' country—this [is] the point in *Mayne* v. *Walter*.

Christie v. *Secretan*, 8 T.R. 192. In that case, the captain [was] an Irishman, but that [was] not insisted on.

Another ground: that [of] the act of property, a construction not sufficient, as it did not appear how the heirs of Christopher Hanson came entitled to it. Third persons can't be bound by such decree.

Another ground: papers thrown overboard, but of this Eggleston [was] acquitted, but if it were otherwise, *Bernardi* v. *Matteux* shows that we are not concluded by this part of the sentence.

Third sentence of the Court of Cassation: That does not conclude this, not to be a Dane.

Mr *Carr*, *contra*: I shall first consider this case independent of the sentences and contend the warranty [was] not complied with.

In this case, the ship [was] liable for detention, and the carrying her in for examination will avoid the policy. Eggleston must be considered as an enemy to France. [He was] not domiciled in Denmark—only a letter of burghership which will not give him Danish privileges as to other nations with us—we do not allow that a foreign captain [is] to navigate British ships, and if so, we can't say it is oppressive in France (we do not condemn, therefore, as prize). Such a captain was a ground of suspicion, and we were to be perfectly free in her navigation.

Rich v. *Parker*, 7 T.R. 705.

As to the sentences:

I shall first consider the rights of the belligerents as neutrals. I admit this [is] a condemnation on ordinances alone, as it is determined that the treaty has expired.

The question, therefore, will be if a nation that has no treaty with a neutral has in any case a right to condemn. These ordinances are consistent with the law of nations and have been acted on for this country. If a neutral is impaired, he must complain through his government; if he does not complain but submits, the individual can't question the acts of a nation, which is only responsible to a nation.[21] Such is the practice in our own country.

Dr Robinson 62, ship *Santa Cruz*.[22] Sir WILLIAM SCOTT says it is the practice of all powers to issue proclamations to which they conform. Now, could a sentence in our courts of Admiralty be questioned here? The regulations send to all, evidently to discover whether a ship be neutral or the trade contraband.[23]

The argument *é contra* would go the length of saying if no treaty, you can't enquire if a ship be neutral or not.

These courts are to distinguish between their own acts and those of unauthorised captors. When they condemn, they adopt the act of the captor, and this sentence is not scrutable by any other.

In *Bernardi* v. *Matteux*, the throwing the papers overboard did not affect the question, and that case only decided that if the foreign court assigns one reason which does not apply to the issue, this court will not imagine others.

Barzillai v. *Lewis*, Park 358, Lord MANSFIELD's opinion.

Salucci v. *Woodmass*, Park 361.

Calvert v. *Bovill*, 7 T.R.[24] That falls within the distinction I have taken as to *Bernardi* v. *Matteux*. There the court would not presume reasons which they have not expressed.

A ship warranted neutral must possess all necessary to show her neutral.

I abandon the first sentence because it condemns on the treaty, and I refer to the second sentence—[that there was] no proper muster roll, therefore a want of documents.

[Re:] Enemy captain: a belligerent may say no enemy shall be a captain.[25] It concludes with saying the captain has broke the whole code of maritime law in France. If you hold regulations of this sort not binding, you will overturn many of our decisions which proceed on particular regulations as rules of evidence to decide on the neutrality. I submit independent of the sentence that she was not navigated according to the contract. And secondly, that the sentence has conclusively determined that she has not been so navigated.

Park, in reply:

Eggleston is an enemy. But no rule adopted by the civilized nations of Europe [says] that ships shall not be navigated by captains of enemies' country. Our Navigation Act against foreign ships only respects the coming into our own ports or our own ship. This, I admit, the French may do. And in this case Eggleston had the authority from the king of Denmark.

---

[21] Lawrence interjects the following note: 'True, but it is against such acts that the underwriters are to indemnify.'

[22] The reference is to The *Santa Cruz* (1798) 1 C. Robinson 49.

[23] Here, Lawrence inserts: 'Then so condemn.'

[24] References to *Calvert* v. *Bovill* (1798) 7 T.R. 523.

[25] Lawrence here inserts the following bracketed note: '(No, unless a treaty to that effect).'

Rich v. *Parker* [was] decided not on the violation of any ordinance of the court of France, but [on] the treaty of his own country. If the courts of France had adopted these *reglement* as media of proof, as rules of evidence from whence they had concluded the ship was enemies' property, I should not have objected. But I object to their taking media of proof as substantive grounds of condemnation.

Bernardi v. *Matteux* [was] decided in favour of plaintiff because they took a medium of proof as a ground of condemnation. Now this differs only in taking many media of proof as ground of condemnation.

Barzillai v. *Lewis*, Lord MANSFIELD. There Lord MANSFIELD did only mean that if a stranger went into a foreign country he was bound by the ordinances. He could not mean that they might condemn on the ground of French ordinances, and in that instance the ship was condemned as an English ship, the *Three Graces*, of Liverpool.

De Souza v. *Ewer*, Park 360, [was] not relied on by Lord KENYON in *Geyer* v. *Aguilar* [but] referred to *Mayne* v. *Walter*, which is in some measure contrary to it.

The French court have drawn no conclusion that Eggleston being a Scotsman, the ship was navigated contrary to the law of nations. The sentences do not state that he has done anything but violated the Marine Code of France.

Ult. Concilium

January 28, 1800

Gibbs, for Plaintiff:

The first sentence is out of the question. The second sentence states an ordinance that a ship which has a captain, supercargo, or chief officer [as] an enemy, it shall be prize.

The result of all three sentences is this: the first condemns because the treaty [was] violated. The second sentence says no treaty. The third sentence adopts some of the grounds and confirms the sentence, therefore, the only question is whether the sentence of the third count can be supported. That states that it is sufficient to legitimate the prize, that Captain Eggleston was a Scotsman.

On the last argument it was said that a sentence proceeding on French ordinances concludes the neutrality. The judgment of the Court of Admiralty according to *Cornelius* v. *Hughes* concludes the property and goes not a step further.

If *res integra*, I should have argued that such sentence did not conclude the question of neutrality. But that is so. I admit [that] if [the ship were] condemned simply as prize, it would have concluded the question of property. But no authority goes the length of what the defendant contends, but expressly excludes it.

Bernardi v. *Matteux*. There [is] no difficulty except in deciding on the ground the court proceeded—whether on an *arrêt* or on the ground of enemies' property. And it being doubtful, a new trial was granted. This case clearly establishes this proposition: that if it clearly appeared that the sentence proceeded on the *arrêt*, it would not be conclusive of the neutrality.

This case is the same thing. It is a condemnation on the ground of the *arrêt* only.

The cases are not distinguishable. *Walter and Mayne* [is] not stronger, because it is more like, for the principle is the same—and there, Lord MANSFIELD observed [that] all turned on the treaties between Spain and Portugal. [It is] absurd to the utmost extent of stateable absurdity to say my contract with a Dane, a Portuguese, or an American shall turn on local ordinances behind our backs in France. The question there was on this same ordinance.

This doctrine [was] recognized in *Geyer* v. *Aguilar*, 7 T.R. 696. Perhaps from loose expressions something like the fabric of an argument may be made, but this [is] to be decided on the principles, not on loose expressions to be found in these cases.

Rous, contra:

I admit this is to be taken as a neutral vessel unless I can show from the sentences that it is not neutral.

A foremasted vessel can escape the ordeal of a court of prize, for [it] would be condemned in a court of law, from the different modes of proceeding. Condemnation as prize generally is to be understood as enemies' property.

Salucci v. *Woodmass*.

Barzillai v. *Lewis*.

The question [is] what is it that the sentences have decided.

In the first sentence the questions are stated: 1st, is the ship *Juliana* Danish property? They then proceed on these grounds: 1st, that the captain is a Scotsman. This [is] a strong presumption.

They state a deviation from the passport, the captain having not been able to justify it as neutral property and gone to London. This [is] a strong presumption.

Appeal abandons the ground of neutrality. Taking all together, it is a condemnation on the ground of the property [being] neutral. But the warranty of neutrality implies she shall conduct herself so as to have all the benefit of a neutral ship.[26]

The ship must be so navigated as to be entitled to the benefit of neutrality, supposing belligerent powers [must] respect neutrality. Yet the circumstances here stated would justify carrying her in, which the ship should not be subject to.

The sentence is conclusive as to what it meant to decide. *Bernardi* v. *Matteux*.

The sentence of the Court of Admiralty [is] conclusive as to the law and the fact. First, because it is a proceeding *in rem*. Such is the practice in our courts on condemnations in the Exchequer. Secondly, because this is an exclusive jurisdiction, and those *ex vi termini* excludes the examination of other courts.

---

[26] Here Lawrence inserts the following: '(How far this goes, the cases cited have determined.)'

So in the case of wills and marriage with us.[27] This [is] grounded in good sense, and if the nation does not question it, it must be taken to be just.[28]

In the case of *Hadogen*, Sir WILLIAM SCOTT says a neutral country can't entertain jurisdiction of the question of prize, except whether the neutrality has been violated.

Robinson's Cases, from 50 to 86.[29]

[On] the distinction betwixt treaties and ordinances, treaties are enforced by force. I have high authority in favour of this obligation of ordinances (*ss.*), Lord MANSFIELD in *Barzillai* v. *Lewis*.

An Order of Council, 8 June 1793, directs all vessels bound to France to be brought in and paid for.

If nations were brought this Order of Council and the decision of the court of prize, [they] would be conclusive for the captors. [And per Order of Council] 6 November 1793, all ships laden with goods the produce of the colonies of France or going there are ordered to be brought in for adjudication. These orders are the text [of] the law of the court of prize.

The whole subject may be comprised in a few sentences. If an individual [is] injured, he may or he must carry his complaint to his sovereign. The sentence of prize [is] conclusive because they decided that the acts are not the unlawful acts of individuals, but the authorized acts of the state.

As to the cases cited, *Walters* and *Mayne* proceeds on the ground that having the supercargo aboard the vessel [was] within the contemplation of the parties. That it does not go to impeach the doctrine of ordinances is established by *Barzillai* v. *Lewis.*

Gibbs, in reply:

Condemnation as good prize is sufficient to negative the neutrality if the particular ground does not appear.

In *Bernardi* v. *Matteux* there was a condemnation of good prize, yet that [was] held not to negative the neutrality.

Barzillai v. *Lewis* has certain contradictory expressions to other cases. You will then look at the principles. My note [of the case] is that Lord MANSFIELD says she was condemned as not being Dutch.

Rous relies on what is stated in the beginning of the claim to show the ground of the judgment. That [is] the statement of the claimant, but that [is] not the ground of the court's judgment. And it is clear in this case that they condemned on the ground of their ordinances. The strongest presumption won't do, unless the court draws the conclusion of enemies' property, and if not, this court [is] not bound by the judgment.

Condemnation in Exchequer is said to be conclusive. That is strange as

---

[27] Lawrence inserts the following note: '(True, it is evidence of the fact that she has violated French ordinances and that violation is a ground of law for condemnation.)'

[28] Lawrence inserts: '(That may be so, but still it may be a risk within the policy not excluded by the warranty.)'

[29] The pages cited in volume 1 of *C. Robinson's Reports* contain two cases decided by Sir William Scott: The *Santa Cruz* (pp. 50–80) and The *Mercurius* (pp. 80–86).

against persons not parties. Judgments of courts of Admiralty [are] conclusive when they act according to the law of nations.

Rous says [there is] no distinction between ordinances and treaties, as both [are] acts of force. So according to him, treaties between nations are not compacts.

As to the argument from our Orders of Council, [that] has nothing to do with the present case.

Question, if a native of this country can controvert the judgment of the Court of Admiralty here—[this] has nothing to [do] with the question whether a Dane is bound by the local ordinances of France.

[There are] only two points in this case, one [of] fact, the other, law. The question of fact [is] if [the ground is] on the *arrêt* or not. I say clearly on the *arrêt* because the last sentence takes notice of nothing else. The text is, whether a local ordinance falsifies the warranty.

Bernardi v. *Matteux*
Mayne v. *Walters*
Salucci v. *Johnson* recognizes it.

[*Opinions of the Justices*]

Lord KENYON: [This is] an action on a policy warranted Dane. The objection [is] that the ship [is] not Dane. She must not only be Dane but must demean itself [*sic*] as a Danish ship.

The question [is] not difficult. But [it is] of importance from the number of questions depending on these sentences.

As far as these sentences go, we must give credit to them, and we can't review them. If, therefore, the French court had condemned it as not being a Danish ship, we must have so decided.

I repeat that I fully agree with the decisions in *Salucci* v. *Johnson* and *Mayne* v. *Walters*. Courts proceeding on these questions act by the law of nations. To these to be added [are] stipulations by the treaties between the parties. Treaties are compacts between the high contracting parties, and ordinances, the particular acts of each state.

One party can't add to the code of the law of nations what they please. What do they do here? They make *arrêt* against the captain of a neutral ship being an enemy. This they have no right to do. They do not condemn as not being Danish property.

The conclusion of the second sentence, and the definitive sentence, shows that they proceeded on the ground of one of their ordinances against a man being captain, when they had no power to prescribe such a thing.

GROSE J.: It is not to be collected from anything that is stated that this ship is not a Dane. [This is] not to be inferred.

Mayne v. *Walters* has determined the case as to a supercargo, and [there is] no difference between a captain and a super cargo.

But it is said that she had not proper documents. We should be bound if this had been found by the French sentence or by necessary inference. To see the ground of condemnation we must look into the sentence of the court of dernier resort.

LAWRENCE J.: Same opinion.

LE BLANC [J.]: Same opinion. Looking into the different sentences, we can't collect that this ship was not condemned as not being a Dane. And unless the court can collect that the Admiralty has so decided, our opinion does not impeach the sentence of the Court of Admiralty abroad. I agree [that] the warranty of neutrality requires [that] she should be so navigated as not to bring her into question.

Question, if the sentence might be law. [It] excluded the party from giving evidence of its being a Dane. The court will look into this sentence to see if it warrants condemnation on that ground, or on a different ground. Though it may justify the condemnation in that country, it will not falsify the warranty of neutrality.

Judgment for Plaintiff

APPENDIX

APPENDIX

[The proceedings below were published by Robert Alderson, student of Lincoln's Inn, from his shorthand notes, reproduced courtesy of John D. Gordan III of New York City, from the copy in his private collection. (Spelling and italics have been retained as in the original.)

According to Foss's biography of Edward Alderson, a nineteenth-century baron of the Court of Exchequer, Baron Alderson's father was Robert Alderson, who became an eminent barrister and recorder of Norwich, Ipswich, and Yarmouth.[1] Robert's grandfather was Samuel Hurry, William Hurry's brother.]

In the Court of Common Pleas
[*1*] PROCEEDINGS at the ASSIZES at THETFORD,
On the 18th of March, 1786, and the 24th of March, 1787,
IN THE
TRIAL of WILLIAM HURRY, Merchant,
Of the Borough of GREAT YARMOUTH,
On an Indictment preferred against him by JOHN WATSON,
Attorney at Law, then
Mayor Elect of the said Borough,
For WILFUL and CORRUPT PERJURY:
AND IN THE
ACTION against the said JOHN WATSON,
Then Mayor of the said Borough,
BROUGHT BY
The said WILLIAM HURRY, for a *malicious Prosecution*
of him by the above Indictment:
WITH
The *Substance* of Mr PARTRIDGE's Opening in the *first* Trial:
AND
The Speeches *at large* of Mess. ERSKINE and HARDINGE in
the *last*.
TO WHICH ARE ADDED

A Relation of the Nonsuit in the *latter* Cause at the Norfolk Assizes in August last; and a Report of the Argument thereupon in the Court of Common Pleas the Michaelmas Term following; and the Judgement of that Court, as delivered by the Lord Chief Justice, when the Nonsuit was set aside, and a new Trial granted.

---

[1] E. Foss, *The Judges of England*, 9 vols. (1848–1854), viii. 130. See also *ODNB, sub nom.* 'Alderson, Sir Edward Hall'.

[2] To the PUBLIC

UNWILLING to break my engagement with the Public, I permitted the Sale of the following Sheets to commence agreeably to my Advertisement, although I had heard that this Day a Motion would be made by Counsel for Mr. Watson for a new Trial.—In consequence, however, of this having actually taken place, I think it right to subscribe my Name to the Work, and to make myself responsible for the Truth of the Facts that are stated in Evidence, for the Justness of the Representation of the Speeches of Counsel, and for the Accuracy of the learned Judge's Address to the Jury.

ROBERT ALDERSON

Saturday, April 28, 1787. Student of Lincoln's Inn

[3] THE Editor of this work dedicates it to the Gentlemen who composed the three respective Special Juries, who attended to decide upon the merits of the various matters which it recalls to their recollection.

Fully conscious to himself that he has done his endeavour to be a faithful Historian, he flatters himself, with the fullest confidence, that he shall be entitled to their *verdict* for a fair, candid, and, as far as the nature of the case will admit of it, accurate statement of facts.

If it should be perceivable that he has some small degree of bias to the side of the Plaintiff in the last action, he begs leave to observe that he does not wish to be considered as a hackney retailer of trials, who recounts the artful sophistry by which villainy is protected, and by which it is rendered successful, and the bold, ingenuous, animated, heart-touching eloquence by which virtue is made conspicuous, and by which virtue is made triumphant, with the same unsympathizing indifference.—What was said of a Roman Annalist, that he related the virtues of Germanicus and the vices of Tiberius, alike unaffected with his subject, the Editor would think a gross satire, if ever, in any case at all analogous, it could be said of him.—His credit, as a regarder of truth, is now with the public; and he trusts it will not be at all injured, because he cannot hide his pleasure at the manifestation of innocence, and the detection and punishment of malevolence.

With respect to the account of the trial upon the indictment, and of Mr. *Partridge*'s speech at the opening, the Editor thinks it right to inform those who may chance to read the following pages, that it is given entirely from memory—but that with respect to the subsequent matter, he has had his recollection much aided by very ample short-hand memorandums, which he took in the course of the proceedings—by means of which he has been enabled, *strictim, uti quaeque memoria digna videbantur, perscribere: eo magis, quod illi a spe, metu, partibus reipublicae, animus liber est.—Igitur de conjuratione, quam verissime poterit, paucis absolvet. Nam id facinus in primis ille memorabile existimat, sceleris atque periculi novitate.*[2]

---

[2] See Sallust, *Bellum Catilinae*, 4.

[4] **Counsel for the Prosecution.**
Messrs. *Partridge*, *Graham*, and *Le Blanc*.
Attorney, Mr. *Berry*.

Counsel for the Defendant.
Messrs. *Erskine*, *Mingay*, and *Murphy*.
Attorney, Mr. *Bell*.

[5] PROCEEDINGS at the ASSIZES at THETFORD, March the 18th, 1786, in the Trial of WILLIAM HURRY, Merchant, for Perjury, on a Traverse of a Bill of Indictment preferred against him by JOHN WATSON, Mayor Elect, at the Quarter Sessions in the Borough Court of Great Yarmouth, whence it was removed by a Writ of Certiorari into the Court of King's Bench, and sent down thence to be tried at Thetford Assizes.

The cause came on before Sir GEORGE NARES, Knt. and a special Jury*, at six o'clock in the evening. An hour and a half before the Judge made his appearance, the court began to fill, so that when the trial commenced, it was so uncommonly crouded, that the Grand Jury in vain applied to the Under-Sheriff, and through him to the Judge himself, to have their own box or gallery cleared. It was, at length, after much bustle, given up as impracticable.

The case was opened by Mr. *Le Blanc*, the junior Counsel, by a bare reading, as usual, of the indictment; in which William Hurry was charged with having caused John Watson, for the purpose of aggrieving and put-[6]-ting him to great expense, to be summoned before a court called the Court of Requests, in the borough of Great Yarmouth; and, not having the fear of God before his eyes, but being instigated by the devil, with having there taken his corporal oath upon the holy gospels of God, falsely, corruptly, wilfully and maliciously deposing, that the said John Watson was indebted to him, the said William Hurry, in the sum of eleven shillings; whereas, in truth and in fact, the said John Watson was not indebted to him, the said William Hurry, in the aforesaid sum, nor in any other sum of money whatsoever; and with having, in consequence of this, been guilty of wilful and corrupt Perjury, to the great displeasure of Almighty God, to the evil example of all others in the like case

---

* Names of the Special Jury:

John Wilson Allen, of Stanhoe, Charles Senkler, of Docking, Edward Parry, of Great Dunham, Hammond Alpe, of East Lexham, Henry William Wilson, of Didlington, Anthony Hammond, of Westacre, Charles Colyer, of East Dereham,	Esqrs.
Samuel Newson, of Roydon, Simon Poole, of Hockwald with Wilton, Richard Tiffen, of Feltwell, Christopher Adcock, of West Bradenham, John Beales, of North Lopham	Tales-men.

offending, and against the peace of our lord the King, in the parish and borough town of Great Yarmouth aforesaid; for which said offence he then stood indicted; and to which indictment he had pleaded not guilty, and had put himself upon his country.

Mr. *Partridge* (the leading Counsel for the prosecution) then got up: his speech was in substance as follows: —

'My Lord, and Gentlemen of the Jury,

I likewise am Counsel on the same side with my learned friend, who has just read the record: The matter in question, as stated by the indictment, which you have heard, is, that William Hurry, of Great Yarmouth, did, on the 12th of September, in a court called the Court of Requests, make an oath before Commissioners duly authorised to administer such an oath, that John Watson was indebted to him in the sum of eleven shillings; whereas the said John Watson was not indebted to him in this sum, nor in any other sum whatsoever; and that he did this to aggrieve the said John Watson, and to put him to expense: for this act the defendant now stands arraigned, on the prosecution of the said John Watson, for the crime of wilful and corrupt Perjury.

It is my duty, then, Gentlemen of the Jury, under his Lordship's correction, to substantiate, in the present case, this fact; it is *your's* [sic] to judge of what may be adduced in evidence, uninfluenced by your feelings, from any fears of the consequences that may, upon the defendant's being fully convicted of the crime in question, fall upon him.

The crime of Perjury, in civil society, is of so heinous and so destructive a nature, that the Legislature has wisely and providently affixed to it a high and severe degree of punishment.

[7] Perjury, Gentlemen, consists in the taking of a judicial Oath, falsely, in a place duly authorised to the taking of it, and for the purpose of answering some corrupt end to the person so taking it.

I think I am pretty accurate in my definition of Perjury; I trust then, Gentlemen, I shall be able to prove, to your satisfaction, that the defendant, William Hurry, stands justly charged with this crime.

It has been industriously circulated through this county, by the friends and favourers of the defendant, that this prosecution is carried on from party motives. I have to declare to you, Gentlemen, that this is not the case, but that Mr. Watson is induced to do this from a pure regard to justice, and to prevent future delinquencies. You must know, Gentlemen, that in the borough of Great Yarmouth, as in many other places in England, there is a Court of Admiralty established, of which court there is an officer, called the Judge, who, in that capacity, is the representative there of the Lord High Admiral of England; and that there is another officer appointed, who is called the Register of this court, which officer is Mr. John Watson, the present prosecutor. The object of this court is to take under its care all anchors and cables, &c. which are lost at sea (and which are taken up by men, who, from their occupation, are called salvors), and to preserve them in a place called the Castle Yard, till they are claimed by the captains or owners of them, who, upon swearing to their property, and paying what is called the salvage, are permitted to take them again.

It is necessary, Gentlemen, in order to make you fully understand the matter, that I should explain to you the nature of the practice or usage in these cases. It sometimes happens that an anchor and cable is taken up with a buoy to it, and sometimes without. In the former case the salvors are entitled to one third only of the value of the anchor and cable so taken up; in the latter to one half. It is likewise an established custom of this court, to pay for the cartage of such anchors, &c. as may be thus taken up, sixpence per hundred weight, let them be brought from any part of the beach or shore to which the jurisdiction of this court extends; a kind of average takes place here, so that, upon the whole, there can be no ground for any one to complain, though in one instance, it may seem too much, and in another too little.

But, besides this court, Gentlemen, there is another court established in Yarmouth, called the Court of Requests, in which a process for the recovery of all debts under the sum of forty shillings may be entered, and upon oath (before Commissioners duly appointed to administer such [*8*] an oath) being made of the sum, redress may be obtained. It was in this court that the transaction upon which the present indictment was founded for Perjury passed. It happened that certain anchors and cables belonging to one Captain Shipley were taken up and put under the care of the Court of Admiralty. The Captain, after a short lapse of time, came, with one Mr. Samuel Hurry, who passed himself off as the agent for Mr. Shipley, and claimed the aforesaid anchors and cables, paid the charges of the court, went away perfectly satisfied, and the matter was supposed to be finally closed.

But, at the end of some weeks, Mr. William Hurry, the defendant, stepped forward, and declared himself not contented with the bill which the Court of Admiralty had made out, respecting the charge of cartage of Mr. Shipley's anchors and cables, for whom he professed himself to be agent. It was not, I repeat, till the end of some weeks—from the 19th of July till the 12th of September—that Mr. Hurry sued for the recovery of this supposed overcharge of cartage. He had an obvious purpose to answer by this delay.

I need not observe to you, Gentlemen, who are well acquainted with the state of the county, that a spirit of opposition much prevails in the town of Great Yarmouth against the corporation, to whom indeed Mr. William Hurry, the present defendant, has ever shewn himself a most determined and a most obstinate antagonist. It was then plainly for the sake of exposing, as he thought, a member of this corporation, that the defendant, Mr. Hurry, delayed his complaint to the date he did, as he knew that, at that time, Mr. John Watson, the Register of the Court of Admiralty, would be nominated to succeed Mr. Reynolds as Mayor; he having frequently expressed his pleasure at the idea of what a pretty figure the Mayor elect would make, when obliged to make his appearance before the Court of Conscience. Can any thing then, Gentlemen, be more evident than the maliciousness of this proceeding? He did it, as the indictment justly states, *to aggrieve Mr. Watson.*

I ought to have observed, in my account of the Admiralty Court, that, besides the Register, there is another officer, called the Chamberlain, who receives all moneys and gives all receipts respecting matters transacted in this court. Had then Mr. Hurry, the defendant, really had any just claim of a debt due to him from this court, the Chamberlain, and not Mr. Watson, was the person against whom he should have sworn it. [9]

But, in fact, it will appear that he had no just claim whatsoever to a debt of eleven shillings.

It is true an account was made out, charging the cartage one pound four shillings; but, upon examining into the business, it was discovered that a wrong statement had been made of the particulars.

Besides the sixpence per cwt. for the cartage of anchors, a shilling is always charged for each cart load of cable. Here, then, were two cables, one of five cwt. making one load, one shilling; another of 22 cwt. making three loads, three shillings; a buoy and buoy-rope, one shilling; *extra help* that was necessary, two shillings; these sums, together with the ten shillings and two pence for the cartage of the anchors, make seventeen shillings and two pence. Upon the face then of this account, it is evident that there is a mistake of only six shillings and ten pence, which, as in every other case of this kind, was to be divided, half of it to be given to the salvors, and the other half to the agent of Captain Shipley; so that it was not possible Mr. Hurry could have a right to swear to more than the small sum of three shillings and fivepence (which was offered to him over and over again, and as often refused), whereas he positively swore to the sum of eleven shillings.*

With the practices and usages of the Court of Admiralty the defendant, Mr. Hurry, from his long residence in Yarmouth, and from his frequent transactions with this court, was fully acquainted; hence, then, it is evident that, from a motive of malice, and for a corrupt end, he did wilfully, deliberately, and knowingly, take a false oath, in a court duly authorised to cause it to be administered as a judicial oath.

I shall now proceed, Gentlemen, to prove to you that this court was duly authorized in this matter.

Here the Counsel for the defendant called out, "We admit it, we admit it."'

Mr. *Partridge*, upon this, omitted entering into the proof of it, and proceeded—

'I should have added, Gentlemen of the Jury, that till the time that Mr. William Hurry stepped forward with his claim on Mr. Watson, his name was never mentioned in the affair; it was another Mr. Hurry, a Mr. Samuel Hurry, a nephew, I believe, of the defendant, who had all [10] along professed himself the agent of Mr. Shipley; quite another house, as we shall fully show, not in the least connected.

---

*The Judge, at this part of the opening, called for the record, and, after looking at it, told Mr. Partridge that he could not find any thing about salvage in the indictment, and that he could not tell what he meant to be at; that if he imagined an indictment for Perjury was to be supported upon a nice calculation of salvage, he was surely mistaken.

If then, Gentlemen of the Jury, these things should appear upon evidence, as I trust they will, and which, if Mr. Hurry is in court, and now hears me, his own feelings must convince him are so, you, Gentlemen of the Jury, cannot, consistently with your duty, help finding him guilty; and, if he be thus found criminal, notwithstanding the former tenour of his life, however fair and upright it may have been (and God forbid that I should say any thing to its detriment), he must undergo that punishment which the laws of his country have assigned to a crime of the nature and magnitude of that for which he is indicted.'

Call William Imms—During the time of this witness's coming and being sworn, Mr. *Erskine* addressed himself to the Judge—'My Lord, I have the highest opinion of Mr. *Partridge*; I shall not be considered as merely complimenting him, when I say, I know he would be obliged to me if I would help him to get rid of this business, which he knows well I could do; but, my Lord, I must wish, for my client's sake, that the cause may be gone into.'

William Imms was sworn.

Mr. *Graham*—You are an officer belonging to the Court of Requests?

I am.

Do you remember a summons being issued out against John Watson?

I do—I served it myself.

Here Mr. *Mingay* interrupted the examination with saying, 'We allow it, we allow all this and much more; we admit the oath to have been taken; we do not come here to ground our objection on trifles, on mere straws; call some of your capital men, I long to see some of their faces.'

Mr. Spurgeon was then called.

Mr. Spurgeon came forward on the bench near the High Sheriff, and, on account of his apparent infirmity, had the oath administered to him in that place.

Mr. *Graham*—Mr Spurgeon, you are the clerk of the Court of Requests?

I am.

Do you remember a summons being issued out against John Watson by William Hurry?

I do.

Did the parties appear?

Mr. Hurry did—Mr. Watson did not. [*11*]

What is the usage of the court in that case?

The officer is sworn to the service of the summons.

Do you remember Mr. William Hurry's taking an oath at that time?

I do—I administered it.

How?

In the usual manner—You shall true answer make to such questions as the court shall demand of you touching the debt in question.

After he was sworn, what did you do?

I asked him, 'Is Mr. John Watson indebted to you, Mr. Hurry, in the sum of eleven shillings?' He answered 'He is.'—I repeated the question.

Upon the witness's being asked respecting who repeated the question, he hesitated whether it was he or Mr. Reynolds; but he said it was either the one or the other.

Mr. *Graham*—Were you not in a situation so as to hear the whole?

Yes.

There being at this time a considerable noise in the court, and the Jury complaining that they could not hear the witness, Mr. *Erskine* declared 'he had no idea of favour in these cases—Why was not the witness in the usual place?—For his part, he did not like being obliged to look over his shoulder every question he wanted to ask.'

Upon Mr. *Graham*'s assuring him, however, that he would repeat the witness's answers to the Jury, Mr. Spurgeon was permitted to keep his station.

Mr. *Graham*—Was what you have told the court the whole of Mr. Hurry's oath?

No.

Upon the question's being repeated, Mr. George Hurry (one of the Commissioners of the court) bending forward, said, 'Brother William, explain yourself.'—Mr. William Hurry then said, 'As Agent for Mr. Shipley.'

Mr. *Graham*—How long might this be after?

Almost immediately.

The Judge, on hearing this, arose, and called for attention: He said, 'It would be hard indeed, if a man were not suffered to explain his own meaning; here is evidently an indictment founded on but *part* of an oath, when that which is most essential to its meaning is left out.'

Messrs. *Erskine* and *Mingay*, observing that the Judge was seizing his opportunity to dismiss the business, both rose up, and, with a truly laudable zeal for the reputation of their client, begged his Lordship to permit [*12*] the cause to go on. The Judge, however, declared, 'he could not in common justice; he hoped future prosecutors would take care, from the present example, to prefer indictments upon juster grounds; it was wonderful!'—'Wonderful, indeed, my Lord' (replied Mr. *Erskine* warmly); 'I do not believe that, in all the annals of human infamy, a parallel case can be found.'

The Judge then said, 'Gentlemen of the Jury, this is an indictment for Perjury on *part* only of an oath, whilst the most material clause has been purposely kept back; you must, of course, find the defendant *not guilty*.'

The Jury turned to one another; and the Judge mentioned to Mr. *Partridge* a particular case, in his recollection, similar to the one that had then happened, but in so low a voice that it was impossible for a by-stander to collect it.

In a very few minutes the Jury returned their verdict—NOT GUILTY. The occasion of their deliberating, even a moment, being a mistake into which one of the Tales-men had fallen, that damages might then be found against the prosecutor. It is worthy of remark that the Jury, when they gave in their verdict, *not guilty*, added (what indeed the acquittal of itself necessarily implied, but which, however, ought to be considered as a marked testimony of their sense of the defendant's innocence) *unanimously*.

Upon this followed—what great sticklers for decency and propriety may carp at, but what honest and good feelings will excuse—*a loud clap of approbation*.

[*13*] PROCEEDINGS

At the last Summer Assizes for the County of Norfolk,
BEFORE
Chief Baron Skynner, and a Special jury,
IN THE CAUSE
HURRY against WATSON,
When the Plaintiff was nonsuited:

With the Argument thereupon, in Michaelmas Term following, in the Court of Common Pleas, and the Judgement of that Court, as delivered by the Lord Chief Justice when the Nonsuit was set aside, and a new Trial granted.

'The Law and the opinion of the Judges are not always convertible Terms, or one and the same thing; since it sometimes may happen that the Judge may mistake the Law.'

BLACKST. COMMENT. vol. I. p. 71, 8vo. edit.

[*14*] Counsel for the Plaintiff.
Messrs. *Murphy*, *Adair*, *Wilson*, and *Preston*.
Attorney, Mr. *Bell*.

Counsel for the Defendant.
Messrs. *Hardinge*, *Partridge*, *Graham*, and *Le Blanc*.
Attorney, Mr. *Berry*.

[*15*] AFTER the acquittal of Mr. Hurry, in the manner which has already been related, paragraphs appeared in the Norwich, Bury, and Ipswich papers, signifying that the trial of the perjury cause went off upon a defect in the indictment, and that a fresh bill would be preferred by the prosecutor.

Upon inquiry of the printers of these papers, it was found that these paragraphs were handed to them by one Mr. Lock, of Norwich, who declared, afterwards, in a subsequent account which he caused to be published, that he had the original, whence he took the copies which he sent to the respective printers, from Mr. Watson, the *Mayor of Yarmouth*, the *late prosecutor of Mr. Hurry*.—Mr. Hurry, learning this circumstance, became fully determined (having had it before recommended to him by his Counsel) to bring his action against Mr. Watson, for a malicious prosecution of him for Perjury.—Accordingly an action was instituted, and the cause came on to be tried at the last Norfolk summer assizes, before Lord Chief Baron SKYNNER, and a Special Jury.*—Messrs. *Erskine* and *Mingay* were retained, conditionally, to attend upon this occasion, if no other indispensible engagement prevented them.—This, however, happened unfortunately, to be the case.—Notwithstanding this, the plaintiff, Mr. Hurry, disappointed as he was of his leading Counsel, still did not hesitate to proceed to lay his case before the court.—It was opened with great precision, fairness, and perspicuity, by Mr. *Murphy*. [*16*]

The Counsel for the defendant, Watson, instead of entering into the merits of the case, laid hold of certain inaccuracies in the pleadings; and, on the plaintiff's producing a copy of the record of acquittal, moved for a nonsuit upon five variances, which were all determined by the Judge for the plaintiff, or given up, except one, and that was this—That in the *declaration* it was stated, that Mr. Hurry was acquitted before Lord LOUGHBOROUGH and Sir GEORGE NARES, Knt. Justices assigned to hold the assizes in and for the said county of Norfolk, *to hear and determine all treasons, felonies, trespasses*, and other misdeeds done and committed; whereas, in the *record* of acquittal, it was before, &c. Justices assigned, &c. *according to the form of the statute in such case made and provided.*—Upon this variance the Judge nonsuited the plaintiff.—The Special Jury, unwilling to aggravate the charges which it was supposed this nonsuit would bring upon the plaintiff, refused, upon this occasion, to accept their usual fee.

The matter afterwards came on to be argued, in Michaelmas Term last, in the court of Common Pleas.

Serjeant *Bolton* showed cause against the nonsuit's being set aside—'That the matter had originated, and was still carried on, from party spirit—that the declaration of the plaintiff stated a commission that never existed, namely, Justices of assize specially assigned *to hear and determine*, &c.—that the record to which they referred for proof of acquittal stated only *Justices of assize*—that this was a material variance—that in many instances where the variance was not so material, the plaintiff had been held to prove what he had stated, and upon failure thereof had been obliged to take the consequence.—In corroboration of

---

*Names of the Special Jury.

Sir John Berney, of Kirby Bedon, Bart.	
Seaman Holmes, of Brooke,	
William Perkins, of Coltishall,	
Thomas Beecroft, of Saxthorpe,	
William Wiggett Bulwer, of Heydon,	Esqrs.
John Custance, of Weston,	
Robert Buxton, of Rushford,	
Thomas Grigson Payne, of Hardingham,	
Hugh Hare, of Hargham,	
James Fox, of Foxley,	
Ropert Rope, of Blofield,	Tales-men.
Richard Francis, of Attleborough	

these opinions, he had recourse to cases: The first he quoted was from 2d Strange, 787. where the word *austriale* being put instead of *australe*, which was the true spelling, it was considered by the court as a sufficient variation on which to ground a non-suit—The next was from Holt, 538. where *Lincoln's Fields* was put for *Lincoln's Inn Fields*.—A third case he produced was from the same reports, where, in referring to a particular act of parliament, the declaration had *unnecessarily* stated the title of it, and had stated it with some trifling variation— A fourth was where a declaration set forth certain money to be paid at four even quarterly payments, whereas it could only be proved that the said money was to be paid within the year.—On the authority of these cases he contended that the nonsuit was a just one; and that the variation upon which the Judge directed it was much more material than any of these.

[*17*] Serjeant *Rook*, on the same side, argued—that this was a prosecution for a malicious prosecution—that it was a prosecution in revenge, and that therefore it ought not to be favoured by the court—that the bill of indictment had been found by a Grand Jury—that the plaintiff, in the present case, was bound to prove his acquittal before a *general* court of assize, but his declaration stated, that he was acquitted before a *special* court of assize, "*Justices of assize, to hear and determine, &c.*"—The record does not prove this, but the contrary—that, from the nature of the suit, the exact rule of law should be observed.

Mr. Serjeant *Adair*, in reply, declared—he did not apply to the court on the ground of having the forms of law given up for the sake of substantial justice— he was certain this nonsuit must be set aside by the plain rules of law. He spoke to the several cases which had been cited, and then contended—that the declaration and record were essentially the same—that a Judge of assize was a Judge who had five commissions—that *oyer and terminer*, &c. was one of these commissions; the commission of assize another; the commission of general gaol-delivery another; the commission of the peace another; and, lastly, the commission of nisi prius, which enables him to try all questions of fact issuing out of the courts of Westminster.—That the record said Mr. Hurry was acquitted before "*Justices of assize;*" that the words added were *insensible, impertinent words*; that the declaration, in stating Justices of assize, had stated every thing that was necessary; that there was no occasion to argue the matter; that there were cases that could not be controverted.—He then produced a case from Crook 2, 32. where Justices of the peace were described as Justices of the peace, with the *additional words to hear and determine, &c.*—When he found this case, he declared, he was quite satisfied, provided he did not, upon inquiry, find it contradicted in any subsequent cases. He assured the court that he had not done this, but quite the contrary. He then quoted another case, where the declaration stated an indictment to have been preferred at the *quarter* sessions, whereas, in fact, it appeared to have been at the *general* sessions.—The nonsuit was set aside upon this principle, that either of the courts was competent to the taking cognizance of the business. He contended that this was a case perfectly in point—that it ran on all fours with the present case—that as the word *quarterly* was a *surplusage*, the court being sufficiently defined without it, so "*Justices of the assize*" was a sufficient description of the persons before whom Mr. Hurry was acquitted, and that the words *to hear and determine, &c.* were insensible and [*18*] impertinent.—Mr. Serjeant *Walker* argued on the same grounds: and the next day the Lord Chief Justice delivered the following judgement.

It is our opinion that the nonsuit ought to be set aside, and a new trial granted.—The question has been argued on two grounds—1st. That the words added in the declaration make nonsense; describe a commission that never existed; and 2dly, That the commission set forth in the declaration differs from that set forth in the record, and that therefore it has not been proved.

The second point is the only one taken notice of at the trial, upon which the learned Judge directed the nonsuit.

If the first point had been made out, it would have been a just ground on which to have moved an arrest of judgement; and if it were clearly to be made out, the court would not set aside a nonsuit on which no judgement could be given.—I shall take notice of this hereafter.

I allow that in this action it is essentially necessary to state an acquittal before persons properly authorised.—If, therefore, the declaration had proceeded to state the plaintiff had been acquitted before Justices of assize, and had set forth all the different commissions under which they acted, and it happened that the record of acquittal had recited likewise all the several commissions, the declaration would not have been bad, and the proof had been complete;—but it is plain that all the words subsequent to Justices of assize would have been perfectly nugatory.—The record of acquittal states only "*Justices of assize.*"—It is not a defective record—it is full proof of the acquittal by due course of law.

The declaration states "*Justices of assize,*" but it goes on to add more words, "*to hear and determine, &c.*" Now it is material to take notice of what is here added.—The addition, in this case, is a description of the persons who held the assize—but this, it has been said, is not proved.—But consider what is to be proved.—It is not every adjective that is substantially to be proved.—You want to prove a proposition, an averment in the declaration, and a necessary one, that the plaintiff was acquitted before Justices of assize; not that Justices of assize are Commissioners of oyer and terminer, to hear and determine, &c. What has this to do with the action? Their having this commission was totally irrelevant to the question.—It might as well be said to be necessary to have declared and proved the names of the Justices as well as their offices.

There are certainly cases of various determination.—I am not sure whether I am able to find any compass by which to steer on to a point through these various determinations.—If the plaintiff chooses to insert circumstan-[*19*]-ces, he may be bound to prove them; but they must be circumstances that bear some relation to his case; they must belong to it, and must not be totally different from it.

In most of the cases where the plaintiff has been nonsuited, this is, or has been supposed to be, the nature of the circumstances, by the court in which the circumstances have been alledged.

In the case of Bristow and Wright, the court had their doubts whether the variation of the evidence, which proved only on a demise *rent to be paid yearly*, was a material one from the declaration, which stated that the *rent was to be paid by four even quarterly payments.*

There were two cases produced from Lord Raymond; the first does not at all apply.—This states that the declaration set forth an agreement for good *merchantable* wheat; whereas it was proved in evidence that only wheat of a *second quality* had been sent.

The second case is undoubtedly rather a nice one.—It was an action of debt for rent.—The plaintiff declared on a demise for a *rent of 15l.* the evidence proved a demise for 15l. and *three fowls.*—Chief Justice HOLT thought this a material variance.—But as a proof that nonsuits are directed just as particular circumstances strike persons at particular times, in the very same case it was urged, as another ground for a nonsuit, that this estate was let by a *special* power of leasing in only a tenant for life, as if he had had a *general* power of leasing; but this, my Lord HOLT, did not think so material a ground for the nonsuit as the other.

It may be difficult to say what is a variance.—I own my Lord HOLT seems to have thought the question was, whether the variance was material or not, and whether the circumstance was relative to the case of the party; which, if he had omitted, would not have hurt him, but not having done so, it became necessary for him to prove.

But I have found many cases where this doctrine seems to be contradicted.—Rolls abridgment 2. 709, Placito 59—This was a case in which there was a variance of date.—When this case occurred it struck me, that all the ground of the doctrine, which is so familiar to the court, is, that it is not necessary to prove every thing under a *videlicet that is not essential to the case*; every *thing essential indeed*, even under a *videlicet* or *scilicet*, it would be necessary to prove.

In the other cases, and in the cases most applicable to the present, where the parties have occasion to refer to a judicial proceeding, the *mode* in which this proceeding is conducted does not make a part of the case, but the result of it does.—See Hobart 79, Hobart 209, Brooke's abridgement, [20] placito 96, title variance.—Here it was urged that the Jury had taken a false oath before *B.* and *R.* Justices of nisi prius, it having been taken before *B.* who had associated to him one who was *R.* the court over-ruled this.—There are several other cases in Dyer's Reports—There is one, Dyer 29, placito 141.—The question here was, whether the writ of attaint shall abate, because of a variance in the writ of attaint, and the proceedings by which the writ is brought.—It was held to be no variance *omitting circumstances* in the description of the writ of attaint in the record of nisi prius, provided the *substance* was well described.—But the case of Busby and Watson, Blackstone 2, 1050, is a stronger case than the present.—The court of *general sessions* and *quarter sessions* are different courts, but still having both the same jurisdiction with respect to the particular matter, the declaration was held to be sufficiently supported.

In the present case, then, it was necessary that the plaintiff should state that there had been a judicial proceeding; the chief thing required was to prove that this judicial proceeding was under competent persons; these were "*Justices of Assize.*"—This authority was sufficiently defined in the *record*; it was sufficiently set forth in the *declaration*; the additional description gave no authority; the *converse* of the *present* case would have stood as well as the *present*.—If the other commissions had been *added* in the *record*, the *leaving them out* in the *declaration*, would not have been a fatal variance.

As to the first objection, that the words are nonsense if taken literally, it admits of this answer—that, be it so, they will not nonsense sense [*sic*]; they do not make the proposition in the declaration nonsense; it is a clear, and explicit, and intelligible proposition.

The difficulty, in all these cases, does certainly enough spring from a desire to accomplish that object which my Lord MANSFIELD has mentioned in the case reported in Douglas.—And I am very apt to think that the ambiguity and prolixity of pleadings arise from the extreme care which practitioners think themselves bound to take, in order to avoid every possibility of the court's stopping their proceedings.—I flatter myself that the best way to avoid any thing of this kind, would be, to trust themselves with confidence to the liberality of the court, rather than stuff their pleadings with unnecessary circumstances; although, it must be confessed, the courts have been more ready to allow objections like the present, than to discourage them.

NOTE

It is hoped that the above account will be read with candour, as the editor is not ashamed to acknowledge that he is but little accustomed to the reporting of law arguments.

[21] PROCEEDINGS
At the Assizes at Thetford, on the 24th of March, 1787,
BEFORE
Mr. Justice Ashhurst and a Special Jury,
IN THE CAUSE
HURRY against WATSON,
With the Speech at length of Mr. *Erskine* for the Plaintiff, And that of Mr. *Hardinge* for the Defendant;
When a Verdict was found for the former. Damages 3000l.

Insidiator superatus—Oppressa virtute audacia est.   Cic. pro Milon.[3]

[22] **Counsel for the Plaintiff.**
Messrs. *Erskine*, *Mingay*, *Murphy*, *Adair*, *Wilson*, and *Preston*.
Attorney, Mr. *Bell*.

Counsel for the Defendant.
Mr. *Hardinge*, Mr. Serjeant *Le Blanc*, Mr. *Partridge*, and Mr. *Graham*.
Attorney, Mr. *Berry*.

[23] Gentlemen of the Jury,*

[Mr *Erskine*]

ALTHOUGH I am totally a stranger in this country, and, consequently, have not the honour to know any of you, yet, I confess, it gives me pleasure to learn from my friend here (Mr. *Mingay*) that I am addressing men of the first distinction, not only for property, but for all those qualities which you will be called upon to exercise upon this occasion.—That I am addressing men who know the value of character—that some of you have been merchants, who must be peculiarly open to the impression of those circumstances, which in honour, duty, and feeling, I am now bound to lay before you.—You know,

---

* Names of the Special Jury.

Sir Martin Brown Folkes, of Hillington, Bart.
Thomas Beecroft, of Saxthorpe,
Richard Wright, of East Harling,
John Lloyd, of Pentney,
Anthony Hammond, of Westacre,   } Esqrs.
George Nelthrope, of Lynford,
Thomas Lobb Chute, of South Pickenham,
William Birch, of Great Cressingham,
Henry William Wilson, of Didlington,
Robert Knopwood, of Threxton,

Zachariah Death, of Diss,   } Tales-men.
William Ripper Coe, of Attleborough,

[3] The reference is to Cicero, *Pro Milone*, xi. 30.

Gentlemen, the nature of that prosecution which now brings you here.—And, perhaps, it is the strongest observation possible with which I can establish its nature, that you know the injury which has given rise to it.—All of you know it.—The sound of it has gone forth into all lands.—There is not a place nor scarce any part of the civilized world where the honor and credit of an English Merchant is of any value, or where the knowledge of a private individual can travel, where this report has not been trumpetted.

There is not a person who now hears me who does not know that the Plaintiff, whom I have now the honor to represent, was, not a twelve-month ago, standing here in a thousand times a worse situation than the felons who have this morning been tried on the other side of the court.

[24] Mr. Hurry, distinguished, and remarkably distinguished, as a man of probity and goodness in every one of the several relations of social life—against whom the breath of slander had never stirred—This Gentleman—never called to account for any thing that disgraced the character of a man, a merchant, a gentleman, or a christian—stood here, I say, in a far worse situation than the commonest felon.—By the instigation of Mr. Watson, he was here arraigned, as a man who had cast off every thing that marks the worthy—branded with the grossest turpitude that can dishonour a human being—and represented as a wretch, that had neither sense of religion, nor fear of shame.

Now, Gentlemen, need I say more to impress you with the justness and propriety of this action, than to assure you that this innocent and injured man does not come here merely to reimburse himself for the expenses to which he has been run—to recover back the money which he has been forced to lay out to defend himself against one of the most flagrant attacks that could possibly be made upon him—but because there is no other way to recover that good name, that peace of mind, that security, that respectability in society, without which even conscious innocence can give but feeble pleasure.

Mr. Hurry, Gentlemen, comes here as a good citizen—to hold out his persecutor as a public example, in order that, by his punishment, the peace and well-being of civil life may be preserved—and that the innocent and the good may enjoy, unmolested, that credit which their conduct merits.

Nothing can be further from my purpose than to misrepresent to you the nature of this action.—It would, indeed, be folly to attempt it—My learned friend (meaning Mr. *Hardinge*) and I shall have no difference on this point.—I am persuaded my observations, in this respect, will every one of them be confirmed by his.—I will give him all the benefit of the observation.—You do not, Gentlemen, sit here to judge of Mr. Hurry's innocence—the record of acquittal marks it—and that it does not follow of course, that because my client is innocent, that therefore Mr. Watson is guilty.—There may be circumstances which may induce the propriety of putting a man upon his trial, which may justly ward off the consequences of an action against his accuser, although he is most honourably acquitted.—I give my learned friend all the benefit of these observations; and therefore, Gentlemen, if, from the evidence that shall be given in the course of this cause, you shall be of opinion—that Mr. Watson, with a pure upright intention, looking only to the rights of mankind, and believing that Mr. Hurry had cast off all sense of duty to his God and his fellow-creatures, [25] endeavoured to bring him to deserved punishment.—If you are of this opinion, I will not call upon you now to convict him.—But should you be of opinion that Mr. Watson was not thus actuated, but that he was influenced by motives of a far less honourable nature, by motives of spleen, resentment and malice, then I am vindicated in saying that there are no damages that can be called severe and exemplary damages, which you, as an English jury, can give to my client—for there is no act that can be marked with worse features of turpitude, than the endeavour to ruin and take away the credit and character of a fellow-being.

It will of necessity happen in small boroughs, such as Yarmouth, that there should, at different times, be a variety of interests.—In such communities it will, it does often, happen that there are differences of opinion, that give rise to bad blood, and to unfavourable wishes, which ought not, however, to break out as they have done, in the instance now before you.—Mr. Watson and Mr. Hurry are, as I am instructed, in different interests.—And though I cannot prove any *expressions* of malice, vulgarly so called; yet, from the circumstances in the conduct of Mr. Watson, which I shall prove, you will be fully able to collect that he must have had it in his heart.

Mr. Watson is Register of the Court of Admiralty—Mr. Reynolds, his partner, was Judge or President of a court call [sic] the Court of Requests, for the adjudication of small debts.—Mr. Watson is an attorney—Mr. Reynolds, as I said, is his partner, not, I hope, Gentlemen, in this iniquitous business—but in trade.

It happened that a ship, called the Alexander and Margaret was obliged, by stress of weather, to leave her anchors and cables in Yarmouth Roads, which were taken up by men employed for that purpose, and lodged, after being paid for the salvage of them, by Mr. Watson, the Register of the Admiralty Court, in the place appointed for their reception.—The plaintiff had no interest originally in these materials—no concern with the ship; which was the property of another; of a Mr. Bartleman; and the captain's name was Shipley.—This Shipley, the captain, was directed, by his owner, to apply to Mr. Hurry, to whom he had previously written, to procure for him again the anchors and cables in question, out of the custody of the Court of Admiralty, and to pay the expenses incurred.—Mr. Hurry did so; but, when he received the bill of charges, he objected to the article of cartage, as being too much.—Most undoubtedly, if there is one thing that requires a scrupulous attention more than another, it is, that persons wrecked should not be imposed upon.— Notwithstanding our na-[26]-tional character for humanity, there are many instances with respect to these matters, which are a disgrace to us.—Now, though I am not instructed to say that Mr. Watson and Mr. Reynolds have been guilty of extortion in these respects; yet, I may say, that it was the duty of Mr. Hurry to take care that they should not.—Mr. Hurry required an account—in consequence of this requisition, a bill was given him, in which bill Mr. Watson, in his own hand-writing, and signed by his own name, makes the following charges:

'Charges on two anchors and cables belonging to captain Shipley.

	£.	s.	d.
Salvage	14	5	0½
Poundage	0	7	0
Cartage	1	4	0
Court Fees	1	12	3
Register	0	12	0
Marshal	0	4	0
	£ 18	4	3½

John Watson'

Mr. Hurry, looking over this bill, takes exceptions to no item in it but one, that was the item for cartage.—And how did this item affect Mr. Hurry?—Was it his own interest that was concerned? No—He was acting as the honest servant of a person who had suffered by distress.—It was his duty to be scrupulous to a farthing.—I own, as to myself, I should not, and would not, be so exact as to trouble myself much for the value of a shilling or two—it might be construed as captious in me if I were—but, as standing in the shoes of another, I would have my demand even to a mite.—Mr. Hurry, then, acted naturally and properly in this case, in objecting as he did.—One feels a reluctance to speak, in the presence of a person so near one, of a transaction which, from its commencement, hath hitherto been so disgraceful to him.—But, let us look to this article in question—for cartage 1l. 4s.—Mr. Hurry said this was an overcharge—not because the weight of the anchors, the quantity of the cable, the distance where they were carried, were not what they were alleged—it was not on any of these accounts.—He admitted the weight, quantity, and distance, &c.—All these things were perfectly understood.—All Mr. Hurry said, was—taking the anchors at the weight stated; the cables at the length mentioned; and the distance as asserted; yet, still I am of opinion that you have demanded more than is reasonable; I think 16s; but I will demand the return of only 11s; because the form of the court where I am to make [27] this demand requires the taking of an oath—And what did Mr. Hurry do before he followed the impulse of this his opinion?—He inquired of his acquaintances—they confirmed him in his opinion.—He made the demand upon Mr. Watson—Mr. Watson refused to grant it.—Mr. Hurry had now nothing to do, but either to abandon his claim altogether, or to summon Mr. Watson into that court, which, by this clause which I will now read to you, has cognizance of small debts under the value of forty shillings—'And be it enacted by, &c. that it shall and may be lawful to and for any person or persons, &c. who now hath, or hereafter shall have any debt, &c. under the value of forty shillings, &c. owing unto him, &c. to apply to any one of the persons mentioned in the commission, who shall immediately make out and deliver to one of the Serjeants at Mace,

&c. a summons in writing, &c. directed to such debtor, &c. expressing the sum, &c. And that, upon proof made that such summons hath been duly served, &c. the Commissioners, any three or more of them assembled in court, &c. are empowered to make due inquiries, &c. and to make such orders and decrees therein, and pass such final judgement or sentence thereupon, and award such costs of suit, as to them shall seem most agreeable to equity and good conscience.'

Mr. Hurry applied to this court thus constituted—a summons was issued.—Before this summons was issued, it was perfectly understood what the nature of the difference was.—I speak it in Mr. Watson's presence, as he there sits.—He knew there was no dispute about a fact—that it was a question that might fairly and honourably have been tried in the Court of Requests—and I have no scruple in asserting, in the face of this multitude that now surrounds me, that there is nothing disrespectful in demanding of another, what you think you have a right to have granted you.—What was the dispute?—It was, whether Mr. Watson should or should not return Mr. Hurry eleven shillings which he had overcharged him.—Mr. Reynolds, the Mayor, was the President of the court where Mr. Hurry made the demand.—If he had thought Mr. Watson ought not to return the money; Mr. Hurry would not have been offended.—He had not charged Mr. Watson with corruptly with-holding it.—He did not hold him out as a man capable of cheating him.—He only wanted the court to determine, which of the two opinions was the just one.—Gentlemen, attend to this.—Mr. Watson was summoned—he did not appear.—Mr. Reynolds, who was his partner, and acquainted with every particular of the transaction before he came into court, sat as Judge.—I speak this in the presence of a Judge who would blush to be instructed by any party before [28] hand.—I speak it in his presence who will feel its weight that; this Mr. Reynolds, President of the Court of Requests, and Judge of the Court of Admiralty, who ought not to have taken up any antecedent opinion upon the case, was fully instructed, as appeared from a written paper which he had in his pocket, in every minutia of this business.—If I say any thing against Mr. Reynolds; he is in court; he maybe [sic] called upon to contradict me: I am not sworn; I am but the representative of another: He may be sworn; and if he is put upon his oath, I shall then, perhaps, be able to strike from him some sparks which will throw still further light upon this dark business.—But why did not Watson attend?—Had he attended, might not he and Mr. Hurry have shaken hands?—What would Mr. Hurry have said?—Would it not have been this?—Mr. Watson, I do not come here to complain of you as a cheat or an extortioner. It is not a fact about which we differ; it is a matter of belief and opinion. this [sic] court shall decide for us.—But it was settled otherwise.—My unfortunate client was marked out for a victim.—They had a snare prepared for him.—He was hunted into the toil, and cruel and persevering was the chace [sic].—Mr. Reynolds, an attorney (take that along with you, Gentlemen) had lying by him, during the time that Mr. Hurry was swearing to his demand, the act of parliament, with the clause, marked ready, which shall be read to you presently.—This Mr. Reynolds, bred an attorney, practising as an attorney, could believe that that court, in consequence of this clause, had no jurisdiction with respect to the matter that formed the foundation of Mr. Hurry's oath.—The clause of the act is this.—'Provided also and be it enacted, by the authority aforesaid, that this act, or any thing herein contained, shall not take away, limit, or lessen the jurisdiction of the Court of Admiralty, held in and for the borough and port of Great Yarmouth aforesaid, by virtue of certain royal grants or charters; but all causes lawfully cognizable in that court, may continue to be commenced, prosecuted and determined therein, according to the usual coarse [sic] and practice thereof, as heretofore hath been; any thing in this act contained to the contrary notwithstanding.'—Now, what does this clause say?—Not what does it say to an attorney; but what does it say even to a common person?—Would not any man clearly perceive, from this clause, that there was, between this Court of Requests and the Court of Admiralty, what we lawyers call a concurrent jurisdiction?

But Mr. Watson did not attend—Mr. Reynolds, with the paper in his pocket in which every particular had been specified to him by Mr. Watson, did—not to determine the case; for, in his then opinion, the [29] court had no jurisdiction.—Would it not have been full as decent if Mr. Watson had attended himself?—Would it not have been full as decent if Mr. Reynolds had produced this paper, which, in his idea, set the whole matter in so clear a light, at the very first?—These events might have frustrated the whole plan.—The Mayor administered the oath—'You say that Mr. Watson is indebted to you in eleven shillings.—To which Mr. Hurry replied—yes.—Now I here lay it down as a point of law, that any man, as an agent for another, may swear to a debt, as due to himself, which has accrued through his agency.—If my servant sells any thing for me upon credit, most undoubtedly, either I or he may swear to the amount of the sum due, upon occasion.—But if it were, that a man could not strictly swear to a debt of this kind, without the additional terms expressive of the agency, what must we think of endeavouring to draw a man into perjury, by tricking him into taking an oath, with the omission of these supposed essential terms?—And was not this the conduct of these men in this case?—They thought Mr. Hurry was in the trap; but to make him still more sure, the question is repeated.—Do you say that Mr. Watson is indebted to you, William Hurry, in the sum of eleven shillings.—Upon this repetition of the question—Mr. George Hurry, one of the Commissioners of the court, said, Brother, explain yourself.—Upon which, Mr. Hurry added—as Agent for Mr. Shipley, and as appears upon the face of this bill (producing this bill, Mr. Watson's own hand-writing) I get nothing by it.—Why, Gentlemen, this is an oath of reference 'as appears by this account.'—I protest to you that the annals of judicature, in high or low tribunals, in those worst of times, which we cannot look back upon without fear and trembling, do, in no instance that I can recollect, exhibit so mischievous and wicked an attempt at injustice, as the one now in prospect before you.—No sooner had these men got this Gentleman, as they thought, into the toil of Perjury, than Mr. Mayor turns to the act of parliament, and says that the court had no cognizance of the matter.—Did he not know this before?—Could he not have informed Mr. Hurry and the Commissioners of this, before Mr. Hurry had taken his oath?—Yes; but then they could not have said, 'We have caught you—we have now an opportunity of reducing you to contempt, of fixing a stain upon you that shall blast you for ever.'—But no indictment can be maintained against a man for an oath taken in a court that has no jurisdiction with respect to the matter of the oath.—Mr. Reynolds, though folly had before, as is frequently the case, blinded wickedness, recollecting that this fact was an absolute ingredient in the constitution of a Perjury—in two [*30*] days—in two days after that he and Mr. Watson had obliged Mr. Hurry to take the oath which he did, and of which they said the court could not take cognizance, when they found it became necessary in order to support the indictment, this mutable and transitory court was by them voted to have jurisdiction.—I do not know how to keep myself in tolerable coolness, when I am stating the matter.—What would have been the conduct of a humane and good magistrate in this business, when it first came before him?—Would he not have advised Mr. Hurry to settle the matter with Mr. Watson when he should be present?—Would he not have endeavoured to mediate justice between the parties, and to have reconciled and composed all their difference?—And did Mr. Reynolds thus act?—No—he suffers Mr. Hurry to take an oath, and then tells him—you can have no redress—the court has no jurisdiction.—On the morning the court has a jurisdiction, and is clothed in all its ancient dignity.—This man was an attorney—he knew, he had studied, the clause of the act.—It was, I doubt not, thumbed over so black that you could hardly read it—yet this man, thus competent to decide, thus varied, as it suited his purpose, his opinion respecting this court—which seems indeed to have had a kind of legal ague—it now had not a jurisdiction, because Mr. Hurry had a claim to establish—it now had a jurisdiction, because Mr. Hurry must be indicted for Perjury.

You have now, Gentlemen, done me the honour to attend to what I have been saying, in proof that there was no fact disputed between the parties, but that it was a mere matter of opinion.—Now I will put it to his Lordship, whether this can possibly be a subject-matter of an indictment for Perjury.—If a man sells me two or more pair of shoes, for which, upon oath, he claims a debt of eighteen shillings, and I am of opinion that the shoes are worth no more than sixteen shillings, shall I indict him for Perjury? The supposition is ridiculous. I repeat it again, and again, that to make an oath a subject-matter for a criminal court, it must be the assertion of a fact, that is known to be false, from a corrupt motive.—Now what fact did Mr. Hurry swear that was not admitted between the parties?—that there were no anchors—no cables—that they were carried no distance, or the like? No such matter.—Or, what object had he in view in taking the oath? Was it to put a large sum of money into his own pocket?—No—it was only to save a very little one in the pocket of another.—Let me suppose Mr. Watson sitting at his desk, in his office, as an attorney, and a countryman coming in, and asking him his opinion respecting prosecution for the crime of perjury, on account of exactly [*31*] similar circumstances as have been stated in this case, a gentleman, a merchant of the first credit and reputation—a person against whom the tongue of slander had never wagged—What would be his advice?—Would he not say—I would advise you to be let blood? Would he not say—attend to this—can there be any malicious, wilful, corrupt, perjury, without motives? Can it be conceived that a man, in flourishing circumstances, can run counter to his conscience, and abandon all his right to the approbation and esteem of his fellow citizens, to put eleven shillings into the pocket of another?—Besides this, my friend, you ought to recollect that it is not a fact about which you are asking my advice, but it is a mere matter of opinion.—I remember that great and august magistrate, who has lived so long to his own credit, and to the benefit of society, and whose loss, in all probability, we shall soon have to deplore—I speak of my Lord MANSFIELD—I remember his saying, when a man was indicted for perjury, for swearing that a wall was seven feet high, whereas it was only six feet—What! indict a man for perjury for a matter which the application of a foot-rule would have settled for the parties! and he instantly threw the record over the table.—There is the case, likewise, of Carnan, the bookseller, who was indicted for swearing to one horse as his, when another, which was proved to be his, was found dead in a ditch.—The learned Judge would not try the cause—He said, the defendant swore certainly to the best of his knowledge at that time, and, no doubt, believed, however mistaken he might be, that he was claiming his own property.—Now, here some motive of interest might be imagined operating, as the value of a horse is something—But in the case of Mr. Hurry, there was nothing upon earth that could be conceived capable of having upon him the least possible degree of influence to commit the act for which he was indicted—Mr. Hurry is a merchant of the first respectability and credit—the sum which he claimed was of the most trivial nature—and he was but an agent in the business.—But, Gentlemen, only conceive how these Attorneys conducted themselves, and what shifts and wiles they had recourse to, in the different stages and management of the business they had taken in hand.—The money claimed was not, say they, due to Mr. Hurry—It was not due from Mr. Watson—it was due from a Mr. Munsor, the carter, to whom Mr. Watson had transferred it.—Good God! how is a man to deal with such persons as these? One is in danger, absolutely, of being indicted by them for being a Lawyer.—But I assert that, if Watson was paid a sum of money of Hurry's, we have a right to look to Watson for that sum. An action would lie against Watson at the suit of Hurry, although [*32*] the money were no longer actually in his hands, but he had paid it over to another. What advice Mr. Watson would give in this case, I will not undertake to say—My learned friend, I doubt not, fully coincides with me in this point.—But it may be said, that the conduct of Mr. Watson, and the bill which he preferred against Mr. Hurry, were left to the consideration of a court of open judicature.—I protest, had he had recourse to a Grand Jury of the county, there might have been some reason to believe that he was actuated by motives not utterly disgraceful to him.—But

Mr. Watson dared not to do this—He was conscious no Jury, but such as was made up, in a great measure, of his relations, friends, and connections, could, or would, answer the purpose he was wishing to get executed.—I do not mean to say that every man that sat upon that Grand Jury, which found the bill against Mr. Hurry, was a corrupt man.—It was, however, the Grand Jury of a Corporation.—It was a limited Jury—of a local jurisdiction.—I wish to God there were fewer of them in these kingdoms.—What would be the consequence, if there was not a power of removing, by writ of Certiorari, any indictment of which these local jurisdictions take cognizance, to the higher and more impartial tribunals of Justice?—What would have been the consequence to my innocent client in the present case?—Would he not have been convicted by the influence of the same men, who, after having hunted him into the toil, would have easily found means to have finished his destruction?—That was their object—We will get, said they, a Petty Jury to second, by their verdict, what the Grand Jury has laid a good foundation for—Then his character is undone—he is cast off, as a stranger to the comforts of society—and we shall rise, triumphant, upon his fall.—The thing was well imagined, and it wanted but little to completion.—But, Gentlemen, what will you say to these men, when you find that they durst not trust even a Jury consisting of their own relations and friends, but with a mutilated and garbled oath?—I do not believe, indeed, that if a man had preferred a bill of indictment for Perjury, upon the grounds of the oath as if it was actually taken by Mr. Hurry, even to a Jury of his own twelve sons, all of whose existences depended upon his absolute will and pleasure, that he could have gotten them, if they had the least degree of regard to honour, or to conscience, to have found the bill.—But Mr. Reynolds did not take a note of all that was sworn—not a word about agency—not a word of an account—nor of 'I get nothing by it'—All he noted was, that Mr. Hurry swore that Mr. Watson was indebted to him eleven shillings—so that even this Grand Jury could be trusted only to a certain extent—only with a mutilated and garbled oath. [33]—When they had thus far succeeded, they did not imagine that they would not have been able, by a Petit Jury, to put a finishing stroke to the matter.—But, thanks to the wisdom and equity of our ancestors, who have so wisely ordered that the operation of local prejudices, in these miserable jurisdictions, may be providently presented, by a reference of our causes to the decision of courts where Justice, indeed, holds an equal balance.—The Borough court of Colchester, very lately exhibited a wretched instance in proof of the propriety of my remark.—A very reputable farmer was actually committed to gaol, as a felon, for having stolen sixpence out of a bag belonging to a gleaner, whom he had desired to go out of his field; and, but for a certiorari, would, in all probability, have been found guilty, as he would have been tried in that court where the recorder, who was principally instrumental in getting him committed, would have sit [sic] as his Judge.—And when the Counsel for the prosecution argued against his being tried in any other court than that in which the indictment was found, Justice GOULD said, 'Good God! he may be tried here, or any where;' and thereupon the matter was given up.—

Certain it is, that some pictures are for one situation—some for another—The bill of indictment that was preferred against my client, was for the meridian of Yarmouth—when it came into this court, it is remembered what a pretty figure these gentlemen then cut—My friend and I were both brought down upon this occasion—My client was put to very great expense; as you are well aware, Gentlemen, we do not attend here for nothing—The case was opened by Mr. *Partridge*, with great clearness and decency—with great force and propriety—I know, and respect his character—I know his mind—I have not a doubt, but that if the cause had gone on then, so as to have given Mr. *Partridge* an opportunity of knowing its real features, he would not have urged the conviction of Mr. Hurry. I have been recently engaged myself, in a similar situation, against the Honourable Henry Hobart, the Foreman of the Grand Jury now sitting in this place.—He has done me the honour, since I have been here, though I never had the pleasure of knowing him before, to thank me for my conduct upon that occasion.—I opened the case which I was called upon to support, with firmness, as Mr. *Partridge* did his—I opened it, with setting forth all those circumstances, in a pointed light, that seemed calculated to bring conviction home to the defendant—so far my duty, as an Advocate, extended.—But when I discovered the nature of the evidence which was adduced—in the face of my clients, who are now, perhaps, cursing me for my conduct, for ought I know—instead of endeavouring to urge the Jury to [*34*] convict the defendant—I shut up my brief, with—God forbid that they should think of convicting him upon any such testimony as they had heard—I hope, never in the Advocate to forget the duty of a Gentleman, or the character or feelings of a Christian.—I would rather lose all my subsistence, all those means by which alone I am enabled to maintain a wife, whom I love, and a numerous family, whom it is my duty to provide for, than give up that benevolence of character (which, I trust, I have hitherto, and which, I hope, it will ever be my pride to maintain) by holding out to shame any man, whom, in my conscience, I know, or believe to be innocent.—But, Gentlemen, then I ask, What must that man be, who, in his own genuine character, does what I cannot do in the character of an Advocate? This may be setting forth a good opinion of myself; but whilst my heart, my feelings, do not contradict me, but bear me out in this respect, I have a right to the boast. I do not think, though I thus lay claim to a large share of good feelings, that I have more than are possessed by my learned friend, who is this day to defend Mr. Watson, and who is, confessedly, not less distinguished for all those brilliant accomplishments which have so deservedly acquired him high reputation as an Advocate, than for all those dearer sensibilities which grace the Gentleman, and characterize the Christian. I am sure, whatever his duty today, as an Advocate, may impose upon him, he will fully accord with me in every thing which, in this respect, I have been saying.—The principal witness called upon when this matter was before this court last year was Mr. Spurgeon.—He proved that Mr. Hurry swore that Watson was indebted to him in eleven shillings.—I thought—I mean no imputation upon Mr. Spurgeon, I thought he was going to stop there.—I called out, let us know all that Mr. Hurry swore.—He then added—as agent for Mr. Shipley, and as appears upon the face of this bill.—I cannot help doing justice to the memory of that pious and good man*—who is now enjoying, I doubt not, the fruit of his labours—who, sitting here as Judge, with a face clouded with the languor of a disease, which, a few weeks afterwards, brought him to an untimely end, instantly, upon hearing this part of Mr. Spurgeon's evidence, had his countenance covered with the blush of indignation; and, with a tone of voice, and manner of address, highly expressive of his feelings, said, turning to the Jury—Gentlemen, you must acquit the Defendant: He has been indicted upon half an oath.—And when I, with a zeal which I thought the honour of my client demanded, not with the borrowed tongue of an Advocate, but with a really excited sen-[35]-sibility, entreated the learned Judge that he would permit the cause to go on, that my client's character might be more fully investigated, and his honour more fully cleared; he, checking the impetuosity of youth, replied to me—What greater honour can your client have than to be acquitted?—The Jury instantly returned their verdict, when plaudits, which were indeed more suitable to a theatre than a court of justice, ensued; but which, as characteristic of honest and good feelings, were, on such an occasion, not much deserving of censure.

Now, Gentlemen, as soon as this event took place, one of these two things must at this moment have been the case—either that Mr. Watson knew the whole of Mr. Hurry's oath when he preferred the indictment, or that he knew it now when he was acquitted.—Attend particularly to this.—Both Mr. Watson and his partner Reynolds were in court at this time.—Let us take the first—that he knew it before.—If he did; what defence can be made for him? He gravely and deliberately garbles and mutilates an oath to make it speak a lie.—There is no speech that can go beyond the bare statement of the case.—There is so much fraud, meanness, and cruelty in this man's conduct, thus viewed, that the English language has not words strong enough to convey my ideas of the abhorrence in which it ought to be held—But, perhaps, it will be said, Mr. Watson was not in the Court of Requests when Mr. Hurry took the oath—that Mr. Reynolds, his partner, had not communicated the whole of it to him—that he did not know but that he had stated the whole when he preferred his bill.— Be it so.—He was certainly in this court when his own witness, Mr. Spurgeon, gave a full detail of Mr. Hurry's oath.—Had he not then had malice in his heart—had he been actuated only by what he pretended to be actuated by, a regard to justice alone, what would he have done?—What would he have done?—Why he would have come forwards in the face of the court, and said, let me make some atonement to Mr. Hurry.—If I had known that these words were in the oath, I would never have taken the step I did.—Do let me embrace this injured man.—Let me fall at his feet—let me implore his forgiveness.— Had he done this, I would myself have been the first to have said—Mr. Hurry, take this man to your arms—he has injured you—but, as a christian, it becomes

---

* Sir GEORGE NARES

you to pardon him.—Remember, Sir, that in the course of justice none of us shall see salvation.—But Mr. Watson did not do this.—No; he, and his partner Mr. Reynolds, left this court with revenge and malice still rankling in their hearts—they went out, like the father of all wickedness into paradise, meditating mischief against the happy and the innocent. Gentlemen, I [*36*] should be ashamed of myself, unless I had the most clear, satisfactory and unequivocal proof of what I am here alleging, to urge a thing so grossly flagrant upon your observation, as that which I am now under the necessity of doing:—Is it credible—Is it to be believed, that Mr. Watson, notwithstanding his being present in court—notwithstanding Mr. Hurry was acquitted upon the oath of the prosecutor's own witness—upon a total variance between the oath proved, and the oath on which the indictment was preferred—that this man should, notwithstanding all these circumstances, instantly upon his leaving the court, cause to be inserted in the public papers that Mr. Hurry was acquitted upon a flaw in the indictment; and that a fresh indictment would be preferred against him?—I need not assert that Mr. Hurry was not acquitted upon a flaw in the indictment.—If this were the case; I have nothing to do but to get my worst enemy accused of the worst crime, and then, when not a shadow of evidence is brought in proof of my allegation, and of course he is decreed innocent, I have only to give it out that he got off by a flaw in the indictment, and that I should commence a fresh prosecution, and thus my end is effectually answered. But, Gentlemen, this was an Attorney who did all this—one who could not be ignorant that, had the case been true respecting the cause of Mr. Hurry's acquittal, he could not be tried again for the same offence. But he was galled at his not succeeding—and he was determined to do something to check the happiness of my client, going home to his house with the honest triumph of integrity.—It is really, Gentlemen, shocking to my feelings to state these matters to you.—I know all the happiness of domestic life—I know all the dear sympathies of the tenderest and dearest of connections—I am alive, therefore, to the joy with which this worthy man hastened to his anxious, disconsolate family.—I can conceive his emotions when he first saw them, trembling between hope and fear, crying out to them—It is over—It is over—oppression is past—and I am restored to my character again. I saw, Gentlemen, I can conceive, I can sympathize with him in this moment of returning happiness. Nor am I less sensible to the reverse that was so soon to follow.—Good God! what must have been the feelings of this man, what of his wife, what of his relatives and friends, thus congratulating each other with the happy termination of their anxiety, when he found in an advertisement in the common news-papers—that he escaped disgrace but by a flaw in his indictment, and that he was still threatened with a fresh prosecution?—that his discredit was chronicled with rewards offered for the recovery of lost pointers, and with notices concerning footmen that were in want of places—nay, that his dis-[*37*]-grace might have the greatest possible notoriety, the PERJURY CAUSE is placed next to the advertisement of the mail coaches, so that no one, who wanted information respecting the best mode of conveyance to London, could look into the paper without this first catching his eye. Nor was the paper, in which this advertisement was first inserted, one of those general papers, such as the Public Advertiser, in which, from the multiplicity of articles, this might chance to have been overlooked; but it was in a paper of the county in which Mr. Hurry resided, in the Norwich Mercury, which, in a single day, perhaps, was read by thousands, all of whom were well acquainted with the character and situation of him, and of all his family.—Give me leave, and I will read you the paragraph—'The Perjury cause which came on to be tried at Thetford, which was supposed to have taken up a long time, took up but a short one, it going off on a defect in the indictment, notwithstanding which, a fresh indictment will be preferred by the prosecutor.'—Going off upon a defect in the indictment—which cleared the Defendant only in such manner that his guilt was still notorious,—and notwithstanding which, a fresh indictment will be preferred by the prosecutor.—I will venture to say, that had this been the case, my client was in a worse situation, than if the charge had been actually brought home to him.—A man, found guilty of a crime, and condemned to the punishment thereto annexed, becomes an object of pity; but when a knave gets off by a trick, by a flaw, by a defect in the indictment, he is more an object of detestation than ever. What a situation then was my unhappy client again thrown into! This paragraph, when printed, had an extensive circulation. News-papers go all over the world.—What was said by the reverend judge goes but a little way—is by folly misunderstood, or by prejudice misrepresented.—This circumstance, then, Gentlemen, must have its weight in impressing you with the conviction of the malicious disposition of the defendant Watson. My Lord will tell you that it is evidence in this cause. It goes to the gist of the action, and whatever tends to the proof of that, is evidence.—How differently constructed must this Mr. Watson be, from any thing that I can conceive of myself! If I thought that a man had robbed my house, and, though I could not swear to him myself, that some of my servants could—and therefore had him apprehended—if, upon his being put upon his trial, it plainly appeared that he was innocent; and that I had injured him in his trade, and had put him to much expense and trouble,—with what pleasure, with what eagerness, would I have put a paragraph into the papers to declare, to publish, his innocence, and to make him all the reparation in my [38] power. But what was the conduct of Mr. Watson? What?—why the man whom he could not convict, he strives to debase—against the authority of the learned Judge—against the decision of a Jury—against the concurrent testimony of a crouded court.—Mr. Hurry shall be a perjured man. I have failed to punish him by wiles, I will punish him by slander—I will blast him with calumny—the slow-moving hand of scorn shall point at him. Thank God, my own heart gives me no image of a man capable of thus acting. I need not tell you, Gentlemen, who have all the relations of life belonging to you—that hence are derived the greatest happinesses that sense produces, and that there are heart-affecting welcomes, which earnestly-wished-for returns occasion. Since I have been in this place, the family of my learned friend here* has exhibited to me a scene of this nature, which filled me with

---

* Mr. *Mingay*

delight.—The joy, the affection, the cheerfulness, which the visit of a brother called up, deeply affected my sensibility; but while thus arrested by the pleasing scene, I confess to you, Gentlemen, I could not help saying to myself—Suppose this happy family, thus cheerful, thus blest, should, in the midst of all their comfort, be, on a sudden, informed by an advertisement in the papers, that this brother, over whom they were so much rejoicing, would be indicted for a horrid crime from which, indeed, he had already escaped but by a flaw. I can feel—I felt—this imaginary transition. I could not bear the image which my own fancy had wrought up—I was obliged to divert my ideas, that I might be enabled to check my emotions.—Mr. Watson, however, was formed after quite a different fashion. He could bear to conjure up, in his own imagination, a similar picture of distressful change; and, what is more, he could coolly endeavour, and take steps, to have it realized. My client had escaped the snare that had been laid for him; but Mr. Watson resolved he should not triumph—he was determined he should not present himself with joy to his wife, whom he had not married many months—to his friends and his relations, who were waiting his return with awful solicitude. He fabricated the libel—that Mr. Hurry was acquitted by a defect in the indictment, and that a fresh bill would be preferred by the prosecutor—and he had it inserted, by means of a Mr. Lock, in four different papers. Upon the appearance of this in the Norwich Mercury, Mr. *Bell*, Mr. Hurry's attorney, with all that good sense and temper, for which, I am told, he is, at all times, conspicuous, wrote a private letter to Mr. Lock, of which the following is a copy:—[39]

'SIR,   Yarmouth, March 30, 1786,

On inquiry of the printer of the Norwich paper, I find that you are the author of the advertisement in last Saturday's paper, purporting that the Perjury cause, tried at Thetford assizes the Saturday preceding, went off upon a defect in the indictment; and that a fresh bill will be preferred. Mr. William Hurry, the defendant in that cause, conceiving that this advertisement is published with a view to injure his character, complains against you for your conduct. It is surely very strange that one, who calls himself a merchant, and must, if he has any feeling, be sensible of the value of a good name, should thus sport with the reputation of another. Mr. Hurry knows not that he ever injured you, and can therefore find no cause for this your attack upon him. At present, he talks to me of calling you before a court to answer for this conduct; and he doubts not but a Jury of Norwich Merchants will think him entitled to some recompense for the injury done him by you. However, Mr. Hurry never acts from sudden impulse, and therefore he will wait for your answer, which I shall expect to receive to-morrow. I am, Sir, your humble servant,

                            JOHN BELL.'

Now this was the most honourable and proper conduct, that could have been pursued by Mr. *Bell*, who, at this time, did not know that Mr. Watson had any hand in the manufacturing of this advertisement. But what does Mr. Lock do?—He publishes this letter in the paper, and, to envenom the sting, that had been fastened in Mr. Hurry's bosom.—He prefaces it with these strictures—'Advertisement to the printer. Sir, that the impartial public may judge of the *malevolence* and persecuting disposition of Mr. Hurry, the following letter is inserted.'—May I ask you, Gentlemen, if there be any evidence of a persecuting disposition in Mr. *Bell*'s letter?—On the contrary, are there not strong marks of a temper just the reverse?—Mr. Lock, feeling that he would be justly dishonoured, and would subject himself to some degree of danger, if he did not give some account of this business, added to Mr. *Bell*'s letter, which he published, the following:

'The paragraph, which, under the name of an advertisement, is alluded to in the above letter, was received by me from the hands of Mr. Watson, and conveyed to the printer by my clerk; and, after the threats, which, since the trial, have been publicly given out by Mr. Hurry and his friends, of bringing his action of damages against Mr. Watson, he has surely little reason to be surprised at the publication of such an advertisement.

Norwich, April 3, 1786.

[40] Now where are those threats of which Mr. Lock complains? Is it a threat, for a man to take steps to get his wrongs redressed? At this time we had been consulted upon this business—the writ was actually sued out, and some advances were made in that action, which, I trust, will have a triumphant effect before this sun is far declined.

Here, then, I fix malice upon the Defendant in this cause. If the fact itself did not do it sufficiently, unconnected with this—this—this does. Whenever a man prosecutes another for a crime, such as that with which my client was charged, from sinister motives, and not from motives of public justice, and this is, by any means, to be made plainly to appear, that man is certainly actuated by malice. If, therefore, I indict a man for what he could not be guilty of, and which I knew was not a subject of perjury—and when he comes down from the bar fairly acquitted, I disappoint his triumph, and turn his libeller;—my motives of conduct in the whole of this business cannot be equivocal. If this be not malice—human nature is subject to worse passions, is infinitely more impure, than I have at present any conception of. Of this malice then, Mr. Watson stands fairly convicted. For this malice, Mr. Hurry took the necessary steps to bring him to a sense of his misconduct, and to clear his own reputation, which, by this man's means was still subject to imputation.

Gentlemen, the action being brought, it was sent down to be tried at Norwich. Mr. *Mingay* and myself were engaged conditionally to have been there. Circumstances occurred that unavoidably prevented us. The cause was opened by my learned friend, across the table, Mr. *Murphy*, with all that strength of language for which his various writings are so conspicuous; and he made, as I am told, a very great impression upon the Jury. Mr. *Hardinge* was brought down to defend his client—and in this, Mr. Watson shew [sic] no small discretion and judgement; for an abler advocate, one, who can make use of more powers of eloquence in support of any cause that he is called upon to maintain, wears not the habit, or the dress of law. But did Mr. *Hardinge* come out with his defence of this man? No.—He knew, he felt, he had nothing upon which to defend him.—He perceived that his client stood naked and indefensible. My learned friends, therefore, fixed upon a variance, a trifling, unimportant, variance (for so it was considered by the court of Common Pleas) between the record of acquittal and the declaration, pointed out to them by Mr. Berry, the clerk of the court. These gentlemen fixed upon a variance, for the defence of their client, who was prosecuted for endeavouring, by the variance of half an oath, instead of a whole one, to trample upon and beat [*41*] down the character and happiness of a fellow-creature. They turned round with this variance to my Lord. His Lordship thought the variance material. Says Mr. *Murphy*—I can resist the Judge: I am convinced there is nothing in the objection. But being rather afraid that it might seem unbecoming him to oppose such authority, he suffered the cause to be stopped; and Mr. *Hardinge* rode away on the back of an attorney. I would beg leave to observe to you, Gentlemen, that the issue of the business, at this time, reflected no discredit upon the learned Judge who was trying the cause. The hurry of a Nisi Prius is very often corrected by the cooler and more solemn determination of the courts during term.

With this same record we are now come down again. We would have amended it; but the court would not even give us leave. Upon this same record we now stand here for judgement.—'The longest day will have an end;'—the race of injustice is almost run.' You are now, Gentlemen, called upon—to protect worth—to uphold honour—to administer comfort to the oppressed. Had an attempt been made to poison or to assassinate my client, and it had been successful, in my opinion, there would have been no comparison between this and the prosecution which the defendant brought against him. He would, in the former case, have been happy—he would have been where the wicked would have ceased from troubling him—he would have slept in quiet; and his friends, however poignant their anguish for his fatal exit might have been, would have comforted themselves with the christian hope of seeing him again in a better world. But if this cruel prosecution had succeeded—the misery would have been, not that he would have died, but that he would have lived— an outcast of society—a wretch disgraced and abhorred by even the lowest of his fellows—bereaved of every privilege of a social being—and what, perhaps, would more than any thing else have pleased the authors of his prosecution— deprived of his franchise to give his vote at the next general election. And if he escaped this cruel prosecution, think, I pray you, of that peace of mind of which he was despoiled—think of all those horrid feelings with which he must have been harassed, whilst his character was uncleared, and his security unestablished.—There is in every man as high sensibility to the opinion which his fellow-creatures may form of him. When he observes the smile of approbation from every quarter, his heart beats with delight; he enjoys a happiness short only of that of heaven itself: Adversity loses all its power to wound him; prosperity still wears a gayer aspect. But take the same man— expose him to the blasts of unmerited detraction—the sunshine of virtue is gone—'this canopy of heaven, fretted with lus-[*42*]-tres, is but a pestilential congregation of vapours.'—He thinks he hears the voice of obloquy in every sound; he imagines himself the sport of the tongue of every one whom he passes; his food digests not in his stomach; and his bed is wetted with his tears. In short, if there be any thing that brings a man down to his grave sooner than another, it is the cruel consequence of slander. But it may be said, that when a man is acquitted, his character is not hurt; he is the same man he was before. I deny this to be fact. Many read the paragraphs which detraction fabricates, that do not hear them contradicted: many have given them a circulation that do not wish to have them contradicted. We have, in this neighbourhood, a most solemn instance to this purpose. The dearest friend I ever had in the world, whose house* I yesterday passed with an aching heart, splendid as his character was, was, nevertheless, exposed to a public trial. I had the honour to attend him during the whole of the painful ordeal to which he was forced to submit. And though he was acquitted, after the most minute and severe investigation, by a court martial of as gallant officers as ever were clothed in a naval suit, in the manner the most honourable that could possibly be imagined; yet has he not ever since been the subject of political squibs? Has he not been censured in magazines, news-papers and pamphlets? Nay, are there not still even many good men, who, looking through the medium of ignorance or of prejudice, yet think that this man, thus acquitted, did tarnish the honour of the British flag? And what is to be done in such a case as this? Who can follow Admiral Keppel in all the manoeuvres of his fleet? Who can point out, whenever they hear the vulgar blasphemy to which his conduct is every day exposed, the various particulars of the complicated transactions of that busy day, which gave rise to his arraignment?[4] Who knows not that there are numbers in the world too lazy to vindicate, where a long detail of circumstances is requisite? Who knows not that there are numbers who are but too fond at least of letting malignity work its own will? I am bold to say, that my friend, great as he was, innocent as he was, never got over the effects of that court-martial—it preyed upon his spirits—and, at last, he died a martyr to its influence. And what is the case of my client? What has he been accused of? He has been accused of one of the worst crimes of society. It is true he has been acquitted; but how is he characterized?—'Is that the Mr. Hurry who was tried for Perjury?' Good God! it is enough to make a man shrink from the light of day. Who will tell the long tale that will wipe off the effect of this trait in his description?

[*43*] Gentlemen, the task is your's [*sic*], and a solemn task it is. Should you find small damages; is not the question obvious?—What has all this fuss been

---

* Eldon-Hall

[4] In a notorious affair of political jealousies involving Lord Sandwich, Admiral Keppel, and Vice-Admiral Palliser, Keppel was court-martialed, but after a five-week trial in early 1779 the charges were roundly refuted and pronounced unfounded. See *ODNB, sub nom.* 'Keppel, Augustus, Viscount Keppel'.

about?—Why all this expence of counsel?—There must certainly be something about this man of, at least, an equivocal nature, if you, a Norfolk Jury, think him entitled only to a trivial compensation. The malice was clear; the want of probable cause is incontrovertible; the subsequent insertion of the libel is an aggravation. If then, notwithstanding these things, your verdict shall be in his favour but a trifling sum, you again blast his credit—you do not do what ought to be done for him—you do not send him forth into the world perfectly cleared of the gross imputation under which he has so long laboured.

It is your duty, Gentlemen, to give Mr. Hurry such damages as you would wish should be given to yourselves, were you in his situation. And believe me—be the compensation you may assign him what it may—he must ever wish that the event, to which that assignment has a reference, had never happened. It must ever recur to him—he will always think it one of the greatest and most serious misfortunes of his life:—For, to adopt the words of a favourite author of my learned friend's—'Ye cannot minister to a mind diseased—pluck from the memory a rooted sorrow—raze out the written troubles of the brain—and with some sweet oblivious antidote, cleanse the stuffed bosom of the perilous stuff, which weighs upon the heart.'[5]

Gentlemen, you may yourselves be the subject of the same wicked attempt: you must offend somebody when you are asserting your own rights, or what you esteem the general rights of mankind. And be the man whom you offend like the prosecutor of my client—he can mark you down for destruction—he can cut you to the earth—and, if you get off, he can say, it was but by a flaw in the indictment. You apply for redress—you complain of the compensation as trivial that is made you. It may then be said to you—why you have set the precedent yourselves—what can you expect?—the measure you meted has been meted to you again.

But, in this case, putting all compensatory damages out of the question, no man will say, the most romantic defender will not pretend, that my client ought not to be reimbursed. Mr. *Bell*, whom I shall call, will tell you—what are the expenses to which Mr. Hurry has been forced—that, independent of all the anxiety, all the oppression, and all the concomitant evils of this prosecution, he has, merely in his defence of that prosecution, laid out between six and 700l. But why all this profusion, it may be said? why were my learned friend and I employed upon this occasion? It is difficult for me to speak on this point, without subjecting myself to the [44] imputation of vanity. But it is well known, that there are some men whom times and chances push more forward into the world than others.

My learned friends (I mean no disparagement to these Gentlemen on my left hand) who are of the first standing in this circuit, were retained on the part of the prosecution, and yet it shall be said the prosecuted shall not go to any other persons. This is just the same as if I should knock a man down, and do him some essential injury, and then prevent him from going to the surgeon, in

---

[5] See Shakespeare, *Macbeth*, act 5, scene 3, lines 4–45.

whose experience and skill he had the fullest confidence, by engaging him before hand, and then complain of the expense which, by my own ill temper at first, and my own persevering malice afterwards, I had unavoidably obliged him to incur, by having recourse to a surgeon at a distance. To the expenses then, Gentlemen, which my client has been at in the progress of this business, he is entitled at your hands, of right. But this is not enough—you must do more for him—you must do that, by your verdict, which will give him the stamp of the opinion you, as his country, entertain of his integrity; of the total want of cause for the prosecution to which he has been subjected; and of the malicious disposition of the defendant, who has so wickedly endeavoured to ruin his character and his happiness. Had I that melody of voice, and that variety of tone, which my learned friend possesses in so eminent a degree, I would again recur to his favourite author, and quote from him those emphatical sentences, which mark a splendidly benevolent mind—'Who steals my purse steals trash, 'tis something, nothing, 'twas mine, 'tis his, and has been slave to thousands; but he that filches from me my good name, robs me of that which not enriches him, and makes me poor indeed.'—Gentlemen of the Jury, I have now finished. If my learned friend means to call no witnesses, which I imagine is the case—if we are to be treated only with what he has to say upon the subject—why what is this but still a fresh trick upon us? But I am under no apprehensions. You, Gentlemen, will undoubtedly be amused with the opportunity that is afforded my learned friend, to display all those brilliant talents for which he is so much and so deservedly renowned. But I beg leave to remind him, that eloquence, when proof is absent, is but a beating of the air—the cause will remain the same. It will, even after the manner in which it will be attempted to be set off, be only like a painted sepulchre, with its rottenness and putrefaction somewhat concealed. But should any witnesses be called, the rule of the profession will then, Gentlemen, entitle me to address you again; and should Mr. Watson put me into that situation—although I have thus long detained the court—and although he may think I can have nothing more to add—he shall find that no discourse can be exhausted, which has his malignity for its subject. [45]

MR. BRADLEY

Mr. *Mingay*—You are agent for Mr. Hurry's attorney?—Yes, sir.
What is that you have in your hand?—The office-copy of the record.
It is a true copy?—Yes.
What is that, Sir?—The examined copy of the indictment.
Is it a true copy?—Yes.
Is Mr. Watson's name on the back?—Yes.

MR. BELL.

Mr. *Mingay.*—You are attorney for Mr. Hurry?—I am.
Were you present at the time he was tried in the other court?—I was.
Did you take an account at the time?—I did not; but as soon as the trial was over, I went to Mr. *Murphy*'s lodgings where I read what he had taken on his Brief, and have read it over many times since.

Will you endeavour to give an account of what passed at the trial?—Mr. *Partridge* opened the case—(Here the witness was interrupted by Mr. *Partridge*, who said there was no occasion for the witness to state his speech.)

Give us an account, Mr. *Bell*, of what evidence, &c.—Mr. Spurgeon was called; he is Clerk of the Court of Requests; he said that Mr. Hurry swore, that Mr. Watson owed him eleven shillings: upon being asked if he said any thing more, Mr. Spurgeon said, yes, Mr. Hurry added, as agent for Mr. Shipley, for an overcharge of cartage. The Judge then took up the record, and, after perusing it, said, They have taken part of his words, can this be an absolute swearing to a falsehood? He then turned to the Jury, and said, Gentlemen, you see the nature of this charge, that the defendant swore that the money was due to him in his own person, whereas he swore it was due to him as agent for another: Will you take a man's words, and not his explanation! Gentlemen, you must acquit the defendant.

Mr. *Bell*, you can tell us what expenses Mr. Hurry was at, at the last trial?—I cannot tell all: My own bill was upwards of 562l.

That included the Counsels [*sic*] fees?—It did: There was 44l. more for the expenses of the witnesses at Thetford; and some of the witnesses were not paid by me.

So that the whole, within your knowledge, was upwards of 600l.?—Yes.

Do you know the hand-writing of Mr. Watson? Look at that bill (this was the salvage bill).—This is Mr. Watson's hand-writing. [46]

ALEXANDER BARTLEMAN.

Mr. *Murphy*—You are owner of a ship called the Alexander and Margaret?—I am.

Did she lie at any time in Yarmouth Roads?—Yes, in July, 1785.

Where do you live?—At North Shields.

Did you hear of any accident which your ship met with?—Yes; she lost two anchors and two cables.

Do you know it of your own knowledge?—Yes.

Did you write to any body about the matter?—Yes, to Mr. Sam. and Wm. Hurry.

What directions did you give?—I wrote to them to procure the anchors and cables, learning from the captain where they lay.

Were you, at any time, at Yarmouth after that?—No.

Did you interfere, and make any explanation to Mr. Watson?—Mr. Hurry claimed the anchors and cables: I know nothing but that he got them.

Can you tell us the weight?—On anchor was 10 cwt. and two quarters; the other 9 cwt. three quarters.

What was the weight of the cables?—I can tell you the length of them; one was between 15 and 16 fathom, the thickness 12 inches; the other between 45 and 50 fathom, the thickness the same.

Being conversant with ship matters, can you form a judgement what was the weight?—Near a ton.

How much is a ton?—Twenty hundred weight,

Cross-Examination.

Mr. *Le Blanc*—Was your letter directed to Samuel and William Hurry?—Yes, it was.

Are those two Gentlemen connected in trade?—I believe so.

SAMUEL HURRY, jun.

Mr. *Adair*—Did you go to Mr. Watson, to pay the salvage to him for the Alexander & Margaret's anchors and cables?—I went with the captain.

Did you ask for a bill?—I did.

Look at that bill: was that the bill?—It was.

You paid the bill?—I did.

Whose money was it?—I had two ten pound notes from Mr. William Hurry, out of which Mr. Watson gave me the change, which I returned to Mr. William Hurry.

When you returned the change, did Mr. William Hurry say any thing?—When I shew him the bill, he objected to the article of cartage, and desired me to go back to Mr. Watson, and tell him so.—I did go.

[47] What past [sic]?—I only told Mr. Watson that Mr. William Hurry objected to the article of cartage: Mr. Watson said it was the usual charge.

He did not return any part of the money?—No.

Was there any thing afterwards that passed between you and Mr. Watson?—I met Mr. Watson upon the quay, and told him he would be summoned to the Court of Requests.

In what respect was the objection stated to Mr. Watson?—In respect to the article of cartage.

What answer did Mr. Watson make you?—Go, and consult your great lawyer *Bell*.

Did you make any reply?—I said he would certainly be summoned to the Court of Requests: To which he said, I shall have no justice there, there are so many of your own family.

Where were the anchors and cables?—In the usual place.

Cross-Examination.

Mr. *Hardinge*—You were sent, you say, by Mr. Hurry: in what character did you apply to Mr. Watson?—As Clerk of the Register Court of Admiralty.

Is it not the duty of this Court to deliver up such things as they have in their custody, upon the salvage being paid?—It is.

You claimed, then, those anchors and cables?—Capt. Shipley swore to the anchors and cables, and I paid the money.

The cartage is included in the bill?—It is.

Do you know the meaning of the term cartage?—It is not a fee, you may make an agreement about it: It is a consideration for labour in carrying, &c.

Are there not certain persons appointed by this court to act as carters?—Mr. Watson told me he usually employed one Munsor.

You have lived as a merchant in Yarmouth?—Yes.

Do you not know that the corporation employ carters of their own?—I know nothing of the matter: I understood so from Mr. Watson: I never did any business of this kind.

Did you not, in the year 1785, for a Mr. James Atty?—I cannot tell: If I did, it was as agent for Mr. Wm. Hurry.

The anchors were returned on the salvage being paid?—They were.

How long after this did you apply to Mr. Watson?—I cannot tell.

Re-examination by the Plaintiff's Counsel.

You recollect that Munsor said it was not usual for him to receive the payment for the cartage at the time?—Yes: he said he generally received it but once a year. [48]

Were you in the Court of Requests?—I was.

How long was it after you had applied to Mr. Watson, that Mr. Hurry made his demand upon Mr. Watson, for the eleven shillings, in the Court of Requests?—It was in *July* that Munsor offered to return me 3s. 5d.

[Observation from the Plaintiff's Counsel—The indictment states, that there was not that debt, nor any other sum, due: We shall prove that they admitted 3s. 5d. overcharge, which was paid.]

MR. SAYERS.

Mr. *Mingay*—Did you attend the Court at Yarmouth, when this business was brought on in the Court of Requests?—I did.

Who presided at that Court?—Mr. Reynolds.

Who is he?—An attorney at Yarmouth.

What was he then?—Mayor.

Who was Mayor Elect?—Mr. Watson.

State what passed—Mr. Hurry was sworn by Mr. Spurgeon, the Clerk of the Court, in the usual manner.

Did Mr. Reynolds ask any thing?—Yes: He said, Do you, Mr. Hurry, swear that John Watson is indebted to you in eleven shillings? To which Mr. Hurry said, Yes.

In the course of this cause before the Commissioners, did Mr. Hurry say any thing by way of explanation?—He did, 'as agent for Mr. Shipley, and as appears by this account,' holding out a paper, adding, 'I get nothing by it.'

What followed upon this?—The Mayor pulled out of his pocket, and produced the Act of Parliament, and said, the Court had no cognizance of the matter: the cause was at an end, and the complaint was dismissed.

Was there not some money returned?—Yes: some explanation took place between themselves about the overcharge, and 3s. 5d. was returned.

To whom was it returned?—They went up to pay it to Mr. Samuel Hurry; but I cannot tell who received it.

How long did the whole of this business take up?—A very few minutes.

Having told us what Mr. Watson is, you can tell us what Mr. Hurry is?—He is a merchant.

[49] A very considerable one?—Yes, a very considerable one.

Are Mr. Watson and his partner, Mr. Reynolds, small Attorneys, or in extensive practice? Are they not as eminent as any in your town?—They are.

Cross-Examination.

Mr. *Hardinge*—You are an Attorney, practising in the Court of Requests?—Yes, I am.

Then you know the method of proceeding? –Yes.

Did you not issue out the summons?—Yes; it bears my signature.

Let me ask you, when a debt is demanded by one person as agent for another, how is the claim made?—There is no usage different in that Court from any other court.

Let me ask you, was not the question put to Mr. Hurry by Mr. Spurgeon, the usual question put to a witness when a debt is claimed? –Yes.

How soon after this proceeding was it that Mr. Watson was Mayor?—This proceeding in the court of Requests was the 12th of September: he was sworn in Mayor on the 29th.

Before this explanation was had, did Mr. Hurry claim as agent? Did he tell you so?—He told it to nobody that I know of.

Let me ask you, was it of his own head, or was it from the prompting of his brother?—It was at his brother's request.

Was he one of the Commissioners?—Yes.

Do you happen to know who the Grand Jury were, or whether there were not some of the Grand Jury who were present in the Court of Requests? Was Richard Miller?—I did not see him in court.

Was Mr. Tolver?—He was.

Re-examination.

Mr. *Mingay*—When Mr. Hurry came into court, did he bring his books with him?—He had his pocket-book in his hand.

Do you recollect who were upon the Grand Jury?—I do not recollect them all.

Then we will endeavour to assist your memory. Do you know John Fisher, was he one?—Yes.

What relation is he to Mr. Watson?—He is cousin to Watson's wife.

Do you know Mr. Cotton?—Yes.

What relation is he to Mr. Watson?—He married Watson's wife's sister.

Do you know Mr. Costerton? What relation is he to Mr. Watson?—Mr. Costerton's wife and Mrs. Watson are cousins.

[50] John Wright, do you know him? Is he any relation to Mr. Watson?—No.

Is he any relation to Mr. Reynolds?—He married his wife's niece.

Mr. Seaman, do you know him? Is he any relation to Mr. Watson?—No.

To Mr. Reynolds?—He married his wife's niece.

Stephen Godfrey, do you know him? Is he any relation to either of these Gentlemen?—No.

Is he not connected with Mr. Reynolds?—He has concerns with him in shipping.

[Here the Counsel finished their inquiry respecting the Grand Jury with observing, that Mr. Watson, by means of his relations, might have shipped off their client to Botany Bay.]

How long have you practised in the Court of Requests?—Five or six years.

Has it not been the custom for the Common-Council-Men to be on the Grand Jury?—Yes.

Do you know Mr. Thomas Dade?—Yes.

Do you know whether or no he used to be on the Grand Jury?—He has been on the Grand Jury: I have seen him.

Your own brother, he used to be on the Grand Jury?—Yes, generally.

Mr. Barker, he used likewise to be on the Grand Jury?—Yes.

They were not upon this Grand Jury?—No.

Does not the Mayor deliver out the list of the Grand Jury?—Yes, he does.

When a person has a charge against any one, and the party summoned does not appear, what is the practice in this court?—An order; *Nisi*, issues to pay the money in ten days, or show cause; in the course of the ten days there is a court-day, on which he may show cause.

Cross-Examination.

Mr. *Hardinge*—In point of practice, after this order, the party making default is liable to an execution, is he not?—Yes.

Is this execution upon his body or goods?—Upon his body. [The witness ought to have said on his body or his goods, that being the real fact.]

And what is the proceeding in this case?—He may be taken either to Bridewell, or the Gaol.

Mr. *Erskine*—There was no order *Nisi* made in this case?—No.

Mr. *Erskine*. My Lord, it being in evidence that Mr. Hurry was the Agent in this business; that an overcharge of three shillings and five pence [*51*] was admitted and actually returned; that the assignment of the Perjury was 'that there was no sum of money whatever due' that no cognizance was taken of the claim upon oath by the Commissioners, but that it was left by them quite undecided; your Lordship will see that it is quite unnecessary to enter into evidence respecting the actual Quantum of this debt, which, as it is a mere matter of opinion, can have no weight in the cause.

The Judge—it does not signify an iota one way or the other.

Mr. DADE.

Mr. *Preston*—How long have you been a Common-Council-Man of Yarmouth?—Twenty years.

Have you generally served on the Grand Jury?—I have very often.

Were you summoned upon this occasion?—No, not that I heard of.

Are you any relation of either Mr. Watson, or Mr. Reynolds?—I have not that honour.

You know Mr. Hurry?—Yes, I know him, and I know him to be a very respectable man.

Mr. LOCK.

What are you, Mr. Lock?—A merchant at Norwich.

You know Mr. Reynolds and Mr. Watson?—I do.

I have a paper here; look at that paragraph; was it put in by you?—No, it was not.

That was not put in by you: look at that; was that?—Yes. I sent it to the printer; I received it from Mr. Watson.

Where is the copy?—I have no copy of it whatever. Mr. Watson wrote it the day of the trial at Thetford, after the trial was over, with an intent to have it inserted in the Norwich papers, and he gave it to me in writing.

Where is that writing?—I gave it to one of the printers.

Mr. BACON.

You are the printer of the Norwich Mercury; that is your paper?—Yes.

Have you a copy of that paragraph or advertisement that is there?—I have; here it is.

Whose hand-writing is it?—I had it from Mr. Lock.

Mr. LOCK.

Is that your hand-writing?—Yes; I had orders to put the account into four papers: I copied this from the one I received from Mr. Watson.

Mr. *Graham.*—Can you undertake to swear that that was a literal copy?—No, I will not swear it: I often make mistakes in copying my own accounts.

[52] Mr. *Graham.*—My Lord, I object to evidence on this kind of loose recollection. The witness will not undertake to swear that this was a literal copy. In this case we have a right to expect the best evidence that the nature of the case will admit of. Mr. Lock should have been applied to; he would have told what he had done with Mr. Watson's copy: the printer to whom he gave it might have been served with a notice to produce it.

The Judge.—In common cases you are certainly right; but in this, Mr. Watson gave Mr. Lock one paper, which was meant to be multiplied. He employed Mr. Lock as his Agent: He entrusted him with Agency, and therefore becomes answerable for his acts.—The paragraph is admissible evidence.

The Clerk of the Court reads.—'The Perjury cause which was was [sic] tried at Thetford on Saturday last, and which was expected to have been a very long one, took up but a short time, it going off on a defect in the indictment; not withstanding which, a fresh bill will be preferred by the prosecutor.'

Mr. *Erskine* now proposed to call evidence as to the property of Mr. Watson, if his learned friend meant to urge *that* in mitigation of damages, but the Defendant's counsel scouting all ideas of this kind, the evidence was here closed on the part of the Plaintiff.

Mr. HARDINGE.

Gentlemen,

I have the honour to attend as counsel for Mr. Watson, who dares, in this his own county of Norfolk, to affirm, that his character is known to be unimpeached. When I say he does this, I must remind you that Mr. Hurry, who is the Plaintiff, has not brought Mr. Watson hither: Mr. Hurry, who is the Plaintiff, thought it would be wiser policy for him to endeavour to wound the character of Mr. Watson at London, than here where he is known.—From this county our enemy had fled: It was by compulsion that Mr. Hurry was obliged to appear in this court. With respect to the Norfolk character of Mr. Hurry, he has thought it wisest to lose and sink it in the universal popularity of my learned friend, Mr. *Erskine*, who, upon this occasion, has rather addressed his indisputed talents to popular favour, than to your dispassionate judgements, and to those grounds of proof and of argument which alone can give sanction to your judgements: yet, in his partial zeal for me, he reminds me, that—'eloquence, when proof is absent, is but a beating of the air'. Gentlemen, I am really at a loss in what light to consider this cause—whether it is an action against Mr. Watson singly; or an action of conspiracy against Mr. Watson, Mr. Reynolds, and the whole Grand Jury, who have all been indifferently represented as combining together in a cold blooded, malicious attack upon Mr. Hurry. Mr. *Erskine*, as is usual with him, has talked [53] much of himself: he has a right to do so; but I must beg leave to correct him in one particular—I mean his benevolence—I give him ample credit for this, out of a cause; but in a cause, that paid, benevolence of his is a benevolence that is perfect ridicule. I flatter myself that as a man, I have some good nature—as a counsel I have none—it is my duty to press forward every topic that can make for my client. I cannot help smiling, when this Gentleman, who has been throwing about his firebrands, and dealing what I will call his envenomed slander, is Gentleman-Usher to so many pathetic appeals to your humanity. Gentlemen, as men of taste, you have heard my learned friend with great pleasure: As men, who feel for public honour, you have heard him safely. Passions you can have none; and if a spirit more implacable than spleen itself, can have kept this action alive till now; it is in your power, this day, perfectly to expel it.

I cannot help recollecting that my learned friend is very partial when he talks of ill blood, which, like a kind of Irish ill blood, he represents as being all on one side. A curious circumstance has dropped from him—'I am afraid', says he, 'you anticipate the whole of what I shall say respecting my client's character, and respecting the injury which he has sustained'—notwithstanding, however, this anticipation, he has made most wonderful exertions upon the occasion. When the indictment first came into this court, his client, conscious of his innocence—what follows—went to sleep—No I sent for Mr. *Erskine* and Mr. *Mingay*. Now what is this, but as if I should say—although I am in perfect good health, I'll have some advice; I'll not be content with such as the country affords; but I'll send to London to Dr. Warren; and, what is more, I'll have John Hunter, the celebrated anatomist come down with him. Gentlemen, mine upon the present occasion is a humble office: I am to connect, by close principles, the law of the country. As Counsel for Mr. Watson, it is matter of perfect indifference to me, whether the learned Judge shall tell you that it is your's [sic] to compare the rule expounded by the law, with the facts before you, or whether he shall explain the rule to you—I can safely entrust it in your hands, or in the hands of his Lordship.

I will not meet my learned friend upon any one of the topics that are foreign to the cause. The whole matter lies in a nut: I will now, as a Lawyer, affirm to you that the law of England does not like this kind of action—It throws upon the plaintiff arduous proof; and, Gentlemen, Mr. *Erskine*, with all his topics of a man's sleeping the worse, of his wetting his bed with his tears, and of the distressful situation of his wife and family, from his having been attempted to be robbed of his good name—by means of which, indeed, he has even, I believe, caused my learned friend here, Mr. *Partridge* to weep more than once—has done nothing for his client—has done, indeed, only what is as old as acting itself—what Mrs. Siddons[6] is in the weekly habit of doing—touched the feelings of his audience with affecting representations. Indeed, what is the rule upon the temper of the law in this case, but this? that for the ends of pub-[54]-lic justice, and for the good of the state at large, no prosecutor of so baneful an offence as perjury ought to be prosecuted: we will guard those against the effects of an error in their judgement, who are necessary instruments of public justice. In felonies, the plaintiff cannot step one foot in the cause, unless he has a copy of the record of acquittal: the same thing cannot be done here. It is very remarkable, to show the jealousy of the law, that a negative proof is thrown upon him who brings an action like the present—he must show that there was malice, and that there was no probable cause. Now, Gentlemen, I take the liberty to assert to you, that this plaintiff has proved neither of these propositions—but if I could admit that he had proved either of the two, and not the other, the action would not lie.

I will begin with the constituent part of this action—malice. I have looked at the various definitions of malice. It is plain it must be somewhat more than mere spleen. I will suggest one definition from an old writer—*Si quis, data opera, male agat*, that is malice. If any man, in a given action, acts wickedly, he is guilty of malice. Implied malice, then, as applicable to this cause, is new; and, in my opinion, extremely inaccurate; for if it be law that both of these propositions must be proved, how can either of them be implied? I understood my learned friend to say, that the want of probable cause does not prove malice, unless the prosecutor knew this: and how is this to be proved? how, if the fact were proved, could it be shewn that the prosecutor was aware of the law upon it? Give me leave to remind you of a very celebrated case—I mean the case of Sir Thomas Davenport—It is so recent, and so well known, that I need but mention it. His was a direct positive oath that a particular man had robbed him; whereas, by the confession of the person who had actually been guilty of the crime, it was plain that he had been mistaken.[7] Gentlemen, it has been said, by a very learned Judge, that the very wildest error, that ever originated, may be consistent with a motive as pure as can be imagined.—But then this is generally very easy of proof.—For malice is not always a thing that skulks—It will betray itself by overt acts.—Hence then it is, that the Judges, HOLT and LEE, have said expressly—that express malice must be proved in all actions like the present.—And is there any such malice as this to be proved in the conduct of Mr. Watson? I allow that he had resentment in his mind; and

---

[6] By the mid-1780s, Sarah Siddons had become 'a cultural icon' as London's most acclaimed actress, regularly appearing at the Drury Lane Theatre, then managed by Richard Brinsley Sheridan. See *ODNB, sub nom.* 'Siddons [*née* Kemble], Sarah'.

[7] See Old Bailey Proceedings Online, <http://www.oldbaileyonline.org/>, case no. t17841208-2, accessed 14 October 2012.

then I ask you, whether you would not have had the same: there is no prosecutor without it: take the case of a rape, where the father is the prosecutor—let me ask, does he bring forward his prosecution from pure motives of regard to public justice, or does he not do it in a great degree from the resentments he feels against the wretch who has injured his child? and yet he is not malicious because he is thus actuated. Gentlemen, you must concede me, that Mr. Watson had a right to resent—he was Mayor Elect—within a month of being Mayor, when he was attempted to be disgraced as a cheat. I remember Mr. *Murphy*, in his opening at Norwich, granted that it was somewhat of an indignity. The case was this—Mr. Watson was summon-[55]-ed by Mr. Hurry to a court for a sum of money, where he was obliged either to submit to the demand, or to subject himself to be sent to Bridewell. On this, then, their own statement of the business, I would be content to rest this part of the cause.— But it is a curious circumstance that Mr. Spurgeon, though subpoenaed by way of finesse, has not been called upon this occasion. It is a singular circumstance that, having produced what this gentleman said upon a former trial, they have not thought proper to bring him forward now. But I have a right to state to you what he would have said. I hold it clear of all doubt that I am at liberty to state, in theory, what Mr. Spurgeon would certainly have proved, had he been called. Let me then assume, for argument's sake, that Mr. Watson, willing to proceed with all due discretion, had recourse to some learned friend, who is a sensible and prudent man, for direction how best to proceed in this business.— I must not presume to hint that he had recourse to Mr. Reynolds; for this gentleman, though of a perfectly unimpeached character, has been shown, by Mr. *Erskine*, to be ten times more wicked than Mr. Watson; and who, though not brought forward upon this occasion, is to be wounded *per obliquum*—is to be grossly calumnized *through* Mr. Watson, and described as a partner in his malice—I must not, therefore, in this case, mention any names; but I must only suppose (what indeed I have much right to suppose) that Mr. Watson, desirous of conducting himself with perfect propriety, applied for advice to a person, who is not the least attainted as to character, and that this person, after having duly considered the matter, gave it as his opinion that there was no occasion to state all the facts in the indictment—and then I beg leave to ask, how can the omission of these facts be any proof of malice in Mr. Watson? And Gentlemen, if Mr. Spurgeon had been called, need I to have had recourse to assumption and supposition upon this matter? Would he not have given a full relation of all the several circumstances relative to this business? It is obvious, therefore, for what reason this gentleman was not called upon for his evidence. I am not to be told that the cause was frivolous; for I answer, who hurried Mr. Watson to that tribunal? Mr. Hurry did: and Mr. Watson had a right to make use of every legal advantage. But we have the sanction of the Grand Jury, that a bill was fit to be preferred against Mr. Hurry for the offence, *as stated to them:* and I now beg leave to assert it as a fact which has been proved, that every part of this case, *including the explanation*, was laid before the Grand Jury; for it has come out, in evidence, that *one* of the *Grand Jury*, at least, was in the Court of Requests. These Gentlemen, then, thus competent to decide upon the propriety of this business, made no hesitation in saying that such an indictment as was preferred was justly preferred—and till this Grand Jury shall, all of them, be proved to be men totally void of all sense and integrity, they are to be considered as having given a sanction to this indictment.* [56]

* The idea which the learned Counsel has here suggested, respecting the privilege of a Grand Juryman, that he has a right to form his judgement not only upon what appears actually in evidence, from the testimony of others, but from what he knows of his own knowledge, touching the matter in question, is undoubtedly perfectly just—It may not be unacceptable to the reader, if I give him here what the author of the book entitled British Liberties has said upon this subject—'In all cases, says he, when a jury is charged with a prisoner, and, after the indictment is read, witnesses fail to appear, the Court always speaks thus to the Jury—*Gentlemen, here is* A. B. [sic] *stands indicted of such a crime, but there are not any witnesses appear against him, so that unless, on your own knowledge, you know him guilty, you must acquit him*—And, certainly, if the Jury's knowledge of a man's guilt is enough to condemn him, why should not their personal knowledge of his innocence, or of the witnesses swearing falsely, be sufficient to acquit him? Let the witnesses be as positive as they will, yet if the jurors have good and reasonable grounds not to believe them, they will, they must remain as ignorant to the party's crime as before. We find this expressly asserted for law in our books, as Style's Reports, lib. 2. 'Though there are witnesses who prove the bill, yet the Grand Inquest is not bound to find it, if they see cause to the contrary;' so Coke, lib. 6. The 'Judges are used to determine who shall be sworn, and what shall be produced as evidence to the Jury; but the Jury are to consider what credit or authority the same is worthy of.'—If a Grand Jury are not judges of evidence, they signify nothing, if (as some allege) because witnesses swear desperately, though the Jury do believe them, they shall be bound to find the bill. This is absurd in the highest degree. Were this admitted, the Grand Jury signify nothing, and are no security to preserve innocence.—We will give an anecdote nearly in Mr. Care's words—A lewd woman once resolved to indict the then Archbishop of Canterbury for a rape: she swore it, no doubt, very heartily. According to *this new doctrine of going according to evidence*, the Jury must presently have found the bill, the Archbishop must have been committed to prison, suspended from ecclesiastical jurisdiction, and his goods and chattels throughout England inventoried by the Sheriff: would it, in that case, have been a good excuse for the Grand Jury, to have said, that though they believed in their consciences the baggage swore falsely, yet swearing it positively, they, as so many parish clerks, were but to say Amen to her oath of the fact, and to find *Billa vera* against that eminent prelate? And if the Jury are judges of the credibility of evidence in this case, and may go contrary to it, why may they not have the same liberty where they find good cause in others? If an indictment is laid against a man for criminal words, said to be uttered in a colloquium, or discourse, though the witnesses positively swear all the express words in the indictment, yet, unless they will relate and fully set forth the substance of the whole conversation, it is impossible the jury should judge of the matter, for expressions that are in themselves, when coupled with other words innocent and loyal, when taken in halves, and separated from those they were so coupled with, become very treasonable; as if one should say, *To affirm the King has no more rights to the crown of England than I have (which is the opinion of the Jesuits with respect to his Majesty, if once excommunicated by the Pope) is detestable treason.*—And two men, at some distance, not well hearing or remembering, or maliciously designing against his life, should swear, that he said, *The King had no more right to the crown than he had.*—Now, that these very words, were uttered is true; but if the evidence are interrogat [sic] as to the rest of the colloquium, they will perhaps

Gentlemen, let me bring to your minds what this oath was—just exactly as false as any one short proposition can be—there was not one part of it true. Mr. Hurry charges Mr. Watson, in a general way, in the Court of Requests, with a debt due to him in a sum specific: Mr. Watson does not attend: the time arrives; he makes default: Mr. Spurgeon puts to Mr. Hurry after he is [57] sworn, this question: what question?—Why, the question he puts to every man that sues for a debt due to himself, *prima facie*—'Do you say that John Watson is indebted to you, William Hurry, in the sum of eleven shillings? And what is the answer?—Yes. A prompter (not a usual thing in a court of Justice) gives a hint—then an explanation follows—"as agent for another." But the explanation is as false as the original oath: In the first place, no such sum as that, which was stated, was due at all: secondly, it was not due to Mr. Hurry, personally: thirdly, it was not due from Mr. Watson; he was the Register; the money had been paid over by him to the carter. In justice to Mr. Watson, I am bold to declare, that if I had been asked my opinion, as counsel, respecting this oath, as it was preferred to the grand Jury, though I do not say I would have said it was advisable to go upon it to the length of an indictment for perjury, I should have had no doubt in saying that the indictment would lie—Nay, I go further—I have no hesitation in saying, that if the whole of the oath had been given, the perjury would still have been of a more flagrant and malignant nature; for, in the first short sentence, he swears to a debt as due to himself; and as such, undoubtedly, he is entitled to some degree of credit, as he must supposed to be well acquainted with his own affairs: But in the two sentences put together, he swears to a sum specific, as due to him for another, *from* a person, from whom it is impossible for him to say he ought to receive it, and who, in fact, was not the person: I do say then, and I will pledge, not only the little reputation I may have acquired, but that which I may at any time hereafter acquire, that, in point of law, this oath of Mr. Hurry's enabled Mr. Watson to prefer a bill of indictment for perjury against him. And can it much be wondered at that he did? Let any man living say, whether there was not a design on the part of Mr. Hurry to injure Mr. Watson. Let any man living say

---

say, there was much more discourse, but they cannot remember it; what satisfaction is this to a Jury? Or would it not be hard for a man to be obliged to hold up his hand at the bar, under the horrid charge of treason in this case? The inquiry of a Grand Jury should be suitable to their title, *a grand inquiry*; or else, instead of serving their country, and presenting real crimes, they may oppress the innocent, as in the case of *Samuel Wright and John Good*, at a sessions in the Old Bailey, about Dec. 1681. *Good* indicts *Wright* for treasonable words, and swore the words positively; but after a grand inquiry, the *Grand Jury* found that *Wright* only spoke the words as of others, thus, *they say so and so*, and concluded with this – *they are rogues for saying it*; and *Good* also at last confessed, that *Wright* was his master, and corrected him for misdemeanors, and then, to be revenged, he comes and swears against him, and which he confessed he was instigated to by one *Powel*; so the Grand Jury, finding it to be but malice, returned the bill *Ignoramus*; whereas, if they had not examined him strictly, they had never discovered the truth, and the master had, without cause, been brought to great charge, ignominy, and hazard.' British Liberties, p. 379.

whether Mr. Watson had not a right to say—I will bind him to his bond—He is the original Shylock.

Gentlemen, I have kept you too long on the article of malice. I will now advert to the want of probable cause. I will suppose, for argument's sake, that there was, in fact and in reality, *no actual probable cause* for the preferring of the indictment in question: but will you say that Mr. Watson had no probable cause for *considering* this as a false oath, intended to prejudice him?—The record of Mr. Hurry's acquittal is produced: but what does this do, but remind me of a case in one of Foote's Farces?[8]—A man swears falsely *now*, and is guilty of perjury: he swore *then*, and was not guilty of perjury: therefore a man that swears *now and then* is not guilty of perjury. Gentlemen, though I do not pretend to describe Mr. Watson as a man of brilliant parts, he is not an idiot; he cannot be imagined to have taken the steps he has, without any motives whatever; he cannot be conceived venturing upon a measure that would subject him to the forfeiture of credit, weakly and foolishly, without even any imaginary grounds whatever. The question to be put in this case is this— Was there, or was there not, a probable cause to strike the mind of [58] Mr. Watson, that Mr. Hurry had, by a false oath, attempted to injure him? Let me put this case—the case, indeed, as it was exactly and precisely put by my learned friend, Mr. *Erskine*. Suppose it was urged against me, that I had sworn to a debt as due to me in one character, whereas, in fact and in truth, it was due in another: would not the substance of this oath be false? Now then, if it was once understood that the substance of it was false, whatever the words are, it is not competent for him to tell me, that there is no probable cause for me to conceive him as perjured from his oath, framed as it was.

I am ashamed, Gentlemen, to detain you so long, because I appeal to the learned Judge for the support of my opinion. The law itself has given Mr. Watson a better counsel than either Mr. *Erskine* or myself. Unless it was clear to a demonstration, that there was, in this case, express malice, and no probable cause whatever, you must acquit—(I use that term, because my learned friend, in his speech, let drop from him this expression, 'convict Mr. Watson') I say, unless these things are proved, you must acquit Mr. Watson. Mr. *Erskine* has drawn a frightful picture of Mr. Hurry's supposed situation, should this be the case, and has strongly urged it upon you as a motive for exemplary damages. But Mr. *Erskine* should remember, that this argument may equally be pressed on the side of Mr. Watson. Is he on a bed of roses, if you, by your verdict, should determine him malicious—should stigmatize him as the revengeful prosecutor of innocence?—*Nemo repente tu[r] pissimus fuit.*[9]

---

[8] The reference is to Samuel Foote, *A Collection of the Most Esteemed Farces and Entertainments Performed on the British Stage*, 3 vols. (1782). Foote was both a playwright and an actor who became the owner of the Haymarket Theatre in the 1770s. Contentious and temperamental, he was falsely accused of sodomy, for which he was tried in a fraudulent prosecution heard by Lord Mansfield and a special jury in the Court of King's Bench in December 1776. Although acquitted, the trial broke Foote's spirit, and he died in 1777. For Lord Mansfield's notes of the trial, see Oldham, *MMSS*, ii. 1004.

[9] See Juvenal, *Satires*, ii. 83.

Supported then, Gentlemen, by the law, you have now an opportunity of closing for ever the differences that have hitherto subsisted between these persons, and of changing all their bad blood into the milk of human kindness. You must be influenced by no preconceptions: you have only to consider whether you are not bound to say, that the man, who preferred the bill of indictment, whence has originated all this long contention, had not grounds for so doing—whether the act, that gave rise to it, was not a case proper to be laid before the bar for the public. Partly in your opinion, and partly in the opinion of the Court, I sit down with perfect confidence that your verdict will be in favor of my client.

No witnesses being called on the part of the defendant, the Judge summed up the evidence on the part of the prosecution, and then addressed the Jury as follows:—

Gentlemen, This is all the evidence on the part of the plaintiff. There have been no witnesses called on the part of the defendant. And as to the general positions, that have been laid down by his counsel, that, in an action of this kind, express malice must be proved, and that any probable cause must be negative, I admit and adopt them as true positions.—As to the express malice, Gentlemen, that to be sure is law; but it is a matter which must be dependant [*sic*] upon facts.—As far as the law is to be considered, the Judge must direct the Jury—As to the facts bearing upon that law, that must be left with you.

[59] In the 1st place then—let us advert to the express malice. As to this—this is a thing which is either to be inferred from the nature of the transaction, or from extrinsical evidence.

Now, Gentlemen, as to the intrinsic evidence, I must say, there does arise a very strong ground whence to infer express malice, from a bare view of this case: for it does appear, from the indictment itself, that Mr. Hurry swore only that Mr. Watson was indebted to him eleven shillings; whereas it comes out in evidence, that he swore this not absolutely, but with this qualification, '*as Agent to Mr. Shipley, and as appears by this account*', in which the matter in question was stated. The varying of the oath thus, for the purpose of preferring the indictment, by a man who, from the nature of his profession, could not be ignorant of the effect which such a variance would make, does certainly argue, very strongly, some degree of malice in the person, who thus acted.

But there is another circumstance, which, undoubtedly, does tend to aggravate his offence. For suppose that the defendant did not know that he had not alleged the whole of the plaintiff's oath when he preferred the bill of indictment against him, when, upon the trial, in which the plaintiff was acquitted, he could no longer be ignorant in this respect, then he ought certainly to have rested content. But you find he did not.—But after the matter has been explained in court, and has had the decision of a Jury, he goes on still, and causes to be published an advertisement, saying that, 'the perjury cause which came on at Thetford, and which was supposed would have taken up a long time, took but a short one, it going off on a defect in the indictment, notwithstanding which a fresh bill will be preferred by the prosecutor.' This proves *persevering* malice.

The next matter is whether, supposing there was malice, there was probable cause. Now, Gentlemen, it was said, in the 1st place, that there was a probable cause, because, even with the explanation, the oath was not true, the money not being due from Mr. Watson, he having paid it over to the carter—supposing there to be any weight in this argument, it came out in evidence, that the money was claimed by the plaintiff in this action, before it was paid over.

The second thing is—It is said, that the defendant was not indebted to the plaintiff in the full sum to which he swore in his affidavit. But this is not necessary—the assignment of the perjury is, that he was not indebted, either in the sum of eleven shillings, or in any sum whatever. An over-charge of six and tenpence has been admitted by the defendant.[10] This then, Gentlemen, I do not think a sufficient probable cause to have induced the defendant to have preferred his indictment. Perjury depends on this—whether the thing was full within the mind of the man who makes the affidavit. Suppose it had been money lent—this would have been within his knowledge; and if his oath, and the fact had varied, there might have been some ground to imagine [60] him perjured. But the plaintiff swore that the Defendant was indebted to him so much as he, the plaintiff, had paid him, the defendant, more money than he ought to have done, according to the common usage. It was a matter of opinion, and not of knowledge—It depended upon circumstances, the price of labour, the distance, the quantity, &c.

From the nature of the case, it does not appear that there was any probable cause to justify the preferring of the indictment.

It being proved that the defendant, Watson, had positive malice, my opinion with respect to which I have given you, the difference in the value, on a question problematical, ought not to shelter him from this prosecution. I shall leave it to your consideration—If you concur with me as to the facts the law is clear. As to damages, that is your province—And as I see so very respectable a Special Jury, I shall not even give a hint with respect to these.

The Jury retired, and the Court was adjourned. In less than an hour, a verdict was delivered to the Judge, at his Lodgings, for the Plaintiff—Damages 3000l.

FINIS

---

[10] See counsel Partridge's explanation, p. [9] above—'there is a mistake of only six shillings and ten pence, which . . . was to be divided, half of it to be given to the salvors, and the other half to be given to the agent of Captain Shipley; so that it was not possible Mr. Hurry could have a right to swear to more than the small sum of three shillings and fivepence'.

SUPPLEMENT
TO THE
TRIAL of HURRY against WATSON
a
REPORT
OF THE
ARGUMENT in the COMMON PLEAS,
UPON A
MOTION FOR A NEW TRIAL,
In TRINITY TERM last.
IN WHICH
The Conduct of the SPECIAL JURY, in the giving of their Verdict, was agitated, and the Doctrine, respecting the Power of the Court to set aside Verdicts for excessive Damages, fully discussed.
TOGETHER WITH
A Relation of the FINAL ISSUE of this long-contested Business.

In the Court of Common Pleas
Easter Term. 27 GEO. III

Mr. Serjeant *Le Blanc*—In Hurry against Watson.

I humbly move your Lordship for a rule to show cause why this verdict should not be set aside and a new trial granted.

This was an action for a malicious prosecution. It was tried at the last Norfolk assizes, before Mr. Justice ASHHURST, at Thetford, when a verdict for 3000l. was given for the plaintiff. I move for this rule upon several grounds.

1st. Upon the ground that in the evidence, which was admitted, the learned Judge admitted a part, which ought not to have been admitted.

2d. That in this kind of action it becomes necessary, in point of law, that the plaintiff shall prove malice and want of probable cause in the conduct of the defendant; that this must be made out by the facts appearing in evidence; that, in the present case, there were not sufficient circumstances, bearing upon this law, to support the action of the plaintiff.

3d. The third ground upon which I submit this case to your Lordship, is the immensity of the damages. I state this as a case, in which they are so flagrantly excessive as to bespeak intemperance in the minds of the Jury, and are such as neither the situation of the plaintiff in the action, nor the circumstances of the defendant at all warrant.

My fourth ground is the improper method, in which these damages were estimated. I mean to lay before the Court, by affidavit, that the Jury, differing with respect to their opinion on this head, came to a determination that the Foreman should permit each Juryman to put down a sum, and, adding all together, should take the medium.

Now I submit to your Lordship that this was a very improper mode of ascertaining the damages. There are the several grounds upon which I submit to your Lordship the propriety of your granting me a rule to show cause.

This action, as I stated, was an action for a malicious prosecution, by an indictment for perjury, found at the sessions, in the Borough Court of Great Yarmouth, and removed by writ of Certiorari into the Court of King's [4] Bench, whence it was sent down to be tried at the Lent Norfolk assizes in eighty-six. The ground of the indictment was, that the defendant swore Mr. Watson was indebted to him in the sum of eleven shillings, when, in fact and in truth, he was not indebted to him in that sum. [Here followed a short recapitulation of the origin of the matter].—The defendant was acquitted; and, at the summer assizes following, he brought his action for damages against his prosecutor, and was nonsuited. At the last Lent assizes for the same county, the cause went down to be tried again. Mr. *Bell*, the plaintiff's attorney, was called, who proved the acquittal of Mr. Hurry at Thetford, and the damages of 600l. and upwards, which he had sustained by maintaining his aforesaid action; and next, Mr. Locke proved, that Mr. Watson brought him a written paragraph in his own hand writing, and directed him to insert it in three different papers—the Norwich, the Bury, and the Ipswich—importing that Mr. Hurry's cause had gone off from a flaw in the indictment, &c. This was brought as a proof of continued malice in Mr. Watson. Mr. Locke did not prove this paper which was given him by Mr. Watson: He had sent it to one of the three printers, but he did not know which. He made a copy of it, and this copy was produced in evidence by the Norwich printer. It was objected here, that if they meant to make any charge against Mr. Watson on this ground, they ought to prove that some endeavour had been made use of to produce that paper, or go further and prove a true copy; but no such evidence was given: on the contrary, Mr. Locke said that he could not say that the paragraph agreed with the original. On this ground, I submit to your Lordship, that this paragraph was improperly admitted as evidence.

I believe, my Lord, that this was the whole of the evidence that was given, except that some evidence was gone into, respecting the Grand Jury, to throw a kind of general slander upon them, that one was related to one man, and one to another, that they were part of the corporation, &c. &c. to prove that this indictment was found by persons improperly influenced.

With respect to the circumstances of the defendant no evidence was given, except that it was said that he was an attorney resident in Yarmouth, and had been Mayor.

I submit, therefore, to your Lordship, in the first place, that this paragraph ought not to have been admitted in evidence—and

2d. That it did appear clear that this gentleman had at first sworn to a debt of eleven shillings as due to him, and that this was the perjury mentioned in the charge in the indictment. That it was a rash oath, and that therefore there was not a want of probable cause in Mr. Watson, when he preferred the indictment. There is a very recent case, which [5] came on in this Court before your Lordship—the case of Kirby and Addington—Here the Justice corrected himself –

Lord LOUGHBOROUGH. No—His mistake was corrected by other witnesses.

What he swore was certainly directly false, but I saw it was not wilful; but I did not recommend when he was acquitted a prosecution on that account.

Judge HEATH. There is the case of the Mayor of Derby, who desired that a fact, that he had stated in his affidavit, might not stand; he was indicted and acquitted, and afterwards recovered upon an action for a malicious prosecution.

Mr. Serjeant *Le Blanc*. The next ground, viz. the damages, it would be sufficient merely to state the sum; but in addition to this I have an affidavit from Mr. Watson himself, that the damages alone, independent of the costs, are more than he is worth in the world. I am aware that the Courts are not inclined to set aside a verdict for excessive damages; but the Courts have always held, that they would not have it understood that they could not set aside a verdict on these grounds. Now I lay it down then, that his case comes within the rule of the Court, and I should hope, on this account, and on account of the affidavits, that the verdict will be set aside. With respect to the conduct of the Jury in giving their verdict, I have an affidavit, as well from one of the Jury, as from two other persons, by which it appears that the Jury put down each a sum, then added the sums together, and then took the medium.

Now the Court has frequently set aside Verdicts that have been formed in an improper manner; as where Juries have drawn lots, tossed up, &c. &c.

Judge WILSON. Do you know, Brother *Le Blanc*, any case where the affidavit of a Juryman has been received in evidence?

Le Blanc. I know it was refused lately in the Court of King's Bench.

Judge GOULD. There was the case of the Polish Jew, Symonds:[11] There the Court received the affidavits of all the Jurors; but, however, after they had done it, there was something like repentance expressed upon the occasion for having received them.

Judge HEATH. The affidavits of the Jury were received in a case, where the coachman of a person was alleged to have said to the Foreman, as he stood by the box 'Now you have a good opportunity of doing a favour to our friend such a one', and that in consequence of this, a verdict was brought in for sixty-pounds only, when much more ought to have been given. But this was to wipe off an aspersion from the Jury.

[6]Mr. Serjeant *Le Blanc*. I think I recollect in the books more cases than one, where a rule was granted to show cause, when it appeared from the affidavit of a Juryman, that the Jury had taken improper methods to form their verdict; that they had tossed up, &c. But in addition to this affidavit of the Juryman, if any objection should be taken to it, I have the affidavit of two other persons, that they have often heard the circumstances which I have mentioned from a juryman himself.

There is a case in Barnes, p. 441, † the case of Philips and Fowler. After a

---

† Mr. Justice *Fortiscue* contra—Vide Lord Fitzwalter's Case—Salkeld 647—This case is not to be found in Salkeld, as mentioned in Barnes.[12]

[11] *R.* v. *Simmons*, 1 Wils. 329 (King's Bench, 1752).

[12] In *Phillips* v. *Fowler*, reporter Barnes (at 441) says to see *Lord Fitzwalter's Case*, Salk. 647, but the case is not in Salkeld. The correct citation should have been 1 Freeman 414.

motion for an arrest of judgement, and pending the consideration of the Court, it being disclosed to the defendant, by two of the Jurors, that they and their fellows, being divided in opinion, had determined their verdict by casting lots; the defendant moved to set aside the verdict, upon an affidavit of the fact made by the two Jurors, and upon hearing counsel on both sides, the question was, whether the defendant in this case could move to set aside the verdict. And the Lord Chief Justice COMYNS and Mr. Justice DORTON[13] were of opinion, that though this motion seemed out of time by the general practice, yet that it being founded upon a matter disclosed to the defendant, and made before judgement pronounced, the Court must receive it, and *the fact as to the Jurors determining by chance being undisputed,* the verdict was set aside.

Lord LOUGHBOROUGH. You have said enough, Brother *Le Blanc*, to induce the Court to call for the Judges report.

A Rule granted.

[7] Trinity Term, Wednesday, June 13, 1787.

The Judges report being read, Mr. Serjeant *Adair* began to show cause against the rule, that had been obtained, in substance, as follows.

My Lord, it becomes now my business to show cause against this rule, and to answer the objections, which have been stated against the verdict, which were divided into four (Vide the motion for the rule).

The first point, my Lord, is that, which appears to be the most material, looking most like a legal ground of objection; that is, the point of evidence. The objection in this case was founded upon the evidence of a Mr. Locke, and upon a strict adherence to what is certainly a rule of law, the admitting only the best evidence, that can be procured. But this rule of law, and what is the best evidence, has always been inferred from the nature of the case, and from the peculiar circumstances of the case. That may be good and admissible evidence against one party, which, on the general rule of law, would not be the best evidence.

I conceive the evidence in question to be of this nature. Mr. Locke was called. He stood in the station of a person, who had been employed by Mr. Watson. He was so employed, and the object for which he was employed was, at the authority of Mr. Watson, to insert a particular paragraph in the public news-papers; and, in order to ascertain what the import of that paragraph or advertisement should be, Mr. Watson furnished him with a draft, with orders to insert it in three different papers. Now the direction of sending it to more papers than one, conveyed with it an authority to Mr. Locke to write over as many more as were necessary. I contend in this case, that between these parties, and for the purpose for which this advertisement was intended, every one of those drafts for this advertisement was in truth an original. They were copies of a paper for the use of a third person. Mr. Locke acted under the

---

[13] Mr Justice Denton.

authority of Mr. Watson; he was his agent; and consequently his act was the act of Mr. Watson.

Mr. Locke swears positively that he fulfilled his agency. Indeed the substance of the advertisement was all that was material. And the imagination of man could not have conveyed Mr. Watson's intentions more fully than Mr. Locke's copy, which were, to impress the public with the idea that Mr. Hurry was not acquitted upon merits, but upon a defect in the indictment. Could it have weighed a feather, either in the action, or in the advancement of the damages, whether an *or*, or an *and* had been [*8*] omitted in the writing of the advertisement? Certainly it could not. Now then, my Lord, as plaintiffs in this cause, we could but go to some one of the printers, and procure the original, whence he printed the advertisement. It was all we could do. It appeared that all the printers had received their advertisements from Mr. Locke. The only way then, to bring the matter home to Mr. Watson, was to call upon one of the printers for his authority. The plaintiff could not have an idea of there being any possible difference, till Mr. Locke had been examined. He saw that all the advertisements were of the same import in the three papers. He may then truly be said to have used all due diligence in procuring the best evidence, in having done what he did, in procuring one of the copies, which Mr. Locke gave to the printer. Supposing that, in fact, that copy had not been a literal copy of the draft, which Mr. Watson gave to Mr. Locke, still, if it had in effect been the same, it would have been enough. Mr. Watson's intention was equally well fulfilled. In the strictest rule of evidence, then, I contend, this was as good evidence as could be produced. But allowing for a moment—but not admitting in fact—allowing, that this paper, which was produced, was but a copy—a copy taken by the party himself will not stand in the same state as one taken by another. Suppose a copy of an account, for instance, in the office of a merchant, taken out by his clerk, under the merchants direction, your Lordship would not suffer him to avail himself of a final *e*, or the omission of an apostrophe,—or because the word honor was spelt without a *u*—Your Lordship would not permit this. I therefore contend, upon the present occasion, 1st. That all the copies in this case were, in fact, originals; and 2d. That if they were copies, there is sufficient evidence, as *against Mr. Watson*, that the one produced was a true copy. Mr. Locke swears that he verily believes it to be such. He ought not to have sworn more. I am sure I would not, in any case, swear more than that I believed such a copy was a literal copy. For your Lordship knows, that in copies even of indictments, where the utmost exactness is required, examined by persons who drew them, by counsel afterwards, variation even of words will sometimes be discovered by another person at the moment. From the very nature then of the thing itself, no other evidence is possible, that what Mr. Locke gave, that he verily believes is to be the true copy. I contend then upon this ground, and upon the ground of the relation of the evidence to the parties, that this was the best evidence upon this occasion, that could be produced.

It seems then to me, that now but little remains to trouble the Court with; for if this is evidence—if it is true that Mr. Watson authorized the insertion of these advertisements in the paper, I am at a loss to put the [9] 2d. objection— That there is not express malice in his conduct towards the plaintiff, and that there was probable cause for it. The facts in this case are extremely few, but they are strong leading facts; they are marked features in the cause; if ever there were a few facts that showed express malice, and proved that there was not the least shadow of probable cause, we shall find them in this case. I will drop those which are mere fringes of the cause; such as the Court where this indictment was preferred; the Grand Jury packed, as I may truly say, for the purpose of finding the bill; these, and such like, as merely (comparatively speaking) trifling circumstances. I shall lay my finger on this fact—that Mr. Watson knew what Mr. Hurry had sworn, and indicted him in the first instance for what he knew he had not sworn—for restraining, restricting, and giving a different meaning to Mr. Hurry's oath, is to all intents and purposes indicting him for swearing what he did not swear. It is impossible any one can be ignorant why the assignment of the perjury was what it was; it was to bring the action. Had Mr. Hurry's oath been stated, the perjury could not possibly have been assigned. Mr. Watson then, clearly, with the fullest knowledge of what Mr. Hurry had sworn, for the sole purpose of subjecting him to the disgrace of an indictment for perjury, perverted justice, and abused the law, and, by the grossest artifice, supported the charge against him. This, my Lord, was the conduct of Mr. Watson in the first instance. But this was not all. Afterwards, when the event of the trial of Mr. Hurry was known to him, when he knew Mr. Hurry was acquitted, instead of learning what he ought to have learned; instead of feeling what he ought to have felt, that he had grossly injured Mr. Hurry; instead of showing an inclination to make a recompence to Mr. Hurry, whose character had never before been blown upon by the breath of slander; instead of doing all this, he proceeds, with all his knowledge in his mind, to plant a new dagger in the breast of Mr. Hurry, by the insertion of the infamous advertisement in the public news papers, through the means of Mr. Locke. It is therefore highly necessary, indeed, for Mr. Watson's counsel to labour the exclusion of this advertisement from the case, which proves in a manner not to be controverted, that Mr. Watson was provoked because Mr. Hurry had escaped his machinations by law, and that therefore he was determined to wound him by another channel. The Court cannot hesitate a moment upon these facts, they are strong and leading facts; they prove malice beyond controversy, and show want of probable cause, without a possibility of doubt. I would ask—Could Mr. Watson be ignorant of what Mr. Hurry swore when he framed the indictment? Can there be a doubt of his malice when he preferred it? Does it not glare upon one when he causes the advertisement to be inserted?

[10] I will not trouble the Court with going into the minutiae. These two facts, which I have mentioned, are in themselves such proofs of malice, so plain, so clear, upon the very face of them, that the Jury, upon this occasion, were not in the situation of many other Juries, obliged to collect their opinion

from a variety of facts, some of which are capable of being tortured by ingenuity into different and doubtful meanings; these facts are not capable of perversion; they speak one uniform language to every person's understanding.

Why need I trouble the Court on the 3d. head? The extreme reluctance which the Court always feel where a verdict is given by a respectable Special Jury, and before one of his Majesty's Judges, render it unnecessary for me to take up your Lordship's time on this point. And if ever there was a case, where it was peculiarly the province of a Jury, according to their own feelings upon the subject, to determine, it was that now before the Court. There can be no case imagined, in which the degree of injury in the person injured, and the degree of malignity in the person injuring, can be carried to greater heights than in this. The total ruin and perdition of any individual may be intended, and may be executed; his character may be blasted; all his prospects be cut off; his health, in consequence of grief and vexation, destroyed; in short, there is no evil that may not with justice be imagined as producible by a *malicious prosecution*. This case, then, now before the Court, is a matter which it was peculiarly the province of a Jury to decide upon; of a Jury of the county, where the conduct of both the parties were under their consideration; of a Jury, composed of gentlemen, who were acquainted with both the parties, who knew the character and circumstances of both the parties. I therefore humbly conceive, that this Court on this third ground, upon which a motion for a new trial has been founded, cannot attend to the application. As to the fourth and last ground of this application, the supposed improper mode of estimating the damages, that, I should think, comes before the Court (viz. upon the affidavit of one of the Jurymen) in a way which the Court will hardly judge admissible.

One reason among many others, for not receiving such evidence as this, is that it is liable to the greatest degree of fallacy, in the present case. The Jury are said each to have put down a separate sum, and then casting them up all together, to have taken the medium or average. But, supposing this to have been the way, to know its effect, the affidavit should have stated what was the lowest sum, that was put down by any individual. I know not indeed expressly that the affidavit has not done this, but I conceive, for very good reasons, that it has not. But supposing the fact –

[*11*] Lord LOUGHBOROUGH. If that was the mode of estimating the damages, the verdict ought not to stand.

Counsel for Defendant. We have an affidavit of one of the Jurors that this was the case, and of two other persons, who heard the Jurymen declare that the Jury did take this mode.

Serjeant *Adair*. Neither the one nor the other of these can be admitted.

The COURT. If the affidavit of the Jurors cannot be received, the other affidavits must be considered as inadmissible likewise.

Lord LOUGHBOROUGH. There are many cases where the improper mode of ascertaining the verdict has been taken cognizance of by the Court.

Judge GOULD. The Court may examine the Jury as to the mode of estimating damages, if they hear of it at the time.

Judge HEATH. How long were the Jury in finding their verdict?—*Ans.*—An hour.—It appears then that they must have considered upon the matter.

Judge WILSON. Suppose all the sums were put down, as has been stated, and the Jury had then looked upon them, and then formed their determination?

Serjeant *Bond*. There is the case of Lawrence and Boswel, in Serjeant Sayer's Reports, p. 100. There is likewise the case of Vasie [*sic*] and Delaval,[14] Term Report, Michael. 26th of the present reign.[15] This was a motion for a new trial upon the affidavit of two Jurors, who swore that the Jury, being divided in their opinions, tossed up, and the plaintiff's friends won. My Lord MANSFIELD said the Court could not receive such an affidavit from any of the Jurymen themselves, in all of whom such conduct is a very high misdemeanour; but in every such case, the Court must derive their knowledge from some other source; such as from some person having seen the transaction through a window, or by some such other means.

There is the case of Quart against Santel. This was an action tried at Exeter. Mr. *Gibbs* moved to set aside the verdict—as, on the bailiff's being called in, one of the Jurymen took up an half-penny, and said, we have won.

Mr. Serjeant *Adair*. I should like to see, my Lord, what this affidavit of the Juryman does state, if my Brother would favour me so far. Mr. Serjeant *Bolton* then read the affidavit of one Zachariah Death, of Diss,[16] the purport of which was, that the Jury did all agree to put down each their separate sums, and having done so, and something being mentioned respecting Mr. Watson's circumstances, they fixed upon 3000l.

[*12*] Lord LOUGHBOROUGH. In the present case, admitting the mode, which the Jury took to estimate the damages, to be an idle one, yet the 3000l. does appear to have been agreed to then by them all. The case of King against Symonds, 1st Wilson, 329, I remember was this—Symonds was indicted for stealing a certain number of dollars; the Jury found a verdict—Guilty of taking away the dollars, but not with a felonious intention. The clerk of assize entered the verdict Guilty. Upon this the oaths of all the Jury were admitted, in order to ascertain their real verdict.

Judge HEATH. I am glad, in the present case, the affidavits are not admissible, on account of the precedent.

Mr. Serjeant *Bond*. My Brother *Adair* has gone so fully into the question now before the Court, that there is but little occasion for me to enter much on the subject. As to the first point, it seems to me that it was strictly –

The COURT. We have no doubts on that head.

Then as to the second point—The malice—It was as gross an instance as ever came before a Jury.

The COURT. You need not labour that matter.

With respect then to the third—Will your Lordship say that 3000l. were too great damages, for being subjected to trial for a crime of the gross nature of

---

[14] (1785) *Vaise* v. *Delaval*, 1 T.R. 11.
[15] Ibid.
[16] Diss was a small town in Norfolk.

perjury; a crime that can scarcely be done away; a crime, which supposes a man totally devoid of every grain of moral honour or honesty. Were it my case, I am sure, I should expect a much greater sum. Your Lordship will recollect the case of Sir Alexander Leith, and Pope,[17] the usurer; there the damages were 10,000l. and the crime, for which Sir Alexander was tried, was of that nature, which, as soon as he was acquitted of it, left no stain on his character.

Lord LOUGHBOROUGH. There is given in evidence upon the prosecution very heavy expences. This I dislike very much. It is probable that the Jury, in estimating their damages, started from the 600l. which was proved upon the trial to have been laid out by the present plaintiff.

Serjeant *Bond*. My Lord, Mr. Hurry had been all this money out of pocket. There is not, I allow, the least analogy between a Jury's assessing damages, and the Prothonotary taxing costs. But when I go to a Jury, I have a right to state to that Jury what damages I have sustained in procuring counsel to protect me, and in taking every necessary step, to which a regard to myself and my family ought to urge me for this purpose. In justice, and in equity, and in conscience, a Jury ought, in such case, to grant a man his charges. If the Jury had said that these charges had been incurred in order to harass the mind, and destroy the peace of ano[*13*]ther, some objection might have been taken to them; but this was not the case: nay, it does not appear that the Jury ever took those charges into consideration at all. If the Counsel for the defendant thought that the expence of 300l. for fees ought not to have been brought in evidence, they ought at the trial to have stated their objections; and the Jury would have been instructed by my Lord to have laid all that out of the question. What evidence is there, that this 600l. was a set off? Certain it is that Mr. Hurry was intitled to a compensation for his expences, and for his feelings. Certain it is that he had a right to his action upon the case for his damages incurred by this malicious prosecution, whether the aggravation of a conspiracy or confederacy were wanting, and the injury came from one only or no; for if this were not so, the legislature would, in instances of this sort, give damages upon indictments. As for the question of the damages—Upon the whole they do not appear to me to be excessive. I will venture to say there is no gentleman who will lay his hand upon his heart, and declare, that he should not mind undergoing all, that Mr. Hurry has undergone, for a similar compensation. I should hope, therefore, that your Lordships will not hesitate to confirm the verdict.

Mr. Serjeant *Lawrence*. My Lord, what is left for me to say upon the subject is reduced to a very narrow compass; namely, to the enquiry—whether or no the damages are excessive, in the present case, and whether on this ground the Court can set aside the verdict.

With respect then to the enormous sum, whence it has been supposed the Jury started on the estimation of their damages, it ought to have been observed upon by the counsel at the trial; not being so, it was admitted by the defendants as fitting and proper. I allow 300l. is a large sum to be given to counsel; but, my

---

[17] (1779) 2 Bl. W. 1327.

Lord, my client was indicted for perjury; a crime, the consequences of which are shocking: It was incumbent upon him, therefore, to use his best exertion to prevent the horrid charge from being brought home to him. I should conceive that Mr. Hurry, when all the leading counsel on the circuit were employed against him, can hardly be deemed profuse in endeavouring, at any price, to procure the best counsel possible. Mr. Hurry's case seems to me to be one of those, about which a man might be justified in laying out his money more than any other. I do not see, therefore, how the Court can think this sum of 300l. was money idly squandered away, or how it can be considered as any ground of objection to the quantum of the damages. I now beg your Lordship's attention to a few cases tending to show, that in questions of Tort, the Jury, and the Jury only, are to determine.

There is a case so long ago as Hil. 28 and 29 Cha. II in Moderna, p. [*14*] 150.[18] This was an action for words spoken by the defendant, that the plaintiff was an unworthy man, and acted against law and reason. The Jury gave a verdict, 4000l. damages. A motion was made for a new trial, upon *three* grounds, but the principal was, that the damages were excessive. Chief Justice NORTH said that, as a Judge, he could not tell what value to set upon the honour of the plaintiff; the Jury have given 4000l. and therefore he could neither lessen the sum, nor grant a new trial, especially since, by the law, the Jury are the Judges of the damages. Now, my Lords, if in those days 4000l. was not considered as too much for such an offence as the one, that has been stated, can the Court think that 3000l. for indicting a man for perjury, now, when money is of so much less value, ought to be looked upon as excessive damages?

Lord LOUGHBOROUGH. The date of your case is against you. Lord NORTH's time was a time of high political ferment.

Mr. Serjeant *Lawrence*. There is the case of Beardmore against the King's Messengers, 2d. Wilson, 244. This was an action for false imprisonment, the damages found by the Jury were 1000l. A motion was made for a new trial, upon the ground of the excessiveness of the damages. It was refused by the Court, Lord CAMDEN presiding, who observed, that they desired it to be understood, that that Court does not say, or lay down any rule, that there never can happen a case of such excessive damages in Tort, where the Court may not grant a new trial; but in that case the damages must be monstrous and enormous indeed, and such as all mankind must be ready to exclaim against at first blush.

Lord LOUGHBOROUGH. My Lord Townshend's case would stand ill by that rule.

Mr. Serjeant *Lawrence*. My Lord, I wish my client's case to stand by this rule. There is the case of Huckle against Money, 2d Wilson, 205. This is an action for false imprisonment, for six hours, by the King's Messenger, upon suspicion of printing the North Briton, number 45, and using him very civilly, by treating him with beef steaks and beer; the damages were 300l. A motion

---

[18] (1677) *Lord Townsend* v. *Hughes*, 2 Mod. 150.

was made for a new trial; it was refused by the Court. The LORD CHIEF JUSTICE observed, that the few cases to be found in the books of new trials for Torts show, that Courts of Justice have most commonly set their faces against them, and the Court interfering in these cases, would be laying aside Juries. It is very dangerous for the Judges to interfere in damages for Torts; it must be a glaring case indeed of outrageous damages in a Tort, and which all mankind at first blush must think so, to induce a Court to grant a new trial for excessive damages. My Lords, I have cited these cases with respect to the amount [*15*] of the damages. With respect to Mr. Watson's circumstances, he gave no proof of his inability, and if he had, the Courts have ever considered it as of no weight. In the famous case of my Lord Grosvenor and the Duke of Cumberland,[19] my Lord MANSFIELD observed, that the rank and situation of the defendant ought not to be taken into consideration: that the Peer and the peasant ought, in the eye of the law, to be looked upon as on a level. There is the case of Wilford and Berkley, 1st. Burrows, 609.[20] A motion was made for a new trial, on the ground of excessive damages. It was an action for crim. con. The defendant was a clerk of the Exchequer, during pleasure, at 50l. a year: the Verdict was 500l. The Court were all clear and unanimous, that although there was no doubt of the power of the Court to exercise a proper discretion in setting verdicts aside for excessiveness of damages, in cases, where the quantum of damage really suffered by the plaintiff could be apparent, or they were of such a nature that the Court could properly judge of the degree of the injury, and could see manifestly, that the Jury had been outrageous in giving such damages as greatly exceeded the injury; yet the case was very different, where it depended upon circumstances, which were properly and solely under the cognizance of the Jury, and were fit to be submitted to *their* decision and estimate. There is the case likewise of Goddart and Grey,[21] in the Court of King's Bench.

Upon the authority of these cases, I conceive, that the Court ought not to lay any stress on the ground of the damages, in this case, being excessive, or be thereby in the least induced to set aside the verdict.

Mr. Serjeant *Adair*. I remember a case in this Court. An action of assault was brought, by a ship's butcher, against the Captain; the Jury gave 400l. damages.[22] The assault proved was only, that the Captain had beaten the man with a rattan, having found him on shore without leave. I made a motion for a new trial, on the ground of the excessiveness of the damages; but the Court would not hear me.

---

[19] See Oldham, *MMSS*, ii. 1281 for Lord Mansfield's trial notes of the case. For the Mansfield observation referenced by Lawrence, see ibid. at 1262, quoting from the verbatim report of the trial (*The Whole Proceedings at Large, In a Cause on an Action Brought by the Rt. Hon. Richard Lord Grosvenor Against His Highness Henry Frederick Duke of Cumberland; For Criminal Conversation With Lady Grosvenor* (1770)).

[20] *Wilford* v. *Buckley* (1758) 1 Burr. 609. For a more expansive version of Lord Mansfield's opinion from a manuscript source, see Oldham, *Trial by Jury*, at p. 71.

[21] Unreported.

[22] Unreported.

Serjeant *Bolton*. Your Lordships will indulge me with a few words in support of this rule. I trust it has appeared to this Court, that there never was a case, in which the cool interposition of the Court was more necessary. It is necessary, in order to allay that fever, if we cannot cure it, which seems to have reigned against the defendant, Mr. Watson, for a long time throughout the whole county of Norfolk. There is no doubt the whole of this business was owing to an election—this Mr. Watson being at the head of the Corporation, and this Mr. Hurry at the head of the Presbyterian Party.

[16] Your Lordship is perfectly apprized from what a contemptible source this contention at first arose. The original demand was but for eleven shillings. This Mr. Hurry, who is represented by the Counsel on the other side as totally pure, as quite free from malice, and as a character that carries about with him nothing but his injuries; this gentleman came into the Court of Conscience, to lodge a complaint against the Mayor Elect of the Corporation of Yarmouth, for the sum of eleven shillings. My Lord, this sum, thus complained of by this gentleman, was not due; all the sum that was due was 6s. 10d. This sum was not due from Mr. Watson; 3s. 5d. of the money had actually been paid over by Mr. Watson to the persons, who took up the ropes and anchor, and the other 3s. 5d. had been tendered over and over again to Mr. Hurry. Nothing was due to Mr. Hurry. If there had been any real ground of a claim at all, it was the owner, or Captain of the ship, who was intitled to make it. Mr. Hurry, therefore, swore to three things, that were not true. He swore to a debt as due to himself, which was in fact due to another—to a larger debt than there were grounds to insist upon—and to a debt, as owing from Mr. Watson, which, in reality, if it was owing at all, was owing from quite another quarter. There certainly then, was probable cause for Mr. Watson to prefer his bill of indictment. But, in order to bolster up this case, the other side pretend to have proved express malice, from a paragraph in the news-papers inserted by Mr. Watson—I must beg your Lordships to attend to the date of that paragraph; you will find it was subsequent, long subsequent to the finding of the bill of indictment: Indeed this paragraph was not inserted till after the trial at Thetford—till after Mr. Watson had been goaded, and provoked, by numberless paragraphs inserted in different Chronicles, to the disadvantage of him and his party, by the friends of Mr. Hurry. Mr. Hurry, my Lord, seems to have acted in this case, like the man, who having done every thing in his power to put another into a passion, and having succeeded, then complains that the man is in a passion. Your Lordship, then, will see no express malice has been proved by the plaintiff against the defendant, and that there was a probable cause for the conduct of the defendant.

Having dwelt thus long on this point, I shall now proceed to the excessive damages. These, my Lord, seem to me such as to stare one in the face; it is a sum which defeats itself; it cannot be paid; the defendant has made an affidavit, that it is much more than he is worth in the world. Your Lordship would do the defendant more injury, and the plaintiff more good, by establishing a less verdict. For the ground of those enormous damages, the plaintiff gave in a sum, called expences, of 620l. in this, 300l. [*17*] was paid for counsel's fees. This ought not to have been done; it was indecent to bring this before the Jury; legal costs and expences are allowed by the proper officer. Now, no officer would have allowed more than five or ten guineas, at most, upon this occasion. The Jury undoubtedly started from this sum, and it is highly probable took into their account likewise the supposed expences of the last trial, the greatest part of which was incurred, in order to bring down Mr. *Erskine* to make a speech, and Mr. *Mingay* to examine the witnesses; for there was nothing in this business, which was not over in half an hour, and which might not have been as well done without those gentlemen as with them. The matter had been very ably conducted, the assizes before, by Mr. *Murphy*; and there were gentlemen upon the circuit, as able and as sufficient for managing this, or any other cause, as go on any circuit whatsoever.

Lord LOUGHBOROUGH. If Mr. *Wilson* was unengaged, I am sure there was no occasion to send for any other counsel.

Mr. Serjeant *Bolton*. My Lord, there was no colour of pretence to send for those gentlemen, nor to purchase their assistance at a sum so enormous. I will admit, indeed, that Mr. *Erskine* earned his fee, for, upon this occasion, he out-Heroded Herod. The effect of Mr. *Erskine*'s speech was such, as to make the Court and Jury madder than a fever.[23] I understand, my Lord, that this Mr. Hurry came to Thetford, more like a conqueror than any thing else; he had all the ladies with him, and all the gentlemen of his acquaintance and neighbourhood: the day of the trial was *a perfect Jubilee of the Hurrys*. And, My Lord, Mr. *Erskine* talked of good name in man and woman, with so sweet an accent and in such moving phrases, that all the men were in tears, and all the women absolutely blubbered. He introduced the old story of his friend Admiral Keppel and Sir Hugh Palliser, and actually declared that the former fell a martyr to the effects of the latter's prosecution of him. He likewise drew a cruel and affecting picture of Mr. *Mingay*'s sisters—who rejoicing at seeing their brother come down in the elegant manner he did, he imagined all of a sudden to be, like Niobes, all tears, from the idea that their brother was accused of stealing a pocket handkerchief, and that of course he was likely to be indicted for a capital offence.

My Lord, by these, and such pictures and pathetic descriptions, he stole into the pockets of the Jury—And my Brother *Adair* is desirous of lending a helping hand, to enable Mr. Hurry to secure the money, which Mr. *Erskine* has thus stolen for him; for he has talked a good deal about the respectability of the Jury, and the deference that of course ought to be paid them. I would wish to know, my Lord, if I am precluded from [*18*] going into the behaviour of the

---

[23] Even the reporter from *The Times* was dazzled by Erskine's speech; he reported that, 'Mr. Erskine (who came down for the express purpose of this cause) in a most animated and masterly speech, pointed out in the strongest manner the aggravation which had been added to the insult, in endeavouring to prepossess the minds of the public against Mr. Hurry, by an advertisement which appeared in the several provincial papers, setting forth, that the said prosecution was set aside only from a flaw in the indictment, and that a fresh bill would be preferred; which said advertisement was proved to originate with Mr. Watson.' *The Times*, 31 March 1787.

Jury. I would always speak with reverence of what falls from the great authority, which has been quoted in the case of Vasie [*sic*] and Delaval; but I really cannot see any thing in that doctrine, that a Juryman shall not be heard to tell his own fault. Why shall he not? A culprit, to convict himself, has his own confession taken against him. Your Lordship has said, that if it was a fact, that the damages were estimated in the manner said, that the verdict ought not to stand. Indeed, by this manner of proceeding, the very principle of a Jury is perverted. You have no one opinion thereby instead of twelve; that is one objection. The next is, that any one man may raise the damages to any height he pleases, and the last the most. And, my Lord, there can, in this case, be no doubt of the fact; we have the affidavit of one of the Jury, and we have the affidavit of two other persons besides, who heard one of the Jurors assert, that each Juryman put down a particular sum, and that then they took the medium, or average. But if your Lordships think that these affidavits are not admissible, I must not go upon it. Certain it is, that the fact was as I have stated; and certain it is, that had this respectable Special Jury, whose credit my brother *Adair* has so much trumpetted, lived in a more early period, they would, for their conduct, have experienced a severe punishment. The law of Attaints would have reached them; their houses would have been razed; their property would have been confiscated, and every one of them, with Sir Martin Folkes at their head, would for ever have been incapable of sitting on a Jury again.

I did not expect upon this argument to hear, that the Court has not authority to mitigate damages. I am surprized to hear, after what so lately happened, in the case of Elliott and Munro,[24] that in matters of Tort this Court has no power to interfere. There is the case of Clarke and Udal—2d Salkeld, 649, and the case of Chambré and Robinson, 1st Shane [*sic*],[25] 691.*

[*19*] And is not the case now before the Court, exclusive of the 300l. counsel's fees, an instance of enormous excess in damages.—Did the plaintiff bring one witness to prove, that any one man upon earth thought him injured? Was he not raised by his prosecution, and is he not now the very idol of the county? What then was the object of this Mr. Hurry, in bringing the last action? Not to clear, as he pretends, his own character, but to asperse and blacken that of Mr. Watson. So far from appearing at Thetford, like an injured man, the day, he

---

* Note, with regard to Chambré and Robinson which seems to be the only case where a new trial was granted merely for the excessiveness of the damages—the Court, in the case of Beardmore, &c. observed—That they were not satisfied with the reason given in that case, and think it of no weight, and want to know the fact, upon which the Court could pronounce the damages to be excessive. The principle on which it was granted, mentioned in Strange, was to give the defendant a chance of another Jury, which is a very bad reason; for if it was not, it would be a reason for a 3d and 4th, and would be digging up the constitution by the roots, and therefore we are free to say, this case is not law, and there is not one single case (that is law) in all the books, to be found, where the Court has granted a new trial for excessive damages, in actions of Tort.

[24] See p. 4, above, for Mr Justice Lawrence's notes of the case of *Monroe* v. *Elliot*.
[25] The reference should have been to *Chambers* v. *Robinson* (1726) 2 Str. 691.

appeared there, was a feast, a festival, and Mr. Watson was the sacrifice. I hope and trust, therefore, your Lordships will set aside the verdict, and send the matter to be reconsidered by another Jury.

Mr. Serjeant *Rooke*. I am of the same side with my brother *Bolton*, and I contend, that his verdict ought to be set aside, on the ground of the excessive damages, and on the ground of the improper evidence, which was admitted. The rule of law is, that the best evidence possible to be procured, shall be procured. This was not the case here. They should have produced the original of Mr. Watson's—whereas Mr. Locke, who was called, produced only a copy, and that a copy too, which he would not swear to be an exact copy; they did not prove that all the advertisements of the papers were the same. There is no necessary implication in the direction, which Mr. Locke is said to have received, to insert the paragraph in more papers than one, that he had authority to multiply the copies; for he might have carried the original to the several printers. Certain it is, however, he was not authorized to make an incorrect copy. So much as to the point of this paper in evidence.

The next great point is the excess of the damages. The Court, in judging of these, will take a variety of circumstances into the account. There was a design in the plaintiff to harass the defendant, by arresting him, and summoning him to the Court of Requests for a debt of 11s—the ground, therefore of this complaint came from Mr. Hurry. The Court will consider, in estimating the damages, what is the sufferance sustained, and how far the defendant can make satisfaction. My Lord, Mr. Hurry came to the trial, as my Brother *Bolton* has described him, like a conqueror. He suffered nothing at all in the business. But how then came these damages to be found by the Jury? A jury, my Lord, how respectable soever they may be, are but men; and men of the best characters are open to impressions; are liable to have their passions heated, by a flummery speech from the counsel: And there cannot be a doubt, but that these damages are owing more to the speech of Mr. *Erskine* than to [20] any thing that Mr. Hurry actually suffered. He is certainly a man of character, and his being such, was probably the reason why the Jury listened to the inflammatory harangues of Mr. *Erskine*. But there is another ground, on which we may account for their conduct in this case. They heard of the enormous expences of the former trial, and of the nonsuit. Now this was evidence, which ought not to have been received; for to have expences brought forward in a Court of law, which a Court of law would not allow, was certainly very improper. They ought not to have had such evidence laid before them. With respect to the power of the Court, to grant a new trial, on the ground of excessive damages; that seems to be settled beyond controversy, by the numerous cases which have been decided; though, undoubtedly they will ever feel tender in using the power. As to the causes which have been produced on the other side; the Court will, I am sure, not fall into the doctrine there laid down.—The instance, in 2d Moderna, of my Lord Townshend, where 4000l. damages were given, the Court will recollect, that that was at a time when parties ran high.

The case cited from Wilson, was a case that happened in the time of General

Warrants, and whoever attends to what was said upon that occasion, will find that it originated from the abhorrence which, at that time, was prevalent in the kingdom against that arbitrary mode of proceeding.

My Lord MANSFIELD has been quoted, as saying, that the circumstances of the defendant ought not to be considered by the Jury, in the case of the Duke of Cumberland and my Lord Grosvenor; but, in that case, his Lordship made this observation, in order to prevent the Jury from giving a verdict beyond what the value of the case demanded, on account of the rank and situation of the Prince defendant.

In the case of Sir Alexander Leith, and Pope, the Court indeed held, that 10,000l. damages were not too much;—but it is to be noted here, that the Court did not go merely upon the degree of the injury sustained by Sir Alexander, but upon the circumstances of Pope. In the report of the case by Mr. Justice BLACKSTONE, it appeared in evidence that the defendant was exceedingly wealthy, and well able to sustain such a verdict: In possession, upon record, of seventy seven judgments, to the amount of more than 100,000l.—and in actual receipt of more than 3000l. per annum annuities, from young gentlemen's lives.

If then the Court will take into consideration the circumstances of the defendant, clear I am, that the circumstances of my client make it mani[*21*]fest, that the verdict should be reconsidered. We have an affidavit, that he is totally unable to sustain the verdict, and there is no affidavit to the contrary. It is then for the Court to determine, whether they will actually ruin this man or not, by the confirming of a verdict, which defeats the very object of the plaintiff, for it is impossible for him to get the money; should the judgment be entered up, my client must be imprisoned for life; for neither the Lords act,[26] nor the insolvent act, extend to this sum of 3000l. In other cases, the Court have considered the damages as to the circumstances of the parties, as well as to the nature of the offence. I submit it then to your Lordships, that the present case, considered in a similar manner, call upon the Court [*sic*] to send it to be reheard before another Jury of the country.

Mr. Serjeant *Le Blanc*, on the same side, followed Serjeant *Rook*, with declaring, that he did not find it incumbent upon him to enter into the motives, which induced the Jury to give the damages which they did; that from the knowledge which he had of them, from his frequent residence in the county, he had not a doubt, that these Gentlemen acted conscientiously in the business, and that they were men of honour; that it was sufficient for him to enquire, whether they have given the verdict rightly upon improper grounds, by having attended more to what was said, than to what was proved: that this was what the most upright man in the world might have done; and that this was all he wished to impute to them upon this occasion: that their Lordships knew it was with a Jury, as it was sometimes with a Judge, that both were liable to mistakes,

---

[26] 32 Geo. II, c. 28. This statute set the amount of groats allowed to imprisoned debtors and mandated they be paid every Monday, 'whatever may be the day on which the defendant is brought up to be discharged, and demanded at the instance of the plaintiff'.

that both, in their conclusion in particular cases, might be wrong. He then entered into the argument against the admission of Mr. Locke's evidence; and into proof of Mr. Watson's having probable cause for this preferring the bill of indictment. With respect to the power of the Court, to set aside verdicts for excessive damages, he forbore to trouble their Lordships with a long string of cases, which were to be found from the times of Stiles, p. 466. in the year 1655, in the case of Wood and Gunston,[27] to the 26th of the present King, in the instance of Ducker and Wood;[28] he remarked in the case of Benson and Sir Thomas Frederick, 3d Burrows, 1846, Lord MANSFIELD said, he had no doubt but it might be right to give an opportunity of reconsidering verdicts, when excessive damages had been given; and that his Lordship seemed to make this observation, on purpose to guard against the idea's prevailing, that the Court had not the power, he was then contending for; and that in the case of Trinity Term, 1785, in Term Reports,[29] the same doctrine is laid down as in Stiles's Reports, Mich. [22] Term, 1655. He then adverted to the excessiveness of the damages; that they were more than the circumstances of the defendant enabled him to pay; that the defendant was, as he always had been, willing, upon oath, to deliver up his *All* to Mr. Hurry; to make him every compensation in his power, to the utmost of his abilities and of his credit; and to add to it any apology, the Court should think proper to prescribe.

Lord LOUGHBOROUGH.

I am of opinion, that the plaintiff in this action was intitled upon the evidence, to substantial and very considerable damages. There was no objection to the admission of Mr. Locke's evidence. I do not think it was necessary to prove the contents of the given paper. It was enough to prove, that the paragraph had been inserted by the direction of the defendant. Now Mr. Locke's evidence was, that he received a paragraph to be inserted in three papers; and that he sent to the papers a writing, containing, to the best of his judgment and belief, a copy of this paragraph. This, I think could have been sufficient evidence to bring the matter home to Mr. Watson. I think, upon the circumstances of the case, it plainly appears, that the indictment was malicious, and without probable cause. That there were no grounds on which Mr. Watson ought to have founded the prosecution of Mr. Hurry for perjury, from the oath which he took; and that the Jury were well warranted in giving him a verdict of damages.

We then come to the excessiveness of these damages. These ought to have been considerable; and to have been given in such a manner, as not to be liable to objection. If they are excessive, the enquiry is open to another Jury; because from the circumstances of the excess, it is to be inferred, that the verdict was given in the hurry of a Nisi Prius; the Court does not arrogate hereby to itself the right of assessing damages, nor does it affect the credit of a Jury. The Court does nothing more, than direct a cooler enquiry should be made. I have

[27] (1655) Style 462.
[28] (1786) 1 T.R. 277.
[29] Ibid.

no doubt that the Court has a power to grant a new trial, in the instance of excessive damages; from the cases, which have been cited from Stiles, in the year 1655, down to the case in the 26th year of his present Majesty, there can be no doubt, that the Court must form a judgement, whether the damages are excessive or not. We did it the other day on a writ of enquiry.[30] In that case, it was pretty obvious what the idea of the Court was—that they considered the damages assessed as too much, so as to desire that the matter [23] might be reheard; what the Court has done in one instance, it may in another. It is very difficult, in a case like the present, to estimate damages, because it must be more the effect of feeling than of any thing else. Where the injury is of a personal nature; where the comfort and happiness of a man are concerned, you have no measure by which to form your judgement. You cannot ascertain a matter of this kind, by pounds, shillings, and pence; nor are the abilities of the defendant to regulate the verdict: for if the plaintiff should be intitled to a particular verdict, the incapacity of the defendant to fulfil it, ought not to be considered as a reason, why it should not be given. But in a case, where the defendant is subjected to no particular injury, in that case, perhaps, some consideration may be thereto had. In a question of this kind coming before me, for the first time, what would have been reasonable to give, might be difficult to say. Three thousand pounds, seems to be an effect of the Jury's being taken by surprize. If the verdict had been a verdict for a thousand pounds, it would have been a verdict, which none could have found fault with. Whether the verdict for three thousand pounds be one of those palpably excessive cases, which would warrant the interference of the Court, I wish for some days to consider. And upon a circumstance thrown out by my Brother *Le Blanc*, it were well if it were considered elsewhere. If my Brothers think with me, *we will take two or three days.*

Mr. Serjeant *Adair* said, that unfortunately Mr. Hurry was not in town.
Mr. Serjeant *Bolton* observed, that a letter might be sent in a day.
Lord LOUGHBOROUGH then said—'It is well worth consideration.'

Mr. Hurry, to whom what thus fell from the Court, was, as speedily as possible, communicated, upon receiving information of it, immediately authorized his attorney, Mr. *Bell*, to send Mr. Watson the following letter:

Mr. JOHN WATSON
SIR,

Finding by my advices this day from London, that on arguing the motion for a new trial, in the action against you, at the suit of Mr. William Hurry, the Court of Common Pleas declared, that my client was intitled to substantial and very considerable damages; and the Court having shown an inclination, that the dispute should be terminated [24] by accommodation, I am authorized by Mr. Hurry to tell you, it always was his intention, when there remained no

---

[30] *Monroe v. Elliott*, p. 4, above.

charge of a stain upon his reputation, to accept of your excuses for your conduct, if you were disposed to make any, and not to insist upon the whole of the damages, which the Jury gave him last Thetford assizes.

Mr. Hurry, desirous to show his respect for the opinion of the Court, and in order to end all legal altercations between you and him, wishes to make two proposals for your choice, viz. either that you pay Mr. Hurry 200l. [*sic*][31] to be applied to such uses as he chuses (not meaning to put one shilling into his own pocket), and all his expences, from the indictment to the final determination of the business; or half the damages fixed by the Jury, with taxed costs.

Mr. Hurry requests your answer by to-morrow, ten o'clock.

> I am, Sir,
> Your very humble servant,
> JOHN BELL

Thursday, Jan. 21, 1787.

To this letter Mr. Watson, in return, pleaded an absolute impossibility to comply with its contents, on account of his circumstances; but offered, at the same time, to pay Mr. Hurry 1000l., and all his taxed costs.

This not being accepted, on Saturday the 23d, the matter came on again before the Court of Common Pleas; when a fresh proposal, which was offered by the friends of Mr. Watson, viz. that he should pay 1500l., and make an apology to Mr. Hurry, was transmitted to the latter; and on Wednesday the 27th, the following rule as drawn up by order of the Court, and served on Mr. Watson's attorney.

> In the Common Pleas, Trinity Term, 27 GEO. III.
> HURRY against WATSON.

Gentlemen, one &c. Wednesday the 27th of June. Upon hearing of counsel on both sides, and by their consent, it is ordered, that the defendant shall pay to the plaintiff, or his attorney, the sum of fifteen hundred pounds, for the plaintiff's damages and costs in this action, within two months next ensuing. And that the defendant do, and shall, make such an apology to the plaintiff, for his conduct, as Mr. Serjeant *Kerby* shall think proper to direct; the same being hereby referred to him, by [25] the consent of both the parties. And it is further ordered, that upon the defendant's paying to the plaintiff the said sum, within the time aforesaid; and upon the defendant's making such apology to the plaintiff, as aforesaid, the verdict found for the plaintiff, at the last assizes held for the county of Norfolk, shall be vacated. But that the Postea do, in the mean time, remain in the hands of the Associate, as a security to the plaintiff for the damages found by the Jury, and for the plaintiff's costs to be taxed by one of the Prothonotaries of this Court: and it is further ordered, that in default of the defendant's paying to the plaintiff the said sum, within the time aforesaid, and making such apology to the plaintiff as aforesaid, the aforesaid

---

[31] This is a typographical error—the entry should have been £2,000.

Postea shall be delivered to the plaintiff, his attorney, or agent, with liberty for him to proceed to judgement and execution thereon.

By the Court,
FOTHERGIL.

On a Motion of Serjeants *Adair*, *Bond*, and *Lawrence*, for the plaintiff.

Serjeants *Bolton*, *Rook*, & *Le Blanc*, for the defendant.

Entered.

BIBLIOGRAPHY, TABLES AND INDEXES

BIBLIOGRAPHY

Note: standard law reports are not included in this bibliography.

MANUSCRIPT SOURCES

United Kingdom

Inner Temple Library, London
 Miscellaneous MS. 96
Lincoln's Inn Library, London
 Dampier MSS.
Middle Temple Library, London
 Lawrence MSS. 20–24, 48–49

United States

Georgetown University Law Library, Washington, D.C.
 Eldon MSS.
Harvard Law School Library, Cambridge, Mass.
 Long Notebooks, collections of notes of cases (various).

NEWSPAPERS, MAGAZINES, AND JOURNALS

The Daily Universal Register (London, 1785–87) (became *The Times*, 1788–).
Espinasse, I. '"My Contemporaries", From the Note-book of a Retired Barrister', *Fraser's Magazine for Town and Country*, 6 (London, 1832).
The London Chronicle (London, 1757–1823).
The London Evening Post (London, 1744–1806).
The Morning Chronicle and London Advertiser (London, 1769–1789) (became *The Morning Chronicle*, London, 1789 1865).

PAMPHLETS AND TRIALS

Alderson, R. *Proceedings at the Assizes at Thetford, On the 18th of March 1786, and the 24th of March, 1787, in the Trial of William Hurry, Merchant, Of the Borough of Great Yarmouth, On an Indictment preferred against him by John Watson, Attorney at Law, then Mayor Elect of the said Borough, for Willful and Corrupt Perjury* (Norwich, 1787).
Old Bailey Sessions Papers: The Proceedings on the King's Commission of the Peace, Oyer and Terminer, and Gaol Delivery of Newgate, Held for the City of London and County of Middlesex at Justice Hall in the Old Bailey, 1729–1888, 167 vols. (1729–1888), available at <www.oldbaileyonline.org>, version 7.0, accessed 26 October 2012.

Seipp, D., *Seipp's Abridgment: An Index and Paraphrase of Printed Year Book Reports, 1268–1535*, available at <www.bu.edu/law/seipp>, accessed 26 October 2012.
The Trial of Henry Yorke, For a Conspiracy, &c. Before the Hon. Mr Justice Rooke, at the Assizes, Held for the County of York, on Saturday, July 10, 1795 (York, 1795).
The Whole Proceedings at Large, In a Cause on an Action Brought by the Rt. Hon. Richard Lord Grosvenor Against His Highness Henry Frederick Duke of Cumberland; For Criminal Conversation With Lady Grosvenor (London, 1770).

BOOKS AND MONOGRAPHS

Anon., *A Treatise on Calico Printing* (London, 1792).
Baker, J. H., *English Legal Manuscripts*, 2 vols. (Zug, Switzerland, 1978, 1990).
——. *English Legal Manuscripts in the United States of America* (London, 1985).
——. *An Introduction to English Legal History*, 4th ed. (London, 2002).
——. *The Order of Serjeants at Law* (London, 1984).
Ballow, H., *A Treatise of Equity, with the addition of marginal references and notes by John Fonblanque, Esq., Barrister at Law*, 2 vols. (London, 1793–1794).
Beattie, J. M., *Crime and the Courts in England 1660–1800* (Princeton, 1986).
Blackstone, W., *Commentaries on the Laws of England*, 4 vols. (Oxford, 1765–69).
Booth, G., *The Law of Real Actions, Etc.* (London, 1704).
Brooke, R., *La Graunde Abridgement*, 2 vols. (London, 1573).
Brougham, H., *Historical Sketches of Statesmen Who Flourished in the time of George III*, 3rd ser., 3 vols. (London, 1843).
Buller, F., *An Introduction to the Law Relative to Trials at* Nisi Prius, 5th ed. (London, 1790).
Campbell, J. C., *Lives of the Chief Justices of England*, 3 vols. (London, 1857).
Chambers, P., *The Cock Lane Ghost: Murder, Sex and Haunting in Dr Johnson's London* (Stroud, 2006).
Clift, H., *A New Book of Declarations, Pleadings, Judgments and Judicial Writs with the Entries Thereupon* (London, 1703).
Coke, E., *The First Part of the Institutes of the Laws of England*, 15th ed. (London, 1794).
A Collection of the Most Esteemed Farces and Entertainments Performed on the British Stage, 4 vols. (Edinburgh, printed for C. Elliot, Parliament-Square, 1782).
Cooke, W., *The Bankrupt Laws*, 4th ed., 2 vols. (London, 1799).
——. *A Compendious System of the Bankrupt Laws* (London, 1785).
Duncan, G. I. O., *The High Court of Delegates* (Cambridge, 1971).
Durston, G., *Crime & Justice in Early Modern England 1500–1790* (Chichester, 2004).
East, E. H., *A Treatise of the Pleas of the Crown*, 2 vols. (London, 1803).
Fearne, C., *An Essay on the Learning of Contingent Remainders and Executory Devises* (London, 1772).
——. *An Essay on the Learning of Contingent Remainders and Executory Devises*, 7th ed. (London, 1820).
Finn, M., *The Character of Credit: Personal Debt in English Culture, 1740–1914* (Cambridge, 2003).
Foss, E., *The Judges of England With Sketches of Their Lives, and Miscellaneous Notices Connected with the Courts at Westminster, from the Time of the Conquest*, vol. 9 (London, 1848).

Gurney, T., *Brachygraphy, or, An Easy and Compendious System of Short-Hand, Adapted to the Various Arts, Sciences, and Professions*, 9th ed. (London, 1778).

Hale, M., *Historia Placitorum Coronae: History of the Pleas of the Crown*, 2 vols. (London, 1778).

Hardcastle, M. S. ed., *Life of John, Lord Campbell, Lord High Chancellor of Great Britain*, 2 vols. (London, 1881).

Hargrave, F., *Collecteana Juridica*, 2 vols. (London, 1791–92).

Holliday, J., *The Life of William Late Earl of Mansfield* (London, 1797).

Holdsworth, W. S., *A History of English Law*, 17 vols. (London, 1903–72).

———. *History of English Law*, 16 vols. (reprint, London, 1966). (London, 1903–72).

Holzmann, G., and Pehrson, B., *The Early History of Data Networks* (Los Alamitos, 1995).

Jacob, G., *A New Law Dictionary*, 10th ed. (London, 1782).

Jenkins, D., *Eight Centuries of Reports*, 3rd ed. (London, 1771).

Langbein, J. H., *The Origins of Adversary Criminal Trial* (Oxford, 2003).

Madox, T., *Firma Burgi* (London, 1726).

Matthew, H. C. G., and Harrison, B. eds., *Oxford Dictionary of National Biography*, 60 vols. (Oxford, 2004).

Moore, W., *Wedlock: How Georgian Britain's Worst Husband Met his Match* (London, 2009).

Musgrave, W., *Obituary Prior to 1800* (London, 1900).

Noy, W. *The Grounds and Maxims, and also An Analysis of the English Laws*, 6th ed. (1794).

Oldham, J., *The Mansfield Manuscripts and the Growth of English Law in the Eighteenth Century*, 2 vols. (Chapel Hill, 1992).

———. *Trial by Jury: The Seventh Amendment and Anglo-American Special Juries* (New York, 2006).

Outhwaite, R. B., *The Rise and Fall of the English Ecclesiastical Courts, 1500–1860* (Cambridge, 2007).

Park, J. A., *A System of the Law of Marine Insurances* (London, 1787).

———. *A System of the Law of Marine Insurances*, 3rd ed. (London, 1796).

Perkins, J., *A Profitable Booke Treating of the Lawes of England* (London, 1545).

Powell, J., *Essay upon the Law of Contracts and Agreements*, 2 vols. (London, 1790).

Rastell, W., *Collection of Entries* (London, 1566).

Redford, A., *Manchester Merchants and Foreign Trade 1794—1858* (Manchester, 1934).

Roberts, R.A. ed., *A Calendar of the Inner Temple Records* (London, 1836).

Sheppard, W., *The Touch-Stone of Common Assurances, or, A Plain and Familiar Treatise, Opening the Learning of the Common Assurances or Conveyances of the Kingdome* (London, 1648).

Simpson, A. W. B. ed., *Biographical Dictionary of the Common Law* (London, 1984).

———. *A History of the Common Law of Contract: The Rise of the Action of Assumpsit* (Oxford, 1975).

Staunford, W., *Pleas of the Crown* (London, 1557).

Swinburne, H., *A Briefe Treatise of Testaments and Last Willes* (London, 1590).

Tidd, W., *The Practice of the Court of King's Bench in Personal Actions*, 2 vols. (London, 1790).

———. *The Practice of the Court of King's Bench, and Common Pleas*, 8th ed., 2 vols. (London, 1828).

Wallace, J. W., *The Reporters Arranged and Characterized with Incidental Remarks*, 4th ed. (Boston, 1882).

Watson, W., *The Clergy-man's Law*, 3rd. ed. (London, 1725).

Woolrych, H.W., *Lives of Eminent Serjeants-at-Law of the English Bar*, 2 vols. (London, 1869).

ARTICLES AND BOOK CHAPTERS

Baker J. 'Le Brickbat Que Narrowly Mist', *Law Quarterly Review* 100 (1984), pp. 544–548.

Ellis, John, 'An Enquiry Whence cometh Wisdom and Understanding to Man?', in W. Jones ed., *The Scholar Armed Against the Errors of the Time* or, *A Collection of Tracts on the Principles and Evidences of Christianity, the Constitution of the Church, and the Authority of the Civil Government*, 2 vols. (London, 1795), vol. 1, pp. 129–191.

Heward, E., 'Dampier Manuscripts at Lincoln's Inn', *Journal of Legal History* 9 (1988), pp. 357–364.

Oldham, J., 'Creditors and the Feme Covert', in M. Dyson and D. Ibbetson eds., *Law and Legal Process: Substantive Law and Procedure in English Legal History* (Cambridge, forthcoming 2013).

——. 'Informal Lawmaking in England by the Twelve Judges in the Late Eighteenth and Early Nineteenth Centuries', *Law and History Review* 29 (2011), pp. 181–220.

——. 'Law-making at Nisi prius in the Early 1800s', *Journal of Legal History* 25 (2004), pp. 221–247.

——. 'Only Eleven Shillings: Abusing Public Justice in England in the Late Eighteenth Century', *The Green Bag*, 15 (2012), pp. 175–188, and pp. 263–273

——. 'Underreported and Underrated: The Court of Common Pleas in the Eighteenth Century', in H. Hartog, W. E. Nelson, and B.W. Kern eds., *Law as Culture and Culture as Law* (Madison, 2000), pp. 119–146.

——. 'Detecting Non-Fiction: Sleuthing Among Manuscript Case Reports for What Was Really Said', in C. Stebbings ed., *Law Reporting in Britain* (London, 1995) pp. 133–155.

Simpson, A. W. B. 'The Penal Bond with Conditional Defeasance', *Law Quarterly Review* 82 (1966), pp. 392–422.

TABLE OF STATUTES

52 Hen. III, c. 6 (1267) (costs) 38
4 Hen. IV, c. 19 (1403) (attorneys) 51
6 Hen. VIII, c. 6 (1514) (felons) . . . . 93 n. 11
23 Hen. VIII, c. 15 (1531) (costs) 39
37 Hen. VIII, c. 9 (1545) (usury) 146
13 Eliz., c. 7 (1571) (bankrupts) 42
18 Eliz., c. 5 (1575) (informers) 39
31 Eliz., c. 5, s. 5 (1588) (limitations) . . . . 99 n. 24
43 Eliz., c. 2 (1601) (poor relief) . . . . 70, 83 n. 94, 167
1 Jac. I, c. 15, s. 2 (1603) (bankrupts) . . . . 42, 152 n. 23
3 Jac. I, c. 4 (1605) (recusants) . . . . 116 n. 58
7 Jac. I, c. 5 (1609) (costs) 178
21 Jac. I, c. 12 (1623) (costs) 178
21 Jac. I, c. 19 (1623) (bankrupts) 42, 156, 244
12 Car. II, c. 18 (1660) (navigation) 307
13 & 14 Car. II, c. 12 (1662) (poor relief) 83
22 & 23 Car. II, c. 10 (1670) (distributions) 66
29 Car. II, c. 3 (1677) (frauds) 123, 129, 130
1 Will. & Mar., c. 16 (1688) (simony) . . . . 26 n. 74
8 & 9 Will. III, c. 11, s. 3 (1697) (*scire facias*, vexatious suits) 244
8 & 9 Will. III, c. 11 (1697) (penal bonds) . . . . 13 n. 21, 18, 19, 247 n. 31
7 Ann., c. 21, s. 11 (1708) (treason) 94
8 Ann., c. 9, s. 43 (1709) (apprentices) 88
9 Ann., c. 14 (1710) (gaming) . . . . liv, 42
12 Ann., st. 2, c. 18 (1713) (salvage) 191
1 Geo. I, private act no. 34 (1714) (Duke of Athol) 72
7 Geo. I, c. 31 (1720) (bankrupts) . . . . 56 n. 48, 244 n. 22
8 Geo. I, c. 11 (1721) (Bridport harbour) 160
9 Geo. I, c. 7, s. 4 (1722) (poor relief) 48, 66
11 Geo. I, c. 4, s. 1 (1724) (Tiverton) . . . . 95 n. 17
2 Geo. II, c. 22 (1729) (set-offs) 245
2 Geo. II, c. 23, s. 6 (1729) (attorneys) 154
2 Geo. II, c. 36 (1729) (seamen) 135
3 Geo. II, c. 25 (1730) (juries) 201
5 Geo. II, c. 24 (1732) (notice) . . . . 3 n. 3
5 Geo. II, c. 30, s. 1 (1732) (bankrupts) . . . . 244 n. 21
6 Geo. II, private act no. 14 (1732) (Duke of Athol) 72
7 Geo. II, c. 8 (1734) (stock-jobbing) . . . . 163 n. 41, 164 n. 44
8 Geo. II, c. 24 (1735) (set-offs) 245
11 Geo. II, c. 19, s. 14 (1738) (distress for rent) 40
12 Geo. II, c. 13, s. 6 (1739) (attorneys' costs) 153
14 Geo. II, c. 17 (1741) (nonsuit) . . . . 164 n. 42

TABLE OF STATUTES

19 Geo. II, c. 32 (1746) (bankrupts) 58
22 Geo. II, c. 46, s. 15 (1749) (attorneys) 81
22 Geo. II, c. 83 (1749) (poor relief) 70
31 Geo. II, c. 10 (1757) (seamen) 11
32 Geo. II, c. 28 (1759) (debtors) .... 64, 146 n. 12, 377 n. 26
8 Geo. III, c. 22 (1768) (Admiralty courts) 119
13 Geo. III, c. 78 (1773) (highways) 164
17 Geo. III, c. 26 (1776) (annuities) 34
21 Geo. III, c. 15 (1781) (prize) .... 85 n. 96
22 Geo. III, c. 47 (1782) (lotteries) .... 99 n. 24
23 Geo. III, c. 58 (1783) (stamp duties) 174
23 Geo. III, c. 88 (1783) (rogues and vagabonds) 191
26 Geo. III, c. 21 (1786) (slaughtering horses) 196
26 Geo. III, c. 60 (1786) (shipping) .... 156 n. 30
27 Geo. III, c. 1 (1787) (lotteries) 8, 100, 143
32 Geo. III, c. 53 (1792) (magistrates, police) 80
33 Geo. III, c. 4 (1793) (aliens) 65
33 Geo. III, c. 52 (1793) (East India Company) 169
34 Geo. III, c. 69 (1794) (insolvency) 78
35 Geo. III, c. 15, c. 80 (1795) (shipping) 168, 169
37 Geo. III, c. 45 (1797) (bank notes) 176
37 Geo. III, c. 97 (1797) (treaty) .... 198 n. 6
43 Geo. III, c. 140 (1803) (*habeas corpus*) .... 78 n. 88
44 Geo. III, c. 102 (1804) (*habeas corpus*) .... 78 n. 88

TABLE OF CASES

References to case notes appear in **bold type**.

—— [sic] v. Highmore (1797)	**165**
—— [sic] v. Manners (1794)	**60**
—— [sic] v. Phillips (1794)	**54**
Acheson v. Fountain (1723)	xxxiv n. 21
Ackland v. Day (1795)	**64**
Acton v. Roberts (1798)	**189**
Aikenhead v. Taylor (1799)	**208**
Alexander v. Ledwick (1795)	**97**
Allam v. Heber (1748)	xxxi n. 2
Allwood v. Henckell (1795)	**266**
Almack v. Chapman (1795)	**87**
Anon. (1612)	228 n. 55
Anon. (1661)	137 n. 93
see also Danell's Case (1661)	
Anon. (1689)	178 n. 67
Anon. (1700)	53
Anon. (1720)	66 n. 71
Anon. (1787)	**36**
Anon. (1794)	**49**
see also Platt v. Knowles (1794)	
Anon. (1794)	**56**
Anon. (1794)	**52**
Anon. (1794)	**52**
Anon. (1794)	**53**
Anon. (1794)	**53**
Anon. (1794)	**56**
Anon. (1794)	**56**
Anon. (1795)	**79**
Anon. (1795)	**80**
Anon. (1795)	**83**
Anon. (1795)	**104**
Anon. (1796)	**159**
Anon. (1797)	**163**
Anon. (1798)	**182**
Anthon v. Fisher (1782)	xxii n. 34
Appleton v. Sweetapple (1783)	xxii n. 33
Apthorp v. Cockerell (1615)	137 n. 94
Ardesoif v. Isaac (1798)	**186**
Aston's Case (1350)	206
Atkins v. Holford Clare (1671)	51 n. 38

Atkinson v. Maylin [Mayling] (1788) 156
Atkinson v. Settree (1744) .... xxiv n. 46, xxxiv n. 20
Attorney-General v. Davy (1741) 48
Attorney-General v. Lade (1746) .... xxxiii n. 19
Attorney-General v. Countess of Portland (1743) xxxviii
Attorney-General v. Scott (1749–50) .... 48 n. 30
Atword v. Burr (1702) .... 101 n. 27
Bagshaw v. Wynn (1739) xxix
Baker v. Jardine (1784) 11
Ball v. Montgomery (1793) .... 225 n. 48, 231 n. 78
Ballard v. Godby [Oddey] (1678) .... 89 n. 4, 98
Bamford v. Burrell (1799) .... xxiv n. 49
Banbury, Corporation, Case of (1706) .... xxiv n. 43
Banbury, Lord, Case of (1716) .... xxiv n. 41, xxxiii n. 19
Banks v. Milward (1796) **133**
Barber v. French (1779) .... 178 n. 67
Barham v. Nethersal (1602) .... 137 n. 91
Barker v. Bishop of London (1790) .... xxiv n. 45
Barrymore, Earl of v. Taylor (1795) **91**
Bartley v. Godslake (1818) .... lv n. 49
Barwell v. Brooks (1784) .... xxii n. 32, 214–215, 224, 226
Barzillai v. Lewis (1782) .... xxii n. 35, xxxvii, 303–304, 307–310
Bates v. Jenkinson (1784) .... 99, 101 n. 27
Baynes v. Forrest (1731) 4
Beardmore v. Carrington (1764) .... xliii, 371, 375
Beatson v. Haworth (1795) xxxiii
Beaty v. Beaty (1795) **78**
Beaufort, Duke of v. Berty (1721) 55
Beaumont, Barony of, Case (1795) **71**
Bedford, Mayor of v. Bishop of Lincoln (1745) .... xxiv n. 46
Belknap, Lady, Case of (1400) .... 227, 229 n. 67, 230, 232
Bennetto v. Elvens [Henry Evans] (1773) xxxvi
Benson v. Frederick (1766) 378
Bernardi v. Matteux (1781) 303, 305–311
Berrie v. Perrie (1615) .... 259 n. 59
Berry v. Herd [Heard] (1632) 135
Best v. Isaac (1796) **156**
Bever v. Tomlinson (1796) **134**
Bewick v. Vaughan (n.d.) 201
Bicknell v. Langstaff (1795) **93**
Billon v. Hyde (1749) 17
Birch v. Triste (1807) .... xxxi n. 2
Bird v. Appleton (1799) **203**
Bird v. Thompson (1795–96) **84**
Bischoff v. Agar (1797) 213, **264**
Blackmore v. Lord Wigtown [Flemyng] (1797) **173**
Blackwell v. Nash (1722) .... 237 n. 4
Blakely v. Vincent (1795) **77**
Blissett v. Hart (1744) .... xxiv n. 46

TABLE OF CASES

Blisset's Case (1831) 55
Blood v. Lee (1769) .... xxiv n. 48
Blumfield's Case (1596) 37
Bodington v. Bodington (1797) 201
Bones v. Booth (1778) 42
Bonsal v. Jones (1795) **61**
Booth v. Cook (1679) 98
Boutflower v. Stafford (1795) **92**
Bowman v. Milbanke (1664) .... 255 n. 43
Bragner v. Langmead (1796) .... xxvi n. 69
Brander v. Robson (1795) **67**
Brandon v. Davis (1807) .... xxvii n. 73
Brandon v. Nesbitt (1794) 195
Brandon v. Pate (1794) **42**
Brickhead v. Archbishop of York (1617) 26
Brier v. Kay (1796) liii
Brigstock v. Stanion (1697) 248
Bristow v. Eastman (1794) 175
Bristow v. Wright (1781) .... xxxv n. 26, 327
Brook, *Ex parte* (1798) **185**
Brooke v. Crowther (1795) 212, **243**
Broughton v. Langley (1702–03) 180
Brown v. Chapman (1763) 257
   see also Chapman v. Brown (1765)
Brown v. Christfeld (1787) 102
   see also Rose v. Christfield (1787)
Browne v. Heathcote (1745) **16**
Brunigg v. Hanger (1659) .... 137 n. 92
Buggin v. Bennett (1767) 138
Burnett v. Kensington (1794–96) .... lii–liii, lx, **104**
Burstall v. Horner (1797) 199
Busby v. Watson (1776) 327
Bush v. Buckingham (1689) .... 89 n. 2, 98 n. 19
Bush v. Green (1787) **4**
Cage v. Acton (1700) .... xxiv n. 41
Caldwell and Co., Case of (1850) 193–194
Callahand v. Skerret (1796) **135**
Calland [Cailland] v. Champion (1797) .... lii, **171**
Calland v. Troward (1794) 111
Callonel v. Brigggs (1703) 238, 241–43
Calvert v. Bovill (1798) 306–307
Calze v. Lyttelton (1774) .... xxx n. 95
Cambridge University Case (1712) .... xxxiv n. 20
Camden, Lord v. Home (1791) .... 85 n. 96
   see also Home v. Lord Camden (1792)
Campbell v. Jones (1796) 242
Camplin v. Bullman (1761) .... xxxiii n. 19
Canterbury, Archbishop of v. Grocers' Company (1771) 117–118
Carey's [Carus] Case (1605) .... 206 n. 17, 207

394 TABLE OF CASES

Carr v. Shaw and Price (1797) **170**
Carrington v. Taylor (1809) .... xxiv n. 41
Carty v. Ashley (1773) 3
Carruthers's Case, *see* Sparrow v. Carruthers (1768)
    see also Pearson v. Carruthers (1768)
Casey v. Donald (1799) lii
Castle v. Litchfield (1668) .... xxxiv n. 20
Caudell v. Shaw (1791) 225, 231
Cave v. Otway (1797) xxviii
Chaloner v. Davis (1704) .... 237 n. 4
Chambers [Chambre] v. Robinson (1726) .... xliii, 375
Chancery v. Needham (1737) .... xxvi n. 69
Chandler v. Blundell (1796) **138**
Chapman v. Brown (1765) .... 256 n. 47, 257, 259–260
    see also Brown v. Chapman (1763)
Chatfield v. Paxton (1798) **192**
Cheap v. East India Co. (1797) **169**
Chelsea Waterworks Co. v. Cooper (1795) **65**
Cherrington v. Abney (1709) .... .20
Chesterfield, Lord v. Janssen (1750) 69
Chichester v. Lethbridge (1738) .... xxxiv n. 20
Child v. Danbridge [Dandridge] (1688) 57
Christian v. Selby (1798) **182**
Christie v. Secretan (1799) .... .306
Church v. Edwards (1787) **35**
Cinque Ports, Case of (1582) .... 150 n. 18
Claire, Earl of v. Perry (1799) **201**
Clarke v. Clement (1796) .... **106,** 162 n. 38
Clarke [Clerk] v. Udal (1702) 375
Clason v. Simmonds (1741) xxxiii
Claxton v. Basty (1703) .... 174 n. 59
Clay v. Willan (1789) 145
Clayton v. Adams (1796) 225–226
Clotworth v. Kingland (1536) .... 48 n. 33
Cock Lane Ghost, Case of (1762) 67, 77
Cole v. Hawkins (1714) xxxv
Colkett v. Freeman (1787) 153
Collet, Lord v. Keith (1798–1802) .... 179 n. 71, 213, 267–273, **273**
Collier v. Butler Danvers (1796) **157**
Collingwood v. Pace (1661–64) 72
Collins v. Collins (1759) .... 19 n. 42
Collins v. Hooper (1796) **136**
Colson v. Telly (1796) **132**
Combe v. Pitt (1763–65) .... xxvii, 136
Compton v. Collinson (1790) 223–224, 227, 229, 232
Conal v. Hawkins (1795) **64**
Cook v. Raven (1787) .... 60, 182 n. 78, 195 n. 4
Cooper v. Chitty and Backiston (1756) .... 57 n. 54, 70 n. 81
Cooper v. Monk (1737) 280

TABLE OF CASES

Corbett [Corbell] v. Poelnitz (1785) 214–215, 223–226, 231–232
Cornelius v. Hughes (1680) 308
Cornwallis v. Savery (1759) 19
Cosser v. Varnham (1794) **58**
Court v. Martineau (1782) . . . . xxii n. 36
Cowan v. Berry (1798) . . . . liv, **183**
Cowan v. Phillips (1797) . . . . liv, 184 n. 80
Cox v. Godsalve (1700) . . . . xxiv n. 41
Crawford [Crauford] v. Hunter (1798–99) **198**
Crepps v. Durden (1777) . . . . xxxiv n. 21
Creswell v. Hoghton (1795) . . . . xxvi n. 68
Crosby v. Wadsworth (1805) . . . . xxiv n. 41
Crossley v. Shaw (1776) . . . . xxxiv n. 21
Cumber v. Wayne [Wane] (1719) 14
Cumberland, Duke of v. Lord Grosvenor (1770) 377
Cutter v. Powell (1795) 135
Dale v. Hall (1750) 86
Dalton v. Lambert (1796) . . . . **146**, 166 n. 46
Danell's Case (1661) . . . . 137 n. 93
 see also Anonymous (1661)
Davenport's Case (1610) 117
Davenport's Case (1784) 355
Davis v. Barbour (1794) **49**
Davis v. Mason (1793) 245, 247
Davis v. Mazzinghi (1787) 8
Davis v. Norton (1726) 256
Davis's [Davy's] Case (1560) . . . . 206 n. 17, 207
Dawson's Case (1566) 207
Dawson v. Myer (1726) . . . . 237 n. 4
Day v. Allen (1798) **190**
Dearly [Deerly] v. Duchess of Mazarine (1696) 223, 226, 228, 230, 232
Deeze, *Ex parte* (1748) 16
De Gaillon v. de Laigle (1798) 228
De Garrow v. Galbraith (1795) **87**
De La Cour v. Read (1794) 53
De Vignier v. Swanson (1798) **191**
Delves v. Franco (1795) **81**
Den, *ex dim.* Gaskin v. Gaskin (1777) . . . . 255 n. 40
Denn, *ex dim.* Webb v. Puckly (1793) . . . . xxvi n. 68
De Pienne Case, *see* Franks v. Duchess de Pienne (1797)
De Souza v. Ewer (1789) 308
Dent v. Weston (1798) **195**
Derby, Mayor of, Case (n.d.) 364
Digby v. Forbes and Grant (1787) **18**
Dod v. Herbert (1655) . . . . 174 n. 59
Dodsworth v. Bowen (1793) 97
Doe, *ex dim.* —— [*sic*] v. Roe (1794) **55**
Doe, *ex dim.* Barnard and Fenton v. Reason (1755) xxviii
Doe, *ex dim.* Bayntun v. Watton (1776) xxxviii

Doe, *ex dim.* Blackborough v. Blackborough (1798) **179**
Doe, *ex dim.* Browne v. Holmes and Longmore (1771) . . . . xxiv n. 42, xxviii
Doe, *ex dim.* Candler v. Smith (1798) . . . . xxxv n. 21, 260 n. 62
Doe, *ex dim.* Church and Phillips v. Perkins (1790) . . . . xxviii n. 79
Doe, *ex dim.* Fenhouse v. Carver (1797) **173**
Doe, *ex dim.* Green v. Taylor (1796) **155**
Doe, *ex dim.* Howe v. Salter (1795) **86**
Doe, *ex dim.* Martin v. Stubbs (1798) **183**
Doe, *ex dim.* Shaw v. Shaw (1796) **156**
Doe v. Davis (1795) . . . . lix n76, **101**
Doe v. Fonnereau (1780) xxvii
Doe v. Kersey (1765) 124
Doe, Lessee of Watson v. Shipphard (1779) . . . . 256 n. 46
Dongel v. Wilson (1769) 188
Dower, Case of (n.d.) 117
Drake v. Mayor of Exon (1666) . . . . 244 n. 21
Dredge v. Bland (1768) 19
Du Bois v. Hole (1708) 228
Ducker v. Wood (1786) 378
Dunnage v. Turton (1797) **170**
Dutch v. Warren (1760) xxiii
Dyke v. Webber (1745) . . . . xxxiv n. 20
Eddowes v. Hopkins (1780) 203
Edie v. East India Co. (1761) . . . . xxxiv n. 21
Eldridge v. Knott (1774) 188
Ellah v. Leigh (1794) 225–226, 232
Ellen v. Rees (1784) 39
Elvis v. Archbishop of York (1619) . . . . 24, 26 n. 71
England, *ex dim.* Syburn v. Slade (1792) . . . . 188 n. 88
Erving v. Peters (1790) . . . . xxiv n. 41
Etriche v. Officer of Revenue (1720) . . . . 70 n. 80
Everingham's Case (1332) 206
Eyre v. Lady Shaftsbury (1722) 48
Farr v. Newman (1792) . . . . 57 n. 54
Farrow v. Chevalier (1700) 248
Feltham v. Cudworth (1702) . . . . 174 n. 59
Fermor's Case (1602) . . . . 24 n. 55
Feron v. Ladd (1799) . . . . 195 n. 2
Ferrers, Lord, Case of (1797) 170
Fitz-Hugh v. Dennington (1704) . . . . 19 n. 43
Fitzwalter, Lord, Case of (1675) 364
Fleetwood v. Eliot (1794) **41**
Folkes v. Chad (1782–83) xxii
Folliott v. Owen (1789) . . . . 27 n. 76
Fonnereau v. Fonnereau (1748) . . . . 6 n. 11
Forward v. Pittard (1785) 86
Fowle v. Newton (1795) **68**
Fowler v. Kimes (1797) **176**
Foxcroft v. Devonshire (1760) 17

Franco v. Franco (1794)	**59**
Franks v. Duchess de Pienne (1797)	224, 226, 228
French, *Ex parte* (1705)	xxiv n. 42
French v. Backhouse (1771)	xxxvi
Frogmorton v. Wharrey (1770)	xxiv n. 51
Fulham v. Downer (1788)	193
Gammon v. Contie (n.d.)	38
Garrells v. Kensington (1799)	**204**, 305 n. 20
Garth v. Cotton (1753)	xxiv n. 43
Geary v. Connop (1693)	136
George v. Baxter (1796)	**146**
Geyer v. Aguilar 1(798)	305, 308–309
Gibbon v. Bond (1731)	23 n. 49
Gibson v. Hearne (1787)	3
Gibson v. Minet (1791)	xl n. 55
Gilchrist v. Brown (1792)	225 n. 47, 231 n. 71
Giles v. Hutchings (1794)	**60**
Gillingham's Case (1631)	207
Gilpin's Case (1629)	xxxi n. 2
Girling's [Gerling's, Griling's] Case (1610)	206 n. 17
see also Oldfield v. Girling (1610)	
Gist v. Mason (1786)	xxiv n. 47, xxv
Glazebrook v. Woodrow (1799)	233, 234 n. 99
Glover v. Stokes (1794)	**61**
Glyn v. Baker (1811)	xxvii n. 73
Goddard v. Vanderheyden (1771)	xxiv n. 49, 244
Goddart v. Grey (n.d.)	372
Goden [Godin] v. Royal Exchange Assurance Co. [London Assurance Co.] (1758)	16
Godwin & Co. v. De Heine *see* Goodwyn v. Dechair	
Goldswain's Case (1778)	52
Goodisson v. Nunn (1792)	238
Goodman v. Goodright (1759)	xxvii
Goodtitle, *ex dim.* Bailey [Bayley] v. Pugh (1787)	**5**
Goodwin v. Crowle (1775)	19 n. 41
Goodwin v. Parry (1792)	100
Goodwyn v. Dechair (1795)	**65**
Gordon v. Harpur (1795)	lx, **134**
Govier v. Hancock (1796)	226, 231 n. 72
Grant v. Vaughan (1764)	xxvi n. 67
Grayson v. Atkinson (1752)	255
Green's Case (1602)	25
Green v. Farmer (1768)	16
Green v. Mayor of Liverpool (1797)	**168**
Green v. Young (1703)	266
Gregson v. Gilbert (1783)	xxii
Grimly v. Fawlkingham (1691)	188 n. 84
Grinham v. Horsfield (1797)	174 n. 58
Groome, *Ex parte* (1744)	244

Grosvenor, Lord v. Duke of Cumberland (1770)	372
Gulston, *Ex parte* (1753)	153
Gurneth v. Derry (1684)	137 n. 90
Hadogen, Case of (n.d.)	310
Hales v. Taylor (1726)	59
Hallet v. Mears (1810)	xxxi n. 2
Hamilton, *Ex parte* (1796)	**139**
Hansel v. Edwards (1796)	**155**
Hardy v. Born (1794)	19 n. 42
Harper v. Carr (1797)	**178**
Harris, *Ex parte* (1796)	**154**
Harris v. Rene (1734)	xxxiv n. 21
Harris v. Woolford (1795–96)	**99**
Hart v. Bassett (1681)	50
Hart v. Lovelace (1795)	186
Hartley v. Smith (1794)	**50**
Harvey v. Rugg (1799)	**208**
Hatchett v. Baddeley (1776)	229, 231–232
Havelock v. Geddes (1810)	xxvii n. 73
Hawkins v. Lukin (1796)	li, **152**
Haycraft v. Creasy (1801)	xlix
Hayford v. Andrews (1599)	14 n. 24
Heathcote v. Crookshanks (1787)	15 n. 33
Heathfield v. Cleland (1799)	**208**
Herring v. Durant (1747)	79 n. 91
Herriot v. Stewart (1796)	liii, **136**
Hickman v. Fish (1624)	162 n. 37
Hier v. Angerstein (1796)	**155**
Hilton v. Smith (1704)	237 n. 4
Hodges [Higden] v. Williamson (1731)	244 n. 21
Hogan v. Jackson (1775)	255
Holbrook's Case (1339)	206
Holditch [Houlditch] v. Mist (1721)	28, 30, 31 nn. 85, 86
Holland v. Jarvis (1799)	**200**
Holland v. Johnson (1792)	53
Holland v. Smith (1787)	**13**
Holman [Holmer] v. Viner (1794)	lix, **56**
Holt v. Scarisbrick (1668)	243
Holt v. Schofield (1796)	**137**
Home v. Lord Camden (1795)	**85**
see also Camden, Lord v. Home (1791)	
Hornby v. Houlditch (1737)	xxiv n. 47
How v. Isaac (1799)	**202**
Howel v. Hanforth (1772)	162
Howell v. Barnes (1634)	48
Hubert v. Groves (1794)	lix, **50**
Huckle v. Money (1763)	371
Hudson v. Hudson (1678)	135
Huggins v. Bumbridge (1740)	xxxiv n. 20

TABLE OF CASES

Hughes v. Mayre (1789) . . . . 167 n. 48
Hughes v. Thomas (1811) . . . . xxiv n. 43
Hulme v. Tenant (1778) . . . . 224 n. 43, 231 n. 79
Hunt v. Bourne (1703) . . . . xxiv n. 41
Hunter v. Lord de Loraine (1772) 131
Huntley v. Roper (1574) 259
Hurry v. Watson (1786–87) . . . . xl–xlvi, lxi n. 91, 5 n. 9, **10, 315**
Hussey v. Wilson (1793) 53
Hutchins v. Kenrick (1760) 202
Hyde v. Price (1797) 231
Hyde v. Whiskard (1800) . . . . xxxiv n. 20
Isaac v. Isaac (1795) **68**
Iveson v. Moore (1698) 50
Jackson v. Gisling (1742) xxvii
Jackson v. Williamson (1788) xliv
James v. Rutlech (1599) . . . . 137 n. 91
Jansen v. Stewart [J'Anson v. Stuart] (1787) 245
Jaques v. Withy [Whithy] (1787) 37, 107
Jewson v. Read (1773) 231
   see also Read v. Jewson (1773)
Jones's Case (1565) 207
Jones v. Barkley (1781) . . . . xxvi, xxxii, xxxiii, 15, 233 n. 84, 242 n. 12
Jones v. Edwards (1787) **9**
Jones v. Roe (1789) . . . . xxvi n. 67, xxxv
Jones v. Lord Say and Seal (1729) 180
Jones v. Sheriffe (1787) **38**
Jones v. Squire (1795) **62**
Jones v. Williams (1779) 246, 248
Jorden v. Atwood (1605) . . . . 177 n. 66
Judd v. Evans (1795) 78
Julian v. Showbrooke (1753) 58
Karlisle's Case (1345) 206
Karver v. James (1741) . . . . xxiv n. 46
Keppel v. Palliser (1779) . . . . 345 n. 4, 374
   see also Palliser v. Keppel (1779)
Kingston v. Preston (1773) . . . . xxxii, xxxiii, 233–234, 242
Kinloch v. Craig (1789) 170
Kinsey v. Heyward (1699) . . . . 99 n. 24
Kirby and Addington (n.d.) 363
Knightly v. Marrow (1682) . . . . 138 n. 98
Koops v. Chapman (1790) liii
Lamii v. Sewell (1750) . . . . 39 n. 13
Lancashire v. Killingsworth (1702) 238, 241
Lane v. Cotton (1702) . . . . xxiv n. 41
Lang, *Ex parte* (1796) **159**
Langston v. Cotton (1795) **78**
Latkow v. Eamer (1795) . . . . 57 n. 53
Lavie v. Phillips (1765) 231
Lawrence v. Boswell (1753) 369

TABLE OF CASES

Layng v. Paine (1745) . . . . xxxiv n. 20
Lea v. Exelby (1602) 239–242
Leacroft, *Ex parte* (1797) **167**
Leak v. Bishop of Coventry and Babington (1601) . . . . 26 n. 70
Leake v. Day (1787) **12**
Leake v. Lord Pigot (1769) 193–194
Lean v. Schutz (1778) 229, 232
Le Cras v. Hughes (1782) . . . . xxii n. 35
Lee v. Raynes (1663) xxxv
Legard v. Johnon (1797) 230
Legatt v. Tollervey (1811) . . . . xxxi n. 2
Leith v. Pope (1779) 370, 377
Le Mesurier v. Parry (1795) **84**
Lewis & Potter, Assignees of v. Assignees of Livesey, Hargrave, & Co.
 (1797) . . . . 162 n. 40
Lewis v. Price (1761) . . . . 189 n. 89
Light v. Middleton (1796) **154**
Lindo v. Corbett (1785) 39
Loddington v. Kime (1695) . . . . xxiv n. 42
London Assurance Co. v. Sainsbury (1783) . . . . xxii n. 35
London Wharfs, Case of (1766) . . . . xxiv n. 51
Lovelace v. Cockett (1627) . . . . 14 n. 26
Lovelace v. Curry (1798) . . . . xxviii n. 79
Lowe v. Peers (1768) 154
Lowndes v. Horne (1778) . . . . xxiii n. 40
Lucky v. Bradley (1786) . . . . 39 n. 17
Ludford v. Barber (1786) . . . . xxiv n. 47
Lumley, Lord, Case of (1609) 72
Luttrel's Case (1601) 188
Mainwaring v. Devon (1787) **36**
Mainwaring v. Sands (1772–73) . . . . 231 n. 73
Maitland v. Graham (1797) **175**
Manning v. Williams (1740) 8
Marlow v. Smith (1723) . . . . 231 n. 77
Marnel, *Ex parte* (1799) **199**
Marriot v. Hanson [Hampton] (1797) 193
Marshall's Case (1773) . . . . 167 n. 48
Marshall v. Rutton (1800) 212–216, **216**
Marryat v. Wilson (1799) . . . . 179 n. 71, 198 n. 6
Martin, *Ex parte* (1795) **89**
Martin v. Smith (1805) xxxix
Martin v. Strachan (1743) . . . . xxvi n. 66
Master v. Fuller (1792) . . . . 231 n. 80
Masterman v. Grant (1794) 92
Matthews v. Phillips (1713) . . . . xxiv n. 42
May v. Shaftoe (1795) **103**
Mayne v. Walter [Walters] (1782) 304–306, 308–311
Maynell v. Saltmarsh (1665) 50
Mazarine, Duchess, Case of, *see* Dearly [Deerly] v. Duchess of Mazarine

TABLE OF CASES

McNeil v. Wiltshire (1796) 1
Mead v. Robinson (1743) .... xxiv n. 46
Mead, Mary, Case of *see* R. v. Mead (1758)
Medcalf v. Hall (1783) .... xxii n. 33
Meekins v. Smith (1791) .... 175 n. 61
Mercer v. Cooke (1787) **14**
Mercurius, The (1798) .... 310 n. 29
Merrit v. Rane (1721) .... 238–239, 241, 242 n. 14
Michel v. Cue [Coe] (1758) 163
Middleton v. Croft (1736) .... xxiv n. 51
Milborn Port, Constables, Case of (1740) .... xxiii n. 40
Milborne v. Dunmow, Inhabitants of (1656) .... 24 n. 60
Milbourn v. Ewart (1793) .... xxiv n. 41
Miller v. Toslin (1795) **80**
Mills v. Head (1817) xxxix
Mitchel v. Edie (1787) 266
Mitchel v. Reynold (1711) 245
Moffat v. Hargraves and Chambers (1795) **88, 97**
Monroe v. Elliot [Elliott] (1787) .... xli, **4**, 10 n. 16, 375 n. 24, 379 n. 30
Montiero v. Clarke (1787) **3**
Moore v. Bishop of Norwich (1585) 24
Morse v. Foote (1794) **41**
Morton v. Lamb (1797) 212, 233–235, **235**
Moses v. MacFerlan (1760) .... xxiii, 194
Moss v. Birch (1794) **53**
Moulin v. Dutton (1795) 201
Munro v. Spinks (1799) **204**
Murray, Case of (1794) **55**, 145
Murray v. Harding (1773) .... 89 n. 5, 98
Nash v. Edwards (1588) 124
Nesbitt v. Lushington (1792) 105
Nevison v. Whitby (1637) 89, 98
Newcoman v. Bethlehem Hospital [Newcoman v. Barkham] (1741) .... 6 n. 11
Newstead v. Keys (1799) **202**
Newton v. Lewis (1741) .... xxxiv n. 20
Nicholas v. Beyer (1787) **12**
Nichols v. Pawlett (1694) .... 37 n. 7
Norris v. Rozle (1787) **20**
Norwood v. Norwood and Reed (1556) 240
Nottingham v. Jennings (1700) .... xxxiv n. 20, 7
Oates v. Miles (1795) **88**
Oldfield and Girling's Case (1610) .... 206 n. 17
    see also Girling's Case (1610)
Oldham v. Hughes (1742) .... 255 n. 37
Oldham v. Peake (1774) .... 138 n. 96
Oswald v. Legh (1786) 188
Owen v. Warburton (1805) xliv
Oxford University, Case of (1613) .... 116 n. 57
Packer v. Welsted (1658) .... 177 n. 65

Palliser v. Keppel (1779)	374
see also Keppel v. Palliser (1779)	
Palmer v. Fletcher (1663)	177 n. 65
Paris v. Stroud & *ux.* (1745)	8
Parke v. Carter (1787)	**16**
Parker v. Nevil and Wood (1614)	37 n. 9
Parkinson, *Ex parte* (1794)	**51**
Parkinson v. Gilchrist (1799)	**197**
Patchett v. Bancroft (1797)	**174**
Paul v. Shaw (1710)	xxxiii n. 19
Peake v. Oldham (1775)	138 n. 97
Pearson v. Carruthers (1768)	223 n. 41
see also Sparrow v. Carruthers (1768)	
Peeters v. Opie (1648)	237 n. 4
Perkins v. Kempland (1776)	244 n. 22
Perry v. Campbell (1789)	182
Perry v. Nicholson (1757)	59
Perryn v. Blake (1770)	71
Peters v. Opie (1671–72)	237 n. 4
Philips v. Cheki (1784)	19
Philips v. Fowler (1735)	364
Phillips v. Lord Falkland (1795)	lv-lvi
Phillips v. Fowler (1735)	364
Phipps v. Burgess (1790)	xlix
Pickering v. Barkley (1648)	134 n. 79
Pigot v. Dunn (1796)	**145**
Piggot v. Penrice (1717)	255
Pitt's Case (1733)	xxiv n. 41, xxxiii n. 19
Platt v. Knowles (1794)	49, **50**
see also Anonymous (1794)	
Pollard v. Bell (1800)	xxxvi-xxxvii, 213, **290**
Pope v. St Leger (1693)	68
Porchester, Lord, Case of (1783)	38
Pordage v. Cole (1668)	237 n. 4, 242
Posthwaite, Case of (n.d.)	227
Potts v. Bell (1800)	xxxiii n. 19
Pouchee v. Lieven (1815)	xxxix
Prescot v. Phillips (1798)	**187**
Preston, *Ex parte* (1772)	228
Preston v. Funnel (1739)	xxxiv n. 20
Price v. Goodrick (1653)	37 n. 8
Priest v. Pidgeon (1772)	xliv n. 81
Pritchard v. Pugh (1779)	xxv, xxvi n. 64
Pritchard v. Stevens (1796)	**147**
Prugnell v. Gosse (1648)	245
Pugh v. Goodtitle (1787)	5 n. 10
Pugh v. Leeds (1777)	xxxviii
Pyke v. Bishop of Bath and Wells (1787)	**20**
Quarrier v. Rousselet (1796)	**119**

TABLE OF CASES

Quart v. Santel (n.d.) 369
Rawlings v. Parry (n.d.) . . . . xxxiv n. 21
Rawson v. Johnson (1801) 233–234, 239
Raynes v. Chevalier (1797) . . . . 164 n. 44
Raynes v. Spicer (1797) **163**
Raynes v. Twogood (1796) . . . . 164 n. 44
Read v. Jewson (1773) 231
Read v. Parsons (1794) **40**
Reading v. Royston (1702) 75
Real v. Macky (1744) . . . . 39 n. 15
Rees v. Rose (1798) **185**
R. v. —— [*sic*] (1795) **83**
R. v. Aitkin (1795) **87**
R. v. Amery (1787) 151
R. v. Anglesey, Justices of (1796) **139**
R. v. Baker (1762) 160
R. v. Barrington (1787) . . . . 93 n. 11
R. v. Bayley (1734) 151
R. v. Beard (1796) **143**
R. v. Beeston (1789) 48
R. v. Bellringer (1792) 151
R. v. Blooer (1760) 160
R. v. Blyer (1797) **170**
R. v. Booth (1796) **106**
R. v. Bosworth (1739) . . . . xxiv n. 51
R. v. Bowes (1796) . . . . xxxii n. 10, **153**
R. v. Boycot (1789) . . . . xxiii n. 40
R. v. Braziers' and Armourers' Co. (1795) **94**
R. v. Bristow (1797) **167**
R. v. Brown (1798) **191**
R. v. Cambridgeshire, Justices of (1795) **66**
R. v. Church Middleton, Inhabitants of (1797) **164**
R. v. Clarkson (1721) . . . . 144, 145 n. 7
R. v. Cole (1796) . . . . xxvi n. 66
R. v. College of Physicians (1796) **140**
R. v. Coombe (1797) **161**
R. v. Cooper (1797) . . . . 161 n. 36
R. v. County of Lancaster, Chancellor of (1794) **52**
R. v. County of Oxford, Inhabitants of (1811) . . . . xxxi n. 2
R. v. Court of Requests of the Tower Hamlet (1795) **102**
R. v. Crossley (1795–96) **103, 148, 158**
R. v. Cudlipp (1796) . . . . 141 n. 3
R. v. Cumberland, Justices of (1795) **70**
  see also R. v. Skelton
R. v. Curtis (1796) **107**
R. v. Cutcliffe (1795) **101**
R. v. Delaval (1763) 145
R. v. Delme (1714) . . . . 150 n. 19
R. v. Doherty (1810) . . . . xxxi n. 2

R. v. Dolben (1796) **139**
R. v. Dorset, Justices of (1797) **160**
R. v. East Rutford, Bailiffs &c. (1796) **151**
R. v. Edie (1795) . . . . 68 n. 77
R. v. England (1795–96) **92, 104**
R. v. Epps (1794) **53**
R. v. Essex, Sheriff of (1796) **106**
R. v. Lord Falkland (1796) **131**
R. v. Fonseca (1757) . . . . xxxiv n. 20
R. v. Foote (1776) . . . . 359 n. 8
R. v. Forey, Steward of the Manor of (1795) **69**
R. v. Fox (1755) . . . . xxvi n. 66
R. v. Gee (1796) **143**
R. v. Gibbon (n.d.) 151
R. v. Ginever (1796) **150**
R. v. Grindley (1796–97) **150, 166**
R. v. Grist (1796) **148**
R. v. Haffendem (1795) **68**
R. v. Hamlyn (1799) **207**
R. v. Harris (1797) . . . . xxvi n. 67
R. v. Head (1770) . . . . 151 n. 20
R. v. Henderson (1798) **191**
R. v. Hills (1796) **147**
R. v. Hooper (1796) **104**
R. v. Horne (1777) . . . . 137 n. 89
  see also R. v. Tooke (1794)
R. v. Isaac and Jacob (1796) **105**
R. v. Jarvis (1756) . . . . xxxv n. 21
R. v. Joden (1795) **63**
R. v. Johnson (1729) . . . . 92, 93 n. 11, 145
R. v. Jones (1703) . . . . xxxiv n. 21
R. v. Jones (1726) . . . . xxvi n. 66
R. v. Kelly (1796) **156**
R. v. Kidd Wake (1795–96) **94, 138**
R. v. Lancaster, Justices of (1795) **83**
R. v. Leigh (1768) . . . . 151 n. 20
R. v. London, Bishop of (1811) . . . . xxxi n. 2
R. v. London, Sheriffs of (1794) **51**
R. v. Luck (1795) **97**
R. v. Luffe (1807) . . . . xxxi n. 2
R. v. Lui (1796) **104**
R. v. Maltravers, Lady (1565) 232
R. v. Mariot (1797) **168**
R. v. Martyr (1810) . . . . xxxi n. 2
R. v. Mawbey (1796) **133, 151**
R. v. May (1770) . . . . xxxiv n. 20
R. v. McCan (1796) **138**
R. v. Mead (1758) 224, 227, 229
R. v. Metcalfe (1794) **61**

TABLE OF CASES

R. v. Middlesex, Sheriff of (1797) **165**
R. v. Middleton (1786) 83
R. v. Monday (1777) 63
R. v. Moseley (1797–98) **172, 179, 181**
R. v. Munday (1794) **51**
R. v. Munoes (1742) . . . . xxxiv n. 21
R. v. Munton (1794) **54**
R. v. Muscle (1795) **69**
R. v. Myers (1786) 132
R. v. Oxford (1795) **65**
R. v. Oxford, Bishop of (1806) xxx
R. v. Parry (1811) . . . . xxxi n. 2
R. v. Parsons (1762) . . . . 67 n. 73
R. v. Pasmore (1789) . . . . xxiv nn. 43, 47
R. v. Preston, Select Vestry of (1797) **167**
R. v. Price (1795) . . . . xxvi n. 66
R. v. Ramsay (1795) . . . . **66, 77,** 157 n. 33
R. v. Reed (1795) **82**
R. v. Rhodes (1721) 143, 161
R. v. Robinson (1765) . . . . xxvi n. 66
R. v. Roddam (1777) 91
R. v. St Andrew's (Holborn), Churchwardens of (1799) **196**
R. v. St Asaph, Bishop of (1752) . . . . 132 n. 76
R. v. St Mary in Cardigan, Inhabitants of (1794) . . . . 55 n. 45
R. v. St Michael, Inhabitants of (1770) xxix
R. v. St Michael's of Bath, Inhabitants of (1781) . . . . xxxiv n. 20
R. v. Sarum, Dean and Chapter of (1795) 91
R. v. Seaforth, Corporation of (1796) **147**
R. v. Sharpness (1787) . . . . xxvii n. 74
R. v. Sidney (1742) . . . . xxxiv n. 20
R. v. Simmons see R. v. Symonds (1752)
R. v. Skelton (1796) . . . . li n. 24, **157**
R. v. Smith (1795) **64**
R. v. Smith (1796) 145
R. v. Smith (1797) **163**
R. v. Soper (1793) 179, 181
R. v. Spettigue (1796) **141**
R. v. Marquis of Stafford (1790) 160
R. v. Stevens (1798) **184**
R. v. Steward (1799) **195**
R. v. Stewart (1796) **143**
R. v. Stone (1795) 93
R. v. Stone (1801) . . . . xxviii n. 79, xxxv n. 21
R. v. Symonds [Simmons] (1752) 364, 369
R. v. Taylor (1765) . . . . xxxiv n. 20
R. v. Lord Thanet (1799) . . . . **200,** 202 n. 11, **205**
R. v. Thirkell (1765) xliv
R. v. Tooke (1794) 61
R. v. Trapshaw (1786) xxv

R. v. Truro, Burgesses of (1794) **60**
R. v. Underwood (1794) **59**
R. v. Uttoxeter (1732) xxx
R. v. Lady Valentia (1796) **144**
R. v. Vipont (1761) .... xxvi n. 67
R. v. Wakefield (1758) .... xxxiv n. 21
R. v. Watts Horton (1786) 83
R. v. Webb (1797) **160**
R. v. Wenfold (1797) **176**
R. v. Willes (1748) .... xxxiii n. 19
R. v. Williams (1796) **145**
R. v. Wooster (1796) **159**
R. v. Wyndham (1716) .... 106 n. 37
R. v. Yorke (1795) **102**
Reynolds v. Berling (1784) 15
Rich v. Parker (1798) 306, 308
Richards v. Bartlett (1584) 14
Richards v. Carvamel (1615) .... 14 n. 25
Richardson v. Cooke (1797) **177**
Ricketts v. Taylor (1798) 1
Riding v. Hayes (1795) **91**
Ringstead v. Lady Lanesborough (1783) .... xxii n. 32, 214–215, 224, 226, 228, 232
Robarts v. Mason (1808) .... xxiv n. 49
Roberts v. Herbert (1660–62) 136
Roberts v. Thomas (1794) **57**
Robertson v. Ewer (1786) 266
Robinson v. Howell (1787) **34**
Roche v. Carey (1772) 8
Rock v. Leighton (1700) .... xxiv n. 41
Rockingham's Case (1664) 207
Roe *ex dim.* Bose v. Blackett (1775) .... 255 n. 41
Roe *ex dim.* Crow v. Baldwere (1793) .... xxvi n. 66
Roe *ex dim.* Dodson v. Grew (1767) .... xxxv n. 21, 256–258
Roe *ex dim.* Nightingale v. Quartley (1787) .... 256 n. 51
Roe *ex dim.* Southall v. Langford (1797) 212, **248**
Roe *ex dim.* Turner v. Doe (1794) **40**
Rogers v. Maylor (1790) 87
Roles v. Rosewell (1794) .... 19 n. 42
Rooswell, *Ex parte* (1795) **80**
Rose v. Bartlett (1633) .... 255 n. 38
Rose v. Christfield (1787) 102
Ross v. Bradshaw (1761) 171
Rotch v. Edie (1795) 265
Russell's Case (1684) .... xxxiii n. 19
Rust v. Cooper (1777) .... xxiv n. 49
Sadler v. Evans (1766) xxix
    see also Windsor, Lady, Case of (1766)
Salucci v. Johnson (1785) 304–305, 311
Salucci v. Woodmass (1784) 307, 309

TABLE OF CASES

Santa Cruz, The (1798)	307, 310 n. 29
Saunders v. Hardinge (1792)	93 n. 12
Savage v. Smith (1775)	xxxv
Sawbridge v. Broughton (1787)	**8**
Sayer v. Verdenhalm (1817)	xxxix
Schinotti v. Bumstead (1796)	**107**
Selby v. Tupper (1787)	**11**
Selwyn v. Selwyn [Selwin v. Selwin] (1760)	xxxv
Servein v. Bishop of Lincoln (*c.* 1597)	26 n. 72
Seven Bishops, Case of the (1688)	201
Shadbolt v. Berthod (1822)	lv n. 49
Sharman v. Strong (1787)	**12**
Shaw v. Hawkins (1736)	**8**
Shaw v. Martin (1795)	**82**
Shipwith [Shipwick] v. Blanchard (1795)	**70**
Shirley v. Wilkinson (1782)	xxii n. 35
Sidney v. Bishop of Gloucester (1564)	116 n. 55
Sikes v. Marshall (1798)	lix n76, **189**
Silvester *ex dim.* Law v. Wilson (1788)	xxxiv n. 20
Simeon v. Thompson (1798)	**195**
Six Carpenters Case (1610)	280
Slade, *Ex parte* (1799)	**197**
Smale v. Hammon (1610)	137 n. 94
Small v. Brackley (1707)	57
Small v. Nairne (1849)	lix n. 75
Smith v. Bowles (1797)	lx, **175**
Smith v. Bromley (1781)	xxvi
Smith v. Hickson (1734)	136
Smith v. Ireland (1787)	**5**
Smith v. Painter (1788)	195 n. 4
Smith v. Parkhouse (1740)	xxiv n. 41
Smith v. Poole (1797)	**162**
Smith v. Shepherd (1795–96)	**85, 132**
Smith v. Woodgale (1797)	**172**
Soulsby v. Neving (1808)	xxxiv n. 20
Sparrow v. Carruthers (1768)	215, 223, 225, 232
see also Pearson v. Carruthers (1768)	
Spiller v. Williams (1795)	**97**
Spires v. Parker (1786)	62 n. 64
Sprigwell v. Allen (1648)	xxiv n. 45, xxxiv n. 20
Spurret v. Spiller (1740)	57
Stanway v. Jennings (1797)	**166**
Stapleton v. Baron de Stark (1754)	8
Stephens v. Tot (1602)	229 n. 66
Stock v. Smith [De Smith] (1735)	59
Stonehouse v. Eliot [Elliot] (1795)	lx, **62**
Stones v. Huertly (1748)	256 n. 49, 258 n. 54
Strathmore, Countess of v. Andrew Robinson Bowles, Esq. (1796)	153 n. 26
Stratton v. Burgiss (1718)	165 n. 45

Strithorst v. Graeme (1770)	39 n. 14
Sullivan v. Montague (1779)	15
Swarbuck v. Wheeler (1749)	8
Sykes v. Potts (1799)	**199**
Syms v. Smith (1629)	248
Tasker v. Geale (1733)	xxiii n. 40
Tassall v. Shane (1590)	14 n. 27
Tatlock v. Harris (1789)	xxvi n. 67
Taylor's Case (n.d.)	134 n. 80
Taylor v. Cole (1789)	280
Tenant v. Hulme (1778)	224
Tench v. Bellis (1797)	**174**
Thompson v. Bristow (1742)	106 n. 38
Thompson v. Buchanan (1782)	17
Thompson v. Hervey (1768)	228
Thorpe v. Clement *see* Clarke v. Clement (1796)	
Thorpe v. Thorpe (1701–02)	237, 242
Thwaits v. Angerstein (1798)	lii
Tinkler v. Poole (1770)	70 n. 82
Tissor's Case *see* Belknap, Lady, Case of (1400)	
Todd [Tod] v. Stokes (1699)	228
Tooke, John Horne's Case *see* R. v. Tooke (1794)	
Torrey v. Adey (1611)	231 n. 70
Townsend, Lord v. Hughes (1677)	xlii, 371
Trent Navigation, Proprietors of the v. Wood (1785)	86
Tribe v. Gaman (1797)	**168**
Troward v. Calland (1795–96)	**111**
Tully v. Sparkes (1728)	244 n. 22
Turner v. Goodwin [Goodwyn] (1713)	xxxiii n. 16, 239
Turner v. Warren (1737)	42 n. 21
Tylle v. Peirce (1634–35)	224 n. 42
Ughtred's [Ughred's] Case (1591)	238
Vaise v. Delaval (1785)	xliv n. 78, xlv, 369, 375
Vaspor v. Edwards [Eddowes] (1702)	xxiv n. 42
Vat v. Green (1726)	39 n. 16
Vigers v. Aldrich (1769)	37, 106
Voght v. Elgin (1798)	**181**
Waddington v. Thellwell (1763)	xxv, xxvi n. 64
Wagstaff, *ex dim.* Tunnent v. Rooke (1787)	**11**
Waller's Case [Sir William] (1634)	206 n. 17, 207
Walter v. Drew (1723)	7
Walwyn v. Thomas (1795)	**81**
Ward v. McCauley (1791)	134
Ward v. Petifer (1634)	202
Ward v. Walthew (1607)	177 n. 65
Warren v. Hall (1787)	9
Watson v. Bingley (1799)	**200**
Webb v. Brown (1797)	**161**
Webb v. Goff (1797)	**174**

Welch v. Hole (n.d.)	63
Weller v. Cheeseman (1787)	**4**
Wellington v. Arters (1792)	189
Wenman v. Taylor (1796)	**120**
Weyland's Case (129)	230
Whitchurch v. Edwards (1787)	**13**
Whitehead v. Vaughan (1785)	16
Whitley v. Learcroft (1796)	**153**
Wilford v. Berkeley [Buckley] (1758)	372
Wiggins v. Ingleton (1705)	136 n. 84
Wilkinson v. Brown (1795)	**102**
Wilkinson v. Wilkinson (1795)	**79**
Williams v. Jacques (1787)	**37**
Williams v. Williams (1795)	**86**
Williamson v. Allison (1802)	xxiv n. 45, xxxiv n. 20
Willis v. Lewis (1743)	3
Willis v. Poole (1780)	171
Wilson v. Campbell (1779)	229
Wilson v. Kensington (1798)	**178, 181,** 198 n. 6, 267 n. 66
Wilson v. Maryat [Maryatt] (1797–99)	179 n. 71, **198,** 267–268, 271–273, 280
Winch v. Keeley (1787)	15
Winchcombe v. Pulleston (1617)	25–26
Winchester, *Ex parte* (1744)	244
Windsor, Lady, Case of (1766)	xxix n. 89
see also Sadler v. Evans (1766)	
Witham v. Hill (1759)	xxvi n. 68
Withnell v. Gartham (1794)	lix, lx n. 82, **47**
Wood v. Gunston (1655)	378
Woodley v. Bishop of Exeter (1624)	114–118
Woodyear's [Woodier's] Case (1743)	152–153
Worley v. Lee (1787)	100 n. 26
Wright v. Good (1681)	358
Wright v. Nutt (1786–87)	**27,** 31 n. 86
Wright v. Simpson (1801)	31 n. 86, 33 n. 3
Wyatt v. Green (1726)	39 n. 16
Wyllie v. Wilkes (1780)	244 n. 22
Wyndham v. Chetwynd (1757)	124
Wynn v. Crowninghshield (1795)	**82**
Yarmouth, Mayor of v. Eaton (1763)	151 n. 20
Yates v. Groves (1791)	58
York, Archbishop of v. Duke of Newcastle (1705)	xvi n. 13

INDEX OF PERSONS AND PLACES

Abbott (Abbot), Charles (later Baron Tenterden, C.J.K.B.), of the Inner Temple, 138
Aberdeen, Aberdeenshire, 141 n. 2
Abingdon, earl of, *see* Bertie, Willoughby
Abney, Sir Thomas, B. Ex., J.C.P., xxiv, xxxiv n. 20
Adair, James
   serjeant-at-law, xlii, xl, xlv, 8–9, 16, 20, 36–38, 40, 42, 60, 93, 158 n. 34, 323, 325, 329, 349, 365, 368–369, 372, 374–375, 379, 381
   chief justice of Chester, 187
Adam, William, of the Inner Temple, 267, 280–286
Adams
   Philip, counsel, 166
   Thomas, 205
Adcock, Christopher, 317
Africa, 119, 270, 288
Alderson
   Edward, B.Ex., 315
   Robert, student of Lincoln's Inn, xl–xli, 10 n. 15, 52, 315–316
Alexander, John Reason, 11–12
Allen, John Wilson, 317
Alpe, Hammond, 317
Ambler, Charles, his reports, xviii
America, 28 n. 80, 29, 32, 38, 93, 198 n. 6, 288
Amory
   Frances, 21
   John, 22–23
   Prudence and husband John, 20–23
   William, 22–24
Anderson, Edmund, C.J.C.P.
   opinion of, 24
   his reports, 259
Andrews, George, of the Middle Temple, his reports, xx
Anstruther, Alexander, of Lincoln's Inn, his reports, xvi, xvii n. 19
Antigua, island of, 54
Armourers and Braziers, Company of, 96 n. 18
Arnold, Dr James Henry, 122, 130
Ashhurst, Sir William Henry
   J.K.B., xxv n. 55, xlvi, liii, lv, 6 n. 11, 15 n. 28, 54 n. 44, 93 n. 11, 119, 211, 214, 215, 233 n. 85, 303–304
   sittings as a justice of the King's Bench (1794) 47–57, (1794–95) 57–76, (1795) 77–103, 195–208, (1796) 104–108, 131–153, (1797) 154–178, (1798) 178–195
   assize judge, xxxvi, xlii, 10 n. 15, 66, 329, 362
   on continuances, 100 n. 24; on deterrence, 143 n. 5; on gender and punishment, 146 n. 11; on imprisonment, 65; on outlawry, 59; on scandalous libel, 107 n. 41; on universal suffrage, 102 n. 29; on usurious bargain, 98
Ashton, —, of the Middle Temple, 34
Asia, 288
Aspinall, Henry, of the Inner Temple, 248
Atcheson, —, counsel, 133
Athol, dukedom of, 72, 74
Atkins (Atkyns), John Tracey, of Lincoln's Inn, 17 n. 38
Attleborough, Norf, 324, 329
Aylesbury, Bucks, gaol, 159
Aylett, Edward, attorney, xli, 4

Babor
   Catherine, 20
   John, clerk, 20
Bacon, John, 179–180
Bahamas, islands of, 84 n. 95
Baker, Sir George, 140
Baldwin, William, of the Middle Temple, lix, 61, 67
Balguy, John, of the Middle Temple, 52
Bangor
   (diocese) bishop of, 165
   diocese of, 150, 166
Barbados, island of, 152
Barkham, Sir Edward, 6 n. 11
Barlow, Henry, secondary of the King's Bench, 201
Barnardiston, Thomas, serjeant-at-law, xviii, xix
Barnes, Henry, his reports, xviii, xx
Barrow, Thomas, of the Inner Temple, lix, 50, 103, 177

411

Barrymore, earl of, 91
Bartleman, Alexander, ship owner, 331, 348
Barton, H., clerk of the rules in the King's Bench, 60
Bassett, Arthur, 117
Batavia, *see* Jakarta
Bath, Som, 145
Bath and Wells (diocese), bishop of, 20–27
Bathurst, Hon. Henry
  J.C.P., xxiv n. 51
  lord chancellor, 224, 228
Battine, Dr William, 122, 129–130
Bayley, John (later J.K.B. and B.Ex.),
  of Gray's Inn xlvii, 57, 137, 163, 170, 174, 176, 186, 215
  serjeant-at-law, 230–231
Beal, Kennet, 196
Beales, John, 317
Bearcroft, Edward, of the Inner Temple, xx, lxi, 47, 49
Beaufort, duke of, 55
Beaumont
  Henry de, first Baron Beaumont, 71, 74, 76
  Joan de, 71, 76
  John de, first Viscount Beaumont, 71, 76
  William de, second Viscount Beaumont, 71, 76
Bedford, Beds
  duke of, 206
  mayor of, xxiv n. 46
Beecroft, Thomas, 324, 329
Bell, John, attorney, 317, 323, 329, 342–343, 346–349, 363, 379–380
Bellecourt, barony of, 74
Bengal, India, 192
Berkshire, county, a magistrate of, 191
Berney, Sir John, 324
Berry, John, attorney, 317, 323, 344
Bertie, Willoughby, earl of Abingdon, 71
Best, William Draper (later C.J.C.P.), of the Middle Temple, 135
Birch
  T., 53
  William, 329
Bird, William, 84
Birmingham, Warks, 145
Biscoe, J. S., 134–135
Blackborough
  John Steele and sons Henry and William, 180
  William and wife Lydia, 179
Blackburne, —, Dr, physician, 121, 125
Blackstone
  Henry, of the Middle Temple, his reports, xviii, xl n. 55, 29 n. 82, 43 n. 23
  Sir William, his commentaries, 93 n. 11, 224; his reports, xviii, xxi, xxix, xxx, 377; J.K.B., xxx; J.C.P. 71
Blencowe, John, B.Ex., J.C.P., xxiv
Bletchingley, Surrey, 114
Blofield, Norf, 324
Bodmin, Cornwall, gaol, 146
Bolton, James, serjeant-at-law, xlii–xliii, xliv n. 78, xl, 3–5, 8–9, 16, 324, 373–374, 376, 379, 381
Bomner, —, president of the Tribunal of Commerce at Bordeaux, 295
Bond
  George, serjeant-at-law, xl, xlii, xliv n. 78, xlv, 16, 18–19, 35, 41–42, 369, 381
  Nathaniel, 42, 142, 176, 207
  Sylvanus, 21–27
Bordeaux, France, 270, 291, 295
Botany Bay, New South Wales, 351
Bowen (Bowin)
  Ann, 249
  Henry, 249
Bowes, Andrew Robinson, 153
Bowyer, Foster, his case notes, xxii
Bozter, Daniel, 91
Bracton, Henry de, 227
Bradley, Abel, 347
Brest, France, 270
Brew House Yard, London, 196
Brewton, Miles, 27, 31, 33
Bridport, Dorset
  mayor of, 160
  town, 160
Brierly, Thomas, master in Chancery extraordinary, 148, 149 n. 14
Brighton (Brighthelmstone), Sussex, 188
Brooke, Norf, 324
Brooke (Brook), Sir Robert, his abridgment, 206 n. 17
Brougham, Henry, Baron Brougham and Vaux, lord chancellor, xlviii
Brown, William, law reporter, 33 n. 3, 35, 111, 224 n. 43
Buckler, —, clerk, 21
Buller, Francis
  J.C.P., 119, 214, 225, 256, 303, 305
  J.K.B, xxxv–xxxvii, xlvi, 6 n. 11, 16, 83, 100 n. 24, 211
  assize judge, liv, 184, 213, 254
  judge delegate, 122
  his notes of cases, xxii, xxiv, xxvi, xxvii n. 72, xxxi, xxxiv n. 20, xliv n. 81, 188 n. 89, 193 n. 97
  his *Trials at Nisi Prius*, 152

on non-performance of an award, 132; on relationship to Lord Mansfield, xxv, xxxii; on testamentary issues, 128–129
Bulstrode, Edward, his reports, 137, 231
Bulwer, William Wiggett, 324
Bunbury, William, his reports, xvi
Burchall, sheriff, 201 n. 10
Burn, Calvert, 6
Burnet, Thomas, J.C.P., his notes of cases, xxiv, xxxi, xxxiv n. 20
Burrough, James (later J.C.P.), of the Inner Temple, 82, 135, 193
Burrow, Sir James
  of the Inner Temple, 99 n. 24
  his notes of cases, xv–xvi, xx–xxi, xxvi–xxix, xxxiv nn. 20–21, xxxv–xxxv
  on cases unreported, xxi n. 26
Burrow, Robert, law reporter, 99 n. 24
Burton, Francis, justice of Chester, 187
Bury (St Edmund's), Suff, 323
Butler, Anthony, 267, 274, 276–279
Buxton, Robert, 324

Cadiz, Spain, lii
Calcutta, India, 293–295, 301, 306
Cambridge, Cambs
  St John's College, vii
  university, 140–141
Cambridgeshire, county of, 66
Camden, Lord, see Pratt, Sir Charles
Campbell
  John, of Lincoln's Inn, 122
  John, Lord Campbell C.J.K.B., lord chancellor, xiii; his notes of cases xxvii n. 75, xxxvii; as counsel xxxix
Canterbury, archbishop of, 357 n. *
Canton, China, 203–204 n. 14
Cape Colony, south Africa, 267 n. 68
Cape Town, south Africa, 267 n. 68, 283–284
Carr
  Ralph, of the Inner Temple, 302, 306
  Thomas, counsel, xxxvii n. 39
Carthew, Thomas, his reports, xix
Castle Hill, Sheffield, Yorks, 102 n. 29
Chambré, Alan, of Gray's Inn (later B.Ex. and J.C.P.), 49, 134, 140, 141 n. 2, 182, 188, 246
Champion, Alexander, as arbitrator, lvi, 131 n. 73
Cheap
  John, 169
  London, ward of, 217–220, 274–277
Chester
  Ches, 79

  chief justice of, 187
Chew Magna, Som, church of, 20
Chute, Thomas Lobb, 329
Clare, earl of, see Fitzgibbon, John
Clarke, Joseph, 248–249
Clayton
  Sir Kenrick, 112–113, 114, 115
  Ralph, serjeant-at-law, 40
Cleaver, William, of Lincoln's Inn, 103
Clerkenwell, London
  bridewell, 68
  parish of, li, 66, 77
Clifford, Henry, 200, 218
Clive, Edward, B.Ex., J.C.P., xxiv
Cock Lane ghost, 67, 77
Cockell, William, serjeant-at-law, liii, 132
Coke, Sir Edward, C.J.C.P. and C.J.K.B.
  attorney-general, 240
  his writings, 183, 215, 224, 229 n. 67, 230–232, 257
Coe, William Ripper, 329
Colchester, Essex, borough court of, 337
Colebrook, Sir George, 70
Collet, John, 267, 274, 276–279, 282–289
Coltishall, Norf, 324
Colyer, Charles, 317
Comyn, Samuel, of the Middle Temple, xxxix
Comyns, Sir John
  C.B.Ex., 365
  his reports, xvi n. 15, xviii, xix, 7
Const, Francis, of the Middle Temple, 67 n. 73, 168, 195
Cooke
  Sir George, his reports, xviii
  William, 162, 235
Copenhagen, Denmark, 203 n. 14, 291–295, 298–301, 306
Cornwall, county of, 50, 105 n. 34, 143, 197
Cory, Michael, clerk, 21
Coventry,
  Lord, 160
  Warks, 63
Cowes, Isle of Wight, 190
Cowper
  Charles, of the Middle Temple, 277, 279
  Henry, of the Middle Temple, his reports, xxi
  William, Earl Cowper, lord chancellor, 6 n. 11
Cox, Samuel, his reports, 27 n. 76, 59 n. 58
Craig, Sir James, major-general, 267, 281
Cricklade, Wilts
  parish of, liv, 101
  town of, 184

Cromwell, Oliver, 80
Cross, John (later serjeant-at-law), of Lincoln's Inn, 265
Crossley, —, solicitor, liii
Cudmore, Prudence and husband Samuel, 21–23
Cumberland, county of, 173
Cunningham, Timothy, his reports, xx
Custance, John, 324

Dade, Thomas, 352
Dampier, Henry
  of the Middle Temple, 106, 142, 200
  J.K.B., 211
Dann, Richard, counsel, 273–274
Darrel (Dayrill), William, counsel, 63, 136
Dauncey, Philip, 189
Davenport, Sir Thomas, xxii, 355
Death, Zachariah, 329, 369
Dealtry, Henry, clerk of the rules in the King's Bench, 90
De Grey, Sir William
  C.J.C.P., xxiv n. 49, xxxv, 117–118, 244
  on libel, 137 n. 89
Denison, Thomas, J.K.B., xxviii
Denman, Thomas, Baron Denman, C.J.K.B., lix
Denmark, 292, 294–295, 298, 302, 306–307
Denton (Dorton), Alexander, J.C.P., 365
Derby, Lord, *see* Smith-Stanley, Edward
Derbyshire, county of, 235–239
Devaynes, —, apothecary, 121, 125, 128
Didlington, Norf, 317, 329
Diss, Norf, 329, 369
Docking, Norf, 317
Doeg, William, ship's officer, 299
Dolben, Sir William, J.K.B., 43 n. 25
Dorchester, Dorset, gaol, 102
Dorset, county of, 160
Douglas, Sylvester, Baron Glenbervie, his reports, xiv–xv, xxi–xxii, xxvi–xxvii, xxx, xxxv n. 26,
Droitwich, Worcs, parish of St Peter's, 249–250
Dudley, Henry Bate, 80
Dundry, chapel of, 20
Dunn, Ralph, counsel, 273
Dunning, John (later Lord Asburton), of the Middle Temple, xxvii–xxviii
Duntzfield & Co., of Copenhagen, 300
Durnford, Charles, of the Middle Temple
  as editor of reports, xvii, xxxiv n. 20
  his reports, xiv, xx, xxvii n. 74, xl n. 55, lxi, 213

Dutch colonies, 286 n. 1
Dyer, Sir James, C.J.K.B., his reports, 116

Eardley, Sampson, Baron Eardley, 191
East, Edward Hyde, of the Middle Temple, law reporter, xiv, xx, xxvii n. 74, xxviii, xxx–xxxii, xxxiv n. 20, xl n. 55, xliv n. 81, lxi, 34 n. 4, 213, 272
East Dereham, Norf, 317
East Harling, Norf, 329
East Indies, 169, 198 n. 6, 213, 267–271, 280, 291–293, 300
East Lexham, Norf, 317
Edgcumbe, George, earl of Mount Edgcumbe, 176
Edinburgh, Midlothian, 140
Edwards, Bezalom and daughters Hannah and Elizabeth, 35
Egerton, Sir Thomas, Lord Ellesmere, lord chancellor, 227
Eggleston, —, ship's master, 291–295, 298–302, 307–308
Ellenborough, Lord, *see* Law, Edward
Ellesmere, Lord, *see* Egerton, Sir Thomas
Ellis, Sir William, J.C.P., 43 n. 25
Elphinstone, Sir George Keith, Viscount Keith, 267, 271–279, 280–289
Elsinore, Denmark, 189
Elsley, Charles, editor of reports, xxix–xxx, xxxv
Erskine, Thomas (later lord chancellor), of Lincoln's Inn
  as counsel, xl n. 58, xlii–xliii, xlvii, l, lvi, lix, 34, 49, 54 n. 44, 55 n. 47, 83, 84, 85 n. 95, 88, 91, 93, 95, 102 n. 29, 122, 133, 142, 149 n. 14, 150, 153 n. 26, 155 n. 29, 194 n. 1, 267, 315, 317, 321, 322, 324, 329–347, 359, 374, 376;
  caseload of, xlvi
  on Admiralty Court prohibition, 190; on advowson, 117; on affidavits, false, 158 n. 34; on assurance, policy of, 208; on attorney apprenticeship, 139; on attorney non-attendance, lviii; on attorney non-performance, 59; on attorney qualifications, 154; on bail, 182, 206; on bankruptcy, 152, 163; on child custody, 144–145; on church vacancies, 111–112; on consolidation rule, 199; on criminal conversation, 144 n. 6; on custom of Court of Livery of Company of Armourers and Braziers, 96 n. 18; on damages, xliii, 157 n. 33; on damages, mitigation of, 353–354, 356; on debt,

INDEX OF PERSONS AND PLACES

172; on gaming, 183, 184 n. 80; on habeas corpus, writ of, 78; on habeas corpus ad testificandum, writ of, 78; on informations, 101, 196; on insurance brokers, 192; on inquiry, writ of, 201; on interrogatories, 61; on juries, use of, 266; on lotteries, 107; on mandamus, writ of, 60, 82, 140, 141 n. 2, 147, 151, 160; on money had and received, action for, 193; on new trials, liii; on non omittas, writ of, 159; on order nisi, 352; on peerage, liability of, 131; on perjury, 137; on perpetual motions, lii; on plaintiffs in error, 112, 115; on possession, 170; on prima facie evidence, 87; on prize, 168–169; on punishment, 191; on rule of attachments, 53; on seamen's articles, 135; on sham pleading, lv; on show cause rule, 203 n. 14; on Sir John Barnard's Act, 164 n. 44; on trespass, action of, 272; on underwriters, 105; on usurious contracts, 89

Espinasse, Isaac, of Gray's Inn, xxv n. 55, xl n. 54, 79, 170, 199
  his reports, xiv, xviii, lviii–lx, 47 n. 27, 54 n. 43, 56 n. 48, 67 n. 73, 175 n. 62
Europe, 269–270, 288, 292
Evance, Thomas, of the Middle Temple, 188
Exeter, Som
  (diocese) bishop of, 114
  city of, 265
Eyre, Sir James
  C.B.Ex., 6
  C.J.C.P., 40–43, 85 n. 96, 111, 119, 170, 179 n. 71, 215, 224–226, 268 n. 72, 271
  on abeyance of inheritance, 74–75; on advowson, 115–116; on citizenship, question of, 271; on succession to office, 115; on testator's meaning, 6

Fabwin, John, clerk, 20
Falkland, Lord, lv
False Bay, south Africa, 286
Farresley, Thomas, his reports, xviii
Feltwell, Norf, 317
Ferguson, Robert, of Lincoln's Inn, 205–206
Ferrand, Jean Baptiste, privateer, 291
Ferrers, earl and countess, see Shirley, Laurence
Fielding, William, of the Middle Temple, 67 n. 73
Fisher, John, 351
Fitzgibbon
  John, earl of Clare, 201
  John, law reporter, xvi–xviii, xix,
Flanders, region of, 60
Flemying, Hamilton, called earl of Wigtown, 173 n. 55
Flint, Flints, 79
Flora, Temple of, disorderly house, 148
Folkes, Sir Martin Brown, 329
Fonblanque, John
  of the Middle Temple, 111
  his treatise of equity, 57
Foote, Samuel, playwright and actor, 359 n. 8
Ford, John, of the Middle Temple, his case notes, xxx–xxxi, xxxiv n. 20
Ford, Randle, of Lincoln's Inn, his case notes, xxx n. 1
Forey, manor of, 69
Fortescue (Fortescue Aland), Sir John, B.Ex., J.K.B., J.C.P., his reports, xviii, xix
Foster
  Sir Michael, J.K.B., 94, 227
  —, master of the King's Bench, 159
Fothergil, Henry, 381
Foulkes, Edward, attorney, 235, 237
Fox, James, 324
Foxley, Norf, 324
France, 38, 213, 267–268, 291–294, 296, 302, 303–311
Francis, Richard, 324
Frederick-nagore, India, see Serampore
Freeman, Richard, his reports, xviii, xix
Frere, William, serjeant-at-law, editor of law reports, xv n. 9, xxi–xxii, xxxiv n. 20
Frost, William, 141–142

Garrow, William (later B.Ex.), of Lincoln's Inn, xlvii–xlviii, 34, 54, 60, 67 n. 73, 78 n. 90, 80, 85 n. 95, 86, 88, 95, 96 n. 18, 131 n. 73, 147 n. 13, 149 n. 14, 152, 158 n. 34, 163, 174 n. 58, 184 n. 80, 192, 196–197, 201, 204, 272
Gaselee, Stephen (later serjeant-at-law), of Gray's Inn, 135, 154, 215, 221, 224–225
Gatty, Robert, attorney, 216
Gawler, John Benjamin, 144 n. 6
Geast, Richard, of the Inner Temple, 212, 254
George III, king of Great Britain and Ireland, 139
Georgia, state of, 27, 28 n. 78, 31, 33 n. 3
Gibbon
  Frances and husband Edward, 22–23, see also Amory, Frances
  Thomas, serjeant-at-law, and son Thomas, 22–23

Gibbs, Sir Vicary (later C.B.Ex. and C.J.C.P.), of Lincoln's Inn, xxxvii n. 39, xlvi–xlviii, lii, 62–64, 77, 81, 83–84, 85 n. 95, 86, 90–91, 95, 96 n. 18, 97–98, 105, 139–140, 142, 144, 150–151, 160, 162–163, 167–169, 171, 177, 181, 184 n. 80, 191–193, 199, 267, 308, 310, 369

Gibraltar, lii, 265

Gibson, Elizabeth, 190

Gilbert, Sir Jeffrey, C.B.Ex., his reports, xvi n. 15, xx

Giles, Daniel, of Lincoln's Inn, 84, 85 n. 95, 267, 272, 277–278

Glamorganshire, county of, 9

Glenbervie, Lord, see Douglas, Sylvester

Gloucester
  (diocese) bishop of, 116 n. 55, 160
  county of, 160

Good Hope, Cape of, 168–169, 198, 267, 274, 280, 287–288

Gould, Sir Henry
  J.C.P., xxv, xliv, 3–39, 337, 364, 368
  his case notes, xxiv

Graham, Thomas, of Lincoln's Inn, 317, 321–323, 329, 353

Gray's Inn, xiii n. 1

Great Cressingham, Norf, 329

Great Dunham, Norf, 317

Great Yarmouth, Norf, xl n. 58, xli, 10, 315, 318–319, 331, 334, 338, 342, 348, 363
  mayor of, xl n. 58, xlv, 323
  mayor-elect of, 10 n. 15

Green, Benjamin (Bengamon), 249

Greenwood, Abraham, attorney, 155 n. 29

Griffin, Nathaniel, 21, 23

Grose, Sir Nash
  J.C.P., xlvi, 10 n. 17, 119, 233–234, 238, 259, 266, 311
  sittings as a justice of the Common Pleas, (1794) 47–56, (1794–95) 57–76, (1795) 77–103, 195–208, (1796) 104–108, 131–153, (1797) 154–178, (1798) 178–195
  on guardianship, 55 n. 47

Guernsey, island of, 290–291, 295, 299–301

Guest
  William, the elder, and wife Martha, 36
  William, the younger, 36

Gurney
  John (later B.Ex.), of the Inner Temple, 90
  Thomas, shorthand writer, 272–273

Haines, Hannah, 248–249

Hale, Sir Matthew
  C.B.Ex., 72

  C.J.K.B., 49, 51, 173
  his case notes and legal writings, xxiv, xxxi, 38, 73, 207
  on effect of attainder, 72

Hamburg, city of, 203 n. 14

Hamilton, William, solicitor, 120–123, 125–128

Hammond, Anthony, 317, 329

Hampshire
  county gaol, 105
  county of, 105 n. 36

Hanson, Christopher, 300–301

Harcourt, Sir Simon, master of the Crown Office, court of King's Bench, xxvii

Hardinge, George, counsel, xl n. 58, 122, 315, 323, 329–330, 343–344, 349, 351–352

Hardingham, Norf, 324

Hardres (Hardress), Sir Thomas (later serjeant-at-law), his reports, 137

Hardwicke, Lord, see Yorke, Sir Philip

Hare, Hugh, 324

Hargham, Norf, 324

Hargrave, Francis, his writings, 38, 71, 73, 224, 228, 229 n. 67

Harris, Thomas, 248–249

Harrison
  Horther, 250
  Mary (Marrey), 249

Harvey, John Springett, of the Middle Temple, 167

Hatch, John, clerk, 21–23, 26

Harwich, Suff, mayor of, 184

Hay, Douglas, xxvi, xlix

Hay, Sir George, 130

Heath, John
  J.C.P., xxxi, xliv, 68, 70 n. 82, 119, 132, 134, 155, 208, 364, 369
  sittings as a justice of the Common Pleas, (1787) 3–39, (1794) 40–43

Henley, Robert, Lord Northington, lord chancellor, 173

Hereford, Heref, gaol, 103

Herod the Great, king of Judea, xliii, 374

Hertford, county of, 6 n. 11

Heydon, Norf, 324

Higby, —, counsel, 100

Hill
  Edward, 21
  George, his case notes, xxviii–xxix, xxx, xxxiv nn. 20–21, xl, 5 n. 10; king's serjeant-at-law, 25, 35
  Richard and daughter Mary, 21–22

Hillington, Norf, 329

INDEX OF PERSONS AND PLACES

Hobart, the Hon. Henry, foreman of grand jury, 338
Hockwald (Hockwold cum Wilton), Norf, 317
Holland, the United Provinces, 38
Holmes, Seaman, 324
Holroyd, George (later J.K.B.), of Gray's Inn, 53, 111, 118, 137, 233–234, 237–239, 243–244, 246
Holt, Sir John
   C.J.K.B. xxiii n. 40, 17, 101 n. 27, 230, 241–242, 327, 355
   his case notes, xxiv, xxxi
   on contracts, 242–243
Hotham, Sir Beaumont
   assize judge, 58, 134, 183
   B.Ex., 119, 122, 127, 128 n. 71
Howell, Richard, 34
Hull (Kingston upon Hull), Yorks, 85, 264–266; harbour of, 132
Hurry
   Samuel, 320, 348–350
   William, xl–xlvi, 5 n. 9, 10, Appendix *passim*
Hutton, Sir Richard, J.C.P., 113, 116
Hyam
   Elizabeth, 252–253, 262, *see also* Liggins, Elizabeth
   William and his wife Ann (formerly Southall), 252, 262

Imms, William, officer of the court of Requests at Great Yarmouth, 321
India, 192–194, 267 n. 68, 295
Inglis, —, merchant of London, 273
Inner Temple, xxxii
   Library, xxiii n. 40, xxxii
Ipswich, Suff, 315, 323
Ireland, 78 n. 88, 93, 176, 201
Ironmongers, Company of, 96 n. 18
Isaac
   Grace and husband Francis, 20–22
   Robert, 21–22
Isle of Man, 284–285

Jakarta (Batavia), Indonesia, 281
Jamaica, island of, 204
Jamson
   Mary, 250
   Richard, 248–249
   Thomas, 250
Jekyll, Joseph, of Lincoln's Inn, xxxv
Jenkins
   David, 206 n. 17, 207
   Sir Leoline, his reports, 206 n. 17
Jephson, William, serjeant-at-law, xxviii

Jervis, Thomas, of the Middle Temple, 188
Johnson
   Dr Samuel, 137 n. 95
   Samuel, attorney, 154
Jones
   Sir Thomas, J.K.B., 43 n. 25
   William, clerk, 20
Joyner, Robert, clerk, 20–22

Keble, Joseph, his reports, 50, 243–245
Keith, Lord *see* Elphinstone, Sir George Keith, 168
Kelyng, Sir John, C.J.K.B., 243 n. 20
Kelynge, William, his reports, xviii
Kent, county of, 167, 205
Kenrick
   Matthew I, 114, 118
   Matthew II, clerk, 114
Kenyon, Sir Lloyd
   master of the rolls, 27 n. 76, 28, 31 n. 86, 32–33, 214
   C.J.K.B., xxxv–xxxvi, xlvii–lxi, 112, 119, 215, 224, 226–229, 232–234, 244, 246, 264, 266, 272–273, 280, 284, 290, 311
   sittings as C.J.K.B., (1794) 47–57, (1794–95) 57–76, (1795) 77–103, 195–208, (1796) 104–108, 131–153, (1797) 154–178, (1798) 178–195; at trial in Westminster Hall, 139 n. 1
   his case notes, xxiii n. 40, xxvi–xxviii, 124 n. 68
   on act of desertion, 135; on act of God, 132; on actions between attorneys, 153; on Admiralty, 52; on Admiralty jurisdiction, 169; on affidavits, 91, 101, 199–200; on affirmative evidence, 85 n. 95; on American citizenship, 268; on annuity, 69; on appeals, 66; on appearance for defendant, 163; on arbitration, 162 n. 40; on arbitration costs, 104 n. 32; on assignment of bail bond, 81; on assurance, policy of, 87, 208; on attorney attendance, lvi–lviii; on attorney qualities, 154–155; on bail practice, 67 n. 75; on bankruptcy, li, 56 n. 48, 57, 61–62, 152–153; on bankrupt's future earnings, 58; on changing venue, 79; on child custody, 172, 179; on child within age of nurture, 181; on choice of umpire, 50; on commission of the peace costs, 157; on common bail, filing of, 147; on common sense, 234; on consequences of ship stranding, 105; on construction of agreement, 238; on construction of policy

Kenyon, Sir Lloyd (*cont.*)
    of assurance, 105; on conversion, 70; on conveyance, 155; on costs, 64, 104; on creditors, 97; on cross interrogatories, 189; on crown rents, 137; on court delays, 163–164; on court discretion, 174; on custody, suspicious, 80; on custom of the realm, 86; on delay of trials, lvi; on descent, laws of, 258–259; on division of offices, 167–168; on ecclesiastical courts, 167; on ejectment, 156; on equitable title, 188; on estate tail, 257; on false imprisonment, 63 n. 65; on fee padding, 136 n. 85; on franchises, 51; on freehold lands, 256–257; on freehold prima tonsura, 202; on general property, 134–135; on habeas corpus, writ of, 52, 78, 89–91, 170; on highway Act, 164; on immoral law, 226; on indemnity, 68; on inquiry, writs of, 201–202; on inquisition de proprietate probanda, 57; on insurable life, lii, 171; on insuring against barratry, 84 n. 95; on intestate, 146; on joint nomination, 63; on latitat, writ of, 79; on law and obligations, xlix; on lease with covenant, 244; on libel informations, 196; on life estates and fees, 190; on Lord Hawkesbury's Act, 156; on malicious charges, 63; on mandamus, writ of, 60, 70, 82, 95–96, 160–161; on mandate to return writ, 52; on married women, 213; on mockery and ridicule, 149 n. 14; on mode of pleading, 151; on money had and received, action for, 193; on moral condemnation, 184 n. 80; on morality, 153 n. 26; on motion for attachment, 49–50; on navigation, lii; on navigation laws, 268; on negligence, lii, 133; on new trials, liii; on nonsuit, 54; on orders of removal, 102; on padded pleadings, liii–lv; on parol evidence, 183; on peerage, privilege of, 131; on penalties, informant's, 184; on perils of the sea, 134; on perjury, 137; on personal notice to attorney, 200; on pleadings, voluminous, 184 n. 80; on possessory action, 176; physicians, admission regulation of, 140–141; on public nuisance, 50 n. 37; on punishment, 68 n. 77, 191, 205; on quo warranto, writ of, 60; on receipt of evidence, 170; on relator, 142; on reviving recognizance, 148; on right of guardianship, 55; on riparian rights, 188; on Seaforth, Lancs, politics of, 147 n. 13;

on settlement, trusts, 186; on sham pleading, lv; on show cause rule, 147; on solvit post diem, 81; on statute of limitations, 188; on stock-jobbing, 164 n. 44; on stoppage in transitu, 175; on testamentary paper, 186; on township, 83; on trespass, 101; on trover, 169; on trustees, 180; on unity of persons, 212; on usury, 89, 97–98; on verdict correction, 203; on vice, l; on want of due service, 81; on warrants, 106, 143; on waste, 173; on writ of error, 49

Keppel, Augustus, Viscount Keppel, 345
Kerby, Cranley Thomas, serjeant-at-law, xl, 9, 13, 36, 380
Keyling (Kelyng), John, Lord Keyling, C.J.K.B., xxxv
Kidd, Stewart, 204
Kiddermarsh (place, not certainly identified), 239
King
    John, clerk, lv–lvi, 65 n. 70, 131 n. 73, 75
    Sir Peter, C.J.C.P., xxiii, xl n. 56,
    Rufus, 178, 181
    —, American minister in London, 178, 181
King's Lynn (Lynn), Norf, 107
Kingston-upon-Hull, Yorks, *see* Hull
Kingston
    Jamaica, 119
    township of, 93 n. 11
Kirby Bedon, Norf, 324
Knopwood, Robert, 329
Knowles, Newman, counsel, 67 n. 73, 78
Kyly, Harriet, 181
Kynaston, John, 248–249

Lamb
    William, 232–237
    (Lambe), William, of Gray's Inn, 50, 178, 234
Lancashire, county of, 83, 235–237
Lancaster, Lancs, corporation of, 51
Lanesborough, Lord, 215, 226
Langford, Thomas, 248–249
Launceston, Cornwall, 141, 207
Law, Sir Edward, Baron Ellenborough,
    of Lincoln's Inn, xlvii, lix, 49, 51, 70, 84, 85 n. 95, 87, 95, 96 n. 18, 107 n. 42, 111, 118, 134, 140, 141 n. 2, 142, 152, 156, 157 n. 33, 162, 169–170, 173–175, 178, 180–181, 193, 201 n. 10, 215, 226–229, 231–232, 234, 237–238, 267, 284
    C.J.K.B., xxiv n. 43, xxxvii, xlvii–xlviii, 215, 267, 272

INDEX OF PERSONS AND PLACES

Lawes, Vitruvius (later serjeant-at-law), of the Inner Temple, liii, 152, 163, 185, 191
Lawrence, Sir Soulden
    life, vii
    serjeant-at-law, 3–39, 370–372
    J.C.P., Part I *passim*
    J.K.B., Parts II–III *passim*
    on advowson succession, 112–114; on consolidation, 190; on covenant, 246–248; on deeds, 174; on habeas corpus, writ of, 89; on King's Bench, xlvi–xlix; on testamentary issues, 129; on unintelligible will, 212; on vendor and vendee, xxxix
Lea, Michael, 248–249
Leach, —, counsel, 147 n. 13
Leach, Thomas, of the Middle Temple, his reports, xviii, xxii, xxv n. 59
Leacroft, —, attorney, 167
Leatherhead, Surrey, manor of, 41
Le Blanc
    Simon, of the Inner Temple, 317; serjeant-at-law, xl, xliii–xlv, 3–5, 13, 19, 38–41, 329, 349, 362–365, 377–379, 381; J.K.B., xxii, xxxiii, 203, 208, 312, 362–365, 377–379, 381; assize judge, 273
    Thomas, master of the court of King's Bench, xxii
Lechmere, Nicholas, of the Middle Temple, xxxiv n. 20
Lee
    (Leigh), John, of Lincoln's Inn, 86
    William, C.J.K.B., xx, xxiv n. 41, xxxiv n. 21, 355
Leeds, Yorks, 264–265
Leghorn, *see* Livorno
Leicester
    Leics, 149
    Fields, London, 92 n. 11
Leiden (Leyden) University of, 141 n. 2
Leith, Sir Alexander, 370
Lensens, Lars, ship builder, 299
Ley, James, 21, 23
Leycester (Leicester), Hugh, of the Middle Temple, 62, 79, 100, 150, 187–188, 257, 258
Liggins
    Edward, 248–249, 262
    Elizabeth, *see also* Elizabeth Hyam, 248–249, 252–253, 260
Lincoln (diocese), bishop of, 26 n. 72
Lincoln's Inn, xxx n. 1, xl, 316
    Library, xiv, xxiv n. 51, xxv, xxx n. 97, xxxvii n. 41, 15 n. 28, 214
    lord chancellor's room in, 43

Lindsay, Thomas, 22
Lisbon, Portugal, 134
Littleton, Sir George, 65
Liverpool, Lancs
    borough of, 16, 84 n. 95, 134, 308
    mayor of, 168
Livorno (Leghorn), Italy, 264–266
Lloyd, John, 329
Lock (Locke), —, merchant of Norwich 323, 342–343, 352–353, 363, 365–366, 376
Lofft, Capel, of Lincoln's Inn, law reporter, xviii, xxi, xxxiii n. 17
London
    (diocese) bishop of, 26 n. 73
    city of, 6 n. 11, 83, 91, 135, 151, 154, 164 n. 44, 168, 191, 204 n. 14, 208, 216–220, 269–270, 273–274, 276–278, 283, 290, 292–295, 299–300, 309, 353–354, 355 n. 6
Loughborough, Lord, *see* Wedderburn, Alexander
Lovell, Joan, Lady, *see* de Beaumont
Luard & Co., 192
Luders, Alexander, of the Inner Temple, 95, 96 n. 18
Ludgate Hill, London, 285
Lumley, Lord, 72
Lushington, Henry Edmund, of the Inner Temple, 66
Lutwyche, Sir Edward, serjeant-at-law, his reports, xvii–xviii
Lynford, Norf, 329

Macclesfield, Lord, *see* Parker, Sir Thomas I
Madeira, island of, 270, 290–291, 294–295, 301, 306
Madras, India, 293–295, 301, 306
Malaga, Spain, lii
Manchester, Lancs, 235–237, 265
Manley, William (later serjeant-at-law), of the Middle Temple, 49, 158 n. 34, 164
Mansfield, earl of, *see* Murray, William
Mariot, G. W., of the Middle Temple, 51, 53, 58, 67, 93, 95, 98, 143, 146–149, 159, 162, 166, 182, 202
Marryat, Samuel, of the Middle Temple, xlvii, 96 n. 18
Marshall, John, 216–219, 221, 223
Marshalsea, marshal of, 235
Masterman, Henry, secondary of the Crown Office, court of King's Bench, xxxi
Martin, John, 89–90
Maule, George, of Lincoln's Inn, his reports, xxiii n. 38

Mauritius, island of, 281
Mawbey, Sir Joseph, 151, 152 n. 22
McDonald, Sir Archibald, C.B.Ex., 86, 118, 119
Mediterranean sea, 264–265
Middle Temple, xiii n. 2, xxx
  Library, xiii
Middlesex, county of, 6 n. 11, 34, 93
Middleton, parish of, 83 n. 93
Miller, Richard, 351
Milles, Thomas, counsel, 175, 191
Mingay, James, of the Inner Temple, xxv, xxvi n. 64, xlvii, liii–liv, lvi, 34, 56, 67 n. 73, 101 n. 28, 102, 131–132, 149 n. 14, 157, 172, 179, 181, 183, 184 n. 80, 317, 321–322, 329, 341, 343, 350–351, 354–361, 374
Mingotti, Regina, singer, 228
Minorca, island of, 18
Mitford, John, solicitor-general, 206, 271 n. 79
Montagu, John, fourth earl of Sandwich, 345 n. 4
Morning Post, newspaper, 80
Morton, William, 235–237
Moseley, —, Dr, 179 n. 73, 181
Mount Edgcumbe, earl of, *see* Edgcumbe, George
Murphy, Arthur, counsel, 317, 329, 343–344, 348, 356, 374
Murray, William, Lord Mansfield, C.J.K.B., xix, xx, xxii–xxiii, xxviii, xxx, xxxii, xxxiv n. 20, xxxv–xxxviii, 5 n. 10, 6 n. 11, 9, 11 n. 18, 15 n. 30, 19 n. 42, 59, 67 n. 73, 101 n. 27, 124 n. 68, 153, 171 n. 53, 194, 214, 228–229, 231–243, 255, 259–260, 307–310, 328, 359 n. 8, 369, 372, 377
  at Guildhall, xxvi
  his trial notes, xxv n.52
  on affidavits, xliv–xlv; on attorney non-attendance, lviii; on attorney quality, 155 n. 29; on continuances, 100 n. 24; on contracts, 233–243; on covenants, types of, xxxii; on devise, xxvii; on foreign country, ordinances of, 308; on French Admiralty court decisions, xxxvii; on lease terms, xxxviii; on mandamus, writ of, 166–167; on nonsuit, xxix; on padded pleadings, liv; on perjury, 336; on qui tam actions, 99 n. 24; on reconsidering verdicts, 378; on relationship with Francis Buller, xxv, xxxi; on Treaty of Utrecht, 303–304; on trover, 70 n. 82
Murray, Sir William, 55

Nantes, France, 203 n. 14
Nares, Sir George
  of the Inner Temple, xxiii n. 40
  J.K.B., xxxiv n. 21, 3 n. 6
  assize judge, xli, 10 n. 15, 317, 324, 339
Neeld, Joseph, counsel, 248
Nelthrope, George, 329
Netherlands, The, 267 n. 68
New Romney, Kent, 151
New York, city of, 14
Newcastle, county of, 83
Newcastle (upon Tyne), Northumberland, 83
Newfoundland, island of, 269
Newgate prison, 69
Newson, Samuel, 317
Nicholl, Sir John, advocate, xxxiii n. 19; king's advocate, 122
Nightinner, Francis, 249
Nolan, Michael, editor of reports, xxii–xxiii, xxx
Norfolk, county of, 323–324, 353, 363, 373, 380
Norris
  Ann, 71, 73
  Sir Edward and wife Frideswide, 71
  Henry and son Henry, Lord Norris of Rycote, 71–73
  Sir John, 71–72, 74–75
  Margaret, 71, 73
North, Sir Francis, C.J.K.B., 371
North Lopham, Norf, 317
North Shields, Northumberland, 208
Northcote, Elizabeth, 22
Northington, Lord, *see* Henley, Robert
Northumberland
  county of, 83
  duke of, 141–142
  earl of, 72, 73
Norwich
  (diocese), bishop of, 24
  Norf, 315, 323, 343, 352–353, 356
Norwich Mercury, newspaper, 341–342
Nunez, A. J., 98

O'Connor, Arthur, 205
Onslow, Arthur (later serjeant-at-law), of the Middle Temple, 184 n. 80
Oracle, The, newspaper, 136 n. 85, 195
Ormond, duke of, 55
Ostend, Southern Netherlands, 52
Outhwaite, Lancs, 83
Owen, Thomas, 206 n. 17, 207
Oxford
  (diocese), bishop of, xxx

INDEX OF PERSONS AND PLACES

county of, xxxi n. 2
Oxford, Oxon
  colleges, Lincoln, 47; Wadham, 165
  university, 47, 116, 121–122, 127, 140–141

Pall Mall, London, 65 n. 70
Palliser (Pallisar), Sir Hugh, 149, 345 n. 4
Palmer, Arthur (later serjeant-at-law), of the Inner Temple, 41
Papal States (Ecclesiastical State), 265
Pardo (Pardoe)
  Ann, 250, 252–253, 255–261
  John, 249–250, 252–254, 260
  Mary, 252, 263
  Sarah (Sarra), 249–250
  William (Willem), 249–250, 252–253, 261, 263
Paris, France, 295, 302
Park, James Allan (later J.C.P)
  of Lincoln's Inn, xxxvii n. 39, xlviii, 175, 192, 266 302, 303 nn. 12 and 14, 305, 307
  his reports, 171
Parke, Rawson, of the Inner Temple, 138, 162, 256
Parker
  E., 250
  Sir Hyde, vice-admiral, 265
  Sir Thomas I, Lord Parker, C.J.K.B., 17, 240; earl of Macclesfield, lord chancellor, 48, 247
  Sir Thomas II, J.C.P., C.B.Ex., his reports, xvi, xvii n. 19, xxi, xxxii, xxxiii n. 19, xxxviii,
  —, attorney, 165
Parry, Edward, 317
Partridge, Henry, of the Middle Temple, xl n. 58, 315–317, 318, 320–321, 323, 329, 338, 348, 355, 361 n. 10
Payne, Thomas Grigson, 324
Paynter, Richard Walter, attorney, 235
Paxton
  A., 192
  & Co., 192–193
  William, 192
Peake, Thomas (later serjeant-at-law), of Lincoln's Inn, 255
Pearce, Mary and husband James, 22
Pennsylvania, state of, 267
Pentney, Norf, 329
Perceval, Spencer (later prime minister), of Lincoln's Inn, 151, 170, 171 n. 51, 203, 208
Perkins, William, 324

Perrens, —, president of the Civil Tribunal of La Gironde, 295
Perryn, Sir Richard
  assize judge, 63, 88, 174, 249
  B.Ex., xl n. 55, 88, 119,223
Philadelphia, Pennsylvania, 154, 213, 267–268, 269 n. 76
Phillips
  Joseph, 252, 263
  Stephen, lv
Pickering, —, counsel, 120, 125–128
Pigot, Lord, 194
Pilkington, Lancs, 83
Pinckney, Charles, 27, 32–33
Plugler, Thomas, 179–180
Plumer, Thomas, of Lincoln's Inn, 71, 99, 258
Plymouth, Devon, lii
Pontefract (Pomfret), honour of, 159
Poole, Simon, 317
Porchester, Lord, liv, 184
Portland, duke of, 119
Portsmouth, Hants, xlvii, 16, 105, 176, 264–265
Portugal, 213, 265, 267, 304, 309
Powis
  barony of, 72 n. 85, 75
  Lord, 72–73
Praed, William Mackworth (later serjeant-at-law), of Lincoln's Inn, 177
Pratt, Sir Charles, earl Camden, C.J.C.P, lord chancellor, xliii, 85, 124 n. 68; on excessive damages, 371
Preston, Isaac, of Lincoln's Inn, 323, 329, 352
Preston, —, recorder of King's Lynn, 107
Price, E., clerk, 196
Pridey
  Benjamin (Bengamin), 249
  Mary (Marre), 249
  Routan, 249
Pyke
  Edward, 24
  Elizabeth and husband Henry, 22
  Elizabeth and husband Thomas, 21
  Humphrey and wife Elizabeth, 21–22, 27
  Robert Isaac, clerk, 21–22
  Robert J. and wife Rebecca, 21

Quarrier, William, ship's master, 119

Ramsgate, Kent, 240
Randall, Thomas, 190
Rashleigh, Charles, attorney, 197

Raymond, Sir Robert, Lord Raymond
C.J.K.B., xvi nn. 14, xliii
   his reports, xvi n. 15, xviii, xix, xx, xxiii
     n. 40, 327
Raymond, Sir Thomas, B.Ex., J.C.P., J.K.B.,
   his reports, xxxv, 43
Reader, William, of the Middle Temple, 52,
   65 n. 70, 164 n. 44
Reynolds, Francis Riddell, judge of the Court
   of Requests at Great Yarmouth, 331,
   333–335, 337, 339–340, 350, 351, 352, 356
Richards, Richard (later C.B.Ex.), of the
   Inner Temple, 122
Richmond, duke of, 147
Roberts
   Richard, 20, 27
   Thomas, 248–249
Robeson
   Henry, 249, 252
   Mary, 248
Robinson
   John, of the Middle Temple, 34
   Thomas, 34
Rochester (diocese), bishop of, 114, 118
Rockingham, marchioness of, 71
Rogers, Robert, clerk, 22–27
Rolls, P. Lee, 92
Rope, Robert, 324
Roper
   William, 252
   —, colonel, 59
Rooke (Rook), Giles
   serjeant-at-law, xl, xlii–xliii, 8–9, 325,
     376–377, 381
   J.C.P., 40–43, 119
   assize judge, 68, 85, 87, 102 n. 29, 103 n. 30,
     200
   Roscoe, Henry, of the Inner Temple, editor
     of law reports, xv, xxi–xxii, xxxvii n. 41
Rous, George, counsel, xxxvii n. 39, 267,
   309–311
Rousselet, John, 119
Roydon, Norf, 317
Runnington, Charles, serjeant-at-law, 42,
   100 n. 24
Rushford, Norf, 324
Russell
   Henry, of Lincoln's Inn, 80, 81, 146,
     158 n. 34
   John, 205
Russell Court, house in, 40
Rutton
   Elizabeth, 220, 222
   Isaac, 218–222

   Mary I, 216–223
   Mary II, 220, 222
   Thomas, 220–222
Ryder, Sir Dudley, C.J.K.B., xx

St Clement Danes, parish of, London, 34
Saint-Domingue (St Domingo), colony of,
   191, 204
St Gilles Croix de Vie (St Giles), France, 269
St Luke's hospital for lunatics, London, 159
St Mary le Bow, parish of, London, 217–220,
   274–277
St Paul's
   cathedral, London, 47
   school, London, vii
St Vincent, island of, 197
Saldanha Bay, south Africa, 283
Salisbury (Sarum), cathedral church of, 91
Salkeld, William (later serjeant-at-law), his
   reports, xviii, xix, xxxiv n. 21, xxxv
Salwarp, Worcs, parish of, 249
Sandown Bay, Isle of Wight, 190
Sandwich, earl of, see Montagu, John
Sargeant Chambers and Company, 14–15
Saville, Sir John, his reports, 24, 150
Saxthorpe, Norf, 324, 329
Sayer, Joseph
   serjeant-at-law, xxviii
   his reports, xx, 369
Scarlett, James (later C.B.Ex., Baron
   Abinger), of the Inner Temple, 237–238
Scilly, Isles of, 105
Scotland, 55, 131 n. 74, 284–285, 291, 298–299,
   301–302
Scott, Sir John
   serjeant-at-law, xl
   attorney-general, 71–72, 94 n. 15, 102 n. 29,
     107 n. 42, 111, 115, 122, 139 n. 1, 271.
     n. 79
   baron Eldon, C.J.C.P., 215, 227–229, 231,
     232
   earl of Eldon, lord chancellor, xlviii n. 1,
     31 n. 86, 33 n. 3
   his anecdote book, xxix n. 87
Scott, Sir William, Baron Stowell
   king's advocate-general, 122, 126–127,
     271 n. 79
   judge of the high court of Admiralty, 307,
     310
Seaforth, Lancs, 147
Selby, Yorks, 85
Selwyn, William, of Lincoln's Inn, his reports,
   xxiii n. 38
Senkler, Charles, 317

INDEX OF PERSONS AND PLACES

Serampore (Frederick-nagore), India, 292 n. 6, 299–300
Shadwell, Midd, magistrates of, 80
Shardlow, Derbs, 235–239
Sheffield, Yorks, 102
Shepherd, Samuel (later C.B.Ex. Scotland)
   of the Inner Temple, xlvii, 51, 53, 56, 58, 60, 67 n. 73, 80–81, 88, 106
   serjeant-at-law, xlvii,134, 147, 183, 202
Sheridan, Richard Brinsley, 355 n. 6
Shipley
   Captain, xli, 319, 322, 331–332, 334, 339, 348–350, 360, 361 n. 10
   William, of Lincoln's Inn, 59
Shirley, Laurence, earl Ferrers and Mary, countess Ferrers, 170
Short, Charles, clerk of the rules, court of King's Bench, his case notes, xxvii
Shropshire, county of, 79
Siddons, Sarah, actress, 355 n. 6
Sills, Henry, 196
Simon's Bay, south Africa, 267 n. 68, 275–276, 286
Simpson, Sir Edward, his case notes, xxxiii n. 19
Skipton, Yorks, lix–lx, 47
Skynner, Sir John, C.B.Ex., assize judge, xlii, 10 n. 15, 323–324
Slade, Thomas, attorney, 197
Sleiber, —, attorney, 155 n. 29
Smith
   Adam, 141 n. 2
   Robert, 21–22
   William, clerk, 21–23, 25–27
Smith-Stanley, Edward, Lord Derby, 206
Snow Hill, London, 285
South Carolina, state of, 27
South Pickenham, Norf, 329
Southall
   Ann, 249–250, 253, 260–262
   Charles, 249
   Edward, 249
   Elizabeth, 252
   Francis I, 249–253, 263
   Francis II, 249, 252–254, 260–262
   John, 249, 262
   Joseph and wife Mary, 248–239, 252–254
   Thomas, 248–249
   William, 248–240, 252, 254, 259–260, 261–262
Spain, 179, 181, 265, 304–305, 309
Spithead, 265
Spurgeon, —, clerk of the court of Requests at Great Yarmouth, 321, 350, 351, 356, 358

Squire
   Christopher, 21
   Elizabeth, 21–22
   Jane and husband William, 20–21
   William, 21
Stafford, county of, 144 n. 6
Standly, H. P., xxii
Stanhoe, Norf , 317
Stanger, Christopher, physician, 140, 141 n. 2
Stapleton
   Brian, 71
   Sir Brian and wife Joan, 71–72
   Thomas, 71, 73–75
Staples & Co., bankers, 175
Stewart
   Anne, pauper, li, 66
   John, 143
Stow, —, counsel, xxxi
Stowell, Lord, see Scott, William
Strange, Sir John, of the Middle Temple, 152 n. 24; his reports, xviii, xx, xxvii–xxviii, xxxiv n. 21
Sun Tavern Fields, London, 196
Surrey, county of, 114, 151, 152 n. 22
Swabey, Dr Maurice, 122
Swinden, Philip, 34

Tame, river, 187
Tasilie, John, 169
Taylor
   M. A., 120
   Sir Robert, 120–121, 127–128
Tenerife (Teneriffe), island of, 290–291
Thanet, Lord, 200, 202 n. 11, 205–206
Tharangambadi (Tranquebar), India, 300
The Times, newspaper, viii, xx, xxviii n. 79, xl, xlv–lvii, lviii nn. 70, 72–74, lx n. 87, lxi, Parts I, II and III, *passim*
Thetford, Norf, 245
Thomas, John, bishop of Rochester, 114, 118
Thompson, Sir Alexander
   B.Ex., 118–119
   assize judge, 99, 133
Threxton, Norf, 329
Thurlow, Edward, baron Thurlow
   lord chancellor, 5 n. 10, 7, 27 n. 76, 28, 31 n. 86, 33, 72 n. 85, 208, 224 n. 43
   on abeyance, 76
Tiffen, Richard, 317
Tooke, J. Horne, 61
Topham, John, counsel, 71
Topping, James, of the Inner Temple, 174, 187
Tothill Fields, Midd, bridewell, 94

Tranquebar, *see* Tharangambadi
Treby, Sir George, C.J.C.P., 118
Tregian, Edward, 205
Trinity House, Corporation of, lii
True Briton, newspaper, 136
Tullibardine, marquis of, 72
Tuscany, Italy, 265

United States of America, 213, 267–271
Uttoxeter, Staffs, xxx

Valentia, Lord and Lady, 144
Vaughan, John (later B.Ex.), serjeant-at-law, 68, 137, 188
Vesey, Francis, his reports, 17 n. 38

Wakefield, Yorks, 245
Wales, 78 n. 88, 120 n. 66
Walker, Thomas, serjeant-at-law, 4, 326
Wallace, John, xv, xviii n. 22, xix n. 23, xxi n. 27, xxviii n. 81, xxxiii n. 17, xl n. 55, lviii, lix
Ward, Sir Edward, C.B.Ex., xxxiii n. 19
Ward, Robert, of the Inner Temple, 265
Washer, John, clerk, 21
Wathen, Josiah-Iles, of Lincoln's Inn, 215, 219, 223–224, 226
Watson, John xl–xlvi, 5 n. 9, 10, 379, Appendix, *passim*
Way, John, custos brevium of the court of King's Bench, 216 n. 37
Wedderburn, Alexander, Lord Loughborough C.J.C.P., xli, lxi, 3–39, 224–225, 363, 365, 368–369, 371, 378–379
    on damages, xlii–xliii; on injunctions, 59 n. 58
West Bengal, India, 292 n. 6
West Bradenham, Norf, 317
West Indies, 135, 269 n. 75
Westacre, Norf, 317, 329
Westby, —, apothecary's assistant, 121–122, 127
Westcott, Mary and husband Thomas, 20–21
Westminster Hall, vii, xvi, xxviii n. 80, xxxii, xlviii–xlix, liii, lv, lviii, 78 n. 90, 136 n. 85, 184 n. 80
    pillory opposite the gate of, 158 n. 34
Weston, Norf, 324
Whitehall Palace, London, 178 n. 70
Whitehaven (Whitshaven), Cumberland, 70, 157
Wigley, Edmund, of the Middle Temple, 53, 202, 256
Wigtown, earl of, *see* Flemyng, Hamilton

Wilkes, John, 227 n. 53
Willes, Sir John, C.J.C.P., his reports, xvii–xviii, xxiv, xxx, 6 n. 11, 303 xxxiv n. 20
Williams, John, serjeant-at-law, 133
Williams (Willeams), William (Willeam), 249
Wilmot, Sir John Eardley
    J.K.B., xxxiv–xxxv n. 21, xliv, 188–189
    C.J.C.P., xxvi n. 68,
    his reports, xxiv
Wilson
    George, serjeant-at-law, his reports, xviii, xxii, xxiv n. 42, xxviii; as counsel, 323, 329, 374
    Henry William, 317, 329
    John, J.C.P., xliv, 122, 130, 364, 369; on affidavits 9; sitting as a justice of the Common Pleas, 3–39
Winch, Sir Humphrey, his reports, 113, 115–118, 162
Winchester (Winton), Hants, 177 n. 64
Windlesham, Surrey, parish of, 151
Wood, George (later B.Ex.), of the Middle Temple, xlvii, lix, 49, 55, 97, 100 n. 24, 107 n. 42, 134, 136, 150, 151, 152, 163, 165, 167, 168, 169, 173, 174 n. 58, 190, 237–238, 245, 247–248
Wooldridge
    Hester, 11–12
    William, 11
Woolwich, London, parish of, li, 66
Worcester
    city, 62, 249
    county of 249
Wright
    Sir James, 27–28, 32–33
    Richard, 329
Wyndham, Sir William, 106 n. 37
Wynne, Sir William, judge of the Prerogative Court, 120, 129–130

Yarmouth, see Great Yarmouth
Yates
    Joseph, of the Inner Temple, 151
    Sir Joseph, J.K.B., and J.C.P., xxxi; assize judge 193 n. 97, 194, 215 n. 35, 223–224 n. 41, 232 n. 82
York
    (diocese), archbishop of, xvi n. 13, 26 n. 71, 75
    county of, 71, 159
Yorke
    Charles, the Rt Hon., xxiv n. 45, xxxi, xxxiv n. 20
    Sir Philip, Lord Hardwicke; his case notes

xxix–xxv, xxxi, xxxiii n. 19, xxxiv n. 20; C.J.K.B. 17; lord chancellor, 6 n. 11, 17, 48–49, 153, 244 n. 22; on goods and chattels, 255; on natural-born subject, 271; on tenancies in common, 258

Yorkshire, county of, 83, 106, 264

INDEX OF SUBJECTS

abandonment, maritime, 265–266
abatement, plea in, 5, 9, 132–133, 173, 223
abeyance of dignities, 71, 72
abjuration of the realm, 223–225, 227, 230–231
ac etiam clause, 53
  absence of, 100
account, 16, 18–19, 84, 150, 160–161, 180, 185, 189, 218–219, 224, 227, 320, 331–332, 334, 337
  action of, 232
ad admittendum clericum (ad admit.), writ of, 25
adjuncts, commission of, 122
administrator, testamentary, 11, 27, 33, 220–222, 252–254
  temporary, 31
Admiralty
  at Copenhagen, 292, 298
  Board of, 52
  court of, at Cape Town, 267, 283, 286; at Great Yarmouth, Suff, xli, 319–320, 331, 333–334, 349
  courts of, xxxiii n. 19, 307–309, 311–312, 318; prohibition to, 138, 168–169, 190–191
  French court of, xxxvi–xxxvii, 213, 290, 302–305
  high court of, appeal to, 119
  lords commissioners of appeal in, 85 n. 96
  solicitor for, 52
  see also vice-admiralty courts
adultery, xlix, 225, 226 n. 51, 228, 231; *see also* criminal conversation
advowson, 20, 111–112, 114–117
  as impartiable inheritance, enjoyed by turns, 75
  as incorporeal hereditament, 117
affidavit
  against requiring security for costs, 155
  against rule for an attachment, 148–150
  application for answer by, 32
  credibility of, 1 (introduction)
  explanatory, 208
  falsehoods in, 158 n. 34, 361
  filed late, admissibility of, 91–92
  habeas corpus, grant of, upon, 78
  in mitigation of damages, 152 n. 22
  in mitigation of punishment, 139 n. 1, 146
  not to be taken off file, 199, 207
  of attempt to collect payment, 131 n. 73
  of belief, 80, 204
  of cause of action on Lottery Act, 99
  of damages sustained, 13
  of government of company, 95
  of grounds to postpone trial, 94
  of inability to satisfy damages awarded, 373, 377
  of insertion of premium in apprenticeship indenture, 88
  of jurors, xliii–xliv, 203, 362, 364–365, 368–369, 375
  of married woman, 49
  of morality of parent, 144
  of parties being alive, 77
  of party being abroad, 166
  of service of process, 182
  of status as township, 83
  of value of cause of action, 3, 189
  of willingness to deliver up items, 87
  of witness character, 67 n. 73;
  of writ being sued out, 86
  proving regular commencement of suit, 100
  rectification of, 79
  to discharge bail, 82, 197
  to hold to bail, 8–9, 43, 53, 181
  to justify bail, 52, 159, 176
  to support habeas corpus application, 103
  to support information in nature of quo warranto, 141–142
  to support mandamus, 140
  to support prohibition, 138
  supplemental, admission of 8–9
  sworn in Hamburg, 181
  time to answer, 101
agent
  action by against principal, 153
  affidavit by, 204
  assurances of, reliance upon, 197
  delivery of conditioned bond by, 14
  for privateer, 11
  general, 16–17
  holding proceeds of sale of prize, 85 n. 96
  insurance broker as, 84, 191
  liability of principal for acts of, 353, 366
  lien on money received in a cause, 185
  making of tender by, 239
  mere, 33

INDEX OF SUBJECTS

passing off as, 319–320
policy of insurance entered into by, 267, 290
service of notice upon, 200
signature by, 166
swearing debt as due to himself, 334, 339, 348, 350–351, 352, 358, 360
voluntary, recovery back of payment by, 193
agreement, special, action on, 40
alias, writ, 86, 99, 100 n. 24
alias and pluries, writ, 25
alien enemy, 195
alimony, 225, 232; *see also under* marriage
American Revolution, 27
ancient lights, *see* lights, ancient
annuity, 6 n. 11, 186, 226, 245
    enrolled memorial of bond for, 34
    motion to set aside, 68
apprenticeship, 88
arbitration, lv–lvi, 17, 41, 59, 79 n. 92, 131 n. 73; *see also under* attachment
arbitrators, lvi, 12, 49
    award of, 49, 50, 54, 59, 155, 173; conclusive, 162
    costs of 104
    means of selection of umpire by, 50
arrest, immunity from, 197
assault
    action for, 60
    by constable, xli
    damages for, liii, 4, 372
    in presence of justices, 205–207
    on married woman, 228 n. 55
    on revenue officer, 69 138, 139, 143, 145
assize
    clerk of, 59–60, 369
    commissions of justices of, 325–329
assizes
    lunatic prosecutrix unable to appear at, 159
    pace of trials on civil side of, xlvii–xlix
    reference to arbitration from, 41
    special verdict at, 23
assizes in
    Bristol, Som, 176
    Carlisle, Cumberland, 224 n. 41
    Cornwall, county of, xl
    Cumberland, county of, 157 n. 33
    Devon, county of, 156
    Exeter, Devon, 369
    Hertfordshire, county of, 86
    Kent, county of, 134
    Lancaster, Lancs, 134
    Lincolnshire, county of, 60
    Maidstone, Kent, 53, 225
    Middlesex, county of, 60, 150 n. 14
    Norfolk, county of, 10 n. 15, 315, 323–324, 328, 362–363, 380
    Oxford, Oxon, 99
    Salisbury, Wilts, 184 n. 81
    Shrewsbury, Salop, 145 n. 8
    Shropshire, county of, 79
    Stafford, Staffs, 133, 200
    Surrey, county of, 58, 99 n. 24
    Thetford, Norf, xl n. 58, xli–xlii, xlvi, 10 nn. 15 and 17, 315, 317, 329, 342, 353, 360, 373, 380
    Warwick, Warks, 63, 68, 136
    Wells, Som, 207
    Winchester (Winton), Hants, 177
    Worcester, Worcs, 155, 189 n. 89, 212, 249, 254, 256 n. 50
    York, Yorks, 70, 85, 102, 103 n. 30, 132
assumpsit, action of
    allegation of tender of plaintiff's performance in, 239–240, 242
    by assignees of bankrupt, 42–43
    declaration in, 62
    evidence of infancy in, 174, 175 n. 60
    on policy of assurance, 290
assurance, policies of
    adjustment of, 87
    alien enemies in action upon, 195
    on neutral shipping, 290–312
    particular average upon, 105
    premium in, 208
    putting off action upon in absence of witnesses, 198
    question of stranding in action upon, 104
    words 'detainment of princes' in, 213, 264
    see also insurance
attachment
    affidavit against, 148–149
    affidavits supporting, 1 (introduction)
    against chancellor of county palatine, 52
    against insane defendant, 103
    against sheriff, 165
    failure to sue out, 25
    for acting as attorney contrary to statute, 51
    for contempt of court, lv–lvi
    for not returning habeas corpus, 82, 90, 170
    foreign, 91
    of goods, 169
    of witness, 53
    premature, 106
    to answer affidavit, 92
    upon arbitration award, 49, 50, 59, 131, 132 n. 76, 168
    where special bail granted, 83

INDEX OF SUBJECTS

attainder, 71, 74–75
attaint, 230 n. 69, 327, 375
attorney
   action against, 97, 200
   articles of clerkship to, 154
   as steward of manor court, 167
   attachment against for contempt, lvi
   bailiff of corporation acting as, 51
   charged with forgery, 1 (introduction)
   clerk of, 92
   convicted of dueling, 143
   convicted of perjury, xli, 4
   lien for costs, 172
   of executor, entitled to probate, 31
   power of, 27
   striking out jurors, 200
   venue in action by, 60
   warrant of, 3–4, 34, 77, 81, 106, 186; given by married woman, 49
   writer of, 154
   see also under Common Pleas
attorneys
   abuse of qui tam actions by, liv–lv
   bills, between, not taxable, 153; of, liii,159
   negligence of, 165
   pettifogging, lv, lxi
   qualification for admittance, 80
   roll of, 139, 154, 197
   striking off, 80, 139, 154–55, 197
   see also under King's Bench; nisi prius
attorney-general
   appointed to the bench, 215
   as counsel, 71–72, 74, 102 n. 29, 107 n. 42, 115, 122, 139 n. 1
   consent of to satisfaction of fine, 153
   in case of outlawry, 59, 92, 93, 104
   in case of quo warranto, 151
   in case of riotous assembly, 94
   in case of treason, 78
   information filed by, 205–206
   see also nolle prosequi
audita querela, writ of, 37–38

bail
   common, 8, 60, 82, 147, 176, 182
   discharge of, 13, 52
   foreign, 197
   in perjury prosecution, 158
   irregular, 182
   justified, 36
   of defendant alien sent abroad, 65
   of one committed on defective warrant, 105
   of one committed for insulting the king, 94
   of one indicted for conspiracy, 104
   on foreign affidavit, 181
   on joint writ, 53
   perfecting, 106, 195 n. 3
   piece, 64, 65
   refusal of, 206
   special, 82–83
   sureties for, sufficiency of, 158 n. 34
   see also under bond
bailiff as attorney, 51
bankrupt
   action against, 244
   breach of covenant not to compete with, 246
bankruptcy
   act of, 17, 152–153
   action for trying questions of, 70 n. 82
   assignees in, action by, 42, 56, 156, 176, 243
   certificate of, 64
   commission of, 56 n. 48, 61–62, 81, 172
   credit due after, 162
   law of, liii
   of firm, 193–194
   of party insured, 16–17
   secret act of, 58
   see also under trover
bargain and sale, *see under* contract
barony in fee
   descent of, 71–76
   escheat of, 72–74
barratry, 84 n. 95
barrister
   as trustee, 144 n. 6
   indicted for assault and battery, 205
   managing an action, 212
   settling a will, 120
barristers
   case notes taken by, xxvi–xxxii
   frequency of appearance, xlvi–xlix
   practising, access to reports, xvii–xxxii, xxxviii
   opinion of sought, by arbitrators, 162; by attorneys, 254
   see also the names of individuals in the index of persons and places
bastardy, li, 179 n. 72
battery, 205, 228 n. 55
benefice, ecclesiastical, 26 n. 73; *see also* advowson
bill
   of exchange, 14, 53, 56
   of lading, 134, 169, 176, 294–296, 299–301
Bodleian Library, Oxford, xiii n. 1; *see also* Oxford University

INDEX OF SUBJECTS

bond
    assignees of, 172
    assignment of, 14
    bail, 13 n. 21, 36, 67, 81, 83
    binding to, 359
    conditional, 13, 14–15, 34, 186, 247 n. 31, 239, 243 248; plea of performance upon, 18–19
    joint, 69
    money, 27
    of arbitration, 59
    of married woman, 224, 226, 229
    of surety, 65
    stamp, 148
    to participate in convoy, 265
    usurious, 88–89, 97–98
Bow Street Criminal Court, 138 n. 1
bribery, liv, 184
brothels, l, 148

Cambridge University, 140–141
    Library, xiii n. 1
capias, special, 170
capias ad satisfaciendum (ca. sa.), writ of, 107 n. 40, 157, 161–162, 182
carrier
    liability of, 145
    lien of, 175
    see also common carrier
case notes
    anonymous, xxii–xxiii, xxxii–xxxiii
    gaps in, xv–xvi
    manuscript, xxiii–xxxvii
case reports, nominate, xiii, xvi, xxvi, xix, xxi–xxiii, xl
cassation, 302
    Supreme Tribunal of, Paris, 302, 306
certiorari, writ of, xxx, 10 n. 15, 92, 93 n. 11, 143, 161, 317, 337, 363
Chancery, xvi n. 12, 27, 214
    bills in, lvi, 79 n. 92
    case in on ancient lights, 20 n. 44
    cases coming from to the court of King's Bench, xxxvi
    cases in on mortgagees, 40
    contempt of, 59 n. 58
    depositions in, 148
    enrolment in, 34
    establishment of will in, 122
    guardianship of child in, 55, 181
    interrogatories in, 189
    jurisdiction of, 150, 166, 173, 182
    master extraordinary in, 149 n. 14
    motion in to take answers off the file, 200

    notes of cases in, xiii n. 2, xiv
    on married women, 227–228
    penalties in, 247
    rules of concerning executors, 66
    suit in concerning annuity, 69
charter party, 154
charter parties, copies of, 211
chattels, as term in will, 255
children, *see* infant
churchwardens, lix–lx, 47 nn. 28, 29, 48–49, 196
Civil Tribunal of La Gironde, France, 295
Cock Lane ghost, 67, 77
Cockpit, the, 178, 181
Colchester, Essex, borough court of, 337
common carrier, 132
    action against on custom of the realm, 85–86
common law, 20 n. 44, 38, 59 n. 58, 130
Common Pleas
    attorney of, sued as attorney of the King's Bench, 56
    Buller, Sir Francis, as justice of, xxxvii n. 40, 214
    cases in, xiii, xxiii, xxxiv n. 20, 82, 85 n. 96, 111, 114–115, 171
    consultation of the judges of, xlv n. 84, 67, 224 n. 41
    justices of as assize commissioners, lx n. 90, 10 n. 15
    Lawrence, Sir Soulden, as justice of, vii, xiii, xiv, 39 n. 18, 43, 111; his notes of cases in, xxxix–xlvi
    monopoly of serjeants-at-law in, 3 n. 2
    practice of, 102; compared with practice of court of King's Bench, xliv, 38
    reports of cases in, xvii–xix, lxi, Part I *passim*, 315–381
common recovery, 35
    uses of, 36
    see also mute person
condemnation of ship as prize, ground of, 308
confederacy, 370, *see also* conspiracy
conscience, *see* equity
Conscience, court of, 10, 319, 373
consent orders, xlv
consideration, *see* contract
consolidation rule, 199
conspiracy
    action of, 354
    for malicious prosecution, 370
    to appoint overseer of township
    to cheat a tradesman, lvi

conspiracy (*cont.*)
   to defraud, 67 n. 73
   to extort money, 191
   to pervert the course of justice, 151
   to prevent grant of administration of will, 104
   to raise wages, xlix
   see also confederacy, Cock Lane ghost
contempt of court, lv–lvi, 54, 156–157
continuances of actions, 86, 99
contract, 41, 233–243
   bilateral, covenants in, xxxii
   bilateral, executory, xiv, 170, 212, 233, 237, 238
   breach of, xxxix, 13, 18–19, 115, 134, 212, 239–240, 243–248
   civil, 225
   consideration, 15
   for factor's lien, 17
   gaming, 43
   joint, 132
   marriage, 215, 232
   non-performance of, 132 n. 76, 233, 237
   of bargain and sale, 238
   of married woman, 232
   ordinary, 268
   performance of, 14–15, 233
   promise, 60, 62, 107 n. 40, 142, 147, 212, 217–221, 233, 235–243; mutual, 237, 241
   property under, xxxix
   specific performance, action for, 227
   tenders, 14–15, 239, 241, 242
   under seal, 14
   usurious, 88, 172
conversion, 70
conveyance
   deed of, 177
   while out of possession, 155
coparceners, 22, 26
   of advowson, 117–118
   of barony in fee, 71, 73, 75
copyhold, 86
   estate, 155
   fine, 194
corporate bodies, 47
   books of, 94–96
corporate by-laws, 140
costs, 12
   award of by arbitrator, 104
   double, 178
   for defendant, by statute, 38–39
   of witnesses, 198
   security for, 38, 155
   taxation of, 53, 199
   upon judgment by default, 164
court officers, case notes taken by, xxvii
courts, *see under individual courts*
covenant
   action of, 154
   bond conditioned for performance of, 19
   breach of, 9, 15,
   dependent, 238
   for rent, 244
   for separate maintenance of wife, 255
   mutual, 242
   not to compete, xiv, 212, 243, 246–247
   types of, xxx–xxxiii
creditors, composition with, 57
criminal conversation, 144 n. 6, 171 n. 51, 201 n. 10; *see also* adultery
cruelty, matrimonial, as ground of separation, 228
curate, not minister of the parish, 196
curia advisari vult, 39
custody
   of child, 55: *see also under* infant
   of document, 80
custom of the realm, *see* common carrier

damages
   actual, 247
   assessment of, 13, 19
   compensatory, 346
   excessive, xli–xlii, liii, 4, 10, 171 n. 51, 362, 370–373, 375–379
   for breach of covenant, 111, 115, 154
   for criminal conversation, 144 n. 6
   for detention of debt, 14
   for harbouring apprentice, 88
   for libel, 201
   for malicious prosecution, 329, 331, 343, 345, 361, 366, 368–369, 380
   for slander, 137, 138 n. 95
   for stopping ancient lights, 189 n. 89
   in assumpsit on separation agreement, 219, 222
   in bankruptcy, 245, 247
   in insolvency, 64, 78–79
   in proceedings for perjury, 322
   in trespass action, 101 n. 28
   in trespass vi et armis, 278–279
   inquisition of, 133
   mitigation of, 152 n. 22, 353
   nominal, 101 n. 28, 154
   on policy of insurance, 203, 204 n. 14, 264, 273, 290
   on sale of goods, 239

INDEX OF SUBJECTS

punitive, xxlix, l, 359
uncertain, 244–245
death, civil, 227, 230, 231
de bene esse, *see under* declaration, information
de homine replegiando, writ of, 55
debt, action of
  against executor, 65
  for rent, 327
  foreign attachment of, 91
  see also bankruptcy
debts
  assignment of, 245
  payment of from confiscated property, 27, 29
debtors
  imprisonment of, 146 n. 12
  payment of groats to, 146
declaration, delivery of de bene esse, 182
deed
  for annuity, 186
  of composition, 56
default, judgment by, 164
defamation, *see* libel; slander
Delegates, high court of, 109 n. 43, 120 n. 64, 130
  commission of adjuncts in, 122
demurrer, 14, 15 n. 28, 19, 24, 111, 211, 216, 221–223, 240, 243, 246, 271, 273, 278
  by the crown in quo warranto, 150–151
  correct response to, xxxv
  joinder in, 20 n. 45, 24, 271
  pleading on, 234
dernier resort, court of, 186, 312
desertion, acts of, 135
detainment, action for, 242
detinue, action of, 239
deviation, maritime, 270
devise, 21–22, 35
  construction of, 117–118
  effect of, 48, 179–180, 252–253, 255–261
  meaning of, 11–12, 114,
  to a woman, 259
  unexecuted, 122–123, 129
  void, 5–7
diplomas, university, purchase of, 141
Directory (Executive Directory), of revolutionary France, 294, 301, 303 n. 13, 306
discovery, of books of lottery commissioners, 107; *see also* interrogatories
disseisin, 227, 230
disseisors, 230–231

distress
  illegal, 70
  warrant of, 174 n. 57
distringas, irregular, 5
divorce
  a mensa et thoro, 226, 229, 232
  a vinculo matrimonii, 214
  custody of children in, 55
  'legal', in consequence of abjuration, profession in religion, or exile, 225
  see also marriage; separation
dueling, 59, 60 n. 61, 143

ecclesiastical
  courts, enforcement of church rate in, 167; jurisdiction of, 225 n. 48; proceedings in for restitution of conjugal rights, 227, 229–230; proof of will in, 120, 122–124, 128, 130; rules of, 66; trial of validity of deeds in, 185–186
  jurisdiction, suspension from, 357 n.*
  law, 228
ejectment
  action of, 38, 55, 101, 155, 173, 183, 190, 212, 254; equitable title examined in, 188; *see also under* lessor
  of mortgagor by mortgagee, 40
election
  municipal, 184
  of a school master, 47
elopement, 228, 229; *see also* marriage, women
embargoes on shipping, 264, 266–267
embezzlement, 246
enclosure Act, 80
enemy alien, *see* alien enemy
enquiry, writ of, *see* inquiry, writ of
entail, 258
equity, 15, 17
  and conscience, 333, 370
  and justice, 113
  bill in, 32, 157
  courts of, 214–215, 228–231, 245; principles of in respect of debts, 29
  effect of proceedings in, 69
  equality as, 137
  natural, 29
  of a point, 33 n. 3
  of our ancestors, 337
  statute construed to avoid recourse to, 19
  statute intended to prevent drawing of defendants into, 247
  suit in, 157, 254
  treatise of, 57

error, writ of, 104
  brought by married woman, 49
  compared to injunction, 182
  execution sued out after, 79–80, 92
  in court of King's Bench, 85 n. 96
  in Exchequer Chamber, 271
  in parliament, 5
  pending, 13, 93
escheat, *see under* barony in fee
estate
  by tenancy in common, 258
  dum casta et sola, 224
  in Georgia, forfeited, 27, 32
estate tail, *see* fee tail
evidence
  affirmative, 85 n. 95
  circumstantial, xlix, 120
  improper, admission of, 376
  parol, 14, 183; of laws of foreign country, 178, 181
  presumptive, 1
  prima facie, 87
  strict rule of, 366
Exchequer (Curia Scaccarium), xxxviii
  barons of, as assize commissioners, lx n. 90; seniority among, 43 n. 25
  bill in, 160
  condemnation of prize in, 309–310
  consultation of the judges of, xlv n. 84, 67, 224 n. 41
  reporting in, xvii, lx
Exchequer Chamber
  court of, 72 n. 84, 179 n. 71, 241, 268 n. 72, 271
  meeting of judges in, 223
excise, 104
excise officer, 64
execution on debt, 81
execution, writ of, 13, 97
Executive Directory, of revolutionary France, *see* Directory
executor, 4, 8, 11, 27
  action by, 91; upon gaming contract, 42–43
  action against, 172
  de son tort, 61–62
  entitlement of, 31
  laches of, 33
  of a married woman, 225
  plea of plene administravit by, 65
  power of sale in, 48
executrix, 21, 22, 190, 251 n. 34, 255
extortion, 191

factor, 16–17, 87, 243, 246,
fee simple, estate in, 35

fee tail
  estate in 7, 256–257, 260
  special, estate in, 35
felon, common, 330
felony
  bail of one committed on suspicion of, 52
  outlawry for, 59
  prosecution for by lunatic, 159
  prosecution for of married woman, 232
  trespass action by one accused of, 62
  witness in custody for, 78 n. 90
felonious intent, 369
feme covert, *see* married woman
feme sole, *see* single woman
feoffment, fraudulent, 24
fieri facias, writ of, 4, 57, 97, 162
final concord, 35, 187
  by married woman, 226, 228
  covenant to levy, 252
fine (conveyancing), *see* final concord
fiscal, officer in Dutch colonies, 286
football match, 68
foreigners, 8, 155
forfeitures, statutory, recovery of, 119
forgery, l, liv, 103, 149 n. 14
franchise
  electoral, 344
  with return of writs, 51
fraud, 54–56, 86, 104, 129, 200, 245
freehold estate, 202
freeholders, as jurors, 94 n. 15

gaming, liv, l, 65 n. 70, 183, 184 n. 80
gaol, *see* prison
gavelkind, custom of, 6 n. 11
goods
  sold and delivered, action for, 41
  stolen, receipt of, 65
Gordon Riots (1780), xxv, xxvi
groats, *see under* debtors
grand juror, *see under* jurors
guardianship, 48
Guildhall, London
  distance to as measurement of length of record, 184
  trials at, xxiii, xxvi, xxxii, xlix, 11, 50 n. 37, 63, 79 n. 92, 95, 97, 105 n. 35, 164 n. 44, 169, 171 n. 53, 175, 179 n. 71, 192, 264, 280

habeas corpus, writ of, 105
  ad faciendum et recipiendum, 82
  ad subjiciendum, 89–91
  ad testificandum, 78

INDEX OF SUBJECTS

cum causa, distinguished from other writs of habeas corpus, 89–90
  on defects in warrant for committal, 143, 161
  on mis-stated conviction, 191
  to keeper of Aylesbury gaol, 159
  to keeper of Newgate gaol, 92, 93
  to keeper of Tothill Fields Bridewell, 94
  to move prisoner to another gaol, 103
  to produce estranged wife, 227 n. 53
  to surrender impressed seaman to bail, 51–52
  see also under infant
Harvard Law School Library, xiii n. 1
heir
  as owner of ship, 300–301, 306
  claim under, 190
  descent to, 22–24, 71–75,
  devise to, 251–252, 254–260
  devise upon trust for, 179–180
  of the body, 35
  see also right heirs
heiress, 22–24
highway repairs, xxxix–xxx, 50
horses,
  racing of, 62
  slaughtering of, 196
housebreaking, 191

impressment of seamen, 51–52, 284–285
imprisonment
  false, 62, 63 n. 65, 371
  leading to breach of covenant, 154
  of French persons in Cape Town, 285
  sureties for good behaviour during, 153
  upon baseless action, 38, 357 n. *
  see also under debtors; prison; punishment
incumbent, ecclesiastical, 20, 24–26, 111–112, 114, 116–117
indemnity
  bond of, 244 n. 22
  contract, 229
  of sheriff, 57, 157 n. 32
  upon payment over by stakeholder, 68
indenture
  of apprenticeship, 88
  of lease and release, 21–23
indictment
  acquittal upon, on condition of reference to arbitration, 131 n. 73
  by lewd woman, 357 n. *
  damages upon, 370
  flaw in, xlvi, 353, 363, 366–367, 374 n. 23

  for assault in the presence of commissioners, 205–207
  for conspiracy to pervert the course of justice, 151 n. 22
  for high treason, 93
  for murder, 59, 60 n. 61
  for neglecting a pauper, 106
  for not repairing highway, 164
  for perjury, xl n. 58, xliii, xlvi, 10 n. 15, 158, 315–320, 322–323, 325, 335, 337–342, 346–347, 350, 356–358, 363, 380
  for public nuisance, 50 n. 37
  for removal of woman in labour to another parish, 66
  for sedition, 102 n. 29
  joint defendants in, 200
  of married woman for felony, 232
  outlawry upon, 92
  probable cause for preferring, 359–361, 373, 378
  record of, 59
infant, 12
  action against, 175 n. 60
  affidavit to hold to bail, 8
  appearing by attorney, 165
  as lessor in ejectment, 38
  custody of, 144, 172, 179, 181
  devise to, 11, 256, 260
  habeas corpus for, 55, 144, 170, 172, 179, 181
  illegitimate, 66–67, 172, 179, 181
  maintenance of, 225
  trusts for, 186
  within the age of nurture, 181
infancy, evidence of, 174
informers, 183
information
  by a lunatic, 159
  change of venue for trial of, 83
  filing of de bene esse, 101
  for assault before commissioners, 205
  for libel, 80, 195–196
  for libel on public justice, xlvi, 10 n. 17,
  in the nature of a quo warranto, 63, 101, 141–143, 147, 151, 184–185
  return of, 52
inheritance, 35, 75
injunctions, 28, 182
inns of court, *see under the names of individual inns in the index of persons and places*
inquiry, writ of, xli, 201, 379
inquisition de proprietate probanda quashed, 57
insanity, 103, 159, 166

INDEX OF SUBJECTS

insolvency, 64, 166; *see also* bankrupt, bankruptcy
insurance, xxii
  average, general and particular, 84
  broker, 16–17, 84
  fire, 6 n. 11
  life, lii, 171
  policy, barratry claim upon, 84–85 n. 95; construction of, lii, 213, 264; copies of, 211; costs in action upon, 199; maritime, deviation on, xxxiii, neutrality of ship insured under, xxxvi–xxxvii, 291–312; payment upon to bankrupt, 16; under-insurance on, 271–272
  see also assurance
interrogatories
  additional, 61
  cross, 189
intestacy, 125, 146
issue, feigned, 212
issue money, in King's Bench, liv–lv

Jews, liv, 158 n. 34, 184
joinder
  in error, 92, 104
  on demurrer, 20 n. 45, 211
jointure, 256
judges, taking opinion of all, 117
judgment
  in autre droit, 172
  irregularity of, 3, 60
  motion in arrest of, 62, 158 n. 34, 235, 237, 239–240, 365
  joint, 37
  on warrant of attorney, 77
  signed irregularly, 53
jury
  assessment of damages by, xli, xliii, liii
  common, 201 n. 10
  good, 201 n. 10
  grand, 317, 325, 336, 338, 351–352, 357–358, 363, 367; common council-men on, 352; of a corporation, 337
  petty, 337
  sequestered, 94 n. 15
  special, xli, xlii, xliii, xlvi, xlviii n. 3, xlix, lviii, 10 n. 15, 78 n. 90, 189 n. 90, 200, 316, 317, 323, 324, 329, 359 n. 8, 361, 368, 375; of merchants, 105 n. 35, 164 n. 44, 194 n. 1, 204 n. 14, 342
  talesmen, 317, 324, 329
  see also jurors; verdict
jurors
  grand, privilege from arrest, 175

  naming on record, xxx
  withdrawal of, 103
  see also under affidavit
justice, natural, 29–31; *see also under* equity
justices of assize, *see* assizes

king, insulting the, 94
king in council, jurisdiction of, 119
King's Bench
  attorneys of, 149
  Buller, Sir Francis, as justice of, xxv, xxxvii n. 40, 214
  cases in, xxx, xxxiii, xxxvi, xxxvii, xxxix, xliv, xlvi, 5–6, 10 n. 17, 27 n. 77, Part II *passim*, Part III, *passim*, 317, 372
  consultation of the judges of, xlv n. 84, 41
  justices of as assize commissioners, xliii n. 63
  Kenyon, Lord, as chief justice of, xxvi
  Lawrence, Sir Soulden, as justice of, vii, xiii, xl, xlvi–lx, 3 n. 2, 43, 111
  paper books in, 211–213
  practice of, xliv; compared with practice of Common Pleas, xliv, 8, 38, 364
  procedure in issuing writs of habeas corpus, 90
  reports of cases in, xiv–xv, xvii, xviii n. 22, xix–xx, xxiii n. 38, xxvii, xxxi–xxxii, lxi
  signer of the writs in, 90
  see also paper books

land tax, 11 n. 18, 136–137, 174
landlord, 101
latitat, writ of, 78, 99–100, 182
law
  'bad', xxxvii–xxxviii
  foreign, xxxvii, 28, 211
  of nations, 213
  positive, 39
  revenue, 51
law students, xvii
lease, 101
  construction of, xxxviii
  reversionary, 183
  with covenant for rent, 244
  see also term of years
lessee, 133, 177, 244 n. 22, 259; encroachment by, 101
lessor, 86, 156; in ejectment action, 6–7, 12, 40, 155, 252, 254–255
libel
  (defamation), xlvi, 80, 107, 136, 195, 199, 245, 342; in corporate book, 94–96
  indecent, 87

INDEX OF SUBJECTS 435

(process) in ecclesiastical court, 185; in vice-admiralty court, 119, 286
licentiousness, 103 n. 29
lien, 16–17, 185
lights, ancient, action for stopping, 177, 188–189 n. 89
limitation of actions, xxxv, 86, 100, 101, 163–164, 183–184, 188
Lords, House of (Domus Procerum), cases in, xiii, 5, 6 n. 11, 30, 71, 85, 109 n. 43, 111, 112, 114, 241; *see also* parliament
lotteries, 8, 99, 107
lunacy, *see* insanity

malice
 implied, 355
 in libel, xlvi, 196
 in malicious prosecution, 331, 339–340, 343, 346–347, 355–356, 358, 359–363, 367, 369, 373
 in perjury, 320
mandamus, writ of
 for disturbance in office, 91
 to admit candidate to examination, 140, 141 n. 2
 to appoint overseers of a township, 83
 to appoint overseers of the poor, 70
 to compel libelous entry in corporate book, 94–96
 to deliver books, to deputy of infant register of a diocese, 150; to committee of lunatic, 166–167
 to elect a bailiff, 147
 to elect a mayor, 60
 to hold court to elect a portreeve, 69
 to hold a vestry, 196
 to justices to hear an appeal, 66, 139
 to license a schoolmaster, 47 n. 28
 to pay penalty from army officer's pay, 82
 to present to a living, 160
 to restore to office of beadle, 102
 to settle an account, 160–161
 to swear into office, 151
manor court, inspection of rolls, 41; *see also under* attorney
marque, letter of, 84 n. 95
marriage
 alimony, 225, 232
 conjugal rights, 222, 227, 230
 contract, *see under* contract
 elopement, 232
 sanctity of, Lord Kenyon on, xlix
 scandalous, 153 n. 26
 see also divorce; separation

married woman
 affidavit of, 49
 assault on, 228 n. 55
 bond of, 224, 226, 229
 Chancery on, 227–228
 confession of judgment by, 49
 contract of, 232
 debts of, xxii; action for, 216
 error, writ of, brought by 49
 executor of, 225
 final concord by, 226, 228
 prosecution for felony of, 232
 property rights of, xiv
 responsibility upon contracts, 213–214
 separated from husband, 216, 223–225, 227–232; chastity of, 225
 separate maintenance of, 232, 232
 trading, 212
 trespass vi et armis, action of, by, 227
 trust for separate use of, 214, 225, 228–229
 validity of will of, 185
 warrant of attorney, given by, 49
 widowhood, 214
mercantile custom, xxii
meum and tuum, cases of, 8
minister of the parish, statutory meaning of, 196
misdemeanour, xxv, 66
mistake
 in affidavit, 207
 in special verdict, 203
 recovery back of money paid by, 192
money had and received, action for, xxiii, 16–17, 42, 87, 192, 193 n. 97, 290
mortgage, 40, 56, 251 n. 34, 254, 256–257
murder, 92, 93 n. 11, 104; *see also under* indictment
mute person, as vouchee in common recovery, 36

National Assembly, of revolutionary France, 306
negligence, lii, lviii, 26, 85–86, 132, 179 n. 71
neutrality in time of war
 forfeiture of, xxxvii
 warrant of, xxxvi, 290, 292, 302–303, 309, 312
new trial, *see* trial
newspaper, 340
 false reports in, xv n. 10
 printer of, in libel action, 195, 201
 proprietor of, in libel action, 80, 136
 see also under names of individual newspapers in index of persons and places

nisi prius, 68, 99 n. 24, 100–101
   absence and unpreparedness of attorneys and counsel at, lvii–lviii
   authority of decision at, 215 n. 35
   commission of, 325
   false oath of jury at, 327
   hurry of, xliii, 344, 378
   impossibility of getting through case at, 79 n. 92
   Kenyon, Lord, at, xlviii, lvii–lviii, 84, 193
   Mansfield, Lord, at, xxv n. 55
   notes of cases at, xxvii n. 75, xxxii, xxxvii, xxxix, lx
   writ of enquiry at, 201, 232
nolle prosequi (non-pross.), 13, 27 n. 77, 59–60, 205–206
non assumpsit, plea of, 174, 240; verdict of, 240
non electus, return of to writ of mandamus, 60
non omittas latitat, writ of, 159
nonsuit, 10 n. 15, 56, 68, 86, 87, 179 n. 71, 180, 190, 208, 254, 272, 315, 363
   costs upon, 174, 199
   entry of directed by arbitrators, 54
   expense of, 376
   for failure to prove handwriting of witness, 39
   for irregular commencement of suit, 101
   judgment as in case of, 41, 53, 163–164
   motion to enter, 62–63, 145, 192, 324–327
   motion to set aside, xlii, liii, 50, 136, 155, 323
   reasons for requesting, lix
   taxing defendant his costs equivalent to, 12
notice of trial, 53; statutory, subscribed on process, 3
nuisance, 133, 148, 188; public, indictment for, 50

oaths, false, 359, 364
obstruction, of revenue officer, 65, 97, 139; of ancient lights, 189 n. 90
Old Bailey sessions house, xlvii, 61, 67 n. 73, 149 n. 14, 358
office, corporate, election to, 63
Office of Classes at Copenhagen, 295
outlawry, xxxiii n. 19, 60 n. 61, 92, 93 n. 11, 104, 170, 202; reversal of, 59
Oxford University, 140–141; *see also* Bodleian Library

paper books, vii–viii, xiv, xxv, xxxvii n. 41, liv, lxi, 15 n. 28, 42, 47, 92–93 n. 11, 97, 111–112, 114, 133–134, 204 n. 14, Part III *passim*
parliament, 94, 102, 138, 268
   privilege of, 274
   rolls of, 229
   Scottish peers in, 131 n. 74
   writ of error in, 5
   see also Lords, House of
parol
   agreement, 14
   licence, 177
   submission, 155
pauper, li, 106
peerage, privilege of, lv, 131
penalty, lenient, circumstances of entered in rule of court, 66, 77
peril of the sea, meaning of, 134
perjury, 315–329
   bail in prosecution for, 158
   bill of indictment for, xlv
   committal to Newgate prison for, 150
   defamatory imputation of, 137, 138 n. 95,
   malicious prosecution for, xli, xliii, 10, 335–336, 340–341, 345, 353, 358, 360–361, 367, 371, 378
   multiple charges of in indictment, liii–liv
   pillory for, 4
   see also under indictment
pick-pocket, 62
pleadings, sham, lv
plene administravit, plea of, 65
pone per vadios, process of against a corporation, 168
poor, overseer of, 106
possessory action, 177
prebendary, 80
precedent, xxi n. 26, xxxii–xxxix
prerogative court of Canterbury, 120, 130
prescription, 187
presentment of highway repairs, xxix
prima tonsura, right of, 202
prison
   Bridewell, London, 356
   debtors', xlix n. 14, 146 n. 12
   Dorchester, Dorset, 102
   Gloucester, Gloucs, 138
   Hereford, Heref, 103
   House of Corrections, 68 n. 77
   King's Bench, 90, 107, 143, 167, 202, 206
   Marshalsea, 235
   Newgate, 64, 69, 78, 92, 93, 97, 103, 106, 107, 138, 139, 143, 150, 158
   Tower of London, 206
   see also under imprisonment; punishment

INDEX OF SUBJECTS

prisoners, poor, relief of, 167
privateers, 11, 16, 296
Privy Council, 119, 178 n. 70
prize of war, 168
prize money, 11
procedure, granting a view, 56
process, irregular, 5, 100, 168
prohibition, writ of, 138, 190
promise, *see under* contract
promissory note, xxxvi, xlviii n. 98
prosecution
    fraudulent, 359 n. 8
    malicious, xli, xliii, 10, 315–329, 362, 363–364, 368, 370
prothonotary of Common Pleas, 12, 38, 39, 370, 380; taxing of costs by, 379, 380
public houses, xxxiv n. 20
punishment
    amputation of a hand, 206 n. 17, 207
    banishment for life, 230
    branding, Lord Kenyon's views on, l
    exile, 223, 224, 225, 227, 231–232
    fine, 38, 87, 102, 104, 143–144, 151, 164, 206, 229, 302; nominal, li, 66–67, 77, 157 n. 33; satisfaction of, 153
    hanging, liv
    hard labour, 138
    imprisonment, 54, 64, 65, 68, 97, 102, 106–107, 138, 139, 143, 146, 148, 206
    in circumstances of compassion, 191
    Lord Kenyon, on, l–li
    mitigation of, 139 n. 1
    pecuniary, 54 n. 44
    pillory, xli, 4, 138, 158 n. 34
    transportation, 223, 225
    whipping, public, 68 n. 77
    see also damages, prison

quare impedit, writ of, 20, 23–25, 116 n. 55, 232
qui tam actions, liv–lv, 8, 99–100, 101 n. 27,
quo warranto, writ of, 60, 63, 101, 141–142, 147, 150–151, 184

rape, 357 n.*
recognizance
    for good behaviour, 64, 143, 153
    of bail, 52, 94
    to appear to receive judgment, 157, 191
    to carry down the record, 147–148
reglements concerning neutrality in time of war (French), 292–294, 306, 308
rejoinder, 12, 26
relators, bona fide, 142

relegation, not civil death, 231
remainders, 258
    contingent, 180, 259
removal, orders of, 102
rent charges, arrears of, 136
replevin, writ of, 70
replication, 26–27, 150–151, 200, 245, 248
    de injuria absque causa, 273
reports, accuracy of, lviii–lx; *see also* case reports, nominate
Requests, Court of, at Great Yarmouth, Norf, xli, 317–319, 321, 331, 333–334, 339, 348–352, 357–358; at Tower Hamlets, Middx, 102
right heirs, meaning of, 5–7
rioting, 205
riotous assembly, 94, 138
riparian rights, 187–189
robbery, l, 43
    on highway, 159, 176
rogue and vagabond, 161, 163, 191
Roman Catholics, 55
Royal Council of Direction and of Commerce, Denmark, 295
rule nisi, 3, 4, 57, 77, 136, 168, 174–175, 352
    for attachment, 168, 170
    granted on ground of judicial misdirection, 63
    refusal of, 131, 133, 155
    to set aside warrant of attorney to confess judgment, 34

salvage, xli, 190, 319, 320 n. *, 331–332, 348–350
scire facias, writ of, 161, 163, 244
scrivener, 98
sea brief, xxxvii n. 38
seamen, wages of, 135
security, negotiable, 146
sedition, 102
seisin in fee, 11, 21–22, 112–114, 249, 259
separation, matrimonial
    articles of, 227 n. 53, 229
    deed of, 222
    legal, 225
    see also divorce, marriage
set off, 15 n. 28, 79, 172, 194, 24
settlement, marriage, 35; strict, 122; portions under, 186
sexual misconduct, Lord Kenyon on, xlix; *see also* adultery, brothels, criminal conversation
sheep stealing, 52
shorthand, case notes in, 272–273

simony, 25–26
single woman, 49, 216, 219, 227, 229, 231–232
slander, 137, 330, 336, 341, 345, 354, 363, 367
solicitor-general, 54, 206, 271 n. 79, 304 n. 17
specific performance, *see* contract
statute
   copies of in paper books, 211
   restricting judicial sentencing discretion, 68 n. 77
   see also under equity
steam engine, *see under* trover
stock-jobbing, 163
suffrage, universal, 102 n. 29
summons, writ of, 72, 74, 75
Supreme Tribunal of Cassation, *see* Cassation

tax, land, *see* land tax
tenancy, 101
   for life, 327
   freehold, of a manor, 41
   joint, 23, 55, 248, 257, 259; of right to present to an office, 48
   in common, 111, 248, 257, 259, 261
   in common and tail, 256–257
   notice to quit, 156
tenant, leasehold, *see* lessee
tenant's title, one coming in privity of, 86
tenements, 41
term of years, 36
testator, 4–7, 31, 65, 117 n. 61, 120–130, 212, 251–259, 260 n. 61
   illiterate, xiv, 212, 248, 258
township, definition of, 83
tort, action for 136; verdict in action for, 10
trade
   international, xiv, 213
   restraint of, 243, 245, 246, 247
   with the enemy, xxv
traverse, 226
treason, high
   bail in cases of, 106 n. 37
   committal for, 78, 93
   delivery of lists of witnesses and jurors to one indicted for, 94 n. 14
   incitement to, 102
   justices assigned to hear, 324
   special commission for trial for, 61
   trial for, 205
treasonable words, 357–358 n. *
Treaty of Amity, Commerce and Navigation 1794, 204 n. 14
Treaty of Utrecht, xxxvii, 303–304
trespass, ab initio, 280
trespass vi et armis, action of
   by bankrupt, 243 n. 20
   by married woman, 227
   change of venue, 60
   for breaking dwelling house, 200
   for false imprisonment, 62
   for seizure of ship, 272, 274, 278–279
   quare clausum (fregit), 208
trespass on the case, action of, 216
trials, jury, at Westminster Hall and Guildhall, xxxii
trial, new, xxxix, xlii–xliii, 49, 223 n. 40, 266, 308, 315–316, 323, 326, 362, 371–372, 379;
   motion for, xxxvi, lii, lix, 40, 47, 56, 58, 63, 68, 70, 78 n. 90, 84, 86, 87, 97–98, 99–100 n. 24, 101, 104–105, 133, 134, 135, 136, 144 n. 6, 152–153, 156, 158 n. 34, 169–170, 170–171, 173, 175, 176, 177, 178, 179 n. 71, 180, 181, 183, 187, 190, 192, 200, 202, 203–204 n. 14, 208, 211;
   unsupportable, liii
   grounds for, 132 207, 254, 368–369, 371–372
   on ground of excessive damages, xli, 10, 375 n.*–376, 379
   postponement of, 98
   refused, 138 n. 95
   rule for, 80, 88, 146
trials, pace of, xlvi–xlix
Tribunal of Commerce at Bordeaux, France, 291, 295, 298
trover, action of, liii, 17, 70, 134, 135, 169, 175, 176, 280
   for steam engine, 56
   in bankruptcy, liii, 56, 156
trust, 26 n. 73, 43, 73, 160, 179–180, 186, 221, 244 n. 21
   deed of, 160, 185
   devise upon, 11
   for separate use of married woman, 214, 225, 228–229
trustees, 15, 56 n. 48, 61–62, 120–122, 144 n. 6, 160, 180, 187, 225, 229, 247

undertaking, peremptory, as reason for not giving judgment, 41
unlivery, writ of issued from court of Admiralty, 168
use and occupation, action of, 40
usurpation of presentment to benefice, 24–25, 27
usury, 88, 97–98, 146, 172

vagabond, *see* rogue and vagabond

INDEX OF SUBJECTS

vagrant, 143
vendor, action by against vendee, xxxix
venire de novo, writ of, 83, 203
venue, change of, 60, 79, 83, 171 n. 52
verdict
   adverse, nonsuit preferable to, liii n. 36, lix
   correction of, 203
   cures defective declaration, 62, 234
   decided by lot, xliv–xlv, 364–365
   set aside, xlii, 10 n. 15, 364, 370, 372, 376, 378
   special, 5–6, 23, 153, 179 n. 71, 269
vice-admiralty courts, 119, 204; appeal from, 204–205
voir dire, 94 n. 15

waiver of irregularity, 53, 56, 60
war, *see* neutrality; prize; reglements; trading with the enemy
warrant
   for commitment into custody, defective, 105, 143, 161; *see also* attorney general, 376–377
warranty of quality of horse, 174
waste, 173, 231
   forfeiture of customary lands for, 173
weir, prescription for, 187
will
   construction of, xxvii

nuncupative, 124, 128
window, new, creating, 20
witness
   attachment for not attending, 53
   coming from abroad, costs of, 198
   false, 357 n.*
words
   action for, 371
   criminal, indictment for, 357 n.*
words and phrases
   animus revertendi, 152
   ex provisione viri, 35
   expedit reipublicae ut sit finis litem, 194
   in propria persona, 39
   noscitur a sociis, 49
   pendent lite nihil innovetur, 24
   pro bono publico, 48
   pro falso clamore, 38
   puis darrein continuance exoneretur, 64
   quod initio non valet tractu temporis non convalescet, 25
   ubi eadem est ratio, eadem lex, 66
   volenti non fit injuria, 194
workhouse, 58, 77, 106
writs
   failure to return, 52
   joint, 53
   see also under names of individual writs